# Lecture Notes in Artificial Intelligence 11741

Subseries of Lecture Notes in Computer Science

More information about this series at http://www.springer.com/series/1244

Haibin Yu · Jinguo Liu ·
Lianqing Liu · Zhaojie Ju ·
Yuwang Liu · Dalin Zhou (Eds.)

# Intelligent Robotics and Applications

12th International Conference, ICIRA 2019
Shenyang, China, August 8–11, 2019
Proceedings, Part II

 Springer

*Editors*
Haibin Yu
Shenyang Institute of Automation
Shenyang, China

Jinguo Liu
Shenyang Institute of Automation
Shenyang, China

Lianqing Liu
Shenyang Institute of Automation
Shenyang, China

Zhaojie Ju
University of Portsmouth
Portsmouth, UK

Yuwang Liu
Shenyang Institute of Automation
Shenyang, China

Dalin Zhou
University of Portsmouth
Portsmouth, UK

ISSN 0302-9743        ISSN 1611-3349   (electronic)
Lecture Notes in Artificial Intelligence
ISBN 978-3-030-27531-0        ISBN 978-3-030-27532-7   (eBook)
https://doi.org/10.1007/978-3-030-27532-7

LNCS Sublibrary: SL7 – Artificial Intelligence

This Springer imprint is published by the registered company Springer Nature Switzerland AG
The registered company address is: Gewerbestrasse 11, 6330 Cham, Switzerland

# Preface

On behalf of the Organizing Committee, we welcome you to the proceedings of the 12th International Conference on Intelligent Robotics and Applications (ICIRA 2019), organized by Shenyang Institute of Automation, Chinese Academy of Sciences, co-organized by Huazhong University of Science and Technology, Shanghai Jiao Tong University, and the University of Portsmouth, technically co-sponsored by the National Natural Science Foundation of China and Springer, and financially sponsored by Shenyang Association for Science and Technology. ICIRA 2019 with the theme of "Robot Era" offered a unique and constructive platform for scientists and engineers throughout the world to present and share their recent research and innovative ideas in the areas of robotics, automation, mechatronics, and applications.

ICIRA 2019 was most successful this year in attracting more than 500 submissions regarding the state-of-the-art development in robotics, automation, and mechatronics. The Program Committee undertook a rigorous review process for selecting the most deserving research for publication. Despite the high quality of most of the submissions, a total of 378 papers were selected for publication in six volumes of Springer's *Lecture Notes in Artificial Intelligence* a subseries of *Lecture Notes in Computer Science*. We sincerely hope that the published papers of ICIRA 2019 will prove to be technically beneficial and constructive to both the academic and industrial community in robotics, automation, and mechatronics. We would like to express our sincere appreciation to all the authors, participants, and the distinguished plenary and keynote speakers.

The success of the conference is also attributed to the Program Committee members and invited peer reviewers for their thorough review of all the submissions, as well as to the Organizing Committee and volunteers for their diligent work. Special thanks are extended to Alfred Hofmann, Anna Kramer, and Volha Shaparava from Springer for their consistent support.

August 2019

Haibin Yu
Jinguo Liu
Lianqing Liu
Zhaojie Ju
Yuwang Liu
Dalin Zhou

# Organization

## Honorary Chairs

Youlun Xiong            Huazhong University of Science and Technology, China

Nanning Zheng       Xi'an Jiaotong University, China

## General Chair

Haibin Yu              Shenyang Institute of Automation, Chinese Academy of Sciences, China

## General Co-chairs

Kok-Meng Lee        Georgia Institute of Technology, USA

Zhouping Yin         Huazhong University of Science and Technology, China

Xiangyang Zhu       Shanghai Jiao Tong University, China

## Program Chair

Jinguo Liu             Shenyang Institute of Automation, Chinese Academy of Sciences, China

## Program Co-chairs

Zhaojie Ju            The University of Portsmouth, UK

Lianqing Liu         Shenyang Institute of Automation, Chinese Academy of Sciences, China

Bram Vanderborght   Vrije Universiteit Brussel, Belgium

## Advisory Committee

Jorge Angeles        McGill University, Canada

Tamio Arai            University of Tokyo, Japan

Hegao Cai             Harbin Institute of Technology, China

Tianyou Chai        Northeastern University, China

Jie Chen              Tongji University, China

Jiansheng Dai       King's College London, UK

Zongquan Deng      Harbin Institute of Technology, China

Han Ding              Huazhong University of Science and Technology, China

| Xilun Ding | Beihang University, China |
|---|---|
| Baoyan Duan | Xidian University, China |
| Xisheng Feng | Shenyang Institute of Automation, Chinese Academy of Sciences, China |
| Toshio Fukuda | Nagoya University, Japan |
| Jianda Han | Shenyang Institute of Automation, Chinese Academy of Sciences, China |
| Qiang Huang | Beijing Institute of Technology, China |
| Oussama Khatib | Stanford University, USA |
| Yinan Lai | National Natural Science Foundation of China, China |
| Jangmyung Lee | Pusan National University, South Korea |
| Zhongqin Lin | Shanghai Jiao Tong University, China |
| Hong Liu | Harbin Institute of Technology, China |
| Honghai Liu | The University of Portsmouth, UK |
| Shugen Ma | Ritsumeikan University, Japan |
| Daokui Qu | SIASUN, China |
| Min Tan | Institute of Automation, Chinese Academy of Sciences, China |
| Kevin Warwick | Coventry University, UK |
| Guobiao Wang | National Natural Science Foundation of China, China |
| Tianmiao Wang | Beihang University, China |
| Tianran Wang | Shenyang Institute of Automation, Chinese Academy of Sciences, China |
| Yuechao Wang | Shenyang Institute of Automation, Chinese Academy of Sciences, China |
| Bogdan M. Wilamowski | Auburn University, USA |
| Ming Xie | Nanyang Technological University, Singapore |
| Yangsheng Xu | The Chinese University of Hong Kong, SAR China |
| Huayong Yang | Zhejiang University, China |
| Jie Zhao | Harbin Institute of Technology, China |
| Nanning Zheng | Xi'an Jiaotong University, China |
| Weijia Zhou | Shenyang Institute of Automation, Chinese Academy of Sciences, China |
| Xiangyang Zhu | Shanghai Jiao Tong University, China |

## Publicity Chairs

| Shuo Li | Shenyang Institute of Automation, Chinese Academy of Sciences, China |
|---|---|
| Minghui Wang | Shenyang Institute of Automation, Chinese Academy of Sciences, China |
| Chuan Zhou | Shenyang Institute of Automation, Chinese Academy of Sciences, China |

## Publication Chairs

Yuwang Liu                    Shenyang Institute of Automation, Chinese Academy
                              of Sciences, China
Dalin Zhou                    The University of Portsmouth, UK

## Award Chairs

Kaspar Althoefer             Queen Mary University of London, UK
Naoyuki Kubota               Tokyo Metropolitan University, Japan
Xingang Zhao                 Shenyang Institute of Automation, Chinese Academy
                              of Sciences, China

## Special Session Chairs

Guimin Chen                  Xi'an Jiaotong University, China
Hak Keung Lam                King's College London, UK

## Organized Session Co-chairs

Guangbo Hao                  University College Cork, Ireland
Yongan Huang                 Huazhong University of Science and Technology,
                              China
Qiang Li                     Bielefeld University, Germany
Yuichiro Toda                Okayama University, Japan
Fei Zhao                     Xi'an Jiaotong University, China

## International Organizing Committee Chairs

Zhiyong Chen                 The University of Newcastle, Australia
Yutaka Hata                  University of Hyogo, Japan
Sabina Jesehke               RWTH Aachen University, Germany
Xuesong Mei                  Xi'an Jiaotong University, China
Robert Riener                ETH Zurich, Switzerland
Chunyi Su                    Concordia University, Canada
Shengquan Xie                The University of Auckland, New Zealand
Chenguang Yang               UWE Bristol, UK
Tom Ziemke                   University of Skövde, Sweden
Yahya Zweiri                 Kingston University, UK

## Local Arrangements Chairs

Hualiang Zhang               Shenyang Institute of Automation, Chinese Academy
                              of Sciences, China
Xin Zhang                    Shenyang Institute of Automation, Chinese Academy
                              of Sciences, China

# Contents – Part II

**Underwater Acoustic and Optical Signal Processing
for Environmental Cognition**

## Piezoelectric Actuators and Micro-Nano Manipulations

## Robot Vision and Scene Understanding

**Visual and Motional Learning in Robotics**

**Signal Processing and Underwater Bionic Robots**

## Soft Locomotion Robot

## Teleoperation Robot

**Autonomous Control of Unmanned Aircraft Systems**

# Power-Assisted System and Control

# Estimation of Knee Extension Force Using Mechanomyography Signals Detected Through Clothing

Daqing Wang[1,2], Chenlei Xie[1,2,3], Haifeng Wu[4],
Dun Hu[1,2], Qianqian Zhang[1,2], and Lifu Gao[1(✉)]

[1] Institute of Intelligent Machines, Chinese Academy of Sciences,
Hefei 230031, China
lifugao@iim.ac.cn
[2] University of Science and Technology of China, Hefei 230026, China
[3] Anhui Province Key Laboratory of Intelligent Building
and Building Energy Saving, Anhui Jianzhu University, Hefei 230022, China
[4] High Magnetic Field Laboratory,
Chinese Academy of Sciences, Hefei 230031, China

**Abstract.** This paper proposes a more flexible method for estimating the knee extension forces using mechanomyography (MMG) signal. We detect the MMG signal of the quadriceps through clothing. Then several features were extracted from three channels. A support vector machine model was applied to generate mapping between the features and the actual forces. Results indicates that the best estimation performance can be obtained using a combination of four features (the mean absolute value (MAV), the sample entropy (SampEn), the mean power frequency (MPF) and the correlation coefficients of 2 different channels (CC2Cs)). Finally, an average coefficient of determination ($R^2$) of 0.799 and a root-mean-squared error (RMSE) of 9.18% of the maximum voluntary isometric contraction (MVC) were obtained. These results are similar to those of earlier studies, which suggests that the information in the MMG signal has not been detectably reduced when measured through clothing. Therefore, the MMG signal through clothing is able to function as a reliable estimator of muscle contraction strength and can be used as the muscle machine interface to control robotics or to monitor human activity.

**Keywords:** Mechanomyography · Force estimation ·
Support vector machines · Quadriceps femoris

## 1 Introduction

The generation of information about the human body is the key in obtaining naturalness and flexibility in human-machine coordinated motion [8]. Muscle contraction strength, which is a primary characteristic of muscle activity, can reflect motion and fatigue status in the human body to some extent and can also be used as an input for control power-assisted devices or devices that monitor human motion. In view of this fact, the

© Springer Nature Switzerland AG 2019
H. Yu et al. (Eds.): ICIRA 2019, LNAI 11741, pp. 3–14, 2019.
https://doi.org/10.1007/978-3-030-27532-7_1

measurement of muscle contraction strength is important for the development of a more advanced robotic system.

Surface electromyography (sEMG) methods were already used in many studies to estimate muscle force [25]. However, their applicability has several limitations due to the electronic origin of the measurements obtained. Similar in scope to sEMG, the mechanomyogram (MMG) records the mechanical vibrations generated by oscillations of contracting skeletal muscle [21]. This vibration is an indicator of the mechanical activity of muscle fibres [10]. Previous studies have proved that the MMG signal provides the same information about muscle activity as sEMG, and it has been considered to be an alternative to sEMG for measuring muscle activity [26, 28]. Several advantages of MMG signal over the sEMG signal have been demonstrated as follows: (1) the maximum intensity of the MMG signal (up to 50 mV using a standard microphone) is generally higher than that of the original sEMG signal, which may reduce hardware requirements; (2) Direct contact with the skin is not necessary for the acquisition of the MMG signal [2], which especially suits for wearable application. Moreover, the ability to recognize knee motion using a MMG signal that is detected through clothing was verified in our previous work [29]. In this way, changes in skin impedance caused by sweat and blood have absolutely no effect on the propagation of the MMG signal due to the origin of the mechanical vibration. Therefore, MMG is more suitable than sEMG for practical engineering applications such as the development of prostheses due to lower hardware requirements, flexible installation and robustness to skin impedance.

Many researchers have focused on the relationship between force and the MMG signal. Overall, as muscle force increases as a result of a high level of contraction, MMG amplitude increases from 0–80% of the maximum voluntary contraction (MVC), then continuously increases [24] or decreases [18] from 80–100% of MVC. This relationship is influenced by several factors, such as motor unit activation strategies and muscle stiffness, and it can be highly nonlinear and complex [3]. Therefore, when compared with polynomial regression, an intelligent algorithm model (e.g., artificial neural network (ANN) or support vector machines (SVM)) may be more capable of describing this relationship. Youn [31] evaluated the feasibility of using an ANN model in combination with the root-mean-square (RMS) and the zero-crossing (ZC) of the MMG signal as inputs to estimate elbow flexion force. The same method was adopted in Lei [17] to estimate the isometric contractions in the biceps brachii, but they chose to use RMS and the frequency variance of MMG as inputs for the ANN model. Fara [9] focused on the prediction of arm end-point force using multi-channel MMG. In their opinion, muscle force can be accurately predicted based on the MMG signal.

In addition to the efforts of improving the accuracy of prediction, issues in the acquisition of MMG may be just as important, as these relate their application in practice. In previous experiments, the sensor was placed in direct contact with the skin using two-sided tape, which may constrain the application of MMG. Also, for the estimation of muscle contraction strength using MMG, researchers have not reached a consensus on which features to focus on; especially there is controversy in regards to whether or not frequency information reflects muscle contraction strength [5] or crosstalk between different channels exists [13]. Consequently, for applications related to the engineering of power-assisted devices, more research is needed to make the use of MMG more flexible and reliable.

The purpose of present study is to examine the features and verify the reliability of estimating muscle contraction strength using MMG signals detected through clothing. To this end, we propose a more flexible method of MMG acquisition, which the sensors were attached with elastic bandages and placed over clothing. For the feature extraction, beside the features used in previous studies such as the mean absolute value (MAV) and the mean power frequency (MPF), the sample entropy (SampEn) was introduced to estimate the muscle force from the perspective of signal complexity; also, a new feature of the correlation coefficient between the 2 different channels (CC2Cs) was proposed. Finally, the potential of the proposed method was demonstrated during isometric contractions of the quadriceps femoris experiments. The block diagram of this study is shown in Fig. 1.

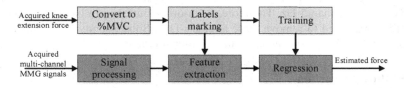

**Fig. 1.** The block diagram of muscle force estimation using MMG detected through clothing

## 2  Methodology

### 2.1  Data Acquisition and Signal Processing

Many different types of sensors have been used to detect MMG signals, including condenser microphones (MIC), piezoelectric contact sensors, accelerometers (ACC), and laser distance sensors. For detecting MMG through clothing, the use of MIC or ACC may be possible due to frequency response, mass and portability of these sensors. ACC was used in this study due a number of factors: (1) ACC sensors are usually lighter and smaller than MIC sensors, making the placement of sensors easier; (2) when cost effectiveness is taken into account, the fact that a triaxial ACC (e.g. ADXL327) costs less than $4 would facilitate the use of multi-channel acquisition (e.g., sensor arrays); (3) ACC is more sensitive than MIC; (4) the feasibility of detecting MMG through clothing using ACC was verified in a previous study.

**Fig. 2.** Illustration of sensor setup

Unlike in previous studies, ACC sensors were placed over clothing on the belly of the muscle and attached to the thigh using elastic bandages, as shown in Fig. 2.

This would serve as a more flexible way of MMG acquisition and expand the possible scope of MMG applications. Also, it was observed that muscle activity would alter the position of clothing and the position of the MMG sensors on the intended muscle during measurement. However, the placement of MMG sensors is not required to be precise or specific [14], and Cescon [6] showed that MMG signals detected by adjacent accelerometers had similar shapes and correlation coefficients that ranged from approximately 0.5–0.9. Therefore, subtle changes in sensor position have little impact on the acquisition of MMG signals in isometric studies.

After the original ACC signal is gained, a signal filter is necessary for the suppression of noise and motion artefact [27]. The peak of the quadriceps femoris MMG signal intensity spectrum occurred at approximately 25–40 Hz [4]. Meanwhile, compared to MIC, the signal detected by ACC inevitably contained data on movement artefacts and gravity in addition to the MMG signal [22], and the artefacts frequencies are typically lower than 5 Hz. Therefore, a 4th-order Butterworth bandpass (5–40 Hz) digital filter was used to remove these artefacts [16]. Subsequently, within this paper, "MMG signal" refers to the signal obtained after filtering.

## 2.2  Feature Extraction

An appropriate feature is crucial for the analysis of the MMG signal. The selection of the extraction algorithm may depend on the type of muscle action and the purpose of the parameter extraction. For the estimation of muscle contraction strength, MMG signals from the vastus medialis corresponding to the changes in contraction strength are shown in Fig. 3. The amplitude of the MMG signal has a strong relationship with the isometric contraction strength. In fact, the amplitude of the MMG signal is correlated with the number of recruited motor units, which determines the contraction strength in the range of 20–80% of MVC. Therefore, the use of the RMS or MAV amplitude has been suggested by many previous researchers for the estimation of the MMG amplitude, which represents the energy of muscle activities [16]; Moreover, the sample entropy (SampEn) was calculated as another feature for use in estimating the complexity and regularity of the signals. In theory, the number of recruited motor units would increase as the contraction strength increased; meanwhile, a greater SampEn value would be generated due to the change of complexity. For detailed steps, please refer to Richman and Moorman [23]. In this paper, SampEn was calculated using N = 500 (number of data points in a moving window), m = 2 (embedding dimension) and tolerance r = 0.2 GSD (global standard deviation; r = 0.025). This means that the tolerance (r) is fixed a priori and does not depend on the standard deviation of each moving window used for the calculation.

A new feature, the correlation coefficient (Spearman rank) between the 2 different channels (CC2Cs), were obtained using (1):

$$\rho = \frac{\sum_{i=1}^{N}(x_i - \bar{x})(y_i - \bar{y})}{\sqrt{\sum_{i=1}^{N}(x_i - \bar{x})^2 \sum_{i=1}^{N}(y_i - \bar{y})^2}} \tag{1}$$

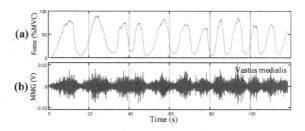

**Fig. 3.** Typical MMG waveform obtained during the isometric contractions: (a) variable force signal; (b) the MMG signal obtained from the vastus medialis

Furthermore, several other common features, including MPF and ZC, were also calculated. To determine whether these features are suitable to describe the changes in muscle contraction, the scatterplot was plotted as shown in Fig. 4 to examine the potential relationship between force value and features. In particular, higher force leads to a larger value of MAV and SampEn, while MPF and CC2Cs appear to have only a qualitative relationship with the force.

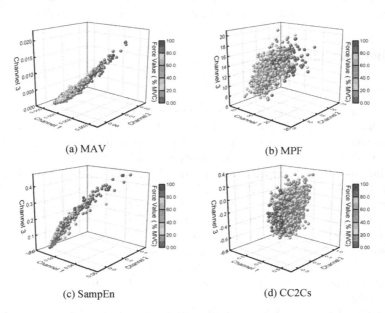

**Fig. 4.** Scatterplots of the extracted features corresponding to the force value: (a) MAV, (b) MPF, (c) SampEn, (d) correlation coefficients of 2 different channels (CC2Cs)

During isometric contraction, a 1000 ms moving window [20] with a 250 ms increment was applied to reduce the transient and stochastic nature of the MMG signal. The normalization of feature vectors is necessary before they are input into the model in order to eliminate the effects of dimension and magnitude among the different features.

## 2.3 Regression and Evaluations

Since the MMG signal has a highly nonlinear and complex relationship with the corresponding forces, the use of SVM to generate the mapping is preferable to polynomial regression.

In this paper, the input vector **x** includes 12 features, along with the corresponding force values as targets t, which were used to establish the SVM model. The input vectors include four features (MAV, MPF, SampEn and CC2Cs) extracted from each 1000 ms MMG signal obtained from three channels. The targets correspond to the mean of force value applied during each second based on our computed force time-series. For establishing the SVM regression model, the LIBSVM software was used and the e-support vector regression (e-SVR) method and the Gaussian radial basis function (RBF-kernel). For more details about SVM regression algorithms, please refer to [7].

Hence, a force-MMG model was generated after training by SVM, and then the continuous force signal was estimated at a temporal resolution of 1000 ms.

The estimation accuracy was evaluated using 10-fold cross validation for each participant, and Root-Mean-Squared Error (RMSE) and coefficient of determination ($R^2$) values for the differences between the predicted values and the actual force measurements were calculated to evaluate the performance of the model.

## 3  Experimental

### 3.1  Experiments Setup

Isometric contractions of the quadriceps femoris were measured, and the experimental setup is shown in Fig. 5; participants were seated on a specially designed chair with their dominant leg fixed at a leg flexion angle of approximately 90°. The isometric strength of knee extension was measured using a force sensor (DYLF-100, Bengbu Sensor, Inc., 0–1000 N) attached to the front of the calf. The MMG signal was detected using ACC sensors (made of ADXL327; size: 27 mm × 22 mm; weight: 2.89 g; 3-axis; measurement range: ± 2 g; bandwidth: 0–100 Hz; Analog Devices, Inc.). An extra circuit for the ADXL327 that used a positive voltage regulator (LM1117-ADJ; Texas Instruments, Inc.) was designed to provide a stable power supply. The signals were sampled at a rate of 500 Hz using a portable data collector (NI USB-6215, National Instruments). A graphical user interface for use in providing visual feedback during data acquisition was programmed by LabVIEW 2015 and the data were acquired using a USB cable.

Since an MMG signal detected from a single location may not be fully representative of the mechanical activity of the entire muscle for large muscles, we used three ACC sensors to detect the MMG from the rectus femoris (RF), vastus lateralis (VL), and vastus medialis (VM) (the vastus intermedius (VI) lies underneath the RF, which cannot be seen without dissection of the RF).

ACC sensors were placed over clothing on the belly the RF, VM, and VL, and attached to the thigh using elastic bandages. The clothes worn by the participants were as follows: 5 pairs of jeans, 1 pair of leggings and 1 pair of trousers.

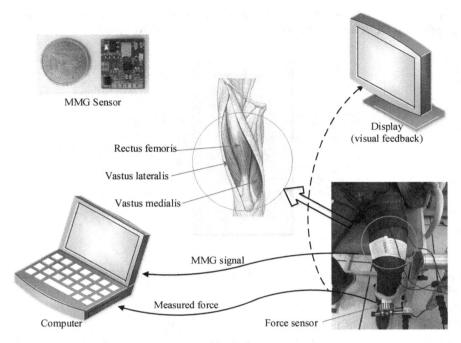

**Fig. 5.** Experimental setup used for the measurement of the quadriceps isometric contraction

At the beginning of the experiment, each participant was asked to perform a maximum voluntary isometric contraction force (MVC) for 4 s. The actual force value during the experiment would be normalized as a percentage of MVC. This is important because the maximum force levels vary across individuals.

During the experiment, the participant performed isometric contractions ranging from 0–100% of MVC with an approximately sinusoidal contraction force value at their personal rhythm based on visual bio-feedback of the applied force level. Each participant was asked to complete the test 4 times for at least 120 s, and a full rest period was allowed before starting the next test.

The ADXL327 is a triaxial device that can measure the acceleration signal in three orthogonal directions (x, y and z). The magnitude of the signal was computed using the Euclidean norm as the raw MMG (prior to filtering) based on the following equation:

$$MMG_{\mathrm{raw}} = \sqrt{\mathrm{ACC}_x^2 + \mathrm{ACC}_y^2 + \mathrm{ACC}_z^2} \qquad (2)$$

### 3.2 Experimental Results

Figure 6 summarizes the estimated results obtained from the SVM model using different inputs. Generally, multiple inputs result in a smaller RMSE than a single input, but some inputs (e.g., ZC) are counterproductive. The selection of inputs calculated from different perspectives appears to produce better results. Ultimately, MAV, MPF, SampEn, and CC2Cs were chosen as the inputs for the SVM model.

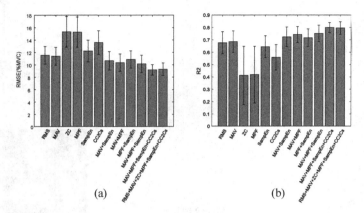

(a)                              (b)

**Fig. 6.** RMSE and $R^2$ values indicating the regression accuracy, using different inputs for same-participant validation

As shown in Table 1, the average same-participant $R^2$ value and RMSE were 0.799 and 9.18% of MVC, respectively, and the cross-participant $R^2$ value and RMSE were 0.431 and 17.20% of MVC, respectively. Compared with the results of previous studies, the accuracy is not decreased even though the MMG signal was measured through clothing.

**Table 1.** RMSE and $R^2$ values indicating regression accuracy[a]

| Participants | Same-participant validation | | Cross-participant validation | |
| --- | --- | --- | --- | --- |
| | RMSE | $R^2$ | RMSE | $R^2$ |
| 1 | 9.29 | 0.815 | 14.62 | 0.583 |
| 2 | 10.59 | 0.807 | 18.69 | 0.527 |
| 3 | 8.82 | 0.828 | 14.66 | 0.526 |
| 4 | 9.28 | 0.723 | 16.95 | 0.374 |
| 5 | 8.68 | 0.771 | 19.08 | 0.206 |
| 6 | 7.89 | 0.807 | 13.69 | 0.635 |
| 7 | 9.68 | 0.843 | 22.74 | 0.170 |
| Total | 9.18 ± 0.847 | 0.799 ± 0.040 | 17.20 ± 3.213 | 0.431 ± 0.185 |

[a]Same-participant validation indicates that the training and the testing data came from the same participant, while cross-participant validation indicates that the data from one of the seven participants was used to test the model established using the data of the remaining six participants.

Figure 7 shows the typical estimated force in comparison to the measured force signal (same-participant validation). The results indicated that estimation could be used to track the trend in the contraction strength, and better estimates were obtained when contraction was smooth and steady.

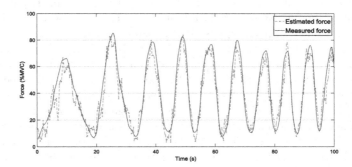

**Fig. 7.** Results of the estimation of the muscle contraction strength (blue line: the measured force; red points: the estimated forces calculated using the proposed method from the MMG signal obtained during the previous second) (Color figure online)

## 4 Discussion

In this study, we demonstrated that the measurement of the MMG signal through clothing to estimate the muscle contraction strength of the quadriceps femoris is feasible.

In a previous work, almost all the ACC sensors were attached to the surface of the skin with two-sided tape. However, this is not reliable or convenient for applying to the study of power-assisted robotics and prosthetic devices. Local elastic compression in the lower extremities has little impact on muscle contraction and MMG signal acquisition [11]. Therefore, the sensors were attached with elastic bandages and the MMG signal was detected through clothing in our study. Based on our results, the information about muscle activity contained in the MMG signal has not been detectably reduced when measured through clothing. Second, our results showed that the MMG signal is of lower frequency, which is in line the results of previous studies. In fact, the tissues of the body including the skin and adipose tissue, act as a low-pass filter [15]. We have tested different sampling frequencies in the range from 500–4000 Hz, and there was no obvious difference in the extracted features. In other words, it is feasible to use a low sampling frequency (e.g., 500 Hz) for the acquisition of the MMG signal, which may improve real-time operational efficiency and reduce hardware requirements.

From our results, the use of the RMS and MAV values to estimate the MMG amplitude seems more suitable for the determination of muscle contraction strength, which is consistent with previous studies that found that the amplitude of the MMG signal is highly correlated with the level of muscle effort [1]. In previous studies, there was controversy as to whether or not the frequency of the MMG signal reflected muscle contraction strength. Our results indicate that MPF also contains useful information that can improve the accuracy of the estimate derived from the SVM model, even if this reflects only qualitative changes. We also observed that some participants experienced muscle tremors between 70 and 100% of MVC, which may have an influence on the decreases in the MMG frequency spectrum. In addition, the muscle contraction strength from 20% to 80% of MVC depends mainly on the number of recruited motor units. The more motor units are recruited, the greater the number of components present in the MMG signal is; thus the signal would become more complex, in theory. Therefore, SampEn was evaluated since entropy is usually used for measuring the complexity and regularity of signals. It is worth noting that SampEn has a higher computational cost than RMS and MAV, but this can be improved with a lower sample frequency.

Based on our results, the RMSE (0.0918) value for the predicted values and the actual measured forces were similar to those obtained in earlier studies (Youn [31], RMSE = 0.141; Fara [9], RMSE = 0.086), even though the methods used to acquire the MMG signal and estimate the values were absolutely different. For the studies using sEMG, the RMSE value are 0.0661 (Huang [12]), 0.12 (Mobasser [19]) and 0.162 (Yokoyama [30]). Although the accuracy is a little lower than the best results of Fara and Huang, the estimation method we proposed is superior regarding lower hardware requirements, flexible installation, and robustness to skin impedance. This indicates that our method, which utilizes sensors that are attached with elastic bandages and placed on clothes, is feasible and can be adopted in future studies.

Also, Table 1 shows that the estimation accuracy of the cross-participant validation test was significantly less than that of the same-participant validation test due to individual differences. This indicated that the MMG-force model should be a subject-specific model. Meanwhile, it may be difficult to obtain better results (e.g., RMSE < 0.05) unless a new suitable feature extraction method or regression algorithm can be proposed. However, for an input control signal for power-assisted robotics, an accuracy of 10% of MVC may be acceptable due to the robustness of a number of control algorithms.

Until now, isometric contractions of the quadriceps femoris has been the only type of muscle activity measured in our experiment; therefore, it is necessary to evaluate the feasibility of this method for use in measuring different real-world activities, such as walking or running. However, the force labelling of training samples would be a key issue since no effective way has been proposed to directly detect muscle contraction strength.

# 5  Conclusion

Based on our results, muscle contraction strength can be accurately estimated from the MMG signal, and the information on muscle activity contained in the MMG signal is not measurably reduced when detected through clothing; thus, our acquisition method can be adopted for use in future applications. Furthermore, the amplitude and entropy of the signal had a strong correlation with contraction strength. The characteristics of the frequency domain and crosstalk can be used as inputs for SVM or ANN in order to improve the accuracy of estimation. Once the general model between muscle contraction strength and the MMG signal is established, the MMG signal will become a valid tool for both investigations of the fundamentals of muscle activity and muscle-machine interfaces for practical engineering applications, such as clinical assessment, rehabilitation, and power-assisted robotics.

# References

1. Alves, N., Chau, T.: Classification of the mechanomyogram: its potential as a multifunction access pathway. In: 2009 Annual International Conference of the IEEE Engineering in Medicine and Biology Society, EMBC 2009, pp. 2951–2954. IEEE (2009)

2. Barry, D.T., Leonard Jr., J.A., Gitter, A.J., et al.: Acoustic myography as a control signal for an externally powered prosthesis. Arch. Phys. Med. Rehabil. **67**, 267–269 (1986)

3. Beck, T.W., Housh, T.J., Cramer, J.T., et al.: Mechanomyographic amplitude and frequency responses during dynamic muscle actions: a comprehensive review. Biomed. Eng. Online **4**, 67 (2005)

4. Beck, T.W., Housh, T.J., Fry, A.C., et al.: A wavelet-based analysis of surface mechanomyographic signals from the quadriceps femoris. Muscle Nerve **39**, 355–363 (2009)

5. Beck, T.W., Housh, T.J., Johnson, G.O., et al.: Does the frequency content of the surface mechanomyographic signal reflect motor unit firing rates? A brief review. J. Electromyogr. Kinesiol. **17**, 1–13 (2007)

6. Cescon, C., Farina, D., Gobbo, M., et al.: Effect of accelerometer location on mechanomyogram variables during voluntary, constant-force contractions in three human muscles. Med. Biol. Eng. Comput. **42**, 121–127 (2004)

7. Chang, C.C., Lin, C.J.: LIBSVM: a library for support vector machines. ACM Trans. Intell. Syst. Technol. **2**, 27 (2011)

8. Dollar, A.M., Herr, H.: Lower extremity exoskeletons and active orthoses: challenges and state-of-the-art. IEEE Trans. Robot **24**, 144–158 (2008)

9. Fara, S., Gavriel, C., Vikram, C.S., et al.: Prediction of arm end-point force using multi-channel MMG. In: 2014 11th International Conference on Wearable and Implantable Body Sensor Networks (BSN), pp. 27–32 (2014)

10. Fara, S., Vikram, C.S., Gavriel, C., et al.: Robust, ultra low-cost MMG system with brain-machine-interface applications. In: 2013 6th International IEEE/EMBS Conference on Neural Engineering, pp. 723–726. IEEE, New York (2013)

11. Fu, W., Liu, Y., Xiong, X.: The influence of external elastic compression on the muscular strength, fatigue and activity of track and field athletes. Chin. J. Sports Med. **29**, 631–635 (2010)

12. Huang, C., Chen, X., Cao, S., et al.: An isometric muscle force estimation framework based on a high-density surface EMG array and an NMF algorithm. J. Neural Eng. **14**, 046005 (2017)

13. Islam, A., Sundaraj, K., Ahmad, R.B., et al.: Analysis of crosstalk in the mechanomyographic signals generated by forearm muscles during different wrist postures. Muscle Nerve **51**, 899–906 (2015)

14. Islam, M.A., Sundaraj, K., Ahmad, R.B., et al.: Mechanomyography sensor development, related signal processing, and applications: a systematic review. IEEE Sens. J. **13**, 2499–2516 (2013)

15. Jaskolska, A., Brzenczek, W., Kisiel-Sajewicz, K., et al.: The effect of skinfold on frequency of human muscle mechanomyogram. J. Electromyogr. Kinesiol. **14**, 217–225 (2004)

16. Krueger, E., Scheeren, E.M., Nogueira-Neto, G.N., et al.: Advances and perspectives of mechanomyography. Revista Brasileira de Engenharia Biomédica **30**, 384–401 (2014)

17. Lei, K.F., Cheng, S.-C., Lee, M.-Y., et al.: Measurement and estimation of muscle contraction strength using mechanomyography based on artificial neural network algorithm. Biomed. Eng. Appl. Basis Commun. **25**, 1350020 (2013)

18. Matheson, G.O., Maffey-Ward, L., Mooney, M., et al.: Vibromyography as a quantitative measure of muscle force production. Scand. J. Rehabil. Med. **29**, 29–35 (1997)

19. Mobasser, F., Hashtrudi-Zaad, K.: A comparative approach to hand force estimation using artificial neural networks. Biomed. Eng. Comput. Biol. **4**, BECB (2012). S9335
20. Nogueira-Neto, G., Scheeren, E., Krueger, E., et al.: The influence of window length analysis on the time and frequency domain of mechanomyographic and electromyographic signals of submaximal fatiguing contractions. Open J. Biophys. **3**(3), 178–190 (2013)
21. Orizio, C.: Muscle sound: bases for the introduction of a mechanomyographic signal in muscle studies. Crit. Rev. Biomed. Eng. **21**, 201–243 (1993)
22. Posatskiy, A.O., Chau, T.: The effects of motion artifact on mechanomyography: a comparative study of microphones and accelerometers. J. Electromyogr. Kinesiol. **22**, 320–324 (2012)
23. Richman, J.S., Moorman, J.R.: Physiological time-series analysis using approximate entropy and sample entropy. Am. J. Physiol. Heart Circ. Physiol. **278**, H2039–H2049 (2000)
24. Smith, T.G., Stokes, M.J.: Technical aspects of acoustic myography (AMG) of human skeletal muscle: contact pressure and force/AMG relationships. J. Neurosci. Methods **47**, 85–92 (1993)
25. Staudenmann, D., Roeleveld, K., Stegeman, D.F., et al.: Methodological aspects of SEMG recordings for force estimation – a tutorial and review. J. Electromyogr. Kinesiol. **20**, 375–387 (2010)
26. Teague, C.N., Hersek, S., Toreyin, H., et al.: Novel methods for sensing acoustical emissions from the knee for wearable joint health assessment. IEEE Trans. Biomed. Eng. **63**, 1581–1590 (2016)
27. Wang, D., Wu, H., Xie, C., et al.: Suppression of motion artifacts in multichannel mechanomyography using multivariate empirical mode decomposition. IEEE Sens. J. **19**(14), 5732–5739 (2019)
28. Wu, H., Huang, Q., Wang, D., et al.: A CNN-SVM combined model for pattern recognition of knee motion using mechanomyography signals. J. Electromyogr. Kinesiol. **42**, 136–142 (2018)
29. Wu, H.F., Wang, D.Q., Huang, Q., et al.: Real-time continuous recognition of knee motion using multi-channel mechanomyography signals detected on clothes. J. Electromyogr. Kinesiol. **38**, 94–102 (2018)
30. Yokoyama, M., Koyama, R., Yanagisawa, M.: An evaluation of hand-force prediction using artificial neural-network regression models of surface EMG signals for handwear devices. J. Sens. **2017**, 1–12 (2017)
31. Youn, W., Kim, J.: Feasibility of using an artificial neural network model to estimate the elbow flexion force from mechanomyography. J. Neurosci. Methods **194**, 386–393 (2011)

# Angular Velocity Estimation of Knee Joint Based on MMG Signals

Chenlei Xie[1,2,3(✉)] ⓘ, Daqing Wang[1,2] ⓘ, Haifeng Wu[4] ⓘ,
and Lifu Gao[1] ⓘ

[1] Institute of Intelligent Machines,
Chinese Academy of Sciences, Hefei 230031, China
xiecl@mail.ustc.edu.cn
[2] University of Science and Technology of China, Hefei 230026, China
[3] Anhui Province Key Laboratory of Intelligent Building and Building Energy
Saving, Anhui Jianzhu University, Hefei 230022, China
[4] High Magnetic Field Laboratory, Chinese Academy of Sciences,
Hefei 230031, China

**Abstract.** Surface Electromyography (sEMG) signal is widely used as a control signal source for wearable power-assisted robots or prostheses. Most sEMG measurement electrodes need to be placed on the skin surface, and the skin should be treated accordingly, which makes the placement of acquisition equipment not convenient enough. To solve the above problems, we use multi-channel human Mechanomyography (MMG) signals to obtain human knee joint motion information, and select SENTOP angle sensor to obtain knee joint angle and angular velocity information. SVM regression model based on MMG signals for estimating knee joint angular velocity is built. In this paper, the root mean square (RMS), mean absolute value (MAV), mean power frequency (MPF), Sample entropy (SampEn) and Spearman's correlation coefficients (SCC) of MMG signal are extracted as input of SVM regression model. Then, the prediction accuracy of SVM regression model used different features are compared. The experimental result shows that the coefficient of determination ($R^2$) of SVM regression model reaches $0.81 \pm 0.02$ when all the above features are selected as input. This paper provides a method for further obtaining torque for motion control of wearable power-assisted robots with lower limbs.

**Keywords:** MMG · SVM · Angular velocity estimation · Knee joint

## 1 Introduction

At present, more and more scholars at home and abroad use wearable robotics technology to develop wearable power-assisted robots or prosthetic limbs in the fields of helping the elderly and rehabilitation training, and provide sports assistance and rehabilitation training for disabled people or the elderly whose limbs are weakened [25], so as to improve their self-care ability and quality of life. One of the key problems is how to realize the coordinated motion between human and robot. To be exact, how does the robot perception system acquire the human motion information as a control

© Springer Nature Switzerland AG 2019
H. Yu et al. (Eds.): ICIRA 2019, LNAI 11741, pp. 15–25, 2019.
https://doi.org/10.1007/978-3-030-27532-7_2

signal source. through analysis and recognition to get the human motion intention, real-time follow and timely help are carried out for the wearer's human motion. One of the hotspots in this field is how to make robot perception system acquire effective human motion information features and control the prosthesis of wearing power-assisted robots [23].

Surface Electromyography (sEMG) signal is widely used as control signal source for wearable force robots or prostheses [17]. The feature of sEMG signals was extracted using time series analysis technology to control prosthetic hand [2]. John et al. [6] used the Sample entropy (SampEn) and zero-crossing rate (ZCR) as time-domain features to control the robot arm. Roman-Liu et al. [16] analyzed the relationship between MDF, average power and muscle contraction from the point of view of power spectrum characteristics. With the increase of muscle contraction intensity, the change of frequency domain characteristics became more intense. Nadeau et al. [12] found that there was an inverse relationship between the power spectrum of sEMG signal and muscle strength level with the increase of muscle contraction force level. In features extraction of sEMG signal, Khezri et al. [7] extracted features using Wigner-Ville distribution method then recognized six movements of hand, and the recognition accuracy reached 91.3%.

However, due to the non-stationarity, weakness, randomness, susceptibility to interference and non-invasiveness of sEMG [5], it is difficult to extract the features of sEMG effectively. Meanwhile, most electrodes for EMG measurement need to be placed on the skin surface, and the skin should be treated accordingly when collecting, which makes the placement of the acquisition equipment not convenient enough [19].

Researchers attempted to use Mechanomyography (MMG) signals [11] as signal sources to control wearable force robots or prostheses [13]. MMG signals record the transverse vibration of muscle during active contraction, which reflects the mechanical characteristics of muscle during movement [20]. Meanwhile, the MMG signal acquisition system has the characteristics of low cost and good anti-interference. More importantly, MMG signal is insensitive to the placement of sensors because of their mechanical vibration characteristics [14]. In addition, when collecting MMG signals, the sensor does not need to contact the skin surface directly, but can still be effectively collected across the clothing, so MMG signal is not affected by the sweat on the skin surface and the impedance changes caused by temperature [10], especially suitable for applications in wearable equipment and other fields.

Barry et al. [1] compared MMG with sEMG and found that the former had more advantages. They proposed that MMG could be used for prosthetic limb control, and made an attempt to prove that the proposed method was feasible. Silva et al. [18] studied the control of bionic prosthesis based on MMG, and built two simple linear classifiers using the root mean square value of MMG signals. Finally, the accuracy rate of opening and closing the prosthetic hand was about 70%. Youn et al. [24] used a neural network model to verify the feasibility of using MMG signals to estimate the muscle strength of the upper limb elbow joint. Kim et al. [8] developed a simple wearable sensor system based on the static optimization method of inverse dynamics, which immediately converted the motion information into muscle force and estimated the muscle strength of the 9 groups of lower limb muscles. Kosaki et al. [9] used a simplified muscle force model, combined with the MMG signals of the biceps and triceps, and proposed an elbow joint torque estimation model. The accuracy of the joint torque estimation model was analyzed through experiments, and compared with torque evaluation model based on the sEMG signals. Dzulkifli et al. [4] designed and deployed a torque monitoring system based on RMS and RMS-ZC of the MMG signals of the quadriceps muscle, which used an artificial neural network model to estimate the knee joint torque in real time to account for the inability to independently quantify muscle torque. It was found that the average correlation coefficients (R) between predicted and actual output torque of knee joint elongation were 0.87 + 0.11 for RMS and 0.84 + 0.13 for RMS-ZC. The average accuracy was 79 ± 14% for RMS and 86 ± 11% for RMS-ZC.

Therefore, this paper proposes a Support Vector Machine (SVM) regression model, which uses multi-channel human MMG signals to estimate angular velocity of knee joint motion. The three-channel MMG signals are detected on the clothes of the thigh muscle, and are input the SVM regression model in the form of a time-series signal for angular velocity estimation. We estimate the knee joint angular velocity which can further obtaining knee joint torque for the lower extremity wearable power-assisted robot motion control.

## 2  SVM Regression Model

SVM based on statistical learning theory is a learning machine based on VC dimension theory and structural risk minimization principle. SVM shows unique advantages in solving small sample, nonlinear and high-dimensional pattern recognition and problems, especially the generalization ability is better than the traditional classification methods, which makes SVM widely used since its introduction.

SVM training is equivalent to solving a quadratic programming problem with linear constraints, which maximizes the distance between the two hyperplanes of the two types of mode points in the separation feature space and ensures that the obtained solution is global optimal. For nonlinear separable samples, the input vector is mapped to a high-dimensional space via a nonlinear transformation, making it linearly separable, finding an optimal hyperplane in the transformed space, and then performing linear classification. The difference of regression SVM is to find an optimal hyperplane to minimize the total deviation between all samples and the hyperplane.

For linear regression problem, N training samples $(x_i, y_i)$ are input, where i = 1, 2, ..., N, feature vector $x_i \in R_n$, output target $y_i \in R$, the optimal hyperplane can be expressed as:

$$f(x) = w^T x + b = 0 \tag{1}$$

Where $\omega$ represents the normal vector of the hyperplane and b is the displacement term representing the distance of the hyperplane spatial position. To solve for $\omega$ and b, the slack variables $\xi$, $\xi^*$, the insensitive parameter $\varepsilon$ and the penalty variable C are introduced to establish the objective function.

$$\begin{cases} \min \ \phi(w, \xi, \xi^*) = \frac{1}{2} w^T w + C \sum_{i=1}^{N} (\xi_i + \xi_i^*) \\ s.t. \quad y_i - w^T x_i - b \le \varepsilon + \xi_i, \\ \qquad w^T x_i + b - y_i \le \varepsilon + \xi_i^*, \\ \qquad \xi_i, \xi_i^* \ge 0, \ \varepsilon, C > 0, \ i = 1, 2, \cdots, N \end{cases} \tag{2}$$

In order to solve the above optimization problem, a Lagrangian function L (3) is introduced.

$$L = \phi(w, \xi, \xi^*) - \sum_{i=1}^{N} \alpha_i (\varepsilon + \xi_i - y_i + w^T x_i + b)$$

$$- \sum_{i=1}^{N} \alpha_i^* (\varepsilon + \xi_i^* + y_i - w^T x_i - b) - \sum_{i=1}^{N} (\gamma_i \xi_i + \gamma_i^* \xi_i^*) \tag{3}$$

Where $\alpha_i$, $\alpha_i^*$, $\gamma_i$ and $\gamma_i^*$ are Lagrange multipliers. According to the necessary conditions for the existence of extremum, the extreme value of the function L (3) should satisfy the condition:

$$\begin{cases} \frac{\partial L}{\partial w} = 0 \Rightarrow w = \sum_{i=1}^{N} (\alpha_i - \alpha_i^*) x_i \\ \frac{\partial L}{\partial b} = 0 \Rightarrow w = \sum_{i=1}^{N} (\alpha_i - \alpha_i^*) = 0 \\ \frac{\partial L}{\partial \xi} = 0 \Rightarrow C = \alpha_i + \gamma_i \\ \frac{\partial L}{\partial \xi^*} = 0 \Rightarrow C = \alpha_i^* + \gamma_i^* \end{cases} \tag{4}$$

Solve Eq. (4) and substitute (3) to solve the quadratic programming problem, as follows:

$$\begin{cases} \max_{\alpha, \alpha^*} \sum_{i=1}^{N} y_i (\alpha_i - \alpha_i^*) - \varepsilon \sum_{i=1}^{N} (\alpha_i + \alpha_i^*) \\ \qquad - \frac{1}{2} \sum_{i=1}^{N} \sum_{j=1}^{N} (\alpha_i - \alpha_i^*)(\alpha_j - \alpha_j^*) K(x_i, x_j) \\ s.t. \quad \sum_{i=1}^{N} (\alpha_i - \alpha_i^*) = 0, \\ \qquad 0 \le \alpha_i, \alpha_i^* \le C, i = 1, 2, \cdots, N \end{cases} \tag{5}$$

Where $k(x_i, y_i)$ is called a kernel function, such as linear kernel function (LINEAR), polynomial kernel function (POLY), radial basis function (RBF), and precomputed kernel, etc. It maps vectors from low-dimensional space to high-dimensional space for solving nonlinear regression problems. The regression function is expressed as:

$$y = f(x) = \sum_{i=1}^{N} (\alpha_i - \alpha_i^*) K(x_i, x) + b \tag{6}$$

The kernel function used in (6) is the RBF. Because the RBF kernel function has good properties, it shows good performance in practical problems. Its expression is:

$$K(x_i, x_j) = \exp(-\gamma \, ||x_i - x_j||^2) \tag{7}$$

Where $\gamma$ is the kernel parameter and represents the width of the radial range of the control function.

## 3   Experiment and Signal Preprocessing

Figure 1 shows the implementation process of SVM regression model. The original MMG signals of three channels are filtered and features are extracted by sliding window in the training stage. The features normalized build the training samples. The normalized training samples are input into SVM regression model for training. The test samples which are filtered, features extracted, normalized are input into the trained SVM regression model for regression testing in the test stage.

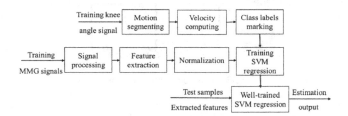

**Fig. 1.** Implementation process of SVM regression model

### 3.1   Data Acquisition and Preprocessing

In order to facilitate sensor placement and signal detection, the superficial muscles which play major role in the corresponding movements are selected according to human motion anatomy for MMG detection. Meanwhile, considering control the muscles of knee flexion and extension into consideration, we select rectus femoris, biceps femoris and semitendinosus from the thigh, as shown in Fig. 2.

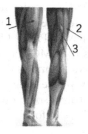

**Fig. 2.** Muscle distribution map: 1 - Rectus femoris, 2 - Biceps femoris, 3 - Semitendinosus

We use the capacitive 3-axis acceleration sensor of ADI company (Model ADXL335, Measuring range: ±3 g, Sensitivity: 300 mV/g) to make MMG sensor. The sensor weighs 2.89 g and has a bandwidth of 50 Hz. Z-axis of the sensor is placed perpendicular muscle surface to measure MMG. Three MMG sensors are placed on the selected muscles and wrapped in the kneepad-like strap. MMG sensor position can be selected in the corresponding muscle area, but should be located in the center of the muscle surface as far as possible. In addition, in order to measure the actual motion angle of the knee joint for further calculate of angular velocity, the angle sensor of SENTOP (Model: WDD35D4-5k) is installed on a joint fixing brace, which is bound to the leg for following rotation. The angular velocity is calculated according to change of angle data in the isokinetic motion knee flexion and extension, which labels velocity category label conveniently. The signal and power line of the MMG sensors and angle sensor are connected to a portable USB collector (Model NI USB-6215, Sampling rate: 500 Hz). The data is collected and stored by interface program of LabVIEW on the computer, as shown in Fig. 3.

**Fig. 3.** Data collection system

Signal flow is continuously read by moving window method for reducing the influence of transient and stochastic characteristics of MMG signals. According to the previous study [22], we choice the 1000 ms (sampling rate 500 Hz, 500 samples) moving window and 250 ms (125 samples) increment. The environmental noise and human motion trajectory are filtered by the 4rd order Butterworth bandpass filter of 5–100 Hz.

## 3.2 Feature Extraction

In order to construct a faster, less expensive prediction model while reducing feature calculation time, the experiment only extracts time domain and frequency domain features from the moving window of each feature. In this paper, root mean square (RMS) and mean absolute value (MAV) of the time domain characteristics of the MMG signals during muscle contraction are selected.

In this paper, mean power frequency (MPF) of MMG signals is used to characterize the frequency domain characteristics of MMG. In addition, as the muscle contraction intensity increases, the number of recruited motion units increases. The MMG signal is generated by the contraction activity of the thousands of motion units, so the components contained in the MMG signal are also gradually increasing. In other words, the complexity of the signal has changed. Therefore, we select SampEn [15] as a feature to measure the complexity of MMG signal.

In practical applications, the acquisition of MMG signals is based on multi-channel data acquisition method, and the amplitude of MMG signals is constantly changing during muscle activity. Therefore, the same components of signals obtained by MMG sensors at different locations are also changing correspondingly, which leads to the change of interference between channels. Therefore, we also select the Spearman's correlation coefficients (SCC) of sample sequence as another feature to measure the interference between MMG signals, as shown in the following formula.

$$\rho_s = \frac{\sum_{i=1}^{N}(rx_i - \overline{rx})(ry_i - \overline{ry})}{\sqrt{\sum_{i=1}^{N}(rx_i - \overline{rx})^2 \sum_{i=1}^{N}(ry_i - \overline{ry})^2}} \tag{8}$$

Where $rx_i$ and $ry_i$ are the ranks of the ith data in the two sequences; $\overline{rx}$ and $\overline{ry}$ are the average ranks of the two sequences.

Meanwhile, the MMG signals are respectively normalized by using the mean and standard before inputting model to eliminate impact of the value range or uniform magnitude of different features.

### 3.3 Experimental Protocol

In this experiment, we attempt to continuously estimate the right knee joint angular velocity when the right knee joint is in the isokinetic motion knee flexion and extension. The experimental method and data is referenced to the experiment in the [21] literature. The experimental participants are 5 healthy young people (aged between 24–36 years old). They fully understand the content of the experiment and agree to participate in the experiment. In the standing position, participants are required to continuously perform a 0–90° angular flexion and extension of the knee joint at least 10 repetitions, each time resting completely, as shown in Fig. 4.

**Fig. 4.** Knee joint motion diagram

More than 700 sets of valid data which include angular velocity and features of MMG signals can be get form each participant. Accuracy of model is tested by 3-fold cross-validation method. The data sets are divided into three equal parts which two of them are used for training and the rest is used for test.

In this paper, the SVM regression model is built by calling LIBSVM 3.22 software [3] in the MATLAB. In this model, C-support vector classification method (c-svc, C is the penalty factor) is applied, and the Gauss radial basis function is adopted as the kernel function. Meanwhile, the optimal kernel parameter $\gamma$ and penalty factor C are ensured by 3-fold cross-validation and grid search.

The estimated accuracy of the angular velocity of knee joint is evaluated by root mean square error (RMSE) and coefficient of determination ($R^2$) which are statistics results based on test sets. The principle of judging the accuracy of the model is that RMSE is smaller and $R^2$ is larger. The mathematical formulas of RMSE and $R^2$ are as follows:

$$RMSE = \sqrt{\frac{1}{N}\sum_{i=1}^{N}(\hat{y}_i - y_i)^2} \tag{9}$$

$$R^2 = \frac{SSR}{SST} = \frac{\sum_{i=1}^{n}(\hat{y}_i - \bar{y})^2}{\sum_{i=1}^{n}(y_i - \bar{y})^2} \tag{10}$$

# 4    Experimental Results and Discussion

The average of $R^2$ and RMSE of 3-fold cross-validation results is used as estimated accuracy of the SVM regression model based on different kind feature subsets for each participant. The experimental results are the average of $R^2$ and RMSE of all participants. Figure 5 shows mean and STD of $R^2$ of the SVM regression model based on different kind feature subsets. We observed that $R^2$ reaches $0.44 \pm 0.07$ used the RMS. $R^2$ reaches $0.33 \pm 0.1$ used the MAV. $R^2$ reaches $0.59 \pm 0.03$ used the MPF. $R^2$ reaches the lowest level ($0.22 \pm 0.05$) used the SampEn. $R^2$ reaches $0.3 \pm 0.03$ used the SCC. $R^2$ reaches $0.74 \pm 0.02$ used the RMS and MPF. $R^2$ reaches $0.75 \pm 0.03$ used the MAV and MPF. $R^2$ reaches $0.79 \pm 0.01$ used the MAV, MPF and SampEn. $R^2$ reaches $0.78 \pm 0.02$ used the MAV, MPF and SampEn. $R^2$ reaches the highest level ($0.81 \pm 0.02$) used the RMS, MAV, MPF, SampEn and SCC. Figure 6 shows mean and STD of RMSE of the estimated angular velocity based on different kind feature subsets. The RMSE reaches lowest level ($0.35 \pm 0.02$) used the RMS, MAV, MPF, SampEn and SCC.

Figure 7 shows the estimated angular velocity of the SVM regression model used the feature subsets which include RMS, MAV, MPF, SampEn and SCC. The blue curve represents the true value measured by the angular velocity, and the red curve means the estimated angular velocity of the SVM regression model.

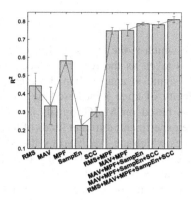

**Fig. 5.** Mean and STD of estimated R2 for all participants

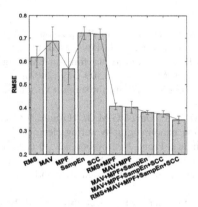

**Fig. 6.** Mean and STD of RMSE for all participants

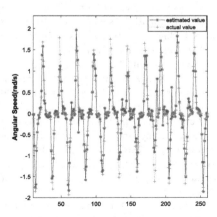

**Fig. 7.** Comparison of the true value and the estimated value of angular velocity (Color figure online)

# 5   Conclusion

In this paper, the knee joint which is the largest and most complex joint of the lower limbs of the human body is taken as the research object. The advantages of MMG signal compared to sEMG signal is analyzed in the theory. We explore a method estimating the angular velocity of knee joint based on multi-channel MMG signals. The SVM regression model based on MMG signals is built for estimating angular velocity of knee joint. In the experiment, different kinds of features are selected to build feature subset. The accuracies which are predicted by the SVM model using different feature subsets are compared. The experimental result shows that the accuracy is higher when the appropriate feature subset is selected as the input, which provides an idea for the application of joint torque estimation in the wearable field.

# References

1. Barry, D.T., Leonard, J.A., Gitter, A.J., Ball, R.D.: Acoustic myography as a control signal for an externally powered prosthesis. Arch. Phys. Med. Rehabil. **67**(4), 267–269 (1986)
2. Boostani, R., Moradi, M.H.: Evaluation of the forearm EMG signal features for the control of a prosthetic hand. Physiol. Meas. **24**(2), 309–319 (2003)
3. Chang, C.C., Lin, C.J.: LIBSVM: a library for support vector machines (2001). http://www.csie.ntu.edu.tw/scjlin/libsvm
4. Dzulkifli, M.A., Hamzaid, N.A., Davis, G.M.O., Hasnan, N.: Neural network-based muscle torque estimation using mechanomyography during electrically-evoked knee extension and standing in spinal cord injury. Front. Neurorobot. **12**, 50 (2018)
5. Ibitoye, M.O., Hamzaid, N.A., Zuniga, J.M., Wahab, A.K.A.: Mechanomyography and muscle function assessment: a review of current state and prospects. Clin. Biomech. **29**(6), 691–704 (2014)
6. John, A., Vijayan, A.E., Sudheer, A.P.: Electromyography based control of robotic arm using entropy and zero crossing rate. In: Proceedings of the 2015 Conference on Advances in Robotics – Air 2015, Goa, India, 02–04 July 2015, pp. 1–6. ACM Press (2015)
7. Khezri, M., Jahed, M.: An inventive quadratic time-frequency scheme based on Wigner-Ville distribution for classification of sEMG signals. In: 2007 6th International Special Topic Conference on Information Technology Applications in Biomedicine. IEEE (2007)
8. Kim, S., Ro, K., Bae, J.: Estimation of individual muscular forces of the lower limb during walking using a wearable sensor system. J. Sens. **2017** (2017)
9. Kosaki, T., Tochiki, A., Li, S., Kanazawa, R.: Torque estimation of elbow joint using a mechanomyogram signal based biomechanical model. In: 2018 12th France-Japan and 10th Europe-Asia Congress on Mechatronics, pp. 260–265. IEEE (2018)
10. Lei, K.F., Cheng, S.C., Lee, M.Y., Lin, W.Y.: Measurement and estimation of muscle contraction strength using mechanomyography based on artificial neural network algorithm. Biomed. Eng. Appl. Basis Commun. **25**(02), 1350020 (2013)
11. Na, Y., Choi, C., Lee, H.D., Kim, J.: A study on estimation of joint force through isometric index finger abduction with the help of SEMG peaks for biomedical applications. IEEE Trans. Cybern. **46**(1), 2–8 (2016)
12. Nadeau, S., Bilodeau, M., Delisle, A.: The influence of the type of contraction on the masseter muscle EMG power spectrum. J. Electromyogr. Kinesiol. **3**(4), 205–213 (1993)

13. Park, J., Kim, S.J., Na, Y., Kim, J.: Custom optoelectronic force sensor based ground reaction force (GRF) measurement system for providing absolute force. In: 2016 13th International Conference on Ubiquitous Robots and Ambient Intelligence (URAI), pp. 75–77. IEEE (2016)
14. Plewa, K., Samadani, A., Orlandi, S., Chau, T.: A novel approach to automatically quantify the level of coincident activity between EMG and MMG signals. J. Electromyogr. Kinesiol. **41**, 34–40 (2018)
15. Richman, J.S., Lake, D.E., Moorman, J.R.: Sample entropy. In: Methods in Enzymology, vol. 384, pp. 172–184. Academic Press (2004)
16. Roman-Liu, D.: The influence of confounding factors on the relationship between muscle contraction level and MF and MPF values of EMG signal: a review. Int. J. Occup. Saf. Ergon. **22**(1), 77–91 (2016)
17. Sensinger, J.W., Schultz, A.E., Kuiken, T.A.: Examination of force discrimination in human upper limb amputees with reinnervated limb sensation following peripheral nerve transfer. IEEE Trans. Neural Syst. Rehabil. Eng. **17**(5), 438–444 (2009)
18. Silva, J., Heim, W., Chau, T.: MMG-based classification of muscle activity for prosthesis control. In: The 26th Annual International Conference of the IEEE Engineering in Medicine and Biology Society, vol. 1, pp. 968–971. IEEE (2004)
19. Takei, Y., Yoshida, M., Takeshita, T., Kobayashi, T.: Wearable muscle training and monitoring device. In: 2018 IEEE Micro Electro Mechanical Systems (MEMS), pp. 55–58. IEEE (2018)
20. Talib, I., Sundaraj, K., Lam, C.K.: Choice of mechanomyography sensors for diverse types of muscle activities. J. Telecommun. Electron. Comput. Eng. (JTEC) **10**(1–13), 79–82 (2018)
21. Wu, H., Wang, D., Huang, Q., Gao, L.: Real-time continuous recognition of knee motion using multi-channel mechanomyography signals detected on clothes. J. Electromyogr. Kinesiol. **38**, 94–102 (2018)
22. Wu, H., Huang, Q., Wang, D., Gao, L.: A CNN-SVM combined model for pattern recognition of knee motion using mechanomyography signals. J. Electromyogr. Kinesiol. **42**, 136–142 (2018)
23. Xie, Q.R., Jiang, Z., Luo, Q.L.: Relationship of root mean square value of electromyography and isometric torque of quadriceps in normal subjects. Rehabil. Med. **26**(3), 25–28 (2016)
24. Youn, W., Kim, J.: Feasibility of using an artificial neural network model to estimate the elbow flexion force from mechanomyography. J. Neurosci. Methods **194**(2), 386–393 (2011)
25. Yu, Y.P.: The research of motion pattern recognition and joint moment analysis of human lower limb based on sEMG. Master's thesis, Soochow University (2016)

# Fingertip Pulse Wave Detection and Analysis Based on PVDF Piezoelectric Thin Film Sensor

Dun Hu[1,2] , Na Zhou[3], Daqing Wang[1,2] ,
Chenlei Xie[1,2,4] , and Lifu Gao[2(✉)]

[1] Institute of Intelligent Machines, Chinese Academy of Sciences,
Hefei 230031, China
[2] University of Science and Technology of China, Hefei 230026, China
lifugao@iim.ac.cn
[3] The Fourth Affiliated Hospital of Auhui Medical University,
Hefei 230000, China
[4] Anhui Jianzhu University, Hefei 230041, China

**Abstract.** The pulse wave contains very rich cardiovascular physiological and pathological information, its waveform amplitude and shape can reflect the physiological and pathological state of human cardiovascular system such as heart rate and blood pressure. Monitoring of pulse wave has important clinical diagnostic value in traditional Chinese medicine and modern medicine. However, the characteristics of weak pulse signal and vulnerable to interference make the extraction of useful fingertip pulse signals a difficult task. Here we propose a type of sensor based on polyvinylidene fluoride (PVDF) piezoelectric thin film that can collect fingertip pulse signal; By zero-phase filtering and denoising, the baseline wander and interference in fingertip pulse signal can be successfully eliminated; In order to verify the validity, practicality of the fingertip pulse signal, the pulse signal with the fingertip is compared with those obtained with the wrist artery, and the characteristics of these two pulse signals are finally further analyzed in time domain and frequency domain. It is shown that the proposed piezoelectric film sensor can effectively detect the pulse fingertip signal. It is also shown the fingertip pulse signal amplitude is smaller than those obtained with the radial artery, but the measured pulse number in unit time with the fingertip is consistent with the radial artery measured result. From the analysis in frequency domain, the pulse fingertip signal focus on the low frequency component, and contains the main physiological information of human body, it is also more convenient access than the radial artery signal.

**Keywords:** Fingertip pulse · PVDF · Cardiovascular · Signal processing · Sensor

## 1 Introduction

The human body pulse system is an important part of the cardiovascular system [1], which can transport nutrients, transmit energy and spread various physiological and pathological information for the human body. Pulse information has important clinical diagnostic value in traditional Chinese medicine (TCM) and modern medicine

© Springer Nature Switzerland AG 2019
H. Yu et al. (Eds.): ICIRA 2019, LNAI 11741, pp. 26–36, 2019.
https://doi.org/10.1007/978-3-030-27532-7_3

(Western medicine). Any viscera (system) in the human body has lesions or is attacked by the outside world, This inevitably changes the vascular properties, function, and blood quality [2], and these changes would appear in the pulse with certain characteristics. Therefore, doing deep research on human pulse information has very important application value.

The pulse is mainly caused by the rhythmic contraction and relaxation of the heart, which continuously squeezes blood into the peripheral blood vessels, causing the blood vessels to continuously expand and retract [3]. The aorta is thus constantly expanding and retracting with the periodic contraction and relaxation of the heart, causing the pulsation of blood vessels, and this pulsation is can be touched in the superficial artery (such as the grid artery, carotid artery, radial artery, etc.). The pulse signal at the superficial artery can be obtained by various sensors, and the pulse wave is a manifestation of the pulse signal.

There are two main arteries at the wrist, the ulnar artery and the radial artery. They branch down on the elbow and reach the wrist on the left and right sides of the forearm. Where the ulnar artery is buried deep, it is not easy to touch, but the radial artery is buried shallow in the wrist, it is easy to touch, and consequently used for consultation. More importantly, the two arteries are not independent of each other, but meet at the palm of the hand and form a loop, like a curved part of a paper clip, from here to the artery of the finger [16–18], as shown in Fig. 1.

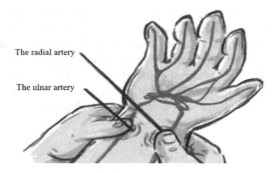

The radial artery

The ulnar artery

**Fig. 1.** The sketch map of the artery of the finger.

In Traditional Chinese Medicine (TCM), TCM practitioners put their three fingers of middle, index and ring fingers on the terminal region of the radial artery to feel the nuances of pulse wave characteristics, which is used to judge the health condition of patients [4, 5]. However, the pulse diagnosis is very difficult to master because of the subjectivity and the strong dependence on experience [6].

With the development of science and technology, the objectification and quantification of pulse diagnosis has become an inevitable trend of diagnosis. In the past decade, a wide variety of sensors have been studied to achieve pulse signal detection. There are two main measurement methods:

1. Pressure detection method: the waveform of sensor pressure F with time is approximated as the waveform of the arterial pressure with time, and the ideal pulse wave waveform can be obtained by subsequent signal processing [7, 15]. Generally, the radial artery at the wrist is a lot more selected as a measuring point.
2. Photoelectric volume pulse wave tracing (PPG): When light is irradiated onto human tissue, the absorption of light by muscles and bones is constant, and the rhythmic beat of blood vessels causes the expansion and contraction of blood vessels, causing the internal blood volume to change periodically. The amount of light absorbed by the blood changes, causing the received light intensity to change periodically, that is, the change in light intensity reflects the change in blood vessel volume. The PPG signal can be obtained by collecting the attenuated light by a photo-detector and converting it into an electrical signal [8]. Generally choose the index finger or middle finger as the test point.

At present, the most common pulse monitoring sensors collect the pulse signal of the radial artery at the wrist. Although the signal amplitude is large, it is necessary to find exactly the radial artery, which would cause inconvenience to the measurement. Besides, the finger-clip photoelectric pulse sensor, which acquires the photoplethys-mogram (PPG) of the blood flow at the fingertip It indirectly measures the pulse signal, and needs to clamp the fingertip to bring a certain degree of discomfort to the monitored person. The obtained pulse wave characteristic point is not obvious and the amplitude is small [9].

PVDF is a piezoelectric material having a solid structure with approximately 50%–65% crystallinity. The morphology consists of crystallites dispersed with amorphous regions [10, 11]. The atoms are covalently bonded, forming long molecular chains. Since the hydrogen atoms are positively and the fluoride atoms negatively charged with respect to the carbon atoms, PVDF is inherently polar. If an external force compresses the film, the dipole orientation is changed and an electrical signal is induced on the electrodes, see Fig. 2. In Fig. 2, a typical charge distribution of the PVDF material is shown.

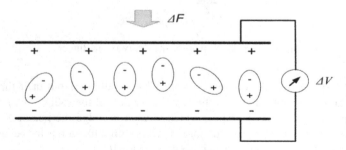

**Fig. 2.** Simplified model structure and typical charge distribution of PVDF material.

Considering that polyvinylidene fluoride (PVDF) piezoelectric film has character-istics of wide frequency response range, soft material, strong anti-interference and easy to use, which is very suitable for doing the monitoring of human physiological signals [10, 11].

Due to the influence of the instrument and the human body, the collected signals are often accompanied by various noises and interference, and the pulse wave signals need to be further processed to extract feature points. In this article a method is proposed for the detection and analysis of the fingertip pulse wave. The fingertip pulse signals were measured by this designed PVDF piezoelectric thin film sensor. After preprocessing the collected signals, the preprocessed signals were further analyzed to realize the features of the fingertip pulse signal in time domain and frequency domain, the proposed method can be applicable to the detection and analysis of the fingertip pulse signal in human body.

## 2   Design and Methods

### 2.1   Configuration of PVDF Film Pulse Wave Sensor

The whole measurement system consists of three following parts. (1) PVDF film pulse sensor. (2) Charge transfer and Amplifier. (3) signal collection. As the human body's itself signal is weak, the charge output of the PVDF sensor needs to be converted into a voltage signal, which can be collected and analyzed after being amplified. The schematic diagram of the system is shown in Fig. 3.

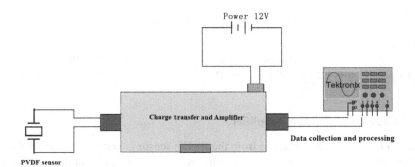

**Fig. 3.** The schematic diagram of the measurement system.

### 2.2   PVDF Film Pulse Sensor

PVDF is a piezoelectric material having a solid structure with approximately 50-65% crystallites. The morphology consists of crystallites dispersed with amorphous regions. The atoms are covalently bonded, forming long molecular chains [9]. If an external force compresses the PVDF film, the dipole orientation is changed and an electrical signal is induced on the electrodes.

In this paper, MEAS's SDT1-028K film is used to collect pulse signals. SDT1-028 piezo film sensor consist of a rectangular element of piezo film together with a molded plastic housing and 18″ of coaxial cable. The film element, screen printed with silver ink, is folded over on itself, given a self-shielding of the transducer area. This is

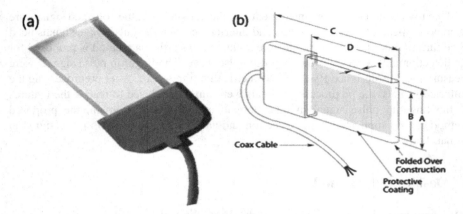

**Fig. 4.** The physical map and simplified model structure of SDT1-028 piezo film sensor: (a) the physical map, (b) the simplified model structure.

important in applications in high EMI environments. Figure 4 shows the physical map and simplified model structure of SDT1-028 piezo film sensors. The SDT1-028K parameters are given in Table 1.

**Table 1.** The parameters of the SDT1-028K.

| DIMENSIONS in INCHES (mm) | | | | | | | |
|---|---|---|---|---|---|---|---|
| Description | A Film | B Electrode | C Film | D Electrode | t (μm) | Cap (nF) | Part number |
| SDT1-028K | .640 (16) | .520 (13) | 1.64 (41) | 1.18 (30) | 75 | 2.78 | 1-1000288-0 |

## 2.3    Charge Transfer and Amplifier

The amount of charge are obtained from the PVDF sensor is very weak and needs to be amplified by a charge amplifier. We employ in the charge amplifier (ICA102c, Vkinging). The ICA102c is a high precision charge amplifier. This product adopts high-precision charge conversion unit, low noise amplification unit, the optimized power supply with low noise power, etc., which makes the product have the advantages of high precision, ultra-low noise, high suppression ratio, wide measurement range and low temperature drift, apply to various occasions of measurement.

The charge amplifier is provided by a charge conversion stage and a voltage amplification stage. The ICA102c charge amplifier module includes a low noise, high input impedance charge conversion circuit and a variable gain precision output amplifier circuit. Figure 5 shows the physical map and the circuit construction of ICA102c charge amplifier.

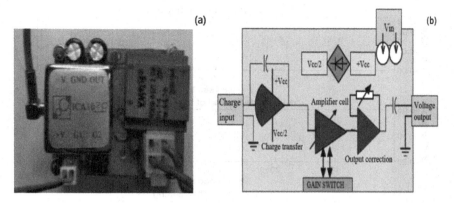

**Fig. 5.** The physical map and the circuit construction of ICA102c charge amplifier: (a) the physical map, (b) circuit construction.

## 2.4  Signal Collection

The amount of voltage from the charge amplifier is an analog signal and needs to be converted into a digital value, and can be stored and processed by the computer. We implemented the signal collection board (VK-701, Vkinging). VK-701 is a signal collection board with 24-bit A/D. It transformed analog pulse signal to digital signal with a maximum sampling frequency (400 KHz). The digital signal obtained from VK-701 are sent to the computer for storage and further processed by MATLAB software.

## 2.5  Data Processing

Because the human body's own signal is weak, and the pulse signal is easily affected by noise such as limb movement, mental stress and power frequency interference [12]. These disturbances make signal analysis difficult and prone to errors. Therefore, signal pre-processing should be performed before feature extraction. The pulse frequency range is within 0–20 Hz, whose spectrum is mainly distributed at 0–10 Hz. The baseline drift is caused by human breathing and electrode movement. The frequency is between 0.05 Hz and 2 Hz. Myoelectric interference is caused by human muscle vibration. As a result, its frequency range is generally between 5 Hz–2 kHz [12–16]. Myoelectric interference, power frequency and multiplier interference, and baseline drift below 0.7 Hz are the main interference sources for body surface pulse signals [13–18]. They are all low frequency interference, so the preprocessing of the pulse signal is actually the filtering of low frequency noise signal [19, 20].

In this study, The zero-phase filtering method is used to remove the baseline drift in the signal, and then the interference signal is filtered by the Butterworth bandpass filter (Wp = [0.4 20]; Ws = [0.1 30]). The wave changes after different signal processing are showed in the Figs. 6 and 7.

In the experiment, in order to collect conveniently, the pulse signals are taken from the left hand. The sampling frequency is 200 Hz, and the data is continuously collected for 60 s. The pulse wave of radial artery and fingertip are collected respectively (see Figs. 6(a), 7(a)).

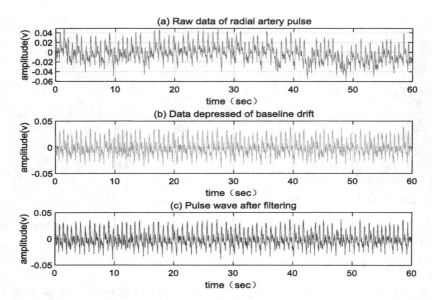

**Fig. 6.** Sample radial artery pulse data processing and measurements for 1-min of data collection at 200 Hz. (a) Raw voltage output from PVDF sensor; (b) Data depressed of baseline drift; (c) Pulse wave after filtering.

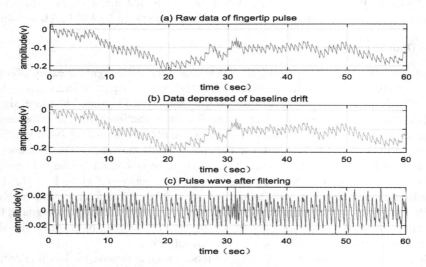

**Fig. 7.** Sample fingertip pulse data processing and measurements for 1-min of data collection at 200 Hz. (a) Raw voltage output from PVDF sensor; (b) Data depressed of baseline drift; (c) Pulse wave after filtering.

From the view of time domain and frequency domain, we analyzed the characteristics of fingertip pulse wave after the baseline drift and filtering. The results are displayed in Figs. 6, 7, 8 and 9.

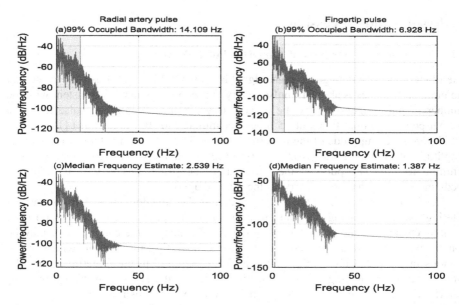

**Fig. 8.** The spectrogram of the radial artery pulse signal: (a) 99% Occupied Bandwidth: 14.1.9 Hz, (c) Median Frequency Estimate: 2.539 Hz. The spectrogram of the fingertip pulse signal: (b) 99% Occupied Bandwidth: 6.928 Hz, (d) Median Frequency Estimate: 1.387 Hz.

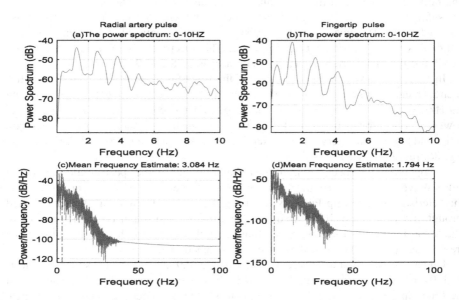

**Fig. 9.** The spectrogram of the radial artery pulse signal: (a) the frequency distribution between 0 and 10 Hz, (c) Mean Frequency Estimate: 3.084 Hz. The spectrogram of the fingertip pulse signal: (b) the frequency distribution between 0 and 10 Hz, (d) Mean Frequency Estimate: 1.794 Hz.

# 3  Results and Discussion

## 3.1  Time Domain Analysis of Fingertip Pulse Wave

The filtered data of the fingertip pulse signal is shown in Fig. 7(c). It is easy to see that the number of pulses is about 13 pulses every ten seconds, which is consistent with the number of pulses measured by the radial artery (78 times/min). The pulse rate of a normal person is equal to about 75 times per minute (60–100 times/min) [15].

The voltage amplitude of the fingertip is about 0.02 V, which is half of the voltage amplitude of the radial artery (0.04 V) (see Figs. 6(c), 7(c)). It is agreement with our intuitive feeling. The pulse at the radial artery is strong, that is why the Chinese medicine chooses the radial artery as the pulse diagnosis.

The fingertip pulse signal has a large change in the time domain waveform after the filtering, as shown in Fig. 7(b) and (c), but the radial artery waveform has no such obvious change, as shown in Fig. 6(b) and (c). To analyze the causes, there may be some kind of low frequency component in the fingertip pulse signal, which is not obvious in the radial artery, this signal is easily acquired in the fingertip pulse. The interference of measuring method and disturbance in the scene may also cause this difference, which is an interesting question that deserves further study.

## 3.2  Frequency Domain Analysis of Fingertip Pulse Wave

The information obtained from the time domain analysis of the fingertip pulse wave is not sufficient to determine the characteristics of fingertip pulse. The Fingertip pulse wave which holds numerous frequency signal is more analyzed in frequency domain compare with the radial artery pulse wave. The spectrograms of the fingertip pulse signal and the radial artery signal are shown in Figs. 8 and 9.

In Fig. 8(b) shows the spectrograph of the fingertip pulse signal. Clearly, the frequency band containing 99% of the signal power is concentrated between 0 and 6.9 Hz. As shown in Fig. 8(a), the radial artery band containing 99% of the signal power is concentrated between 0–14.1 Hz. The Median frequencies of the fingertip pulse and the radial artery pulse signal are 1.38 Hz (see Fig. 8d) and 2.53 Hz (see Fig. 8c) respectively.

Compared to the spectrogram of the radial artery pulse, the spectrogram of fingertip Pulse Wave is more concentrated in the lower frequencies, as shown in Fig. 8. The characteristics of fingertip Pulse Wave in the frequency domain can further reflected through the view the 0–10 Hz frequency distribution and Mean Frequency in Fig. 9. The Mean Frequency Estimate of the fingertip pulse and the radial artery pulse signal are 1.79 Hz (Fig. 9d) and 3.08 Hz (Fig. 9c) respectively.

Under normal circumstances, the heart rate is 0.9–2.5 Hz, and respiratory rate is 0.13–0.45 Hz. The noise signal is mostly high frequency signal [11]. It is shown that the fingertip pulse low frequency component is able to reflect the main physiological information of human body (heart rate and respiratory rate). Through spectrum analysis, the designed PVDF piezoelectric film sensor in this paper can effectively monitor the physiological signals of the human body by measuring the fingertip pulse.

# 4  Conclusion

PVDF piezoelectric film has been widely used because of its softness and convenience, and it has developed a sensor that can collect fingertip pulse based on PVDF piezoelectric film. The characteristics of the fingertip pulse signal are further analyzed by comparing the pulse signals collected by the radial artery. The time domain and frequency domain analysis of the fingertip pulse signal shows that the sensor can effectively collect the pulse signal of the human body. Compared to the pulse of the radial artery, the fingertip pulse signal amplitude is small, but the low frequency component is more concentrated. The physiological signals of the human body are mostly low frequency. The fingertip pulse signal contains the main human physiological signal information, but it is more convenient to obtain than other parts. Through the PVDF piezoelectric film sensor, the human physiological signal can be monitored for a long time without interference. The difference between the low-frequency component signal of the fingertip pulse and the radial artery pulse is worthy of further study. Improving the performance of PVDF piezoelectric sensors and reducing the impact of body shake and respiratory interference on the measurement is the key to achieving fingertip pulse measurement and needs to be optimized.

# References

1. Hu, C.-S., Chung, Y.-F., Yeh, C.-C., Luo, C.-H.: Temporal and spatial properties of arterial pulsation measurement using pressure sensor array. Evid. Based Complement. Altern. Med. **2012**, 9 (2012)
2. Lee, J.-Y., Jang, M., Shin, S.-H.: Study on the depth, rate, shape, and strength of pulse with cardiovascular simulator. Evid. Based Complement. Altern. Med. **2017**, 11 (2017)
3. Shen, Y.: Analysis of cardiovascular basic parameters based on brachial artery pulse wave. Northeastern University (2012)
4. Chu, Y.W., Luo, C.H., Chung, Y.F., et al.: Using an array sensor to determine differences in pulse diagnosis—three positions and nine indicators. Eur. J. Integr. Med. **6**(5), 516–523 (2014)
5. Wang, D., Zhang, D., Lu, G.: A robust signal preprocessing framework for wrist pulse analysis. Biomed. Signal Process. Control **23**, 62–75 (2016)
6. Liu, S., Hua, L., Lv, P., Yu, Y., Gao, Y., Sheng, X.: A pulse condition reproduction apparatus for remote traditional Chinese medicine. In: Chen, Z., Mendes, A., Yan, Y., Chen, S. (eds.) ICIRA 2018. LNCS (LNAI), vol. 10984, pp. 453–464. Springer, Cham (2018). https://doi.org/10.1007/978-3-319-97586-3_41
7. Ting, L., Gang, Y.: Development of a non-invasive pulse wave detection and analysis system. Biomed. Eng. J. **25**(5), 1059–1062 (2008)
8. Ding, X.Y., Chang, Q., Chao, S.: Study on the extract method of time domain characteristic parameters of pulse wave. In: IEEE International Conference on Signal and Image Processing (2017)
9. Xing, X., Sun, M.: Optical blood pressure estimation with photoplethysmography and FFT-based neural networks. Biomed. Opt. Express **7**(8), 3007–3020 (2016)
10. Li, Z.: Design and implementation of PVDF-based sleep monitoring system (2015)
11. Ma, Y., Wang, Y., Zhang, H., et al.: Real-time monitoring of heart rate respiration rate based on piezoelectric thin film sensor. Sens. Microsyst. **37**(316(06)), 124–126 (2018)

12. Liu, Q.: Research on sleepiness detection method based on ECG pulse signal. Lanzhou University of Technology (2012)
13. Han, Q.: Nonlinear analysis of pulse signal and its influence on different emotions and environment. Zhejiang University (2007)
14. Abulkhair, M.F., Salman, H.A., Ibrahim, L.F.: Using mobile platform to detect and alerts driver fatigue. Int. J. Comput. Appl. **123**(8), 27–35 (2015)
15. Wang, W., Xu, Y., Zeng, G., et al.: Extraction and dual domain analysis of pulse wave signals. Electron. Technol. Appl. (2019)
16. Sun, Y., Yu, X.: An innovative non-intrusive driver assistance system for vital signal monitoring. J. Biomed. Health Inf. **18**(6), 1932–1939 (2014)
17. Yao, C., Zhong, J., Liu, H., et al.: Human pulse diagnosis for medical assessments using a wearable piezoelectret sensing system. Adv. Funct. Mater. **28**(40), 1803413 (2018)
18. Jayasenan, J.S., Smitha, P.S.: Driver drowsiness detection system. IOSR J. VLSI Sig. Process **4**(1), 34–37 (2014)
19. Zhou, Y., Xu, Q., Kong, W.: Study on analysis and identification of pulse characteristics. J. Biomed. Eng. **23**(3), 505–508 (2006)
20. Ye, N., Sun, Y.G., Yang, D.: Noninvasive heart rate variability detection device for fatigue driving detection system. Appl. Mech. Mater. **246–247**, 194–198 (2012)

# Basic Research on Wireless Remote Control Rabbit Animal Robot Movement

Yong Peng$^{(\boxtimes)}$, Zilin Wang, Qian Zhang, Shaohua Du, Yang Zhao,
Luonan Yang, Jianing Liu, Yawei Cheng, Aidi Wang,
and Yingjie Liu

Department of Biomedical Engineering, School of Electrical Engineering,
Yanshan University, Qinhuangdao 066004, Hebei, China
PY81@sina.com

**Abstract.** Bio-robots are emerging and forward-thinking high-tech fields in the world today. However, the research on rabbit animal robots has not yet been reported in detail, so this study conducted an exploratory study on the exercise control of adult rabbits (n = 20). The tungsten as the electrode material was selected, and the implanted brain electrode was fabricated by electrochemical corrosion and insulation treatment. The brain electrode was implanted into the rabbit brain movement area by means of the brain stereotaxic instrument; the wireless remote control system was independently developed, and the wireless remote control system was applied. Control experiments were performed on rabbit robots. The results showed that the left side of the cerebral cortex of the rabbits could control the movement of the right leg and the right turn of the rabbit; the right side of the cerebral cortex of the rabbit could stimulate the left leg movement and turn to the left. Control the rabbit robot left and right steering success rate is 90%. The stimulation mode is continuous stimulation, and the stimulation parameters are: pulse interval 1–255 ms, pulse number 1–50, pulse width 1–10 ms, voltage intensity 10 V. In this study, the wireless remote control system is used to electrically stimulate the rabbit brain motion zone, which can initially control the movement of rabbit robots.

**Keywords:** Rabbit animal robot · Implanted brain electrode ·
Brain stereotaxic instrument · Wireless remote control system

## 1 Introduction

The use of biological control technology to develop animal robots began in the 1990s. In the past 20 years, animal robots have become one of the most active frontiers in the world's technological development. With the in-depth study of life science and technology, molecular biology, electronic technology, complex and applicable systems, and the interdisciplinary integration of various disciplines, the development of nature-based animal robots has made great progress [1]. The University of Tokyo in Japan conducted research on silkworm moth robots, sweet potato moth robots, and scorpion robots from 1995 to 1997, and opened the prelude of animal robots [2–4]. The State University of New York Talwar et al. implanted microelectrodes into the rat brain and

© Springer Nature Switzerland AG 2019
H. Yu et al. (Eds.): ICIRA 2019, LNAI 11741, pp. 37–43, 2019.
https://doi.org/10.1007/978-3-030-27532-7_4

successfully developed a robotic rat (robo-rat) based on the reward mechanism, which controls its advancement, left turn, right turn, over obstacles or climbing by electrical signal coding [5]. China Shandong University of Science and Technology has successfully developed a mouse-based robot based on the reward mechanism, which can remotely control its left and right rotation, advancement, and rotation [6]. Zhejiang University of China successfully controlled the rats to turn around, climb the stairs, circle the "8", and even jump to the platform of 30 cm [7]; and integrate the machine intelligence with the biological intelligence to develop a "visually enhanced rat". On the big sand table, the white rats follow the road signs to accurately find the target photo [8]. Nanjing University of Aeronautics and Astronautics also developed a large gecko robot [9].

At present, representative animals of animal robot research include rats, geckos, sea turtles, sharks, goldfish, squid, etc., and the research on rabbit animal robots has not been reported in detail, so this study is for adult rabbits (n = 20). An experimental study of motion control was conducted. The rabbit brain was implanted into the brain electrode, and the wireless remote control electrical stimulation experiment was performed on the rabbit robot using a self-made wireless control system. The results showed that the left ventricle of the cerebral cortex of rabbits could control the right leg movement and right steering behavior of rabbits; stimulate the right side of the cerebral cortex of rabbits to control the left leg movement and leftward steering behavior of rabbits. The research work in this paper provides a certain experimental basis for the in-depth research and practical application of rabbit animal robots.

## 2    Materials and Method

### 2.1    Instruments

Digital display brain stereotaxic instrument (Stoelting, USA), Micro thruster, P-600 miniature hand drill (China Cixi Baohe Tools Co., Ltd.), tungsten wire (d = 0.1 mm), BL-420E biological function experimental system (China Chengdu Taimeng) Technology Co., Ltd. products, self-made wireless remote control system device.

### 2.2    Reagent

Reagents: Lu Mianning II (China Jilin Province Huamu Animal Health Products Co., Ltd., batch number: 201203), absolute ethanol, polyimide (Durimide 7510, 2100 Series).

### 2.3    Test Animal

Choose 20 healthy adult rabbits, weighing 1.5 kg–2.5 kg, male or female (provided by the Laboratory of Biomedical Engineering, Yanshan University).

## 2.4    Electrode Preparation

Select tungsten as the electrode material, straighten the tungsten wire (d = 0.1 mm), fix the two ends of the tungsten wire horizontally, one end can be stretched, and the tungsten wire is uniformly heated by the alcohol lamp, while at the same time Stretch one end and pull it hard. After cooling, a section of tungsten wire is taken, and the straightened tungsten wire is vertically fixed, so that it is in a natural vertical tensile state, the upper end is fixed, the lower end is suspended from the weight, and then annealed (Fig. 1).

**Fig. 1.** Stimulating electrode

## 2.5    Localization of Brain Electrode Implantation Sites

The rabbits were anesthetized with Lu Mianning II, and the anesthetized rabbits were fixed on a digital display stereotaxic apparatus. According to the three-dimensional positioning method of the rabbit brain, the skull surface is divided into twelve regions according to the dotted line of the rabbit brain skull mark. Adjust the brain stereotaxic instrument and point the tip of the electrode to the skull of the rabbit skull, so that the herringbone tip is just 1.5 mm below the center of the anterior iliac crest. According to the rabbit brain function partition map, the three-dimensional digital display of the brain stereotaxic apparatus is used to mark the implantation sites A (RL2, P2, H8), B (LL2, P2, H8), D (RL3, P3, H8), E (LL3, P3, H8), four points and a reference point C outside the brain (Fig. 2).

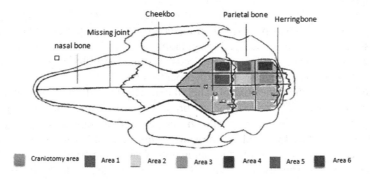

**Fig. 2.** Line-drawing Zoning Map

## 2.6    Development of Wireless Remote Control System

Independently developed wireless remote control system, the system consists of three parts: PC control terminal, wireless transmitter (composed of STC12C5410AD microcontroller and transmitter chip Nrf905), stimulator (composed of STC12C54 10AD microcontroller and nRF905). The main working mode is: setting the program stimulation parameter and issuing control command through the PC console, transmitting the wireless signal after receiving the signal by the wireless transmitter, and then receiving by the receiver device carried by the rabbit robot, the receiver transmits the signal to the C8051 based micro. The processor is then pulsed by the stimulator to the brain electrode, and the simulated electrical signal stimulates the cerebral cortex motor area through the brain electrode, thereby intervening in the rabbit cortical motor area to achieve control of the rabbit robot motion.

## 2.7    Rabbit Robot Wireless Control Experiment

### 2.7.1    Rabbit Anesthesia
Rabbits were weighed and weighed. Lu Mianning II was injected into the ear of the rabbit ear at a dose of 0.1–0.2 kg to enter the anesthesia.

### 2.7.2    Implantation and Fixation of Brain Electrodes
According to the coordinate value obtained by locating the stimulation site, the craniotomy drill is used to drill the corresponding position on the surface of the skull, and the drilled point is aligned with the stereotactic locator, and the self-made tungsten wire electrode is obtained according to the positioning stimulation site by using the micro thruster. Coordinate values are implanted into rabbit brain tissue, and the dental cement seals the skull to create an area. At the same time, the implanted electrode is fixed, and penicillin is partially disinfected to prevent infection.

### 2.7.3    Wireless Control Experiment
Put a special vest on the rabbit. The device has obtained the national patent (publication number; CN204518794U [10], the wireless stimulator is fixed on the vest, and the electrodes are implanted at two points A and B. The adjustment of the parameters of the stimulus signal generator is performed on the control panel on the PC. The stimulation intensity starts from a weak one. Each stimulation lasts for 10 s, and each stimulation is intermittent for 10 min to prevent rabbits from adapting to electrical stimulation signals and nerve fatigue, thus affecting the experimental results.

Through the switch on the control panel, the on/off of the stimulation signal on each stimulation electrode is controlled, and the brain function area is stimulated by different parameters to observe the reaction and the corresponding motion action. When the parameter is small, the threshold value of the action potential is not reached, and it is not easy to cause the rabbit to produce an action. When the parameter is too large, the rabbit may react too strongly, and may cause certain damage to the brain tissue of the rabbit, because the nerve has certain Adaptability and fatigue, should not be stimulated for a long time, should also adjust the stimulation parameters moderately.

Stimulation mode: single stimulation. Stimulus parameters: pulse interval 1–255 ms; number of pulses: 1–50; pulse width 1–10 ms, voltage intensity 10 V. Since the stimulation voltage is constant 10 V, the stimulation intensity is changed by the control program to adjust the pulse number, interval and width to achieve the optimal stimulation parameters (Fig. 3).

**Fig. 3.** Wireless remote control device

## 3   Experimental Result

The results showed that the results of different regions of the cerebral cortex of rabbits were different, stimulating the functional area on one side of the cortex, and the rabbits showed leg movement and turning on the opposite side of the body, that is, when stimulating the A-point (right side) of the brain layer. The rabbit turned to the left, controlling the rabbit robot to turn left successfully 90%; when stimulating the home to avoid the B layer (left side) of the brain, the rabbit turned to the right, and the right steering success rate of the control rabbit robot was 90%. Among the 20 rabbit robots in this experiment, 18 rabbit robots have obvious control effects; one rabbit robot died after implanting the electrodes, suspected to be caused by improper operation; the other can not appear significant when controlling Sports behavior. Experiments show that the pulse interval of 10 ms, the number of pulses of 10, and the pulse width of 5 ms are the optimal stimulation parameters for rabbit robot motion control (Figs. 4 and 5).

**Fig. 4.** Control rabbit right turn          **Fig. 5.** Control rabbit left turn

## 4   Conclusion and Discussion

In this study, the electrical stimulation method was used to electrically stimulate the brain movement area through the implanted brain electrode, and the wireless remote control of rabbit animal robot movement was initially realized.

.

This research, implanted brain electrodes were fabricated using tungsten as a preparation material, and tungsten filaments were processed and processed from three aspects: physical, electrochemical and insulating treatment. The bending of the tungsten wire is changed by the method of hot working straightening, so that the pen is directly inserted into the animal body, and the experimental error is reduced. The density of the tungsten wire becomes uniform by the method of passing the direct current voltage and straightening, which is favorable for uniform corrosion of the needle tip. The anhydrous ethanol and the polyimide are uniformly coated on the surface of the tungsten wire in a volume ratio of 2:1 for insulation treatment. By implanting the electrodes without craniotomy, the rabbits did not die within one week from the survival of the rabbits, indicating that the self-made implanted brain electrodes have better biocompatibility.

In the research of animal robot wireless remote control system, Nanjing University of Aeronautics and Astronautics has developed a micro-small animal robot remote control stimulation system, which can realize the requirements of lightweight, miniaturization and low energy consumption of wireless stimulator [11]. The animal robot remote control stimulation system based on 3G network communication developed by Nanjing University of Aeronautics and Astronautics can be applied in places with 3G network, and the remote control range is expanded [12]. These remote control systems are well suited for wireless control of animal robots. The wireless remote control system designed in this paper, wherein the system hardware includes a wireless communication module, an electrical stimulation signal generation module, and a power module; the system software includes a serial communication setting and a motion mode selection. In use, according to the PC control panel of the rabbit animal robot behavior control system designed in this paper, the stimulation channel and the stimulation parameters are selected, and the electric stimulator mounted on the rabbit robot is remotely controlled by the upper computer to perform electrical stimulation, and the stimulator is emitted. The signal stimulates the brain movement zone through the brain electrode, and wireless remote control experiments are performed on the rabbit robot (n = 20). The results show that the control rabbit robot completes the left and right steering success rate is 90%. It shows that the wireless remote control system of this research can realize wireless remote control of rabbit robots.

In the experiment, we found that rabbits are fatigued and adaptable to long-term electrical stimulation, so the experimental parameters can be adjusted in time according to the situation of home exemption, and the stimulation time and intensity need to be controlled within the tolerance range of the rabbit. This paper only conducts preliminary research on wireless remote control of rabbit robot motion, and there are many scientific and technical issues to be further studied in the future.

**Acknowledgement.** This project was supported by the project of National Natural Science Foundation of China (project number: 61573305), and the project of PhD Foundation in Yanshan University in China (project number: B702).

# References

1. Wang, W., Dai, Z.: Research status and development of animal robots. Mach. Manuf. Autom. **39**(2), 1–7 (2010)
2. Hadfield, P.: Robot Roach is born. New Sci. Mag. **2074**, 26 (1997)
3. Kuwana, Y., Ando, N., Kanzaki, R., et al.: A radiotelemetry system for muscle potential recordings from freely flying insects. In: IEEE BMES/EMBS Conference, Atlanta, GA, October 1999, p. 846 (1999)
4. Holzer, R., Shimoyama, I.: Locomotion control of a bio-robotic system via electric stimulation. In: Proceedings of the IEEE International Conference, France, pp. 1514–1519 (1997)
5. Talwar, S.K., Xu, S.H., Hawley, E.S., et al.: Rat navigation guided by remote control. Nature **417**(6884), 37–38 (2002)
6. Wang, Y., Su, X., Zhai, R., et al.: Animal robot remote navigation system. Robot **28**(02), 183–186 (2006)
7. Zheng, Y., Zhang, W., Wang, P., et al.: Research on remote navigation and behavior training system in rats. J. Biomed. Eng. China **26**(6), 830–836 (2007)
8. Zhou, W.: "Grafting" machine vision for rats [EB/OL], 23 May 2013. http://www.news.zju.edu.cn/news.php?id=37289. Accessed 10 Apr 2015
9. Guo, C., Dai, Z., Sun, J.: Research status and future development of animal robots. Robot **27**(2), 188–192 (2005)
10. Peng, Y., Su, Y., Ju, Y., Shen, W., Guo, C.: A rabbit animal robot backpack. CN204518794U, Hebei, 05 August 2015
11. Zhang, C., Guo, C., Cai, L.: Development of micro-miniature animal robot remote sensing system. Comput. Technol. Appl. **37**(5), 134–137 (2011)
12. Chen, X.: Development of rat nerve stimulation system based on constant current source. Zhejiang University, Hangzhou (2014)
13. Zhu, Z., Wang, H., Han, J.: Development of animal robot remote control stimulation system based on 3G network communication. Autom. Instrum. **10**, 71–74 (2017)

# Bio-inspired Wall Climbing Robot

# Design and Realization of a Bio-inspired Wall Climbing Robot for Rough Wall Surfaces

Jinfu Liu[1,2], Linsen Xu[1,3(✉)], Shouqi Chen[2], Hong Xu[2],
Gaoxin Cheng[2], Tao Li[1], and Qingfeng Yang[1]

[1] Institute of Advanced Manufacturing Technology, Hefei Institutes of Physical
Science, CAS, Hefei, China
lsxu@iamt.ac.cn
[2] University of Science and Technology of China, Hefei, Anhui, China
liujinfu@mail.ustc.edu.cn
[3] Anhui Province Key Laboratory of Biomimetic Sensing and Advanced Robot
Technology, Hefei, Anhui, China

**Abstract.** As a special robot in extreme environment, wall-climbing robot can be used in bridge detection, signal collection, disaster search and rescue, and mine inspection. However, existing wall-climbing robots can only climb on one or several kinds of wall surfaces carrying a lighter load. Inspired by the structure characteristics of flies and clingfish, a wall-climbing robot with microspines and suction cup is proposed. Microspines are beneficial to the contact between the hook tip and the wall surface. Suction cup including flexible skirt edge and high-speed eddy fans, can avoid the robot overturning due to failing in the gripping. In addition, the relationships of adsorption force and pressure versus the distance between suction cup and wall surface are measured. Furthermore, the kinematic of robot is analyzed and the force of wall to the robot and motor torque are evaluated respectively. Finally, the prototype of the wall-climbing robot is manufactured and tested on a variety of rough wall surfaces, and the experimental results show that the robot climbs stably with a larger load.

**Keywords:** Wall-climbing robot · Microspines · Suction cup ·
Flexible skirt edge

## 1 Introduction

The emergence of wall-climbing robot can help humans avoid engaging in dangerous high-altitude work, which not only increases work efficiency and saves costs, but also improves the working environment of operators. It is widely applied in a variety of fields, including chemical and infrastructure maintenance of nuclear industry, surface cleaning of tall building, high-altitude rescue, anti-terrorist detection and so on. The traditional wall-climbing robots mostly employ magnetic adsorption, vacuum adsorption, dry adhesion and et al., all of which have their own application scope [1–3]. The method of magnetic adsorption can generate a large adsorption force, but the wall surface is required to be magnetic material. Negative pressure adsorption has a good adaptability to the wall surfaces, but when there are bugles or pits on the wall surface, the adsorption condition

© Springer Nature Switzerland AG 2019
H. Yu et al. (Eds.): ICIRA 2019, LNAI 11741, pp. 47–59, 2019.
https://doi.org/10.1007/978-3-030-27532-7_5

will be broken due to air leakage. Dry adhesion and electrostatic adsorption are new types of adsorption method, and the material is vulnerable to the influence of dust, then they are mainly applied to smooth and clean wall surfaces. Compared with adsorption and adhesion, microspines has incomparable advantages on rough wall surface. To date, various climbing robots with grippers installed have been proposed [4–7]. Through the interlocking force formed between the spines and the wall surface, Stanford University has developed a wall-climbing robot with parallelogram structure, named spiny-II [8–10], which can only achieve one directional movement on one surface and has a relatively slow speed. Considering the requirements of robot speed and adaptability on different wall surfaces, Boston dynamics, has successively developed a series of robots for trees, building external walls and wooden power poles [11–14], based on the directional spines research of Stanford University. This series of robots can not only realize the fast climbing on a single vertical wall, but also switch smoothly among various walls. However, because the spines can not adapt to the wall completely, then the movement is not stable. None of the above robots can climb on ceiling wall. NASA proposed a wall-climbing robot with four mechanical arms based on flexible spine plates [15], which is mainly used for climbing on rough ceiling surface. Due to the uniform distribution of spines and excellent adaptability, therefore, the robot move extremely stable and also has a large carrying capacity, but its climbing speed is relatively low. In domestic, Prof. Mei has developed a "T" shape wall-climbing robot, which is similar to DROP robot of Caltech [16, 17]. Nanjing University of aeronautics and astronautics and Beihang University have developed separately four-legged wall-climbing robots by referring to the structural characteristics of "Rise" robot [18, 19]. Note that, these robots are unable to climb steadily for a long time and also not carry a larger load.

According to the above reviews and design requirement on rough wall surface, a bio-inspired wall climbing robot with microspines and suction cup is proposed. The organization of this paper is given as: Sect. 2 illustrates the methods and materials used for microspines and suction cup. Section 3 provides the design of wall-climbing robot. Section 4 describes kinematics analysis, Sect. 5 shows the evaluation of forces and motor torque and experimental testing on different wall surfaces, and conclusion is presented in Sect. 6.

## 2  Microspines and Suction Cup

Inspired by the structure of fly's feet, Microspines are developed, shown in Fig. 1, including six flexible arms made from polyurethane materials, no barbed fish hooks, as well as wheel hub. Due to the adaptive characteristics of the flexible arm, therefore, it can provide the maximum contact between the spines and the wall surface. The connection of spines and substrate is cast by hot melt nylon, which is more conducive to the fixation of spines than 502 glue or other adhesive material. The wheel hub whose material is nylon 6600 having higher tensile and bending resistance, affords a rigid supporting that holds flexible arms and connects the external transmission shaft.

Figure 2 shows the new eddy suction cup including an eddy fan, a vacuum chamber and a soft skirt edge. The structure principle of the eddy vacuum suction cup is similar to that of the centrifugal pump. The inner air is discharged through the

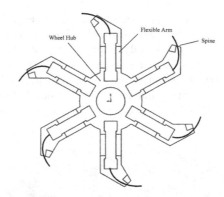

**Fig. 1.** A structure schematic of microspines.

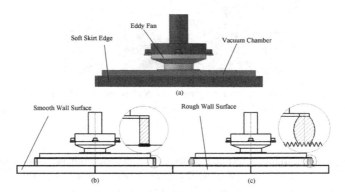

**Fig. 2.** The eddy suction unit. (a) Physical model of eddy suction unit, (b) adsorption state of eddy suction unit on smooth wall surface, (c) adsorption state of eddy suction unit on rough wall surface.

rotation of the impeller, thus forming differential pressure ensures that the robot is attached to the wall surface. The only difference lies in the structure design of flexible skirt edge, which can effectively reduce the air into the negative pressure chamber. When the suction cup is in contact with the smooth wall surface, the profile of skirt edge is shaped like a drum, and the lower edge is closely fitted with the wall surface. While the suction cup contacts with the rough wall surface, since there are many particles on the surface. Therefore, the flexible skirt edge is embedded into the gap among these particles by its own adaptability, shown in Figs. 2(b) and (c).

## 2.1  Rapid Microspines Manufacturing and Performance Analysis

It is very difficult to model the microspines with rigid wheel hub and flexible support arm due to the difference of their material. The manufacture technology of microspines is made by shape deposition manufacturing (SDM) [20]. First, cut the hook into the desired shape with scissors and place the it in a specific position at the end of the spine housing. Turn the heater to 500 °C and melt the nylon at the end of spine to integrate them together. Next, place the fishhook with nylon handle and the wheel hub in the mould. According to the ratio of 1:1, polyurethane materials of smooth cast-65A and 65B are mixed together, then stirred uniformly in a beaker. In addition, remove air bubbles in the mixed material by negative pressure pump, and use a disposable straw to suck out the mixture and pour along one end of the mould. At last, put the mould into the holding furnace with 80 °C temperature for three hours, shown in Fig. 3.

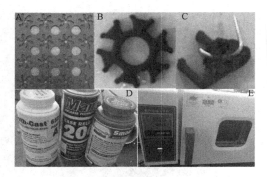

**Fig. 3.** Manufacturing process of microspines. (a) Nylon mould, (b) the center wheel hub, (c) the composite of nylon and fishhook, (d) polyurethane material and mold release agent, (e) holding furnace.

Shape deposition manufacturing can use a variety of high polymer materials for microspine. However, because of their different material properties, so it has a great influence on the grasping performance. Taking polyurethane for example, As the serial number of the product is relatively low, the flexibility of the material is better. With the increase of the serial number, the rigidity of the material becomes higher and higher [21]. As the number reaches 70, the material basically has no elasticity. Since the robot requires relatively rigid microspines, therefore, we choose the Smooth-Cast 65 as the material of flexible arm. The relationship between material serial number and performance is shown in Fig. 4.

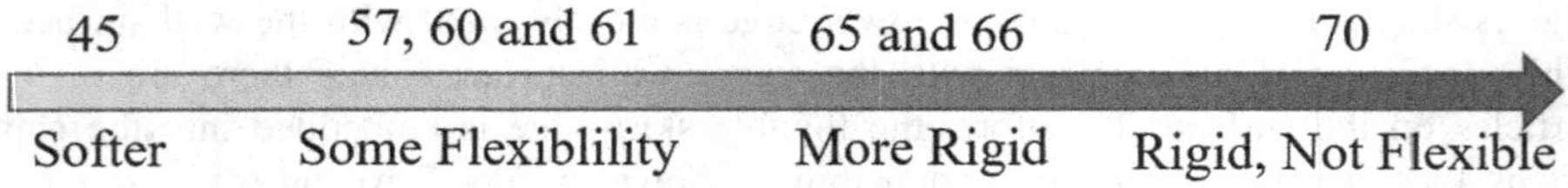

| 45 | 57, 60 and 61 | 65 and 66 | 70 |
|---|---|---|---|
| Softer | Some Flexiblility | More Rigid | Rigid, Not Flexible |

**Fig. 4.** The relationship between serial number and material properties for polyurethane

The expected motion modes of the microspines are "contact-bending-overlap", In the initial state, the grappling hook contacts particle on the wall surface, with the rotation of the spine wheel, the flexible arm is gradually bent and the direction of the grasping force is also gradually parallel to the wall surface. Finally, under the action of tangential force and motor torque, the flexible arm is partly overlapped with spine wheel, shown in Fig. 5. With the rotation of the wheel, the contact angle between the spine wheel and the wall surface gradually decreases, therefore, the spine also gradually begins to separate from the wall surface. In this process, the flexible arm needs to bear large bending stress. Bending stiffness is an important parameter to resist the deformation of flexible arm, which is determined by the material and designed structure. The larger stiffness will cause the collision between the spine and wall surface, then the front end of microspines will fail to grip the wall surface. Inadequate stiffness will cause the microspines to slip along wall surface and never grip any wall surfaces. Consequently, the analysis of bending stiffness can give an estimate to carrying load and grasping ability.

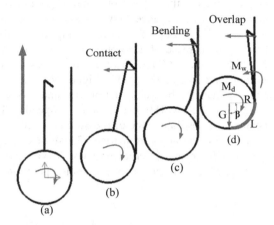

**Fig. 5.** Designed motion modes of flexible arm during a cycle period.

According to Euler beam bending theory, we can obtain the rotation angle $\beta/2$ for solving the maximum moment of flexible arm.

$$\frac{\beta}{2} = \frac{M_W L}{6EI}, \tag{1}$$

where $M_w$ is the bending moment applied by wall surface, $\beta$ is the central angle of the overlapping flexible arm, L is the wrapped length, E is elasticity modulus of polyurethane, I is the area moment of inertia.

As can be seen from Fig. 5, $L/\beta$ is equal to the wheel hub radius R, therefore, Eq. (1) can be rearranged as

$$M_w = \frac{3EI}{R}, \tag{2}$$

According to the balance condition during grasping, the moment equation can be known as

$$M_w \leq M_d - GR)/n. \tag{3}$$

where n is the number of microspines sheet. Substituting Eq. (3) to Eq. (2), we can know that

$$n \geq \frac{M_d - GR}{3EI} R. \tag{4}$$

## 2.2  Experimental Testing of Suction Cup

The distance between the suction cup and the wall surface and the speed of the fan are the most important factors affecting the adsorption force. Figure 6(b) shows the curve of the adsorption force versus the distance between suction cup and wall surface, measured by the experimental apparatus described in Fig. 6(a). When the distance changes from 0 to 4 mm, the decrease of adsorption force is not obvious at different rotation speeds (5000, 10000 and 15000 rpm) respectively. As the distance is more than 4 mm, the adsorption force decreases rapidly. Figure 6(c) shows the curve of the internal pressure versus the distance between suction cup and wall surfaces with different slope angle (45°, 90°, 135°, and 180°) at the rotation speed of 15000 rpm. With the increase of the distance, the absolute value of pressure gradually decreases, and the change trend is consistent with the adsorption force. Therefore, using the curve can easily obtain the adsorption force and internal pressure of vacuum chamber at any rotation speed and distance, which will be useful for stable operation of wall climbing robot in the future.

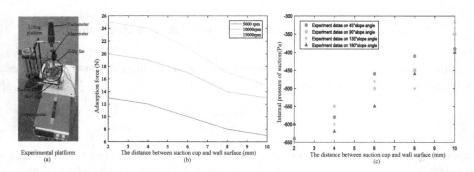

**Fig. 6.** Adsorption force and pressure testing. (a) Testing platform, (b) the relationship of adsorption force versus the distance between suction cup and wall surface, (c) the relationship of pressure versus the distance between suction cup and wall surface.

## 3   Robot Design

Figure 7 shows the schematic diagram of the wall-climbing robot, which includes spine wheels composed of microspines, transmission belts, and vacuum suction cup composed of eddy fans, as well as power system. The spine wheels and transmission belts on the single side of the robot are driven by one motor, which greatly improves the energy utilization rate and saves the installation space. The eddy suction cup is separately controlled by a brushless DC motor, which can adjust the rotation speed in real time by the change of internal negative press. By controlling the speed of the motors on the both sides, the robot can move forward, backward and turn according to different motion trajectory. The parameters of the robot are presented in Table 1.

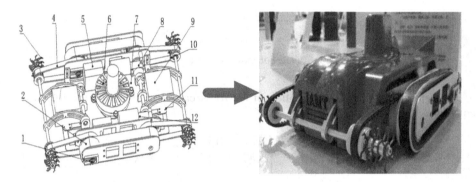

**Fig. 7.**  Design of robot body. 1 - adjustment mechanism; 2 - synchronous belt; 3 - spine wheel; 4 - driving belt; 5 - control board; 6 - highspeed vortex fan; 7 - negative press cavity; 8 - left driving motor; 9 - battery; 10 - synchronous pulleys; 11 - tension spring; 12 - left driving motor.

**Table 1.**  The parameter of the wall-climbing robot.

| Mass | Length | Width | Height | Speed |
|---|---|---|---|---|
| 1.3 kg | 35.5 cm | 24.8 cm | 9.5 cm | 5−10 cm/s |

## 4   Kinematics Analysis

In the global coordinate system XOY, shown in Fig. 8, the position A of the robot can be represented by the vector $p_a = [x_a, y_a, \theta_a]^T$, where x and y is the center coordinate of the robot, $\theta_a$ is the movement direction counterclockwise around x axis. The motion of a mobile robot is expressed by the robot's linear speed $v_a$ and angular speed $\omega_a$.

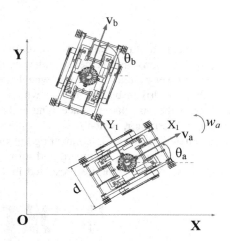

**Fig. 8.** Robot movement diagram.

Therefore, the kinematics equation of the robot can be obtained by the following equation.

$$\dot{p}_a = \begin{bmatrix} \dot{x}_a \\ y_a \\ \theta_a \end{bmatrix} = \begin{bmatrix} \cos\theta_a & 0 \\ \sin\theta_a & 0 \\ 0 & 1 \end{bmatrix} \begin{bmatrix} v_a \\ \omega_a \end{bmatrix} = \mathbf{J}q_a, \qquad (5)$$

where $\mathbf{J}$ is jacobian matrix, $q_a$ is the matrix including linear speed and angular speed. The position parameter of point B in coordinate system XOY, is set to $p_b = [x_b, y_b, \theta_b]^T$. In the coordinate system $X_1AY_1$, the motion error $p_e = [x_e, y_e, \theta_e]^T$ can be obtained.

$$p_e = \begin{bmatrix} x_e \\ y_e \\ \theta_e \end{bmatrix}_{(X_1AY_1)} = \begin{bmatrix} \cos\theta_a & \sin\theta_a & 0 \\ -\sin\theta_a & \cos\theta_a & 0 \\ 0 & 0 & 1 \end{bmatrix} \begin{bmatrix} x_b - x_a \\ y_b - x_a \\ \theta_b - \theta_a \end{bmatrix}_{(XOY)}. \qquad (6)$$

The differential equation of position error of robot which is used to solve tracking control problem, can be deduced as

$$\dot{p}_e = \begin{bmatrix} \dot{x}_e \\ y_e \\ \theta_e \end{bmatrix}_{(X_1AY_1)} = \begin{bmatrix} \omega_a y_e - v_a + v_b\cos(\theta_b - \theta_a) \\ -\omega_a x_e + v_b\sin(\theta_b - \theta_a) \\ \omega_b - \omega_a \end{bmatrix}_{(X_1AY_1)}. \qquad (7)$$

Through experimental testing shown in Fig. 9, the relationship between the wheel speed n and voltage U is as follows

$$n = 1.875U + 1.25. \tag{8}$$

The robot's linear speed $v_a$ and angular speed $\omega_a$ can be obtained as

$$\omega_a = \frac{(n_2 - n_1)D\pi}{d}, \tag{9}$$

$$v_a = \frac{(n_2 + n_1)D\pi}{2}, \tag{10}$$

where $n_1$ and $n_2$ are the left and right wheel speeds respectively, D is the diameter of wheel speed, d is the distance between left and right wheels.

Substituting Eqs. (8), (9) and (10), we can obtain

$$\omega_a = \frac{1.875(U_2 - U_1)D\pi}{d}, \tag{11}$$

$$v_a = \frac{1.875(U_2 + U_1)D\pi}{2} + 1.25D\pi, \tag{12}$$

where $U_1$ and $U_2$ are left and right input voltage of the motors.

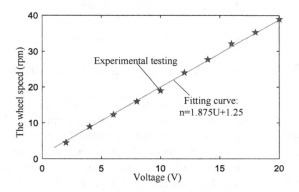

**Fig. 9.** The relationship between wheel speed and voltage.

# 5   Mechanical Analysis and Experimental Testing

## 5.1   Quasi-static Analysis on Rough Wall Surface

The climbing movement of robot on the rough wall mainly relies on the locking force formed by the microspines and the wall surface, as well as the negative pressure of the eddy fan, the quasi-static analysis diagram is shown in Fig. 10.

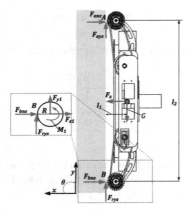

**Fig. 10.** Free body diagram of the climbing robot.

Quasi-static analysis is usually adequate as the wall-climbing robot moves at a low speed or uniform motion. In addition, assuming the left and right structure are symmetric, then the system of equations for equilibrium during climbing rough wall surface is obtained by

$$\sum F_x = 0 = F_{ans} + F_{bns} - Gcos\theta - F_s, \tag{13}$$

$$\sum F_y = 0 = F_{ays} + F_{rys} - Gsin\theta, \tag{14}$$

$$\sum M_B = 0 = F_{ans}l_2 - F_s l_2/2 + Gl_1 sin\theta - Gcos\theta l_2/2, \tag{15}$$

where $F_{ans}$ is the normal force of wall surface to the front spine wheel, $F_{bns}$ is the normal force of wall surface to the rear spine wheel, $\theta$ is the climbing slope angle, G is gravity of the wall climbing robot, $F_{ays}$ is the tangential force of wall surface to the front spine wheel, $F_{rys}$ is the tangential force of wall surface to the rear spine wheel, $F_s$ is the suction force, $l_1$ is the distance between the center of gravity and wall surface, and $l_2$ is the distance between the front and rear spine wheels.

## 5.2    The Evaluation of Forces and Motor Torque

In order to obtain the torque of the motor, the force of the free body of the spine wheel and the adhesive belt was analyzed respectively, shown in Fig. 11. When climbing on the rough wall, the motor torque is mainly used to overcome the tangential force of the wall surface to the spine wheel. To further verify the normal force and the driving torque of the motor, which are required by the robot in real time, tension and pressure sensors are laid under the wall surface. Meanwhile, in the experiment, the slope angles of 45°, 90°, 135°, and 180° wall surface were used as testing platform. The changing curves of theoretical and experimental normal force with the slope angle are shown in Fig. 11(a). Based on the experimental results, we can know that the experimental values have a certain deviation with theoretical value, due to different features on wall surfaces. However, their changing trend is consistent, and the maximum deviation is around 2N, but it can meet our design requirement.

At the same time, based on the selected angle above, we installed a torque sensor at the end of the motor to detect the torque changing plot of the motor. According to the analysis results, the maximum deviation of torque is about 0.1 Nm, shown in Fig. 11 (b). Therefore, when selecting the motor, the safety factor of the robot should also be considered carefully.

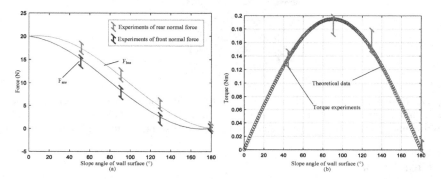

**Fig. 11.** (a) The force plots of experimental and theoretical normal force at different slope angles, (b) the torque plots of experimental and theoretical normal force at different slope angles.

### 5.3  Climbing Experiments on Rough Wall Surfaces

In order to verify the motion performance of the robot on the rough wall surface, sandpaper wall surfaces with roughness of 0–5 mm, 0–2 mm and 0–1 mm were selected as the test platform. The experimental testing pictures on rough wall surfaces are shown in Fig. 12. The dimensioning at the bottom of the below figure represents the distance from the ground.

As shown in Fig. 12(a)–(c), the wall surface with larger asperities can provide much grabbing point, which ensure full contact between microspines and wall surface. So it is hard to hard to see any slippage during movement for the robot. In addition, it also can carry external battery with 500 g weight and detection instruments with 600 g weight. For the wall surface with relatively smaller asperities, shown in Fig. 12(d)–(f), the maximum load capacity of the robot is 300 g, with the exception of 500 g external battery. Furthermore, the robot will slip a little during the movement. However, when the robot climbs on the wall surface shown in Fig. 12(g)–(i), the microspines are often unable to grasp asperities whose diameter is relatively small. Therefore, when the wall features are not obvious, the robot will slip due to the lack of proper grasping position.

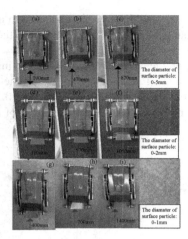

**Fig. 12.** Experimental tests on three types of rough vertical wall surfaces. (a)−(c) represent the coarse sandpaper surface with roughness of 0−5 mm, (d)−(f) represent the fine sandpaper surface with roughness of 0−2 mm, (g)−(i) represent the concrete surface with roughness of 0−1 mm.

## 6  Conclusion

According to motion principle of special animals, bionic flexible microspines and eddy suction cup were developed to apply in the virtual prototype. Based on Euler beam bending theory, the bending moment under maximum bending deformation was analyzed. Furthermore, by analyzing the characteristics of the wall surface, an adaptive eddy suction cup with flexible skirt edge was designed, then the relationships of the adsorption force and vacuum chamber pressure versus the distance which is between the suction cup and wall surface were obtained respectively. With the two structures, a novel bio-inspired wall-climbing robot was brought out. In addition, the kinematic of robot was analyzed, and the forces of wall to the robot and the motor torque were evaluated respectively on the rough wall surface. Finally, the prototype of the wall-climbing robot was manufactured and tested on different slopes, and then experiment results showed that the robot could climb stably on rough wall surfaces.

**Acknowledgments.** This work was supported by grants from Science and Technology Major Project of Anhui Province (17030901034), Jiangsu Key Research and Development Plan (BE2017067).

## References

1. Sato, E., Eriko, S., et al.: Dismantlable adhesion properties of reactive acrylic copolymers resulting from cross-linking and gas evolution. J. Adhes. **93**(10), 811–822 (2017)
2. Tavakoli, M., Carlos, V., Neto, P., et al.: The hybrid omni climber robot: wheel based climbing, arm based plane transition, and switchable magnet adhesion. Mechatronics **36**, 136–146 (2016)

3. Julia, P., Frensemeier, M., Kroner, E.: Switchable adhesion in vacuum using bio-inspired dry adhesives. ACS Appl. Mater. Interfaces **7**(43), 24127–24135 (2015)
4. Rosa, G.L., Messina, M., Muscato, G., Sinatra, R.: A low-cost lightweight climbing robot for the inspection of vertical surfaces. Mechatronics **12**(1), 71–96 (2002)
5. Balaguer, C., et al.: A climbing autonomous robot for inspection applications in 3D complex environments. Robotica **18**(3), 287–297 (2000)
6. Daltorio, K.A., et al.: A small wall-walking robot with compliant, adhesive feet. In: IEEE/RSJ International Conference on Intelligent Robots and Systems, Edmonton, Alta, Canada, pp. 1268–1273. IEEE (2005)
7. Hawkes, E.W., Christensen, D.L., Cutkosky, M.R.: Vertical dry adhesive climbing with a 100x bodyweight payload. In: International Conference on Robotics and Automation, Seattle, WA, USA, pp. 3648–3653. IEEE (2015)
8. Kim, S., Asbeck, A.T., Cutkosky, M.R., et al.: Spinybotll: climbing hard walls with compliant microspines. In: International Conference on Advanced Robotics, Seattle, WA, USA, pp. 601–602. IEEE (2005)
9. Asbeck, A.T., Kim, S., McClung, A., et al.: Climbing walls with microspines. In: Proceedings of the IEEE International Conference on Robotics and Automation, Orlando, FL, USA, pp. 4315–4317. IEEE (2006)
10. Kim, S., Asbeck, A.T., Cutkosky, M.R., et al.: Scaling hard vertical surfaces with compliant microspine arrays. Int. J. Robot. Res. **25**(25), 1165–1179 (2006)
11. Saunders, A., Goldman, D.I., Full, R.J., et al.: The RiSE climbing robot: body and leg design. In: Unmanned Systems Technology VIII - International Society for Optics and Photonics, Orlando, FL, USA, pp. 623017-1–623017-13 (2006)
12. Autumn, K., Buehler, M., Cutkosky, M., et al.: Robotics in scansorial environments. In: Unmanned Ground Vehicle Technology VII - International Society for Optics and Photonics, Orlando, FL, USA, pp. 291–303 (2005)
13. Spenko, M.J., Haynes, G.C., Sanders, J.A., et al.: Biologically inspired climbing with a hexapedal robot. J. Field Robot. **25**(4–5), 223–242 (2008)
14. Haynes, G.C., Khripin, A., Lynch, G., et al.: Rapid pole climbing with a quadrupedal robot. In: International Conference on Robotics and Automation, Kobe, Japan, pp. 2762–2772. IEEE (2009)
15. Parness, A., Frost, M., Thatte, N., et al.: Gravity-independent rock-climbing robot and a sample acquisition tool with microspine grippers. J. Field Robot. **30**(6), 897–915 (2013)
16. Chen, D.L., Zhang, Q., Liu, S.Z.: Design and realization of a flexible claw of rough wall climbing robot. Adv. Mater. Res. **328**, 388–392 (2011)
17. Liu, Y.W., Sun, S.M., Wu, X., Mei, T.: A wheeled wall-climbing robot with bio-inspired spine mechanisms. J. Bionic Eng. **12**(1), 17–28 (2015)
18. Wang, W., Wu, S., Zhu, P., et al.: Analysis on the dynamic climbing forces of a gecko inspired climbing robot based on GPL model. In: 2015 IEEE/RSJ International Conference on Intelligent Robots and Systems, Hamburg, Germany, pp. 3314–3319 (2015)
19. Ji, A., Zhao, Z., Manoonpong, P., et al.: A bio-inspired climbing robot with flexible pads and claws. J. Bionic Eng. **15**(2), 368–378 (2018)
20. Dollar, A.M., Howe, R.D.: A robust compliant grasper via shape deposition manufacturing. IEEE/ASME Trans. Mechatron. **11**(2), 54–161 (2006)
21. Kalind, C., Wiltsie, N., Parness, A.: Rotary microspine rough surface mobility. IEEE/ASME Trans. Mechatron. **21**(5), 2378–2390 (2016)

# The Graspable Algorithm for a Wall-Climbing Robot with Claws

Fanchang Meng[1,2] (iD), Yiquan Guo[1,2] (iD), Fengyu Xu[1,2(✉)] (iD),
Guoping Jiang[1,2] (iD), and Bei Wang[1,2] (iD)

[1] College of Automation, Nanjing University of Posts and Telecommunications,
Nanjing, China
xufengyu598@163.com
[2] Jiangsu Engineering Lab for IOT Intelligent Robots (IOTRobot),
Nanjing, China

**Abstract.** Wall-climbing robots have been widely used in the inspection of smooth walls. However, no satisfactory adhesion methods have been developed for robots that will allow them to climb rough walls. This paper proposes a suitable adhesion method that employs grappling-hook-like claws arranged in a cross shape. First, we address the implementation mechanism required. Then, a method of extracting the parameters characterizing a rough wall is devised, and 3D profiles of rough walls simulated. A method of triangulation is proposed to judge which regions of a 3D wall can be gripped, and we subsequently present a grasping discrimination algorithm for the interaction between the miniature claws and 3D wall profile. Finally, the simulation proves the validity of the discriminant algorithm for gripping 3D walls. It provides a more reliable method of adhesion for robots on rough walls.

**Keywords:** Flexible grasping claw · Grasping discrimination algorithm · Asperity of rough wall surfaces

## 1 Introduction

The surfaces of high-altitude buildings constructed using stone, concrete, and rough bricks generally show signs of serious ash deposition. This means that more stringent requirements are placed on the adhesion methods used by the wall-climbing robots employed. Traditional magnetic methods are extensively used to inspect magnetic walls [1, 2]. Vacuum suction (adhesion due to negative pressure) methods can be adapted to different walls [3, 4], but are essentially limited to the inspection of smooth walls. Methods employing vibrating suckers [5], highly-efficient negative-pressure suckers with a centrifugal impeller [6], and electrostatic adhesion also have their own scopes of application [7], but do not adapt well to walls that are dusty and have high humidity.

One of the 'RiSE' robots proposed by Spenko et al. uses tiny hooks to allow the robot to cling to a wall. A modular method of combination allowed these to be combined to form a tree-climbing robot with ground walking capability based on 6 modular feet [8]. Goran designed a kind of biomimetic climbing robot, 'DynoClimber' [9], according to biological climbing models which was able to dynamically climb vertical walls with

© Springer Nature Switzerland AG 2019
H. Yu et al. (Eds.): ICIRA 2019, LNAI 11741, pp. 60–71, 2019.
https://doi.org/10.1007/978-3-030-27532-7_6

climbing speeds that were significantly faster than previous prototypes. A climbing robot has also been designed by Provancher based on the methods of energy conservation and optimization design [10]. This robot climbs by alternately grasping uplifts on the wall with a pair of mechanical hooks driven by a swinging balancing weight. Researchers at Stanford University developed a bioinspired wall-climbing robot, 'Spinybot', whose feet have micro-spines which allow it to climb rough wall surfaces using hooking protuberances [11]. Using the method of gripping walls with tiny hooks, Xu designed a multi-legged wall-climbing robot with claws and established a mechanical climbing model for it [12–14]. This robot is able to climb static walls but the hooks, unfortunately, are likely to become detached from the wall under large external disturbances (*e.g.* wind loads and wall vibrations).

In summary, wall-climbing robots have been extensively studied and many successful applications have been achieved. However, in general, the various approaches to adhesion of the robots have their own limited scope of application. In this research, we aim to design a new grappling-hook-like claw and present a discriminating algorithm to allow the claws to grip rough protuberances on 3D walls.

The rest of the paper is arranged as follows. Section 2 proposes the adhesion method for the grappling claws and extracts the characteristic parameters of rough wall surfaces using a 3D scanner. In Sect. 3, we propose a discriminant algorithm for the claws to stably grip the 3D rough walls. The simulation experiment proves the feasibility of the algorithm in Sect. 4. The conclusions and future research directions are summarized in Sect. 5.

## 2 Interaction Mechanism Between a Bionic Hook and Rough Bulge on a Wall Surface

### 2.1 Mechanical Structure of the Grappling-Hook-Like Claws

When designing wall-climbing robots, two key issues need to be considered: mobility and adhesivity. Based on the characteristics of cockroach claw, a grappling-hook-like claw is proposed here that is arranged in the shape of a cross (Fig. 1). Two pairs of secondary claws are fixed on the main structure, each containing an actuating cylinder and multiple elastic hooks. The claws are fixed onto the main structure by various means. The pair of longitudinal claws play the primary grasping role by gripping the wall using the two upper and lower secondary claws. This not only improves the grasping force, but also enhances the adaptability of the claw system to the wall. The pair of transverse claws are mainly designed to assist gripping and prevent rollover.

### 2.2 Method of Extracting the Characteristic Parameters of the Rough Wall Surface

Parameters characterizing the roughness of the wall are critical to the grasp stability of the claws. A 3D scanner was used to scan the wall to extract data to characterize the roughness of the wall and allow 2D and 3D profiles of the rough wall to be simulated.

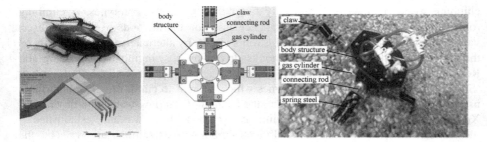

**Fig. 1.** The structure of the gripper

The process used to extract the surface features of the wall is shown in Fig. 2. The rough wall used in the experiment (measuring 650 mm × 450 mm × 20 mm) was built using sand and stones and the scanning range used was 250 mm × 250 mm (Fig. 3). Due to the unevenness of the wall, all the data could not be obtained in one measurement. Instead, the experiment was carried out through a series of overlapping scans using marked points. The initial sample data obtained for the feature points was divided into several sets and separately imported in the Geomagic Studio software package (Fig. 4a displays data on 13,386 feature points). In this way, a 3D point cloud model of the rough wall was constructed. After filtering the point clouds using Geomagic Studio, a 3D wall profile was generated (Fig. 4b).

**Fig. 2.** The feature extraction procedure used on the rough wall surface.

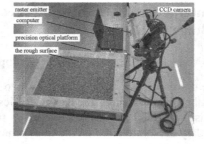

**Fig. 3.** The measurement experiment and rough wall.

(a) 3D point cloud model

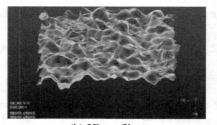

(b) 3D profile

**Fig. 4.** The 3D features of the rough wall

## 2.3     Discriminant Condition for the Hooks to Stably Grip Rough Protuberances on the Wall Surface

Curves describing the protuberances on an arbitrary rough wall can be drawn according to the 3D surface profile data presented in Fig. 4. Depending on the characteristics of the curves, the separation between two peaks is taken to be the period. Two typical curve types, labeled A and B, can be found by summarizing the characteristics of each period (Fig. 5). For A-type curves (Fig. 5a), there is a groove present so the claws can hook onto the groove directly. For B-type curves (Fig. 5b), the upper hooks cannot grasp the protuberance while the lower hooks can easily do so.

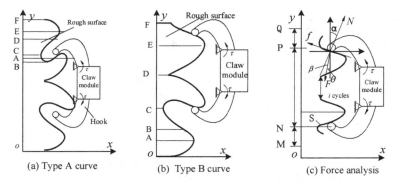

(a) Type A curve          (b)  Type B curve          (c) Force analysis

**Fig. 5.**  Analysis of hooks gripping protuberances on the wall

A force analysis is shown in Fig. 5c for when the hooks are attached to convex points. In the figure, $\alpha$ represents the normal angle (i.e. the angle between the direction of the contact normal between the hook and protuberance and the vertical plane), $\mu$ is the friction coefficient, and $\theta$ the grasping angle (i.e. the angle between the grasping force $F$ and the negative $y$ direction). The analysis reveals that the situation is stable if $F \sin \beta < N\mu$ and $F \cos \beta = N$. Thus, $\beta < \arctan \mu$, implying that the stability condition is

$$\alpha < \theta + \arctan(\mu) \tag{1}$$

The condition given in Eq. (1) is the same as that for friction self-locking. For the B-type curve shown in Fig. 5b, FD is the period and it is clear the upper hooks cannot grasp the wall in section ED while they may slide down along the wall in section FE. When Eq. (1) is satisfied, the claws will successfully grip the wall.

## 3   Discriminant Algorithm for the Graspable Positions on 3D Walls

Given point cloud data describing a 3D wall profile, the triangle formed by three adjacent points is used in place of the wall profile of the region. The places that can be contacted with the hook can therefore be judged by partitioning the point cloud data into a myriad of triangular regions. Then, all the contactable regions identified can be checked to see whether they can be grasped according to the discriminant conditions for gripping.

## 3.1  Triangulation Strategy

Each point in the data has coordinate information related to a set of $x$-, $y$-, and $z$-axes and the points collectively form a surface that is spatially curved. In this research, a triangular-combination strategy is proposed to deal with the point cloud.

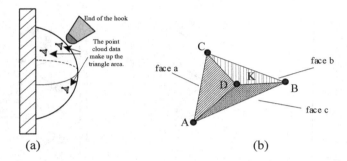

**Fig. 6.** Contact models for the hook–wall contact: (a) contact model of the spherical asperity composed of point clouds, (b) contact model of the hook and a pyramid convex to the wall.

The contact between the hook and the wall surface can be treated as being equivalent to that between the hook and triangles formed by the point clouds of the wall (Fig. 6). In Fig. 6b, the triangle $\triangle ABC$ formed by the points A, B, and C is regarded as representing the appearance of the surface in this region. If there is a point D above $\triangle ABC$, then the region $\triangle ABC$ can be partitioned into a protuberance in the form of a triangular pyramid. As the hook slides in the region, it makes contact with faces $a$, $b$, and $c$. The point cloud data are subjected to triangular combination. According to the radius of the tip of the hook, all the contactable triangular combinations are found via a process of traversal based on the coordinates of the points. On this basis, the contact angles between the hook and each triangle are computed. Then, in accordance with Eq. (1), it is determined whether the triangle can be grasped or not.

## 3.2  Judging If a Region Is Graspable or Not

In 3D space, the tip of the hook is a hemisphere and the 3D wall profile is equivalent to the spatial point cloud data. The contactable condition in this case can be expressed in the form: if three points can be contacted with the tip of the hook, then the triangle formed by the three points is a contactable triangle.

A spherical model is employed to analyze the contact between the tip of the hook and the spatial point cloud (Fig. 7). Seven points, A–G, are randomly selected from the surface. It is further assumed that any arbitrary set of three of these points are not collinear, so that the seven points form 35 unique triangles. The contact between the multitude of spatial points and the sphere can therefore be decomposed into that with several triangles. Taking the triangle $\triangle ABC$ formed by the contact points A, B, and C as an example, the constraints for contact being made between the three vertexes of the triangle and a sphere of given radius are as follows:

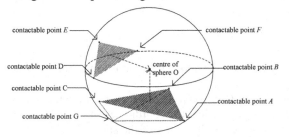

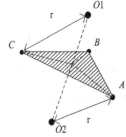

**Fig. 7.** Contact model of the spatial points and a sphere.

**Fig. 8.** Position of the center of the sphere corresponding to the triangle.

**Constraint 1:** The length of each arbitrary side (AB, AC, or BC) of triangle $\triangle ABC$ should not be longer than the diameter of the sphere, 2r, that is,

$$\begin{cases} (x_A - x_C)^2 + (y_A - y_C)^2 + (z_A - z_C)^2 \le 4r^2 \\ (x_A - x_B)^2 + (y_A - y_B)^2 + (z_A - z_B)^2 \le 4r^2 \\ (x_B - x_C)^2 + (y_B - y_C)^2 + (z_B - z_C)^2 \le 4r^2 \end{cases} \tag{2}$$

**Constraint 2:** The area of $\triangle ABC$ needs to be smaller than or equal to the largest area of an inscribed triangle of the sphere. The inscribed triangle that passes through the center of the sphere has the largest area. Suppose that the central angles corresponding to each side of an inscribed triangle are $\alpha_0$, $\beta_0$, and $\gamma_0$ ($\alpha_0 > 0$, $\beta_0 > 0$, $\gamma_0 > 0$, and $\alpha_0 + \beta_0 + \gamma_0 = 2\pi$). Then, the area of the triangle is $S = r^2(\sin \alpha_0 + \sin \beta_0 + \sin \gamma_0)/2$ and the extremum is obtained when $\alpha_0 = \beta_0 = \gamma_0 = 2\pi/3$, in which case $S = 3r^2(2\pi/3)/2 = 3\sqrt{3}r^2/4$. According to Heron's formula, the area of a triangle is given by $S = \sqrt{p(p-AB)(p-AC)(p-BC)}$ where $p = (AB + AC + BC)/2$. Therefore, the three sides of $\triangle ABC$ need to obey the relationship

$$0 < \sqrt{p(p-AB)(p-AC)(p-BC)} \le 3\sqrt{3}r^2/4 \tag{3}$$

**Constraint 3:** Points inside deep grooves or small cracks are probably not contactable. The contact points A, B, and C are all located at a distance r away from the center of the sphere and the sphere does not contain any other spatial points inside. That is, an arbitrary point in the space, $p(x_i, y_i, z_i)$, must lie a distance away from the center of the sphere of at least $r$. Overall, we have

$$\begin{cases} \sqrt{(x-x_A)^2+(y-y_A)^2+(z-z_A)^2}=r \\ \sqrt{(x-x_B)^2+(y-y_B)^2+(z-z_B)^2}=r \\ \sqrt{(x-x_C)^2+(y-y_C)^2+(z-z_C)^2}=r \\ \sqrt{(x-x_i)^2+(y-y_i)^2+(z-z_i)^2}\geq r \end{cases} \tag{4}$$

Three spatial points simultaneously meeting the above three constraints constitute a contactable triangle.

In the above analysis, the precondition of Constraint 3 is that the coordinates of the center of the sphere are known. However in practice, the coordinates of the center are unknown. A method of finding the coordinates of the center of the sphere based on the coordinates of three spatial points and the radius r is described as follows.

Figure 8 shows the location of the center of the sphere corresponding to the spatial triangle. In the algorithm, the solve function in MATLAB is used to convert the problem to finding the symbolic analytical solution of a set of algebraic equations. The procedure in MATLAB is written as:

$syms$   $x, y, z$;

$$[x,y,z]=solve(r^2-(x-x_A)^2-(y-y_A)^2-(z-z_A)^2, r^2-(x-x_B)^2$$
$$-(y-y_B)^2-(z-z_B)^2, r^2-(x-x_C)^2-(y-y_C)^2-(z-z_C)^2);$$

When merely Constraints 1 and 2 are met, the solutions found for the coordinates of the center of the sphere will probably not be real. For this reason, imaginary solutions need to be eliminated during the computation. In this research, the coordinate information relating to the z-axis of the point clouds reflects the fluctuations in the wall profile. As the hook tip contacts the point clouds in a downwards manner, the solution with the largest $z$ value is always taken if there are multiple solutions.

After solving for the coordinates of the center of the sphere, the angle between the normal vector of the contact triangle (pointing towards the center of the sphere) and the reverse direction of the movement of the hook is the contact angle. The normal vector of $\Delta ABC$ is written as

$$\overrightarrow{n}=\frac{[(x_B,y_B,z_B)-(x_A,y_A,z_A)]\times[(x_C,y_C,z_C)-(x_A,y_A,z_A)]}{\|[(x_B,y_B,z_B)-(x_A,y_A,z_A)]\times[(x_C,y_C,z_C)-(x_A,y_A,z_A)]\|} \tag{5}$$

To guarantee that $\overrightarrow{n}$ always points to the center of the sphere, an arbitrary point on $\Delta ABC$ is selected. Taking the vertex A as an example, the vector $\overrightarrow{AO}$ connecting A to the center of the sphere O is constructed. If the angle between $\overrightarrow{AO}$ and $\overrightarrow{n}$ is less than $90°$, then we set $\overrightarrow{n_{ABC}}=\overrightarrow{n}$; otherwise, we set $\overrightarrow{n_{ABC}}=-\overrightarrow{n}$. The angle between the resulting vector and the reverse direction of the movement of the hook (supposing that the hook moves in the negative direction of the y-axis) is the contact angle between the hook tip and the triangle. Then, whether or not the triangle meets the gripping constraints can be judged based on Eq. (1).

### 3.3    Procedural Steps and Algorithm

First, we outline the steps involved in the discrimination process, and then present the corresponding algorithm.

**Step 1:** The hook size $r$ and minimum graspable angle $\theta_{min}$ are defined. To prevent an overlarge space between adjacent points, the final point cloud sample $M_{21}[x_{set}, y_{set}, z_{set}]$ is obtained by conducting interpolation on the initial set of point clouds based on the hook size $r$.

**Step 2:** All three-point combinations probably forming contactable triangles are acquired by traversal through the point cloud sample $M_{21}[x_{set}, y_{set}, z_{set}]$ and using Eqs. (2) and (3)—put them into $M_{22}[x_{combine}, y_{combine}, z_{combine}]$.

**Step 3:** Then, each combination in $M_{22}[x_{combine}, y_{combine}, z_{combine}]$ is tested to see if it satisfies Constraint 3: (1) The three points in the current combination (and radius $r$ of the hook tip) are used to find the corresponding center of the sphere. If the result is real, move on to (2); otherwise, go back to Step 3 to test the next combination. (2) Using the center of the sphere derived (taking the one with larger z-coordinate, if there are two solutions), the distances of the points in $M_{21}[x_{set}, y_{set}, z_{set}]$ to the center of the sphere are calculated through traversal. If there is no point whose distance to the center of the sphere is shorter than r, the current three points and the corresponding center of the sphere are placed in matrix $M_{23}$ and then the next combination is judged by returning to Step 3. This is continued until all combinations in $M_{22}$ have been tested.

**Step 4:** The vector normal to the contact triangle is derived according to Eq. (5) and checked to make sure it points to the center of the sphere—then the contact angle $\theta$ between the hook and the contact triangle is calculated. Using the condition $\pi/2 - \theta > \theta_{min}$, it is found that the angle satisfies the grasping constraint. If it does, the group of points are put into matrix $M_{24}$.

**Step 5:** The next group of points in $M_{23}$ is taken and judged as in Step 4. Judgment continues until all the combinations have been judged and all graspable positions acquired.

## 4    Simulations

To check the performance of the algorithm with respect to the numbers and positions of graspable points discovered, simulations were performed using the MATLAB software package. Some of the initial point clouds in Sect. 2.3 are selected as experimental data and interpolation conducted using a cubic method. Theoretically, the smaller the space between points after interpolation the better. However, a spacing that is too small will lead to an excessive number of calculations being undertaken. In this work, the wall surface is profiled according to the hook size ($r \geq 10\,\mu m$) of the claw tip and so an interpolation spacing of $4\,\mu m$ is adopted (Figs. 9, 10 and 11). As the wall profile appears as point clouds, the change in the $z$-coordinates of the data points reflects the fluctuations in the wall surface. We also assume that the hook always moves along the negative direction of the $y$-axis.

The number of graspable points is used as the measurement criterion when analyzing the simulations. The point clouds making up the wall surface are shown in Fig. 9 (1,176 points are shown) and black asterisks are used to represent the graspable points. The heights of the wall surface are represented using different colors. It can be seen from the simulations that the lower and upper regions of convex peaks cannot be grasped when a hook moves in the negative y-direction. Near the bottoms of the pits in the wall surface, there are some regions that do satisfy the grasping angle condition but cannot contain the hook. Therefore, these regions are regarded as not satisfying the contact conditions.

Comparing Figs. 9a and b, it can be seen that the number of graspable points is significantly reduced when the value of $r$ is increased. By comparing the $M_{24}$ matrices in these two simulations, the numbers of graspable points are found to be 104 ($r = 10\,\mu m$ and $\theta_{min} = 40°$) and 46 ($r = 20\,\mu m$ and $\theta_{min} = 40°$). The reason for the difference in graspable point is that, for a given wall surface, the region between two convex peaks and pits will be less likely to accommodate the hook when the latter grows in size. Thus, the number of contactable regions and graspable positions is reduced accordingly. Comparing Figs. 9a and c, the number of graspable points is also significantly decreased if $\theta_{min}$ is made larger (the $M_{24}$ matrices indicate that there are 104 graspable points in Fig. 9a, where $\theta_{min} = 40°$, and 73 in Fig. 9c, where $\theta_{min} = 50°$).

The three simulations in Fig. 9 also show that there are multiple ungraspable points near the boundary region corresponding to $y = 120\,\mu m$. This is because we have assumed that the hook moves in the negative y-direction during the simulations and $y = 120\,\mu m$ corresponds to the initial position. Therefore, Constraint 3 partially fails.

Further simulations were made using diverse wall surfaces with different asperity. The simulation results using the same parameters as before are shown in Figs. 10 and 11 (Fig. 10 consists of 1,436 point clouds and Fig. 11 - 1,176). Comparing the $M_{24}$ matrices, as before, it is found that the numbers of graspable points in Fig. 10 are 272, 114, and 191 for cases (a)–(c) (corresponding to $r = 10\,\mu m$, $\theta_{min} = 40°$; $r = 20\,\mu m$, $\theta_{min} = 40°$; and $r = 10\,\mu m$, $\theta_{min} = 50°$), respectively. The corresponding numbers in Fig. 11 are 67, 46, and 56, respectively.

In light of the simulation results, the following conclusions can be drawn: (1) the smaller the radius $r$ of the hook, the greater the number of graspable points; and (2) the smaller the minimum graspable angle $\theta_{min}$, the greater the number of graspable points.

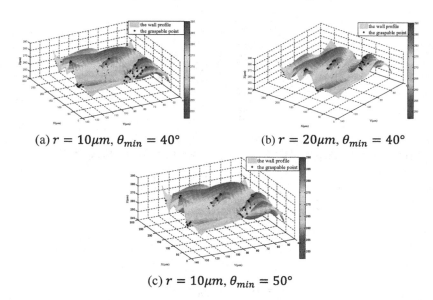

(a) $r = 10\mu m$, $\theta_{min} = 40°$    (b) $r = 20\mu m$, $\theta_{min} = 40°$

(c) $r = 10\mu m$, $\theta_{min} = 50°$

**Fig. 9.** Simulation results obtained using the algorithm (1,176 points). (Color figure online)

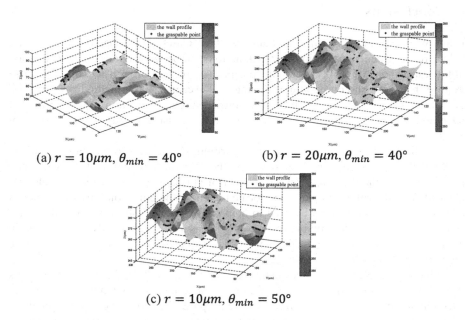

(a) $r = 10\mu m$, $\theta_{min} = 40°$    (b) $r = 20\mu m$, $\theta_{min} = 40°$

(c) $r = 10\mu m$, $\theta_{min} = 50°$

**Fig. 10.** Further simulation results obtained using the algorithm (1,436 points).

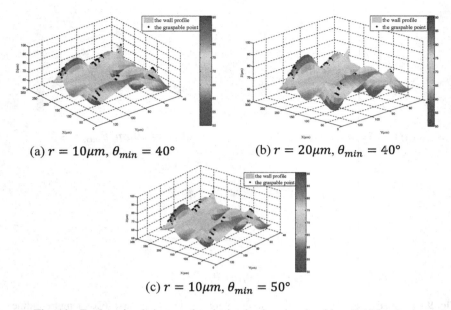

(a) $r = 10\mu m$, $\theta_{min} = 40°$        (b) $r = 20\mu m$, $\theta_{min} = 40°$

(c) $r = 10\mu m$, $\theta_{min} = 50°$

**Fig. 11.** Further simulation results obtained using the algorithm (1,176 points).

## 5 Conclusions

In this work, we put forward a structure in which claws are arranged in a cross and deduce the mechanical conditions for locking to occur between hooks on the claws and protuberances on the walls from the perspective of friction self-locking. We also propose that walls should be scanned using a 3D scanner and a method of extracting the roughness characteristics of the wall is provided. Our simulation results imply that 3D morphologies of rough walls can be reproduced using profile curves and point clouds.

The effectiveness of the discriminant algorithm with respect to graspable positions on 3D walls was verified via simulations and the effect of the radius r of the hooks and minimum graspable angle $\theta_{min}$ on the number of graspable points found on walls was deduced. The algorithm can judge and locate the graspable points on rough walls and is a practical algorithm that can be used to help wall-climbing robots grasp walls. Thus, we must design the wall-climbing robot so that it has a reasonable body size, a hook tip that is as small as feasible, and a friction coefficient (between the hook and wall surface materials) that is as large as possible.

In the future, we plan to investigate methods for identifying the graspable regions of a wall more thoroughly. As part of this investigation, it is intended that a visual detection algorithm will be employed to more purposefully look for graspable points. If the algorithm is applied to a climbing robot, it is necessary to carry a micro-scanner on the robot, scan the wall with a micro-scanner, determine the grabbing point, and adjust the posture to achieve the grab. This is one of our next major research directions.

**Acknowledgments.** This research is supported by National Natural Science Foundation of China (51775284), Primary Research & Development Plan of Jiangsu Province (BE2018734), Joint Research Fund for Overseas Chinese, Hong Kong and Macao Young Scholars (61728302), and Postgraduate Research & Practice Innovation Program of Jiangsu Province (SJCX18_0299).

# References

1. Gao, X., Xu, D., Wang, Y.: Multifunctional robot to maintain boiler water-cooling tubes. Robotica **27**(6), 941–948 (2009)
2. Tavakoli, M., Viegas, C., Marques, L.: OmniClimbers: omni-directional magnetic wheeled climbing robots for inspection of ferromagnetic structures. Robot. Auton. Syst. **61**(9), 997–1007 (2013)
3. Li, J., Gao, X., Fan, N., Li, K., Jiang, Z.: Adsorption performance of sliding wall climbing robot. Chin. J. Mech. Eng. **23**(6), 733–741 (2010)
4. Hu, B., Zhao, Y., Fu, Z.: A miniature wall climbing robot with biomechanical suction cups. Ind. Robot Int. J. **36**(6), 551–561 (2009)
5. Wang, W., Wang, K., Zong, G., Li, D.: Principle and experiment of vibrating suction method for wall-climbing robot. Vacuum **85**(1), 107–112 (2010)
6. Koo, I.M., et al.: Development of wall climbing robot system by using impeller type adhesion mechanism. J. Intell. Robot. Syst. **72**(1), 57–72 (2013)
7. Liu, R., Chen, R., Shen, H., Zhang, R.: Wall climbing robot using electrostatic adhesion force generated by flexible interdigital electrodes. Int. J. Adv. Robot. Syst. **10**(36), 1–9 (2013)
8. Spenko, M.J., Haynes, G.C., Saunders, J.A.: Biologically inspired climbing with a hexapedal robot. J. Field Robot. **25**(4–5), 223–242 (2008)
9. Lynch, G.A., Clark, J.E., Lin, P.C., Koditschek, D.E.: A bioinspired dynamical vertical climbing robot. Int. J. Robot. Res. **31**(8), 974–996 (2012)
10. Provancher, W.R., Jensen-segal, S.I., Fehlberg, M.A.: ROCR: an energy-efficient dynamic wall-climbing robot. IEEE/ASME Trans. Mechatron. **16**(5), 897–906 (2011)
11. Asbeck, A.T., Kim, S., Cutkosky, M.R., Provancher, W.R., Lanzetta, M.: Scaling hard vertical surfaces with compliant microspine array. Int. J. Robot. Res. **25**(12), 1165–1179 (2006)
12. Xu, F., Wang, X.: Design method and analysis for wall-climbing robot based on hooked-claws. Int. J. Adv. Robot. Syst. **9**(3), 1–12 (2012)
13. Xu, F., Shen, J., Hu, J., Jiang, P.: A rough concrete wall climbing robot based on grasping claws: mechanical design. Analysis and laboratory experiments. Int. J. Adv. Robot. Syst. **13**(5), 1–10 (2016)
14. Xu, F., Wang, B., Shen, J., Hu, J., Jiang, G.: Design and realization of the claw gripper system of a climbing robot. J. Intell. Robot. Syst. **89**, 301–317 (2018)

# Improved CPG Model Based on Hopf Oscillator for Gait Design of a New Type of Hexapod Robot

Xiangyu Li[1,2], Hong Liu[2], Xuan Wu[2(✉)], Rui Li[1], and Xiaojie Wang[2]

[1] Engineering Research Center of Automotive Electronics
and Embedded System, Chongqing University of Posts and Telecommunications,
Chongqing 400065, China
[2] Institute of Advanced Manufacturing Technology,
Hefei Institute of Physical Science, Chinese Academy of Sciences,
Changzhou 213164, China
xwu@iamt.ac.cn

**Abstract.** We proposed and designed a new type of hexapod robot leg structure with four-bar linkage mechanism to replace the most used bare joints for hexapod robots. The new design reducing the weight of the legs as well as the robot body inertia could offer a way to control the hexapod robot easily by using the knee joints. Based on this design, we developed CPG (central pattern generator) model using Hopf oscillator for a multi-leg coupling model which possesses a ring-type CPG network composed of six CPG units. The advantage of the improved CPG model needs one Hopf oscillator for each leg that could improve the stability of the model. The model output signals are converted to the angular trajectories of the hip joint and the knee joint through a mapping function. Simulation and experiment show that the CPG network outputs stable and smooth signals with steady phase differences, which can achieve a smooth walking statue for the hexapod robot under the triangular gait mode.

**Keywords:** Hexapod robot · Four-bar linkage mechanism ·
Central pattern generators · Hopf oscillator

## 1 Introduction

Hexapod robot with its stable mechanical structure, flexible walking and limb redundancy makes it valuable for applications in harsh environment such as irregular terrains and aerospace. The common hexapod robot has three degrees of freedom in the legs. The legs of the robot are relatively bulky, and the leg inertia is large during the crawling process. Since hexapod robot has the characteristics of multiple degrees of freedom of joints and flexible gaits among the legs, it is difficult to obtain a general control law for motion control of multi-legged robot that meets the requirements through simple analytical method. In view of the problem, inspired by studying the laws of animal movement, it is found in nature that the animal rhythm movement is controlled by the CPG (central pattern generator) located in the spine. The CPG-based bionic control method has good self-stability and adaptability [1–4]. At present, the CPG model has

© Springer Nature Switzerland AG 2019
H. Yu et al. (Eds.): ICIRA 2019, LNAI 11741, pp. 72–83, 2019.
https://doi.org/10.1007/978-3-030-27532-7_7

been widely used in robot control fields such as robot fish, machine snakes, and machine turtles [5–8]. Compared with the traditional model-based robot control method, the CPG control method does not need to build the model of robot body and environment, and it does not rely on external feedback and high-level commands to generate stable rhythmic motion, which can adapt to the unstructured environment, and it has advantages in diverse motion modes and tight joint connection [9].

Serving for different application scenario, CPG models can be divided into several types [10], such as biological neuron models, semi-central models, and coupled oscillator models. The commonly used CPG models are semi-central model and coupled oscillator model. The semi-central model simulates alternating movements of the extensor and flexors. Among them, the Kimura oscillator has been widely used for motion control of multi-legged robot. The Kimura oscillator adds sensor feedback based on the Matsuoka oscillator model, and uses two mutually inhibited flexor and extensor neurons to form an oscillator model. The oscillator improves the stability of the motion of the quadruped robot, but the model has disadvantages in control algorithm which is too complicated to be implemented, and the parameters are also difficult to be adjusted. The coupled oscillator model consists of a nonlinear oscillator that has a clearly physical meaning for model parameters. The amplitude and phase of the oscillator are directly adjustable, making it easy to control the multi-legged robots. The most commonly used oscillator models include the Kuramoto oscillator model, the Hopf oscillator model, and the Wilson-Cowan oscillator model [11, 12].

In this paper, we developed CPG model using Hopf oscillator for motion control of a hexapod robot. The new type of hexapod robot has legs with four-bar linkage mechanism to replace the most used bare joints. The new design reducing the weight of the legs as well as the robot body inertia could offer a way to control the hexapod robot easily by using the knee joints.

## 2   The Structure and Gait of a Hexapod Robot

### 2.1   Structure of Hexapod Robot

As shown in Fig. 1, the hexapod robot is divided into two parts: the body and the legs. As shown in Fig. 2, each leg of the hexapod robot consists of a hip joint, a knee joint, and a four-bar linkage mechanism, each leg having three degrees of freedom. The hip joint is parallel to the ground, and the hip joint controls the horizontal swing of the single leg in the horizontal direction. The knee joint rotates by itself to drive the four-bar linkage mechanism to have two degrees of freedom, and the knee joint and the four-bar linkage mechanism drive the robot leg to swing in the vertical direction.

The common hexapod robot has three degrees of freedom in the legs, namely hip joint, knee joint and bare joint. The legs of the robot are relatively bulky, and the leg inertia is large during the crawling process. When using the CPG model control, the control model algorithm is complicated due to the excessive number of joints of the robot, and it is also difficult to generate a stable and smooth output signal. In this study, the bare joint of the hexapod robot is replaced by a four-bar linkage mechanism, as shown in Fig. 3. The link $L_3$ is rotated by the knee joint link $L_4$, so that the B point is also rotated as bare joint. From this design, the robot legs still have three degrees of freedom. The $L_2$ connecting rod is equipped with a spring device, which has a buffering effect on the robot crawling. Compared with the three-joint leg design, the mechanism of such design has a reduced range of rotation at point B, but it still satisfies the degree of freedom of rotation of the leg. This design makes the robot control simpler and the legs more lightweight.

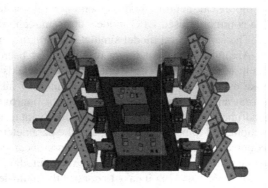

**Fig. 1.** Schematic design of hexapod robot

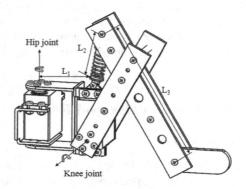

**Fig. 2.** Schematic structure of the robot leg

## 2.2 Hexapod Robot Triangle Gait Description

Gait refers to the movement of each leg of the robot in a certain order and trajectory. The robot can adjust the posture of the body by stepping and frequency.

The gait cycle T is the time required for the robot to complete a full gait. The gait duty cycle is $\varepsilon$, which is the ratio of the time of the supporting phase to the entire gait cycle in one gait cycle.

The hexapod robot gait is usually divided by the number of contact angles with the ground. Commonly there are triangular gait, follow-up gait and wave gait. Triangle gait is the fastest gait for multi-legged robots to walk. Figure 4 is a schematic diagram of the triangular gait supporting phase and the oscillating phase of the hexapod robot. White indicates the swing phase, black indicates the support phase, leg 1, leg 3, and leg 5 are a group, leg 2, leg 4, and leg 6 are a group, the same group legs have the same phase, and the different groups have a phase difference of $\pi$. In this paper, the triangular gait of $\varepsilon = 0.5$ is selected. When the robot walks, the support phase of each leg is equal to the swing phase time. One leg supports and the other leg swings, so that the robot alternately walks according to the prescribed gait.

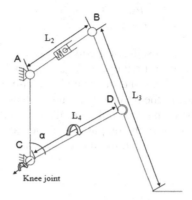

**Fig. 3.** Four-bar linkage diagram

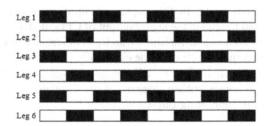

**Fig. 4.** Timing diagram of triangle gait

# 3   CPG Oscillator Network Model and Simulation

## 3.1   CPG Oscillator Model

The central mode generator is a discrete neural network that is commonly used in biological rhythmic motion control to generate complex high-dimensional signals to control animal motion [13]. The CPG model is often referred to as a nonlinear oscillator model. The spontaneous oscillation of CPG neurons is similar to conventional mechanical vibrations, simulating CPG generation signals by using single or multiple non-linear oscillators connected to each other. The nonlinear oscillator has a limit loop. If the limit loop is stable, all the traces in the system will be close to the limit loop, so that even if there is a small disturbance in the system, the system can still return to a stable state.

The Hopf oscillator has a stable limit cycle, and the trajectories in the field are spiraled close to the limit ring, which has good stability. Compared with other oscillators, the main advantage of Hopf oscillator is that it can easily control the amplitude and frequency of the oscillator output signal. The model parameters have clear physical meaning, so we choose Hopf oscillator as the basic model of CPG theory. The mathematical model of the Hopf oscillator is described by Eq. (1) [13]:

$$\begin{cases} \dot{x} = \alpha(\mu - x^2 - y^2)x - \omega y \\ \dot{y} = \beta(\mu - x^2 - y^2)y + \omega x \\ \omega = \frac{\omega_{stance}}{e^{-bx}+1} + \frac{\omega_{swing}}{e^{bx}+1} \end{cases} \tag{1}$$

where the amplitude is $\mu$, the oscillator frequency is $\omega$, $\alpha > 0$ and $\beta < 0$ are the convergence speeds of the control limit cycle; $\omega_{stance}$ and $\omega_{swing}$ respectively represent the frequency of the support phase and the swinging phase, and b is a large positive value, ensuring the frequency of the oscillator different values can be taken between the support phase and the wobble phase. x and y are the two state variables of the oscillator, specifying the output of y as the output of the oscillator.

Let $x = r\cos\varphi, y = r\sin\varphi, \gamma = \omega t$, the model presented in polar coordinate form is described by Eq. (2):

$$\begin{cases} \dot{r} = r(\mu - r^2) \\ \dot{\varphi} = \omega \end{cases} \tag{2}$$

According to the system simulation, when $\mu > 0$, Hopf oscillator bifurcates, and the system has a stable limit cycle. In this paper, the limit cycle characteristics of the system at $\mu > 0$ are used to realize the signal output of CPG model. Figure 5 shows the phase plan of Hopf oscillator state variables x and y at different initial values. It can be seen from the figure that the Hopf limit cycle eventually tends to be stable regardless of the initial value. As shown in Fig. 6, take $\omega_{stance} = \omega_{swing}$, $\mu = 0$ and the output waveform represents the output phase diagram of the oscillator y at the same time of the swing phase and the supporting phase.

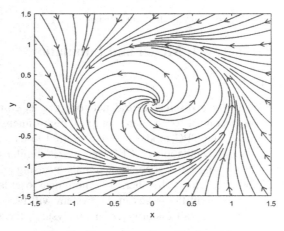

**Fig. 5.** Phase plane diagram of x and y

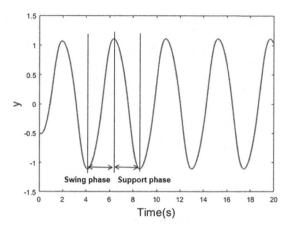

**Fig. 6.** Hopf oscillator's output curve y

As can be seen from Fig. 6, the oscillator can spontaneously generate a stable periodic oscillation signal, which is a good simulation of CPG neurons in biological systems.

In order to achieve coordinated motion among the legs of the hexapod robot, the mutual coupling of the oscillators is required to ensure the synchronization and coordination of the motion. The coupling relationship between the CPG model oscillators is modeled by the Eq. (3).

In the Eq. (3), $\delta$ represents the coupling strength between the oscillators, indicating the phase difference between the i oscillator and the j oscillator. Take $\omega_{stance} = \omega_{swing}$. The convergence coefficient $\alpha = \beta = 1$. By setting different phase differences, the values are taken as $\pi/2$ and $\pi$ respectively. Figure 7 shows the obtained output curves of two oscillators.

$$\begin{cases} \dot{x}_i = \alpha(\mu - r_i^2)x_i - \omega_i y_i \\ \dot{y}_i = \beta(\mu - r_i^2)y_i + \omega_i x_i + \delta \cdot \sum_j \Delta_{ji} \\ \Delta_{ji} = (y_j \cdot \cos\theta_j^i - x_j \sin\theta_j^i) \\ \omega = \frac{\omega_{stance}}{e^{-bx}+1} + \frac{\omega_{swing}}{e^{bx}+1} \end{cases} \tag{3}$$

## 3.2 Ring CPG Network Model Construction

The CPG network topology of the hexapod robot consists of six CPG units. Each CPG unit corresponds to one leg of the hexapod robot and consists of a Hopf oscillator. A weighted directed graph is used to form a mesh structure, and six CPG units are used as six vertices of the directed graph, and full symmetric two-way connections are used between adjacent vertices. The CPG network topology is shown in Fig. 8. In the robot's triangular gait, the legs are divided into two groups: {1, 3, 5} and {2, 4, 6}. The legs of the same group have the same phase, and the legs of the different groups are opposite in phase.

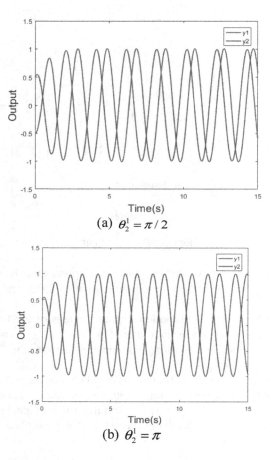

(a) $\theta_2^1 = \pi / 2$

(b) $\theta_2^1 = \pi$

**Fig. 7.** Phase difference output waveform of two coupled oscillators

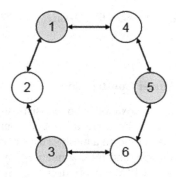

**Fig. 8.** The ring-type network topology of CPG

### 3.3    Joint Trajectory Design

In the case of three joint controls, the robot needs two oscillators for output on one leg, and the hexapod robot requires a total of 12 oscillators. It will result in more oscillators needed for the model, the CPG network is more complicated, and the parameter adjustment is difficult. In this paper, the number of single-leg joints is reduced by the mechanism design, so that the CPG model requires only six oscillators for gait output. It is convenient for the later design of various gait and gait conversion experiments.

During the walking of the hexapod robot, the angle of the joint of the single leg has the following rule: when in the swing phase, the leg swings forward, the angle of the hip joint increases, and when the maximum value is reached, the support phase enters. at the same time, the knee joint angle increases first. Raise the leg and then reduce it to the swing of the support phase. When the phase is supported, the hip joint angle is reduced, the robot body moves forward, and the knee joint remains basically unchanged. As shown in Fig. 9, the phase relationship between the hip joint and the knee joint of the robot is the output y of the single oscillator that is used as the hip joint input signal, and the output x is transformed by the function as the input signal of the knee joint. The rising section of the output curve represents the swing phase of the robot's leg motion, and the falling section represents the support phase.

According to the change rule of the joint angle of the hip joint and the knee joint, the angle trajectory of each joint in the leg is generated by the mapping function method. As shown in Eq. (4), the hip joint angle is obtained by multiplying the oscillator output y by the proportional coefficient $k_0$, and the knee joint angle is obtained by the piecewise function of the oscillator output x. The angle function of each joint of a single leg is defined as follows:

$$\begin{cases} \theta_1 = k_0 y \\ \theta_2 = \begin{cases} k_1 x + b_1 \, (\dot{y} \geq 0) \\ k_2 x + b_2 \, (\dot{y} < 0) \end{cases} \end{cases} \tag{4}$$

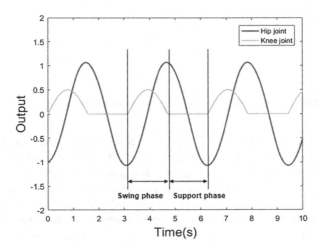

**Fig. 9.** Triangle gait's phase curve between hip and knee joint

where $k_i$ (i = 0, 1, 2) is the proportionality factor and $b_j$ (j = 1, 2) is a constant. Adjusting $k_0$, $k_1$, $k_2$, $b_1$, $b_2$ causes the oscillator to output the angle value of the hip joint.

Combined with the parameters of the hexapod robot mechanism, $k_0 = 0.52$, $k_1 = 0.26$, $k_2 = 0.01$, $b_1 = 0$, $b_2 = 0$. To distinguish the different joint angles of different legs, define each joint angle for each leg: denoted by $\theta_j^i$, where i is the number of the leg (i = 1, 2, 3, 4, 5, 6), j = 1 indicates the hip joint, and j = 2 indicates the knee joint. Figure 10 is the joint angle output curve of the two legs in the triangular gait.

## 4   Experimental Validation

In order to verify the effectiveness of the hexapod robot gait adjustment algorithm based on Hopf oscillator, a prototype of hexapod robot is designed and assembled as experimental platform shown in Fig. 11. The length, width and height of the robot are 300 mm * 150 mm * 90 mm and the weight is 3.18 kg. The hexapod robot is driven by the DS3120 high-torque servo. The STM32 processor is used as the main controller control chip and driven by the PCA9685 servo control chip. It mainly includes power buck-boost module, controller module and servo control module.

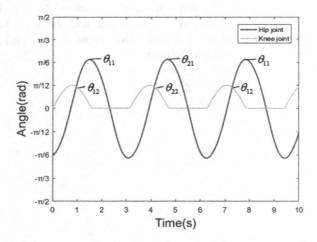

**Fig. 10.** Triangle gait single leg two joints output angle curve

By using the mapping function to transform the output of simulation results as the angle of movement of each leg, and using the ring CPG network model to construction the robot overall motion frame. The Fig. 12 shows the measured angle curves of the two joints in the leg under the triangular gait in experiments. By discretizing the experimental data and running it through the controller, the gait experiment is carried out on the experimental platform of the hexapod robot. When the robot legs are in the swing phase, collision may occur between the adjacent two legs. Therefore, during the

**Fig. 11.** Hexapod robot prototype

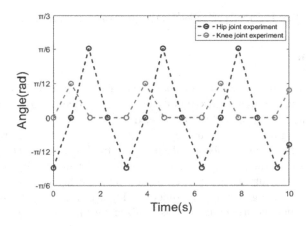

**Fig. 12.** Experimental angle curve of two joints in the leg under triangular gait

swing phase, the limit angle of the hip joint is not set to - Π/6, and the actual angle is - Π/9. Figure 13 is a triangular gait Hexapod test. According to the measurement, the hexapod robot took 43 s to walk 480 mm distance, with an average speed of 11.16 mm/s. Due to the slight error between the mechanical structures of the robot during the walking, the robot will shift to the right by 56 mm during the straight 480 mm process. The experimental results show that the hexapod robot moves smoothly and the gaits are coordinated with each other.

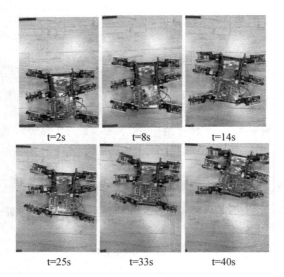

t=2s        t=8s        t=14s

t=25s        t=33s        t=40s

**Fig. 13.** Hexapod robot triangle gait walking experiment

## 5 Conclusion

A CPG model using Hopf oscillator for motion control of a hexapod robot is proposed and studied on a new design of hexapod robot. The proposed hexapod robot has four-bar linkage mechanism instead of the most used bare joints for driving multi legs. The new design reducing the weight of the legs as well as the robot body inertia could offer a way to control the hexapod robot easily by using the knee joints. Through such leg structure, the hexapod robot CPG gait control model is established by Hopf oscillator, and the CPG model output signal is converted into the hexapod robot joint angle trajectory by establishing a mapping function. Finally, the smooth walking of the hexapod robot under the triangular gait is realized by the prototype of the hexapod robot.

## References

1. Taga, G., Yamaguchi, Y., Shimizu, H.: Self-organized control of bipedal locomotion by neural oscillators in unpredictable environment. Biol. Cybern. **65**(3), 147–159 (1991)
2. Miyakoshi, S., Taga, G., Kuniyoshi, Y., Nagakubo, A.: Three dimensional bipedal stepping motion using neural oscillators - towards humanoid motion in the real world. In: International Conference on Intelligent Robots and Systems, pp. 84–89. IEEE (1998)
3. Kimura, H., Fukuoka, Y., Nakamura, H.: Biologically inspired adaptive dynamic walking of the quadruped on irregular terrain. In: Hollerbach, J.M., Koditschek, D.E. (eds.) Robotics Research, pp. 329–336. Springer, London (2000). https://doi.org/10.1007/978-1-4471-0765-1_40

4. Morel, Y., Porez, M., Leonessa, A., Auke, J.: Nonlinear motion control of CPG-based movement with applications to a class of swimming robots. In: Conference on Decision and Control and European Control Conference, pp. 6331–6336. IEEE (2011)
5. Wu, Z., Yu, J., Tan, M.: Comparison of two methods to implement backward swimming for a carangiform robotic fish. Acta Automatica Sinica 39(12), 2232–2242 (2013)
6. Wu, X., Ma, S.: Adaptive creeping locomotion of a CPG-controlled snake-like robot to environment change. Auton. Robots 28(3), 283–294 (2010). https://doi.org/10.1007/s10514-009-9168-1
7. Gao, Q., Wang, Z., Zhao, H.: Gait control for a snake robot based on Hopf oscillator model. Robot 36(6), 688–696 (2014)
8. Seo, K., Chung, S., Slotine, J.: CPG-based control of a turtle-like underwater vehicle. Auton. Robots 28(33), 247–269 (2010)
9. Ren, J., Xu, H., Gan, S., Wang, B.: CPG model design based on Hopf oscillator for hexapod robots gait. CAAI Trans. Intell. Syst. 11(5), 627–634 (2016). (in Chinese)
10. Ijspeert, A.J.: Central pattern generators for locomotion control in animals and robots: a review. Neural Netw. 21(4), 642–653 (2008)
11. Liu, C., Fan, Z., Seo, K., Tan, X., Goodman, E.D.: Synthesis of Matsuoka-based neuron oscillator models in locomotion control of robots. In: Proceedings of the Third Global Congress on Intelligent Systems (GCIS), pp. 342–347. IEEE (2012)
12. Matsuoka, K.: Sustained oscillations generated by mutually inhibiting neurons with adaptation. Biol. Cybern. 54(6), 367–376 (1985)
13. Yu, J., Tan, M., Chen, J., Zhang, J.: A survey on CPG-inspired control models and system implementation. IEEE Trans. Neural Netw. Learn. Syst. 25(3), 441–456 (2014)

# A Novel Tracked Wall-Climbing Robot with Bio-inspired Spine Feet

Yanwei Liu[1]([⊠]) [ID], Sanwa Liu[1], Limeng Wang[1], Xuan Wu[2], Yan Li[1], and Tao Mei[3]

[1] School of Mechanical and Precision Instrument Engineering,
Xi'an University of Technology, Xi'an 710048, China
liuyw@xaut.edu.cn
[2] Institute of Advanced Manufacturing Technology, Hefei Institutes of Physical Science, Chinese Academy of Sciences, Changzhou 213164, China
[3] Suzhou Rongcui Special Robot Co. Ltd., Suzhou 215004, China

**Abstract.** This paper proposes a novel tracked wall-climbing robot with bio-inspired spine feet. The robot's track is composed of a dozen spine feet, which are used to attach on rough surfaces. Compared with legged climbing robots, tracked climbing robots have more spines and the adhesion property could be improved, but their rotary movements make it difficult for spines to detach from surfaces. To address this problem, a mechanism with two circular guides is introduced in the robot design to imitate the foot attaching and detaching movements of insects. Driven by the mechanism, the spine foot begins to attach on the surfaces when it locates at the front of the robot, and detaches from the surface when it locates at the rear of the robot. Some climbing experiments have been conducted, and the robot is capable of climbing on sandpaper, brick, coarse stucco, and pebble walls.

**Keywords:** Tracked climbing robot · Spine foot · Rough surface

## 1 Introduction

In nature, many animals possess the outstanding ability of climbing on vertical and inverted surfaces. Nearly all adult insects possess claws which can be used to cling on asperities distributed over rough and hard surfaces or penetrate in soft surfaces [1]. Geckos and some insects used hairy adhesive to adhere to smooth surfaces due to van der Waals forces [2, 3]. The stable attachment of adhesive plays a critical role in the climbing performances. In addition, the detachment from the climbing surface must be easy and rapid for efficient locomotion. The claws in these insects' legs are obviously directional, and the branched setae arrays in gecko toes are directional [4]. Due to the directional property of adhesives, the adhesion forces between substrate surfaces and adhesives are controllable. Therefore, insects and geckos are able to detach their feet easily and rapidly by manipulating their legs or feet as they climb [4, 5].

Inspired by claws and spines of insects, many wall-climbing robots have been developed. For legged robots with spines or other directional adhesives, the attachment and detachment can be controlled by manipulating the movements of their legs and

© Springer Nature Switzerland AG 2019
H. Yu et al. (Eds.): ICIRA 2019, LNAI 11741, pp. 84–96, 2019.
https://doi.org/10.1007/978-3-030-27532-7_8

feet. Spinybotll utilized a fixed alternating tripod gait, and each spine foot was driven by a RC servo to attach and detach [6]. Similar attaching and detaching movements were employed in other climbing robots [7, 8]. Rise V2, a hexapod robot, used similar spine feet to climb on rough surface, and a four-bar leg mechanism was used to generate proper foot trajectory for attachment and detachment [9]. LWbot employed a modified Chebyshev four-bar linkage mechanism to imitate the attaching and detaching movements of insects by generating "D" shaped foot trajectory, and could climb on vertical brick surfaces and cloth curtains using spine feet [10]. LEMUR 3 employed spine grippers to climb on the rough rock surface, and each gripper possessed two actuators used to control the gripper's operations of attachment and detachment [11]. An inchworm-like robot with two spine grippers was able to climb on vertical and inverted brick surfaces, and each spine gripper was controlled by a RC servo and two springs to achieve attaching and detaching movements [12].

Compared with legged robots, wheeled and tracked robots have many advantages, including high speeds, simple structures, minimal actuators, and high efficiencies. Several wheeled wall-climbing robots with spines have been developed. The wheeled robot, DROP, could climb 85° inclines [13], and the climbing performances were improved with new configurations [14]. With insect-inspired compliant spine mechanisms, the wheeled robot, Tbot, could climb on 100° inclined brick surfaces [15]. However, DROP and Tbot cannot achieve the detaching movement employed in legged robots described above, and the detachment of spine in those wheeled climbing robots is an enforced operation. The spine detaches from the surface when it rotates nearly parallel to the climbing surface or reaches the adhesion limitation. During the detachment, the spine may be stuck in a narrow crack, and the compliant suspensions, spines or surface asperities could be damaged.

This paper contributes a novel tracked wall-climbing robot with bio-inspired feet, aims to achieve efficient locomotion with stable attachment and easy detachment. Section 2 presents the robot design. Section 3 presents the design and analysis of the mechanism with dual guides. Section 4 shows the prototype and experiment of this robot. Section 5 presents conclusions and future work.

## 2   Robot Design

### 2.1   Mechanical Design

The tracked wall-climbing robot mainly consists of robot frame, tread, sprocket wheel, tails and rear wheels, as shown in Fig. 1. And the tread consists of 18 spine feet and a chain structure, as shown in Fig. 2. The tread is driven by a single DC motor through a sprocket wheel. Using the spine feet, the robot is able to climb up and down on rough surfaces. The long tail could reduce the adhesion force needed to balance the pitch back torque produced by the robot weight. The rear wheels could reduce the friction force acting on tail during climbing.

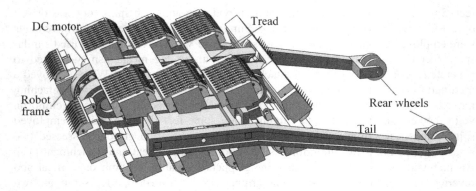

**Fig. 1.** Overall structure of the robot.

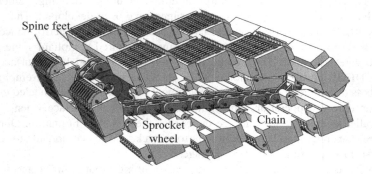

**Fig. 2.** The tread structure of the robot.

## 2.2 Bio-inspired Spine Foot

The compliant spine mechanism is a critical part in the design of wall-climbing robots with spines. With the compliant spine mechanism, more spines could be involved to provide adhesion and share the load.

The tarsus plays a critical role in the climbing performance of insects. The segmented structure of tarsus makes it more flexible to suit irregular surfaces, and makes the attachment more reliable [16]. Only utilizing claws and sharp spines on the tarsomeres distal and tibia distal, *Serica orientalis* Motschulsky, a leaf-feeding insect, can climb on leaves, tree trunks and rough outer wall surfaces. The tarsal chain of the insect has been studied in [15]. As shown in Fig. 3a, the tarsus of the insect consists of five tarsomeres (Ta1–Ta5), linked via flexible joints, and all these tarsomeres are ventrally movable.

As shown in Fig. 3b, inspired by the flexible tarsal chain, a compliant spine toe has been designed to suit irregular surfaces, and makes more spines attach the surface to share load. The compliant spine toe consists of a spring-like suspension and a miniature spine. Considering the difficulty in controlling a large number of toes, the current toe design is a passive version, different from the controllable tarsal chain of insects. However, dozens of compliant spine toes would improve the attachment. The bio-inspired compliant spine toe owns normal and tangential flexibilities. The normal flexibility of the spine toe enables spine toe arrays to adapt to the uneven wall surface morphology. The tangential flexibility makes the suspensions stretchable, and more spines have opportunities to engage on the surface asperities, and the adhesion property of spine toe arrays could be improved.

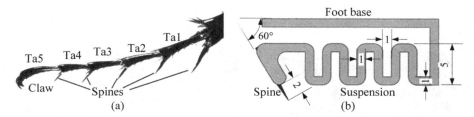

**Fig. 3.** The design of a bio-inspired spine toe. (a) The tarsal chain of the insect *Serica orientalis* Motschulsky; (b) The compliant spine toe.

As shown in Fig. 4, a spine foot consists of ten compliant spine toes. And spacers prevent two adjacent compliant spine toes from interference. With a stop pin, the stiffness of the compliant spine toe is directional, and the spine could be pulled off the surface without large deformation of the suspension. The spine foot was made from SLS (Selective Laser Sintered) PA2200 nylon (ESO). The spine was approximately 2 mm long outer the suspensions, and made of disposable acupuncture needles (HUANQIU brand) with 180 μm shaft diameter and 30 μm–60 μm tip radius.

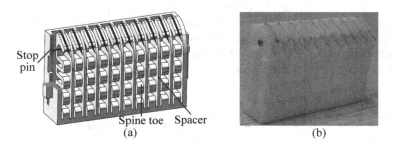

**Fig. 4.** Structure of the bio-inspired spine foot. (a) The CAD model of spine foot; (b) A spine foot prototype.

## 3 Design and Analysis of the Dual-Guide Mechanism

Legged wall-climbing robots could employ articulated legs or linkage mechanisms to achieve stable attachments and easy detachments. This section focuses on the design of analysis of a dual-guide mechanism employed to imitate the attaching and detaching movements of insects.

## 3.1   Mechanism Design

The dual-guide mechanism consists of the robot frame and spine foot unit, similar to the track system and steps in escalator. As shown in Fig. 5, there are four symmetrical circular guides in the robot frame, two inner guides and two outer guides. As shown in Fig. 6, the spine foot unit consists of two spine feet and foot frame, and there are two outer pins and an inner pin. The inner pin moves along the inner guides, and the outer pins move along the outer guides.

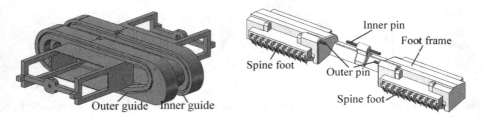

**Fig. 5.**  The structure of robot frame.       **Fig. 6.**  The structure of spine foot unit.

As shown in Fig. 7, the dual-guide mechanism can be simplified as a linkage moving along two guides. The yellow dashed line and the blue solid line represent outer guide and inner guide respectively. The linkage has two sliding joints, one moves along the inner guide (the blue solid line), and another moves along the outer guide (the yellow dashed line). The spine foot unit and the linkage are assembled together as a whole part. When the spine foot unit moves along the two guides, the position and posture of the spine foot can be controlled by the relative position between the two guides. A proper guide design could be used to achieve imitate the attaching and detaching movements of insects. Figure 8 shows the schematic diagram of the robot model with nine spine foot units. They are connected with each other via a chain structure, and driven by a DC motor.

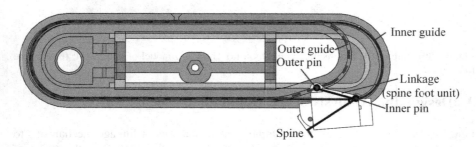

**Fig. 7.**  The simplified model of the dual-guide mechanism. (Color figure online)

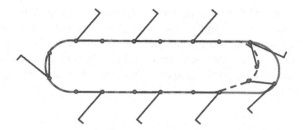

**Fig. 8.** The schematic diagram of the robot model. (Color figure online)

## 3.2 Analysis of Attaching and Detaching Movements

Figure 9 shows the attaching and detaching movements of a spine foot during forward climbing. The colored and grey lines represent the initial and final positions of the guides with spine foot units respectively. The black dotted lines represent the final positions of spine foot units. As shown in Fig. 9a, the spine foot at the front of the robot tries to contact the surface, and achieves the attachment with anticlockwise rotation around the fixed center $O_1$. As shown in Fig. 9b, the spine foot at the rear of the robot tries to leave the surface, and achieves the detachment with clockwise rotation around the fixed center $O_2$. The detachment of spine foot is just the inverse operation of its attachment, and the velocity direction of the spine during the rotation is concordant with the spine direction. It means that the spine is pulled out from the surface by the force parallel to the spine direction. Therefore, the detachment of the spine foot could be easy and rapid.

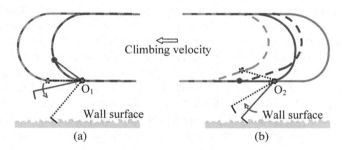

**Fig. 9.** The schematic diagrams showing the attaching and detaching movements of the spine foot during forward climbing. (a) Attaching movement; (b) Detaching movement. (Color figure online)

Thanks to the dual-guide mechanism, the robot can not only climb forward but also climb backwards. Figure 10 shows the attaching and detaching movements of a spine foot during backward climbing. The colored and grey lines represent the initial and final positions of the guides with spine foot units respectively. The black dotted lines represent the final positions of spine foot units. As shown in Fig. 10a, the spine foot at the front of the robot tries to leave the surface, and achieves the detachment with clockwise rotation around the fixed center $O_1$. As shown in Fig. 10b, the spine foot at the rear of the robot tries to contact the surface, and achieves the attachment with anticlockwise rotation around the fixed center $O_2$. The detachment of spine foot is just the inverse operation of its attachment, and the velocity direction of the spine during the rotation is concordant with the spine direction. So, the detachment of the spine foot could be easy and rapid.

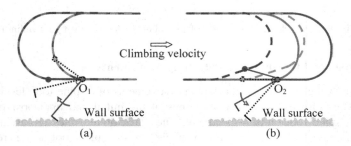

**Fig. 10.** The schematic diagrams showing the attaching and detaching movements of the spine foot during backward climbing. (a) Detaching movement; (b) Attaching movement. (Color figure online)

## 3.3   Force Analysis During Detachment

The detachment property of the spine foot is critical in the tracked robot, this section focuses on the forces analysis of the spine foot during detachment. When the robot climbs forward, the outer guide and inner guide move forward, and under the guidance of outer and inner guides, the spine foot at the rear of the robot starts to detach from the wall surface. As shown in Fig. 11a, the spine foot begins to detach from the surface, the outer pin starts to move onto the inclined line, $\theta$ is the incline angle, and the inner pin is still on the horizontal line, $N_1$ and $f_1$ are the normal force and friction force acting on the outer pin by outer guide respectively, $N_2$ and $f_2$ are the normal force and friction force acting on the inner pin by inner guide respectively, $F$ is the pulling force acting on inner pin by the chain structure. With the spine foot rotates clockwise, the tangential force $F_T$ and the adhesion force $F_A$ acting on the spine drop to zero. In order to rotate the spine foot, the moment $M$ action on point O must be clockwise, the equation is given as:

$$M = N_1 L_1 \cos \theta - f_1 L_1 \sin \theta > 0 \tag{1}$$

Where $L_1$ is the distance between the inner pin and outer pin, $f_1 = \mu N_1$, $\mu$ is the coefficient of friction, and the requirement constraint can be simplified as:

$$\tan \theta < \frac{1}{\mu} \tag{2}$$

As shown in Fig. 11b, the spine foot rotates clockwise around the fixed center O to a maximum angle, the outer pin keeps moving on the inclined line, and the inner pin starts to move onto the curved line, $N_1'$ and $f_1'$ are the normal force and friction force acting on the outer pin by outer guide respectively, $N_2'$ and $f_2'$ are the normal force and friction force acting on the inner pin by inner guide respectively, $F$ is the pulling force acting on inner pin by the chain structure. In order to avoid friction self-locking of the outer pin, the requirement constraint is given as:

$$\tan \gamma < \frac{1}{\mu} \tag{3}$$

Where the angle $\gamma$ can be given as:

$$\gamma = \arcsin \frac{L_3 \sin \theta}{L_1} \tag{4}$$

Where $L_3$ is the distance between the right ends of the horizontal sections of two guides. Here, $\theta$ is 18°, $L_1$ is 12 mm, $L_3$ is 20 mm, and the distance between spine tip and the inner pin $L_2$ is 17 mm, the angle between the spine and the normal direction of wall surface $\alpha$ is 50°. According to Eq. (4), the angle $\gamma$ is 31°. According to Eqs. (2) and (3), the coefficient of friction $\mu$ should be small than 1.67, the requirement constraint easy to satisfy.

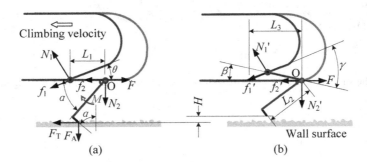

**Fig. 11.** Free-body diagrams of the spine foot during detachment. (a) The spine foot begins to detach from the surface; (b) The spine foot rotates clockwise around the fixed center O to a maximum angle.

During the detachment (from Fig. 11a to b), the spine foot has rotated clockwise with an angle $\beta$ of 11°, and the height $H$ that the spine has been lifted away from the wall surface can be given by Eq. (5), $H$ is 2.3 mm.

$$H = L_2(\sin \alpha - \sin(\alpha - \beta)) \tag{5}$$

## 3.4  Simulation of Detaching Movement

The attaching movement is an inverse operation of detaching movement. Here, the detachment of a spine foot during forward climbing has been simulated via ADAMS. Figure 12 is the simulation result of a spine foot detaching movement, and the blue curve presents the trajectory of the spine tip, and the detailed trajectory is drawn in Fig. 13. Figure 14 is the simulation result of spine foot rotation angle during detachment, the abscissa is the y-direction displacement, and the rotation angle is defined as anticlockwise positive and clockwise negative. The detachment can be divided into three phases. In the first phase (as shown in Fig. 12a–b), the spine foot rotates clockwise around the inner pin with a rotation angle of 11°, and the spine tip moves upward 2.3 mm. In the second phase (as shown in Fig. 12b–c), the inner pin moves on the curved line, and the spine foot firstly rotates clockwise to a maximum angle of 14.8°, the spine tip is 3.3 mm away from the wall surface. In the third phase, the spine foot rotates anticlockwise to the initial attitude with the rotation angle of 0°, and the spine tip is 5.8 mm away from the wall surface. Consider the worst situation that the whole body of the spine (2 mm long) has penetrated in the surface. In the first detachment phase, the spine is pulled out from the surface completely, and in the second detachment phase, the spine does not have chance to contact with the surface any more. It means that the detachment of the spine foot is reliable.

**Fig. 12.**  The simulation results of the detaching movement of a spine foot. (Color figure online)

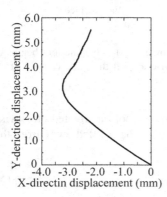

**Fig. 13.**  The trajectory of the spine tip.

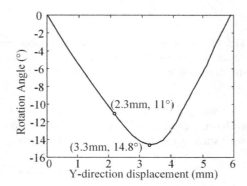

**Fig. 14.**  The rotation angle of the spine foot.

# 4 Experiments

As shown in Fig. 15, a robot prototype was built. The current prototype possesses 18 spine feet, and more spine feet would be involved to achieve larger adhesion. The robot prototype is 200 g in weight, 126 mm in width, and 186 mm in length. With an onboard lithium battery (3.7 V and 680 mAh), the robot is capable of climbing up and down on rough surfaces via remote radio controller.

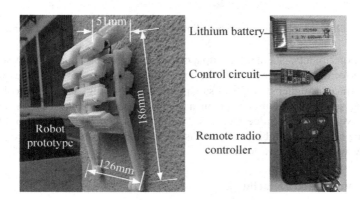

**Fig. 15.** The robot prototype.

## 4.1 Climbing Experiments

As shown in Fig. 16, several climbing experiments of the robot on different vertical surfaces have been conducted. Due to the dual-guide mechanism, the robot is capable of climbing on sandpaper (Fig. 16a), coarse stucco (Fig. 16b), pebble wall (Fig. 16c) and other hard and rough surfaces. For soft surfaces, such as net curtains, spines are easy to be stuck and difficult to detach. As shown in Fig. 16d, the proposed robot can climb on a net curtain. It means that the dual-guide mechanism is effective, and the detachment is easy.

**Fig. 16.** Climbing experiments on several surfaces. (a) Sandpaper; (b) Coarse stucco wall; (c) Pebble wall; (d) Net curtain.

**Fig. 17.** Still frames showing the robot climbing upward on real building exterior wall.

In the experiments, standard sandpapers were chose as standards to judge the climbing performance of the robot. The experiment results show that the robot can climb on surfaces rougher than P120 sandpaper surfaces (Fig. 16a). Figure 17 shows the climbing sequences of the robot on a coarse stucco building exterior wall. The distance between adjacent spine feet $L$ is 25.6 mm, and the robot takes 1.6 s to climb up a distance of $L$. The climbing speed of is about 16 mm/s, and it would be increased significantly with a high power motor.

## 4.2    Attachment and Detachment

Figure 18 shows the attachment and detachment of spine feet when the robot climbed upward on sandpaper surfaces. The attaching and detaching movements are the same as what described above in Sect. 3. The upper spine foot rotates in clockwise direction to attach on the surface, and the lower spine foot firstly rotates in anticlockwise direction to pull the spine off the surface, and then rotates in clockwise direction to leave away from the surface. Climbing results show that the attachment is stable and the detachment of a spine is easy and rapid.

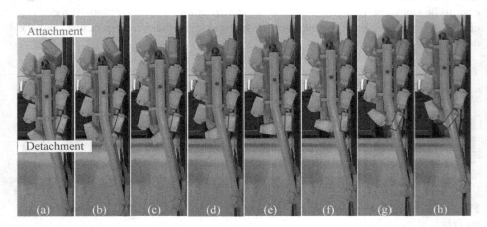

**Fig. 18.** The attaching and detaching movement sequences of the spine feet when the robot climbing upward on vertical sandpapers.

# 5   Conclusion

The robot demonstrates a dual-guide mechanism that achieves easy and rapid detachment for tracked wall-climbing robots with spines. Simulation and experiment results show that the proposed mechanism is effective. With the mechanism, the attachment is stable and the detachment is easy, and the tracked robot is capable of climbing on sandpaper, brick, coarse stucco, pebble walls and other rough vertical surfaces.

**Acknowledgment.** This research was supported by National Natural Science Foundation of China (No. 51805431) and Natural Science Basic Research Plan in Shaanxi Province of China (No. 2018JQ5062).

# References

1. Bußhardt, P., Kunze, D., Gorb, S.N.: Interlocking-based attachment during locomotion in the beetle Pachnoda marginata (Coleoptera, Scarabaeidae). Sci. Rep-UK. **4**(6998) (2014)
2. Autumn, K., Sitti, M., Liang, Y.A., et al.: Evidence for van der Waals adhesion in gecko setae. PNAS **99**(19), 12252–12256 (2002)
3. Eisenhaure, J., Kim, S.: A review of the state of dry adhesives: biomimetic structures and the alternative designs they inspire. Micromachines **8**(4), 125 (2017)
4. Autumn, K., Dittmore, A., Santos, D., et al.: Frictional adhesion: a new angle on gecko attachment. J. Exp. Biol. **209**(18), 3569–3579 (2006)
5. Tian, Y., Pesika, N., Zeng, H., et al.: Adhesion and friction in gecko toe attachment and detachment. PNAS **103**(51), 19320–19325 (2006)
6. Asbeck, A.T., Kim, S., Cutkosky, M.R., et al.: Scaling hard vertical surfaces with compliant microspine arrays. Int. J. Robot. Res. **25**(12), 1165–1179 (2006)
7. Ji, A.H., Zhao, Z.H., Manoonpong, P., et al.: A bio-inspired climbing robot with flexible pads and claws. J. Bionic Eng. **15**(2), 368–378 (2018)
8. Xu, F., Wang, X., Jiang, G.: Design and analysis of a wall-climbing robot based on a mechanism utilizing hook-like claws. Int. J. Adv. Robot. Syst. **9**(6), 261 (2012)
9. Spenko, M.J., Haynes, G.C., Saunders, J.A., et al.: Biologically inspired climbing with a hexapedal robot. J. Field Robot. **25**(4–5), 223–242 (2008)
10. Liu, Y., Sun, S., Wu, X., et al.: A leg-wheel wall-climbing robot utilizing bio-inspired spine feet. In: 2013 IEEE International Conference on Robotics and Biomimetics (ROBIO), pp. 1819–1824. IEEE (2013)
11. Parness, A., Abcouwer, N., Fuller, C., et al.: Lemur 3: a limbed climbing robot for extreme terrain mobility in space. In: 2017 IEEE International Conference on Robotics and Automation (ICRA), pp. 5467–5473. IEEE (2017)
12. Liu, G., Liu, Y., Wang, X., et al.: Design and experiment of a bioinspired wall-climbing robot using spiny grippers. In: 2016 IEEE International Conference on Mechatronics and Automation (ICMA), pp. 665–670. IEEE (2016)
13. Parness, A., McKenzie, C.: DROP: the durable reconnaissance and observation platform. Ind. Robot Int. J. **40**(3), 218–223 (2013)
14. Carpenter, K., Wiltsie, N., Parness, A.: Rotary microspine rough surface mobility. IEEE/ASME Trans. Mechatron. **21**(5), 2378–2390 (2016)

15. Liu, Y.W., Sun, S.M., Wu, X., et al.: A wheeled wall-climbing robot with bio-inspired spine mechanisms. J. Bionic Eng. **12**(1), 17–28 (2015)
16. Frantsevich, L., Gorb, S.: Structure and mechanics of the tarsal chain in the hornet, Vespa crabro (Hymenoptera: Vespidae): implications on the attachment mechanism. Arthropod Struct. Dev. **33**(1), 77–89 (2004)

# A Wall Climbing Robot Arm Capable of Adapting to Multiple Contact Wall Surfaces

Shiyuan Bian[1,2,3], Dongyue Xie[4], Yuliang Wei[1,2,3], Feng Xu[1,2,3],
Min Tang[1,2,3], and Deyi Kong[1,2,3,4(✉)]

[1] State Key Laboratory of Transducer Technology,
Institute of Intelligent Machines, Hefei Institutes of Physical Science,
Chinese Academy of Sciences, Hefei 230031, China
kongdy@iim.ac.cn
[2] Key Laboratory of Biomimetic Sensing and Advanced Robot Technology
of Anhui Province, Institute of Intelligent Machines, Hefei Institutes of Physical
Science, Chinese Academy of Sciences, Hefei 230031, China
[3] University of Science and Technology of China, Hefei 230026, China
[4] Hefei University of Technology, Hefei 230601, China

**Abstract.** The wall climbing robot is widely used in a great many fields. There are more and more technical requirements for wall-climbing robots, such as better load, more stability and adapt to multiple environments. This paper studies a composite wall climbing robot palm for a wall climbing robot to adopt multiple environments. The palm consists of a suction cup, five hooks, and bionic setae array materials. The body of the palm is produced by 3D printing and the bionic materials are fabricated by polymer print lithography technology inspired by the gecko. The edge of the suction cup has cured a circle of bionic setae array materials to enhance the adhesion force. The bionic setae array materials on the palm for better adapt to the smooth surface and the hooks are used to attach on the rough surface. The composite palm is well tested in smooth, wet and rough surfaces. Moreover, the composite palm is fixed on the arm of the wall climbing robot. The arm of the wall climbing robot is proposed by a new type of gear transmission system.

**Keywords:** Wall climbing robot · Bionic setae array · Adhesion ·
Lithography technology

## 1 Introduction

Around the investigates of wall climbing robot, many adhesion ways were proposed, such as magnet, pneumatic (negative pressure), claw, and bionic adhesive. Since the 90s, the electromagnets and permanent magnets wall-climbing robots with legs, wheels, tracks were investigated. Grieco [1] investigated a six-leg wall climbing robot with a four-phase discontinuous sawing gait for controlling itself. Berengueres [2] proposed a semi-compliant distributed adhesion magnetic pad for adhering on the wall. This pad replaced the sticky material similar to the bristles of gecko with some small magnets. Peters [3] introduced a four-legs magnetic wall climbing robot with 3DOF legs were controlled by two identical walking modules. Kamagaluh [4] proposed a

© Springer Nature Switzerland AG 2019
H. Yu et al. (Eds.): ICIRA 2019, LNAI 11741, pp. 97–109, 2019.
https://doi.org/10.1007/978-3-030-27532-7_9

crawling and wall climbing four-legs robot Winspecbot with magnetic feet for climbing on the steel pipe. Fei [5] investigated four wheels climbing robot with four optic fiber sensors for inspecting the weld seam. Fischer [6] proposed an only 8 mm high wall-climbing robot to inspect the stators or rotors of power generator which can move in any direction by flexible magnetic rollers. Tavakoli [7] investigated a wall climbing robot could adapt to non-flat surfaces by the omnidirectional wheels and the permanent magnet units. Xu [8] presented a track wall climbing robot with an elastic brace mechanism, a load-scatter mechanism and parallelogram mechanism to inspect the oil tank's volume. Shen [9] proposed a permanent magnetic tracks wall climbing robot with the adhesion mechanism and the anti-toppling mechanism to inspect the water tube. Lee [10] investigated a wall climbing robot could move from the horizontal to the vertical surfaces by flexible magnetic treads, torque-controlled motors, elastic connecting links, and an active tail.

In the industrial field, the pneumatic climbing robot was used for smooth non-magnetic surface, which adhesion ways include the type of suction cup and the chamber. Kim [11] proposed a four-legs walking and climbing robot with a suction cup to adapt the 3D environment by the algorithms of the boundary transition region. Tlale [12] investigated a four-legs wall climbing robot with two modules, which movement by distributed mechatronics controller. Wile [13] presented a two-legs climbing robot with suction cups, which could walk on a smooth surface and a 70-degree angled surfaces. Shang [14] studied a wall-climbing robot that used two pairs of the pneumatic suction cup to drive in two directions. Luk [15] presented two types of pneumatic adhesion wall-climbing robots that used the sliding frame walking mechanism to move on the surface. The vacuum gripping was used to adhere to uneven or rough surfaces. Zhang [16] proposed a fully pneumatic sliding frame climbing robot with X and Y cylinders, which moves by the improved FA compensating variable bang-bang control algorithm. Apostolescu [17] investigated a climbing robot that used belt-screw mechanisms to move on horizontal and vertical surfaces and used vacuum cups to attach on the surface. Yu [18] proposed a type of climbing robot that used tracks to move on the surface and used suction cups to adhere to the smooth surfaces. Nishi [19] studied a climbing robot, which used a fan to form negative pressure adsorption and crawler to move on the wall. Longo [20] investigated a double-legs wall climbing robot, which consisted of three modules driven by three pneumatic cups. Qian [21] designed a wall climbing robot with sliding suction cup that used fluid network theory for adhering on the surfaces more stability. Miyake [22] studied a wall climbing robot with vacuum-based wet adhesion system, which was driven by wheels. The comparison experiments of the smooth and rough surface were studied. Song [23] investigated a climbing robot with impeller and two-layer suction seals system to enhance the adhering capability on the non-smooth vertical wall and a horizontal ceiling. Li [24] proposed a wall-climbing robot that used a centrifugal fan to adhere on the surface and movement by wheels.

In order to climbing on the rough surfaces, some researchers had done these works. Kim [25] studied a wall climbing robot for rough surface by a Parallel four-bar machine with six special claw toes. Clark [26] investigated a climbing robot with two legs with claws inspired by the cockroach and gecko. Schmidt [27] proposed a wall climbing robot with three steerable wheels for omnidirectional locomotion, which used negative pressure chamber to adhere on the wall. Saunders [28] proposed a six-legged climbing robot that can climb on the tree by the claws on the tip of the toes. Provancher [29] studied a type of climbing robot ROCR that used alternating hand-holds and an actuated tail to drive itself upward inspired by climbers and brachiating gibbons. Birkmeyer [29] presented a climbing robot that had six legs driven by an actuator. The robot can climb on the cloth by the claws on the feet. Daltorio [30] presented a leg-wheel type of climbing robot that can climb at 60° inclined concrete surfaces. Liu [31] proposed a leg-wheel wall climbing robot with a four-bar linkage mechanism and spine foot that can climb on the cloth and brick surfaces.

Moreover, some researchers investigated the robots with adhesion material inspired by gecko to climb on the smooth surfaces. Unver [32] investigated a tank-like climbing robot, which can climb on any degree from 0 to 360 on smooth surfaces. Unver [33] proposed a four-legged climbing robot that used the diagonal gait to move on the smooth surfaces. The power is provided by the steering gear at the joint between the front and rear legs. Moreover, a climbing robot with the four-bar-based legged-body climbing robot with polyurethane adhere materials was proposed [34]. Murphy [35] investigated a leg-wheel climbing robot that was consisted of a, a body, a tail, and two wheel-legs. Each leg of the wheel had three feet fixed with polyurethane adhere materials. Cutkosky [36] presented a four-legged wall climbing robot called Stickybot that relied on the servos to drive the four-bar mechanism moving in the plane. The wire was pulled by the servos to realize the toe peeling inspired by the real large gecko peeling action. Menon [37] proposed a wall-climbing robot that had six legs and 18 actively controlled joints. The adhesion force based on the micro setae array inspired by the toe of gecko. Wu [38] investigated a track wall climbing robot with adhering materials that can climb from the vertical surface to the ceiling surface. Most of the above wall-climbing robots are only adapting to a type of surface.

In order to investigate a wall-climbing robot that has the capability of adapting multiple environments, this paper proposes a composite wall climbing robot palm includes bionic adhesion material, bionic suction cup, and bionic hooks can adapt rough, wet and smooth surfaces. The bionic adhesion material is fabricated by polymer print lithography technology inspired by the gecko. The bionic suction cup is produced inspired by clingfish to enhancing the adhesion force. The hooks are used to attach on the rough surfaces inspired by the toe of the gecko. This composite bionic palm is assembled to the arm of the wall climbing robot for multiple environments. The new type of arm with a gear transmission is studied.

## 2  Design and Analysis of the Robot

### 2.1  The Palm of the Wall Climbing Robot

#### A. Bionic setae array

The other, known as the animal gecko, is capable of rapidly crawling on vertical or even inverted dry walls, relying on the dense "setae–claw" micro-nano composite array and the sharp hooks on its toes (Fig. 1).

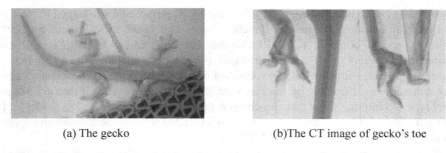

(a) The gecko                    (b)The CT image of gecko's toe

**Fig. 1.** The image of gecko's toes on the gecko toe.

Polymer print lithography technology is used to produce the setae array inspired by the gecko. Before the photoresist coating processing, the silicon wafer must be cleaned and dried. A photoresist is coated on the silicon wafer, and the photoresist solvent is removed by soft baking. By stepping down the projection exposure, the wafer is exposed to form the desired pattern. Then remove the exposed portion by development, leaving the unexposed portion. After hard-baking, the photoresist film adheres more firmly. Afterwards, permanently retain the pattern on the silicon wafer by wet etching. At the same time, thermal diffusion and ion implantation are used for doping. It is performed by thermal diffusion and ion implantation, and the photoresist film is removed by a glue-dispenser to form a multi-aperture pattern on the silicon wafer. Finally, uncovering the PDMS uniformly coat on the above-mentioned completed silicon wafer can obtain seta array adhesive material similar to that on the toe of gecko (Fig. 2).

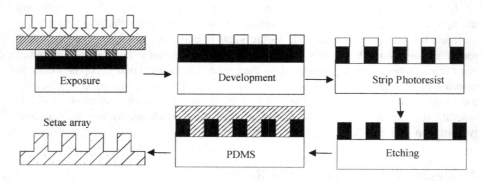

**Fig. 2.** The manufacturing process of bionic setae array

By the polymer print lithography technology method mentioned above, two different scales of bionic setae array materials are fabricated as Fig. 3. The diameter of the Fig. 3(a) and (b) are 30 μm and 10 μm, respectively. The length of the two type materials are 40 μm and 20 μm, respectively. These materials are fabricated for the bionic suction cup in next section.

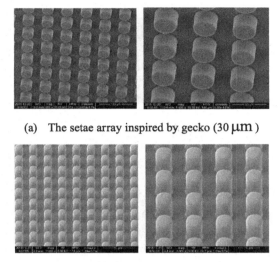

(a)    The setae array inspired by gecko (30 μm )

(b)    The setae array inspired by gecko (10 μm )

**Fig. 3.**  The different scales of bionic setae array.

## B. Bionic suction cup

In this paper, a bionic "suction cup-setae-claw" composite attachment structure for wall climbing robots that can crawl on both dry and wet walls was proposed by studying the structural characteristics of the corresponding functional organs of the cling-fish and gecko. The cling-fish can adsorb on rough and slippery surfaces such as seaweed, reef, and shells firmly, mainly due to its special "suck-bristle" composite structure (Fig. 4a). The suction disk formed by the pelvic fin and pectoral fin of the cling-fish is mainly on the scale of several centimeters. The millimeter-scale surface is distributed on the edge of the suction cup with a large number of micron-scale bristle, which plays a key role in adsorption and prevents tangential slip between the suction cup and the wall (Fig. 4b). The special suction cup with the micron-scale bristle on the edge was manufactured by lithography technology as Fig. 4c. This bionic suction cup is composed of suction cup in the center and setae array on the side.

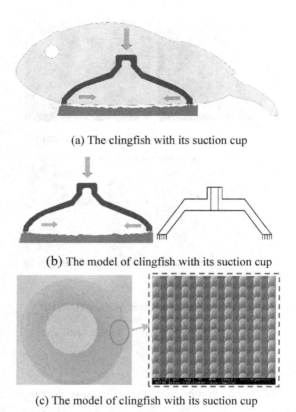

(a) The clingfish with its suction cup

(b) The model of clingfish with its suction cup

(c) The model of clingfish with its suction cup

**Fig. 4.** The bionic suction cup inspired by cling-fish.

In order to investigate the adhesion characteristic of the bionic suction cup on the different surfaces (acrylic plate and PTFE plate), the tangential adhesion forces of the bionic suction cup with setae array and without are measured as shown in the following Figures.

As shown in Fig. 5, the dry tangential adhesion force of the bionic suction cup with setae array on side is higher than the bionic suction cup without. As shown in Fig. 5(a) and (c), or Fig. 5(b) and (d) the dry tangential adhesion force of the suction cup is higher than the wet tangential adhesion force. The tangential adhesion force of the bionic suction cup on the Acrylic plate is higher than the adhesion force on the PTFE plate, as Fig. 5(a) and (b) or Fig. 5(c) and (d).

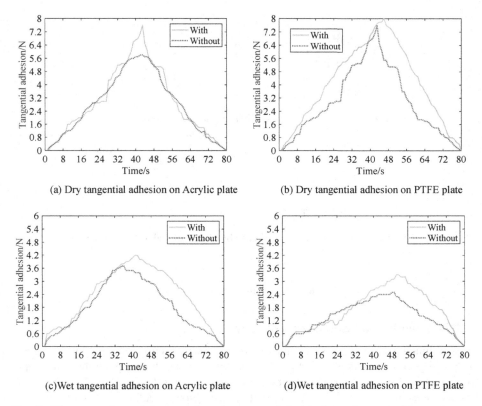

(a) Dry tangential adhesion on Acrylic plate

(b) Dry tangential adhesion on PTFE plate

(c)Wet tangential adhesion on Acrylic plate

(d)Wet tangential adhesion on PTFE plate

**Fig. 5.** The comparison of the normal suction cup and the bionic suction cup with setae array. The solid line represents the suction cup with the setae array on side, while the dotted line represents without it.

## C. Gecko bionic toe

The bionic toes (as Fig. 6) are proposed due to the behavior of the gecko using the hook on the wall. The toe includes two parts: one is the part has a bionic hook on the tip of the toe (as Fig. 6a), the other part with adhering setae array material on the surface (as Fig. 6d). The hook on the tip of the toe can be extended and closed for the different touch surface. The adhere part with materials are fabricated by the lithography technology as the Part B. This part is used for climbing on the smooth surface. The hooks on the tip are used for attaching on the rough surface. These two parts are adapted to suit two different wall surfaces, respectively.

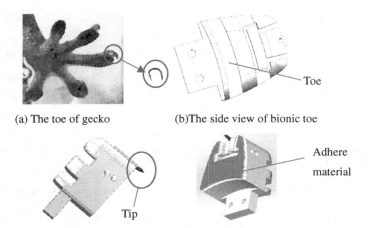

(a) The toe of gecko            (b)The side view of bionic toe

(a) The side view of the bionic toe (b)The bionic toe of wall climbing robot

**Fig. 6.**  The details of the bionic toe.

## D. Composite wall climbing robot palm

Combined with the above-mentioned bionic suction cup, imitation gecko setae array and gecko's hooks, this part proposes a 'three-in-one' bionic palm that can adapt to various wall surfaces inspired by the gecko and the cling-fish (as Fig. 7). This palm has five toes which are described as Part C. The bionic suction cup is applied for increasing the adhesive force on the center of the palm (Fig. 8).

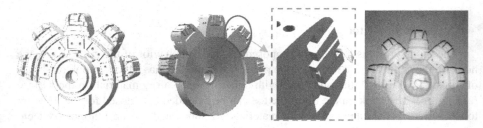

**Fig. 7.**  The 'three-in-one' bionic palm

The 'three-in-one' bionic palm can carry 1 kg weight in three different surfaces, rough, dry smooth surface, and wet smooth surface.

(a) Rough surface          (b) Dry smooth surface          (c) Wet smooth surface

**Fig. 8.** The adhesion performance test of the 'three-in-one' bionic palm.

## 2.2 The Arm of the Wall Climbing Robot

This arm of wall climbing robot combines four legs with five linkages which are driven by the gear transmission system. Every leg includes two motors, one (Motor 1) drives the leg to stretch out and the other (Motor 2) lifts the leg up. Taking a leg of a wall climbing robot as an example, the gear 3 fixed is fixed together with the link 1 and the gear 4 is fixed together with link3. The link 1 is driven by the gear 2 and the link 2 is driven by gears the gear 1 (Figs. 9, 10 and 11).

$$\theta_1 = \omega_1 t, \quad \theta_2 = \omega_2 t \tag{1}$$

$$D_1 = mZ_1, \quad D_2 = mZ_2 \tag{2}$$

$$\frac{Z_1}{Z_2} = \frac{D_1}{D_2} = \frac{\omega_1}{\omega_2} = \frac{\theta_1}{\theta_2} = k \tag{3}$$

In order to ensure the wall climbing robot crawling in a line, the gear 3 and gear 4 should rotate according to a certain transmission ratio as the function (3). The gears are produced by 3D printing as the transmission ratio as Fig. 12.

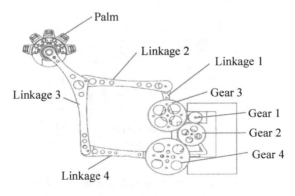

**Fig. 9.** The arm of the wall climbing robot

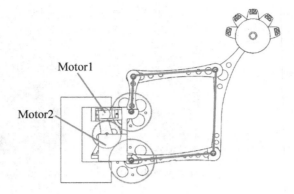

**Fig. 10.** The arm of the wall climbing robot

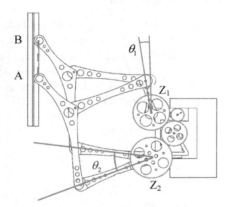

**Fig. 11.** Motion position of the arm

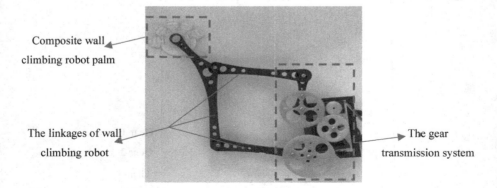

**Fig. 12.** The arm of the wall climbing robot

# 3 Conclusions

The multiple scales of the bionic materials are fabricated by polymer print lithography technology inspired by the gecko. The bionic suction cup is produced with adhesion array setae inspired by clingfish to enhance the adhesion force. The hooks are assembled on the bionic palm to attach on the rough surfaces inspired by the toe of the gecko. This paper proposes a composite wall climbing robot palm includes adhesion array setae, bionic suction cup, and bionic hooks can adapt rough, wet and smooth surfaces. This composite bionic palm is assembled to the new gear transmission arm of wall climbing robot for multiple environments.

# References

1. Grieco, J., Prieto, M., Armada, M., Gonzalez de Santos, P.: A six-legged climbing robot for high payloads. In: Proceedings of the International Conference on Control Applications, CCA, Trieste, Italy, pp. 446–450 (1998)
2. Berengueres, J., Tadakuma, K., Kamoi, T., Kratz, R.: Compliant distributed magnetic adhesion device for wall climbing. In: Proceedings of the International Conference on Robotics and Automation, ICRA, pp. 1256–1261 (2007)
3. Peters, G., Pagano, D., Liu, D.K., Waldron, K.: A prototype climbing robot for inspection of complex ferrous structures. In: Proceedings of the 13th International Conference on Climbing and Walking Robots, CLAWAR, Nagoya, Japan, pp. 150–156 (2010)
4. Kamagaluh, B., Kumar, J.S., Virk, G.S.: Design of a multi-terrain climbing robot for petrochemical applications. In: Proceedings of the 15th International Conference on Climbing and Walking Robots, CLAWAR, Baltimore, USA, pp. 639–646 (2012)
5. Fei, Y., Zhao, X., Wan, J.: Motion analysis of a modular inspection robot with magnetic wheels. World Congr. Intell. Control Autom. 2, 8187–8190 (2006)
6. Fischer, W., Caprari, G., Siegwart, R., Moser, R.: Compact climbing robot rolling on flexible magnetic rollers, for generator inspection with the rotor still installed. In: Proceedings of the 14th International Conference on Climbing and Walking Robots, CLAWAR, Paris, France, pp. 384–391 (2011)
7. Tavakoli, M., Marques, L., de Almeida, A.T.: OmniClimber: an omnidirectional light weight climbing robot with flexibility to adapt to non-flat surfaces. In: International Conference on Intelligent Robots and Systems, IEEE, pp. 280–285 (2012)
8. Xu, Z., Ma, P.: A wall-climbing robot for labelling scale of oil tank's volume. Robotica 20(02), 209–212 (2002)
9. Shen, W., Gu, J.: Permanent magnetic system design for the wall-climbing robot. In: International Conference on Mechatronics and Automation, Niagara Falls, Canada, no. July, pp. 2078–2083 (2005)
10. Lee, G., Kim, J., Seo, T.: Combot: compliant climbing robotic platform with transitioning capability and payload capacity. In: International Conference on Robotics and Automation, ICRA, IEEE, Saint Paul, Minnesota, USA, pp. 2737–2742 (2012)
11. Kim, H., Kang, T., Choi, H.: Walking and climbing robot for locomotion in 3D environment. In: International Symposium on Automation and Robotics in Construction, ISARC (2004)

12. Tlale, N.S., Bright, G.: Distributed mechatronics controller for modular wall climbing robot. In: International Conference on CAD/CAM, Robotics and Factories of the Future, India, no. July, pp. 740–752 (2006)
13. Wile, G., Aslam, D.M.: Design, fabrication and testing of a miniature wall climbing robot using smart robotic feet, Technical Report. Servo 1, Micro and NanoTechnology Laboratory, Michigan State University, E. Lansing, Michigan, USA (2007)
14. Madsen, O., Shang, J., Sattar, T., et al.: Design of a climbing robot for inspecting aircraft wings and fuselage. Ind. Robot Int. J. **34**(6), 495–502 (2007)
15. Luk, B.L., Collie, A.A., Cooke, D.S., Chen, S.: Walking and climbing service robots for safety inspection of nuclear reactor pressure vessels. J. Measur. Control. **39**(2), 43–47 (2006)
16. Zhang, H., Wang, W., Zhang, J.: High stiffness pneumatic actuating scheme and improved position control strategy realization of a pneumatic climbing robot. In: Proceedings of the International Conference on Robotics and Biomimetics, IEEE, Bangkok, Thailand, pp. 1806–1811 (2009)
17. Apostolescu, T.C., Udrea, C., Duminica, D., Ionascu, G., Bogatu, L., Cartal, L.A.: Development of a climbing robot with vacuum attachment cups. In: International Conference on Innovations, Recent Trends and Challenges in Mechatronics, Mechanical Engineering and New High-Tech Products Development, MECAHITECH, p. 3 (2011)
18. Yoshida, Y., Ma, S.: Design of a wall-climbing robot with passive suction cups. In: Proceedings of the International Conference on Robotics and Biomimetics, ROBIO, IEEE, Tianjin, China, pp. 1513–1518 (2010)
19. Nishi, A., Wakasugi, Y., Watanabe, K.: Design of a robot capable of moving on a vertical wall. Adv. Robot. **1**(1), 33–45 (1986)
20. Longo, D., Muscato, G.: Simulation and locomotion control for the Alicia3 climbing robot. In: 22nd International Symposium on Automation and Robotics in Construction, ISARC, Ferrara (Italy), 11–14 September 2005
21. Qian, Z.-Y., Zhao, Y.-Z., Fu, Z., Wang, Y.: Fluid model of sliding suction cup of wall-climbing robots. Int. J. Adv. Robot. Syst. **3**(3), 275–284 (2006)
22. Miyake, T., Ishihara, H., Yoshimura, M.: Basic studies on wet adhesion system for wall climbing robots. In: Proceedings of the International Conference on Intelligent Robots and Systems, IROS, San Diego, USA, pp. 1920–1925 (2007)
23. Song, Y.K., Lee, C.M., Koo, I.M., Tran, D.T., Moon, H., Choi, H.R.: Development of wall climbing robotic system for inspection purpose. In: Proceedings of the International Conference on Intelligent Robots and Systems, IROS, Nice, France, pp. 1990–1995 (2008)
24. Li, J., Gao, X., Fan, N., Li, K., Jiang, Z.: Adsorption performance of sliding wall-climbing robot. Chin. J. Mech. Eng. **23**, 1 (2010)
25. Kim, S., Asbeck, A.T., Cutkosky, M.R., et al.: SpinybotII: climbing hard walls with compliant microspines. In: Adsorption performance of sliding wall-climbing robot Advanced Robotics, 2005, ICAR 2005, Proceedings, pp. 601–606 (2005)
26. Clark, J., Goldman, D., Lin, P.-C., et al.: Design of a bio-inspired dynamical vertical climbing robot. In: Robotics: Science and Systems (2007)
27. Schmidt, D., Hillenbrand, C., Berns, K.: Omnidirectional locomotion and traction control of the wheel-driven, wall-climbing robot. CROMSCI Robotica J. **29**(7), 991–1003 (2011)
28. Saunders, A., Goldman, D., Full, R., et al.: The rise climbing robot: body and leg design. In: Defense and Security Symposium, p. 623017 (2006)
29. Birkmeyer, P., Gillies, A.G., Fearing, R.S.: CLASH: climbing vertical loose cloth. In: 2011 IEEE/RSJ International Conference on Intelligent Robots and Systems (IROS), pp. 5087–5093 (2011)

30. Daltorio, K.A., Wei, T.E., Gorb, S.N., et al.: Passive foot design and contact area analysis for climbing mini-whegs. In: 2007 IEEE International Conference on Robotics and Automation, pp. 1274–1279 (2007)
31. Liu, Y., Sun, S., Wu, X., et al.: A leg-wheel wall-climbing robot utilizing bio-inspired spine feet. In: 2013 IEEE International Conference on Robotics and Biomimetics, ROBIO, IEEE (2013)
32. Unver, O., Sitti, M.: Tankbot: a palm-size, tank-like, climbing robot using soft elastomer adhesive treads. Int. J. Robot. Res. **29**(14), 1761–1777 (2010)
33. Unver, O., Uneri, A., Aydemir, A., et al.: Geckobot: a gecko inspired climbing robot using elastomer adhesives. In: Proceedings of the 2006 IEEE International Conference on Robotics and Automation(ICRA), Orlando, USA, IEEE, pp. 2329–2335 (2006)
34. Unver, O., Sitti, M.: Flat dry elastomer adhesives as attachment materials for climbing robots. IEEE Trans. Robot. **26**(1), 131–141 (2010)
35. Murphy, M., Kute, C., Menguc, Y., et al.: Waalbot II: adhesion recovery and improved performance of a climbing robot using fibrillar adhesives. Int. J. Robot. Res. **30**(1), 118–133 (2011)
36. Kim, S., Spenko, M., Trujillo, S., et al.: Smooth vertical surface climbing with directional adhesion. IEEE Trans. Robot. **24**(1), 65–74 (2008)
37. Menon, C., Li, Y., Sameto, D., et al.: Abigaille-I: towards the development of a spider-inspired climbing robot for space use. In: Proceedings of the 2nd Biennial IEEE/RAS-EMBS International Conference on Biomedical Robotics and Biomechatronics, Sottsdale, USA, IEEE, pp. 384–389 (2008)
38. Wu, X., Wang, D., Zhao, A., et al.: A wall-climbing robot with biomimetic adhesive pedrail. In: Zhang, D. (ed.) Advanced Mechatronics and MEMS Devices, pp. 179–191. Springer, New York (2013). https://doi.org/10.1007/978-1-4419-9985-6_9

# Development of Control System
# with Double-Closed Loop for a Multi-mode
# Wall-Climbing Robot

Hong Xu[1], Linsen Xu[2,3(✉)], Gaoxin Cheng[1], Shouqi Chen[1],
and Jinfu Liu[1]

[1] University of Science and Technology of China, Hefei, Anhui Province, China
xuhong94@mail.ustc.edu.cn
[2] Institute of Advanced Manufacturing Technology,
Hefei Institutes of Physical Science, CAS, Hefei, China
lsxu@iamt.ac.cn
[3] Anhui Province Key Laboratory of Biomimetic Sensing
and Advanced Robot Technology, Hefei, Anhui Province, China

**Abstract.** The paper proposes a multi-mode wall-climbing robot, for the requirements of bridge detection, disaster search and rescue. Firstly, according to the biomimetic mechanism, the claw wheels, adhesive tracks and eddy vacuum fans are designed respectively. With these bionic structures the robot can climb on a variety of complex walls. Secondly, by virtue of the spatial layout characteristics of the mechanical structure of the robot, the unconventional shaped control circuit board of the BLDC motor is designed independently. At the same time, due to different wall roughness, the robot will not move stably, then the speed of the motor needs to be adjusted in real time. Therefore, the double-closed loop control system of BLDC motor has been designed, which is simulated and analyzed based on SIMULINK. The results show that the designed control system has excellent dynamic performance and steady-state performance, meeting the working requirements of wall-climbing robots on various wall surfaces.

**Keywords:** Wall-climbing robot ·
Unconventional shaped control circuit board · BLDC motor

## 1 Introduction

The wall-climbing robot, which is a robot different from the traditional humanoid, can be used for wall cleaning, inspection, spray maintenance and other operations. Researchers have developed a series of biomimetic prototypes of crawler robots based on different attachment mechanisms. For the claw attachment mechanism, DROP, a rotating robotic mechanism, tiny thorns, was designed at the California Institute of Technology's Jet Propulsion Laboratory. It can move to concrete surfaces at an angle and is capable of rapid transition from horizontal to vertical [1]. Lam et al. designed a tree climbing robot that can climb from the trunk to the branches. The robot has a wide clamping curvature and its payload weight is almost three times its own. At the same

H. Yu et al. (Eds.): ICIRA 2019, LNAI 11741, pp. 110–122, 2019.
https://doi.org/10.1007/978-3-030-27532-7_10

time, through the global path and motion planning algorithm, the robot can navigate and crawl on the branch [2, 3]. For the adhesion mechanism, Rui Chen designed a wall-climbing robot by studying the wall-climbing mechanism of the gecko. Its wall climbing mechanism is different from gecko, but it uses static adhesion generated by a specific electrostatic pad [4]. Michael. Murphy designed a small wall-climbing robot that uses a viscous elastomeric material to move the robot in a smooth vertical plane [5]. For the adsorption mechanism, Shanqiang Wu of China Jiliang University designed a vacuum adsorption wall-climbing robot that can run on brick walls and concrete walls [6]. Andreas Papadimitriou designed a wall-climbing robot based on a vortex fan that is connected to the wall by an electric ducted fan (EDF) [7].

Traditional wall-climbing robots can only perform well on the specific wall because they only use an attachment mechanism, which is not suitable for all walls. Combined with the characteristics of claw, adhesion and vacuum adsorption, a new type of wall-climbing robot was designed, which has a good performance on various wall surfaces.

In order to drive the three mechanical mechanisms of the wall-climbing robot so that the wall-climbing robot can climb on various wall surfaces, we chose brushless DC (BLDC) motor as the power source. Compared with the traditional brush DC motor, the BLDC motor has the advantages of simple structure, small size, stable operation, simple and convenient maintenance, high work efficiency, large output torque, smooth and stable speed regulation.

At the same time, with the improvement of manufacturing process and the application of various excellent control algorithms in the motor, the performance of BLDC motor has been greatly improved, so it has been widely used in various industries. R. Shanmugasundram designed a fuzzy controller for BLDC motor, which achieves better perfomance compared with conventional PID controller, under different working conditions [8]. Kamil Plachta presented a new method of controlling BLDC motor, which is a kind of current controlling method. This method can increase the starting torque and eliminate dead zone of torque in the entire engine operating range [9]. The BLDC motor is often used fan applications. It can reduce power consumption and improve high motor efficiency by choosing optimal commutation angle [10].

However, there are few researches on the control system of BLDC motor for the wall-climbing robots. At the same time, the BLDC motor controllers on the market need to have enough three-dimensional space for placement, which is not suitable for compact wall-climbing robots. Therefore, it is necessary to design a new BLDC motor controller based on the available space of the wall climbing robot.

This article will introduce mechanical structures, control system design and experiments. The rest of this article is organized as follows. The second part introduces the mechanical structure. The third part details the design of the control system, including the mathematical model of the BLDC motor, the design of the hardware circuit board and the speed and current double-closed loop. The fourth part introduces simulation and data analysis based on SIMULNK. The conclusion is shown in the fifth part.

## 2  Mechanical Structure

A new type of bionic wall-climbing robot has been designed, which can move on different walls, as shown in Fig. 1. The wall-climbing robot is mainly composed of three parts: the adsorption mechanism, the adhesion mechanism and the claw mechanism.

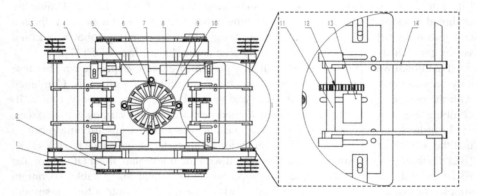

**Fig. 1.** The design of wall-climbing robot:1-adjustment mechanism, 2-adhesive tracks, 3-claw wheels, 4-driving tracks, 5-right driving motor, 6-eddy vacuum fans, 7-driving motor, 8-vacuum chamber, 9-battery, 10-left driving motor, 11-rotational shaft, 12-transmission system, 13-switching motor, 14-swing rod.

### 2.1  The Adsorption Mechanism

Figure 2 shows the adsorption mechanism, including a eddy vacuum fans, vacuum chamber and flexible skirt.

**Fig. 2.** The adsorption mechanism

The eddy vacuum fans is placed at the geometric center of the vacuum chamber. When the wall-climbing robot is climbing on different wall surfaces, the outside air enters, and the air inside the vacuum chamber is discharged, generating air negative pressure, enabling the wall-climbing robot be attracted to the wall and prevent overturning.

Air negative pressure adsorption is a special adsorption method different from the traditional contact adsorption, which can make the wall-climbing robot have good adsorption effect on the wall with different roughness and different vertical Angle [7]. By adjusting the motor speed, different air negative pressure thrust is obtained, so that the wall-climbing robot is able to carry load under different conditions.

## 2.2   The Adhesion Mechanism

The adhesion mechanism mainly includes two adhesive tracks, which are distributed symmetrically on the left and right sides of the wall-climbing robot, as shown in Fig. 3. The adhesive tracks are driven by the master-slave synchronous wheels, and the pre-tightening force of the tracks is also related to the center distance of the two synchronous wheels [11].

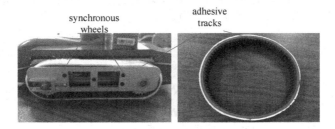

**Fig. 3.**  The adhesion mechanism

When the wall-climbing robot climbs on a smooth surface, such as glass surface, the adhesion mechanism plays a major role. The adsorption mechanism keeps the robot attached to the wall without overturning. Without the adhesive tracks, the wall climbing robot will slide down on the wall due to gravity. The adhesion force is not only related to the adhesive material, but also has a power exponential relationship with the negative pressure of the air generated by the adsorption mechanism.

## 2.3   The Claw Mechanism

Figure 4 shows the claw mechanism of the wall-climbing robot. The claw mechanism is mainly composed of four claw wheels, driving tracks and swing rod.

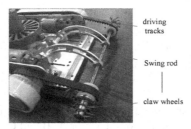

**Fig. 4.**  The claw mechanism

In the grabbing mode, the most important mechanical structure is the claw wheels which is composed of the claw and the wheel body [1]. The positions of the claw on the wheels are arranged in a certain rule. The material of claw must have a certain strength and stiffness, otherwise the claw is easy to deform and damage.

On the rough wall surface, the locking force be formed by claws and the raised particles on the wall surface, enables the wall climbing robot to crawl normally. At the same time, due to the inconsistency of the raised particles on the wall, the adsorption mechanism needs to be assisted in the climbing process.

## 3    Development of Control System

### 3.1    The Mathematical Model of BLDC Motor

The equivalent circuit of the BLDC motor drive system, which is composed of IGBT inverter and BLDC motor, is shown in Fig. 5.

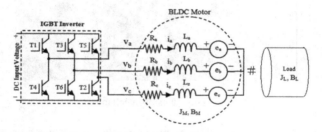

**Fig. 5.** The equivalent circuit of BLDC motor drive system

In order to facilitate the analysis of the mathematical model of BLDC motor, we make the following assumptions:

(1)  Ideal power semiconductor devices;
(2)  Constant inductances and resistance;
(3)  Ignore changes in magnetic field and temperature during motor operation;
(4)  The motor is unsaturated.

Based on the above assumptions, the voltage balance equation of the motor can be expressed in matrix form as:

$$\begin{bmatrix} U_a \\ U_b \\ U_c \end{bmatrix} = \begin{bmatrix} R_s & 0 & 0 \\ 0 & R_s & 0 \\ 0 & 0 & R_s \end{bmatrix} \begin{bmatrix} i_a \\ i_b \\ i_c \end{bmatrix} + \begin{bmatrix} L_s - L_m & 0 & 0 \\ 0 & L_s - L_m & 0 \\ 0 & 0 & L_s - L_m \end{bmatrix} p \begin{bmatrix} i_a \\ i_b \\ i_c \end{bmatrix} + \begin{bmatrix} e_a \\ e_b \\ e_c \end{bmatrix}$$

$$(1)$$

Where: $U_a$, $U_b$ and $U_c$ are the voltage (V) of the A, B and C wire windings on the stator; $i_a$, $i_b$ and $i_c$ are the current (A) of the stator A, B and C wire windings; $e_a$, $e_b$ and

$e_c$ are the electromotive force (V) of the stator A, B and C wire windings; $L_s$ is the self-inductance (H) of the winding; $L_m$ is the mutual inductance (H) generated by the current flowing through each winding; $p$ is the differential operator: $d/dt$.

When the BLDC motor is running smoothly, its electromagnetic torque equation is:

$$T_e = \frac{e_a i_a + e_b i_b + e_c i_c}{w} \qquad (2)$$

Where $w$ is the angular velocity (*rad/s*). The equation of mechanical motion is:

$$T_e - T_l = J \frac{dw}{dt} + Bw \qquad (3)$$

Where $T_l$ is the load torque, $J$ is the rotor inertia, and $B$ is the viscous damping coefficient of BLDC motor [8].

### 3.2   The Control System Design

In the actual crawling process, as the wall features change, in order to prevent over-turning, sufficient air negative pressure thrust is required, and the motor speed can be quickly adjusted in real time. Therefore, we designed a double-closed loop control system for speed and current [12]. By adjusting the controller parameters, the BLDC motor can respond quickly.

In the double-closed loop control system of BLDC motor, when the motor starts, the current loop makes the winding current increase rapidly to the set maximum value and keeps it constant, so that the motor can reach the set speed quickly. After the speed is stable, as the inner ring, the current loop mainly plays the role of current limiting protection, and the speed outer loop keeps the maintaining speed constant. The Fig. 6 is a general block diagram of the BLDC motor control system.

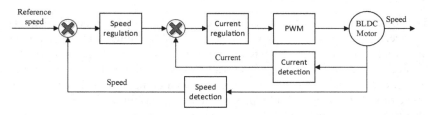

**Fig. 6.** The control system structure

The BLDC motor control system consists of two parts: hardware circuit and software program. The core of the hardware circuit is TI's TMS320F28069 main control chip, which outputs PWM wave. After being amplified by the driver, the PWM wave is input into the motor to control the start and stop of motor, speed and electromagnetic torque. In the self-designed control circuit board, in addition to the peripheral pin circuit of the main control chip, it also includes hardware circuits such as an AD sampling circuit, a Hall sensor interface circuit, and an encoder interface circuit. The software program is mainly divided into two parts: the setting of the main control chip register and the algorithm design. It mainly outputs PWM waves of different duty ratios according to the feedback signals of various detecting devices through the control algorithm.

### (1) The hardware design of BLDC motor control system

The Fig. 7 shows the overall hardware design of the BLDC motor control system.

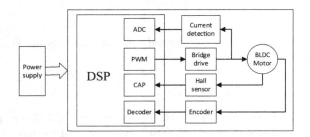

**Fig. 7.** The hardware design of BLDC motor control system

In the hardware circuit, the power supply module supplies power to the entire circuit system. The PWM module of the DSP chip outputs PWM wave, and the PWM wave is amplified by the power amplification system (bridge drive). Finally, PWM is input into the motor to control the speed [13]. The Hall sensor detects rotor position signal, the encoder detects the motor speed, and the ADC module collects the winding current signal. These detection feedback signals are fed back to the DSP chip, and processed by the algorithm to obtain PWM waves of different duty ratios [14, 15].

### (2) The control board design

The common BLDC motor drives consist of rectangular circuit boards that take up extra space. Three drives are required to drive the wall-climbing robot, which not only requires a lot of space, but also increases the weight of the wall-climbing robot.

In order to reduce the weight of the wall-climbing robot and make full use of the space between the mechanical structures of the wall-climbing robot, according to the prototype of self-designed wall-climbing robot, an unconventional shape of the control board has been designed, whose second generation is the same shape as the first generation, as shown in Fig. 8(a). The width of the board is slightly smaller than the width of the base, and the front and rear notches are to match the spatial position of the mechanical structure. Figure 8(b) shows the spatial position of this unconventional shaped circuit board placed on the wall-climbing robot.

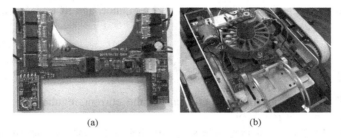

(a)                              (b)

**Fig. 8.** (a) The first generation of unconventional shaped circuit board; (b) Placement of unconventional shaped circuit board on wall-climbing robot.

### 3.3    The Control Algorithm Design

The PID control is a classic control algorithm. Because of its simple structure, high reliability and robustness, it is widely used in various control systems. In this paper, the incremental PID control algorithm is used in the BLDC motor control system of wall-climbing robot.

The expression for the discrete PID control is:

$$u(k) = k_p(error(k)) + k_i \sum_{j=0}^{k} error(j) + k_d(error(k) - error(k-1)) \quad (4)$$

Where $k_p$, $k_i$, and $k_d$ are the proportional coefficient, the integral coefficient, and the differential coefficient, respectively; $k$ is the sampling time. $error(k-1)$ and $error(k)$ are the deviations obtained at the $(k-1)th$ and $kth$ times, respectively.

According to the principle of recursion:

$$u(k-1) = k_p(error(k-1)) + k_i \sum_{j=0}^{k-1} error(j) + k_d(error(k-1) - error(k-2))$$
$$(5)$$

Then the incremental PID control algorithm is [12]:

$$\Delta u(k) = k_p(error(k) - error(k-1)) + k_i error(k) + k_d(error(k) - 2error(k-1) + error(k-2)) \quad (6)$$

### 3.4    The Speed and Current Double-Closed Loop Design

#### (1) The Current Loop Design

In the design of the current regulator, when the current loop has no steady-state error, good locked-rotor characteristic can be obtained. At the same time, when the control signal is suddenly applied, the winding current cannot exceed the allowable value to prevent damage to the motor. Therefore, we design the current loop as a type I system, the current regulator is designed as a PI regulator, and its transfer function can be written as:

$$W_{ACR}(s) = \frac{K_i(\tau_i s + 1)}{\tau_i s} \tag{7}$$

Where $K_i$ is the proportional coefficient of the current regulator; $\tau_i$ is the time constant of the current regulator.

According to the actual parameters, the transfer function of each device in the current loop is approximated [16]. Finally, the dynamic structure of the current loop is as shown in the Fig. 9.

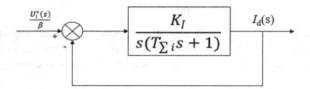

**Fig. 9.** The dynamic structure of the current loop

## (2) The Speed Loop Design

In order to achieve no steady-state error in speed and good dynamic anti-interference performance, the speed loop is designed as a type II system, and the speed regulator is designed as a PI speed regulator [16]. Its transfer function is:

$$W_{ASR}(s) = \frac{K_n(\tau_n s + 1)}{\tau_n s} \tag{8}$$

Where $K_n$ is the proportional coefficient of the speed regulator; $\tau_n$ is the time constant of the speed regulator.

After combining the transfer functions of the various devices in the speed loop, the resulting dynamic structure diagram is shown in Fig. 10.

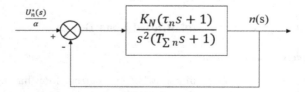

**Fig. 10.** The dynamic structure of the speed loop

# 4  Simulation Experiment and Result Analysis

The parameters of the BLDC motor for the wall-climbing robot are shown in Table 1.

**Table 1.** The BLDC motor parameters.

| Parameters | Value | Unit |
|---|---|---|
| Nominal torque | 0.413 | N.m |
| Nominal current | 5.7 | A |
| Nominal voltage | 48 | V |
| Motor constant | 0.097 | N.m/W |
| Terminal resistance | 0.771 | Ω |
| Terminal inductance | 0.36 | mH |
| Number of pole pairs | 12 | pairs |

According to the previous analysis, a simulation model of the speed and current double-closed loop BLDC motor control system has been established on SIMULINK, as shown in the Fig. 11.

The reference speed of BLDC motor was set to 2000 rpm, and the simulation duration was set to 0.4 s to obtain the simulation results.

As shown in Fig. 12, the motor speed increases rapidly from zero to the set value, the rise time is short, and the start-up is rapid. This is because when the motor starts, the speed value is very small, the speed loop is equivalent to the open loop, and the current loop is adjusted to make the winding current rapidly increase to the maximum value, so that the motor speed can increase rapidly. At the same time, since the output of the current PI regulator is set within a certain range, the speed, without overshoots, can be quickly stabilized at the set value without steady-state error.

As shown in the Fig. 13(a), at the initial time, the winding has a large initial current. This is because the speed is low and the back electromotive force is too small. As the speed increases, the phase current gradually decreases and eventually enters the steady state. The three-phase winding of the motor is turned on according to a certain rule, so that the current of each phase winding fluctuates periodically. At the same time, the electromagnetic torque of BLDC motor will also fluctuate with the fluctuation of the motor current, as shown in Fig. 13(b).

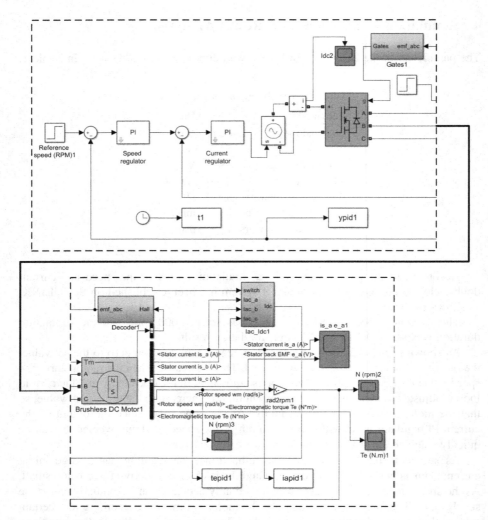

**Fig. 11.** The simulation model of the double-closed loop control system of BLDC motor

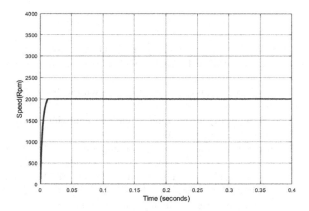

**Fig. 12.** The speed waveform

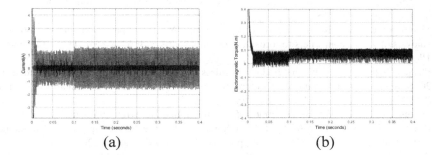

**Fig. 13.** (a) The current waveform; (b) The torque waveform.

## 5 Conclusion

It can be seen from the simulation experiment that the motor speed increases rapidly in the step response, the rise time is short, without overshoots. when the speed is stable, there is no steady-state error, and the adjustment time is short. The control system has excellent dynamic performance and steady-state performance. In order to further improve the compactedness of the wall-climbing robot, we will continue to expand the function of the controller to complete the goal of one controller simultaneously controlling the operation of multiple motors.

**Acknowledgements.** This work was supported by grants from Science and Technology Major Project of Anhui Province (17030901034), Jiangsu Key Research and Development Plan (BE2017067).

# References

1. McKenzie, C., Parness, A.: Video summary of DROP the durable reconnaissance and observation platform. In: 2012 IEEE International Conference on Robotics and Automation, pp. 3535–3536. IEEE, Saint Paul (2012)
2. Lam, T.L., Xu, Y.S.: Motion planning for tree climbing with inchworm-like robots. J. Field Robot. **30**(1), 87–101 (2013)
3. Lam, T.L., Xu, Y.S.: Biologically inspired tree-climbing robot with continuum maneuvering mechanism. J. Field Robot. **29**(6), 843–860 (2012)
4. Chen, R.: A gecko-inspired electroadhesive wall-climbing robot. IEEE Potentials **34**(2), 15–19 (2015)
5. Murphy, M.P., Sitti, M.: Waalbot: an agile small-scale wall-climbing robot utilizing dry elastomer adhesives. IEEE/ASME Trans. Mechatron. **12**(3), 330–338 (2007)
6. Wu, S., Wu, L., Liu, T.: Design of a sliding wall climbing robot with a novel negative adsorption device. In: 2011 8th International Conference on Ubiquitous Robots and Ambient Intelligence (URAI), pp. 97–100. IEEE, Incheon (2011)
7. Papadimitriou, A.: Modeling, Identification and Control of a Wall Climbing Robot Based on Vortex Actuation (2018)
8. Shanmugasundram, R., Zakariah, K.M., Yadaiah, N.: Implementation and performance analysis of digital controllers for brushless DC motor drives. IEEE/ASME Trans. Mechatron. **19**(1), 213–224 (2012)
9. Plachta, K.: A new control method of brushless DC motor to maximize starting torque. In: 2016 IEEE 16th International Conference on Environment and Electrical Engineering (EEEIC), pp. 1–5. IEEE, Florence (2016)
10. Lelkes, A., Bufe, M.: BLDC motor for fan application with automatically optimized commutation angle. In: 2004 IEEE 35th Annual Power Electronics Specialists Conference (IEEE Cat. No. 04CH37551), vol. 3, pp. 2277–2281. IEEE, Aachen (2004)
11. Wu, X., Wang, X., Mei, T., et al.: Mechanical analyses on the digital behaviour of the Tokay gecko (Gekko gecko) based on a multi-level directional adhesion model. Proc. R. Soc. **471** (2179), 1–20 (2015)
12. Xu, C., et al.: Digital PID controller for Brushless DC motor based on AVR microcontroller. In: 2008 IEEE International Conference on Mechatronics and Automation, pp. 247–252. IEEE, Takamatsu (2008)
13. Demirtas, M.: Off-line tuning of a PI speed controller for a permanent magnet brushless DC motor using DSP. Energy Convers. Manage. **52**(1), 264–273 (2011)
14. Wu, H.-C., Wen, M.-Y., Wong, C.-C.: Speed control of BLDC motors using hall effect sensors based on DSP. In: 2016 International Conference on System Science and Engineering (ICSSE), pp. 1–4. IEEE, Puli (2016)
15. Liu, C.S., Hwang, J.C., Chen, L.R., et al.: Development of new structure of brushless DC servo motor for ceiling fan. In: 2009 4th IEEE Conference on Industrial Electronics and Applications, pp. 2640–2643. IEEE, Xi'an (2009)
16. Yu, C.H.E.N., Ri-tu, W.U.: Double closed loop speed regulation system of BLDC motor. Light Ind. Mach. **7**(1), 76–79 (2009)

# Design of a Master-Slave Composite Wall Climbing Robot System for Penstock Assembly Welding

Jiashe Zhu, Zhenguo Sun[✉], Wei Huang, and Qiang Chen

Department of Mechanical Engineering,
Tsinghua University, Beijing 100084, China
nbzhzjs@163.com, sunzhg@tsinghua.edu.cn

**Abstract.** Nowadays, the penstock assembly welding of hydroelectric power stations is carried out by manual arc welding. In order to improve the working environment and raise the welding efficiency, this paper proposed a master-slave composite wall-climbing robot system based on gapped permanent magnet adhesion. With the master-slave composite design idea, the payloads of welding robot are shared and the flexibility and stability of the robot are improved. As a key mechanism of wall-climbing robot, the design and layout of the permanent magnetic adhesion module is studied. According to the result of static analysis and dynamic analysis of the welding robot, an optimized layout for adhesion module design is found. A Prototype of the robot system is built and experiments on the adhesion ability and motion ability of the robot system are carried out.

**Keywords:** Wall climbing robot · Welding robot · Penstock assembly

## 1 Introduction

Aqueduct penstock is a key component of the diversion system of hydroelectric power stations. Its installation and field assembly welding have the characteristics of heavy workload, long pipeline length, and limited work space. The common method of field assembly welding is manual arc welding (MAW) [1]. Although the welding procedure has been matured, but it still faces the problem of high labor intensity, low efficiency and high requirements for welders. And the quality of the weld seam is greatly affected by the welder's status. Application of robot welding can improve the working environment of workers, reduce labor intensity and improve welding efficiency. In this paper, a master-slave composite wall climbing welding robot system based on gapped permanent magnet adhesion is designed to replace manual welding and improve the efficiency.

## 2 Robot System Design

### 2.1 Working Environment

With the increase of the capacity of hydroelectric power station, the water head of hydropower station increases gradually, and the strength and specifications of diversion

© Springer Nature Switzerland AG 2019
H. Yu et al. (Eds.): ICIRA 2019, LNAI 11741, pp. 123–134, 2019.
https://doi.org/10.1007/978-3-030-27532-7_11

penstock have been improved. With the increase of the water flow, the nominal diameter of the penstock can reach more than 10 m, and the thickness increases correspondingly according to the increase of the pressure. Welding robot should be designed to adapt the increasing scale of the penstock.

The assembly welding of penstock can be divided into the longitudinal weld and circumferential weld. Longitudinal welding may be completed in the workshop or on-site according to different specifications and conditions, while circumferential welding is an indispensable link in the field installation of the penstock. In this paper, the author takes circumferential welding of penstock as the operational objective, and puts forward the following requirements for the welding robot according to the conditions:

(1) The robot should have the ability to operate in all positions and all attitude of 12–15 m diameter penstock and to complete the circumferential seam welding. Since there may be longitudinal seams excess height of penstock after rounding, the robot should have the ability to move over the height of 4 mm.
(2) In order to make the robot reach the target position quickly, it should also have the ability of fast movement. Therefore, the maximum speed of the robot is required to be no less than 2 m/min in the design.

## 2.2    Design of Master-Slave Composite Robot

In order to carry out the assembly welding, the robot needs to carry relevant equipment including welding torch, clamping mechanism, wire feeder, wire reel, driving part, and control system, etc. In addition, there is a cable connection between the robot and the monitoring station. With the change of working height, the robot will be affected by different cable weight.

**Table 1.** Robot load statistics

| Payloads | Size/mm | Weight/kg |
| --- | --- | --- |
| Welding torch and clamping mechanism | 270 × 240 × 125 | 5.4 |
| Wire feeder | 250 × 185 × 110 | 5.0 |
| Wire reel | 54 × $\phi$200 | 5.3 |
| Cables | 250 × 200 × 100 | 0–2.4 |
| Body Structure and other parts | / | 14.8 |
| Total | / | 30.5–32.9 |

As shown in Table 1, the total weight of the welding robot is more than 30 kg, which puts a higher requirement for the robot's adhesion ability and may reduce the flexibility of the robot's movement greatly. Among them, the weight of the cable varies with the height of welding position and the cable may be swaying in the wind at any time, which has an impact on the stability of the robot operation. Besides, the overall size of the robot is quite big with all these equipments, which reduces the adaptability of the robot to curved surfaces.

To solve the above problems, a master-slave composite robot is proposed in this paper. As shown in the Fig. 1, the system consists of a master welding robot, a slave robot, and a monitoring station. Among these components, two sub-robots attach to the surface of the penstock and complete welding work, while the monitoring station is used to monitor and control the robot system by operators.

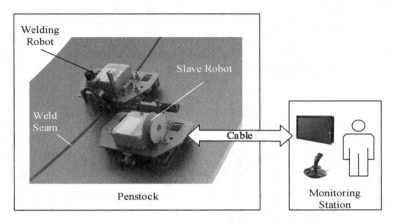

**Fig. 1.** A master-slave composite robot system

The master welding robot is responsible for the implementation of circumferential welding. It takes flexibility and stability as design characteristic. Besides motion mechanism and adhesion mechanism, the master robot only carries a welding torch, clamping mechanism, and necessary control system to minimize its load for flexibility (see Fig. 2). According to the research of Gui [3], the motion mechanism of the robot adopts a three-wheel structure of rolling steering, which is realized by a differential motion of two driving wheels, so as to reduce the steering power and improve the flexibility. The whole width and length of the master welding robot are 620 mm and 502 mm, respectively.

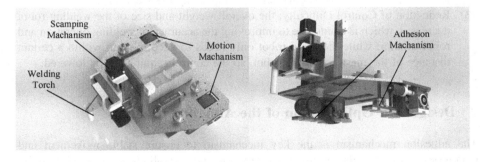

**Fig. 2.** Design of the master welding robot

Slave robot is mainly responsible for the load of welding-related equipment and interact with the monitoring station. Its design is aimed at heavy load and stabilization. The main load includes wire feeder, wire reel and control system (see in Fig. 3). It also bears the towing force of the cables connected to the monitoring station. In the process of assembly welding, the slave robot follows the master robot to support the operation. In the design of the main body, motion mechanism, and adhesion mechanism, the slave robot adopts a similar design of the master robot. It greatly reduces the complexity of the development of control system. The whole width and length of the slave robot are 560 mm and 400 mm, respectively.

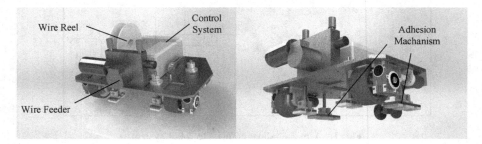

**Fig. 3.** Design of the slave robot

With the master-slave composite design, the welding robot system has the following advantages compared with a single welding robot:

(1) Adhesion ability requirement: the master welding robot no longer loads wire feeder, wire reel and most part of the control system. Its overall weight is reduced to 18.7 kg, which is 43.4% lower than that of a single welding robot. The weight reduction greatly reduces the requirement of adhesion force and improves the flexibility of the welding robot.
(2) Improvement of stability: The cables between the robot and the monitoring station are completely borne by the slave robot, which makes the welding robot run under a more stable state, and is conducive to improving the weld quality.
(3) Reduction of Control Difficulty: the overall weight and size of the welding robot decreases, which is conducive to improving the accuracy of welding operation and robot motion; while the slave robot only needs to keep moving within a certain distance of the master welding robot, so the control requirement is lowered.

## 3   Design and Optimization of the Adhesion Module

The adhesion mechanism is the key mechanism to ensure stable movement and operation. At present, the common adhesion method of wall-climbing robot includes magnetic adhesion and vacuum adhesion [4]. The penstock is made of magnetic material with sufficient thickness, and it is suitable for magnetic adhesion [5]. Magnetic adhesion includes permanent magnet adhesion and electromagnetic adhesion. In order to ensure the safety of field operation, permanent magnet adhesion is used as a robot adhesion method [6].

## 3.1 Design of Gapped Permanent Magnet Adhesion

Most of the permanent magnet wall-climbing robots use magnetic wheels and crawlers [7], which have the problems of low utilization of magnetic field and high resistance to motion. Therefore, the gapped permanent magnet adhesion is used in the welding robot system to separate the permanent magnet adhesion from the motion mechanism, so as to improve the utilization of the permanent magnet adhesion and reduce the influence on the motion resistance. In this paper, a yoke permanent magnet adhesion module is used, and the designed magnetic circuit is shown in Fig. 4.

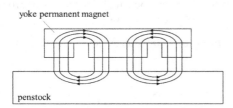

**Fig. 4.** Magnetic circuit of yoke permanent magnet module

**Fig. 5.** Adaptable adhesion mechanism

For the gapped permanent magnet adhesion module, when the air gapped increases, the adhesion force decreases rapidly, which affects adhesion stability. In order to adapt to the wall of pipe with different curvature radius, a connecting mechanism of adhesion module is designed as shown in Fig. 5. The connecting mechanism of the adhesion module consists of a helical pair and a rotating pair. The helical pair adjusts the height between magnetic module and penstock and the rotating pair adjusts the angle between magnetic module and penstock, making the magnetic adhesion module adaptable for different curvature radius of the surface and different robot attitudes.

## 3.2 Layout Optimization of Adhesion Module

In welding process, there are requirements in preheat temperature, interpass temperature and post-heat temperature. Before welding, all seams connected with high strength steel need to be preheated to 80–120 °C for 30 min. The interpass temperature during welding is required to be higher than the preheating temperature which keeps between 80–200 °C. These temperature requirements are close to or even exceed the maximum operating temperature of most Nd–Fe–B magnets. Therefore, the adhesion module is designed to keep a sufficient distance from the weld seam, so as to avoid the demagnetization (Fig. 6).

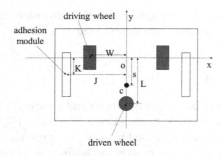
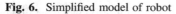
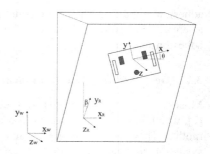

**Fig. 6.** Simplified model of robot          **Fig. 7.** Mechanical analysis model

In order to further study and optimize the design of adhesion force and layout of adhesion module, static and dynamic analysis of the welding robot is carried out. Since the curvature radius of the penstock exceeds 12 m, the penstock surface is approximated to a straight surface in the mechanical analysis (see in Fig. 7).

**Static Analysis.** The force analysis of the robot in static state is shown in Fig. 8.

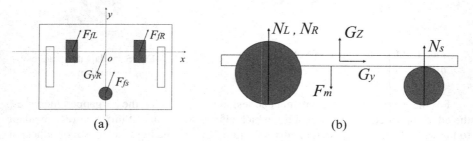

**Fig. 8.** Force analysis of the robot

The force balance relations and moment balance relations are as follows:

$$
\begin{cases}
G_{yR} = F_{fL} + F_{fR} + F_{fs} \\
G_z + N_L + N_R + N_s = 2F_m \\
2F_m K + G_y H = G_z s + N_s L
\end{cases}
\tag{1}
$$

The robot subjected to gravity may fail in the static state as follows: overall slip, normal detachment, longitudinal overturning and side overturning.

*Overall Slip.* When the static friction force on each wheel is insufficient, robot may slip along the surface affected by gravity component $G_{yR}$. The critical conditions for the failure are as follows:

$$F_{fL} + F_{fR} + F_{fs} \leq G_{yR} \tag{2}$$

The permissible adsorptive force conditions are as follows:

$$F_m \geq \frac{1}{2\left(\mu_s \cdot \frac{L-K}{L} + \mu_R \cdot \frac{K}{L}\right)} \left[\left(\mu_s \cdot \frac{L-s}{L} + \mu_R \cdot \frac{s}{L}\right)G_z + (\mu_s - \mu_R)G_y \cdot \frac{H}{L} + G_{yR}\right] \tag{3}$$

Where $\mu_s$ and $\mu_r$ are the static and rolling friction coefficient between the wheel and the surface; $H$ is the height of the center of gravity of the robot.

*Normal Detachment.* Normal detachment refers to the fact that the robot is subjected to the normal component $G_z$ of gravity and has the possibility of disengagement failure as a whole in the normal direction. The critical conditions for its occurrence are as follows:

$$2F_m \leq G_z \tag{4}$$

*Longitudinal Overturning.* Longitudinal overturning refers to the possibility of longitudinal overturning failure along the driven wheel or along the driving axle of the robot under the action of gravity components $G_y$ and $G_z$. The critical conditions for the occurrence of longitudinal overturning failure are as follows:

$$\begin{cases} 2F_m \cdot (L - K) \leq G_y H + G_z(L - s) \\ 2F_m \cdot K \leq G_y H + G_z s \end{cases} \tag{5}$$

The permissible adsorptive force conditions are as follows:

$$\begin{cases} F_m \geq \frac{1}{2(L-K)}[GH \cos \beta \cos \theta + G \sin \beta(L - s)] \\ F_m \geq \frac{1}{2K}(GH \cos \beta \cos \theta + Gs \sin \beta) \end{cases} \tag{6}$$

*Side Overturning.* Side overturning refers to the failure of single driving wheel disengagement caused by gravity components $G_x$, $G_y$ and $G_z$ (see in Fig. 9), i.e. the overturning occurs along the line between driving wheel and driven wheel on one side. The critical conditions for the overturning are as follows:

$$F_m(2l_1 + l_2) \sin \alpha \geq G_z(L - s) \cdot \cos \alpha + F_m l_2 \sin \alpha + G_x H \sin \alpha + G_y H \cos \alpha \tag{7}$$

The permissible adsorptive force conditions are as follows:

$$F_m \geq \frac{1}{2(L - K)} G\left[(L - s) \cdot \sin \beta + H \cos \beta\left(\frac{L}{W} \sin \theta + \cos \theta\right)\right] \tag{8}$$

It can be seen that the above failure conditions are related to the tilt angle $\beta$, the robot attitude angle $\theta$ and the longitudinal position $K$ of the adhesion module. In order to ensure the full attitude operation of the robot, i.e. $\theta \in [-\pi, \pi]$, the permissible

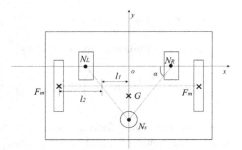

**Fig. 9.** Static analysis for side overturning

adsorptive force $[F_m](\beta, K)$ under each failure condition is simulated numerically (see in). The parameters of robot in the calculation are as follows: $L = 300$ mm, $W = 250$ mm, $s = 200$ mm, $\mu_s = 0.5$, $\mu_r = 0.05$, $m = 20$ kg, $H = 200$ mm.

**Dynamic Analysis.** When the robot moves on the surface of the penstock, the common failure modes are the skidding of driving wheel and the insufficient driving force of the motor. According to the experimental results, the maximum driving torque of a single driving mechanism occurs when the robot is turning in situ, which is the most prone to motion failure. Dynamic analysis of the welding robot in this situation is shown in the Fig. 10, where $F_L$ and $F_R$ are the driving forces provided by the two driving wheels respectively, $F_{frL}$ and $F_{frR}$ are the rolling friction resistance on the two driving wheels, and $F_{fs}$ is the rolling friction resistance on the driven wheels (Fig. 11).

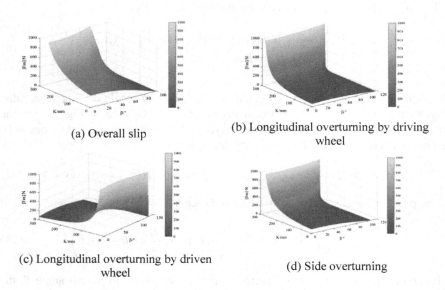

(a) Overall slip

(b) Longitudinal overturning by driving wheel

(c) Longitudinal overturning by driven wheel

(d) Side overturning

**Fig. 10.** Numerical simulation of adhesion capacity conditions

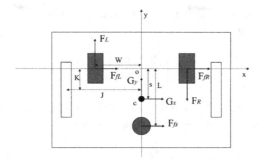

**Fig. 11.** Dynamic analysis model

The dynamic equation of the steering process of the welding robot is obtained as follows:

$$\begin{cases} \dot{V}_x = \frac{1}{m}\left(F_{fL} + F_{fR} + F_{fs} - G_x\right) - \omega V_y \\ \dot{V}_y = \frac{1}{m}\left(F_L - F_R - G_x\right) + \omega V_x \\ \dot{\omega} = \frac{1}{I_z}\left[W(F_L + F_R) - LF_s - sG_x\right] \end{cases} \tag{9}$$

Where $I_z$ is the rotational inertia of the welding robot centered on the origin o of coordinate oxyz. The forces can be expressed as follows:

$$\begin{cases} F_L = \frac{M_L}{R} - F_{frL} \\ F_R = \frac{M_R}{R} - F_{frR} \end{cases} \tag{10}$$

According to the balance relationship, the support forces of each wheel have the following relations:

$$\begin{cases} N_L = F_m\frac{L-K}{L} - G_z\frac{L-s}{2L} - G_y\frac{H}{2L} - G_x\frac{H}{2W} \\ N_R = F_m\frac{L-K}{L} - G_z\frac{L-s}{2L} - G_y\frac{H}{2L} + G_x\frac{H}{2W} \\ N_s = \frac{2F_mK + G_yH - G_zs}{L} \end{cases} \tag{11}$$

Based on the analysis of the actual motion of welding robot, the following assumptions can be made: (a) The welding robot moves in a straight line with uniform speed and does not slip. It can be considered that $\dot{V}_x$, $\dot{V}_y$, $\dot{\omega}$ are equal to 0; (b) Since the welding robot moves along the circumferential seam, the rotational angular velocity and linear velocity are small, and the centrifugal force is far less than the robot weight, the influence of centrifugal acceleration is neglected. According to the above assumptions, formula (9) can be modified to the following equations:

$$\begin{cases} F_{fL} + F_{fR} + F_{fs} - G_x = 0 \\ F_L - F_R - G_y = 0 \\ W(F_L + F_R) - F_{fs}L - G_xs = 0 \end{cases} \tag{12}$$

The following conditions must be met if the driving wheel does not slip when the welding robot is turning in situ:

$$\begin{cases} \frac{M_L}{R} \le \mu_s N_L \\ \frac{M_R}{R} \le \mu_s N_R \end{cases} \tag{13}$$

By substituting formula (11) and formula (12), the permissible adsorptive force to prevent the robot from skidding is obtained as follows:

$$F_m \ge \frac{1}{\left[(\mu_s - \mu_r)\frac{L-K}{L} - \mu_r \frac{K}{W}\right]} \left\{ \begin{array}{l} \left[(\mu_s - \mu_r)\frac{H}{2W} + \frac{s}{2W}\right]G\cos\beta\sin\theta \\ + \frac{1}{2}\left[(\mu_s - \mu_r)\frac{H}{L} + 1\right]G\cos\beta\cos\theta \\ + \frac{1}{2}\left[(\mu_s - \mu_r)\frac{L-s}{L} - \mu_r \frac{s}{W}\right]G\sin\beta \end{array} \right\} \tag{14}$$

It can be seen that the occurrence conditions of the driving wheel skidding are also related to the tilt angle $\beta$, the attitude angle $\theta$ and the longitudinal position $K$ of the adhesion module. As the robot moves along the circumferential seam, the numerical simulation analysis is carried out by taking $\theta = 0°$ (see in Fig. 12). It can be concluded that the most probable wall angle of driving wheel skidding failure is $\beta = 4.84°$.

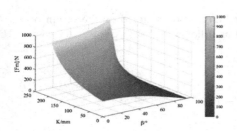

**Fig. 12.** Numerical simulation of adhesion capacity condition

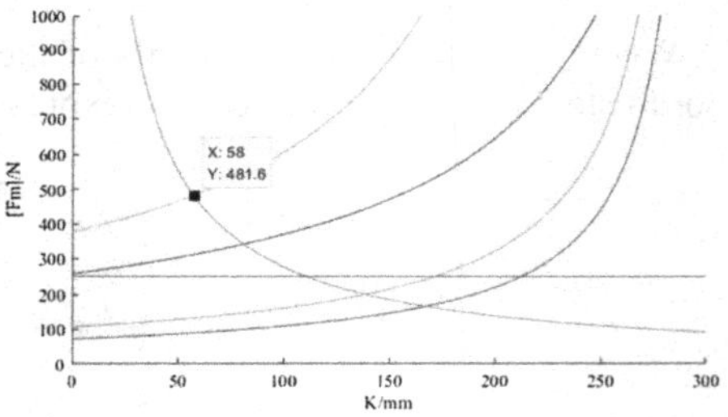

**Fig. 13.** Effect of layout parameter K on permissible adsorptive force

**Layout Optimization of Adhesion Module.** By integrating the numerical simulation results under the above failure conditions and choosing the maximum permissible adsorptive force at each tilt angle and attitude angle, the relationship between the permissible adsorptive force $[F_m]_M$ of the permanent magnet adhesion module and the layout parameter $K$ of the adhesion module can be obtained (see in Fig. 13).

The results show that the location of the adhesion module is mainly determined by the overturning failure conditions and the skidding conditions. When the distance between the adhesion module and the driving wheel axle is $K = 57.5$ mm, the permissible adhesion force is minimized and the permissible adhesion force is $[F_m] = 486.1$ N.

## 4   Prototype Experiment

As the slave robot's mechanism design is similar to the master robot and its load is heavier than the master robot, the motion ability of the robot system is limited by the slave robot. The kinematic performance of the slave robot is tested on a vertical wall (see in Fig. 14). According to the experiment, the robot has the ability to adhere to the steel surface in full attitude. The maximum linear velocity of slave robot is 3.6 m/min and the maximum angular velocity of in situ steering is 0.3 rad/s.

**Fig. 14.** Experiment on the slave robot: (a), (b) linear velocity experiment; (c), (d) angular velocity of in situ steering experiment

According to the above design, a prototype of the robot system (see in Fig. 15) is built. A cooperative motion experiment is carried out on a vertical wall (see in Fig. 16). The linear velocity of the robot system is 3 m/min.

**Fig. 15.** Prototype   of   the   robot system

**Fig. 16.** Cooperative motion experiment of the robot system

## 5  Conclusion

In this paper, a wall-climbing welding robot system based on gapped permanent magnet adhesion is proposed for field assembly welding of the water diversion penstock. The master-slave design improves the flexibility of the robot motion and the stability of the welding operation. Through mechanical analysis of the robot, a permissible adhesion force model is established, and the layout design of the permanent magnet adhesion mechanism is optimized. Finally, in the prototype test, the adhesion capacity and movement ability of the robot at various wall angles and postures are verified.

## References

1. Chen, G.-X., Lei, X.-M., Zeng, Z.-L., Chen, Z.-G.: Analysis on weld deformation of penstock. Hot Working Technol. **35**(3), 41–42 (2006)
2. Jian-Feng, C., Chuan-Bao, M., Ning, L.: Influence of wall thickness of steel penstock on sharing ratio of internal pressure in bedrock for pumped storage power station. Water Resour. Power (2017)
3. Gui, Z., Chen, Q., Sun, Z., Zhang, W.: Turning power losses in the wheeled locomotion mechanism for a wall climbing robot. J. Tsinghua Univ. (Sci. Technol.) **48**(2), 161–164 (2008)
4. Nansai, S., Elara, R.: A survey of wall climbing robots: recent advances and challenges. Robotics **5**(3), 14–28 (2016)
5. Lee, G., Kim, H., Seo, K., et al.: Series of multilinked caterpillar track-type climbing robots. J. Field Robot. **33**(6), 737–750 (2016)
6. Shang, J., Bridge, B., Sattar, T., et al.: Development of a climbing robot for inspection of long weld lines. Ind. Robot **35**(3), 217–223 (2008)
7. Zeliang, X., Ma, P.: A wall-climbing robot for labelling scale of oil tank's volume. Robotica **20**, 209–212 (2002)

# Underwater Acoustic and Optical Signal Processing for Environmental Cognition

# Numerical Prediction of Self-propulsion Point of AUV with a Discretized Propeller and MFR Method

Lihong Wu[1]([⊠]) [iD], Xisheng Feng[2], Xiannian Sun[1],
and Tongming Zhou[3]

[1] Ship Building and Ocean Engineering College, Dalian Maritime University,
No. 1 Linghai Road, Dalian, China
wlh@sia.cn
[2] State Key Laboratory of Robotics, Shenyang Institute of Automation,
Chinese Academy of Sciences, No. 114 Nanta Road, Shenyang, China
[3] School of Civil and Resource Engineering, The University of Western
Australia, 35 Stirling Highway, Crawley, WA 6009, Australia

**Abstract.** It is important to determine the self-propulsion point for marine vehicles to evaluate the approaching velocity output from a determined propeller. A method is presented that significantly reduces the computational cost by coupling a discretized propeller with a MFR (Multiple Frames of Reference) method for evaluation of the propulsion factors of AUV (Autonomous Underwater Vehicle). The predicted approaching velocity in this study was approximately 2.8% lower than the design value of 1.0 m/s obtained using nominal wake fraction, which can be attributed to increased energy dissipation for the water at the wake caused by the propeller. The effective wake fraction was 0.303 and the thrust deduction was 0.163.Vortex pairing was found at the blade tip and developed downstream of the propeller. In addition, the hull and tail-planes were beneficial for improving the thrust of the propeller. The proposed method is a viable option to validate fluid dynamics analyses of the unsteady motion of self-propelled marine vehicles simulated with physics-based methods, particularly for cases which have a shortage of experimental data.

**Keywords:** Self-propulsion point · AUV · Discretized propeller · MFR

## 1 Introduction

It is necessary to determine the self-propulsion point of an AUV to predict its position, power consumption, and the duration it can work underwater with a limited power source capacity. Currently, the self-propulsion point of a marine propeller can be obtained with ship model tests and numerical methods. The latter method is cost-effective and can provide various flow conditions and flow field analysis results.

There are three methods to explore the self-propulsion point of marine vehicles: a coefficient-based method, a physics-based method and a MFR method. The coefficient-based simulation method (Ueno and Nimura [1], Azarsina and Williams [2]) has traditionally been used to determine the self-propulsion point, which is based on the

© Springer Nature Switzerland AG 2019
H. Yu et al. (Eds.): ICIRA 2019, LNAI 11741, pp. 137–147, 2019.
https://doi.org/10.1007/978-3-030-27532-7_12

available hydrodynamic coefficients obtained from model tests or empirical estimates. A physics-based simulation method has been proposed by McDonald and Whitfield [3] and further developed by Pankajakshan [4], Lübke [5], Bhushan et al. [6], Carrica [7–9], Chase and Carrica [10], and Mofidi and Carrica [11]. Carrica used a dynamic overset mesh method to calculate flow fields for the self-propulsion motion of the DARPA Suboff submarine, the turning and zigzag maneuvers of a surface combatant, and the sink and trim motions of a container ship. The simulation results included prediction of the self-propulsion point, isosurfaces of the axial velocity, propeller blade tip vortices, and hub vortex development. These simulations are particularly complex owing to the disparity in length and timescale between the propeller and the ship itself, as well as the evolving mesh, which varies as the computation progresses. As a result, these simulations require the calculation to be performed in a supercomputer center and require approximately 1 month of wall clock time with 50–160 processors.

A detailed development of the unsteady flow field is not always necessary, such as for acquiring the self-propulsion point, investigating the interaction between the propeller and ship hull under working conditions, or validating a propeller design. Thus, the MFR method is presented, which employing a fixed mesh during the simulation (Choi et al. [12], Wei and Wang [13]). This has the important benefit of maintaining a high-quality CFD (Computational Fluid Dynamics) mesh without concern for the severe mesh distortion that can occur with the moving mesh method or the interpolation problems that can occur with the overset mesh method.

In this study, the MFR method was applied to investigate the self-propulsion point of a fully appended AUV with a discretized propeller. And the unsteady condition of the propeller blades at the self-propulsion point was simulated, illustrating the thrust variation of the blades resulting from the wake of the tail-planes. The vortex structure downstream of the propeller in an unsteady condition was also investigated.

## 2  Geometry

The selected AUV was designed and produced by SIA (Shenyang Institute of Automation), China. The AUV has a designed velocity of 1.0 m/s with a propeller rotation of 300 rpm under the designed loadings. As shown in Fig. 1, the AUV hull is composed of three parts: a nose section with a semi-elliptical radius, a middle section with a constant radius, and a tail section with a semi-conical radius. Four identical tail-planes arranged in a symmetrical "+" configuration and the tested propeller are attached to the tail section. The tested propeller has four blades with a diameter of 0.216 m. As shown in Fig. 1, viewing the propeller from the stern, Blade1 is at the top at 0°, while Blades 2, 3, and 4 are at 90°, 180°, and 270°, respectively. Two reference frames are defined on the AUV: the global frame of reference, OXYZ, and the local frame of reference, oxyz. OXYZ is fixed at the outer domain and is stationary, while oxyz is fixed at the inner domain and rotates together with the propeller. Both reference frames have an identical axis coinciding with the longitudinal axis of the AUV hull, which are defined as Z and z in the two reference frames, respectively.

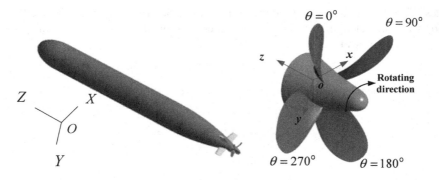

**Fig. 1.** Geometry of a fully appended AUV and two reference frames

## 3   Numerical Methods

Analysis of the self-propulsion point of a fully appended AUV was based on RANS (Reynolds Averaged Navier-Stokes) equations. It should be noted that there are many turbulence models available to solve propeller rotation problems, including RNG (Renormalization Group) k-ε (Wang et al. [14]), RSM (Reynolds Stress Model) (Huang et al. [15]), k-ω sst (Menter [16], Ji et al. [17]), and DDES (Delayed Detached Eddy Simulation) based on k-ω sst (Chase and Carrica [10]). In this paper, k-ω sst was used to model the Reynolds stress tensor.

MFR allows for analyses involving a single domain or multiple domains. As shown in Fig. 2, two domains, i.e., an inner domain and outer domain, were defined in this simulation. The inner domain includes the propeller and a finite part of the wake, and is rotating with the propeller. The rest of the body, including the AUV and rudder, are defined as the outer domain, which is stationary. Between the rotating and stationary domains, there are three interfaces, which are located at the top, bottom, and circumferential surface of the inner domain. At each interface, the mesh connection method is General Grid Interface (GGI). Steady simulation was conducted using the Frozen Rotor model, and the Transient Rotor Stator was employed to simulate the transient characteristics at the self-propulsion point. The transient computation is initialized using a steady-state solution result.

The mesh system was built in response to the domain topology. A tetrahedral grid was built for the inner domain, and a hybrid grid (Wu et al. [18]) was generated for the outer domain. The tetrahedral grid includes the surface grids on the four blades and hub and the volume mesh filling in the wake field of the propeller and the remaining domain. Line density was set on thin areas including the blade tip, leading edge, trailing edge, and the connecting curves between the propeller and hub. The blade was meshed with a grid size of 0.008D (where D is the diameter of the propeller), while the refinement line on the blade tip, leading edge, and trailing edge was meshed with a curve element size of 0.002D. The hybrid grid in the outer domain includes triangle grids on the surface of the hull and tail-planes, a ten-layer prismatic mesh at the near wall region, and tetrahedral grids filling in the remaining domain. To capture the wake, a mesh density region was built downstream of the propeller blades with size 0.025D, a ratio of 1.2, and a length of 5 D. The whole mesh system and close-up views of specific parts are shown in Fig. 3.

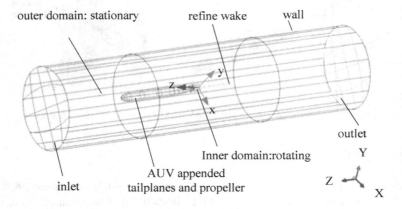

**Fig. 2.** Two domains in MFR model and boundary conditions

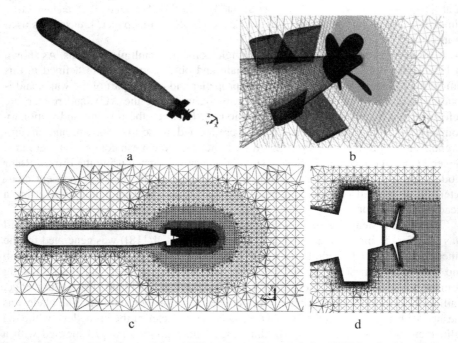

**Fig. 3.** Mesh for the self-propulsion AUV (a, the surface mesh for AUV fitted with tail-planes and propeller; b, details of wake grids; c, mesh at symmetry plane; d, close-up view of stern mesh)

To solve the momentum equations, a second-order centered scheme was used for diffusion and a second-order backward discretization was used in time. For the turbulence equations, a second-order upwind scheme was used for convection. No-slip boundary conditions were assigned to the blades, hub, tail-planes, and AUV hull. The incoming velocity was defined at the inlet, zero static pressure was defined at the outlet, and free-slip conditions were defined for the walls of the outer domain. In the steady simulation, the time step was selected based on a physical time step. In the unsteady simulation of self-propulsion, a total time of 0.6 s was set for three complete cycles. The interval time for the output was defined as every time step, during which the simulation results were monitored at the time for a rotation of 1°. Transient results for the pressure and velocity were output at each time step.

## 4 Prediction of Self-propulsion Point

At a prescribed advance velocity for a constantly rotating propeller at 300 rpm, the resistance R and thrust T of the propeller are first calculated. The new incoming velocity is then interpolated according to the difference between the calculated R and T. The calculated T–V and R–V curves for the selected AUV are shown in Fig. 4. The self-propulsion point of this AUV is determined as the intersection of these two curves, at which the approaching velocity is 0.972 m/s for the propeller rotating at 300 rpm. The predicted approaching velocity is thus approximately 2.8% lower than the designed value of 1.0 m/s.

Comparison of the hydrodynamics in self-propulsion tests and relative open water tests can be used to determine the effective wake fraction $W_e$, relative rotation efficiency $\eta_R$, and thrust deduction factor t. At the self-propulsion point, the rotation speed of the propeller is measured as n. The thrust and torque are measured as $T_B$, $Q_B$, respectively. The speed of hull is $V_S$. Correspondingly, the thrust $T_0$ is defined as that resulting from the propeller rotating at a speed of n in open water, where:

$$T_B = T_0 \tag{1}$$

The current advance velocity is then calculated in open water as $V_{A0}$. The effective wake and wake fraction can be determined as follows:

$$u = V_S - V_{A0} \tag{2}$$

$$w_e = \frac{V_S - V_{A0}}{V_S} \tag{3}$$

The relative rotative efficiency, $\eta_R$, is given by the following:

$$\eta_R = \frac{Q_0}{Q_B} \tag{4}$$

At the same time, the resistance of the AUV without the propeller when cruising at the same velocity, $V_S$, is recoded as R. The thrust deduction factor, t, is then given by the following:

$$t = \frac{T_B - R}{T_B} \tag{5}$$

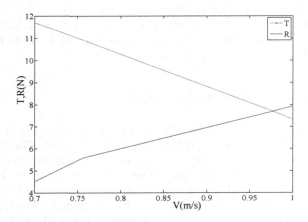

**Fig. 4.** Propeller thrust (T) and total resistance (R) versus hull cruising velocity (V) in self-propulsion

The effective wake fraction We, obtained for the selected propeller caused by the AUV in this study is 0.303, which is close to the values of 0.31 for the same-shape AUV reported by Bettle et al. [19] and 0.30 reported by Allmendinger [20] and Cairns et al. [21]. The calculated rotative efficiency $\eta_R$ is 1.008, which is close to unity. The obtained thrust deduction is 0.163, which deviates slightly from the value of 0.1338 determined experimentally by Bettle et al. [19] for a submarine. This deviation may be due to the different shape resulting from the sail installed on the top of the submarine, which increases the resistance percentage.

## 5  Flow Field

The interaction between the hull, tail-planes, and propeller in the flow field at the self-propulsion point is investigated in this section. Figure 5 shows a view of the pressure contours at different locations, including the hull, tail-planes, propeller, and several axial slices downstream of the propeller, labeled with different legends. There is an evident decrease in pressure with acceleration of the flow behind the propeller, induced by both the propeller and the convergence of the flow behind the hull.

Figure 6 shows the wake contours at the self-propulsion point at a cross section on the plane x = 0 as the propeller rotates through different positions of 0°, 18°, 36°, 54°, 72°, and 90°. The far field velocity for this computation is the approaching velocity. Vortex pairing appeared at the blade tip and developed downstream of the propeller. In addition, the vortex pairing vanished rapidly along the propeller wake, showing that although the MFR can predict the self-propulsion point, the rotating flow is restricted in the rotating domain, and cannot describe the pre-swirl flow upstream of the rotating propeller or the after-rotating flow downstream of the rotating propeller. This is a result of its dynamic interface, which cannot model the transient effects.

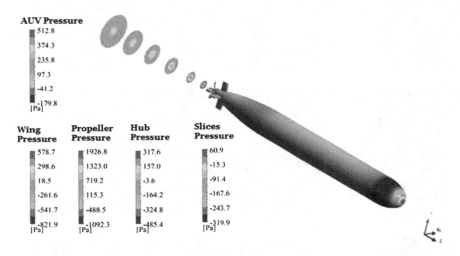

**Fig. 5.** Local pressures of AUV with tail-planes and propeller at self-propulsion point (Pressure variation along axis Z of AUV, each with the different legend to make contour variation clear in local position)

The non-uniform inflow from the tail-planes causes significant transient loads on the propeller blades, which are obtained with the unsteady self-propulsion simulation and shown in Fig. 7. Owing to the symmetry of the propeller, the thrust coefficient for only one blade is given. It is evident that the blade produces thrust in a periodic oscillation. With each revolution of the blade, four periods of thrust can be identified due to the symmetrical propeller and tail-planes, which correspond to the four tail-planes. When the blade is located with an angle of about 7.0° between the blade and its adjacent tailplane, the thrust coefficient provided by the blade has a maximum value of 0.0423. Correspondingly, the minimum thrust coefficient occurs at an angle of about 3.0° from the center position between two adjacent tail-planes.

Figure 8 shows cross-sections of the wake at two positions downstream of the propeller for the AUV two bodies. At the close location (z = 0.03 m), the wake of the four blades is obvious. At the faraway location (z = −0.1 m), the wake is decayed. The tip vortex pairing is strengthened more for AUV_tailplane_propeller (AUV with tail-planes and propeller) than for AUV_propeller (AUV appended with only propeller) at both locations. However, the hub vortex is the opposite. This strengthened tip vortex indicates that the amplitude of the thrust for each blade is larger for the AUV with tail-planes than that without tail-planes.

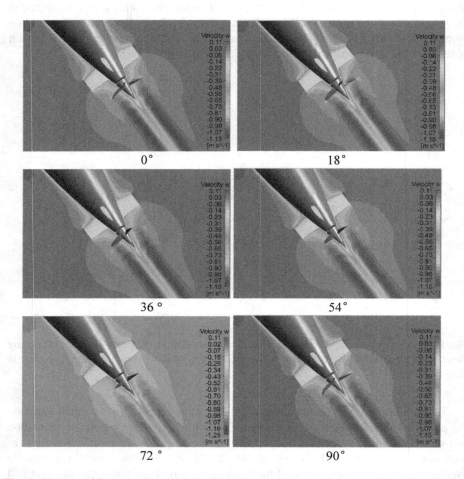

**Fig. 6.** Vortex pairing at wake region in the self-propulsion point at a cut plane through the rotation axis z (x = 0)

## 6 Conclusions

The self-propulsion point of a fully appended AUV was successfully modeled using the MFR method and a discretized propeller. The simulation was conducted on a work-station with 8 nodes and took approximately 7 d using the following specifications:

Intel (R), Xeon(R), CPU E5-1620 0@3.60 GHz, 3.60 GHz, RAM 16.0 GB. The approaching velocity, propulsion factors, and interaction among the hull, tail-planes, and propeller at the self-propulsion point of the AUV were obtained and discussed. The results shows that:

(1) The effective wake fraction is 0.303 and the thrust deduction, t, is 0.163.
(2) The predicted approaching velocity is 0.972 m/s with 2.8% lower than the design value of 1.0 m/s.
(3) Vortex pairing appeared at the blade tip and developed downstream of the propeller.
(4) The hull and tail-planes are beneficial for improving the thrust of the propeller.
(5) The blade produces thrust in a periodic oscillation. With each revolution of the blade, four periods of thrust can be identified due to the four tail-planes.
(6) Although the MFR method can predict the self-propulsion point, the rotating flow is restricted in the rotating domain, which cannot describe the pre-swirl flow upstream of the rotating propeller or the after-rotating flow downstream of the rotating propeller. This is a result of its dynamic interface, which cannot model the transient effects.

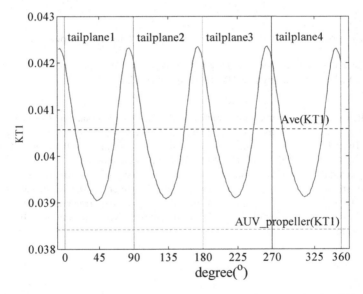

**Fig. 7.** Thrust coefficients of one blade at a full revolution in unsteady simulation of AUV appended tail-planes and propeller

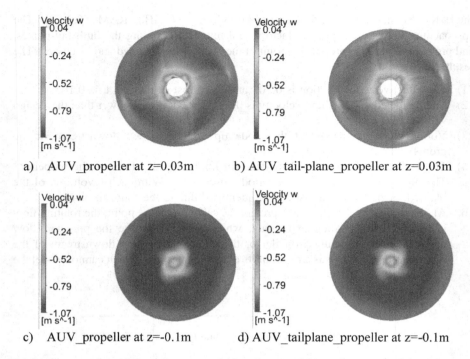

a)   AUV_propeller at z=0.03m      b) AUV_tail-plane_propeller at z=0.03m

c)   AUV_propeller at z=-0.1m      d) AUV_tailplane_propeller at z=-0.1m

**Fig. 8.** Cross sections of the wake at two positions (up, z = 0.03 m; down, z = −0.1 m) for two bodies (left, AUV_propeller; right, AUV_tail-plane_propeller)

**Acknowledgement.** The authors are grateful to the Chinese Scholarship Council (CSC), the State Key Laboratory of Robotics, the Natural Science Foundation of China (with Grant No. 51009016 and 51409047) and the Fundamental Research Funds for the Central Universities (with Grant No. 3132017030, 3132018206) for their financial support, as well as the University of Western Australia (UWA in Australia) for providing facilities for simulations. In addition, many thanks should be given to the underwater vehicle center of SIA (Shenyang Institute of Automation, China) for providing the AUV model and some experimental data for validation. Grateful acknowledgement should also be given to Professor Xiannian Sun, who helped a lot in editing the manuscript.

# References

1. Ueno, M., Nimura, T.: An analysis of steady descending motion of a launcher of a compact deep-sea monitoring robot system. In: OCEANS 2002 MTS/IEEE, pp. 277–285 (2002)
2. Azarsina, F., Williams, C.D.: Maneuvering simulation of the MUN explorer AUV based on the empirical hydrodynamics of axi-symmetric bare hulls. Appl. Ocean Res. **32**, 443–453 (2010)
3. McDonald, H., Whitfield, D.: Self-propelled maneuvering underwater vehicles. In: Proceedings of 21st Symposium on Naval Hydrodynamics, Throndheim, Norway (1996)

4. Pankajakshan, R., Remotigue, S., Taylor, L., et al.: Validation of control-surface induced submarine maneuvering simulations using UNCLE. In: Proceedings of 24th Symposium on Naval Hydrodynamics, Fukuoka, Japan (2002)
5. Lübke, L.O.: Numerical simulation of the flow around the propelled KCS. In: CFD Workshop Toykyo, Tokyo, Japan (2005)
6. Bhushan, S., Xing, T., Carrica, P., et al.: Model-and full-scale URANS simulations of athena resistance, powering, seakeeping, and 5415 maneuvering. J. Ship Res. **53**(4), 179–198 (2009)
7. Carrica, P.M., Castro, A.M., Stern, F.: Self-propulsion computations using a speed controller and a discretized propeller with dynamic overset grids. J. Mar. Sci. Technol. **15**, 316–330 (2010)
8. Carrica, P.M., Fu, H.P., Stern, F.: Computations of self-propulsion free to sink and trim and of motions in head waves of the KRISO Container Ship (KCS) model. Appl. Ocean Res. **33**, 309–320 (2011)
9. Carrica, P.M., Hosseini, H.S., Stern, F.: CFD analysis of broaching for a model surface combatant with explicit simulation of moving rudders and rotating propellers. Comput. Fluids **53**, 117–132 (2012)
10. Chase, N., Carrica, P.M.: Submarine propeller computations and application to self-propulsion of DARPA Suboff. Ocean Eng. **60**, 68–80 (2013)
11. Mofidi, A., Carrica, P.M.: Simulation of ZigZag maneuvers for a container ship with direct moving rudder and propeller. Comput. Fluids **96**, 191–203 (2014)
12. Choi, J.E., Min, K.S., Kim, J.H., et al.: Resistance and propulsion characteristics of various commercial ships based on CFD results. Ocean Eng. **37**, 549–566 (2010)
13. Wei, Y.S., Wang, Y.S.: Unsteady hydrodynamics of blade forces and acoustic responses of a model scaled submarine excited by propeller's thrust and side-forces. J. Sound Vib. **332**, 2038–2056 (2013)
14. Wang, C., Huang, S., Xin, C.: Research on the hydrodynamics performance of propeller-rudder interaction based on sliding mesh and RNG k-ε model. J. Ship Mech. **15**(7), 715–721 (2011)
15. Huang, S., Xie, X.S., Hu, J.: Effect of fin on podded propeller hydrodynamic performance. J. Naval Univ. Eng. **21**(2), 50–54 (2009)
16. Menter, F.R.: Two-equation eddy-viscosity turbulence models for engineering applications. AIAA J. **32**(8), 1598–1605 (1994)
17. Ji, B., Luo, X.W., Peng, X.X., et al.: Numerical analysis of cavitation evolution and excited pressure fluctuation around a propeller in non-uniform wake. Int. J. Multiph. Flow **43**, 13–21 (2012)
18. Wu, L.H., Li, Y.P., et al.: Hydrodynamic analysis of AUV underwater docking with a cone-shaped dock under ocean currents. Ocean Eng. **85**, 110–126 (2014)
19. Bettle, M.C., Gerber, A.G., Watt, G.D.: Unsteady analysis of the six DOF motion of a buoyantly rising submarine. Comput. Fluids **38**, 1833–1849 (2009)
20. Allmendinger, E.: Submersible Vehicle Systems Design. The Society of Naval Architects and Marine Engineers, New Jersey (1990)
21. Cairns, J., Larnicol, E., Ananthakrishnan, P.: Design of AUV propeller based on a blade element method. In: OCEAN 1998 Conference, Nice, France, pp. 672–675 (1998)

# Underwater Image Restoration Based on Red Channel and Haze-Lines Prior

Dabing Yu[1], Guanying Huo[1(✉)], Yan Liu[1], Yan Zhou[1,2],
and Jinxing Xu[1]

[1] College of Internet of Things Engineering,
Hohai University, Changzhou 213022, China
huoguanying@hhu.edu.cn
[2] Changzhou Key Laboratory of Sensor Networks
and Environmental Sensing, Changzhou 213022, China

**Abstract.** Due to the scattering and absorption of light while it propagates in the water, underwater images often suffer from low contrast and color distortion. In order to solve this problem, we propose an underwater image restoration algorithm based on red channel and haze-lines prior in this paper. Firstly, the red channel prior is used to estimate veiling-light. Secondly, according to the characteristics of red channel attenuation in water, the attenuation ratio of red-blue channel and red-green channel are introduced to estimate the transmission by using haze-lines prior. Finally, the transmission is corrected by the red channel boundary constraint. In addition, for underwater artificial illumination, we introduce saturation as the low bound of the transmission estimation to reduce the impact of artificial light. The experimental results show that the proposed algorithm can restore image color information, improve image clarity and obtain better visual quality. The quantitative analysis indicates that the proposed algorithm performs well on a wide variety of underwater images and is competitive with other state-of-the-arts.

**Keywords:** Underwater image restoration · Red channel · Haze-lines ·
Saturation · Artificial illumination · Transmission

## 1 Introduction

In recent years, underwater image sensing and analysis technology has developed rapidly and has been widely used in marine geological surveys, marine biological detection and protection, marine military and other fields. However, underwater images are essentially characterized by their poor visibility, especially the low contrast and inaccurate color, due to the strong attenuation and light scattering in water. the degraded images have serious impact on the subsequent image analysis task.

Underwater image restoration is usually based on the underwater image imaging models [1], which is mainly composed of forward scattering component, backward scattering component and direct component. Forward scattering component results in blurred details and lack of texture information in underwater images. To solve this problem, Hou et al. [2] combine the point spread function of light in water with the

© Springer Nature Switzerland AG 2019
H. Yu et al. (Eds.): ICIRA 2019, LNAI 11741, pp. 148–158, 2019.
https://doi.org/10.1007/978-3-030-27532-7_13

modulation transfer function to remove the effects of forward scattering. For the underwater imaging, there is a short distance between the object and the camera, the influence of forward component can be neglected, and the removal of back scattering becomes a crucial problem. Due to the low contrast caused by backscattering, image exhibits foggy effects. He *et al.* [3] propose the dark channel prior (DCP) dehazing model, which has been widely used to underwater image restoration [4–6]. Sathya *et al.* [4] propose a variant of DCP, which equalizes the different color channels to achieve a better visual effect on the restored image. However, when light travels through the water, the red light with long wavelength has the largest attenuation and the shortest propagation distance. Galdran *et al.* [7] suggest the red channel prior (RDCP) to estimate the transmission by using the saturation correction when handing the artificially illuminated underwater images.

Berman *et al.* [8–10] innovatively propose the haze-lines prior dehazing model, in which they find each color cluster in the clear image becomes a line in RGB space. Using these haze-lines, we can recover both the distance map and the haze-free image. Haze-line clusters and restores each pixel in the image, so the color recovery of the image is more complete. Jerlov [11] developed a frequently used classification scheme for oceanic waters. The Jerlov water types are I, IA, IB, II and III for open ocean waters, and 1 through 9 for coastal waters. For different types of water, the attenuation coefficient ratios of blue-red and blue-green channels are obtained, so the haze-lines model is applied to underwater image restoration. However, the transmission of blue channel is the empirical value estimation without taking into account the characteristics of the red channel, so it often results in the inaccurate low bound estimation. Furthermore, for artificial illuminated underwater images it does not perform well.

Considering the advantages of the red channel and haze-lines model in image restoration, we propose an underwater image restoration algorithm based on red channel and haze-lines prior, which can cope efficiently with artificial light sources possibly present in the scene. Firstly, we use the red channel prior to obtain an accurate estimation of the veiling-light. Then we introduce the attenuation coefficient ratios of the red-blue channel and red-green channel, and apply the haze-lines dehazing model to underwater image restoration. meanwhile we estimate a more accurate transmission by using the red channel prior to perform a low bound constraint. Finally, the image is restored according to the underwater imaging model. In addition, for the underwater image with artificial light, the saturation is used as the threshold value to correct the transmission based on the above algorithm.

## 2 Proposed Algorithm

### 2.1 Underwater Image Degradation Model

According to Jaffe-McGlamery model [1], by travelling the light from the source to the image plane of the camera, there are three components: the light going through the camera without scattering (direct component); the light going through the camera with a small angle scattering (forward component) and the veiling-light going through the camera reflecting by the suspended particles (backscatter component). Due to the short distance between the camera and the object, the forward scattering component can be ignored. So the acquired image can be defined as:

$$I_\lambda(x) = t_\lambda(x)J_\lambda(x) + A_\lambda(1 - t_\lambda(x)) \tag{1}$$

Where $x$ is the pixel coordinate, $\lambda \in \{r, g, b\}$ represents RGB three color channels. $I_\lambda$ is the acquired image value in color channel, $t_\lambda$ is the transmission of that color channel, and $J_\lambda$ is the object radiance that we wish to restore. The global veiling-light component $A_\lambda$ is the scene value in areas with no objects.

The transmission for each channel:

$$t_\lambda(x) = e^{-\beta_\lambda d(x)} \tag{2}$$

Here $d(x)$ denotes the object distance and the $\beta_\lambda$ depicts water attenuation coefficient for each channel.

## 2.2    Veiling-Light Estimation

DCP model is used for underwater image restoration, it neglects that the transmission $t_\lambda$ is wavelength-dependent. We have to take into account that red intensity decays faster as distance increases. When the distance increases, the intensity of the red channel is close to zero, we could estimate a smaller result of the dark channel. To solve this problem, Galdran [7] suggest the following modification of the dark channel prior, which it denotes as red channel prior (RDCP). It notes that:

$$J^{RDCP}(x) = \min\left(\min_{y \in \Omega(x)}(1 - J_R(y)), \min_{y \in \Omega(x)}(J_G(y)), \min_{y \in \Omega(x)}(J_B(y),)\right) \approx 0 \tag{3}$$

Where, $\Omega(x)$ is a neighborhood of pixels around the $x$ location. Notice that for a degraded image near the observer, the red channel still keeps some intensity, so its reciprocal $(1 - J_R(y))$ is low, and the prior is still true. As distance increases, red intensity rapidly decays, and its weight in the red channel decreases near to zero, while $(1 - J_R(y))$ is close to 1.

Since the red channel has the fastest underwater attenuation, the value of the red channel is close to zero at infinity, the pixel value at infinity is the veiling-light, so we denote $H(x)$:

$$H(x) = (1 - I_R(x)) - \max(I_B(x), I_G(x)) \tag{4}$$

The veiling-light $A_\lambda$ is then estimated [3] by the pixel values that are below 10% $H(x)$.

## 2.3    Transmission Estimation

The transmission of a foggy image is only related to distance, while the transmission of underwater images is related to not only distance but also the attenuation coefficients of RGB channels.

By Eqs. (1) and (2), for underwater images we can get the equations for the RGB channel separately:

$$A_R - I_R = e^{-\beta_R d(x)}(A_R - J_R) \tag{5}$$

$$A_G - I_G = e^{-\beta_G d(x)}(A_G - J_G) \tag{6}$$

$$A_B - I_B = e^{-\beta_B d(x)}(A_B - J_B) \tag{7}$$

Introducing the haze-lines model into the water adds three unknown variables $\beta_R, \beta_G, \beta_B$, so we introduce two crucial variables $\beta_{RB}, \beta_{RG}$:

$$\frac{\beta_R}{\beta_B} = \beta_{RB}, \quad \frac{\beta_R}{\beta_G} = \beta_{RG} \tag{8}$$

We multiply both sides of Eqs. (6) and (7) by the parameter $\beta_{RG}$, $\beta_{RB}$ respectively, then we get:

$$(A_G - I_G)^{\frac{\beta_R}{\beta_G}} = e^{-\beta_G d(x) \cdot \frac{\beta_R}{\beta_G}}(A_G - J_G)^{\frac{\beta_R}{\beta_G}} \tag{9}$$

$$(A_B - I_B)^{\frac{\beta_R}{\beta_B}} = e^{-\beta_B d(x) \cdot \frac{\beta_R}{\beta_B}}(A_B - J_B)^{\frac{\beta_R}{\beta_B}} \tag{10}$$

Then, we achieve a form similar to Eq. (1),

$$\begin{bmatrix} A_R - I_R \\ (A_G - I_G)^{\beta_{RG}} \\ (A_B - I_B)^{\beta_{RB}} \end{bmatrix} = t_R(x) \begin{bmatrix} A_R - J_R \\ (A_G - J_G)^{\beta_{RG}} \\ (A_B - J_B)^{\beta_{RB}} \end{bmatrix} \tag{11}$$

We similarly cluster the pixels to haze-lines and obtain an initial estimation of the transmission of the red channel $t_R(x)$. In the haze-lines dehazing model, we first cluster the pixels to form haze-lines in the RGB space, then assume that at least one pixel of each pixel cluster is haze-free pixel. However we cannot find an unattenuated pixel through the haze-lines in underwater images. The attenuation coefficients measured by Jerlov indicate that even scene points are located at a distance of only one meter from the camera have a $t_B$ of about 0.9. There are differences in the attenuation coefficients of different water bodies, so we consider the fast decay characteristics of the red channel. Based on the fast attenuation characteristic of the red channel, we take $t_R^* = 1 - t_R(x)$ and choose the appropriate threshold to constrain.

For underwater images, there must be $J_\lambda \geq 0, \forall \lambda \in \{R, G, B\}$, so the transmission can not be zero. We obtain a lower bound $t_{LR}$ on the transmission of the red channel. Combined with Eqs. (1) and (3), and considering the different attenuation coefficients of the different color channels:

$$t_{LR} = \max\left\{ 1 - \frac{1 - I_R}{1 - A_R}, (1 - \frac{I_G}{A_G})^{\beta_{RG}}, (1 - \frac{I_B}{A_B})^{\beta_{RB}} \right\} \tag{12}$$

Finally, we get the transmission of the red channel as $\bar{t}_R(x)$:

$$\bar{t}_R(x) = \max\{t_R^*, t_{LR}\} \tag{13}$$

Considering that the haze-lines prior is superior to the DCP prior, it is performed per-pixel. Without imposing spatial coherency, the pixels of these clusters are non-local, and can be located anywhere in the image. This estimation can be inaccurate if a small amount of pixels were mapped to a particular haze-line, the noise can affect the angles significantly. The transmission map should be smooth, we assume that there is a smooth transmission map $\hat{t}_R(x)$. We can get a smooth transmission map $\hat{t}_R(x)$ similar to the transmission map $\bar{t}_R(x)$:

$$\hat{t}_R(x) = \arg\min\left\{ \sum_x \frac{[\hat{t}_R(x) - \bar{t}_R(x)]}{\sigma^2(x)} + \delta \sum_x \sum_{y \in N_x} \frac{[\hat{t}_R(x) - \hat{t}_R(y)]^2}{\|I(x) - I(y)\|} \right\} \tag{14}$$

Where $\hat{t}_R(x)$ is the smooth transmission map, $\delta$ is a parameter that controls trade-off between the data and the smoothness terms, $N_x$ denotes the four nearest neighbors of $x$ in the image plane and $\sigma(x)$ is the standard deviation of $\bar{t}_R(x)$, which is calculated per haze-line.

Once $\hat{t}_R(x)$ and $A_\lambda$ is estimated, we can recover underwater images using Eq. (15):

$$J_\lambda = \frac{I_\lambda - A_\lambda}{\hat{t}_\lambda} + A_\lambda \tag{15}$$

$$\hat{t}_G = \hat{t}_R^{\beta_G/\beta_R}, \quad \hat{t}_B = \hat{t}_R^{\beta_B/\beta_R} \tag{16}$$

According to the water classification proposed by Jerlov [11], we choose the appropriate attenuation coefficient ratios $\beta_{RB}, \beta_{RG}$, we can obtain the recovery image $J_\lambda$. Equation (15) compensates for the intensity changes that happen in the path between the object and the camera. we perform a global white-balance on the result.

## 2.4   Handling Artificial Illumination

The artificial light increases the intensity of the pixel, which cause the over compensation of the pixel during the image restoration, so the image will be distorted. Therefore, we introduce the saturation to the haze-lines model when the artificial light exists in image. Constraint is made to improve the compensation for pixels in artificial illumination. Saturation is defined as:

$$\text{Sat}(I(x)) = \frac{\max(I^R(x), I^G(x), I^B(x)) - \min(I^R(x), I^G(x), I^B(x))}{\max(I^R(x), I^G(x), I^B(x))} \tag{17}$$

Saturation can effectively separate areas with artificial light from the rest of the image. For the underwater image with artificial light, Saturation is introduced to correct the estimation of transmission. Then a new low bound is obtained for the underwater image with artificial light, Eq. (12) is converted into:

$$t_{LR} = \max\left\{ 1 - \frac{1 - I_R}{1 - A_R}, (1 - \frac{I_G}{A_G})^{\beta_{RG}}, (1 - \frac{I_B}{A_B})^{\beta_{RB}}, (1 - \alpha Sat) \right\} \qquad (18)$$

where $\alpha \in [0, 1]$ is a scalar multiplier that can be manually adjusted to suit the amount of artificial light we want to take into account.

(a)      (b)      (c)

**Fig. 1.** Result of considering the saturation. (a) Underwater image with artificial illumination, (b) Underwater image restoration without saturation, (c) Underwater image restoration with saturation.

As shown in Fig. 1, we get the two results of considering the saturation prior or not. without the saturation prior, the algorithm uses the intensity value compensated by the artificial light for image restoration, we get an overcompensation result with a layer of red fog around the artificial light. When we add the saturation prior to the algorithm, saturation can effectively separate the pixels with artificial light from the rest of the image, the influence of the artificial light on the image restoration is eliminated, so the restored image has better visual effect.

Our method is summarized in Algorithm 1.

---

**Algorithm 1  Underwater image recovery**

---

**Input:** $I(x)$

**Output:** $J(x), \hat{t}(x)$

1. Estimate the veiling light $A_\lambda$ using RDCP[7]

2. For each $(\beta_{RB}, \beta_{RG})$ values of water type[11] do

3.  For each $\lambda \in \{R, G, B\}$ do

   $I_\lambda(x) = sign(I_\lambda(x) - A_\lambda) \cdot abs(I_\lambda(x) - A_\lambda)^{\beta_{RC}}$ ( $\beta_{RC}$ is defined in Eq.8 )

4. Cluster pixels to 1000 Haze-Lines as in [8] and estimate an initial transmission $t_R$

and $t^*_R = 1 - t_R(x)$

5. Get the lower bound using Eq.(12) based on RDCP, If the input $I(x)$ is an underwater image with artificial illumination, do Eq.(18)

6. Perform regularization by calculating $\hat{t}_R(x)$ that minimizes Eq. (14)

7. Calculate the restored image Eq. (15)

8. Perform a White Balance on the restored image

---

## 3   Experiment Results

A wide variety of underwater images in different environment obtained from websites and papers [12, 13] are used for the experiments. These images are divided into two categories, low-quality underwater images and low-illumination deep water images. The low-quality underwater images have obvious color cast, detail blurring, image distortion and so on. Low-illumination deep water images have problems such as low brightness and poor visual effects. In this section, the proposed algorithm is compared with the state-of-the-arts. The comparative algorithms are DCP [3], UDCP [14], RDCP [7], HL [8], UHL [10]. Qualitative analysis and quantitative analysis are used to evaluate the effectiveness of algorithms. All the implementations are implemented under MATLAB R2017 environment on a PC platform with a 2.2 GHz Intel Core i5 CPU, 3.9 GB RAM and 64-bits OS.

### 3.1   Qualitative Analysis

We use the images in the underwater data set for comparative experiments. The comparison of the experimental results is shown in Fig. 2.

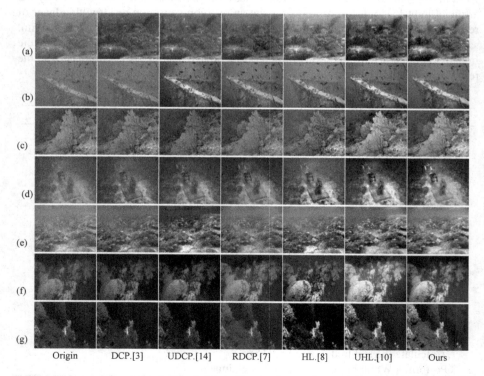

**Fig. 2.** Comparison on low-quality and low-illumination underwater image. (a), (b), (c), (d), (e) are low quality images, (f), (g) are low illumination underwater images.

In Fig. 2, the algorithm used in DCP [3] directly applies DCP to underwater image restoration. Although DCP can eliminate the influence of backscattering to some extent, it does not consider the difference in attenuation coefficient of each channels. The restoration images are bright by the algorithm in UDCP [14], there is color distortion in the image restoration results, and the low-illumination underwater image all have poor performances. The algorithm proposed in [7] considers the selective absorption of light waves by water and corrects the transmittance estimation. The processed images are clearer and have a certain color recovery, but their recovery effect on low-illuminance images is not good. The haze-lines dehazing model proposed in [8] has a good effect on image dehazing, it is unsuitable for underwater image restoration without considering the selective absorption of light by water. The underwater images restored by the algorithm proposed in [10] is reddish overall, and the restored images still have the problem of blurred details. Our method can remove most any color cast, restrain the backscattering while maintaining the color balance of the image. Even for the low-illumination images, the results have a better visual effect with an obviously improved brightness and clear details.

### 3.2 Quantitative Analysis

In this section, we use four objective evaluation measures to quantitatively evaluate the images using each algorithm. They are the average gradient [15], image information entropy [16], underwater image evaluation index UCIQE (underwater color image quality evaluation) [17], and UIQM (underwater image quality measures) [18]. The average gradient measures the sharpness of the image. The image information entropy measures the information level of the image. UCIQE and UIQM are two non-reference image quality evaluation methods for underwater images. UCIQE is based on CIE Lab color space, with chromaticity, saturation and contrast as the measurement parameters. UIQM is based on human eye vision system excitation, taking color, sharpness and contrast in RGB color space as the measurement parameters. UCIQE and UIQM linearly combine the respective measurement indicators to obtain the evaluation index. The larger the value, the better the color balance, saturation, sharpness, contrast, and the subjective visual effect. We perform objective quality evaluation on the images in Fig. 2, and obtain four tables with the optimal values in bold. Table 1 is the UCIQ evaluation index, Table 2 is the UIQM evaluation index, Table 3 is the average definition evaluation index, and Table 4 is information entropy evaluation index. The results of each evaluation index are as follows.

The four evaluation indices of the restored images by proposed algorithm have significant improvement compared with original images. The proposed algorithm obviously improves the values of UCIQE, UIQM and information entropy compared with other algorithms. These evaluation indices show that the proposed algorithm has a good effect on underwater image restoration.

To further illustrate the effectiveness of our method, the average values of each evaluation index for algorithms are selected for comparison. To better show the contrast, we plot the results into a histogram as shown in Fig. 3.

It can be concluded from the Fig. 3 that our algorithm is superior to the other five algorithms under the evaluation indicators UCIQE, UIQM, and Information entropy. That is to say, the chromaticity, saturation, contrast and other indicators of the images restored by the proposed algorithm are better than other algorithms.

**Table 1.** UCIQE indices of underwater image restoration

|     | Origin | DCP. [3] | UDCP. [14] | RDCP. [7] | HL. [8] | UHL. [10] | Ours |
|-----|--------|----------|------------|-----------|---------|-----------|------|
| (a) | 0.2990 | 0.5138 | 0.4843 | 0.4216 | 0.4246 | 0.5557 | **0.5683** |
| (b) | 0.3103 | 0.3172 | 0.5173 | 0.4386 | 0.4758 | 0.5266 | **0.5712** |
| (c) | 0.4521 | 0.4810 | 0.6086 | 0.5320 | 0.6103 | 0.5775 | **0.6249** |
| (d) | 0.4158 | 0.5013 | **0.6491** | 0.4544 | 0.4518 | 0.4896 | 0.6037 |
| (e) | 0.3444 | 0.4515 | 0.4720 | 0.3490 | 0.5366 | 0.4991 | **0.5703** |
| (f) | 0.3974 | 0.5516 | 0.6355 | 0.4434 | 0.5359 | 0.5392 | **0.6569** |
| (g) | 0.4985 | 0.6469 | 0.4994 | 0.4685 | 0.52505 | **0.6543** | 0.5865 |

**Table 2.** UIQM indices of underwater image restoration

|     | Origin | DCP. [3] | UDCP. [14] | RDCP. [7] | HL. [8] | UHL. [10] | Ours |
|-----|--------|----------|------------|-----------|---------|-----------|------|
| (a) | 2.3759 | 3.8777 | 4.7281 | 3.4797 | 2.8733 | 4.5876 | **4.4990** |
| (b) | 0.5182 | 0.4817 | 1.7988 | 1.9328 | 0.9226 | **3.1582** | 2.1357 |
| (c) | 3.2841 | 3.2074 | 3.6592 | 4.4859 | 1.5838 | 4.3901 | **5.0019** |
| (d) | 1.7011 | 2.0265 | 3.1563 | 4.3115 | 2.1767 | 4.3465 | **5.2180** |
| (e) | 2.5730 | 2.8542 | 4.6068 | 4.3583 | 1.3612 | 4.6147 | **5.1825** |
| (f) | 0.3974 | 4.2633 | 4.5334 | 4.3929 | 2.7547 | **5.3539** | 4.1837 |
| (g) | 0.4958 | 2.8033 | 2.3529 | 2.7842 | 0.9014 | 2.6901 | **3.4915** |

**Table 3.** Average gradient indices of underwater image restoration

|     | Origin | DCP. [3] | UDCP. [14] | RDCP. [7] | HL. [8] | UHL. [10] | Ours |
|-----|--------|----------|------------|-----------|---------|-----------|------|
| (a) | 1.9101 | 3.3007 | 3.8479 | 2.9073 | 4.4822 | 5.3920 | **5.5259** |
| (b) | 2.0507 | 2.1953 | 5.2913 | 4.3084 | 3.8013 | **6.0844** | 5.3244 |
| (c) | 9.2549 | 10.1996 | 10.3490 | 9.1940 | 16.6636 | 15.2686 | **16.1136** |
| (d) | 2.1274 | 2.9131 | 3.5290 | 3.4776 | **5.1630** | 4.8100 | 4.6312 |
| (e) | 5.9047 | 7.6511 | 10.3289 | 7.1842 | 11.3302 | 11.4976 | **11.8776** |
| (f) | 0.3974 | 2.9493 | 3.0474 | 3.1500 | **5.4696** | 5.1391 | 4.3826 |
| (g) | 0.4958 | 2.5123 | 2.3049 | 2.5536 | 4.1351 | **5.9221** | 4.9220 |

**Table 4.** Information entropy indices of underwater image restoration

|     | Origin | DCP. [3] | UDCP. [14] | RDCP. [7] | HL. [8] | UHL. [10] | Ours |
|-----|--------|----------|------------|-----------|---------|-----------|------|
| (a) | 6.3023 | 6.6684 | 6.6957 | 7.0244 | 7.4519 | 7.4114 | **7.6800** |
| (b) | 5.7574 | 5.8077 | 6.8082 | 6.9430 | 5.6053 | **7.2913** | 7.1469 |
| (c) | 7.1426 | 7.1752 | 6.8316 | 7.2225 | 7.1590 | 7.7085 | **7.7315** |
| (d) | 6.6305 | 6.4777 | 6.5989 | 6.9462 | 7.1465 | 7.4187 | **7.5127** |
| (e) | 6.8681 | 6.9674 | 7.1484 | 7.1065 | 7.1269 | 7.4955 | **7.6843** |
| (f) | 6.6162 | 6.4382 | 6.2251 | 7.1098 | 6.9124 | **7.8142** | 7.2809 |
| (g) | 5.8618 | 5.5613 | 4.9158 | 5.8882 | 3.1624 | 6.1909 | **6.7996** |

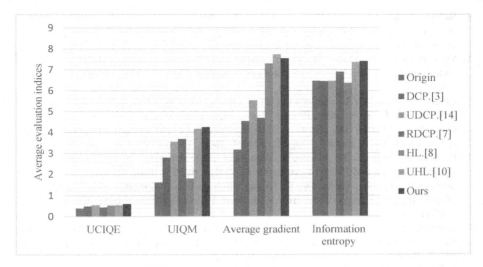

**Fig. 3.** Average evaluation indices of state-of-the-arts and ours.

## 4 Conclusions

In this paper, we propose an underwater image restoration algorithm based on red channel prior and haze-lines prior. By combining the attenuation characteristics of red channel with haze-lines prior. the red channel prior is used to perform a low bound to correct the estimation of the transmission. For the underwater image with artificial light, the saturation is introduced and added as a part of the low bound of the transmission estimation. The saturation can effectively separate the pixels with artificial light from the rest of the image. The transmission estimation of the underwater image with artificial light source is corrected. Our algorithm has a certain effect on artificially illuminated underwater images. Our future work will focus on how to further improve our algorithm and attain more accurate estimation of veiling-light.

**Acknowledgments.** This work was partially supported by the National Key R&D Program of China (2018YFC0406903), the National Natural Science Foundation of China (No. 41706103) and the Natural Science Foundation of Jiangsu (No. BK20170306).

## References

1. Jaffe, J.S.: Computer modeling and the design of optimal underwater imaging systems. IEEE J. Oceanic Eng. **15**(2), 101–111 (1990)
2. Hou, W., Gray, D.J., Weidemann, A.D., et al.: Automated underwater image restoration and retrieval of related optical properties. In: IEEE International Geoscience and Remote Sensing Symposium, pp. 1889–1892 (2008)
3. He, K., Sun, J., Tang, X.: Single image haze removal using dark channel prior. IEEE Trans. Pattern Anal. Mach. Intell. **33**(12), 2341–2353 (2011)

4. Sathya, R., Bharathi, M., Dhivyasri, G.: Underwater image enhancement by dark channel prior. In: International Conference on Electronics and Communication Systems, pp. 1119–1123 (2015)
5. Wen, H., Tian, Y., Huang, T., et al.: Single underwater image enhancement with a new optical model. In: IEEE International Symposium on Circuits and Systems, pp. 753–756 (2013)
6. Chiang, J.Y., Chen, Y.C.: Underwater image enhancement by wavelength compensation and dehazing. IEEE Trans. Image Process. **21**(4), 1756–1769 (2012)
7. Galdran, A., Pardo, D., Picon, A., et al.: Automatic red-channel underwater image restoration. J. Vis. Commun. Image Represent. **26**(1), 132–145 (2015)
8. Berman, D., Treibitz, T., Avidan, S.: Non-local image dehazing. In: IEEE Conference on Computer Vision and Pattern Recognition (CVPR), pp. 1674–1682 (2016)
9. Berman, D., Treibitz, T., Avidan, S.: Diving into haze-lines: color restoration of underwater images. In: Proceedings of the British Machine Vision Conference (BMVC), vol. 1, no. 2 (2017)
10. Berman, D., Levy, D., Avidan, S., et al.: Underwater single image color restoration using haze-lines and a new quantitative dataset. In: IEEE Conference on Computer Vision and Pattern Recognition (CVPR), arxiv:1811.01343 (2018)
11. Jerlov, N.G.: Marine Optics, vol. 14. Elsevier, Amsterdam (1976)
12. Park, D., Han, D.K., Jeon, C., Ko, H.: Fast single image dehazing using characteristics of RGB channel of foggy image. IEICE Trans. Inform. Syst. **96**(8), 1793–1799 (2013)
13. Bryson, M., Johnson-Roberson, M., Pizarro, O., Williams, S.B.: True color correction of autonomous underwater vehicle imagery. J. Field Robot. **33**(6), 853–874 (2015)
14. Drews, P.L.J., Nascimento, E.R., Botelho, S.S.C., et al.: Underwater depth estimation and image restoration based on single images. IEEE Comput. Graph. Appl. **36**(2), 24–35 (2016)
15. Jiang, Z.X., Pu, Y.: Underwater image color compensation based on electromagnetic theory. Laser Optoelectron. Prog. **55**(08), 237–242 (2018)
16. Xie, H.L., Peng, G.H., Wang, F., et al.: Underwater image restoration based on background light estimation and dark channel prior. Acta Opt. Sinica **38**(01), 18–27 (2018)
17. Yang, M., Sowmya, A.: An underwater color image quality evaluation metric. IEEE Trans. Image Process. **24**(12), 6062–6071 (2015)
18. Panetta, K., Gao, C., Agaian, S.: Human-visual-system-inspired underwater image quality measures. IEEE J. Oceanic Eng. **41**(3), 541–551 (2016)

# A Survey of Underwater Acoustic SLAM System

Min Jiang[1,2,3], Sanming Song[1,2(✉)], Yiping Li[1,2], Wenming Jin[1,2], Jian Liu[1,2], and Xisheng Feng[1,2]

[1] State Key Laboratory of Robotics, Shenyang Institute of Automation, Chinese Academy of Sciences, Shenyang 110016, China
{jiangmin,songsanming,lyp,jinwm,liuj,fxs}@sia.cn
[2] Institutes for Robotics and Intelligent Manufacturing, Chinese Academy of Sciences, Shenyang 110169, China
[3] University of Chinese Academy of Sciences, Beijing 100049, China

**Abstract.** Due to the unavailability of GPS signal, it is more urgent to develop the autonomous navigation capability for the underwater vehicles. In this paper, we summarize the development status of underwater SLAM (simultaneous localization and mapping) system. Different from the terrestrial or aerial SLAM that largely depends on the optical sensors, the underwater SLAM system mainly uses the acoustic sensors, i.e., sonars, to watch the environment. With respect to the general SLAM system, which is mainly composed of the front-end local data-association and the back-end global error adjustment, we briefly survey recent progress in sonar image registration and the loop closure detection. Furthermore, some heuristic problems are posed in the conclusion.

**Keywords:** Data association · Underwater SLAM · Underwater vehicle

## 1 Introduction

Maps are essential for marine scientifically interesting sites analysis and helpful to improve the underwater vehicle's autonomy. Usually, the accuracy of the generated map is heavily dependent on the accuracy of the underwater vehicle localization, other than the accuracy of the exteroceptive sensors, for example, the single line laser-based structured light system can generate millimeter resolution seafloor bathymetry [27]. The GPS (global position system), which is commonly used by the terrestrial and aerial robot, is not available for underwater applications because of the strong attenuation of the electromagnetic wave underwater. Without GPS, there are two methods to localize an underwater vehicle. One is the acoustic localization system, the other is based on the inertial information.

According to the length of the baseline, the acoustic localization system can be categorized into three types, i.e., Long Baseline (LBL), the Short Baseline (SBL), and the Ultra Short Baseline (USBL). Among them, the LBL system

H. Yu et al. (Eds.): ICIRA 2019, LNAI 11741, pp. 159–170, 2019.
https://doi.org/10.1007/978-3-030-27532-7_14

is the most popular one because it can provide very good position accuracy. High-frequency (300 kHz) LBL provides sub-centimeter localization accuracy but restricting the underwater vehicle to operate within the maximum range of 100 meters. Long-range localization up to 10 km can also be achieved by the standard low-frequency (12 kHz), but tradeoff the accuracy to 0.1 to 10 m depending on the range and beacon geometry [2]. The main drawback of the LBL system is the cost and time required to deploy a set of acoustic beacons on the seafloor in predefined locations and later recovery them. Those operations can be quite cumbersome for adverse environments. In addition, if the acoustic beacon is deployed on the sea floor with complex structure, multipath and occlusions may be suffered. The other problem is the slow update rate because the vehicle location is calculated based on the measured roundtrip travel time between the vehicle and acoustic beacon.

Without deploying the acoustic beacon on the sea floor, the transducers of SBL system are mounted on the ship hull as far from each other as possible. On the other hand, USBL systems have the transducers mounted closely to each other. Both systems can provide the relative range and bearing to an acoustic beacon. On the other hand, LBL can only provide ranges to a set of acoustic beacons and multilateration technique must be used to estimate the vehicle's location. One problem of USBL is the ship to vehicle bearing measurements degrade as a function of the water depth. It has been shown in the task of visually mapping the RMS Titanic that the USBL estimation cannot navigate the vehicle with enough accuracy in deep sea [9]. The common problem of the acoustic localization system is that confining the vehicle operation to the area of coverage of the system [26].

Localizing the underwater vehicle with the inertial information is another common practice in underwater vehicle community. It does not require any external aids and thus is self-contained. It does not emit or receive any external signal making it a good choice for the stealthy purpose mission without the risk of being interfered or jammed. Dead reckoning estimates the vehicle position and orientation by integrating the vehicle's velocity and acceleration provided by the inertial sensor. In fact, dead reckoning can also be carried out based on the bottom tracking velocity provided by the DVL (Doppler Velocity Loggers) and orientation measured by the AHRS (Attitude and Heading Reference System). With high end inertial sensor, the dead reckoning can achieve a drift of 0.1% of the distance travelled. However, with more typical and modestly priced units, it can easily achieve a drift of 2% to 5% of the distance travelled [36]. Hence, one drawback of the dead reckoning estimates is that the accuracy of the estimation will degrade with increasing mission time. Although regularly surfacing to get GPS correction can bound the accumulated error, it is unachievable in military or deep sea survey mission.

Using environmental information to localize an underwater vehicle is also a feasible method. In terrain based navigation, localization is achieved by matching sensor data with an a prior environment map. The advantage of the map-based navigation method is the fact that it is a completely onboard navigation, without the need for external devices, granting the vehicles a large operational range [28]. However, same as the planet surface exploration, a prior map often cannot be obtained before the mission is executed. In those situation, SLAM (simultaneous localization and mapping) system which can concurrently estimate the vehicle position and maintain environmental map becomes an alternative option. It is a key prerequisite for truly autonomous navigation. Notwithstanding there are a few surveys [22,28,36] related to the underwater SLAM methods, they are not dedicated to the underwater SLAM. SLAM framework is usually composed of two parts, front-end part and back-end part. In this paper, we focus on the underwater SLAM method survey with special emphasis on the SLAM front-end part including sonar image registration methods and loop closure detection methods. The commonly used sensors for underwater SLAM are briefly introduced, too.

## 2   Proprioceptive Sensors

Underwater vehicles are often equipped with proprioceptive sensors including compass, DVL, IMU (Inertial Measurement Unit), and depth sensor to estimate the vehicle's pose and location without external aids.

The DVL determines the underwater vehicle surge, sway, and heave velocities by transmitting acoustic pulses and measuring the Doppler shifted returns from these pulses off the seabed [36]. DVL has been widely equipped by small-scale unmanned underwater vehicles[e.g. small AUV (autonomous underwater vehicle) and ROV (remote operated vehicle)] because of its relative low cost [28].

The compass provides the vehicle's bounded heading reference. The magnetic compass measures the magnetic field vector, making the sensor reading be easily affected by the objects with a strong magnetic signature. On the other hand, gyrocompass has the advantage of being unaffected by metallic objects. It measures heading using a fast spinning disc and the rotation of the earth and points to true north, other than earth's magnetic north pole (like magnetic compass does) [36].

The IMU provides the estimates of vehicle orientation, velocity with a combination of accelerometers and gyroscopes [36]. Usually, the more expensive, the better performance can be achieved.

In cases where 3-dimensional map needed to be constructed, the $z$ component of the vehicle location is essential [10] and can be directly measured by a barometer or pressure sensor with enough accuracy [36]. Comparatively, the estimations of $x$, and $y$ components are more difficult. As stated in Sect. 1, they can be provided by the dead reckoning method using the IMU measurements or DVL and AHRS measurements. The pose displacement estimated by the dead reckoning can be used to seed the registration algorithms which will be detailed in Sect. 4.

## 3   Exteroceptive Sensors

Exteroceptive sensors are used to sense the environment. In clear water and short range applications (e.g., underwater archaeological sites imaging [5], ship hull inspection [34]), optical sensors can provide rich information of the underwater environment. However, they suffer from the turbidity and illumination condition of the ambient water column. In those cases, acoustic sensors are often employed. Below, the commonly used sonars for underwater SLAM are briefly introduced.

## Multibeam Echosounder (MBE)

MBE is often used to generate bathymetry maps of the seafloor. MBE is composed of one projector and one hydrophone responsible for transmitting and receiving the echo sounding to measure the terrain. The first is oriented longitudinally and the latter is oriented transversally to the vehicle's bow. MBE can ensonify multiple locations on the seafloor with a single ping benefiting from the advanced beam forming and beam steering techniques. A swath usually composes an area of points in a direction along the vehicle track. An MBE can have more than 400 beams, making it nearly optimal sonar sensors for bathymetric terrain applications [28].

## Sidescan Sonar (SSS)

Compared to the MBE which only interprets the time-of-flight of acoustic waves to obtain terrain measurements, SSS also interprets the acoustic backscatter intensity of the returned signal. After each pulse emissions, SSS listens to the echo intensities at fixed time intervals, until a new pulse is emitted. Same as the MBE, swath refers to the recorded data array containing the received intensities. Because the acoustic echo intensity is mainly influenced by the reflectivity of the sea floor, SSS provides a relatively high definition acoustic image of the seabed other than bathymetric data. Many factors can influence the seabed acoustic image formation, such as grazing angle, terrain surface, and local water properties [28]. MBE and SSS can only provide a swath of seafloor measurement at one time. Keeping vehicle in motion is necessary to acquire successive swaths of terrain measurement. The final bathymetric map or acoustic image can be generated using the mapping sensor data and associated vehicle pose and location.

## Mechanical Scanning Sonar (MSS)

Due to its compact size, low cost and low energy-consumption, MSS is widely equipped by small AUVs, ROVs and energy budget restricted vehicles. The MSS works as follows. The transducer head transmits an acoustic beam in a certain direction and waits for the bounced back acoustic wave if objects are in this direction. The echoic response will be subsequently quantized into a series of discrete intensity values referred to bins with each bin corresponding to a predefined distance. Then, the transducer head will change the transmitting direction by a predetermined angle, emits another beam, and waits for the corresponding response. This process is repeated until the entire scan sector is covered. The scanning period often lasts few to dozens of seconds inducing the motion distortion problem of the MSS image if the vehicle's pose and location alters during the scanning process [18].

## Electronic Scanning Sonar (ESS)

ESS is a kind of sonar that can provide high-definition acoustic imagery at a fast refresh rate. Because of its high resolution, it is even referred to as acoustic cameras, sometimes. A fan shaped acoustic wave spanning the sonar's view in the azimuth and elevation directions is transmitted to insonify the scene and then the acoustic return is sampled by an array of transducers as a function of range and bearing. One problem is that the reflected echo could have originated anywhere along the corresponding elevation arc. Hence, the height information of obstacles is lost when the 3D fan shaped acoustic wave is squashed into a 2D image [16].

**Dual-Frequency Identification Sonar (DIDSON)**
Conventional sonars generally transmit one wide beam covering the entire field of view and use delay lines or digital beamforming techniques on reception. DIDSON uses acoustic lenses to form very narrow beam which can ensonify stripe along the bottom and receives the corresponding echo whose amplitude varies in time as the reflectance varies with range along the ensonified surface. Sound is transmitted only in these beam directions, and the sonar is sensitive to only these directions during a single transmit/receive cycle. This feature makes the DIDSON image be sharper and less noisy than those produced by sonars with one broad transmitting beam and receiving beam. Echoes from 96 adjacent lines are processed to map the reflectance of the ensonified sector-shaped area, forming a DIDSON image. In most cases, DIDSON provides unambiguous, near photographic quality images [3].

## 4  Sonar Image Registration

Because much research endeavor has been dedicated to the vision image registration, we focus on the sonar image registration method in this paper. In SLAM framework, the sonar image registration can improve the dead reckoning estimation between consecutive vehicle poses and refine the loop closure constrain transformation parameters between nonconsecutive poses. Consider two partially overlapping sonar images $f(x)$ and $g(x)$ that are taken by the sonar at different times. There exists an unknown transformation matrix $T$ which is determined by a vector of parameters, which typically includes translation $(\Delta x, \Delta y)$, elevation $\Delta z$, rotation $\theta$, tilt $\phi$, and roll $\varphi$ , mapping pixel $x_1$ in image $f$ to its counterpart in image $g$. Sonar image registration aims at finding the optimal transformation matrix minimizing the matching error within the overlapping area

$$T^* = \arg\min \sum_{(x_1, x_2)} |f(x_1) - g(x_2)|$$

In terms of point cloud registration, ICP(Iterative Closet Point) [4] method has been regarded as the golden metric. Many ICP variants have been proposed during past few decades. pIC (Probabilistic Iterative Correspondence) method [29] is a probabilistic variant of the ICP. It explicitly deals with sensor measurement uncertainty to decide which point in the reference scan is statistically compatible with a certain point of the floating scan. Later, works of [14,26] successfully apply the pIC algorithm to the MSS image registration taking the motion induced distortion problem into consideration. Further, [18] proposed to model both the reference scan and floating scan as Gaussian mixture models and used the symmetrical Kullback-Leibler divergence as the distance measure between two Gaussian mixture models. It was validated that this method could dramatically reduce the computational cost without compromising the estimation precision allowing lower intensity threshold to be applied to segment the MSS image.

The method (called MSISpIC) proposed by [13,14] was claimed to be suitable for the uncertainty inherent in sonar data. Although it was dedicated to the MSS sonar image registration, it was extended to register 3-dimensional point clouds which were generated by the multibeam sonar mounted on a pan and tilt unit in [35]. The registration process was divided into two steps (1) point-to-point association for coarse registration and (2) point-to-plane association for fine registration. The multibeam sonar is usually mounted looking down in order to measure the terrain generating the 2.5D bathymetric point cloud. To register the bathymetric point clouds, [38] used the 2D correlation to determine the $(\Delta x, \Delta y)$ translation and fully 3D ICP alignment to create a 6 DOF terrain relative measurement. In fact, the structured light imaging can provide 3D measurements of the seafloor with higher resolution than stereoscopy or multibeam sonar [27]. Reference [17] proposed to minimize the Sum of Squared Differences error surface to compute the $(\Delta x, \Delta y)$ translation, once overlapping sub-maps are identified and then gridded.

Compared to optical images, acoustic images suffer problems to their construction and the physical effects of the acoustic waves such as: inhomogeneous resolution, acoustic distortion, loss of three-dimensional information, nonuniform pixel intensities, acoustic reverberation, acoustic shadow, and noise increasing the difficulty of registration [40]. Due to those inherent characteristics of sonar data, pixel-level features, for example Harris corner [20,31], extracted in sonar images suffer from low repeatability rates and instability. Other researchers proposed alternatives involving features at region level rather than at pixel scale [1,19]. A Fourier-based technique was further proposed by [16] which takes into account the whole image content, thus contributing to the minimization of ambiguities in the registration. Later, this method was successfully applied to the underwater chain inspection by mosaicking the sonar images gathered along the chain trajectory for visual inspection [15]. The Fourier-based method needs to convert the raw sonar data into a Cartesian format, introducing an interpolation error at the very beginning of the processing pipeline which is undesirable. Hence, the algorithm based on optical flow between consecutive sonar frames was proposed to register the sonar image in [12]. With the fact that neighboring pixels of sonar image show dependencies due to acoustic reverberation and dispersion, [41] only used the peripheral information in the neighborhood of a pixel to calculate the mutual information. The transformation parameters were pursued by maximizing mutual information.

## 5   Loop Closure Detection

Loop closure detection is the task of identifying the same place using sensory information generated from different viewpoints and timestamps. It is a central part of SLAM framework, as it is often the only source of new information that can be used to correct accumulated dead reckoning error. The specific loop closure detection method employed in a SLAM approach often relies on the map representation which can be categorized into three types, i.e., feature-based, location-based, or view-based [6].

Feature based map often consists of a collection of predefined geometric primitives in specific locations. Commonly used feature types are line feature, point feature, and corner feature, etc. The choice of the feature type often depends on the environment. A feature extraction algorithm must be employed to extract features from the raw sensor data. One notable example is the line feature [37] extracted from the MSS image captured from the man-made abandoned marina. The relationship between the measured line feature and the features already existing in the map was determined by the Joint Compatibility Branch and Bound (JCBB) [32]. If the measured line feature corresponded to one of the already mapped features, this measured line feature was used to update the system, else the measured line feature was new and needed to be incorporated into the map. The work of [44] tried to extract point features from the sonar images with the artificial sonar targets being deployed at the field test site a prior. On the other hand, point feature extracted from MSS image was used to describe natural bay environment in [11]. One main drawback of feature based approaches is that loop closure detection relies on the dead reckoning estimate because of that features are distinguishable only by their global or relative locations. Further, feature based map is not very suitable for unknown environments. Worse still, autonomous feature extraction from sonar data and the associated classification problem is difficult because of the typically low resolution of the sensors and amorphous shape of natural features [42].

Location-based maps which is independent of feature extraction discretize the environment into a number of regions, each of which is labelled with a value indicating the probability or degree of belief in some property. The most common property is occupancy, so the location-based map can also be called occupancy grid map. It was firstly introduced by Elfes [8] and then received a wider acceptance in robotics because it was commonly used as input to algorithms for path planning, collision avoidance, sensor fusion etc. Occupancy grid map has been adopted in several marine tasks. In mapping a flooded sinkhole, 3D evidence grid was chosen as the basic world representation. An array of 54 pencil-beam sonars could provide a constellation of range measurements around the vehicle. Those sonars were in the shape of three great circles which enabled the vehicle to observe previously mapped regions while exploring. Although the specific loop closure detection method was not mentioned, improvement over dead-reckoning was validated when the vehicle returning to a previously mapped path [10]. In the task of exploring and mapping the ancient cisterns, considering very little was known about the cisterns under investigation (i.e., size, types of features, number of features, etc.), an occupancy grid map was used to represent the belief state of the environment [43]. However, the specific loop closure detection method was also not mentioned. Other applications of occupancy grid map include the bathymetric mapping [2] and iceberg mapping [33] where there are often no clearly identifiable features. In those applications, closing large loops was usually avoided by specially designing the vehicle trajectory [39]. By the way, location-based maps are resolution-dependent, can be cumbersome to update, can have high memory requirements, and discard information by assigning a single value to each cell.

In view-based approaches, maps are composed of a collection of full sensor readings, including raw data and the sensor pose where the data were collected (e.g., a laser scan with the location and orientation of the sensor). Compared to feature-based map, since there is no feature extraction algorithm required, no information is lost or misinterpreted in the process. Compared to location-based map, view-based map is more expressive since they represent arbitrary shapes in the environment without aggregating all measurements in a given region into a single value. In [26] and [25], pose threshold method was proposed, i.e., each new pose of a scan was compared against the previous scan poses that were in the nearby area defined by a threshold. Whenever enough sonar points were overlapping, a loop closure constrain was added between those two poses. Further, [7] proposed to combine the Mahalanobis distances between poses and shape matching together to give reliable loop closure detections, taking the uncertainty of poses into consideration. In the process of mapping a floating iceberg by moving around it, loop closure can also be detected by using the ICP algorithm to align multibeam ranges from the beginning and end of the circumnavigation [21].

Without using dead reckoning estimates to generate loop closure candidates, there exists brute force method to detect loop closures, i.e., current view is compared to all historical views with corresponding similarity measure. For instance, in a partially structured environment, like harbor area, composed of piers, boats and ships, the topological relationship between them should remain constant and can be adopted as a landmark which can be identified on the next robot visit. Santos et al. [40] proposed to describe the sonar image as a topological graph by establishing the relationships between each Gaussian function which was used to fit the image segments. This description is translation and rotation invariant and graph comparison can be carried out to detect loop closures. Other brute force methods are the works of [24,30,35]. A disadvantage of view-based maps is that they can be memory and computationally intensive if all sensor data is saved and processed.

All in all, one loop closure detection method is to simply compare current view to all historical views. False loop closure constrain maybe generated, because there exist very similar scenes which are the most common in natural underwater environment. Although, using the dead reckoning estimates can generate loop closure candidates, the estimates suffer from the drift over time.

Thus, the advantages of generating the loop closure candidates with only sonar images independent of dead reckoning estimates appear clear.

## 6    Conclusion

This paper has surveyed recent techniques of sonar image registration and loop closure detection dependent on different sonar sensors used. The initial transformation parameters are important to make the sonar image registration method converge to the global extreme value. Although the dead reckoning estimate can seed those registration methods, it suffers from drift overtime and maybe not accurate enough. Hence, the global extreme value searching ability of the optimization method should be improved. On the other hand, better parameter initialization procedure should also be designed to reliably seed the registration methods. The commonly used loop closure detection methods in underwater environment have been categorized according to the map type used. From the surveyed papers, it is apparent that view and location based approaches have wide applications because they are much more suitable for unknown environments which are common in underwater missions. No matter how better the loop closure detection method can perform, false positive loop closure constrain maybe unavoidably generated. Hence, robust SLAM back-end should be developed to recognize, remove false positive loop closure constrains and re-compute the state estimation. Although pioneering works, such as [23, 45] have emerged, more studies are still required to make them be practicable for underwater tasks. Not only the sonar image registration method but also the loop closure detection methods reported are mostly tested on the collected sonar data. Much more endeavour should be made to increase their robustness and reduce the computational cost to make them run onboard in the future.

**Acknowledgements.** The work is supported by the Strategic Priority Program of the Chinese Academy of Sciences (No. XDC03060105, No. XDA13030203), the State Key Laboratory of Robotics of China (No. 2017-Z010), the National Key Research and Development Program of China (No. 2016YFC0300801, No. 2016YFC0300604, No. 2016YFC0301601), the project of "R&D Center for Underwater Construction Robotics", funded by the Ministry of Ocean and Fisheries (MOF) and Korea Institute of Marine Science & Technology Promotion (KIMST), Korea (No. PJT200539), the Public science and technology research funds projects of ocean (No. 201505017).

## References

1. Aykin, M., Negahdaripour, S.: On feature extraction and region matching for forward scan sonar imaging. In: 2012 Oceans, pp. 1–9. IEEE (2012)
2. Barkby, S., Williams, S.B., Pizarro, O., Jakuba, M.V.: A featureless approach to efficient bathymetric SLAM using distributed particle mapping. J. Field Robot. **28**(1), 19–39 (2011)
3. Belcher, E., Hanot, W., Burch, J.: Dual-frequency identification sonar (DIDSON). In: Proceedings of the 2002 Interntional Symposium on Underwater Technology (Cat. No. 02EX556), pp. 187–192. IEEE (2002)

4. Besl, P.J., McKay, N.D.: Method for registration of 3-D shapes. In: Sensor Fusion IV: Control Paradigms and Data Structures, vol. 1611, pp. 586–607. International Society for Optics and Photonics (1992)
5. Bingham, B., et al.: Robotic tools for deep water archaeology: surveying an ancient shipwreck with an autonomous underwater vehicle. J. Field Robot. **27**(6), 702–717 (2010)
6. Bosse, M., Zlot, R.: Map matching and data association for large-scale two-dimensional laser scan-based SLAM. Int. J. Robot. Res. **27**(6), 667–691 (2008)
7. Chen, L., Wang, S., Hu, H., Gu, D., Liao, L.: Improving localization accuracy for an underwater robot with a slow-sampling sonar through graph optimization. IEEE Sens. J. **15**(9), 5024–5035 (2015)
8. Elfes, A.: Sonar-based real-world mapping and navigation. IEEE J. Robot. Autom. **3**(3), 249–265 (1987)
9. Eustice, R.M., Singh, H., Leonard, J.J., Walter, M.R.: Visually mapping the RMS titanic: conservative covariance estimates for SLAM information filters. Int. J. Robot. Res. **25**(12), 1223–1242 (2006)
10. Fairfield, N., Kantor, G., Wettergreen, D.: Real-time SLAM with octree evidence grids for exploration in underwater tunnels. J. Field Robot. **24**(1–2), 03–21 (2007)
11. He, B., et al.: Autonomous navigation based on unscented-FastSLAM using particle swarm optimization for autonomous underwater vehicles. Measurement **71**, 89–101 (2015)
12. Henson, B.T., Zakharov, Y.V.: Attitude-trajectory estimation for forward-looking multibeam sonar based on acoustic image registration. IEEE J. Oceanic Eng. **99**, 1–14 (2018)
13. Hernández, E., Ridao, P., Ribas, D., Mallios, A.: Probabilistic sonar scan matching for an AUV. In: 2009 IEEE/RSJ International Conference on Intelligent Robots and Systems, pp. 255–260. IEEE (2009)
14. Hernàndez Bes, E., Ridao Rodríguez, P., Ribas Romagós, D., Batlle i Grabulosa, J.: MSISpIC: a probabilistic scan matching algorithm using a mechanical scanned imaging sonar. J. Phys. Agents **3**(1), 3–11 (2009)
15. Hurtós, N., Palomeras, N., Carrera, A., Carreras, M.: Autonomous detection, following and mapping of an underwater chain using sonar. Ocean Eng. **130**, 336–350 (2017)
16. Hurtós, N., Ribas, D., Cufí, X., Petillot, Y., Salvi, J.: Fourier-based registration for robust forward-looking sonar mosaicing in low-visibility underwater environments. J. Field Robot. **32**(1), 123–151 (2015)
17. Inglis, G., Smart, C., Vaughn, I., Roman, C.: A pipeline for structured light bathymetric mapping. In: 2012 IEEE/RSJ International Conference on Intelligent Robots and Systems, pp. 4425–4432. IEEE (2012)
18. Jiang, M., Song, S., Tang, F., Li, Y., Liu, J., Feng, X.: Scan registration for underwater mechanical scanning imaging sonar using symmetrical Kullback-Leibler divergence. J. Electron. Imaging **28**(1), 013026 (2019)
19. Johannsson, H., Kaess, M., Englot, B., Hover, F., Leonard, J.: Imaging sonar-aided navigation for autonomous underwater harbor surveillance. In: 2010 IEEE/RSJ International Conference on Intelligent Robots and Systems, pp. 4396–4403. IEEE (2010)
20. Kim, K., Neretti, N., Intrator, N.: Mosaicing of acoustic camera images. IEE Proc.-Radar Sonar Navig. **152**(4), 263–270 (2005)
21. Kimball, P.W., Rock, S.M.: Mapping of translating, rotating icebergs with an autonomous underwater vehicle. IEEE J. Oceanic Eng. **40**(1), 196–208 (2015)

22. Kinsey, J.C., Eustice, R.M., Whitcomb, L.L.: A survey of underwater vehicle navigation: recent advances and new challenges. In: IFAC Conference of Manoeuvering and Control of Marine Craft, vol. 88, pp. 1–12 (2006)
23. Latif, Y., Cadena, C., Neira, J.: Robust loop closing over time for pose graph SLAM. Int. J. Robot. Res. **32**(14), 1611–1626 (2013)
24. Ma, T., Li, Y., Wang, R., Cong, Z., Gong, Y.: Auv robust bathymetric simultaneous localization and mapping. Ocean Eng. **166**, 336–349 (2018)
25. Mallios, A., Ridao, P., Ribas, D., Carreras, M., Camilli, R.: Toward autonomous exploration in confined underwater environments. J. Field Robot. **33**(7), 994–1012 (2016)
26. Mallios, A., Ridao, P., Ribas, D., Hernández, E.: Scan matching SLAM in underwater environments. Auton. Robot. **36**(3), 181–198 (2014)
27. Massot-Campos, M., Oliver, G., Bodenmann, A., Thornton, B.: Submap bathymetric SLAM using structured light in underwater environments. In: 2016 IEEE/OES Autonomous Underwater Vehicles (AUV), pp. 181–188. IEEE (2016)
28. Melo, J., Matos, A.: Survey on advances on terrain based navigation for autonomous underwater vehicles. Ocean Eng. **139**, 250–264 (2017)
29. Montesano, L., Minguez, J., Montano, L.: Probabilistic scan matching for motion estimation in unstructured environments. In: 2005 IEEE/RSJ International Conference on Intelligent Robots and Systems, pp. 3499–3504. IEEE (2005)
30. Muhammad, N., Fuentes-Perez, J.F., Tuhtan, J.A., Toming, G., Musall, M., Kruusmaa, M.: Map-based localization and loop-closure detection from a moving underwater platform using flow features. Auton. Robots **43**(6), 1419–1434 (2019)
31. Negahdaripour, S., Firoozfam, P., Sabzmeydani, P.: On processing and registration of forward-scan acoustic video imagery. In: The 2nd Canadian Conference on Computer and Robot Vision (CRV 2005), pp. 452–459. IEEE (2005)
32. Neira, J., Tardós, J.D.: Data association in stochastic mapping using the joint compatibility test. IEEE Trans. Robot. Autom. **17**(6), 890–897 (2001)
33. Norgren, P., Skjetne, R.: A multibeam-based slam algorithm for iceberg mapping using auvs. IEEE Access **6**, 26318–26337 (2018)
34. Ozog, P., Carlevaris-Bianco, N., Kim, A., Eustice, R.M.: Long-term mapping techniques for ship hull inspection and surveillance using an autonomous underwater vehicle. J. Field Robot. **33**(3), 265–289 (2016)
35. Palomer, A., Ridao, P., Ribas, D.: Multibeam 3D underwater slam with probabilistic registration. Sensors **16**(4), 560 (2016)
36. Paull, L., Saeedi, S., Seto, M., Li, H.: Auv navigation and localization: a review. IEEE J. Oceanic Eng. **39**(1), 131–149 (2014)
37. Ribas, D., Ridao, P., Tardós, J.D., Neira, J.: Underwater SLAM in man-made structured environments. J. Field Robot. **25**(11–12), 898–921 (2008)
38. Roman, C., Singh, H.: A self-consistent bathymetric mapping algorithm. J. Field Robot. **24**(1–2), 23–50 (2007)
39. Roman, C.N.: Self consistent bathymetric mapping from robotic vehicles in the deep ocean. Ph.D. thesis, Massachusetts Institute of Technology (2005)
40. Santos, M.M., Zaffari, G.B., Ribeiro, P.O., Drews-Jr, P.L., Botelho, S.S.: Underwater place recognition using forward-looking sonar images: a topological approach. J. Field Robot. **36**(2), 355–369 (2019)
41. Song, S., Herrmann, J.M., Si, B., Liu, K., Feng, X.: Two-dimensional forward-looking sonar image registration by maximization of peripheral mutual information. Int. J. Adv. Robot. Syst. **14**(6), 1–17 (2017)

42. Stutters, L., Liu, H., Tiltman, C., Brown, D.J.: Navigation technologies for autonomous underwater vehicles. IEEE Trans. Syst. Man Cybern. Part C (Appl. Rev.) **38**(4), 581–589 (2008)
43. White, C., Hiranandani, D., Olstad, C.S., Buhagiar, K., Gambin, T., Clark, C.M.: The malta cistern mapping project: underwater robot mapping and localization within ancient tunnel systems. J. Field Robot. **27**(4), 399–411 (2010)
44. Williams, S.B., Newman, P., Rosenblatt, J., Dissanayake, G., Durrant-Whyte, H.: Autonomous underwater navigation and control. Robotica **19**(5), 481–496 (2001)
45. Xie, L., Wang, S., Markham, A., Trigoni, N.: GraphTinker: outlier rejection and inlier injection for pose graph SLAM. In: 2017 IEEE/RSJ International Conference on Intelligent Robots and Systems (IROS), pp. 6777–6784. IEEE (2017)

# Improved Multi-object Tracking Algorithm for Forward Looking Sonar Based on Rotation Estimation

Xiufen Ye[(⊠)] and Xinglong Ma

Harbin Engineering University, Harbin, China
{yexiufen, mxll2138}@hrbeu.edu.cn

**Abstract.** Multi-object tracking algorithm for forward-looking sonar (FLS) often requires carrier motion information, in order to correct the tracking error caused by the carrier motion. However, it is sometimes difficult to obtain carrier information or synchronize the sonar image with carrier attitude sensor data. Therefore, it is still meaningful to study tracking multiple objects without using carrier motion information. In this paper we focus on improving the performance of multi object tracking without navigation data when the sonar carrier is rotating. The traditional detection-by-tracking framework was improved by rotation estimation. A linear motion model in polar coordinate system was used, and both detection and data association were performed in polar coordinates system. Phase correction was used to estimate the rotation velocity. The velocity was added to the motion model as a control. The improved method was tested on real sonar sequence obtained in conditions which carrier rotated several times. For evaluating the algorithm, we presented a simple approach for object detection. Finally, the results of several tracking metrics show better performance compared with conventional tracking method.

**Keywords:** Forward looking sonar · Multi-object tracking · Motion estimation

## 1 Introduction

Multi-objects tracking of underwater environment using forward-looking sonar can be used for collision avoidance of underwater vehicles, underwater security [1], helping robots understand underwater environment better, etc. In the field of computer vision using optical image, multiple tracking benchmark have been developed, such as MOT17 [2], KITTI [3], etc. However, the underwater acoustic image dataset is precious and sonar data is more difficult to collect. And it is necessary to make a further study on multi-object tracking for sonar image. Tracking-by-detection framework is still a popular field in object tracking such as IOU Tracker [4]. The framework uses the detections directly, and assigns them to tracks. Because of the simple architecture, we could acquire high real-time performance. Track-by-detection framework is also widely used in the forward-looking sonar for multi-object tracking, such as [5] detect obstacle signatures first and then uses Kalman filter and joint probability data association algorithm to track multiple targets. Some researches combine navigation data with sonar data. [6] uses Partical-PHD filter to track the multiple targets of the sonar, and

© Springer Nature Switzerland AG 2019
H. Yu et al. (Eds.): ICIRA 2019, LNAI 11741, pp. 171–183, 2019.
https://doi.org/10.1007/978-3-030-27532-7_15

uses the inertial navigation devices to compensate motion on the forward-looking sonar image, and then threshold segmentation of the sonar image is performed. [7] proposes a nonlinear model based on navigation data, and uses unscented Kalman filter to estimate the motion state of the target.

We cannot rely on the navigation data in some cases, such as when synchronizes sonar data with navigation data, or the carrier's motion status is hard to obtain. However, in these cases, if we associate data between tracks with measurements directly with no compensation of the carrier motion, the tracking continuity will decline when the sonar's carrier rotates. Targets near the rotation center move more slowly than those far away from the center. It will cause target loss and false association in data association process. It is necessary to estimate the rotation of the sonar carrier by using the sonar image sequences, when there is no motion information of the vehicle.

Global feature-based method is often used to estimate the rotation or match two sonar images but not feature-based method [8], because that are robust to noise in FLS image. [9] uses a graph descriptor to represent the topologic relationship between the observed targets. And use the descriptor to detect a loop closure. Deep learning is used to match the sonar image in [10], the method uses the navigation data as labels, inputs two frames which need to match to a CNN model, and outputs a score to represent the overlapping the area of the two frames. Experiment shows that the matching performance of their proposed method is higher than the feature-based method. [8] compares three global registration methods based on phase correlation for mosaicking sonar images, and shows that using phase correlation in polar coordinate directly is better than others under most cases. [11] uses the phase correction method to estimate the rotation and translation of the carrier, and makes them as feedback to compensate the drift error of AUV. Considering the robustness and real-time requirement, this paper used the phase correction method based on Fourier transform to estimate the rotation of the carrier.

Figure 1 shows the tracking-by-detection framework. The improved framework of this paper is shown on the left side, and the traditional multi-target tracking method [11, 12] is shown on the right side. The traditional framework detects the objects in cartesian coordinates system, and associates the detections with the predictions of the tracks in cartesian coordinates. Then updates the tracker use the assigned pair of detection and track. Finally, outputs the cartesian coordinates of the objects in the tracker list.

In order to suppress the tracking performance degradation caused by the rotation of sonar carrier, the improved multi objects tracking framework used phase correction to estimate the rotation velocity, and added it to the motion model as a control. For keeping the model linear, we used the motion model in polar coordinate system. The data association process is also performed in this system. Finally, coordinates were converted to cartesian coordinate system for output. The rest of this paper is organized as follows. Section 2 presents the brief description of the improved tracking method. Section 3 shows the experiments results on a real sonar image sequence. Finally, Sect. 4 is the conclusion.

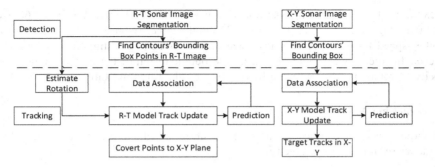

**Fig. 1.** Overview of proposed method and traditional method.

## 2 Method

### 2.1 Rotation Estimation

We compensated the prediction in the model by the estimation of rotation velocity. Phase correlation [13, 14] was used to estimate the rotation velocity of the carrier. Table 1 shows the process of phase correlation algorithm to estimate the rotation angle between two frames in sonar image sequences.

**Table 1.** Algorithm of rotation estimation based fourier transform.

---

1: **Inputs:**
   R-Theta image $I_{n-1}$ in frame $n-1$ with size $h_R$ and width $w_T$
   R-Theta image $I_n$ in frame $n$ with height $h_R$ and width $w_T$
   R-Theta image bearing resolution ratio $Res_b$
2: **Outputs:**
   The angle $\omega$ of rotation between frame $n-1$ and frame $n$
3: Resize $I_{n-1}$ and $I_n$ to square with size $s \times s$
4: Applies a Hanning window to $I_{n-1}$ and $I_n$
5: Computes the 2D Discrete Fourier Transform (DFT) $G_{n-1}$ and $G_n$ of the two frames
6: Computes the normalized cross power spectrum
   $$C = \frac{G_{n-1}G_n^*}{|G_{n-1}G_n^*|}$$
7: Computes the inverse DFT $r$ of $C$
8: Find the peak location $(\Delta x, \Delta y)$ in $r$
9: Computes the rotation angle $\omega$ by
   $$\omega = \Delta x \cdot Res_b \cdot \frac{w_T}{s}$$
10: Return $\omega$

---

The raw sonar data is a rectangle matrix called R-Theta image, where every column contains the measurements within the measurement range in one bearing. In line 3, the input images have been resized to square for stable of the phase correction algorithm.

For example, the height of our sonar image $h_R$ was 1219, and the width $w_T$ was 768, we resize the image to $312 \times 312$, where s is 312 in the table. We use smaller size 312 for a higher speed boost. Under our test, size 312 is enough for estimating the rotation angle $\omega$. In line 9, we should also scale the output to return the correct angle. The velocity of rotation $\dot{\omega}$ is computed by dividing by the sampling time.

## 2.2    Tracking Model

Each target is assigned a tracker. The state transition model and measurement model of the tracker in time step $t$ is given by:

$$\mathbf{x}_{t+1} = \mathbf{F} \cdot \mathbf{x}_t + \mathbf{v}_t + \mathbf{B} \cdot \mathbf{u}_t \tag{1}$$

$$\mathbf{z}_t = \mathbf{H} \cdot \mathbf{x}_t + \mathbf{w}_t \tag{2}$$

where $\mathbf{x}_t$ is the state vector, $\mathbf{F}$ is the state transition matrix, $\mathbf{H}$ is the measurement matrix, $\mathbf{v}_t$ and $\mathbf{w}_t$ are Gaussian white noise with covariance matrix $\mathbf{Q}_t$ and $\mathbf{R}_t$ respectively. The state transition matrix is given as follows, where $T$ is the sampling time:

$$\mathbf{F} = \begin{bmatrix} 1 & 0 & T & 0 \\ 0 & 1 & 0 & T \\ 0 & 0 & 1 & 0 \\ 0 & 0 & 0 & 1 \end{bmatrix} \tag{3}$$

measure matrix:

$$\mathbf{H} = \begin{bmatrix} 1 & 0 & 0 & 0 \\ 0 & 1 & 0 & 0 \end{bmatrix} \tag{4}$$

In cartesian coordinate system model state $\mathbf{x}_t$ is often chosen by $[\begin{array}{cccc} x_t & y_t & \dot{x}_t & \dot{y}_t \end{array}]^T$, where $x_t$ and $y_t$ is the target coordinates, cartesian coordinate system $\dot{x}_t$ and $\dot{y}_t$ was the speed of the target in $x$ and $y$ direction.

Adding the rotation velocity to the model in cartesian coordinate system directly is difficult, so we use a linear model in polar coordinate system, so the state vector $\mathbf{x}_t$ is chosen by $[\begin{array}{cccc} r_t & \theta_t & \dot{r}_t & \dot{\theta}_t \end{array}]^T$, where $r_t$ and $\theta_t$ is target coordinates in polar coordinate system, $\dot{r}_t$ and $\dot{\theta}_t$ are the speed in the direction of $r$ and $\theta$ respectively, and due to the influence of vehicle velocity $\dot{\omega}_t$, $\theta_{t+1}$ can be given by the state transition equation as follows:

$$\theta_{t+1} = \theta_t + \dot{\theta}_t T + \dot{\omega}_t T \tag{5}$$

Therefore, the control vector $\mathbf{u}_t$ is given by:

$$\mathbf{u}_t = [\dot{\omega}_t] \tag{6}$$

and the control matrix $\mathbf{B}$:

$$\mathbf{B} = [\, 0 \quad T \quad 0 \quad 0 \,]^T \tag{7}$$

Each tracker is predicted and updated using Kalman filter equations, the prediction step:

$$\hat{\mathbf{x}}_t = \mathbf{F} \cdot \mathbf{x}_{t-1} + \mathbf{B} \cdot \mathbf{u}_t \tag{8}$$

$$\hat{\mathbf{P}}_t = \mathbf{F}\mathbf{P}_{t-1}\mathbf{F}^T + \mathbf{Q} \tag{9}$$

and the update step:

$$\mathbf{K}_t = \hat{\mathbf{P}}_t\mathbf{H}^T \left( \mathbf{H}\hat{\mathbf{P}}_t\mathbf{H}^T + \mathbf{Q} \right)^{-1} \tag{10}$$

$$\mathbf{x}_t = \hat{\mathbf{x}}_t + \mathbf{K}_t(\mathbf{z}_t - \mathbf{H} \cdot \hat{\mathbf{x}}_t) \tag{11}$$

$$\mathbf{P}_t = (\mathbf{I} - \mathbf{K}_t\mathbf{H})\hat{\mathbf{P}}_t \tag{12}$$

## 2.3   Tracking

We used the detection-by-tracking framework [12]. Each target was assigned a tracker, the following steps are performed during every sampling time: Get a frame from the image sequences. Estimate the rotation velocity and perform the prediction step for all trackers in the tracker list use the velocity. Detect objects and get measurements. And then associate predictions and measurements. We could get pairs of assigned predictions and measurements, unassigned predictions and unassigned measurements in this data association step. Then use the assigned measurements to update the tracker respectively, create new tracker using the unassigned measurements and the losing time of the tracker corresponding to the unassigned prediction should increase one. Hungarian algorithm was used to solve the cost matrix for data association. The cost matrix was filled with the Euclidean distance in polar coordinate system between predictions and measurements in polar coordinate system. Table 2 shows the algorithm for computing the distance. We normalize the range of prediction and measurement in line 4 and line 5 for numerical stability. The law of cosines is used for calculate the distance in line 6.

There are three parameters in the tracking part need to set, the maximum matching distance $D_{th}$, the minimum survival time $L_{min}$, and the maximum loss time $L_{max}$. If the distance between the prediction and measurement is further than $D_{th}$, this pair will not be considered as matched pair. If the object appears more than $L_{min}$ frames, a target id will assign to the object and the tracker will be deleted if it has lost more than $L_{max}$ frames.

**Table 2.** Compute distance in polar coordinates.

---

1: **Inputs:**
    Prediction: $r_p, \theta_p$ and Measurement: $r_m, \theta_m$
2: **Outputs:**
    Distance between prediction and measurement: $D$
3: $R_{max} = \max(r_p, r_m)$
4: $r_p = r_p/R_{max}$
5: $r_m = r_m/R_{max}$
6: $D = \sqrt{r_p^2 + r_m^2 - 2r_pr_m \cos(\theta_p - \theta_m)}$
7: $D = D \cdot R_{max}$
8: Return $D$

---

### 2.4    Coordinate Transform

We detect objects in polar coordinate system and the corrections of the model presented in Sect. 2.1 is also in polar coordinate system. We should convert them to cartesian coordinate system. Figure 2 shows the coordinate transformation from polar to cartesian. The left shows the R-Theta image, and the cartesian coordinate system is shown on the right.

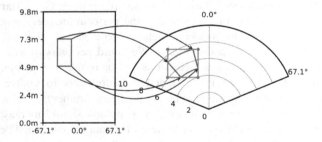

**Fig. 2.** Coordinate transformation.

Each object in the polar system is represented by $r, \theta, w, h$, where $r$ and $\theta$ are the center of the target's border box, $w$ is the width of the bounding box in polar sonar image, and $h$ is the height of the bounding box. In the polar coordinate system, the coordinates of the four vertices of the bounding box can be expressed as $P_i = (r_i, \theta_i)$, where $i = 1, 2, 3, 4$, we could get them as follows:

$$\begin{cases} P_1 = \left(r - \frac{1}{2}h, \theta - \frac{1}{2}w\right) \\ P_2 = \left(r - \frac{1}{2}h, \theta + \frac{1}{2}w\right) \\ P_3 = \left(r + \frac{1}{2}h, \theta + \frac{1}{2}w\right) \\ P_4 = \left(r + \frac{1}{2}h, \theta - \frac{1}{2}w\right) \end{cases} \tag{13}$$

The final tracking results are shown in the cartesian coordinate system, which requires coordinate transformation. We take the following approach: first, convert the four vertices to the cartesian coordinate system by:

$$\begin{cases} x = r \sin \theta \\ y = r \cos \theta \end{cases} \tag{14}$$

We could get $P_i' = \{x_i, y_i\}$, where $i = 1, 2, 3, 4$. Then the four vertices of the bounding box in cartesian coordinates shown on Fig. 2 right filled with red color is given by:

$$\begin{cases} x_{min} = \min\{x_i; i = 1, 2, 3, 4\} \\ y_{min} = \min\{y_i, i = 1, 2, 3, 4\} \\ x_{max} = \max\{x_i, i = 1, 2, 3, 4\} \\ y_{max} = \max\{y_i, i = 1, 2, 3, 4\} \end{cases} \tag{15}$$

So the output vertices of the bounding box in cartesian coordinate system are $P_1^c = (x_{min}, y_{min}), P_2^c = (x_{max}, y_{min}), P_3^c = (x_{max}, y_{min}), P_4^c = (x_{max}, y_{max})$. The object is represented by $P_1^c, P_2^c, P_3^c, P_4^c$.

## 3  Experiments

### 3.1  Dataset

We validated the tracking algorithm using real sonar data. The dataset contains 663 images. Each image is a R-Theta sonar image with width 768 and height 1219. The range resolution is 10 m per pixel, and the bearing resolution is 10 degree per pixel. The frame rate of the dataset is 7 fps. The sonar carrier rotated several times with different rotation velocity in order to test the robustness of the algorithm to rotation. We annotated the images in the sequence followed the annotation rules in MOT16 [2] strictly, and 52 tracks were labeled with 4077 bounding boxes appeared in the sequences totally. The annotations were labeled on R-Theta sonar images, and converted to cartesian coordinate system by the method presented in Sect. 2.4. The evaluation of metrics was performed in cartesian coordinate system.

### 3.2  Object Detection

Figure 3(b) shows a R-Theta sonar image. We proposed a simple method for object detection to validate the tracking model. The objects in R-Theta sonar image are often accompanied by shadows. This feature was used to detect objects. Figure 3(a) shows the method, A is a point in sonar image, B is a point at a distance of $d$ from point A away from the sonar, we compute the mean value $m_A$, $m_B$ in window A and window B with a constant window size respectively. If the difference between $m_A$ and $m_B$ is greater than threshold, then label the point A using one, otherwise, label the point A using zero. We could get the binary image by traversing the whole image, and then erode and dilate the binary image to remove noise. In our test, the window size is set to

34, the threshold is set to 24, and the distance is set to 26. Figure 3(c) show the binary segment results, then we find contours in the binary image and get the bounding boxes of contours. Figure 3(d) shows the bounding boxes. We ignored the noise boxes near the sonar head. Figure 3(e) shows the boxes in cartesian coordinate system converted by the method presented in Sect. 2.4.

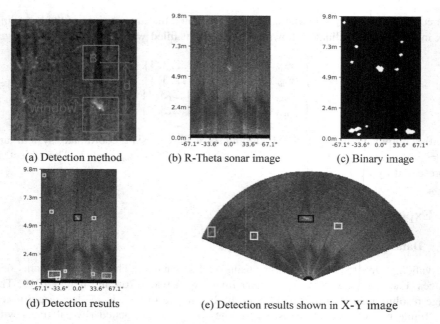

(a) Detection method          (b) R-Theta sonar image          (c) Binary image

(d) Detection results          (e) Detection results shown in X-Y image

**Fig. 3.** Object detection results. (Color figure online)

### 3.3 Parameter Settings

We compared the tracking performance of three methods: cartesian model with status vector $\begin{bmatrix} x_t & y_t & \dot{x}_t & \dot{y}_t \end{bmatrix}^T$ which represented by XYKF, and polar coordinate model with status vector $\begin{bmatrix} r_t & \theta_t & \dot{r}_t & \dot{\theta}_t \end{bmatrix}^T$, without compensation of rotation estimation, which represented by RTKF and the improved polar coordinate model using the rotation estimation described in Sect. 2.1, represented by RTWKF. All the method used the same detector presented in Sect. 3.2 for fair. We chose same tracker parameter described in Sect. 2.3 in order to compare the three trackers, the minimum survival time $L_{min}$ was 10 frames, the maximum loss time $L_{max}$ was 5 frames, and the minimum loss distance $D_{th}$ was 0.5 m.

**Kalman Filter Parameters Selection.** Process noise $\mathbf{Q}$ and measurement noise $\mathbf{R}$ is given by $diag\{Q, Q, Q, Q\}$ and $diag\{R, R, R, R\}$ respectively, we used the grid search method to determine the filter parameters $Q$ and $R$. Parameters were selection from the interval between 0.00001 to 10, increasing by a factor of 10. Figure 4 shows the recall rate (Recall), MOTA [15] (multi-target tracking accuracy), the total number of identity switches IDs [16] with different $Q$ and $R$. In the process of parameter selection, we found that RTWKF is more robust to parameters. The best results all appear in the RTWKF method represented by the red curve, and the RTWKF method is less affected by parameter changes and can maintain higher performance compared with the other two methods. We set both $Q$ and $R$ to 0.0001.

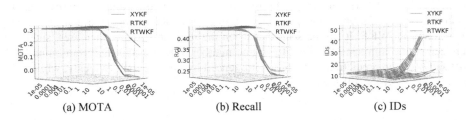

(a) MOTA        (b) Recall        (c) IDs

**Fig. 4.** Comparison of MOTA, recall and IDs for different $Q$ and $R$.

### 3.4 Performance

**Multi-object Tracking Performance.** We should choose intersection-over-union threshold (IOU) threshold for the evaluation method. It is common to choose between 0.25 to 0.5 [2]. There is inherent bias between the detections and the annotations, because we use a traditional segmentation method to detect the objects. Higher threshold is strict for the detection method, so we used IOU threshold 0.3 to perform all the metrics, that is, if the IOU between bounding box of prediction and annotation is smaller than 0.3, the prediction is a true positive (TP). The evaluation results are shown in Table 3, the metrics were computed followed by [2] strictly. It can be seen from the table that except for FP (number of false alarms), which is slightly higher than the other two methods, other performance has been improved obviously. We used a standard computer with a 3.7 GHz AMD CPU and programmed with Python and OpenCV library [17] to compare the frequency (Hz) metrics. The time cost by detection is not included same as MOT benchmark. The metric Hz shows that all the three method meet the real-time requirements. We will show how the rotation estimation improve the performance in the following parts.

**Table 3.** Multi-object tracking metrics (best performance is marked in **bold**).

| Tracker | MOTA % (↑) | IDF1 % (↑) | MT (↑) | ML (↓) | FP (↓) | FN (↓) | IDs (↓) | FM (↓) | IDP % (↑) | IDR % (↑) | Rcll % (↑) | Prcn % (↑) | Hz (↑) |
|---|---|---|---|---|---|---|---|---|---|---|---|---|---|
| XYKF | 29.8 | 47.7 | 6 | 22 | 805 | 3401 | 10 | 145 | 65.9 | 37.4 | 43.4 | 76.4 | 37.0 |
| RTKF | 29.9 | 47.7 | 6 | **21** | **803** | 3396 | 10 | 147 | 65.8 | 37.4 | 43.5 | 76.5 | **38.2** |
| RTWKF | **30.8** | **52.1** | **7** | **21** | 805 | **3340** | **9** | **142** | **71.1** | **41.1** | **44.4** | **76.8** | 33.0 |

**Tracking Performance on Single Object.** We evaluated on tracking single object to see how the model improved the tracking performance. The tracking process assigned tracks and objects using predictions and measures as presented in Sect. 2.3. For single object, if the prediction is more accurate, the tracker is better. We can use the error between the prediction and measurement called prediction error to compare tracking performance. As shown in Fig. 5(a) and (b) are the two targets appeared in the sequence, with ID of 2 and 29, appearing at frame 217 and 558, and disappearing at frame 593 and 663, respectively. The red line is the absolute value of the estimated rotation velocity, the blue line is the prediction error of RTKF, and the orange line is the error of RTWKF. It can be seen that when the rotation velocity increases, such as between frame number 210 and 240, frame number 320 and 350, and frame number 640 and 660, the prediction of RTKF is influenced by the rotation obviously, while the error of RTWKF is still lower.

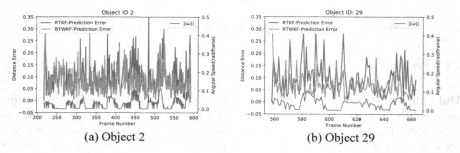

**Fig. 5.** Comparison of single target prediction error. (Color figure online)

**Comparison of Tracking Performance for Different Distance Threshold $D_{th}$.** If the distance between the prediction and the measurement is greater than the $D_{th}$ presented in Sect. 2.3, the pair of the prediction and measurement is considered to be mismatched. So smaller $D_{th}$ is stricter for the tracker. Figure 6 shows the multi-target tracking precision MOTA [15] (combines false positives, missed targets and identity switches), recall rate (successfully detected rate), IDs [16] (target identification switching number) scores for different $D_{th}$.

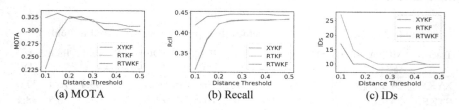

**Fig. 6.** Effects of different distance thresholds on tracking performance.

It shows that the performance of RTKF and XYKF is close to each other, and the they drop significantly when sets $D_{th}$ between 0.1 and 0.2, while RTWKF maintains a good performance. Figure 7 shows the tracking results from frame 439 to frame 445 when the $D_{th}$ was 0.15 m. We could see the stability comparison of the three methods when sonar rotated. It can be seen from the red curve in Fig. 5(a) that the estimated rotation velocity of the carrier starts to increase around frame 439. At frame 442, the target far from the sonar center has lost or deviated in XYKF and RTKF, while RTWKF still tracks the targets. This will cause low recall rate and identity switches. At frame 445, The targets have been lost completely and the target in the central of visual field has deviated. However, one target has deviated while other targets is still tracked well in RTWKF. So as shown in Fig. 7 the recall rate and IDs of RTWKF is more stable than RTKF and XYKF.

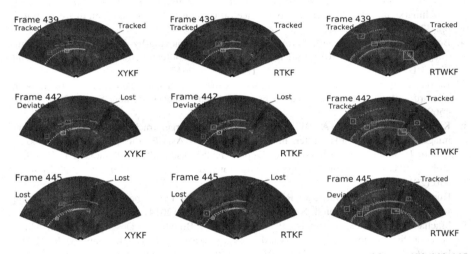

**Fig. 7.** Tracking results. The three columns of are the tracking sequence of frame 439,442,445 of XYKF, RTKF and RTWKF respectively. The rectangle shows the tracking results in this frame, and the points with the same color shows the tracks of the objects. (Color figure online)

## 4   Conclusion

In this paper, we focused on multi-object tracking using forward-looking sonar without carrier motion information. The proposed estimated the rotation of sonar carrier using phase correction and added the rotation to the motion model in polar coordinate system as control. We validated the method on a real sonar dataset. As a result, MOT metrics show that the proposed method has more accuracy and multiple experiments show that the method is more stable than traditional approaches when the carrier of sonar is rotating.

**Acknowledgments.** This work was supported by the National Natural Science Foundation of China (Grant No. 41876100), the State Key Program of National Natural Science Foundation of

China (Grant No. 61633004), the National key research and development program of China (Grant No. 2018YFC0310102 and 2017YFC0306002), the Development Project of Applied Technology in Harbin (Grant No. 2016RAXXJ071) and the Fundamental Research Funds for the Central Universities (Grant No. HEUCFP201707).

# References

1. DeMarco, K.J., West, M.E., Howard, A.M.: Sonar-based detection and tracking of a diver for underwater human-robot interaction scenarios. In: 2013 IEEE International Conference on Systems, Man, and Cybernetics, pp. 2378–2383, October 2013
2. Milan, A., Leal-Taixé, L., Reid, I.D., Roth, S., Schindler, K.: MOT16: a benchmark for multi-object tracking. CoRR abs/1603.00831 (2016), http://arxiv.org/abs/1603.00831
3. Geiger, A., Lenz, P., Urtasun, R.: Are we ready for autonomous driving? The kitti vision benchmark suite. In: 2012 IEEE Conference on Computer Vision and Pattern Recognition, pp. 3354–3361, June 2012
4. Bochinski, E., Eiselein, V., Sikora, T.: High-speed tracking-by-detection without using image information. In: 2017 14th IEEE International Conference on Advanced Video and Signal Based Surveillance (AVSS), pp. 1–6, August 2017
5. Karoui, I., Quidu, I., Legris, M.: Automatic sea-surface obstacle detection and tracking in forward-looking sonar image sequences. IEEE Trans. Geosci. Remote Sens. 53(8), 4661–4669 (2015)
6. Kalyan, B., Balasuriya, A., Wijesoma, S.: Multiple target tracking in underwater sonar images using particle-PHD filter. In: OCEANS 2006 - Asia Pacific, pp. 1–5, May 2006
7. Quidu, I., Jaulin, L., Bertholom, A., Dupas, Y.: Robust multitarget tracking in forward-looking sonar image sequences using navigational data. IEEE J. Oceanic Eng. 37(3), 417–430 (2012)
8. Hurtós, N., Cufí, X., Salvi, J.: Rotation estimation for two-dimensional forward-looking sonar mosaicing. Adv. Intell. Syst. Comput. 252, 69–84 (2014)
9. Machado, M., Zaffari, G., Ribeiro, P.O., Drews-Jr, P., Botelho, S.: Description and matching of acoustic images using a forward looking sonar: a topological approach. IFAC-PapersOnLine 50(1), 2317–2322 (2017). http://www.sciencedirect.com/science/article/pii/S2405896317308364. 20th IFAC World Congress
10. Cardozo de Souza Ribeiro, P.O., Machado dos Santos, M., Lilles Jorge Drews, P., Silva da Costa Botelho, S.: Forward looking sonar scene matching using deep learning. In: 2017 16th IEEE International Conference on Machine Learning and Applications (ICMLA), pp. 574–579, December 2017
11. Cho, H., Pyo, J., Yu, S.: Drift error reduction based on the sonar image prediction and matching for underwater hovering. IEEE Sens. J. 16(23), 8566–8577 (2016)
12. Hamuda, E., Ginley, B.M., Glavin, M., Jones, E.: Improved image processing-based crop detection using kalman filtering and the hungarian algorithm. Comput. Electron. Agric. 148, 37–44 (2018). http://www.sciencedirect.com/science/article/pii/S0168169917307718
13. Hurtós, N., Romagós, D., Cufí, X., Petillot, Y., Salvi, J.: Fourier-based registration for robust forward-looking sonar mosaicing in low-visibility underwater environ-ments. J. Field Robot. 32, 123–151 (2015)
14. Kim, B., Cho, H., Yu, S.: Development of imaging sonar based autonomous trajectory backtracking using AUVs. In: 2016 IEEE/OES Autonomous Underwater Vehicles (AUV), pp. 319–323, November 2016

15. Bernardin, K., Stiefelhagen, R.: Evaluating multiple object tracking performance: the clear mot metrics. EURASIP J. Image Video Process. **2008**(1), 246309 (2008). https://doi.org/10.1155/2008/246309
16. Ristani, E., Solera, F., Zou, R.S., Cucchiara, R., Tomasi, C.: Performance measures and a data set for multi-target, multi-camera tracking. CoRR abs/1609.01775 (2016). http://arxiv.org/abs/1609.01775
17. Bradski, G.: The OpenCV Library. Dr. Dobb's J. Softw. Tools **25**, 120–125 (2000)

# Numerical Simulation of Collision Between an Oil Tanker and Ice

Aifeng Zhang$^{(\boxtimes)}$ ⓘ, Lihong Wu, Lanxuan Liu,
Xiong Chen, and Xinyu Zhao

Naval Architecture and Ocean Engineering College,
Dalian Maritime University, Dalian 116026, China
afzhang@dlmu.edu.cn

**Abstract.** The ice floe has a great influence on the speed and navigation safety of polar ships. Whether it is the exploitation of oil and gas or the opening of new lanes, the problems of ship-ice collisions should be paid close attention to. In order to further study the collision response of the side structure under ice loads, the finite element technology is used to simulate the collision process between the ship and ice in this paper. The crashworthiness is compared and analyzed according to the results of stress, strain of side structure and energy absorption during ship-ice collisions by selecting different ice impact speeds. The numerical results provide certain technical supports for the structural damage prediction and evaluation of ships sailing in the ice areas.

**Keywords:** Ship-ice collision · Side structure · Collision response ·
Numerical simulation

## 1 Introduction

The assessment report on the Arctic Circle of 2008 US Geological Survey shows that the Arctic Circle contains the world's 13% of untapped oil resources and 30% of natural gas resources. It will be Persian Gulf in the future. The problem of ship-ice interaction is a critical issue in ships working around ice. Since the material properties of sea ice are complex, it is of critical importance to develop effective material constitutive models to improve numerical methods for ice-ship interaction analysis [1–3]. In recent years, many scholars have studied the physical properties of ice and the structural response of ship-ice collision based on collision experiments and finite element method. The ice load forecast of ship in ice-breaking process is a scientific problem to be solved [4–6]. The influence rule of ship-ice floe collision is a reference for anti-ice load structural design of ships [7]. Finite element method is used to numerically analyze the collision between ship-ice, the results of hull structural deformation, and collision force and energy absorption in references [8–10]. In this paper, ship and ice floe are in motion that is different from others. The finite element technology is used to simulate the collision process between the ship and ice in order to further study the collision response of the side structure under ice loads.

© Springer Nature Switzerland AG 2019
H. Yu et al. (Eds.): ICIRA 2019, LNAI 11741, pp. 184–194, 2019.
https://doi.org/10.1007/978-3-030-27532-7_16

## 2  Theoretical Basis of Finite Element Simulation

The collision between the ship-ice is a transient nonlinear response process under a large impact load. The components of the collision area generally go beyond the elastic phase and enter the plastic flow state, and may suffer various forms of damage and failure such as buckling and tearing. The finite element software used in this paper can simulate a variety of high transient nonlinear events. The module uses an explicit integration algorithm that is ideal for analyzing highly nonlinear dynamic problems.

When using the explicit algorithm to solve the dynamic problem, the first is to carry out the relevant spatial discrete processing, and then the Newton's second law is used to obtain the motion equation of the collision [11]. For the overall coordinate system, the equation of motion of the collision can be expressed as:

$$[M]\{a\} + [C]\{v\} + [K]\{d\} = \{F^{ex}\} \tag{1}$$

where $[M]$ is the mass matrix, $[C]$ is the damping matrix, $[K]$ is the stiffness matrix, $\{a\}$ is the acceleration vector, $\{v\}$ is the speed vector, and $\{d\}$ is the displacement vector, $\{F^{ex}\}$ is an external force vector including collision force. The collision equation can be written as:

$$[M]\{a\} = \{F^{re}\} \tag{2}$$

$$\{F^{re}\} = \{F^{ex}\} - \{F^{in}\} \tag{3}$$

$$\{F^{in}\} = [C]\{v\} + [K]\{d\} \tag{4}$$

If the mass matrix $[M]$ is transformed into a diagonal matrix using concentrated mass, the equations for each degree of freedom will be independent of each other, namely:

$$M_i a_i = F_i^{re} (i = 1, 2, \ldots) \tag{5}$$

To use the explicit algorithm to solve the collision equation, first calculate the acceleration from Eq. 5, as shown in Eq. 6:

$$a_i = F_i^{re} / M_i \tag{6}$$

Then, the speed is obtained by integrating the time, the displacement is obtained by integrating the time again. Time integration is performed using a central differential display format, the display format of the center difference is as shown in Eq. 7:

$$\begin{cases} V_{n+1/2} = V_{n-1/2} + a_n \left( \Delta t_{n+1/2} + \Delta t_{n-1/2} \right)/2 \\ d_{n+1} = d_n + V_{n+1/2} \cdot \Delta t_{n+1/2} \\ \Delta t_{n+1/2} = \left( \Delta t_n + \Delta t_{n+1} \right)/2 \end{cases} \tag{7}$$

Therefore, the displacement, speed, and acceleration at each discrete time point can be obtained from Eq. 7 over the entire time domain.

# 3  Geometry and Simulation Conditions

In this paper, finite element software is used as the pre-processing tool which establishes the side structure of the tanker strengthened by the IACS ice class rules and the cube ice model with a side length of 12 m in ice areas. The shapes of ice floe exhibit different collision properties, but it is more dangerous for the angular geometries. The condition of collision is that the edge of the ice floe collides with the side of the ship, as shown in Fig. 1.

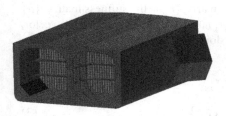

**Fig. 1.** Collision finite element model

**Fig. 2.** Collision damage deformation

## 3.1  Material Properties of the Model

The ideal elastic-plastic model and the Cowper-Symonds [12] constitutive equation is used for the ship material as shown in Table 1.

**Table 1.** The model parameters of strengthening ship

| Steel grade | Material density Kg/m$^3$ | Yield stress MPa | Elastic modulus N/m$^2$ | Strain rate parameter $D$ | Strain rate parameter $P$ | Maximum plastic strain | Poisson's ratio |
|---|---|---|---|---|---|---|---|
| A32 | 7850 | 315 | $2.06 \times 10^{11}$ | 3200 | 5 | 0.167 | 0.3 |
| A36 | 7850 | 315 | $2.06 \times 10^{11}$ | 3200 | 5 | 0.15 | 0.3 |

The difference in mechanical properties of sea ice under different conditions leads to the complexity of its materials. It is generally defined as a typical elastic-plastic material according to the characteristics of sea ice ductile-brittle transition. The specific parameters are shown in Table 2 [13].

**Table 2.** The model parameters of ice

| Material density Kg/m$^3$ | Shear modulus GPa | Yield stress MPa | Hardening modulus GPa | Bulk modulus GPa | Plastic failure strain | Fission pressure MPa |
|---|---|---|---|---|---|---|
| 900 | 2.2 | 2.12 | 4.26 | 5.26 | 0.35 | −4 |

### 3.2 Solving Parameter Settings

The ship surges freely and while the other five degrees of freedom are constrained. The type of contact used on the ship-ice model is face-to-face contact, known as master-slave contact, where the ship side is the master face and the ice is the slave face. In order to avoid the occurrence of sand leakage during the modeling process, the slave face mesh is finer than the master face.

## 4   The Numerical Results of Ship-Ice Collision

### 4.1   The Influence of Ice Speed on Ship-Ice Collision

The finite element simulation model of the ice floe and the ship side structure is built when the edge of the ice floe collides with the middle part of the ship. According to the control variable method, the initial speeds of the ice floe are 4 m/s, 6 m/s and 8 m/s, respectively. The outer plate thickness, side impact location and other simulation parameters are not changed. The damage of the ship's side structure, von-Mises stress, the effective plastic strain and the energy absorption of the components of the side structure during the collision are analyzed and compared under different ice floe impacts speeds. The collision positions of the three working conditions are located between the vertical stringer and strong frame, as shown in Fig. 2.

The stress color maps of ship's side structure after collision under three conditions are compared, as shown in Fig. 3. It can be seen that the damage area of the structure is concentrated in the contact area. The structure far from the collision area is not affected by the force. This phenomenon shows strong locality. Under three working conditions, the vertical truss structure undergoes large lateral extrusion deformation with the increase of impact speed. Table 3 shows the penetration and stressed area of the ship's side structure under three working conditions.

**Table 3.** The penetration and stressed area of the ship's side structure

| Initial speed of ice floe (m/s) | Penetration (mm) | Stressed area (m$^2$) |
|---|---|---|
| 4 | 269 | 38.65 |
| 6 | 446 | 43.48 |
| 8 | 868 | 54.36 |

It can be seen that the penetration and stressed area of the structure are proportional to the increase of the impact speed. The different degrees of deformation and damage occur for ship side component during the collision. The shell plating of side is the first

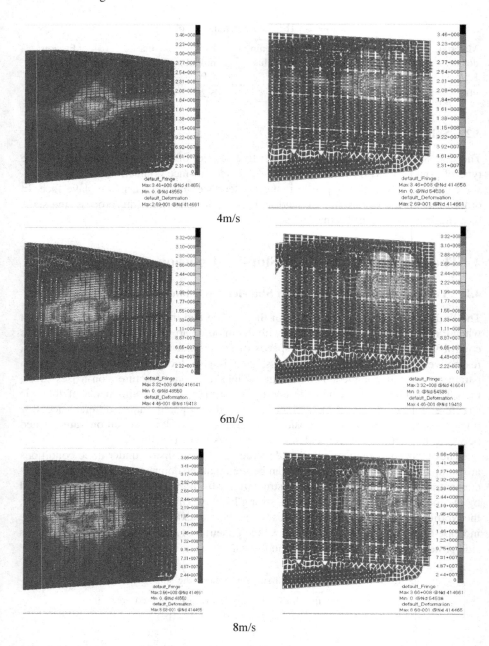

4m/s

6m/s

8m/s

**Fig. 3.** Ship side structural damage at different ice floe speeds (outer view (left) and inner view (right))

contact area in the collision. The membrane tension deformation mainly occurs in the contact area of the shell. With the continuous cutting of the ice edges, the plastic deformation of the shell increases. Therefore, producing the maximum plastic strain is viewed as rupture of the side plating. At same time the corresponding shell elements are deleted by the program.

Since longitudinal beam is an important component of the side structure, it is necessary to observe its deformation form during collision. Figure 4 shows the stress color-maps of the side longitudinal at different time points within 1 s of the collision process when the ice floe speed is 6 m/s.

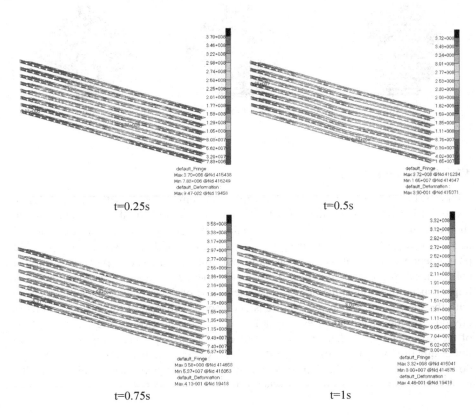

**Fig. 4.** Stress color maps of side longitudinal at different times

Figure 4 shows that the web of the profile has a smaller crushing deformation and the face plate has not been bent from the beginning of the collision to 0.25 s when the side longitudinal is under surface load. Its maximum deformation at node 19458 and the amount of deformation is 94.7 mm. The edge of ice cuts the side longitudinal directly with the penetration increasing and the rupture of the side plating. From 0.25 s to the end of the collision, the side longitudinal has obvious bend deformation and the form also changed to lateral extrusion deformation. The deformation gradually increases to 446 mm. During the collision process, the ice absorbs part of the energy and transforms it into its own deformation energy. Figure 5 shows the damage of ice after collision for three working conditions. In the process of collision, some elements of ice edge are deleted because of the maximum plastic failure strain. The main deformation form of ice is extrusion deformation. The greater the speed of the ice is, the more damage elements of the ice edge is, which indicates that the deeper the ice body penetrates the ship's side structure, the more fully it contacts the internal components.

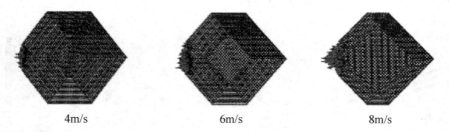

| 4m/s | 6m/s | 8m/s |

**Fig. 5.** Ice floe damage

### 4.2  Stress-Time Curve

Figure 6 shows the change of von-Mises stress of element 17836 with time at different speeds. It is inspected that the stress-time curve has obvious nonlinear fluctuations. It should be noted that the stress of side structures changes with the increasing time and has a downward trend after rising at the beginning, and then remain steady. The phenomenon shows that force produces loading-unloading-loading process during the collision. During the period from 0 s to 0.4 s, the stress value corresponding to the impact speed of 8 m/s is the largest. The rate of rise of the curve becomes more severe with the increase of the speed. The transient response change of the structure is more obvious. As the speed increases, the earlier of stress peak appears, the earlier the time of the side plating unit damage occurs. However, the side plating component may not fail at this time when the impact speed is 4 m/s. On the one hand the maximum stress does not exceed the yield limit, and on the other hand it produces unloading phenomenon because of the failure of other structural components.

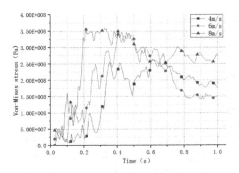

**Fig. 6.** Von-Mises stress time curve          **Fig. 7.** Effective plastic strain-time curve

### 4.3  Strain-Time Curve

The effective plastic strain-time curve of the collision at different impact speeds is shown in Fig. 7. It shows the strain of the same element. The points corresponding to the maximum strain are not same for the different speeds when the collision process finishes. Table 4 lists the maximum effective plastic strain values of the side structures after the end of the collision. It should be noted that this value is the maximum strain of the entire side node at different speeds.

It can be seen from Table 4 that the greater the impact speed of the ice floe is, the more severe the side structural response is, and the greater the maximum plastic strain value of the structure is.

**Table 4.** Maximum effective plastic strain at the end of collision

| Working condition | 4 m/s | 6 m/s | 8 m/s |
|---|---|---|---|
| Maximum effective plastic strain | 0.0636 | 0.0903 | 0.152 |

### 4.4  Energy Absorption

The total energy is of constant in the ship-ice collision. The damping energy, friction energy and hourglass energy are small proportion in the total energy. Most of initial kinetic energy of the side and the ice is transformed into the elastic-plastic deformation energy of the side and the deformation energy of the ice (The internal energy). Therefore, it is necessary to compare the energy absorption of various components on the side of the ship at different impact speeds.

The energy absorption is analyzed for some components of the side structure to know clearly the energy conversion during the ship-ice collision. Figure 8 shows the internal energy-time curve of the collision for the outer panel, the longitudinal beam, the strong frame, the vertical girder and the ice at different ice floe speeds. It can be concluded at once from Fig. 8 that for the ice floe speeds of 4 m/s, 6 m/s, and 8 m/s, the internal energy for the outer panel is 0.528 MJ, 1.541 MJ, and 9.427 MJ, respectively. When the impact speed doubles, the energy absorption of the outer panel increases by 16.85 times. It shows that the penetration increases, the outer panel absorbs more energy at the same time with the increasing of speed. The outer plate becomes the main component to prevent the edge of the ice cutting inner of side structure at speed of 8 m/s.

In addition, the energy absorption trend of the longitudinal beam, the strong frame and the vertical girder is similar. They get also more energy with the increasing of speed. But its energy absorption ratio gradually decreases. This is affected by the penetration after the outer plate rupture. When the penetration is gradually increasing, the outer panel absorbs more energy, which results in a decrease in the ratio of energy absorption. The energy absorption ratio of the longitudinal beam for the first two working conditions is the highest in the whole internal energy system. It indicates that the longitudinal beam plays an irreplaceable role in the collision. Therefore, the longitudinal beam should be considered of strengthening component to improve the crashworthiness of the side structure.

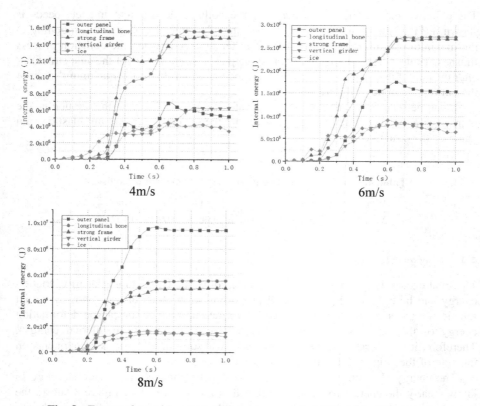

**Fig. 8.** Energy absorption curve of each component at different ice floe speeds

## 5  Conclusions

The process of ship-ice collision is very complex. It is associated to many other factors, such as the properties of sea ice material properties, ice shape and collision location. The changes of speed are only considered in this paper. A numerical simulation method using finite element was performed to identify the structure response at different speeds during ship-ice collisions. The research results show the process of ship-ice collision and indicate the response of side structures. It can provide guidance for the crashworthiness of polar ship structure design. The following conclusions can be drawn from the numerical simulations:

First, the damage and deformation of the side components become more serious with the increase of collision speed. The collision depth for side structure increases by 2.23 times if the collision speed doubles. When the side structure stress in the collision area exceeds the yield limit, plastic deformation occurs. If the outer plate is no breakage, the membrane tension deformation will occur in the contact area of outer plate. And the conquassation and extrusion bending deformation in the transverse frames and longitudinal beams will occur with varying degrees.

Second, ice will be damaged because of the different impact speed between ship and ice. As the speed increasing, the more kinetic energy is converted into the internal energy of ice, which results in the damage and deformation of ice.

Third, different collision speeds will affect the response of ship structures. The strain of side structure increases with the increase of the speed. The stress curve is more complex with the speed and shows obvious nonlinear characteristics.

**Acknowledgement.** The authors are grateful to the State Key Laboratory of Robotics, the Natural Science Foundation of China (with Grant No. 51009016) and the Fundamental Research Funds for the Central Universities (with Grant No. 3132017030) for their financial support.

## References

1. Xu, Y., Hu, Z.Q., Chen, G., et al.: Overview of the investigating methods for ship-ice interaction analysis. J. Ship Mech. **23**(1), 110–124 (2019)
2. Zhai, S.S., Li, H., Wang, C., et al.: The effect of different constitutive modeling on ship-ice interaction. Ship Sci. Technol. **36**(6), 20–25 (2014)
3. Hu, Z.Q., Gao, Y., Yao, Q.: A new constitutive model of ice material for Ship-ice interaction based on ideal elastic-plastic property. Naval Archit. Ocean Eng. **32**(1), 65–73 (2016)
4. Zhang, J., Wang, K.M., He, W.X.: Study on ice load calculation method of polar icebreaker bow under continuous ice breaking. Shipbuild. China **59**(3), 155–163 (2018)
5. Wang, L., Shen, W.W.: Research of structure failure mode and damage mechanism under interaction of ice-breaking structure and ice load. Ship Eng. **38**(11), 11–16 (2016)
6. Wang, W.Y., Tang, W.Y., Yang, C.J.: Rapid calculation method of ice loads considering structural deformation energy. Ship Ocean Eng. **46**(2), 38–43 (2017)
7. Zhang, J., Chen, C., Zhang, M.R.: Research on structure dynamic response in Ship-ice floe collision. Ship Eng. **36**(6), 24–27 (2014)
8. Xu, S.D., Hu, Z.Q., Chen, G.: Numerical simulation of strengthening side crashworthiness of LNG ships in ice zone. Ship Eng. **38**(6), 1–6 (2016)

9. Jin, Y., Hu, J.J., Liu, J.J.: Structural dynamic response of the ice navigating ship in level ice. Ship Sci. Technol. **39**(6), 33–37 (2017)
10. Yang, J.C., Zhu, F.X., Wu, W.F., et al.: Numerical analysis on ship-ice collision based on ANSYS/LS-DYNA. Marine Technology **3**, 30–34 (2007)
11. Jing, L.P.: Condition of stability of explicit finite element step integral pattern for wave motion. Chin. J. Rock Mechan. Eng. **24**(A01), 5120–5124 (2005)
12. Kee, P., Pedersen, P.T.: Modeling of the internal mechanics in ship collisions. Ocean Eng. **23**(2), 107–142 (1996)
13. Song, Z.C., Chn, J.M.: Dynamic analysis of the collision between sea-ice and single-pile simple platform. China offshore Platf. **24**(2), 19–22 (2009)

# Underwater De-scattering Range-Gated Imaging Based on Numerical Fitting and Frequency Domain Filtering

Minmin Wang[1,2], Xinwei Wang[1,2,3(✉)], Yuqing Yang[1,2], Liang Sun[1], and Yan Zhou[1,2,3]

[1] Optoelectronic System Laboratory, Institute of Semiconductors, CAS, Beijing 100083, China
wangxinwei@semi.ac.cn
[2] College of Materials Science and Opto-Electronics Technology, University of Chinese Academy of Sciences, Beijing, China
[3] School of Electronic, Electrical and Communication Engineering, University of Chinese Academy of Sciences, Beijing, China

**Abstract.** One of the major challenges of underwater imaging is its sensitivity to water scattering. In this paper, a method of underwater de-scattering range-gated imaging based on numerical fitting and frequency domain filtering is developed to suppress scatter effect and improve image quality. The backscatter noise is eliminated by using its numerical fitting value after measuring a sequence of water scattering maps. The Jaffe-McGlamery computer model and the light propagation property in water are introduced, and forward-scatter noise is reduced by filtering process in the frequency domain. After removing the backscatter and forward-scatter noise, the resolution and contrast of gated images are improved. A range-gated imaging system is established, and experiments are conducted in pools to prove the effectiveness and superiority of the proposed method. Compared with traditional range-gated imaging, the results demonstrate that the proposed method increases the image entropy by about 69%. The research is beneficial for enhancing underwater range-gated active imaging.

**Keywords:** Underwater range-gated imaging · Laser imaging ·
Water scattering · Forward scatter · Backscatter · Image enhancement

## 1 Introduction

Underwater range-gated imaging has been used in applications of subsea detection [1–4], underwater navigation [5], and fisheries stock assessment [7, 8]. As we all know, when light is propagating underwater, it is absorbed and scattered by water. If there is only the absorption in the water, increasing the light source luminance or the receiver sensitivity will increase operation range. Scattering is a process that redirects the light of illuminator into the unwanted directions, which includes backscatter and forward-scatter noise. The backscatter noise limits the apparent target-to-background contrast, while the forward-scatter noise causes blurring of the image features. For the range-gated imaging,

© Springer Nature Switzerland AG 2019
H. Yu et al. (Eds.): ICIRA 2019, LNAI 11741, pp. 195–204, 2019.
https://doi.org/10.1007/978-3-030-27532-7_17

the light that arrives within the gate time, namely the sampling volume of interest contributes to the imaging process, as shown in Fig. 1. The scatter noise outside the gate time is blocked. However, the scatter noise inside the sampling volume also contributes to the imaging, so images of underwater scene are degraded, especially in turbidity environment [2, 8]. The underwater gated images may suffer one or some of the following problems: blurring, low contrast, low resolutions, limited range visibility, non-uniform light, and so forth. Therefore, it is urgent to remove the scatter noise and improve the image quality for underwater range-gated imaging applications.

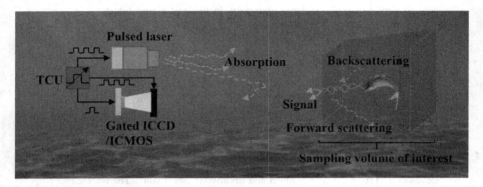

**Fig. 1.** Principle of underwater range-gated imaging and light propagation in water.

In this paper, we present a method of underwater de-scattering range-gated imaging based on numerical fitting and frequency domain filtering, for improving the resolution and contrast of gated image by eliminating the scatter noise. Experiments show that the proposed method achieves higher accuracy compared with the traditional range-gated method.

## 2    Underwater De-scattering Range-Gated Imaging Method

A typical range-gated imaging system consists of a pulsed laser, a gated ICCD/ICMOS and a time control unit (TCU), as depicted in Fig. 1. The TCU synchronizes the gated camera and the pulsed laser. For the range-gated imaging, the light that arrives within the gate time contributes to the imaging process, including the water scatter in the sampling volume. This part of scattering is capable of contaminating and deteriorating gated images.

To remove the scatter noise for the range-gated imaging, we analyze the basic physics of light propagation in the water medium and the model developed by McGlamery and Jaffe [9–12], the radiance received by the sensor is mathematically expressed as

$$E_0(x, y) = E_d(x, y) + E_b(x, y) + E_f(x, y) \qquad (1)$$

where $(x, y)$ is the Cartesian coordinates, $E_d(x, y)$ is the direct signal, $E_b(x, y)$ is the backscatter noise and $E_f(x, y)$ is the forward-scatter noise. To recover the useful information of underwater images, the forward-scatter and backscatter noise should be reduced, as shown in Fig. 2.

**Gated image with scattering noise**      **De-scattering gated image**

**Fig. 2.** Illustration of the process of scatter noise removal.

### 2.1   Backscatter Noise Removal

Before measuring the scene underwater, we capture a sequence of images containing only the backscatter of water and background. The background in the captured images, namely the ambient light noise and device noise can be eliminated by background subtraction where the background image is obtained when the laser light is turned off. The average value of backscatter noise captured at different range can be calculated. The relation between the backscatter noise and the whole range can be fitted with a poly-nominal function. Therefore, the value of backscatter noise at different range can be obtained and removed from the gated images.

### 2.2   Forward-Scatter Noise Removal

After reducing the backscatter noise, we obtain

$$E(x, y) = E_0(x, y) - E_b(x, y) = E_d(x, y) + E_f(x, y) \tag{2}$$

The forward-scatter noise can be obtained by

$$E_f(x, y) = E_d(x, y) * g\left(x, \frac{y}{R}, G, c, B\right) = e^{-cR} E_d(x, y, 0) * g\left(x, \frac{y}{R}, G, c, B\right) \tag{3}$$

Here, $g\left(x, \frac{y}{R}, G, c, B\right) = (e^{-GR} - e^{-cR})F^{-1}e^{-BRf}$, where $R$ is the range from the system to the object, $c$ is the total attenuation coefficient, $B$ is an empirical factor, $G$ is an empirical constant with the value $|G| \leq$ c, * denotes the convolution, $F^{-1}$ denotes the inverse Fourier transform. The 2D FFT is applied to Eq. (3) as shown in Eq. (4),

$$E(f) = S(f)E_d(f) \tag{4}$$

where $S(f) = (e^{-GR} - e^{-cR})e^{-BRf} + e^{-cR}$. It is simplified as $S(f) = Ke^{-BRf} + e^{-cR} = e^{-cR}(k'e^{-BRf} + 1)$, and $k' = K/e^{-cR}$. The water is divided into several layers with the thickness of $\Delta R$. Suppose that each layer between the sensor and objects scatters the same amount of light and light is scattered by every layer behind the layer, we can get the formula of scatter noise as

$$E_f(f) = E_d(f)\left(k'e^{-B\Delta Rf} + k'e^{-B2\Delta Rf} + \ldots + k'e^{-BRf}\right) = k\frac{1-e^{-bf}}{f}E_d(f) \quad (5)$$

where $k = k'/B$ and $b = BR$. $S(f)$ is re-expressed as

$$S(f) = 1 + k\frac{1-e^{-bf}}{f} \quad (6)$$

Finally, the relationship between the direct signal noise and the irradiance captured by the sensor is expressed as

$$E_d(f) = \frac{1}{1 + k\frac{1-e^{-bf}}{f}}E(f) \quad (7)$$

The model shown in Eq. (7) represents a high-pass filter in the frequency domain. One aspect to note is that the infinite value of the filter should be avoided in practice. The values of parameters $k$ and $b$ will affect the performance of the model. Figure 3 shows the shape of the model curve with different parameters $k$ and $b$. The value of $b$ weakly affects the value of model in low frequency, and the slope of the curve is mainly affected by parameters $k$. Therefore, we should choose $k$ and $b$, especially $k$ appropriately to remove the forward-scatter noise and obtain higher quality images.

## 3  Experimental Result and Discussion

In order to verify the effectiveness of the method, we established a range-gated imaging system named as Fengyan, which consists of a pulsed laser illuminator, a gated camera, and a TCU. The laser illuminator has a center wavelength of 532 nm, and its laser pulse width is about 1 ns. The typical operating frequency for the laser is 30 kHz, and its average power is about 0.5w. The gated camera has a gated GEN II intensifier, which is coupled to a CCD with 1360 × 1024 pixels and acts as a gate with a minimal gate time of 3 ns. The experiment under triangular RIPs is performed, where the laser pulse width and the gate time are both set as 3 ns.

We perform the experiment in a pool when the total attenuation coefficient is 0.4/m, as shown in Fig. 4. The object underwater is a standard pyramid target, of which the height and width increase by the step of 1 cm. The largest side length of the step is 12 cm. Before we begin the measurement, the background image is captured. We capture a sequence of gated images containing only the water scattering. After reducing the background, the mean values of each gated images and its numerical fitting curve are shown in Fig. 5(a), from which the backscatter noise of the medium can be obtained. A gated image located at the object is captured when the time delay is set as 25 ns, as shown in Fig. 5(b). The areas marked by red rectangle in the captured images

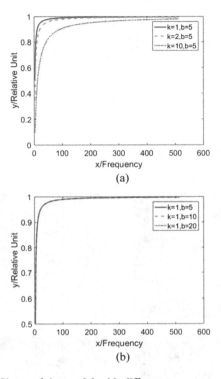

(a)

(b)

**Fig. 3.** Shape of the model with different parameters $k$ and $b$.

Standard pyramid target

Fengyan

**Fig. 4.** Experimental scene.

are enlarged to see the difference more clearly. Removing the backscatter noise darkens the edges to some extent, as shown in Fig. 5(c). To remove the forward-scatter noise and obtain the resultant image, 2D FFT, frequency shifting and inverse FFT are applied, which not only reduces the forward-scatter noise, but can also improve the

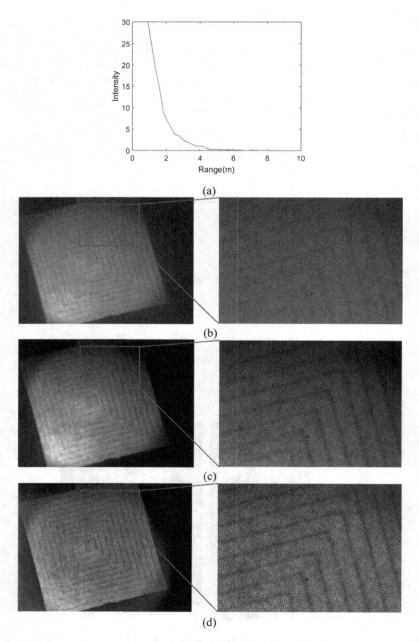

**Fig. 5.** Experimental results when the total attenuation coefficient is 0.4/m: (a) backscatter noise at different range; (b) the original image obtained using the traditional range-gated imaging; (c) the image after removing the backscatter noise using the proposed method; (d) the image after removing the forward-scatter noise using the proposed method.

image quality of edges, as shown in Fig. 5(d). The parameters $k$ and $b$ for the band-pass filter are set as 1 and 5, respectively. The contrast and resolution of the whole images are improved, which means that the proposed method can effectively achieve clearer and sharper image compared with traditional range-gated imaging. Besides, the median filtering, mean filtering and Gaussian filtering are also used here to remove the noise, as shown in Fig. 6. Obviously, the median filtering and mean filtering fail in improving the image contrast, while the Gaussian filtering destroys the image with uneven intensity distribution.

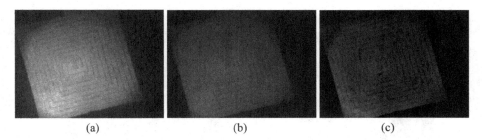

    (a)                          (b)                          (c)

**Fig. 6.** Processing results of Fig. 5(b) using: (a) median filtering; (b) mean filtering; (c) Gaussian filtering.

To better illustrate the difference, the image entropy of these images is shown in Table 1. $I_0$ represents the original image. $I_b$ represents the image after removing the backscatter noise using the proposed method. $I_f$ represents the image after removing the forward-scatter noise using the proposed method. $I_{mean}$, $I_{median}$ and $I_{Gaussian}$ represents the image processed by median filtering, mean filtering and Gaussian filtering, respectively. Median filtering and mean filtering reduce the image entropy. Even though Gaussian filtering improves the image entropy, it darkens parts of the image. Compared with traditional rage-gated image $I_0$, the entropy of image obtained using the proposed method ($I_f$) is improved by about 69%.

**Table 1.** Image entropy when the attenuation coefficient is 0.4/m.

|  | $I_0$ | $I_b$ | $I_f$ | $I_{mean}$ | $I_{median}$ | $I_{Gaussian}$ |
|---|---|---|---|---|---|---|
| Image entropy | 0.7402 | 0.9468 | 1.2510 | 0.6534 | 0.5361 | 1.3744 |

In order to further test the performance of the proposed method, we measure a standard pyramid target when the water quality gets worse with the attenuation coefficient of 0.7/m. The time delay is also set as 25 ns. The mean values of the captured gated images are shown in Fig. 7(a). A gated image is captured as shown in Fig. 7(b). Spiky noisy points are apparent on the image, which limit the contrast and resolution of image. Figure 7(c) and (d) show the image after reducing the backscatter and forward-scatter noise using the proposed method, respectively. Figure 8 shows the images processed by

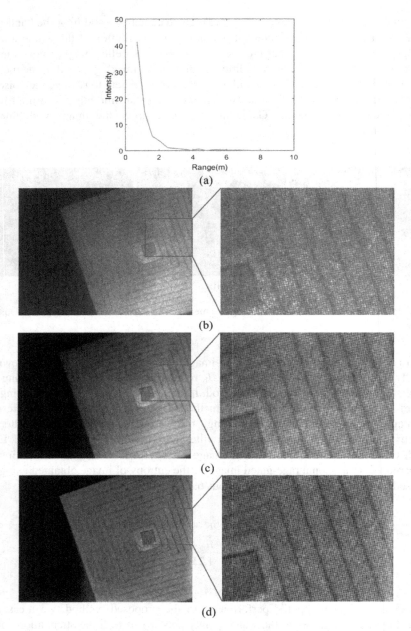

**Fig. 7.** Experimental results when the total attenuation coefficient is 0.7/m: (a) backscatter noise at different range; (b) the original image obtained using the traditional range-gated imaging; (c) the image after removing the backscatter noise using the proposed method; (d) the image after removing the forward-scatter noise using the proposed method.

the median filtering, mean filtering and Gaussian filtering, respectively. Obviously, the proposed method deals better with scatter noise compared with other methods. The image entropy is shown in Table 2. Compared with traditional range-gated imaging, the image entropy is improved about 71% using the proposed method. The image entropy also shows the superiority of the proposed method over other filtering methods.

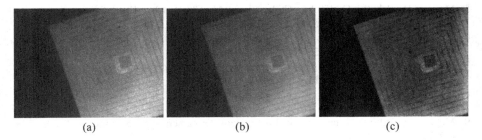

      (a)            (b)            (c)

**Fig. 8.** Processing results of Fig. 7(b) using: (a) median filtering; (b) mean filtering; (c) Gaussian filtering.

**Table 2.** Image entropy when the attenuation coefficient is 0.7/m.

|  | $I_0$ | $I_b$ | $I_f$ | $I_{mean}$ | $I_{median}$ | $I_{Gaussian}$ |
|---|---|---|---|---|---|---|
| Image entropy | 0.6517 | 0.8539 | 1.1181 | 0.5013 | 0.4917 | 1.3406 |

# 4 Conclusion

In this paper, we propose a method of underwater de-scattering range-gated imaging based on numerical fitting and frequency domain filtering. It is an extension of the Jaffe-McGlamery computer model and the light propagation property in water. The backscatter and the forward-scatter noise are removed from the gated images respectively. Experiments demonstrate that the proposed method outperforms the traditional range-intensity correlation range-gated algorithm quantitatively and visually. The research result is also valuable for underwater 3D imaging.

**Funding.** The authors acknowledge the financial funding of this work by the National Key Research and Development Program of China (Grant 2016YFC0302503), the National Natural Science Foundation of China (NSFC) (Grant 61875189), and the Youth Innovation Promotion Association CAS (No. 2017155), the Strategic Priority Program of the Chinese Academy of Sciences (No. XDC03060102).

# References

1. Weidemann, A., Fournier, G. R., Forand, L., Forand, L., Mathieu, P.: In harbor underwater threat detection/identification using active imaging. In: Proceedings of SPIE - The International Society for Optical Engineering, vol. 5780, p. 14 (2005)

2. Church, P., et al.: Overview of a hybrid underwater camera system. Proc. SPIE **9111**, 91110O (2014)
3. Christnacher, F., Laurenzis, M., Monnin, D., Schmitt, G., Metzger, N., Schertzer, S., Scholtz, T.: 3D laser gated viewing from a moving submarine platform. Proc. SPIE **9250**, 9250F (2014)
4. Wang, X., et al.: Underwater 3D triangular range-intensity correlation imaging beyond visibility range (invited). Infrared Laser Eng. **47**(9), 0903001 (2018)
5. Monnin, D., Schmitt, G., Fischer, C., Laurenzis, M., Christnacher, F.: Active-imaging-based underwater navigation. Proc. SPIE **9649**, 96490H (2015)
6. Liu, X., Wang, X., Zhou, Y., Liu, Y.: In situ planktons and fishes detection based on optical gated sampling. Appl. Opt. **55**(18), 4850–4855 (2016)
7. Mariani, P., et al.: Range-gated imaging system for underwater monitoring in ocean environment. Sustainability **11**, 162 (2019)
8. Laurenzis, M.: Investigation of range-gated imaging in scattering environments. Opt. Eng. **51**(6), 061303 (2012)
9. Mcglamery, B.L.: A computer model for underwater camera systems. Proc. SPIE **208**, 208 (1979)
10. Jaffe, J.S.: Computer modeling and the design of optimal underwater imaging systems. IEEE J. Ocean. Eng. **15**(2), 101–111 (1990)
11. Hou, W., Gray, D.J., Weidemann, A.D., Arnone, R.A.: Comparison and validation of point spread models for imaging in natural waters. Opt. Express **16**(13), 9958–9965 (2008)
12. Lu, H., Li, Y., Uemura, T., Kim, H., Serikawa, S.: Low illumination underwater light field images reconstruction using deep convolutional neural networks. Future Gener. Comput. Syst. **82**, 142–148 (2018)

# Threshold-Dependent Joint Bilateral Filter Algorithm for Enhancing 3D Gated Range-Intensity Correlation Imaging

Yuqing Yang[1,2], Xinwei Wang[1,2,3(✉)], Liang Sun[1], Jianan Chen[1], Han Dong[1], Minmin Wang[1,2], Shaomeng Wang[1,2], and Yan Zhou[1,2,3]

[1] Optoelectronic System Laboratory, Institute of Semiconductors, CAS, Beijing 100083, China
wangxinwei@semi.ac.cn
[2] College of Materials Science and Opto-Electronics Technology, University of Chinese Academy of Sciences, Beijing, China
[3] School of Electronic, Electrical and Communication Engineering, University of Chinese Academy of Sciences, Beijing, China

**Abstract.** Three-dimensional gated range-intensity correlation imaging (GRICI) can acquire three-dimensional information of targets with high range resolution in real time. In practical applications, the intensity distribution of laser illumination, light propagation property and target optical reflectivity lead to data holes for 3D images. In this paper, we proposed an improved threshold-dependent joint bilateral filter (TJBF) algorithm based on the characteristics of 3D GRICI to fill data holes and reduce noise. In our method, the composite intensity image obtained by adding two overlapped gate images is used as the gray-domain guidance image for the joint bilateral filter of 3D images. The threshold of 3D reconstruction is used to determine the pixels to be filled and the calculation weight to ensure the accuracy of filling holes and denoising. Experiments show that the holes of 3D images are effectively filled, the whole 3D image is smooth and target edges are clear, and the range resolution is improved after repaired. The research is beneficial for enhancing 3D GRICI in applications of underwater imaging and 3D measurement.

**Keywords:** Three-dimensional imaging ·
Gated range-intensity correlation imaging · Joint bilateral filtering · Filling holes

## 1 Introduction

Three dimensional range-gated imaging (3DRGI) [1–4] not only has the characteristics of high spatial resolution and long detection range, but also can acquire target three-dimensional information with large depth of field and high range resolution in real time. At present, 3DRGI mainly include time slicing method [5], and gated range-intensity correlation imaging (GRICI) (also known as super-resolution three-dimensional laser imaging) [1, 3]. Compared with the time slicing method, the GRICI only needs to modify the delay to obtain two gated images under different delays, and use the relationship between range and intensity to calculate the range information of targets.

© Springer Nature Switzerland AG 2019
H. Yu et al. (Eds.): ICIRA 2019, LNAI 11741, pp. 205–214, 2019.
https://doi.org/10.1007/978-3-030-27532-7_18

GRICI has low complexity, low data volume (minimum two images), and higher range resolution under the same parameters. Therefore, it becomes the main technique for real-time 3DRGI.

In practical applications, due to the intensity distribution of laser illumination, light propagation property and target optical reflectivity, 3D images acquired by GRICI may have holes and noise disturbance. These will result in loss of targets, and low range resolution, and thereby affect target detection and recognition. Therefore, it is an urgent problem to fill the holes and remove noise from 3D images

In order to repair the holes and suppress noise of depth images, many researchers have made important contributions. Ming Zhang et al. used a layered bilateral filter to repair 3D images [6]. Park et al. repaired 3D images by adding edge information and weights to the non-local mean filtering [7]. Matyunin et al. used inter-frame motion compensation and median filtering to fill holes in 3D images [8]. Liu improved Telea's fast marching method [9, 10], using color images as guiding information for hole filling. Camplani uses the adaptively weighted joint bilateral filter alternate iterative to repair 3D images [11]. At present, these algorithms for repairing 3D images are mainly aimed at binocular stereo vision, structured light three-dimensional imaging, time-flight three-dimensional imaging, etc., and are not fully applicable to 3D images acquired by 3D GRICI.

In this paper, a threshold-dependent joint bilateral filter(TJBF) algorithm is proposed based on the characteristics of 3D GRICI to fill the holes and suppress noise of 3D images. The schematic diagram of the algorithm is shown in Fig. 1. Firstly, the original 3D image is generated based on the original two-dimensional slice images A and B via 3D GRICI. Then the original image A and B are added to obtain a composite image. Finally, the holes and noise in the original 3D image are repaired according to the composite image using the TJBF algorithm.

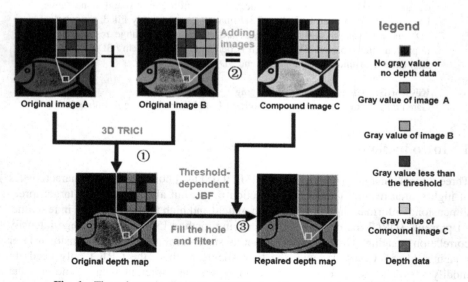

**Fig. 1.** The schematic diagram of TJBF algorithm to repair the 3D image

The remainder of this paper is organized as follows. In Sect. 2, we describe the related theories and proposed method in detail. Section 3 shows the experiments of the proposed method, and Sect. 4 is the conclusion of this paper.

## 2  Theory and Method

### 2.1  Principle of 3D GRICI

At present, two kinds of 3D GRICI are developed, including 3D trapezoidal GRICI [1] and triangular GRICI [3]. The former has a trapezoidal range-intensity profiles (RIPs) of gate images, and the latter has a triangular RIPs of gate images. Taking the triangular algorithm as an example, A schematic diagram of triangular GRICI is shown in Fig. 2(a). In the algorithm, the gate width is equal to the laser pulse width. Under the convolution, the RIPs of the space sampling region of interest are triangles. The rising edge of the triangular envelope is called as the head signal area, and the falling edge is called as the tail signal area. As shown in Fig. 2(a), the tail signal of the gate image A overlaps with the header signal of the gate image B, and the distance information r of the target can be obtained by establishing the intensity relationship between the gate image A and the gate image B.

For triangle 3D GRICI, the target range can be denoted as

$$r = \frac{\tau_A c}{2n} + \frac{I_{head,B}}{I_{head,B} + I_{tail,A}} \frac{t_L c}{2n} \tag{1}$$

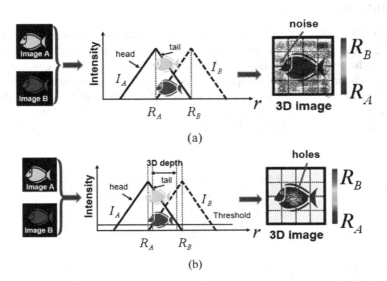

(a)

(b)

**Fig. 2.** Triangular range-intensity correlation algorithm: (a) without threshold set and noise in the 3D image, (b) with threshold set to remove noise and there are holes in the 3D image

where $r$ is the target range, $\tau_A$ is the time delay between the laser pulse and the gate pulse in the gate image, $c$ is the light speed in vacuum, $t_L$ is the laser pulse width which equals the gate time, $I_{tail,A}$ is the gray value of the gate image A with a time delay of $\tau_A$, $I_{head,B}$ is the gray value the gate image B with a time delay of $(\tau_A + t_L)$. $n$ is the refractive index of the medium. The depth of field of 3D imaging is

$$D = \frac{t_L c}{2n} \tag{2}$$

Equation (2) shows that the laser pulse width determines the depth of field of the triangle 3D GRICI.

In the practical application, due to the influence of background light and scattering medium and the noise of the imaging system itself, there will be noise interference in the gate images in Fig. 2(a). As shown in Fig. 2(b), in order to remove the noise interference, a threshold equivalent to the noise intensity is set in the triangle 3D GRICI, and the pixel whose gray value is lower than the threshold does not participate in the three-dimensional reconstruction. From the Fig. 2(b) we can see that the part of the tail signal of gate image A and the head signal of gate image B that is below the threshold does not participate in the three-dimensional reconstruction, which will result in the lack of depth data near $R_A$ and $R_B$, thus resulting in data holes in the 3D image. The lack of depth data will result in the loss of the corresponding depth of field. Since the noise is unavoidable in practical applications, the threshold must be set to suppress the noise disturbance to 3D images. When the target signal is equivalent to the noise, the threshold may cause holes in 3D images. Therefore, it is necessary for removing noise and filling holes in 3D GRICI.

## 2.2    TJBF for 3D GRICI

The bilateral filter (BF) algorithm was originally proposed by Tomasi and Manduchi in 1998 [12], which is a nonlinear filtering algorithm where the output value is a weighted average of the input values, and the weight of each input value is combined. The weight of each input value is a compromise between the spatial proximity of the image and the similarity of the pixel values. The algorithm considers the spatial distance information and color similarity between the pixels, which achieves the purpose of edge preservation and denoising. The formula for the bilateral filter algorithm is as follows:

$$I'(x,y) = \frac{1}{w_p} \sum_{i,j \in \Omega} w(i,j) \cdot I(i,j) \tag{3}$$

$$w_p = \sum_{i,j \in \Omega} w(i,j) \tag{4}$$

Where $I'(x,y)$ is the filtered output value, $\Omega$ is the domain range of the pixel point $(x,y)$, $w(i,j)$ is the weight coefficient at the point $(i,j)$ which consisted of the image spatial domain weight and the gray domain weights, $w_p$ is the normalization parameter, and $I(i,j)$ is the depth data value in the neighborhood.

Since the weights of the spatial domain and gray domain of the BF are all from the same image, the filling effect on the 3D image is not obvious. Petschnigg et al. proposed a joint bilateral filter (JBF) in 2004 [13], which improves the bilateral filter by taking the gray domain weights from another guide image. When another image is a high quality reference image, JBF can be used to fill the holes. Our algorithm is based on the JBF, and combined with the unique properties of 3D GRICI.

The JBF algorithm must have a high quality boot image. Unlike other three-dimensional imaging methods, the 3D GRICI cannot obtain high-quality color images, and can not fill the holes of 3D image according to the color similarity in color images. Since the 3D image acquired by 3D GRICI according to the gated adjacent two-dimensional slice images, the high-quality guide image can only be generated from the original slice images.

The proposed algorithm proposes a composite image C = A + B formed by adding two original gated image A and B as the guidance image of the JBF, as shown in Fig. 3. The RIPs of C is trapezoid, which is equivalent to the convolution result when the gate width is twice the laser pulse width. The grayscale value of the C is enhanced, and the target information is more complete, so it can be used as a guide image of the JBF to fill holes of the original 3D image.

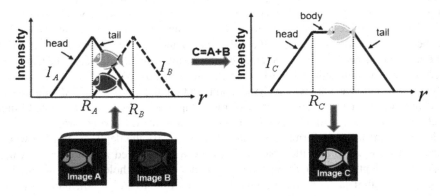

**Fig. 3.** Composite image C by adding gated image A and B

Since range-gated imaging only focus on target in a certain distance slice, the target may occupy only a portion of the entire image and the other portion has no depth data. Since the threshold is set in the 3D inversion so that the holes appearing at the target also have no depth data, it is the key to determine whether the pixels with no depth data need to fill. To this end, we propose a TJBF algorithm, which uses the three-dimensional inversion threshold constraint JBF to make it suitable for inpainting 3D image acquired by 3D GRICI. The algorithm can be expressed by the following formula:

$$D'(x,y) = \frac{w_{A,B}(x,y)}{w_p} \sum_{i,j \in \Omega} w_s(i,j) \cdot w_r(i,j) \cdot w_C(i,j) \cdot D(i,j) \tag{5}$$

$$w_p = \sum_{i,j \in \Omega} w_s(i,j) \cdot w_r(i,j) \cdot w_C(i,j) \tag{6}$$

$$w_s(i,j) = \exp(-\frac{(i-x)^2 + (j-y)^2}{2\sigma_s^2}) \tag{7}$$

$$w_r(i,j) = \exp(-\frac{(I_C(i,j) - I_C(x,y))^2}{2\sigma_r^2}) \tag{8}$$

$$w_{A,B}(x,y) = \begin{cases} 0, I_A(x,y) < Th \ \&\ \& \ I_B(x,y) < Th \\ 1, I_A(x,y) \geq Th \ || \ I_B(x,y) \geq Th \end{cases} \tag{9}$$

$$w_C(i,j) = \begin{cases} 0, I_C(i,j) < 1 \\ 1, I_C(i,j) \geq 1 \end{cases} \tag{10}$$

In Eqs. (5)–(10), $D'(x,y)$ is the filtered output depth value, $D(i,j)$ is the depth data in the neighborhood, $I_A$, $I_B$ and $I_C$ represent the gray value of original gate image A, B and composite image C, respectively. Th represents the threshold value when generating the 3D image in three-dimensional inversion. $w_{A,B}$ and $w_C$ respectively indicate whether the adjustment pixel needs to fill the depth data and whether the weight coefficient at the pixel point needs to be calculated, $\sigma_s$ and $\sigma_r$ are standard deviation of Gaussian function, other parameters are consistent with those in Eqs. (3)–(4).

From Eq. (5), we add two weights compared to the traditional JBF algorithm. These two weights can just answer the two most important questions in the hole filling-which holes need to be filled and what kind of data is filled to be accurate?

It can be known from formula (9) that when $w_{A,B} = 0$, the depth data of the whole filtered output is zero, and the hole does not need to be filled at point $(x,y)$; when $w_{A,B} = 1$, the depth data output after filtering is not zero, the hole need to be filled or the original depth data is filtered at point $(x,y)$. According to the judgment condition of $w_{A,B}$, when the gray values of the original images A and B are simultaneously smaller than the threshold, point $(x,y)$ is a hole in the 3D image, and the intensity information at the point is considered to be caused by noise, so there is no need to fill the hole. When one of the original images A or B has a gray value greater than the threshold and the other is less than the threshold, point $(x,y)$ is still a hole in the 3D image. But at this time, point $(x,y)$ can be considered to have the target information, and the hole need to be filled. When the gray values of both of the original images A and B are greater than the threshold, point $(x,y)$ is not a hole in the 3D image, so the depth data at the point is filtered.

It can be seen from Eq. (10) that when $w_C = 0$, the total weight at point $(i,j)$ is 0, and the weight is not included at this point; when $w_C = 1$, the total weight at point $(i,j)$ is the weight of the original JBF, which is included in the weighted average. According to the judgment condition of $w_C$, when there is no pixel value in the C, it means that there is no target at the point, so the point does not participate in the calculation of the weight; on the contrary, the weight of the point is taken into account.

From the above analysis, the role of the weight $w_{A,B}$ ensures that the filling will not be excessively filled and not filled properly, the effect of the weight $w_C$ ensures the accuracy of the filling data, and reducing the use of unusable data leads to inaccuracies in the filling of depth data. Therefore, compared with the traditional JBF, the improved TJBF algorithm combined with the characteristics of 3D GRICI is more accurate and effective for filling and filtering the 3D image.

## 3   Experiments and Results

For experimental research, an underwater GRICI system named as Fengyan is established. A 532 nm laser is used as the illuminator, and its full width at half-maximum (FWHM) is 1 ns at a pulse repetition frequency of 30 kHz. For the gated camera, a gated GEN III intensifier is coupled to a CCD with $1360 \times 1024$ pixels. The image lens has a focal length of 240 mm. The TCU realized by the field-programmable gate array (FPGA) can provide the desired time sequence for the pulsed laser and the gated camera.

The experiment scene is shown in Fig. 4. The Fengyan is under water, and the Pyramid target is at a distance of 3 m from Fengyan. By using multi-pulse time delay integration method [14], the pulse width of the laser can be set to 3 ns, the pulse repetition frequency is 30 kHz, the gate width is also 3 ns. The frame rate of the CCD is 10 frames per second. Adjust the spot size, image intensifier gain, and CCD receive lens field of view size, and set the system delay to 25 ns and 28 ns according to the distance between the target and the system, respectively. Obtain the adjacent gate images A and B of the target as Fig. 5(a) and (b).

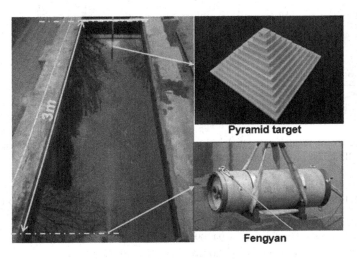

**Pyramid target**

**Fengyan**

**Fig. 4.** Experiment scene and target

After obtaining the original images, offline processing was performed using MATLAB software. Firstly, according to the method in Fig. 1, the gated image A and B are used to generate a original depth image using the 3D GRICI algorithm via set the threshold to 25 as shown in Fig. 5(d). Then, the gated image A and B are added to obtain a composite image C as shown in Fig. 5(c). Finally, the holes and noise in the original depth image are repaired according to the composite image using the threshold-independent joint bilateral filtering algorithm. The repaired image is shown in Fig. 5(e).

As can be seen from Fig. 5(c), the gradation value is significantly enhanced and the target information is more complete with respect to the gate images A and B. It can be seen from Fig. 5(d) that there are a lot of holes and noise in the original 3D image. After filling the holes and denoising, the repaired 3D image shows that the target is complete, the 3D image is smooth, the edge is clear, and the image quality is greatly improved. In order to quantify the effects before and after the 3D image inpainting, the depth data amount, range resolution and distance signal to noise ratio (DSNR) before and after the depth image inpainting are calculated separately as shown in Table 1.

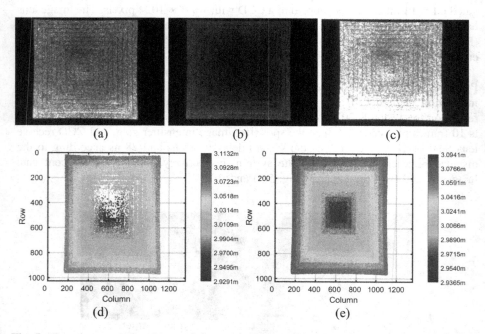

**Fig. 5.** Experiment results: (a) gated image A, (b) gated image B, (c) composite image C, (d) original 3D image, (e) repaired 3D image.

**Table 1.** Depth data amount, range resolution and distance signal to noise ratio (DSNR).

| Comparison project | Original 3D image | Repaired 3D image |
|---|---|---|
| Depth data amount | 943096 | 1068992 |
| Range resolution (m) | 0.0074 | 0.0042 |
| DSNR (dB) | 27.0880 | 33.7048 |

As can be seen from Table 1, compared with the original depth image, the lost data was retrieved, and a total of 125,896 depth data were filled; the range resolution was increased by 3.2 cm, and the DSNR was increased by 6.7 dB. The above experimental results show that the proposed method can accurately and effectively repair the hole and noise of depth images acquired by 3D GRICI.

## 4 Conclusion

In this paper, we proposed an improved threshold-dependent joint bilateral filter (TJBF) algorithm which based on the characteristics of 3D GRICI to fill the hole and denoising. In our method, the composite image obtained by adding the adjacent two gate images is used to the gray domain guidance image of the joint bilateral filter. The threshold of the 3D image is used to determine whether a pixel is a hole to be filled and whether it participates in the weight calculation, thereby the accuracy of filling holes and denoising can be effectively ensuring. Experiments show that the holes of 3D image are effectively filled, the whole 3D image is smooth and the edge is clear, and the range resolution is greatly improved after repaired.

**Acknowledgements.** The authors acknowledge the financial funding of this work by the National Natural Science Foundation of China (NSFC) (Grant 61875189),, the National Key Research and Development Program of China (Grant 2016YFC0500103 and 2016YFC0302503), the Strategic Priority Program of the Chinese Academy of Sciences (No. XDC03060102), and the Youth Innovation Promotion Association CAS (No. 2017155).

## References

1. Laurenzis, M., Christnacher, F., Monnin, D.: Long-range three-dimensional active imaging with superresolution depth mapping. Opt. Lett. **32**(21), 3146–3148 (2007)
2. Christnacher, F., et al.: 3D laser gated viewing from a moving submarine platform. In: Proceedings SPIE, vol. 9250, p. 9250F (2014)
3. Xinwei, W., Youfu, L., Yan, Z.: Triangular-range-intensity profile spatial-correlation method for 3D super-resolution range-gated imaging. Appl. Opt. **52**(30), 7399–7406 (2013)
4. Xinwei, W., et al.: Underwater 3D triangular range-intensity correlation imaging beyond visibility range (invited). Infrared Laser Eng. **47**(9), 0903001 (2018)
5. Busck, J., Heiselberg, H.: Gated viewing and high-accuracy three-dimensional laser radar. Appl. Opt. **43**(24), 4705–4710 (2004)
6. Yang, Q.Q., Wang, L.H., Li, D.X., et al.: Hierarchical joint bilateral filtering for depth postprocessing. In: IEEE International Conference on Image and Graphics, pp. 129–134 (2011)
7. Park, J., Kim, I.I., Tai, Y.W., et al.: High quality depth map upsampling for 3D-TOF cameras. In: IEEE International Conference on Computer Vision, pp. 1623–1630 (2011)
8. Matyunin, S., Vatolin, D., Berdnikov, Y., et al.: Temporal filtering for depth maps generated by Kinect depth camera. in: 3DTV Conference, pp. 1–4 (2011)
9. Liu, J., Gong, X., Liu, J.: Gded inpainting and filtering for Kinect depth maps. In: IEEE International Conference on Pattern Recognition, pp. 2055–2058 (2012)
10. Telea, A.: An image inpainting technique based on the fast marching method. J. Graph. Tools **9**(1), 23–34 (2004)

11. Camplani, M., Mantecon, T., Salgado, L.: Accurate depth-color scene modeling for 3D contents generation with low cost depth cameras. In: IEEE International Conference on Image Processing, pp. 1741–1744 (2012)
12. Tomasi, C., Manduchi, R.: Bilateral filtering for gray and color images. In: IEEE International Conference on Computer Vision, pp. 839–846 (1998)
13. Petschnigg, G., Szeliski, R., Agrawala, M., et al.: Digital photography with flash and no-flash image pairs. ACM Trans. Graph. 23, 661–672 (2001)
14. Xinwei, W., Youfu, L., Yan, Z.: Multi-pulse time delay integration method for flexible 3D super-resolution range-gated imaging. Opt. Express 23(6), 7820–7831 (2015)

# A Launch and Recovery System for Unmanned Surface Vehicle Based on Floating Bracket

Junjie Chen, Yang Yang, Xingang Jiang, Xiaolong He,
Shaorong Xie, Yan Peng, and Dong Qu[✉]

Shanghai University, Shanghai 200444, China
dongqu@shu.edu.cn

**Abstract.** In recent years, many countries have increasingly invested in the marine industry, thus greatly improving the level of ship automation. As the new favorite in the field of reconnaissance, survey and rescue, unmanned surface vehicle (USV) has been widely used. Generally, the USV is carried out by mother ship when performing tasks, which poses great challenges to the launch and recovery of USV in a harsh marine environment. To resolve these problems, this study develops a floating bracket type launch and recovery system (L&RS). When the USV is far away from the floating bracket, it is homing by GPS navigation. As the distance is close, the floating bracket can regulate the direction by the real-time visual information and then the USV travels into floating bracket. This method can improve the accuracy and stability of the USV in the process of entering the floating bracket, which improves the success ration of recovery operation.

**Keywords:** Unmanned surface vehicle (USV) ·
Launch and recovery system (L&RS) · Floating bracket · Visual

## 1 Introduction

In recent years, the USV has been developed from the upgrade of the traditional manned boats. It has various functions such as information collection, maritime rescue, bottom survey, target tracking, real-time monitoring. It can be used to implement path planning and information collection according to different mission arrangements. Due to many advantages of USV, many countries have begun to conduct in-depth research and functional development of USV. Through the design and analysis of the hull shape, Brizzolara develops a catamaran that can keep running smoothly and perform tasks in the case of medium waves [1]. To protect and monitor ports in real time, the United States has developed a threat interception system for using on USV [2]. In addition, many USVs have also been successfully applied to the fields of marine engineering, such as the Charlie [3], the 'JingHai-I', the kayak SCOUT and others [4–7].

The launch and recovery is a key technology for the application of the marine robot, such as USV, AUV, etc. Sarda and Dhanak designed a device for USV to deploy and recycle AUV. They put two winches on the USV and a set of docking devices at the end of the winch rope, to recover AUV by retracting the docking device [8]. Palomeras and Vallicrosa designed a funnel-type AUV recovery unit by using visual

© Springer Nature Switzerland AG 2019
H. Yu et al. (Eds.): ICIRA 2019, LNAI 11741, pp. 215–223, 2019.
https://doi.org/10.1007/978-3-030-27532-7_19

technology. AUV recognizes the position of the entrance signal light to accurately entry into the funnel [9]. For the recovering of USV, Harbin Engineering University has proposed a slide-type launch and recovery device. Moreover, they studied the impact of the waves on the device. By the proposed wave compensation technique, it can reduce the impact of sea conditions effectively and complete the recovery of USV [10].

Within the process of launching and recovering, the challenge is to dock the USV into the floating bracket. Due to the influence of the waves, the violent relative motion between the USV and the floating bracket occurred, and thus the USV is difficult to enter the floating bracket. Cowen has proposed an optical docking method of achieving high-precision docking between underwater vehicles and underwater nodes, to enable the underwater charging and data transmission [11]. Park has proposed an under-actuated AUV underwater docking method to guide AUV docking by switching two controllers [12]. In addition to the docking systems in the marine engineering, there are also some docking systems of space robot are useful for reference [13–15].

In order to solve the problem of USV deployment at sea, this paper proposes to recycle USV by floating bracket. The article mainly consists of the following parts. The second section mainly introduces the principle and operation process of the L&RS. The recovery strategy and kinematic model of floating bracket are introduced in the third section. The fourth section describes the field experiments and verify the feasibility of the system. Finally, this paper is summarized and the future work is prospected.

## 2    Launching and Recovery System

To solve the problem of launch and recovery for the USV, this study develops an automatic launch and recovery system based on the floating bracket.

### 2.1    Concept and Mechanism

As shown in Fig. 1, the target USV is made of PE material and has a length of 2.6 m, a width of 1.4 m and a height of 0.5 m. It has various characteristics, such as light weight, corrosion resistance and maneuverability. Moreover, the USV adopts modular design and is equipped with communication antenna, laser, inertial navigation combination instrument, camera and other sensors, which is suitable for mapping and surveying in the sea, ponds and rivers.

**Fig. 1.** USV.

The L&RS consists a bracket mechanism and a propulsion system.

(1) **Bracket mechanism:** the overall structure of the launch and recovery system is shown in Fig. 2. The floating bracket is constructed with stainless steel profiles. The floating bracket is slightly larger than the USV shape, and two buoyancy tanks are fixed at the bottom of the float bracket. A guiding design is installed at the entrance of the floating bracket to increase the catering area between floating bracket and USV.

(2) **Propulsion system:** there are four underwater thrusters around the bracket. The two thrusters are respectively mounted on two sides of the floating bracket, and the two thrusters are mounted on the front of the bracket. When the USV approached to the floating bracket, the propulsion device works to provide thrust for the floating bracket to move and rotate.

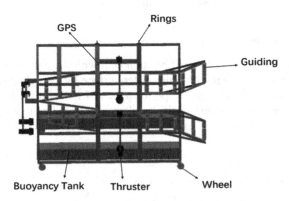

**Fig. 2.** Floating bracket.

## 2.2 Control System

Figure 3 shows the control system of the launch and recover system, which includes the floating bracket control system and the USV control system. The floating bracket control system is mainly including an Industrial Personal Computer for analyzing various sensor data and a stm32 for driving the motor. The USV receives the positioning information of the floating bracket to start the path planning for homing. After receiving the GPS information of the USV, the floating bracket begins to regulate its orientation to face the USV.

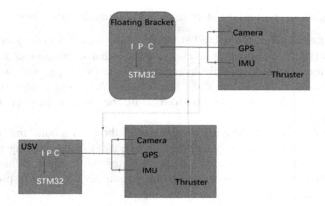

**Fig. 3.** Control system.

## 2.3   Operation Process

After the USV arrives at the designated mission area with the mother ship, the floating bracket and the USV are lowered onto the water surface by a single point boom. Then the USV reverses the floating bracket to perform the tasks. As shown in Fig. 4, after the mission is completed, the USV automatically plans a straight line to home according to the longitude and latitude of itself and the floating bracket.

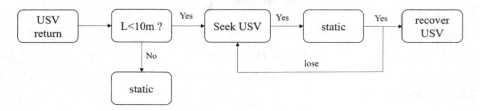

**Fig. 4.** Recovery process.

After the USV closes to the floating bracket, the recovery process is as follows.

1   When the USV is ready to return, the floating bracket adjusts its own guiding direction align with the path line.
2   Due to the influence of the waves, the floating bracket needs to keep the position and posture stable.
3   When the USV arrives about ten meters away from the front of the floating bracket, it activates the camera and begins to select the information for the floating bracket, and then keeping its direction aligned with the float bracket in real time.
4   The floating bracket keeps the guiding direction to the direction of the USV.
5   The USV drives into the floating bracket and the recovery operation is completed (Fig. 5).

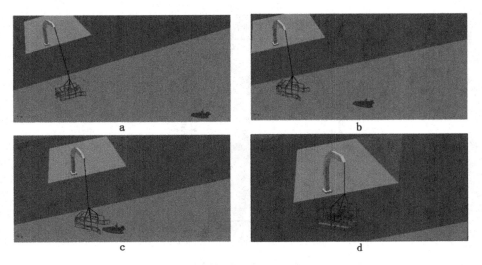

**Fig. 5.** Recovery process.

## 3  Recovery Strategy

In the high-seas, the mother ship will shake violently under the action of the waves, which is not conducive to the launch and recovery of the USV. To improve the safety and high efficiency of the USV recovering operation, this paper proposes a real-time adjustment strategy to ensure that USV can be successfully driven into the floating bracket.

### 3.1  Kinematics of the Floating Bracket

The floating bracket regulates its guiding direction towards the route line according to the straight route planned by the USV. Because the floating bracket is also affected by the waves and wind, it is also necessary to perform real-time direction regulation to improve the success rate of recovering operation.

As shown in Fig. 6, $\theta$ represents the angle at which the platform rotates, $M$ represents the horizontal actual distance between the thruster 1 and the thruster 4 to the center of mass; $R$ represents the distance from thruster 2 and thruster 3 to the center of mass; $\beta$ represents the angle between the center of mass and the thruster connection and the $Y$-axis. From the actual speed of the thruster, the speed in the $X$-axis direction can be obtained.

$$
\begin{bmatrix} v_{1x} \\ v_{2x} \\ v_{3x} \\ v_{4x} \end{bmatrix} = \dot{X} \begin{bmatrix} 1 \\ 1 \\ 1 \\ -1 \end{bmatrix} - \dot{\theta} R \cos \beta \begin{bmatrix} 0 \\ -1 \\ -1 \\ 0 \end{bmatrix} \tag{1}
$$

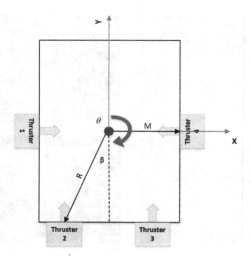

**Fig. 6.** Motion model.

Similarly, the speed in the $Y$-axis direction can be obtained.

$$
\begin{bmatrix} v_{1y} \\ v_{2y} \\ v_{3y} \\ v_{4y} \end{bmatrix} = \dot{Y} \begin{bmatrix} 1 \\ 1 \\ 1 \\ 1 \end{bmatrix} + \dot{\theta} \begin{bmatrix} M \\ R\sin\beta \\ -R\sin\beta \\ -M \end{bmatrix}
\tag{2}
$$

According to (1) and (2), (3) can be obtained.

$$
\begin{bmatrix} \dot{X} \\ \dot{Y} \\ \dot{\theta} \end{bmatrix} = \begin{bmatrix} \frac{1}{2} & 0 & 0 & -\frac{1}{2} \\ 0 & \frac{1}{2} & \frac{1}{2} & 0 \\ 0 & \frac{1}{2R\sin\beta} & -\frac{1}{2R\sin\beta} & 0 \end{bmatrix} \begin{bmatrix} v_{1x} \\ v_{2y} \\ v_{3y} \\ v_{4x} \end{bmatrix}
\tag{3}
$$

where $v_1$, $v_2$, $v_3$, $v_4$ represent the speeds of the four thrusters; $X$ and $Y$ represent the distance that the floating bracket moves in the $X$-axis and $Y$-axis direction.

From the kinematic analysis, the relationship between the translational and rotational motion of the floating bracket and the four thrusters can be obtained.

## 3.2   Docking Strategy

In the recovering operation, the sailing direction of the USV is $V1$; the guiding direction of the floating bracket is $V2$; the distance between the USV and the floating bracket is $L$; the heading angle of USV is $\eta$. Due to the influence of the sea surface waves, the sailing direction of the USV changes to $V1'$, the deflection angle is $\beta$; the guiding direction of the floating bracket changes to $V2'$, the deflection angle is $\alpha$.

To stably enter the floating bracket, the traveling distance and rotational angle can be regulated as (4) and (5) respectively (Fig. 7).

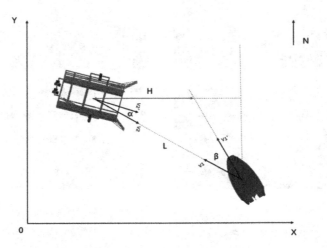

**Fig. 7.** Docking adjustment strategy.

$$H = L \cdot (\sin \eta - \cos \eta \tan(\eta - \beta)) \qquad (4)$$

$$\theta = \beta + \alpha \qquad (5)$$

## 4   Experiments and Discussion

The experiment was performed in a circular pool about 30 m in diameter and 10 m deep. There is a large crane near the pool that can imitate the process of launch and recovery the USV from the mother ship.

At the beginning of the experiment, the USV planned a track point through the longitude and latitude points of USV and floating bracket, then slowly approached to the floating bracket at a speed of 0.3 m/s. To increase the success rate, the USV had been designed two navigation methods: path planning and visual navigation. When the USV was far away from the floating bracket, the floating bracket transmitted the GPS position information to the USV by the antenna for path planning. After traveling to the distanced floating bracket for 10 m, USV would send its own position signal to the floating bracket and enter the search mode. The camera installed on the USV faced to the floating bracket. When the vision system searched for the floating bracket, the heading was adjusted so that the floating bracket was always at the center of the screen, then the USV could travel toward the floating bracket. Screenshot of launch and recovery process as show in Fig. 8.

**Fig. 8.** Experiments in the pool.

## 5 Conclusion

This paper developed a launch and recovery system composed of bracket mechanism and propulsion system. The bracket mechanism was used for lifting the USV, and the propulsion system was used for controlling the position and posture of the floating bracket to ensure that the USV could enter the floating bracket smoothly. During the process of launch and recovery, the posture of the floating bracket was adjusted in real time through an adaptive docking strategy. From the poor experiments, the validity of the system and the accuracy of the docking strategy were verified. The floating bracket would be used as a platform for offshore refueling and information transmission.

**Acknowledgment.** This study was supported by National Natural Science Foundation of China (Grant No. 61773254), Shanghai Sailing Program (Grant No. 17YF1406200), Shanghai Young Eastern Scholar Program (Grant No. QD2016029), and Shanghai civil-military integration program (Grant No. JMRH-2018-1043).

# References

1. Brizzolara, S., Curtin, T., Bovio, M.: Concept design and hydrodynamic optimization of an innovative SWATH USV by CFD methods. Ocean Dyn. **62**(2), 227–237 (2012)
2. Simetti, E., Turetta, A., Casalino, G.: Towards the use of a team of USVs for civilian harbour protection: the problem of intercepting detected menaces, Oceans. IEEE (2010)
3. Caccia, M., Bono, R., Bruzzone, G.: Sampling sea surfaces with SESAMO: an autonomous craft for the study of sea-air interactions. IEEE Robot. Autom. Mag. **12**(3), 95–105 (2005)
4. Yang, W.R., Chen, C.Y., Hsu, C.M.: Multifunctional inshore survey platform with unmanned surface vehicles. Int. J. Autom. Smart Technol. **01**(2), 19–25 (2011)
5. Peng, Y., Yang, Y., Cui, J.: Development of the USV 'JingHai-I' and sea trials in the Southern Yellow Sea. Ocean Eng. **131**, 186–196 (2017)
6. Bertaska, I.R., Shah, B., Von Ellenrieder, K.: Experimental evaluation of automatically-generated behaviors for USV operations. Ocean Eng. **106**, 496–514 (2015)
7. Curcio, J., Leonard, J., Patrikalakis, A.: SCOUT - a low cost autonomous surface platform for research in cooperative autonomy, Oceans. IEEE (2006)
8. Sarda, E.I., Dhanak, M.R.: A USV-based automated launch and recovery system for AUVs. IEEE J. Oceanic Eng. **42**(1), 37–55 (2017)
9. Palomeras, N., Vallicrosa, G., Mallios, A.: AUV homing and docking for remote operations. Ocean Eng. **154**, 106–120 (2018)
10. Zheping, Y., Haitao, S., Honghan, Z.: On wave compensation control technology of stinger-principle-based launch and recovery device for UUV. In: Control Conference. IEEE (2012)
11. Cowen, S., Briest, S., Dombrowski, J.: Underwater docking of autonomous undersea vehicles using optical terminal guidance. In: MTS/IEEE Conference Proceedings, Oceans 1997, pp. 1143–1147. IEEE (1997)
12. Park, J.Y., Jun, B.H., Lee, P.M.: Underwater docking approach of an under-actuated AUV in the presence of constant ocean current. IFAC Proc. Vol. **43**(20), 5–10 (2010)
13. Pavlich, J., Tchoryk, P., Ritter, G.: Autonomous satellite docking system (2001)
14. Feng, F., Tang, L.N., Xu, J.F.: A review of the end-effector of large space manipulator with capabilities of misalignment tolerance and soft capture. Sci. China Technol. Sci. **59**(11), 1621–1638 (2016)
15. Romano, M., Friedman, D.A., Shay, T.J.: Laboratory experimentation of autonomous spacecraft approach and docking to a collaborative target. J. Spacecraft Rockets **44**(1), 164–173 (2007)

# Piezoelectric Actuators and Micro-Nano Manipulations

# Finite Element Analyses of Working Principle of the Ultrasonic Needle-Droplet-Substrate System for Multiple-Function Manipulation

Xiaomin Qi[1,2], Qiang Tang[3], Pengzhan Liu[1], and Junhui Hu[1(✉)]

[1] State Key Laboratory of Mechanics and Control of Mechanical Structures,
Nanjing University of Aeronautics and Astronautics, Nanjing 210016, China
ejhhu@nuaa.edu.cn
[2] School of Mechanical and Automotive Engineering,
Anhui Polytechnic University, Wuhu 241000, China
[3] Faculty of Mechanical and Material Engineering,
Huaiyin Institute of Technology, Huaian 223001, China

**Abstract.** Convenient and high-efficiency manipulation of nanoscale materials has huge potential applications in nano assembly and biomedical technology. We have reported an ultrasonic needle-droplet-substrate system to aggregate and then transport the nanoscale materials freely at the interface between the substrate and water droplet. In the manipulation method, the ultrasonic needle is inserted into the water droplet of nanoscale material to generate a controlled ultrasonic field for the manipulations. In this paper, we report the detailed method and results of FE (finite element) analyses for the investigation of working principle of the manipulation system. The FE analyses show that the ultrasonic needle can generate an acoustic streaming field around the ultrasonic needle to implement the nano aggregation and transportation. The computational results can well explain the experimental phenomena of multiple-function manipulation.

**Keywords:** Finite element · Ultrasonic needle-droplet-substrate system · Manipulation · Multiple-function

## 1 Introduction

Manipulation of nanoscale materials has huge potential applications in the fabrication of nano-sensing materials and nano-electrode, nano decoration, micro/nano assembly [1–3], etc. Several existing methods for the manipulation of micro/nanoscale materials have been reported. They include the magnetic method [4, 5], dielectrophoresis method [6, 7], optical method [8, 9], and acoustic method [10, 11]. Compared to other methods, the acoustic method has the following merits. It is not selective to the material properties of manipulated samples, and has little thermal damage to the manipulated samples (in some methods). Its devices can be very simple and compact. Therefore, the acoustic method is very competitive in nanoscale material manipulations.

© Springer Nature Switzerland AG 2019
H. Yu et al. (Eds.): ICIRA 2019, LNAI 11741, pp. 227–233, 2019.
https://doi.org/10.1007/978-3-030-27532-7_20

In order to implement the aggregation and transportation of nanoscale materials at a droplet-substrate interface by the same ultrasonic device, an ultrasonic needle-droplet-substrate system, which can aggregate and then transport the nanoscale materials freely at the interface between the substrate and water droplet, was proposed [12, 13]. In the manipulation method, the ultrasonic needle is inserted into the water droplet of nanoscale material to generate a controlled ultrasonic field for the manipulations. This new strategy for multiple-function manipulation of nanoscale materials, combined with other technologies, has potential applications in nano assembly, biomedical technology and so on.

In this paper, we report the detailed method and results of FE (finite element) analyses for the investigation of working principle of the manipulation system. The FE analyses show that the ultrasonic needle can generate an acoustic streaming field around the ultrasonic needle to implement the nano aggregation and transportation. The computational results can well explain the experimental phenomena of multiple-function manipulation. The FE analyses method also provides an effective way to design and optimize the multiple-function manipulation system.

## 2 Experimental Setup and Manipulation Functions

Figure 1 shows the experimental setup of the ultrasonic needle-droplet-substrate system for multiple-function manipulation nanoparticles. The experimental setup consists of three main components: ultrasonic needle, vibration transmission rod (VTR) and piezoelectric plate. The ultrasonic needle made of fiberglass is bonded onto the tip of the VTR by the 502 glue, the VTR made of stainless steel is bonded onto the edge of the long side of the piezoelectric plate by epoxy resin adhesive, and the VTR's end is fixed with a special fixture. The VTR has a uniform diameter of 1 mm, and is 26 mm long out of the piezoelectric plate. The ultrasonic needle and the piezoelectric plate are in the same plane, the ultrasonic needle has a uniform radius of 10 μm, and is 3 mm long, the angle between the VTR and the ultrasonic needle is about 90°. The length, width and the thickness of the piezoelectric plate are 20 mm, 10 mm and 0.78 mm, respectively. The piezoelectric constant $d_{33}$, electromechanical coupling factor $k_{33}$, mechanical quality factor $Q_m$, dielectric dissipation factor $tan\delta$, and density are $200 \times 10^{-12}$ C/N, 0.60, 800, 0.5%, 7450 kg/m$^3$, respectively. The piezoelectric plate is used to generate the vibration, which passes through the VTR to excite the ultrasonic needle. The droplet is formed by DI water and ultrasonically dispersed nanoscale samples, and the ultrasonic needle can be positioned by the xyz platform. In the experiments, Si nanoparticles with a diameter of 500 nm was used as the manipulated sample, and the ultrasonic needle, inserted into the water droplet, was perpendicular to the substrate made of silicon. In the manipulation, the ultrasonic needle was moved to the adjacent of the droplet-substrate interface, on which there were nanoscale samples, to carry out the manipulation.

Images a–d in Fig. 2 show a multiple-function manipulation process for the Si NPs on the silicon substrate surface. In the experiments, the operating frequency and voltage are 75.5 kHz and 25 $V_{p-p}$, respectively. In image a, the Si NPs are uniformly dispersed in the water droplet. The micro-size nano spot in image b is formed by 120 s sonication. From image *b* to *d*, the aggregated micro-size nano spot is transported freely at the interface between the silicon substrate and water droplet.

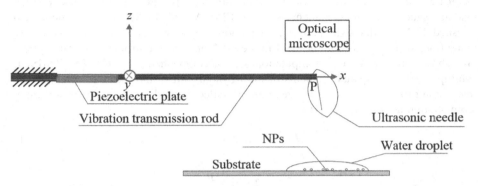

**Fig. 1.** Schematic diagram of the ultrasonic needle-droplet-substrate system for the multiple-function manipulation.

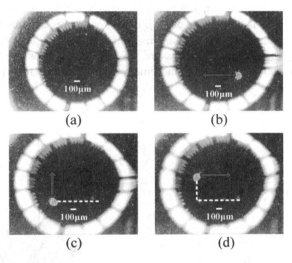

**Fig. 2.** Aggregation and transportation of the micro-size nano spot at the interface between the silicon substrate and water droplet.

In the experiments, the orthogonal vibration velocities at the ultrasonic needle's root $V_x$, $V_y$ and $V_z$ were 5.2 $\angle$ −13.8° mm/s, 61.6 $\angle$ −12.5° mm/s and 2.2 $\angle$ 172.5° mm/s, respectively. As the magnitude of the y-directional vibration velocity was much larger than that of the x- and z-directional vibration velocities, vibration trajectory at the ultrasonic needle's root was approximately linear.

## 3  FE Computational Model and Method

In order to investigate the manipulation mechanism, ultrasonic vibration and the acoustic streaming of the ultrasonic needle-droplet-substrate system were computed and analyzed by the finite element method (FEM). A mathematical-physical model and meshed FEM model used in the computation are shown in Fig. 3. The boundary conditions of the acoustofluidic field in the ultrasonic needle-droplet-substrate system are shown in Fig. 4. The computation was accomplished by software COMSOL Multiphysics. The spatial gradients of the Reynolds stress and mean 2$^{nd}$ pressure are the driving force of the acoustic streaming. Detailed method for the acoustic streaming computation as follows [14–16].

$$F_j = -\partial \langle \rho_0 u_i u_j \rangle / \partial x_i \tag{1}$$

$$\overline{p_2} = \frac{1}{2\rho_0 c_0^2} \frac{B}{A} \langle p^2 \rangle \tag{2}$$

$$\rho_0 (\overline{u}_i \partial \overline{u}_j / \partial x_i) = F_j - \partial \overline{p}_2 / \partial x_j + \eta \nabla^2 \overline{u}_j \tag{3}$$

where $u_i$ and $u_j$ are the vibration velocities of the sound field, $\rho_0$ is the fluid density without sound field, $c_0$ is the sound speed, $p$ is the sound pressure (the first order), $\frac{B}{A}$ is the nonlinear parameter of the acoustic medium, $F_j$ is the spatial gradient of the Reynolds stress, $\overline{p_2}$ is the mean 2$^{nd}$ pressure, $\eta$ is the shear viscosity coefficient of the acoustic medium, and < > represents the time average over one time period.

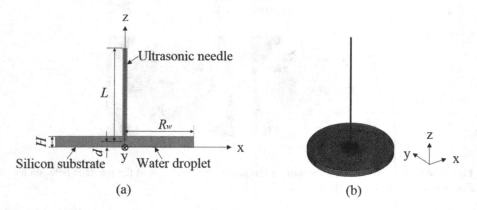

**Fig. 3.** (a) Math-physical model for the ultrasonic needle-droplet-substrate system. (b) Meshed model for the ultrasonic needle-droplet-substrate system.

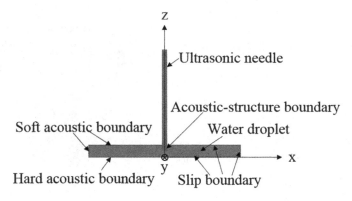

**Fig. 4.** Boundary conditions for the acoustofluidic field of the ultrasonic needle-droplet-substrate system.

## 4   Results and Discussion

The parameters of the ultrasonic devices and experimental system, used in the FEM computation, are listed in Table 1. The computed acoustic streaming on the substrate surface is shown in Fig. 5. It can be seen that the acoustic streaming on the substrate surface flows inward from the all-around, and the NPs are flushed to the location under the ultrasonic needle's tip. This explains the formation of the micro-size nano spot with a round shape shown in Fig. 2. The location of the acoustic streaming field is determined by the ultrasonic needle. Thus, the acoustic streaming can be shifted by moving the ultrasonic needle, which can be implemented by moving the ultrasonic device. Thus the micro-size nano spot can be transported freely at the droplet-substrate interface.

**Table 1.**   Parameters of the ultrasonic devices and experimental system.

| Device dimensions & experimental setup parameters | Material constants |
|---|---|
| Ultrasonic needle length $L$ (mm): 3 | Water density $\rho$ (kg/m$^3$): 1000 |
| Ultrasonic needle radius $R$ (μm): 10 | Sound velocity in water $c$ (m/s): 1500 |
| Water film thickness $H$ (mm): 0.15 | Shear viscosity of water $\eta$ (Pa s): 0.001 |
| Water film radius $R_W$ (mm): 3.5 | Ultrasonic needle density (kg/m$^3$): 2200 |
| Distance $d$ between the ultrasonic needle's tip and substrate (μm): 40 | Poisson's ratio of the ultrasonic needle: 0.3 |
| Angle $\theta$ between the ultrasonic needle and the VTR (°): 90 | Young's modulus of the ultrasonic needle (Pa): 7.4 × 10$^{10}$ |

In the above computation, the ultrasonic needle vibrates in the direction parallel to the substrate. Our computation shows that if the vibration of ultrasonic needle is not parallel to the substrate, the desired acoustic streaming field shown in Fig. 5 cannot be generated, which means that the aggregation and transportation functions cannot be realized by the device.

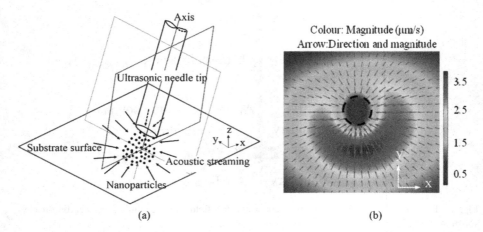

**Fig. 5.** (a) Schematic diagram of the acoustic streaming on the substrate surface. (b) Computational acoustic streaming on the substrate surface.

## 5 Summary

With the FEM computation, we have analyzed the aggregation and transportation mechanism in the ultrasonic needle-droplet-substrate system proposed by our group. The computation indicates that the acoustic streaming, which is generated by the linear vibration of the ultrasonic needle parallel to the substrate, can result in the multiple-function manipulation. The FE analyses method also provides an effective way to design and optimize the multiple-function manipulation system.

**Acknowledgements.** This work is supported by the following funding organization in China: the National Basic Research Program of China (973 Program, Grant No. 2015CB057501), State Key Lab of Mechanics and Control of Mechanical Structures (Grant No. MCMS-0318K01), and Higher Education Promotion Project of Anhui (Grant No. TSKJ2016B20).

## References

1. Dash, S.P., Patnaik, S.K., Tripathy, S.K.: Investigation of a low cost tapered plastic fiber optic biosensor based on manipulation of colloidal gold nanoparticles. Opt. Commun. **437**, 388–391 (2019)
2. Rajput, N.S., Le Marrec, F., El Marssi, M., Jouiad, M.: Fabrication and manipulation of nanopillars using electron induced excitation. J. Appl. Phys. **124**(7), 074301 (2019)
3. Zhang, B., Meng, F.S., Feng, J.G., Wang, J.X., Wu, Y.C., Jiang, L.: Manipulation of colloidal particles in three dimensions via microfluid engineering. Adv. Mater. **30**(22), 1707291 (2018)
4. Agiotis, L., Theodorakos, I., Samothrakitis, S., Papazoglou, S., Zergioti, I., Raptis, Y.S.: Magnetic manipulation of superparamagnetic nanoparticles in a microfluidic system for drug delivery applictions. J. Magn. Magn. Mater. **401**, 956–964 (2016)

5. Huang, C.Y., et al.: Magnetic micro/nano structures for biological manipulaition. Spin **6**(1), 1650005 (2016)
6. Han, S.I., Kim, H.S., Han, A.: In-droplet cell concentration using deelectrophoresis. Biosens. Bioelectron. **97**, 41–45 (2017)
7. Liu, L.B., Chen, K., Xiang, N., Ni, Z.H.: Dielectrophoretic manipulation of nanomaterials: a review. Electrophoresis **40**(6), 873–889 (2019)
8. Grier, D.G.: A revolution in optical manipulation. Nature **424**(6950), 810–816 (2003)
9. Kumar, S., Wittenberg, N.J., Oh, S.H.: Nanopore-induced spontaneous concentration for optofluidic sensing and particle assembly. Anal. Chem. **85**(2), 971–977 (2013)
10. Mao, Z.M., et al.: Enriching nanoparticles via acoustofluidics. ACS Nano **11**(1), 603–612 (2017)
11. Li, N., Hu, J.H., Li, H.Q., Bhuyan, S., Zhou, Y.J.: Mobile acoustic streaming based trapping and 3-dimensional transfer of a single nanowire. Appl. Phys. Lett. **101**(9), 093113 (2012)
12. Hu, J.H.: Ultrasonic Micro/Nano Manipulations: Principles and Examples. World Scientific, Singapore (2014)
13. Zhou, Y.J., Hu, J.H., Bhuyan, S.: Manipulations of silver nanowires in a droplet on a low-frequency ultrasonic stage. IEEE Trans. Ultrason. Ferroelectr. Freq. Control **60**(3), 622–629 (2013)
14. Tang, Q., Hu, J.H.: Analyses of acoustic streaming field in the probe-liquid-substrate system for nanotrapping. Microfluid. Nanofluid. **19**(6), 195–1408 (2015)
15. Tang, Q., Hu, J.H.: Diversity of acoustic streaming in a rectangular acoustofluidic field. Ultrasonics **58**, 27–34 (2015)
16. Lighthill, J.: Acoustic streaming. J. Sound Vib. **61**(3), 391–418 (1978)

# Research on HDD-UJ Robot Joint Structure Design and Motion Regulation Strategy

Zhongtao Li[1] and Tianhong Luo[2(✉)]

[1] School of Mechatronics and Vehicle Engineering,
Chongqing Jiaotong University, Chongqing 400074, China
[2] School of Mechanical-Electrical Engineering,
Chongqing University of Arts and Sciences, Chongqing 402160, China
20180012@cqwu.edu.cn

**Abstract.** A heterogeneous double-drive universal joint (HDD-UJ) that can realize yaw motion and pitching motion is proposed. The virtual prototype model of the HDD-UJ is designed to determine the driving mechanism and motion form of the joint. By deducing the mathematical model of the displacement field of the "C"-shaped electrostrictive driving block, combined with the structural characteristics of the HDD-UJ, a motion regulation strategy is proposed and its mathematical model is established. Finally, in order to verify the rationality and effectiveness of the motion regulation strategy, the simulation experiments under three conditions of ideal, error, and regulation are carried out. The experimental results show that the HDD-UJ combines the electrostrictive material with the motion regulation strategy, which greatly reduces the joint motion error and improves the motion stability.

**Keywords:** Robot joint · Electrostrictive material · Motion regulation strategy · Heterogeneous double drive

## 1 Introduction

As a combination of drive, transmission, sensing, and regulation of robot joints, new functional joints are widely used in aerospace, industrial medical, and interstellar exploration [1–3]. It is the mainstream trend of robot joint development to integrate new functional materials with traditional joints to improve joint performance. New functional materials applied to robot joints and other mechanisms include pneumatic artificial muscles [4, 5], shape memory alloys [6] and electrostrictive materials [7]. Luo et al. [5] proposed a new type of driven bionic shoulder joint structure driven by pneumatic artificial muscle and motor. The mechanism has good precision, dexterity, and carrying capacity. Among many new functional materials, electrostrictive materials are often used as high precision actuators because of their small size, light weight, high energy density, high precision, high resolution, high frequency response, and large output [7–9]. In order to better control the motion of the robot mechanism, many intelligent control models such as proportional integral control (PI) [8], neural network control [10], robust control [11], and impedance control [12] are applied to the field of motion control. These control methods have also been improved and matched [4].

© Springer Nature Switzerland AG 2019
H. Yu et al. (Eds.): ICIRA 2019, LNAI 11741, pp. 234–244, 2019.
https://doi.org/10.1007/978-3-030-27532-7_21

At the same time, many scholars have proposed many new bionic control models for unique institutions. In reference [5], the influence of time-delay nonlinearity and multi-factor coupling of SMA-motor composite driven bionic elbow joint on motion accuracy is proposed. A spatio-temporal coupling model based on biological gene regulation network, which effectively improves the accuracy of joint motion.

In this paper, the universal coupling is used as the prototype of the machine, and the motor and electrostrictive material are used as the dual drive source. A heterogeneous double-drive universal joint (HDD-UJ) driven by motor and electrostrictive material is designed. The virtual prototype model of the HDD-UJ is established, the driving mechanism is expounded, and the displacement field of the "C"-shaped electrostrictive driving block (C-EDB) as the auxiliary driving source is derived. Based on this, the motion regulation strategy of the HDD-UJ is proposed and its mathematics model is established. Finally, in order to verify the rationality of the HDD-UJ structure design and the effectiveness of the motion regulation strategy, the motion simulation experiment is carried out and the experimental results are analyzed. This has important reference value for the research of new functional joints of robots in the future.

## 2 HDD-UJ Design and Displacement Field of the C-EDB

### 2.1 HDD-UJ Virtual Prototype Model

Due to the structural characteristics of the universal joint, it has two degrees of freedom. The research object of this paper is the HDD-UJ with the universal coupling as the prototype, and we design the virtual prototype model of the HDD-UJ by computer. The 3D illustration is shown in Fig. 1. It has two independent driving sources, a driving motor as a main driving source and a "C"-shaped electrostrictive driving block as an auxiliary driving source by $n$ pieces of "C"-shaped electrostrictive sheet. The main function of the driving motor is to provide the main driving force, and the main function of the C-EDB is to assist the driving motor to micro-drive, so as to achieve the high-precision positioning of the transmission integration joint.

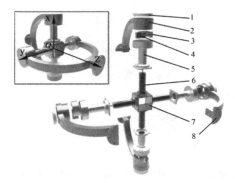

**Fig. 1.** HDD-UJ 3D illustration 1 end cover; 2 insulating transmission ring; 3 C-EDB; 4 insulating transmission block; 5 supporting tube; 6 driving motor; 7 pedestal; 8 arched beam

The insulating transmission block is connected to the output shaft of the driving motor, and the insulating transmission ring is matched with the end of the supporting tube. The arched beam is fixed on the outer side of the insulating driven ring so as to the HDD-UJ connects the manipulator big arm and forearm. Both end faces of the C-EDB are respectively fixed to the insulating transmission block and the insulating transmission ring, so that the driving force of the insulating transmission block is transmitted to the insulating transmission ring. The end cover cooperates with the end of the insulating transmission ring to form an enclosed space for the insulating transmission ring. The joint can generate up and down pitching motion around the Y-axis and produce left and right yaw motion around the X-axis. The coordinate system of sides wing motion around the X-axis and pitching motion around the Y-axis of the joint is shown in Fig. 1.

The HDD-UJ has a range of motion from $-129°$ to $+129°$ in both directions of rotation. The specific payload of the HDD-UJ depends on the rotation parameters of the drive source (motor and the C-EDB).

## 2.2    Stress Field and Displacement Field of Electrostrictive Materials

The electrostrictive material block coated with flexible electrode (size $b \times c \times h$) above by Wei et al. [13] was used as the theoretical calculation model (as shown in Fig. 2). The displacement and stress fields of the model are calculated while considering the coupling between the electric field bulk force and the dielectric constant and deformation. For the above model, the potential difference between the upper and lower surfaces of the electrostrictive material block is constant $U$, the electric field and stress field in the model are evenly distributed throughout the model, the mathematical formula of the displacement field is as follows

$$\begin{cases} u_x = \frac{-\varphi_1\lambda + 2\varphi_2\mu + \varepsilon_0(\lambda+\mu)}{4h^2\mu(2\mu+3\lambda)} U^2 x = \gamma_x x \\ u_y = \frac{-\varphi_1\lambda + 2\varphi_2\mu + \varepsilon_0(\lambda+\mu)}{4h^2\mu(2\mu+3\lambda)} U^2 y = \gamma_y y \\ u_z = \frac{\varphi_1(\lambda+\mu) + \varphi_2\mu - \varepsilon_0(2\lambda+\mu)}{2h^2\mu(2\mu+3\lambda)} U^2 z = \gamma_z z \end{cases} \tag{1}$$

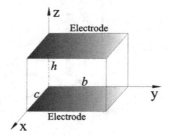

**Fig. 2.**  Electrostrictive material square model with coated electrodes [13]

where $u_x$, $u_y$ and $u_z$ are displacement fields in all directions; $\gamma_x$, $\gamma_y$ and $\gamma_z$ are undetermined constants; $\varphi_1$ and $\varphi_2$ are two electrostrictive constants independent of each other; $\varepsilon_0$ is the dielectric constant when there is no strain; $\mu$ and $\lambda$ are Lame constants, which are expressed as Young's elastic modulus $Y$ and poisson's ratio $v$ as follows

$$\lambda = \frac{Yv}{(1+v)(1-2v)}, \ \mu = \frac{Y}{2(1+v)} \tag{2}$$

### 2.3  Displacement Field of the C-EDB

The C-EDB model of the HDD-UJ based on electrostrictive material-assisted driving is shown in Fig. 3, with electrodes on both sides (each "C"-shaped electrostrictive driving sheet coated with the same electrode). Considering that the C-EDB is a three-quarter ring structure with a "C" shape, there is a certain difference from the standard electrostrictive material block shown in Fig. 3. Now it mainly analyzes Eq. (1) and simplifies the C-EDB model to derive its displacement field.

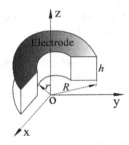

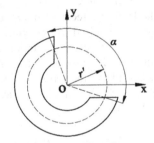

**Fig. 3.** C-EDB model with coated electrode          **Fig. 4.** C-EDB simplified model

We simplify the C-EDB model. Without considering the radial displacement field and stress field, we take the average value of the outer radius and inner radius of the C-EDB ring as the original length in the driving direction, as shown in Fig. 4. We can obtain the length of the arc on the average radius as follows

$$L = \frac{360 - \alpha}{180} \pi r' \tag{3}$$

where $L$ is the arc length on the average radius; $\alpha$ is the arc opening angle on the average radius; $r'$ is the average radius of the C-EDB, $r' = (R+r)/2$, $r$ is the inner radius of the C-EDB; $R$ is the outer radius of the C-EDB.

We can obtain the elongation or shortening length of the C-EDB under voltage $U_C$ as follows

$$u_C = \frac{-\varphi_1\lambda + 2\varphi_2\mu + \varepsilon_0(\lambda+\mu)}{4(h/n)^2\mu(2\mu+3\lambda)}$$

$$U_C^2 L = \frac{(360-\alpha)(R+r)\pi[2\varphi_2\mu - \varphi_1\lambda + \varepsilon_0(\lambda+\mu)]}{1440(h/n)^2\mu(2\mu+3\lambda)}U_C^2 \tag{4}$$

## 3  HDD-UJ Motion Regulation Strategy

### 3.1  Motion Regulation Strategy

There are two driving sources for the HDD-UJ: One is the main driving force of the driving motor as the main driving source, and the fast positioning of the joint forearm end; the other is the C-EDB as the auxiliary driving source provides an auxiliary driving force to offset the driving error of the driving motor, so that the positioning accuracy of the joint forearm end is within the error tolerance.

When the HDD-UJ receives the motion command, the driving motor rotates by one working angle as required by the command. During the driving process of the driving motor, the sensor detects the rotation error of the joint, and transmits the detection result back to the joint control system. At this time, the control system makes different responses according to the error. As shown in the HDD-UJ motion regulation strategy flow chart in Fig. 5. The schematic diagram of the HDD-UJ motion regulation strategy is shown in Fig. 6.

### 3.2  Mathematical Model of the Motion Regulation Strategy

Based on the mathematical model of the displacement field of the standard elec-trostrictive material block, combined with the characteristics of the C-EDB itself, the displacement field mathematical model of the C-EDB is derived. Based on the above theoretical basis, the mathematical model of the HDD-UJ regulation is established. For the regulation of the C-EDB, the external control system will send an action command to the joint at $t$. The joint theoretical (i.e. "set point") side swing angle is $\theta_{theo}^x(t)$ and the pitch angle is $\theta_{theo}^y(t)$. The main driving source of the HDD-UJ is servo motor, and the motor itself has a certain rotation error, so the actual side yaw angle $\theta_x(t)$ and pitch angle $\theta_y(t)$ of the joint at this time are expressed as follows

$$\begin{cases} \theta_x(t) = \theta_{theo}^x(t) + \Delta_x(t) = \theta_{motor}^x(t) + \theta_{u_c/2} + \Delta_x(t) \\ \theta_y(t) = \theta_{theo}^y(t) + \Delta_y(t) = \theta_{motor}^y(t) + \theta_{u_c/2} + \Delta_y(t) \end{cases} \tag{5}$$

where $\Delta_x(t)$ and $\Delta_y(t)$ are rotation errors generated by the driving motor of the yaw motion and the pitching motion at the time of $t$, respectively; $\theta_{motor}^x(t)$ and $\theta_{motor}^y(t)$ are the theoretical value of the yaw state and the state of the pitch state that the motor

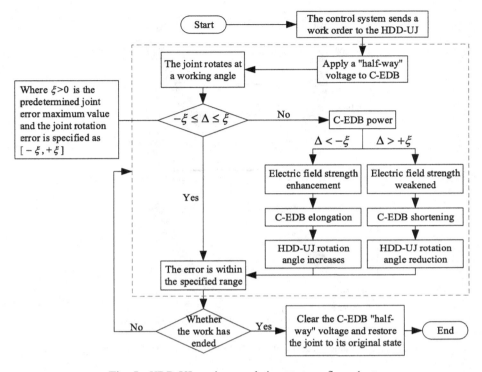

**Fig. 5.** HDD-UJ motion regulation strategy flow chart

should output under the command; $\theta_{u_c/2}$ is the driving angle value of the C-EDB under the "half-way" voltage state, $\theta_{u_c/2} = 6u_r/\pi$.

At the time of $t$, when the HDD-UJ rotation angle exceeds the standard error range, the external control system will issue a corresponding command to apply voltage to the C-EDB to offset the rotation error of the driving motor by the elongation/shortening length of the C-EDB.

$$\begin{cases} \theta_x(t) = \theta_{theo}^x(t) + \Delta_x(t) + \omega_x(t)d_x(t) \\ \theta_y(t) = \theta_{theo}^y(t) + \Delta_y(t) + \omega_y(t)d_y(t) \end{cases} \tag{6}$$

where $\omega_x(t)$ and $\omega_y(t)$ are the regulation factors of the yaw motion and the pitching motion at the time of $t$, respectively; $d_x(t)$ and $d_y(t)$ are the regulation values of the yaw motion and the pitching motion at the time of $t$, respectively.

$$\omega_x(t) = \omega_y(t) = \begin{cases} +1, & \Delta_{x,y}(t) < -\xi \\ 0, & -\xi \leq \Delta_{x,y}(t) \leq +\xi \\ -1, & \Delta_{x,y}(t) > +\xi \end{cases} \tag{7}$$

where $\xi$ is the maximum error allowed by the joint, and $\xi > 0$.

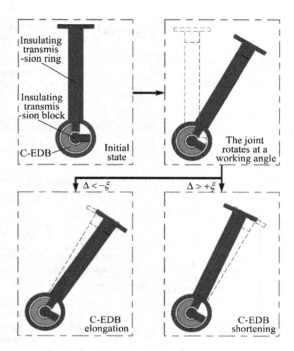

**Fig. 6.** Schematic diagram of the HDD-UJ motion regulation strategy

It can be seen from the foregoing derivation that the regulation value $d_{x,y}(t)$ of the C-EDB has the following relationship with the elongation/shortening length $u_{Cx,y}$ under the corresponding voltage $U_{Cx,y}^2$.

$$d_{x,y}(t) = \frac{180u_{Cx,y}}{\pi r'} \tag{8}$$

## 4    Simulation and Discussion

In order to prove the effectiveness of the motion regulation strategy to improve the joint positioning accuracy and reduce the error rate after introducing the new functional material-electrostrictive material, the following three states are simulated and analyzed: (1) the joint positioning accuracy characteristic under the ideal state (the state without considering any error), and calculate the value of the joint rotation angle and the end space coordinate under the theoretical state; (2) Introduce the motor driving error, but do not consider the influence of electrostrictive materials and motion regulation strategy on joint positioning accuracy characteristics, calculate and analyze the value of joint motion under the error state; (3) Introduce the motor drive error, consider the influence of electrostrictive materials and motion regulation strategy on the accuracy of joint positioning, and calculate and analyze the value of joint motion under the regulation state.

### 4.1   Preparation Before Simulation

For the HDD-UJ, there are two degrees of freedom in the direction of rotation, which are the yaw motion around the $x_H$-axis and the pitching motion around the $y_H$-axis, as shown in Fig. 7.

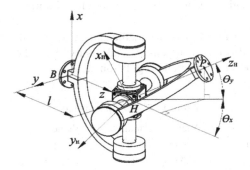

**Fig. 7.**  HDD-UJ space rotation diagram

According to the geometric relation, we can calculate the spatial coordinate value of $P(p_x, p_y, p_z)$ at the fixed reference coordinate system $\{B\}$ as follows

$$(p_x \quad p_y \quad p_z) = (l \quad l \quad l)\begin{pmatrix} \sin\theta_y & 0 & 0 \\ 0 & \cos\theta_y \sin\theta_x & 1 \\ 0 & 0 & \cos\theta_y \cos\theta_x \end{pmatrix} \tag{9}$$

where $l$ is the distance from the center point of the big arm or forearm end of the HDD-UJ, $l = 324$ mm.

In this simulation experiment, the HDD-UJ uses Kollmorgen's AKM2 servo motor as the main driving source, and the AKM2 servo motor's multi-turn absolute positioning accuracy is 8′ (the data from Kollmorgen AKM synchronous servo selection guide). The structural and physical parameters of the C-EDB are shown in Table 1.

### 4.2   Simulation Experiment

Here, we use MATLAB for simulation analysis, and the simulation parameters are set as follows: the total time of simulation is set as 3.6 s, the time step is 0.1 s, and there are 37 time nodes from 0.0 s to the cut-off of 3.6 s. The values of the functions $\theta^x_{motor}(t)$ and $\theta^y_{motor}(t)$ for the time $t$ are as follows

$$\begin{cases} \theta^x_{motor}(t) = 0.5\sin(5\pi t/9) \\ \theta^y_{motor}(t) = 0.5\cos(5\pi t/9) \end{cases} \tag{10}$$

We use the "rands" function in MATLAB to randomly generate two out-of-order error matrices in $[-8/60, +8/60]$. The number of data in each error matrix is the same as the number of time nodes in the simulation. and the data corresponds to the yaw motion error value and pitching motion error value of each time node, respectively.

$$\Delta_{x,y}(t) = \frac{h_f \times \text{rands}(n)}{60} \tag{11}$$

where $h_f$ is the positioning accuracy (rotation error) of the motor, and the unit is "arc minute".

Bring the data in Table 1 into the mathematical model of the HDD-UJ motion regulation strategy and perform simulation analysis to obtain the rotation angle values under theoretical state, error state and regulation state.

**Table 1.** C-EDB parameters

| Parameters | Value | Parameters | Value [13] |
|---|---|---|---|
| $\alpha$ (°) | 129.000 | $U$ (V) | $2.000 \times 10^4$ |
| $h$ (mm) | 30.000 | $\varphi_1$ (Fm$^{-1}$) | $-9.798 \times 10^{-6}$ |
| $n$ | 60.000 | $\varphi_2$ (Fm$^{-1}$) | $-4.899 \times 10^{-6}$ |
| $r$ (mm) | 20.000 | $Y$ (MPa) | 100.000 |
| $R$ (mm) | 40.000 | $v$ | 0.260 |
| $r'$ (mm) | 30.000 | $\text{Log}(|\varepsilon_0/\varphi_2|)$ | 1.00 |

### 4.3  Discussion and Analysis

In order to intuitively see the relationship between the rotation angle values of the HDD-UJ under theoretical state, error state and regulation state (including yaw motion and pitching motion), we drew the curve of rotation angle as shown in Fig. 8.

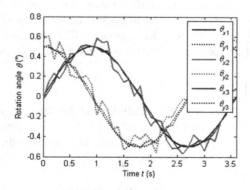

**Fig. 8.** The curve of the HDD-UJ rotation angle value under each state

We first solved the error value before and after the regulation and drew the corresponding curve as shown in Fig. 9. It can be seen intuitively from Fig. 9 that the yaw error value and the pitching error value have large fluctuations before the regulation, and most of the rotation angle values exceed the error limit range [−0.05°, +0.05°]. However, the fluctuation of the error value after the regulation is significantly smaller, and both are distributed within the error limit range [−0.05°, +0.05°]. According to the analysis of the data, the maximum absolute error values of the yaw and the pitching motion are 0.13268276 mm and 0.125491408 mm before the regulation, respectively, and the maximum absolute error values of the yaw and pitching motion are 0.04475401 mm and 0.043232946 mm after the regulation, respectively.

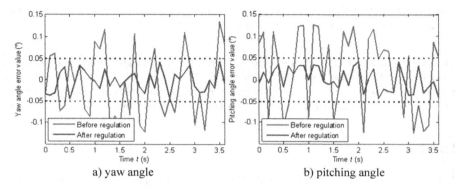

a) yaw angle                b) pitching angle

**Fig. 9.** HDD-UJ angle error value curve

By calculating the mean and variance of the error value before and after regulation, we can see that: the absolute error mean of each time node before the regulation of the yaw motion is 0.067361491 mm, and the absolute error mean of the each time node after the regulation is 0.020060173 mm, it is reduced by 70.22%; the absolute error mean of each time node before the regulation of the pitching motion is 0.081934691 mm, and the absolute error mean of the each time node after the regulation is 0.023729961 mm, it is reduced by 72.26%. The error variance of each time node before the regulation of the yaw motion is 0.005952287, the error variance of each time node after the regulation is 0.000572492, it is reduced by 90.38%; the error variance of each time node before the regulation of pitching motion is 0.007742546, the error variance of each time node after the regulation is 0.000693937, it is reduced by 91.04%.

## 5 Conclusion

In this paper, we designed a HDD-UJ robot joint, and proposed a motion regulation strategy for the HDD-UJ. By analyzing the regulation strategy and studying the displacement field of the C-EDB, we established the motion regulation strategy mathematical model. Finally, we obtained the following conclusions through the research and simulation experiment analysis of the HDD-UJ:

(1) The C-EDB composed of electrostrictive materials is introduced into a robot joint to form a new type of functional material joint, the HDD-UJ, which is a transmission integration joint and has two degrees of freedom. It can carry out yaw motion and pitching motion, and can achieve large-scale space operations.

(2) According to the simulation experiment results, under the given voltage $U_{x,y} = 2 \times 10^4$ V, the rotation error mean of the HDD-UJ after regulation decreased by 70.22% (yaw) and 72.26% (pitching).

(3) The results of simulation analysis also found that the rotation error variance of the HDD-UJ after regulation was reduced by more than 90%, and the motion stability of the joint was significantly improved, which provided important reference value for the study of new functional joints.

**Acknowledgements.** This work was supported by Chongqing Graduate Research and Innovation Project (Grant No. CYS18223), Chongqing Technology Innovation and Application Demonstration Project (Grant No. cstc2018jszx-cyzdX0175) and Chongqing University of Arts and Sciences Graduate School Research Project (Grant No. M2018 ME16).

# References

1. Chen, Q.Z., Chen, W.H., Liu, R., et al.: Mechanism design and tension analysis of a cable-driven humanoid-arm manipulator with joint angle feedback. J. Mech. Eng. **46**(13), 83–90 (2010)
2. Ying, S.S., Qin, X.S., Ren, Z.G., et al.: Design and research of robot driving joint based on artificial muscles. Robot **30**(2), 142–146 (2008)
3. Ma, J., Wu, Y.H., Xu, M., et al.: Study on the joint driver of micro robot based on piezoelectric element for celiac operation. Robot **25**(4), 335–338 (2003)
4. Xie, S.L., Mei, J.P., Liu, H.T., et al.: Hysteresis modeling and trajectory tracking control of the pneumatic muscle actuator using modified Prandtl-Ishlinskii model. Mech. Mach. Theory **120**, 213–224 (2018)
5. Luo, T.H., Li, H.L.: Study on structural design and dynamic characteristics of bionic shoulder joint driven by PAM-motor. Mech. Sci. Technol. Aerosp. Eng. **38**(2), 170–177 (2019)
6. Luo, T.H., Guo, Y., Ma, X.Y., et al.: Spatiotemporal coupling model of SMA-motor compound drive joint based on gene regulatory network. Comput. Integr. Manuf. Syst. **23**(4), 815–824 (2017)
7. Wang, N.F., Cui, C.Y., Guo, H., et al.: Advances in dielectric elastomer actuation technology. Sci. China Technol. Sci. **61**(10), 1512–1527 (2018)
8. Zheng, J.H., Cui, Y.G., Lou, J.Q., et al.: Model and experiments for compound control of a piezoelectric micro-gripper. Robot **37**(3), 257–263 (2015)
9. Liu, Y.F., Li, J., Hu, X.H., et al.: Modeling and control of piezoelectric inertia-friction actuators: review and future research directions. Mech. Sci. **6**(2), 95–107 (2015)
10. Liu, X., Yang, C.G., Chen, Z.G., et al.: Neuro-adaptive observer based control of flexible joint robot. Neurocomputing **275**, 73–82 (2018)
11. Yeon, J.S., Yim, J., Park, J.H.: Robust control using recursive design method for flexible joint robot manipulators. J. Mech. Sci. Technol. **25**(12), 3205–3213 (2011)
12. Semini, C., Barasuol, V., Boaventura, T., et al.: Towards versatile legged robots through active impedance control. Int. J. Rob. Res. **34**(7), 1003–1020 (2015)
13. Wei, H.E., Jiang, Q., Zhou, Z.D.: Some problems of nonlinear mechanics for electrostrictive materials. J. Nantong Univ. (Natural Science Edition) **10**(3), 46–52 (2011)

# A Composite Controller for Piezoelectric Actuators Based on Action Dependent Dual Heuristic Programming and Model Predictive Control

Shijie Qin[1,2] and Long Cheng[1,2(✉)]

[1] State Key Laboratory of Management and Control for Complex Systems, Institute of Automation, Chinese Academy of Sciences, Beijing 100190, China
long.cheng@ia.ac.cn
[2] School of Artificial Intelligence, University of Chinese Academy of Sciences, Beijing 100049, China

**Abstract.** Piezoelectric actuators (PEAs) have been widely applied in nanopositioning applications due to the advantages of the rapid response, large mechanical force and high resolution. However, due to the inherent hysteresis nonlinear property, the high-precision control of PEAs is challenging. To achieve the goal of high-precision motion control, various control methods have been reported in the literature. Recently, adaptive dynamic programming (ADP) has gained much attention to solve optimal control problems. Action dependent dual heuristic programming (ADDHP) is one of the effective structures of ADP, which can estimate the gradient of the cost function by using both the control action and the state as the input of the critic networks. In addition, model predictive control (MPC) is a form of control that uses the current state and the model predicted states to obtain the control action. In this paper, a composite controller is designed for the tracking control of PEAs with ADDHP and MPC. A multilayer feedforward neural network (MFNN) is proposed to model PEAs and is then instantaneously linearized for real-time finding the solutions to the optimization problem in MPC. Experiments are designed to verify the effectiveness of the proposed control method and some comparative experiments with other control methods are also conducted to show that the proposed method can achieve a better tracking performance.

**Keywords:** Action Dependent Dual Heuristic Programming (ADDHP) · Model Predictive Control (MPC) · Instantaneous linearization · Piezoelectric Actuators (PEAs)

## 1 Introduction

With the advantages of the rapid response, large mechanical force and high resolution, the piezoelectric actuators (PEAs) have gained much attentions in

© Springer Nature Switzerland AG 2019
H. Yu et al. (Eds.): ICIRA 2019, LNAI 11741, pp. 245–256, 2019.
https://doi.org/10.1007/978-3-030-27532-7_22

nanopositioning applications [1]. The PEAs are usually used in the high-precision equipments such as micromanipulators [2], vibration assisted polishing device [3] and atomic force microscopes [4]. However, the inherent nonlinearities of PEAs (i.e., the creep, hysteresis and vibration) bring much difficulties in achieving the goals of high-precision motion control. To address these challenges, various efforts have been made for the control of PEAs. There are basically three types of controllers: the feedforward control method with dynamic models [5], the feedback control method and the feedforward-feedback control method.

Model predictive control (MPC) is a form of control method where the current state of the system is regarded as the initial state to solve the finite-horizon open-loop optimal control problem for obtaining the control action online at each sampling time [6]. MPC uses a pre-computed control law and can achieve an effective control performance when the dynamic model is able to fit the physical system well. In [7], a multilayer feedforward neural network (MFNN) model is used to approximate the behavior of PEAs and a nonlinear MPC (NMPC) is adopted to realize the tracking control. After that, the instantaneously linearized MFNN model is proposed in [8] to simplify the computation for solving the nonlinear optimization problem in MPC. Some other MPC-based controllers include [9–11]. However, all MPC methods just utilize finite states of the predictive model and obtain the sub-optimal control action in a short run. Different from the MPC method, the adaptive dynamic programming control (ADP) can obtain the optimal action in a long run.

ADP is first proposed by Werbos based on the principle of the reinforcement learning (RL). Every living organism obtains information by interacting with environment and improves their actions to survive. The change of actions based on interactions with the environment is called RL. And the mathematical formulations for RL and a practical implementation method is described as ADP [12]. In 1977, Werbos proposed heuristic dynamic programming (HDP) and dual heuristic programming (DHP) [13] and then proposed action dependent HDP (ADHDP) and action dependent DHP (ADDHP) in 1992 [14]. The basic structure of the ADP consists of three networks: model network, critic network and action network. The critic neural network is used to approximate the cost function (HDP) or the gradient of the cost function (DHP), while the action neural network is used to obtain the optimal control actions. Different from the HDP and DHP, the ADHDP and ADDHP take both the current control action and the current state, rather than the current state only, as the input of the critic network. The ADP utilizes an iterative method to solve the optimal control problem and the weights of the action and critic networks should be updated at each iteration. After sufficient iterations, the sub-optimal control action and the cost function can be convergent to the optimal control action and cost function, respectively.

In this paper, a composite controller with ADDHP and MPC is proposed for the tracking control of PEAs. In MPC, a MFNN model is used to approximate the behaviour of PEAs and then is instantaneously linearized to simplify the computation of solving the optimization problem in MPC. Then the MFNN is also adopted in ADDHP as the model network and two back-propagation (BP) neural networks are used as the critic network and the action network, respectively. In the following paper, the details of the MFNN model for PEAs and its linearized version are to be introduced. Then the basic knowledge of dynamic programming (DP), the basic structure of ADP and the structure of the ADDHP which are used for tracking control of PEAs are to be introduced in details. After that, experiments are designed to validate the effectiveness of the proposed method on the piezoelectric nanopositioning stage (P-753.1CD, Physik Instrumente, Karlsruhe, Germany) and some comparisons are made with other control methods.

## 2   A Composite Controller for PEAs Based on ADDHP and MPC

The ADDHP consists of three neural networks: model network, action network and critic network. A MFNN model is used to model for PEAs and is trained off-line as the model network. Two BP networks are trained on-line as the action network and the critic network, respectively. Moreover, the MFNN is then instantaneously linearized to avoid computing the complicated optimization problem at each sampling instant in MPC.

### 2.1   MFNN Model for PEAs

In [8], the MFNN model of PEAs has three layers: the input layer, the hidden layer and the output layer. In the hidden layer, each neuron adopts the tangent sigmoid function as the activation function. While the neurons in the input and output layers choose the linear unit function as the activation function. Then the input-output relationship of the network can be written as follows:

$$y(k) = H[\varphi(k)] = \sum_{j=1}^{n} w_j^o \sigma \left( \sum_{i=1}^{m} w_{ji}^h \varphi_i(k) + w_{j0}^h \right) + w_0^o, \tag{1}$$

where $m = n_a + n_b$ and $n$ are the number of neurons in the input and hidden layer, respectively. There is only one neuron in the output layer. $\varphi(k) = [y(k-1), ..., y(k-n_a), u(k-1), ..., u(k-n_b)]$ is the input vector of the MFNN ($\varphi_i(k)$ is the $i$th element of $\varphi(k)$). $w_{ji}^h$ is the weight between the $j$th neuron in the hidden layer and the $i$th neuron in the input layer and $w_j^o$ is the weight between the neuron in the output layer and the $j$th neuron in the hidden layer. $\sigma(x)$ is the tangent sigmoid function and

$$\sigma(x) = \frac{e^{2x} - 1}{e^{2x} + 1}. \tag{2}$$

The Levenberg-Marquardt (L-M) training method is used to obtain the weight of this network.

## 2.2    Action Dependent Dual Heuristic Programming

Dynamic programming is a very useful method to solve the optimal control problems by using the principle of optimality [15]. For a general nonlinear (time-varying) discrete-time dynamic system

$$x(k+1) = F[x(k), u(k), k], \quad k = 0, 1, \ldots \tag{3}$$

where $x \in \mathbb{R}^n$ and $u \in \mathbb{R}^m$ are the state vector of the system and the control action, respectively. $F$ denotes the system function. Then consider the following cost function $J$

$$J[x(i), i] = \sum_{k=i}^{\infty} \gamma^{k-i} U[x(k), u(k), k], \tag{4}$$

where $U[x(k), u(k), k]$ is the utility function and $0 < \gamma \le 1$ is called the discount factor. To solve the optimal control problem, a control sequence $u(k), k = i, i + 1, \ldots$ should be chosen to minimize the cost function. According to Bellman's optimality principle, there are two following equations to describe the optimal control solution

$$J^*(x(k)) = \min_{u(k)} \{ U(x(k), u(k)) + \gamma J^*(x(k+1)) \}, \tag{5}$$

$$u^*(k) = \arg\min_{u(k)} \{ U(x(k), u(k)) + \gamma J^*(x(k+1)) \}. \tag{6}$$

Equation (5) is the principle of optimality and one can solve the two equations to obtain the optimal control sequence. If the system can be modeled by linear dynamics and the cost function is quadratic, the control action can be obtained by solving a standard Riccati equation [16]. However, the system is often modeled by the nonlinear dynamics and the control action is dependent on the solutions to the Hamilton-Jacobi-Bellman (HJB) equation [17].

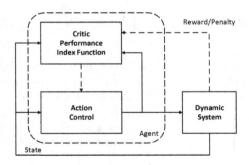

**Fig. 1.** Learn from the environment [15].

Unfortunately, the HJB equation is often difficult to be solved due to the well-known "curse of dimensionality". In order to overcome this challenge, the ADP is proposed to approximate solutions to the HJB equation. The basic structure of the ADP is shown in Fig. 1.

There are three main parts: the critic performance index function, action control and dynamic system, which are usually three neural networks called critic network, action network and model network. The action network is used to obtain the approximate solutions to the Eq. (6) and the model network is used to approximate the behavior of the dynamic system. It is worth noting that the critic networks are normally different in various structures of ADP.

The dual heuristic programming (DHP) is a common structure of the ADP, in which the output of the critic network is the approximation of the gradient of the cost function rather than the cost function $J(x(k))$ itself. The basic principle of the action dependent DHP (ADDHP) is similar to that of the DHP, while the ADDHP takes both the current state $x(k)$ and the control action $u(k)$ as the input of the critic network. The ADDHP structure is shown in Fig. 2.

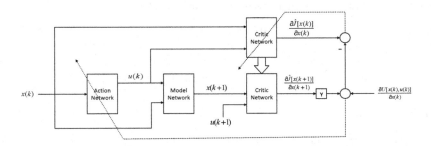

**Fig. 2.** The structure of the ADDHP.

The model network is the MFNN model, which is trained off-line, while the action and critic networks are trained on-line. According to [18] and [19], the critic network is trained by minimize the error as follows

$$\|E_c\| = \sum_k E_c(k) = \frac{1}{2} \sum_k \sum_{j=1}^l E_j^2(k), \tag{7}$$

$$E_j(k) = \lambda_j(k) - \frac{\partial^+ U(k)}{\partial x_j(k)} - \gamma \frac{\partial^+ J(k+1)}{\partial x_j(k)}, j = 1, 2, ..., l, \tag{8}$$

where $l$ is the number of neurons in the hidden layer of the critic network. Then the objective of the training of the action network is minimize the cost function $J(k)$. The training method of the action network and the critic network is the gradient descent method described as follows:

$$\Delta W_c(k) = -l_c(k) \frac{\partial E_c(k)}{\partial W_c(k)},$$

$$W_c(k+1) = W_c(k) + \Delta W_c(k),$$

$$\Delta W_a(k) = -l_a(k) \frac{\partial J(k)}{\partial W_a(k)},$$

$$W_a(k+1) = W_a(k) + \Delta W_a(k),$$

where $W_c$ and $W_a$ are the weights of the critic and action networks, respectively; $l_c$ and $l_a$ are two positive learning rates.

## 2.3  Instantaneously Linearized MFNN Model for MPC

According to [8], at each sampling instant, the instantaneously linearized MFNN model can approximate the behavior of PEAs and simplify the computation in MPC. The Taylor expansion of the dynamic linearized MFNN model is as follows:

$$y(k) - y(p) = a_1(y(k-1) - y(p-1)) + ... + a_{n_a}(y(k-n_a) - y(p-n_a)) + b_1(u(k) - u(p)) + ... + b_{n_b}(u(k-n_b) - u(p-n_b)),$$

where $p$ is the current operating sampling time, and

$$a_i = \left.\frac{\partial H(\varphi(k))}{\partial \varphi_i(k)}\right|_{\varphi(k)=\varphi(p)}, i = 1, ..., n_a,$$

$$b_j = \left.\frac{\partial H(\varphi(k))}{\partial \varphi_{j+i}(k)}\right|_{\varphi(k)=\varphi(p)}, i = n_a + 1, j = 1, ..., n_b.$$

With a bias term

$$\zeta(p) = y(p) - a_1 y(p-1) - ... - a_{n_a} y(p-n_a) - b_1 u(p-1) - ... - b_{n_b} u(p-n_b),$$

the Taylor expansion can be rewritten as

$$y(k) - y(p) = a_1 y(k-1) + ... + a_{n_a} y(k-n_a) + b_1 u(k) + ... + b_{n_b} u(k-n_b) + \zeta(p). \quad (9)$$

By adopting the dynamic linearized MFNN model, the control law of model predictive controller can be formulated in an explicit form at each sampling instant.

## 2.4  The Composite Control Method with ADDHP and MPC

The ADP can obtain the optimal action in a long run while MPC can only obtain this action during a period of time from the current state on. Inspired by that, a composite controller is proposed to obtain the higher control accuracy based on ADDHP and MPC. The structure of the composite controller is shown in Fig. 3.

In MPC, the details of how to solve the control action of the predictive controller $u_{MPC}(k)$ can refer to [8] and the $u_{MPC}(k)$ is the same as $u(k)$ in [8], while the $u_{ADDHP}(k)$ is the output of the action network in the ADDHP. Then the actual control input of PEAs can be obtained by

$$u(k) = a \times u_{MPC}(k) + b \times u_{ADDHP}(k),$$

where $a$ and $b$ are the weights associated with the control action in MPC and the control action in ADDHP, respectively.

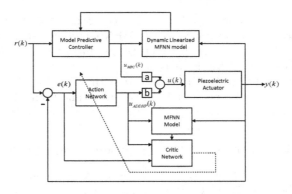

**Fig. 3.** The structure of the composite controller

# 3   Experimental Results and Comparisons

Experiments are designed to verify the effectiveness of the proposed method and to compare the proposed composite controller with the PID controller and the predictive controller. These experiments are conducted on the commercial piezoelectric nanopositioning stage (P-753.1CD, Physik Instrumente, Karlsruhe, Germany). The diagram of the field experiment device is shown in Fig. 4.

## 3.1   MFNN Model for PEAs

To get a high-precision MFNN model, the neurons of the network should be sufficient, while the computation burden increases with the increase of the number of neurons. To balance the contradiction, the parameters of the MFNN model are chosen as $n_a = 2$, $n_b = 2$, and $n = 5$. A white noise signal is used to excite the PEA to generate the data for training MFNN model. The L-M training

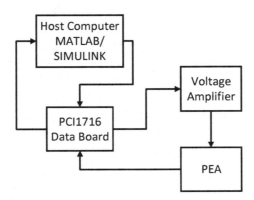

**Fig. 4.** The diagram of the field experiment device

method is used to training approach. Then the sinusoidal signals with different frequency are used to excite both the MFNN model and the physical PEA simultaneously. The comparison between the output of the MFNN model and the actual displacement of the PEA is shown in Fig. 5.

It can be seen that the MFNN model can fit the actual PEA well and then it can be applied to the model network in the ADDHP and then be instantaneously linearized for the MPC.

## 3.2   Control Performance of the Proposed Composite Controller

In MPC, the penalty parameter $\rho = 30$ and the predictive and control horizons are both set to be 7 [8]. In ADDHP controller, the aim of the control is to track the sinusoidal signals and the utility function is defined as follows

$$U(k) = \frac{1}{2}e(k)^2,$$

where $e(k) = r(k) - y(k)$ is the tracking error between the reference signal $r(k)$ and the output of the PEA $y(k)$. In addition, as shown in Fig. 3, $e(k)$ is chosen to be the input of the action network and the critic network for achieving the satisfactory control performance. The tracking profile of the proposed composite controller is shown in Fig. 6.

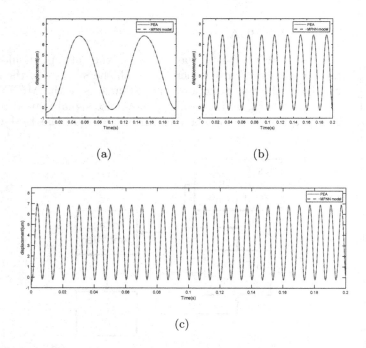

(a)                                        (b)

(c)

**Fig. 5.** The comparisons between the output of the MFNN model and the actual displacement of the PEA under sinusoid signals with different frequencies: (a) 10 Hz (b) 50 Hz (c) 150 Hz

The steady-state tracking error between the sinusoidal reference ($4sin(2\pi ft - \frac{\pi}{2} + 4)(\mu m)$) and the actual output of the PEA is extremely small at a low frequency. The steady-state tracking error for 10 Hz reference signal is within the range of $[-0.0124, 0.0127]\,\mu m$. Then with the increase of the frequency, the error becomes larger. For example, the range of the steady-state tracking error with the 150 Hz reference signal is $[-0.1792, 0.1817]\,\mu m$, which is still acceptable.

## 3.3    Comparisons with Other Control Methods

To validate the effectiveness of the proposed composite controller, some comparative experiments are conducted under the same piezoelectric nanopositioning stage.

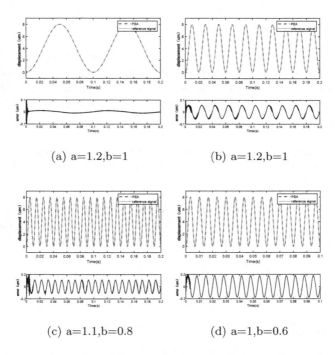

(a) a=1.2,b=1                    (b) a=1.2,b=1

(c) a=1.1,b=0.8                  (d) a=1,b=0.6

**Fig. 6.** Tracking performance of the proposed composite controller under sinusoid signals with different frequencies: (a) 10 Hz; (b) 50 Hz; (c) 100 Hz; (d) 150 Hz.

**Comparison with the Servo PID Method.** There is one commercial PID control function available in the piezoelectric nanopositioning stage provided by PI company. With the same the sinusoidal reference signal, the tracking performance comparisons between the servo PID controller and the proposed controller are shown in Fig. 7. It can be seen that the proposed controller has smaller tracking errors.

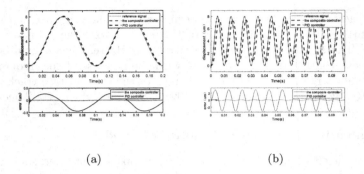

(a)                                            (b)

**Fig. 7.** The tracking performance comparisons between the servo PID controller and the composite controller under sinusoid signals with different frequencies: (a) 10 Hz; (b) 100 Hz.

**Comparison with MPC.** The performance comparison between the proposed composite controller and the inversion-free predictive controller proposed in [8] has been made as well. The comparison results are as shown in Table 1. It is apparent that the proposed composite controller can reduce the tracking errors at low frequencies.

**Table 1.** Performance comparison between the proposed composite controller and the controller proposed in [8]: RMSE (Root mean square error) and MAXE (Maximum error)

| Reference frequency | The composite controller (RMSE/MAXE, $\mu$m) | The controller in [8] (RMSE/MAXE, $\mu$m) |
|---|---|---|
| $f = 5\,\text{Hz}$ | 0.0036/0.0068 | 0.0042/0.0125 |
| $f = 10\,\text{Hz}$ | 0.0073/0.0127 | 0.0080/0.0184 |
| $f = 50\,\text{Hz}$ | 0.0380/0.0579 | 0.0395/0.0618 |

## 4    Conclusion

In this paper, a composite controller with ADDHP and MPC has been proposed to control the piezoelectric actuator. The predictive control predicts the next few steps to obtain a local optimal control, while the adaptive dynamic programming controller can obtain the optimal control action in a long run. The MFNN model is used to fit the PEA physical system and it is also used as the model network in the ADDHP, which is trained off-line. The critic network and the action network in ADDHP are trained on-line to get the gradient of the cost function and the control action, respectively. The MFNN model is then instantaneously linearized in the predictive control. The composite controller with these two control methods has obtained a satisfactory tracking performance. The experiments on the piezoelectric nanopositioning stage (P-753.1CD) have shown that the tracking errors are smaller compared with the servo PID controller and the MPC controller especially for the low-frequency reference signals.

**Acknowledgement.** This work was supported in part by the National Nature Science Foundation under Grant 61873268, Grant 61421004, and Grant 61633016, in part by the Research Fund for Young Top-Notch Talent of National Ten Thousand Talent Program, in part by the Beijing Municipal Natural Science Foundation under Grant L182060, and in part by the Major Science and Technology Fund of Beijing under Grant Z181100003118006.

# References

1. Gu, G.-Y., Zhu, L.-M., Su, C.-Y.: Modeling and control of piezo-actuated nanopositioning stages: a survey. IEEE Trans. Autom. Sci. Eng. **13**(1), 313–332 (2016)
2. Xu, Q.: Robust impedance control of a compliant microgripper for high-speed position/force regulation. IEEE Trans. Ind. Electron. **62**(2), 1201–1209 (2015)
3. Wang, G., Zhou, X., Ma, P., Wang, R., Meng, G., Yang, X.: A novel vibration assisted polishing device based on the flexural mechanism driven by the piezoelectric actuators. AIP Adv. **8**(1), 015012 (2018)
4. Wu, J., et al.: Effective tilting angles for a dual probes AFM system to achieve high-precision scanning. IEEE/ASME Trans. Mechatron. **21**(5), 2512–2521 (2016)
5. Clayton, G.M., Tien, S., Leang, K.M., Zou, Q., Devasia, S.: A review of feedforward control approaches in nanopositioning for high-speed SPM. J. Dyn. Syst. Meas. Contr. **131**(6), 061101 (2009)
6. Mayne, D.Q., Rawlings, J.B., Rao, C.V., Scokaert, P.O.M.: Constrained model predictive control: stability and optimality. Automatica **36**(6), 789–814 (2000)
7. Cheng, L., Liu, W., Hou, Z.-G., Yu, J., Tan, M.: Neural network based nonlinear model predictive control for piezoelectric actuators. IEEE Trans. Ind. Electron. **62**(12), 7717–7727 (2015)
8. Liu, W., Cheng, L., Yu, J., Hou, Z.-G., Tan, M.: An inversion-free predictive controller for piezoelectric actuators based on a dynamic linearized neural network model. IEEE/ASME Trans. Mechatron. **21**(1), 214–226 (2016)
9. Cheng, L., Liu, W., Yang, C., Hou, Z.-G., Huang, T., Tan, M.: A neural-network-based controller for piezoelectric-actuated stick-slip devices. IEEE Trans. Ind. Electron. **65**(3), 2598–2607 (2018)
10. Cheng, L., Liu, W., Hou, Z.-G., Huang, T., Yu, J., Tan, M.: An adaptive Takagi-Sugeno model based fuzzy predictive controller for piezoelectric actuators. IEEE Trans. Ind. Electron. **64**(4), 3048–3058 (2017)
11. Cao, Y., Cheng, L., Peng, J., Chen, X.: An inversion-based model predictive control with an integral-of-error state variable for piezoelectric actuators. IEEE/ASME Trans. Mechatron. **18**(3), 895–904 (2013)
12. Lewis, F.L., Vrabie, D.: Reinforcement learning and adaptive dynamic programming for feedback control. IEEE Circ. Syst. Mag. **9**(3), 32–50 (2009)
13. Werbos, P.: Advanced forecasting methods for global crisis warning and models of intelligence. Gen. Syst. Yearb. **22**, 25–38 (1977)
14. Werbos, P.: Approximate dynamic programming for real-time control and neural modeling. In: White, D.A., Sofge, D.A. (eds.) Handbook of Intelligent Control: Neural, Fuzzy and Adaptive Approaches, Chap. 13, pp. 493–525. Van Nostrand, New York (1992)

15. Wang, F.-Y., Zhang, H., Liu, D.: Adaptive dynamic programming: an introduction. IEEE Comput. Intell. Mag. **4**(2), 39–47 (2009)
16. Lewis, F.L.: Applied Optimal Control and Estimation. PrenticeHall, Upper Saddle River (1992)
17. Lewis, F.L., Syrmos, V.L.: Optimal Control. Wiley, New York (1995)
18. Prokhorov, D.V., Wunsch, D.C.: Adaptive critic designs. IEEE Trans. Neural Netw. **8**(5), 997–1007 (1997)
19. Lendaris, G.G., Shannon, T.T., Schultz, L.J., Hutsell, S., Rogers, A.: Dual heuristic programming for fuzzy control. In: Proceedings Joint 9th IFSA World Congress and 20th NAFIPS International Conference, Vancouver, pp. 551–556. IEEE (2001)

# Regenerative Chatter Control
# with Piezoelectric Actuator for Micro-structure
# Surface Turning

Yang Wang, Lue Zhang$^{(\boxtimes)}$, Tao Chen, and Lining Sun

School of Mechanical and Electric Engineering,
Soochow University, Suzhou 215000, China
zhanglve@suda.edu.cn

**Abstract.** Micro-structure surface is widely used in optics and industry because of their excellent optical properties, wear resistance, adhesion and lubricity. At present, there are many methods for micro-structure surface processing, among which the ultra-precision machining is commonly used processing method. In the process of micro-structure surface manufacturing, the dynamic change of cutting depth can cause instability in the machining process, resulting in the generation of chatter, which is one of the most important factors affecting the quality of machining in the declination of surface quality and generation of noise and tool wearing. The study of regenerative chatter has become a focus in the current manufacturing industry. Ultra-precision diamond cutting by using Fast Tool Servo (FTS) structure is a widely used microstructure surface processing method. In this paper, the chatter of turning process using FTS is modeled, and the occurrence of chatter is simulated and analyzed. Then BP neural network is applied for the chatter control of the proposed FTS system, the corresponding vibration curves are obtained.

**Keywords:** Regenerative chatter · Piezoelectric actuator ·
Micro-structure turning · BP neural network

## 1 Background

Micro-structured surface refers to a surface with a surface accuracy from micron to nano and ultraprecision surface roughness. It can realize many new functions such as micro, array, integration, and imaging, which are difficult to achieve with common components. It has important application value in the fields of biology, optics, mechanics, etc. For example, microlens and pyramid array can be used for liquid crystal display illumination [1, 2], and the microstructure surface also has good application on the optical surface of the structure. For example, the surface of a compound-eye structure with thickness of 1.6 mm can be easily integrated with commercial CCD (Charge coupler devices) to obtain a compact structure. And it has potential application prospects in the fields of machine vision and motion recognition [3].

There are many processing methods for micro-structured surfaces, such as electron beam writing, lithography, etc. The diamond ultra-precision machining has become a hot research technology for the fabrication of micro-structured surfaces because of its

© Springer Nature Switzerland AG 2019
H. Yu et al. (Eds.): ICIRA 2019, LNAI 11741, pp. 257–265, 2019.
https://doi.org/10.1007/978-3-030-27532-7_23

ability to process smooth and continuous non-rotationally symmetrical three-dimensional structures, diverse processing materials, high processing efficiency. Ultra-precision machining of microstructures with diamond tool includes: flying cutting, slow skate servo machining and Fast Tool Servo (FTS). The fast tool servo machining technology is to add an FTS module to the ordinary T-type lathe. This module drives the tool to generate high-frequency, short-stroke fast and precise feed motion in the Z direction during the machining process, in conjunction with the movement of other axes of the machine tool to complete precision and efficient machining of complex surface parts. The processing accuracy of diamond machining can up to micron level, surface roughness up to nanometer. In the processing of micro-structured surfaces, since the cutting speed and the amount of cutting depth are a time variable, it causes a dynamic change of the cutting force, so the cutting process is unstable, and the chatter is generated, resulting in the processing accuracy being less than demanded. In severe cases, it can cause the tool damage, so it is necessary to suppress the chatter vibration generated during the processing of microstructure surfaces.

At present, the methods of chatter suppression can be mainly divided into three types: passive control, active control and semi-active control. Passive control means that the processing system does not accept the input energy from the outside, the purpose of reducing the vibration of the tool or the workpiece is achieved by increasing the rigidity or damping of the system. For example, Yang et al. designed a tuned mass damper (TMD) with the same mass and optimized the damping and stiffness values using the minimax numerical optimization algorithm to improve the chatter resistance [4]. Active vibration control uses a certain actuator to directly apply force to the vibrating body to achieve the purpose of reducing vibration. Sinawi et al. studied the method of suppressing tool vibration by using Kalman filter on the basis of isolating other cutting disturbances affecting the tool, and it proved that this control strategy can greatly improve the machine tool turning workpiece surface roughness [5]. Semi-active control is based on passive control theory. At the same time, the energy required for external control is less than that of active control. Yao et al. proposed a method of generating parametric excitation using a magnetorheological fluid damper to suppress chatter and verifying its effectiveness by experiments [6]. Since the piezoelectric materials have been discovered, the research on active vibration control by using piezoelectric materials has gradually increased. The main difference between these schemes is the control algorithm. Osama Abdeljaber et al. developed a neural network based algorithm to control the voltage signal applied on the piezoelectric patches to control the vibration of flexible cantilever plates [7]. Xie et al. presented a new active vibration control method by using the fractional order $PD^{\mu}$ algorithm, and the method was proved to reduce the vibration of lattice grim beam more rapidly than integer order PD algorithm [8]. Therefore, it is of great practical significance to use the piezoelectric actuator to actively control the chatter during cutting. In this paper, a method for chatter suppression in micro-structure surface processing by using piezoelectric actuator is proposed.

## 2 Model Description

The turning process can be simplified as a single degree of freedom (SDOF) 2D model shown in the Fig. 1.

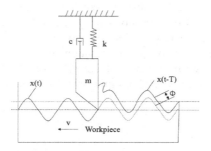

**Fig. 1.** The turning modal

During the cutting process, every time the tool passes over the surface of the workpiece, it will leave a wave on the surface of the workpiece due to some external perturbation. The tool parameters $m$, $k$, $c$ are the mass, stiffness and damping coefficient of the tool system. The $v$ indicates the direction of workpiece. The mathematical model of cutting model is:

$$m\ddot{x}(t) + c\dot{x}(t) + kx(t) = F(t)\cos\theta \tag{1}$$

$F(t)$ is the dynamic cutting force, $\theta$ is the cutting angle. The dynamic cutting force $F(t)$ can be expressed as followed:

$$F(t) = k_f b h(t) \tag{2}$$

Where $k_f$ is the cutting stiffness coefficient, the unit is N/mm$^2$; $b$ is the cutting width, the unit is mm; $h(t)$ is the dynamic cutting thickness, the unit is mm. The dynamic cutting thickness $h(t)$ can be expressed as followed:

$$h(t) = h_0 - [x(t) - x(t - T)] \tag{3}$$

Here $h_0$ is the theoretical cutting thickness, $x(t - T)$ is the wave generated during the previous revolution and $x(t)$ is the wave generated during the current revolution, $T$ is the time when the machine tool spindle rotates for one week, the unit is s. Combined with the above formulas, the system's turning chatter equation can be obtained as followed:

$$m\ddot{x}(t) + c\dot{x}(t) + kx(t) = k_f b[h_0 - x(t) + x(t - T)]\cos\theta \tag{4}$$

# 3  Control Algorithm

The experimental platform designed to achieve the chatter control is shown in Fig. 2. The FTS used the piezoelectric ceramics as driving component which have the advantages of fast response, high acceleration and wide frequency response range. Since piezoelectric ceramics are sensitive to tensile force, torsion and shearing force, it is not possible to directly drive the tool with piezoelectric ceramics. Therefore, the piezoelectric ceramic and the tool holder are connected by a floating joint, and the feeding of the tool is realized by the deformation of the flexible hinge. The piezo-electric ceramic is prevented from being subjected to a radial force. The piezoelectric actuator attached to the tool is used for suppression of chatter.

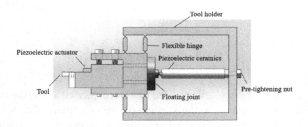

**Fig. 2.**  The structure diagram of FTS

By applying Laplace transform and using relations to Eq. (4), $\gamma$ is turning vibration system damping rate, $\omega_n$ is the natural frequency of turning system,

$$\gamma = \frac{c}{2\omega_n m} \tag{5}$$

$$\omega_n^2 = \frac{k}{m} \tag{6}$$

The Eq. (7) can be obtained:

$$(s^2 + 2\gamma\omega_n s + \omega_n^2)x(s) = \frac{\omega_n^2}{k}F(s)cos\theta \tag{7}$$

The strain can be converted to voltage by piezoelectric materials. The strain equation of the piezoelectric actuator is:

$$\varepsilon_p = U(t)\frac{d_{31}}{t_p} \tag{8}$$

$\varepsilon_p$ is the strain of piezoelectric actuator, $d_{31}$ is the piezoelectric coefficient, $t_p$ is the thickness of piezoelectric actuator, $U(t)$ is the voltage applied to the actuator. The output force of piezoelectric actuator can be calculated as Eq. (9), $k_{PZT}$ is the stiffness of piezoelectric actuator:

$$F_{PZT} = \varepsilon_p k_{PZT} = U(t) \frac{d_{31}}{t_p} k_{PZT} \tag{9}$$

The output force of piezoelectric actuator is requested to suppress the vibration of tool, it satisfies the Eq. (10):

$$\ddot{x}(t) + 2\gamma\omega_n\dot{x}(t) + \omega_n^2 x(t) = \frac{\omega_n^2}{k} U(t) \frac{d_{31}}{t_p} k_{PZT}cos\theta \tag{10}$$

By applying Laplace transform to Eq. (10), Eq. (11) can be obtained:

$$(s^2 + 2\gamma\omega_n s + \omega_n^2)x(s) = \frac{\omega_n^2}{k} U(s) \frac{d_{31}}{t_p} k_{PZT}cos\theta \tag{11}$$

Then the transfer function of voltage and displacement can be obtained:

$$\emptyset(s) = \frac{x(s)}{U(s)} = \frac{\omega_n^2 d_{31} k_{PZT}cos\theta}{kt_p(s^2 + 2\gamma\omega_n s + \omega_n^2)} \tag{12}$$

The control method used in this paper is feedforward control based on BP neural network. Firstly, the tool path of the micro-structure surface is calculated, and the machining process is simulated by the finite element simulation software. According to the stability analysis principle, the track point of the chatter can be predicted during the whole process. The desired voltage applied to the piezoelectric actuator can be calculated by BP neural network algorithm to achieve the effect of chatter control. The most commonly used neural network is a multilayer feedforward neural network. The training process can be divided into two stages: sample data forward propagation and training error back propagation. The structure of the neurons is shown in Fig. 3(a), the structure of BP neural network is shown in Fig. 3(b). The input of each neuron is linearly summed by the connection weights, then output is obtained through the transfer function of neurons of next layer.

$$y_j = f(\Sigma) = f(x_1 w_{1j} + x_2 w_{2j} + \ldots + x_i w_{ij}) \tag{13}$$

If the actual output does not match the expected output, the error is propagated backwards to adjust the connection weights of each layer. In the training, all connection weights are adjusted by following the principle that the actual output is closest to the ideal output. The actual output is calculated according to forward propagation (from input to output), and the adjustment of weight is propagated in the opposite direction (from output to input).

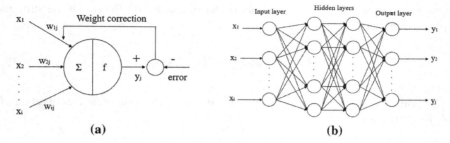

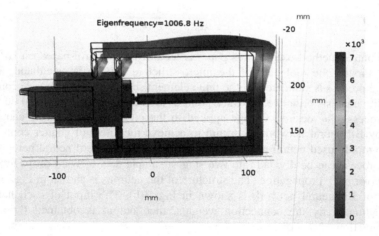

**Fig. 3.** (a) The structure of neurons (b) The structure of BP neural network

## 4  Current Results

The modal analysis of the FTS structure shows that the first-order natural frequency is 1006.8 Hz as shown in Fig. 4, so this working frequency should be avoided during actual processing. The natural frequencies of the first six orders are respectively 1006.8, 1067.9, 1446.9, 1756.8, 2168.6 and 2245.2 Hz.

**Fig. 4.** The natural frequency of FTS

It is necessary to simulate to know the performance of FTS. When the piezoelectric ceramic travels the maximum stroke 90 μm, the stroke of the tool is 90.03 μm as shown in Fig. 5, and the maximum stress on the FTS structure is 351.0 MPa.

Now the actual cutting process of the tool is simulated to observe the performance of chatter suppression. The cutting force is:

$$F = 243 a_p^{X_F} f^{YF} v_c^{ZF} K_F \tag{14}$$

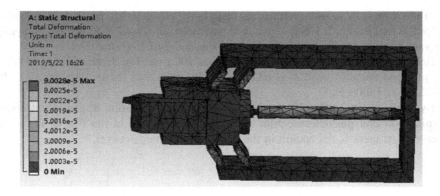

**Fig. 5.** The maximum stroke of FTS

The parameters $X_F$, $Y_F$, $Z_F$ and $K_F$ are the correction factors of the cutting force, $f$ is the feed rate taken as 0.4 mm/r. The formula for cutting speed $v_c$ is:

$$v_c = \pi dN/1000 \tag{15}$$

The parameter $d$ is the diameter of the workpiece, $a_p$ is the depth of cut, $N$ is the spindle speed.

By analyzing the stability of the cutting, the stability lob can be obtained as Fig. 6.

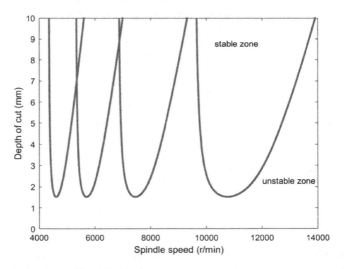

**Fig. 6.** The stability lob of turning

In this paper, PZT-5H is selected as material of piezoelectric actuator, diamond is selected as tool material. The tool dynamic parameters are mass, stiffness and damping. The values are respectively 0.5 kg, 3.06e6 N/m and 240.4 N*s/m.

Here the diameter of workpiece $d$ is taken as 100 mm. The depth of cut $a_p$ is taken as 2 mm and spindle speed $N$ is taken as 10000 rpm, then the cutting force can be calculated as 15000 N.

By applying the cutting force on the knifepoint, the vibration displacement image of knifepoint and piezoelectric film are obtained as shown in the Fig. 7. It can be observed that there is fluctuation in the displacement image curve.

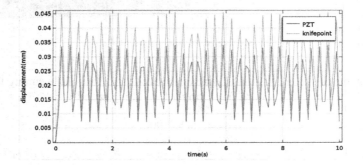

**Fig. 7.** The vibration displacement of the knifepoint and piezoelectric

The desired voltage can be obtained through BP Neural network by using the displacement information. The voltage curve image is shown in Fig. 8.

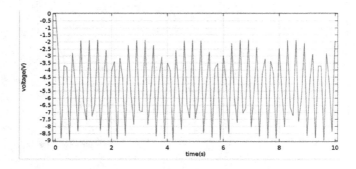

**Fig. 8.** The voltage curve image

After obtaining the output voltage of the piezoelectric actuator, the reverse voltage value is added on the piezoelectric actuator. Then the vibration displacement of knifepoint is obtained as shown in the Fig. 9.

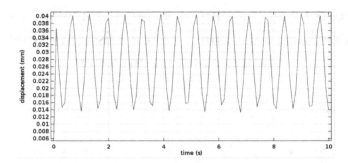

**Fig. 9.** The vibration displacement of the knifepoint after voltage application

## 5 Conclusions

In this paper model of regenerative chatter for the occurrence of chatter in microstructure surface processing using FTS is established. One BP neural network based algorithm was developed to control the voltage applied on the piezoelectric actuator. After simulation, it can be found that the amplitude of vibration displacement of knifepoint reduced about 11.1% and the vibration frequency has increased after applying the voltage on piezoelectric actuator. It showed a good vibration suppression effect. It is proved that the feedforward control method based on BP neural network is feasible.

**Acknowledgments.** The project is supported by National Natural Science Foundation of China (Grant No. 51505313) Natural Science Foundation of Jiangsu Province of China (Grant No. BK20150340).

## References

1. Liu, C.F., Pan, C.T., Chen, Y.C., et al.: Design and fabrication of double-sided optical film for OLED lighting. Opt. Commun. **291**, 349–358 (2013)
2. Tsai, J.Z., Chang, R.S., Li, T.Y.: LED backlight module by a light guide-diffusive component with tetrahedron reflector array. J. Disp. Technol. **8**(6), 321–328 (2012)
3. Li, L., Yi, A.Y.: Design and fabrication of a freeform microlens array for a compact large-field-of-view compound-eye camera. Appl. Opt. **51**(12), 1843–1852 (2012)
4. Yang, Y., Munoa, J., Altintas, Y.: Optimization of multiple tuned mass dampers to suppress machine tool chatter. Int. J. Mach. Tools Manuf **50**(6), 834–842 (2010)
5. El-Sinawi, A.H.: Active vibration isolation of a flexible structure mounted on a vibrating elastic base. J. Sound Vib. **271**(1–2), 323–337 (2004)
6. Yao, Z.H., Mei, D.Q., Chen, Z.C.: Chatter suppression by parametric excitation: model and experiments. J. Sound Vib. **330**(13), 2995–3005 (2011)
7. Abdeljaber, O., Avci, O., Inman, D.J.: Active vibration control of flexible cantilever plates using piezoelectric materials and artificial neural networks. J. Sound Vib. **363**(17), 33–53 (2016)
8. Xie, C.H., Wu, Y., Liu, Z.S.: Modeling and active vibration control of lattice grid beam with piezoelectric fiber composite using fractional order $PD^{\mu}$ algorithm. Compos. Strut. **198**, 126–134 (2018)

# Control and Testing of a Serial-Parallel XYZ Precision Positioner with a Discrete-Time Sliding Model Controller

Yanling Tian[1,2], Yue Ma[1], Fujun Wang[1(✉)], Kangkang Lu[1],
Xiaolu Zhao[1], Mingxuan Yang[1], and Dawei Zhang[1]

[1] Key Laboratory of Mechanism Theory and Equipment Design
of Ministry of Education, School of Mechanical Engineering,
Tianjin University, Tianjin 300054, China
wangfujun@tju.edu.cn
[2] School of Engineering, University of Warwick, Coventry CV4 7AL, UK

**Abstract.** This paper reports the control and testing of a serial-parallel piezo-actuated XYZ precision positioner. The XYZ positioner mainly consists of a Z stage connected with the parallel XY stage in series. The XYZ positioner was fabricated through wire electrical discharge machining, and system identification was performed to obtain the dynamic model of the system. In order to further improve the performance of positioner, a discrete-time sliding model (DSM) controller with PID sliding surface is proposed to achieve precision position control. The proposed controller has the advantage of fast response, strong robustness. A number of experiments have been carried out to verify the performance of positioner and effectiveness of proposed DSM controller. The results indicate that the positioner can implement a workspace of $85.4 \times 87.5 \times 11.9 \ \mu m^3$ with coupling errors less than 1.56% in the non-working direction, and good spatial trajectory tracking performance and high positional accuracy can be realized through the proposed control strategy.

**Keywords:** Precision positioner · Piezoelectric actuators ·
Discrete-time sliding model control

## 1 Introduction

In recent years, with the rapid development of micro/nano technology, precision positioning is widely used in some fields such as semiconductor manufacturing, microelectronics industry, and biological engineering [1–3]. The three degree of freedom (3-DOF) translational XYZ positioner plays an increasingly important role in positioning systems, such as scanning probe microscopy for nanoscratching and nanoimaging [4, 5]. The performance of the positioner is closely related to the accuracy of micro/nano manipulation and manufacturing [6]. For the demand of micro/nano devices manufacturing with high density and high integration, it is necessary to develop and control the high performance 3-DOF translational precision positioner.

The 3-DOF translational micro-nano positioner has attracted considerable attention from both researchers and manufacturers. In the literatures, there has been two main

© Springer Nature Switzerland AG 2019
H. Yu et al. (Eds.): ICIRA 2019, LNAI 11741, pp. 266–276, 2019.
https://doi.org/10.1007/978-3-030-27532-7_24

structures for 3-DOF translational micro/nano positioner, namely, serial and parallel nano-positioners. The series mechanism has no coupling error and is simple to control [7], and parallel mechanism has a compact structure and high loading capability [8]. Serial-parallel XYZ positioners, in terms of a parallel XY platform connecting with Z platform in series, has the advantages of both serial and parallel structures, provide a suitable configuration for 3-DOF translational micro/nano positioners [9].

The static and dynamic characteristics of precision positioner are mainly dependent on the structure of the mechanism and the performance of the actuator [10]. At present, piezoelectric actuator (PEA) is one of the best choices to drive positioners due to the infinite resolution, high stiffness, and large bandwidth. However, the hysteresis, creep, and external disturbance generally exist in positioners driven by PEA. The hysteresis and creep arise from the inherent nonlinearities of employed PEAs, and external interference is the problem that must be considered in precision positioning systems, which all will lead to poor positioning accuracy [11]. To improve the positioning performance, many control methods have been proposed. Among them, proportional-integral-derivative (PID) controller have been widely applied in micro-nano manipulating application. Some advanced control theories including the adaptive control [12], iterative learning control [13], robust control [14], and neural networks control [15], were presented to control precision positioning systems. However, complicated calculations and parameters tuning process make the applications of these controllers limited [16]. Because the discrete-time sliding mode (DSM) controller with PID sliding surface can achieve a fast response, strong robustness and less steady-state error [17], DSM control is an effective control method to improve the positioning accuracy.

The major contribution of this paper is the control and testing of a serial-parallel XYZ precision positioner. To achieve high operation accuracy and compact structure, the Z stage is serially connected with the parallel XY stage where PEAs are embedded in the end-effector. A DSM controller is designed to control the position of the developed mechanism with high accuracy and fast response.

The remainder of this paper is organized as follows: Sect. 2 introduces the mechanism of the XYZ precision positioner. Prototype development and system identification are presented in Sect. 3. The DSM control design is described in Sect. 4. The experimental tests and conclusion are summarized in Sect. 5 and Sect. 6, respectively.

## 2 Mechanism

The overall mechanism of the XYZ positioner is shown in Fig. 1. PEA is chosen as the driver for the precision positioner. In order to expand the motion stroke, a hybrid amplification mechanism with a pair of rotating lever mechanism and a half-bridge mechanism is utilized. By adopting a pair of rotating levers, the lateral error can be offset while the space is effectively saved attributing to changing the displacement output direction. In addition, the displacement ratio is further improved by connecting a half bridge mechanism. In order to prevent the PEA from being destroyed, a hemisphere ceramic adapter is introduced to transform the concentrated force into distributed force on the piezoceramic plate. What's more, the input mechanism is machined as a concave surface cooperated with hemisphere surface to provide excellent limit and automatic centering function, which will effectively ensure motion decoupling property.

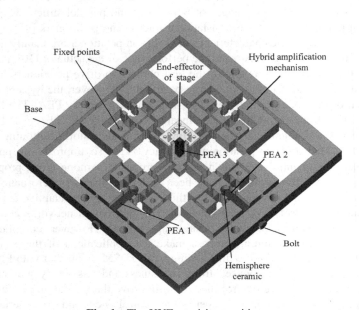

**Fig. 1.** The XYZ precision positioner

In order to obtain high stiffness and compact structure, the Z stage is embedded in the output end of the parallel XY stage. The XY stage is connected symmetrically by four hybrid amplification mechanisms to prevent parasitic displacement. In addition, the effects of thermal deformation and external interference can be reduced, and same performance can be achieved in X and Y directions by the fully symmetrical structure. The positioner also introduces leaf-type double parallelogram mechanism to further improve the dynamic property of positioner.

## 3  Prototype Development and System Identification

### 3.1  Prototype Development and Experimental Setup

A prototype of the positioner was fabricated through wire electrical discharge machining. The overall dimension of the positioner is $134 \times 134 \times 27 \text{ mm}^3$. Three PEAs were used to generate high precision input displacement. A dSPACE DS1103 controller was utilized to output analog voltages, which were then amplified by THORLABS voltage amplifier to provide voltages of 0–100 V for the actuation of PEAs. Input displacement, output displacement, and coupling error were measured by five capacitive sensors, whose outputs were collected in real time by dSPACE controller. To prevent external disturbance, all the devices were mounted on a vibration isolation Newport RS-4000 optical table. The experimental setup is shown in Fig. 2.

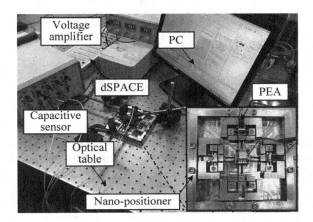

**Fig. 2.** Experimental setup

## 3.2 System Identification

Based on the frequency response, system identification was adopted to obtain the dynamic model of positioner for the design of the controller. Sine swept signals with the amplitude of 0.1 V and frequency varying from 0.1 Hz to 2500 Hz were produced by a dSPACE DS1103 controller to actuate the PEA. The resonance amplitude was captured by capacitive sensors with sample frequency 10 kHz. Then the Matlab System Identification Toolbox was utilized to process the data, and the results are shown in Fig. 3. The transfer functions of position are obtained from the input-output sequences, and they are expressed as

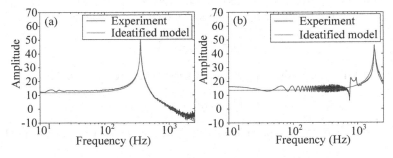

**Fig. 3.** Results of system identification in (a) the X-direction and (b) the Z-direction

$$G_x(s) = \frac{-2.068 \times 10^7}{s^2 + 22.94s + 5.178 \times 10^6}$$

$$G_y(s) = \frac{-2.101 \times 10^7}{s^2 + 37.62s + 5.237 \times 10^6}.$$

(1)

$$G_z(s) = \frac{-5.505 \times 10^8}{s^2 + 113.7s + 1.3 \times 10^8}$$

## 4  Controller Design

PID-type DSM controller is used to control the positioner, and diagram of DSM controller is shown in Fig. 4. According to the identified transfer function, the discrete state equation of positioner can be written as

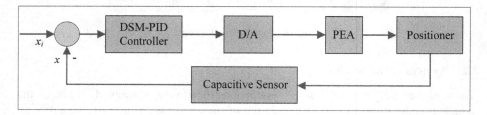

**Fig. 4.**  DSM control diagram.

$$x(k) = \sum_{i=1}^{n} a_i x(k-i) + \sum_{i=0}^{m} b_i u(k-i).$$

(2)

The control objective is to make the actual trajectory $x(t)$ close to the ideal trajectory $x_i(t)$, and the tracking error of the system can be defined as

$$e(k) = x_i(k) - x(k).$$

(3)

Then the PID-type sliding mode control surface can be expressed as

$$s(k) = c_1 e(k) + c_2 \varepsilon(k) + e(k) - e(k-1).$$

(4)

where $c_1$ and $c_2$ are positive parameters and should be chosen to satisfy the Hurwitz condition.

The accumulative error item $\varepsilon(k)$ is defined as

$$\varepsilon(k) = \sum_{i=1}^{k} e(i) = \varepsilon(k-1) + e(k).$$

(5)

Designing the sliding control law as

$$u(k) = \frac{1}{b_0}\left(x_i(k) - \sum_{i=1}^{n} a_i x(k-i) - \sum_{i=1}^{m} b_i u(k-i) - \right)$$
$$-\frac{(c_1+2)e(k-1) - e(k-2)}{b_0(c_1+c_2+1)} - \text{slaw} \tag{6}$$

where $\text{slaw} = \frac{-\lambda_1 T \text{sgn}(s(k-1)) - \lambda_2 Ts(k-1)}{b_0(c_1+c_2+1)}$, $\lambda_1$ and $\lambda_2$ are positive constant parameters, $T$ is the sampling time, sgn is sign function.

Substituting (6) into (2), the following equation can be obtained:

$$x(k) = x_i(k) - \frac{(c_1+2)e(k-1) - e(k-2)}{c_1+c_2+1} + \frac{\lambda_1 T \text{sgn}(s(k-1)) + \lambda_2 Ts(k-1)}{c_1+c_2+1}. \tag{7}$$

Substituting (7) into (4) yields

$$s(k) = s(k-1) - \lambda_1 T \text{sgn}(s(k-1)) - \lambda_2 Ts(k-1). \tag{8}$$

To demonstrate the stability of the control system, a Lyapunov function is adopted as follows:

$$V(k) = \frac{1}{2}s^2(k). \tag{9}$$

Then, the following conditions should be satisfied:

$$\Delta V(k) = s^2(k+1) - s^2(k) < 0, \qquad s(k) \neq 0. \tag{10}$$

On account of the short sampling time $T$, the existing and reachable condition can be written as

$$\begin{cases} (s(k+1) - s(k))\text{sgn}(s(k)) < 0 \\ (s(k+1) + s(k))\text{sgn}(s(k)) > 0 \end{cases}. \tag{11}$$

Based on (11), the following relationship can be deduced:

$$\begin{aligned} (s(k+1) - s(k))\text{sgn}(s(k)) \\ = -\lambda_1 T - \lambda_2 T|s(k)| < 0 \end{aligned} \tag{12}$$

$$\begin{aligned} (s(k+1) + s(k))\text{sgn}(s(k)) \\ = -\lambda_1 T \text{sgn}(s(k)) - \lambda_2 Ts(k) > 0 \end{aligned} \tag{13}$$

Based on (12) and (13), it can be concluded that the controller is stable, and the trajectory can reach the sliding surface in finite time and remain on the sliding surface.

Due to the use of the symbol function, when $s$ closes to zero, chattering phenomenon will appear. In order to avoid this problem, the sign function is substituted by a saturation function which can be expressed as

$$\text{sat}(s) = \begin{cases} 1, & s > \Delta \\ \frac{s}{\Delta}, & |s| \leq \Delta \\ -1, & s < -\Delta \end{cases} . \tag{14}$$

Among them $\Delta$ is the boundary layer thickness. The switching control is employed to make the system quickly move toward the sliding mode when the position is outside the boundary layer. The feedback control is used to reduce the chattering generated during the sliding mode switching within the boundary layer.

## 5    Experiment

### 5.1    Open-Loop Experiment

At first, open-loop experiments were performed to test the performance of positioner. The PEA was actuated by a triangular input signal with frequency of 1 Hz and maximum voltage of 100 V under open-loop condition. The displacements of input and output ends in $x$ axis were measured by two sensors, and at the same time three sensors were fixed up orthogonally to collect information of the input-output coupling in the $y$ direction and the output coupling in the $z$ direction, respectively. The experiment was repeated in the $y$ and $z$ directions, and the results are illustrated in Fig. 5(a)–(c). It can be observed that the workspace of the stage is $85.4 \times 87.5 \times 11.9 \ \mu m^3$. The amplification ratio in the $x$- and $y$-axis are 8.54 and 8.58 respectively. What's more, the measured coupling ratios are relatively small as shown in Table 1, which shows good decoupling properties.

Due to the use of PEAs, the hysteresis and nonlinearity of the positioner is apparent under open-loop condition, as depicted in Fig. 5(d). It can be found that during the extension and retraction process of the PEA, a voltage signal is input corresponding to two different output displacements, which indicates the hysteresis of the positioner needs to be compensated by controller.

### 5.2    DSMC Experiment

DSM controller was carried to compensate the hysteresis and obtain a precision positioning. To test the tracking capability, a spherical curve contouring was applied, which can be mathematically expressed by

$$x(t) = R(\sin(s_r t) \cos(2\pi f t) + 1)$$
$$y(t) = R(\sin(s_r t) \sin(2\pi f t) + 1) \tag{15}$$
$$z(t) = R(\cos(s_z t) + 1)$$

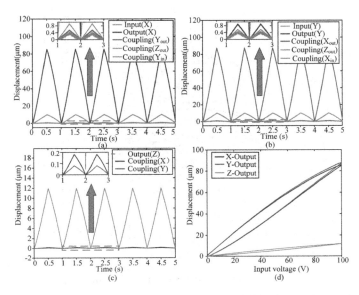

**Fig. 5.** Open loop test results for the workspace, amplification ratio, and decoupling performance in the (a) X axis, (b) Y axis and (c) Z axis (d) Hysteresis curve

**Table 1.** Experimental results of decoupling property test

| Driving direction | X | Y | Z |
|---|---|---|---|
| Output coupling along X axis | — | 1.01% | 1.56% |
| Output coupling along Y axis | 0.52% | — | 0.66% |
| Output coupling along Z axis | 1.06% | 0.47% | — |
| Input coupling along X axis | — | 0.52% | — |
| Input coupling along Y axis | 0.54% | — | — |

where $R$ is the radius of spherical curve; $f$ is rotational frequency of the spiral; $s_r$ is the feed rate along the radial direction; $s_z$ is the feed rate along the Z-direction.

At a maximum tracking speed of 60 μm/s, the spatial trajectory and errors of the three axes are shown in Fig. 6. The $x$, $y$, and $z$-axis tracking errors are within 3.2%, 3.6% and 2.2%, respectively, which proves DSM controller greatly reduce the effects of hysteresis and external disturbances, enabling the positioner to achieve high trajectory tracking accuracy.

The resolution of the XYZ positioner is tested by a stairway-type signal with an 8 nm height, and the experimental results are shown in Fig. 7. It can be found that the position resolution of the XYZ positioner can reach 8 nm under DSM control.

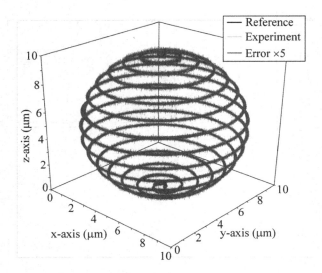

**Fig. 6.** The result of three-axis trajectory tracking

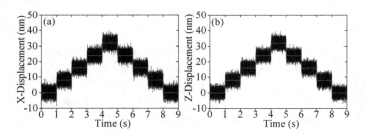

**Fig. 7.** Motion resolution: (a) for X axis and (b) for Z axis

## 6 Conclusion

This paper presents the control and testing of a serial-parallel XYZ precision positioner. The XYZ positioner was fabricated through wire electrical discharge machining, and the system identification was carried to obtain the reliable system model. Then a novel DSM controller was designed to improve the performance of positioner. A series of experiments were performed to examine performance of positioner and validity of the controller. The results show that the travel range of the stage is $85.4 \times 87.5 \times 11.9$ m$^3$, where the amplification ratios in X- and Y-axis are 8.54 and 8.58, respectively. The natural frequencies were tested to be 362.8 Hz, 365.9 Hz and 1861.4 Hz. Finally, the spatial trajectory tracking performance of positioner is tested under DSM controller. The result indicates that the positioner can accurately follow a spherical trajectory, and an 8 nm position resolution can be obtained in three work directions.

**Acknowledgments.** This research was supported by National Natural Science Foundation of China (Grant nos. 51675371, 51675376 and 51675367), National Key R&D Program of China (nos. 2017YFB1104700, 2017YFE0112100, and 2016YFE0112100), Science & Technology Commission of Tianjin Municipality (Grant no. 18PTZWHZ00160), China-EU H2020 MNR4SCell (no. 734174).

# References

1. Qin, Y., Shirinzadeh, B., Tian, Y., Zhang, D., Bhagat, U.: Design and computational optimization of a decoupled 2-DOF monolithic mechanism. IEEE-ASME Trans. Mechatron. **19**(3), 872–881 (2014)
2. Wang, F., Liang, C., Tian, Y., Zhao, X., Zhang, D.: Design and control of a compliant microgripper with a large amplification ratio for high-speed micro manipulation. IEEE-ASME Trans. Mechatron. **21**(3), 1262–1271 (2016)
3. Colom, A., Casuso, I., Rico, F., Scheuring, S.: A hybrid high-speed atomic force-optical microscope for visualizing single membrane proteins on eukaryotic cells. Nat. Commun. **4**, 2155 (2013)
4. Gozen, B., Ozdoganlar, O.: Design and evaluation of a mechanical nanomanufacturing system for nanomilling. Precis. Eng. J. Int. Soc. Precis. Eng. Nanotechnol. **36**(1), 19–30 (2012)
5. Cai, K., Tian, Y., Wang, F., Zhang, D., Shirinzadeh, B.: Development of a piezo-driven 3-DOF stage with T-shape flexible hinge mechanism. Robot. Comput. Integr. Manuf. **37**, 125–138 (2016)
6. Li, Y., Xu, Q.: A totally decoupled piezo-driven XYZ flexure parallel micropositioning stage for micro/nanomanipulation. IEEE Trans. Autom. Sci. Eng. **8**(2), 265–279 (2011)
7. Shan, Y., Leang, K.: Design and control for high-speed nanopositioning serial-kinematic nanopositioners and repetitive control for nanofabrication. IEEE Control Syst. Mag. **33**(6), 86–105 (2013)
8. Zhang, X., Xu, Q.: Design and testing of a new 3-DOF spatial flexure parallel micropositioning stage. Int. J. Precis. Eng. Manuf. **19**(1), 109–118 (2018)
9. Nagel, W., Leang, K.: Design of a dual-stage, three-axis hybrid parallel-serial-kinematic nanopositioner with mechanically mitigated cross-coupling. In: IEEE International Conference on Advanced Intelligent Mechatronics, pp. 706–711. IEEE (2017)
10. Guo, Z., et al.: Design and control methodology of a 3-DOF flexure-based mechanism for micro/nano-positioning. Robot. Comput. Integr. Manuf. **32**, 93–105 (2015)
11. Qin, Y., Shirinzadeh, B., Tian, Y., Zhang, D.: Design issues in a decoupled XY stage: static and dynamics modeling, hysteresis compensation, and tracking control. Sens. Actuator A Phys. **194**, 95–105 (2013)
12. Xu, Q., Jia, M.: Model reference adaptive control with perturbation estimation for a micropositioning system. IEEE Trans. Control Syst. Technol. **22**(1), 352–359 (2014)
13. Helfrich, B., Lee, C., Bristow, D., Xiao, X.: Combined H-infinity-feedback and iterative learning control design with application to nanopositioning systems. IEEE Trans. Control Syst. Technol. **18**(2), 336–351 (2010)
14. Li, Y., Xu, Q.: Design and robust repetitive control of a new parallel-kinematic XY piezostage for micro/nanomanipulation. IEEE-ASME Trans. Mechatron. **17**(6), 1120–1132 (2012)

15. Dinh, T., Ahn, K.: Radial basis function neural network based adaptive fast nonsingular terminal sliding mode controller for piezo positioning stage. Int. J. Control Autom. Syst. **15**(6), 2892–2905 (2017)
16. Wang, F., et al.: Dynamic modeling and control of a novel XY positioning stage for semiconductor packaging. Trans. Inst. Meas. Control. **37**(2), 177–189 (2015)
17. Xu, Q.: Design, testing and precision control of a novel long-stroke flexure micropositioning system. Mech. Mach. Theory **70**, 209–224 (2013)

# Modeling and Testing of a Novel Decoupled XY Nano-positioning Stage

Fujun Wang[1(✉)], Xiaolu Zhao[1], Zhichen Huo[1], Yanling Tian[1,2], Yue Ma[1], and Dawei Zhang[1]

[1] Key Laboratory of Mechanism Theory and Equipment
Design of Ministry of Education, School of Mechanical Engineering,
Tianjin University, Tianjin 300054, China
wangfujun@tju.edu.cn
[2] School of Engineering, University of Warwick, Coventry CV4 7AL, UK

**Abstract.** This paper reports the modeling and experimental testing of a novel XY flexure-based nano-positioning stage. The stage is driven by two piezo-electric actuators, and a novel compound decoupling-guiding mechanism is designed. The mechanism mainly features with the series connection of separated prismatic join and parallelogram, which reduces the parasitic displacement of the actuator and guides the motion of end-effector. A compound bridge type amplifier and centrosymmetric mechanism are adopted to obtain decoupled large range motion. A kinematics model using the compliance matrix method is established to describe the characteristics of stage. Finite element analysis is also conducted to evaluate the performance of the nano-positioning stage. A prototype of the stage has been fabricated by the wire electro discharge machining method. Experimental verification is further carried out, the results demonstrate that the proposed stage has a working stroke of $40.2 \times 42.9~\mu m^2$ corresponding to the applied voltage of 100 V, and it has a cross-axis coupling ratio of 0.6% and an input coupling ratio of 3.5%.

**Keywords:** Nano-positioning stage · Decoupling-guiding mechanism · Kinematics model · Flexure-based mechanism

## 1 Introduction

Nano-positioning stages with microscale level stroke and nanoscale accuracy have been an essential technique for scanning probe microscopy, nano-fabrication and biomedicine [1–5]. As an important part of the precision manipulation and positioning systems, the characteristics of the stage have crucial effects on the accuracy and efficiency of these systems [6].

Up to date, many flexure-based stages have been developed for nanoscale positioning. The actuator is a crucial portion of nano-positioning stage. Among the numerous kinds of actuators, the piezoelectric actuator (PEA) is widely used owing to its unique properties [7]. Besides, the piezo-driven flexure-based stages can be divided into two categories, i.e. serial kinematic structures and parallel kinematic structures. Serial structures can be easily manufactured and controlled, but such kinematic

© Springer Nature Switzerland AG 2019
H. Yu et al. (Eds.): ICIRA 2019, LNAI 11741, pp. 277–284, 2019.
https://doi.org/10.1007/978-3-030-27532-7_25

mechanisms are limited by cumulative error and diverse dynamic characteristics along different axes [8]. In contrast, parallel mechanisms are adopted extensively due to compact structure and impressive stiffness [9]. However, the decoupling ability is a high demand for parallel kinematic stages to reduce the control complexity [10]. Decoupling refers to eliminating cross-coupling between different axes, thus the motion of end-effector along one axis is not affected by another. In addition, input decoupling capability is also crucial for parallel mechanisms. Since PEA cannot suffer from lateral loads, eliminating the effect of end-effector on the actuator is indispensable [11]. Developing a decoupling mechanism with good property has become the demand to enhance the performance of nano-positioning stages.

Based on the above discussion, a piezo-driven XY precision flexure-based positioning stage is proposed. A novel compound decoupling-guiding mechanism (CDGM) is employed to eliminate input and output coupling, and a compound bridge type mechanism is adopted for amplification. The remainder of this paper is organized as follows: Sect. 2 introduces the mechanical design of XY stage, and analytical modelling of the stage is carried out in Sect. 3. In Sect. 4, finite element analysis (FEA) is conducted, and experimental test is conducted in Sect. 5. Finally, the conclusion is drawn in Sect. 6.

## 2   Mechanical Design

PEA is adopted to drive the stage, and thus amplifier is required due to the small stroke of actuator [12–14]. Bridge type amplifier has been widely used for displacement amplification due to its large amplification ratio and compact size, and the compound bridge type amplifier (CBTA) is further adopted because of a significantly increased lateral stiffness [15]. Four CDGMs featured with the series connection of separated prismatic join and parallelogram are used to isolate the actuator, transmit the driving force and sustain the intermediate end-effector.

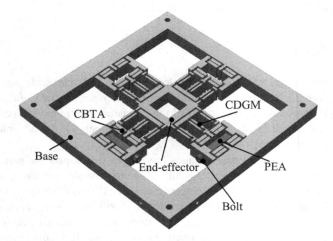

**Fig. 1.** Schematic diagram of the proposed XY nano-positioning stage

The proposed piezo-driven XY precision flexure-based positioning stage is depicted in Fig. 1. A new type of compound decoupling-guiding mechanism is employed to eliminate input coupling, and a bridge type mechanism is used for displacement amplification. The end-effector is supported by CDGM. These mechanisms are arranged symmetrically, which ensures output decoupling and similar performance along two axes. A bolt is installed to adjust the preloading on the PEA. The series of aforementioned configuration are conducive to improve the performance of the stage.

## 3 Kinematic Modeling

Based on the above design, the stiffness model needs to be established for statics modeling afterwards. In this part, the compliance matrix method is employed. The $3 \times 3$ matrix $C_r$ refers to the compliance of a right-angle flexure hinge in the local coordinate system:

$$C_r = \begin{bmatrix} \frac{L}{Ebt} & 0 & 0 \\ 0 & \frac{4L^3}{Ebt^3} & \frac{6L^2}{Ebt^3} \\ 0 & \frac{6L^2}{Ebt^3} & \frac{12L}{Ebt^3} \end{bmatrix} \qquad (1)$$

where only the in-plane deformation is considered. The parameters L, b, t represents the length, width and thickness of hinge, and E is the young's modulus of the material.

The compliance matrix of a hinge in the local coordinate system can be transferred into a global coordinate system by

$$C_r^o = (TR)C_r(TR)^T \qquad (2)$$

where $T$ and $R$ represents the transformation matrix and rotation matrix from the local to the global coordinate system, respectively.

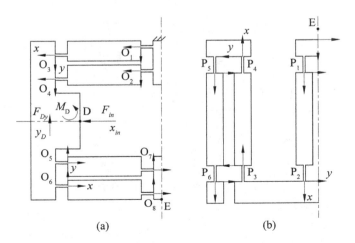

**Fig. 2.** Parameters and coordinates for (a) half of BTDA and (b) CDGM

Due to the symmetry of the mechanism, half of a CBTA is firstly analyzed, as depicted in Fig. 2. According to the relationships of hinges in half of the CBTA, the compliance of the mechanism in the global coordinate system E-xy can be derived as follows:

$$C_l^E = \left( \left( C_1^E + C_3^E \right)^{-1} + \left( C_2^E + C_4^E \right)^{-1} \right)^{-1} + \left( \left( C_5^E + C_7^E \right)^{-1} + \left( C_6^E + C_8^E \right)^{-1} \right)^{-1} \quad (3)$$

where $C_i^E$ ($i = 1, 2, 3, \ldots, 8$) represents the compliance of hinge-$i$ in the global coordinate system:

$$
\begin{aligned}
C_i^E &= \left( T_i^E R_{z\_\pi} \right) C_r \left( T_i^E R_{z\_\pi} \right)^T, i = 1, 2, 3, 4 \\
C_i^E &= \left( T_i^E R_{z\_0} \right) C_r \left( T_i^E R_{z\_0} \right)^T, i = 5, 6, 7, 8
\end{aligned}
\quad (4)
$$

Therefore, the compliance of the amplifier is calculated as

$$C_B^E = \left( \left( C_l^E \right)^{-1} + \left( C_r^E \right)^{-1} \right)^{-1} \quad (5)$$

where $C_r^E$ represents the compliance of the right half of that amplifier, which can be derived on account of the vertical symmetry. Likewise, the compliance of the CDGM is obtained as follows:

$$C_C^E = \left( \left( \sum_{i=1}^{6} C_i^M \right)^{-1} + \left( \left( T_i^E R_{y\_\pi} \right) \sum_{i=1}^{6} C_i^M \left( T_i^E R_{y\_\pi} \right)^T \right)^{-1} \right)^{-1} \quad (6)$$

where $C_i^M$ ($i = 1, 2, 3, 4, 5, 6$) represents the compliance of CDGM hinge-$i$ in the global coordinate system.

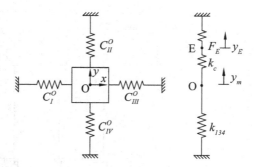

**Fig. 3.** Stiffness model of the stage

As shown in Fig. 3, the centrosymmetric mechanism is be divided into four units, and each of them is composed of CDGM and CBTA in series. Hence, the compliance of the mechanism except the CBTA of unit-II can be derived by

$$C_{down}^O = \sum_{i=1}^{3} \left( \left( T_i^O R_{z\_\frac{i\pi}{2}} \right) \left( C_B^O + C_C^O \right) \left( T_i^O R_{z\_\frac{i\pi}{2}} \right)^T \right)^{-1} + C_C^O \qquad (7)$$

where $C_B^O$ and $C_C^O$ represents the compliance of amplifier and CDGM of unit-II in the global coordinate system O-xy, respectively, and both can be derived by the transformation matrix. According to the Hooke's law, the lower left quarter of the amplifier at point D can be analyzed by

$$X_D = C_{ll}^D F_D \qquad (8)$$

where $C_{ll}^D$ is the compliance of the lower left quarter of the amplifier in the coordinate system D-xy, and $X_D$ and $F_D$ represent the deformation matrix and force matrix at point D, respectively:

$$X_D = [x_{in} \quad y_D \quad \theta_D]^T, F_D = [F_{in} \quad F_{Dy} \quad M_D]^T. \qquad (9)$$

In addition, the boundary conditions of the lower left quarter of the amplifier is written as

$$\theta_D = 0, y_D = 2y_E, y_E = C_{down}^O(2,2)F_{Ey}, F_{Ey} = F_{Dy}. \qquad (10)$$

From the above, the stroke of the stage $y_E$ is derived. And the input stiffness of the mechanism is derived by

$$k_{in} = \frac{F_{in}}{2x_{in}}. \qquad (11)$$

## 4 Finite Element Analysis

In order to further study the performance of the developed stage, ABAQUS is employed for finite element analysis. Based on the geometric model in Fig. 1, the finite element model of mesh generation using C3D10 is established, which is a 10-node quadratic tetrahedron element. The mesh density nearby the flexure hinge is increased to obtain higher accuracy.

The theoretical stroke PEA is 20 μm at the maximum voltage of 150 V, so an attainable input displacement of 10 μm is applied to the input end of CBTA, as shown in Fig. 4. It can be observed that the stroke of the stage along X-axis is 68.4 μm, and the amplification ratio is 6.84. In addition, the parasitic displacement of stage along Y-axis is less than 0.04 μm, and the parasitic displacement of the bridge type mechanism is only about 1.7 μm, which can be ignored. Therefore, the proposed mechanism can be considered as completely input and output decoupled. The input stiffness of the mechanism is evaluated to be 6.90 N/μm by applying a concentrate force of 70 N at the input end of CBTA. All the FEA results prove the effectiveness of the developed mechanism.

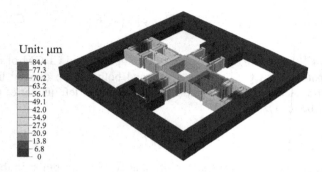

**Fig. 4.** Deformation result of stage

## 5    Experimental Evaluation

The prototype of the proposed stage is fabricated by wire electrical discharge machining (WEDM) method to ensure the processing accuracy, and AL7075 is selected as the material. The overall size of the mechanism is $142 \times 142 \times 10$ mm$^3$. The experimental system is shown in Fig. 5, mainly includes positioning mechanism, capacitive displacement sensor (C8-2.0), THORLABS voltage amplifier, dSPACE DS1103 controller and PC. Two PSAs (Type PSt150/5 × 5/20L) implanted in BTDA are used to generate input displacements with high precision and high resolution. Sensor targets are installed at the mobile platform and input end of BTDA, respectively. To restrain the interference of external vibration, all the instruments are installed on an optical isolation platform.

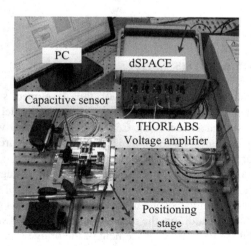

**Fig. 5.** A prototype of the XY stage

In order to test the static performance of the proposed stage, a triangular wave signal with 10 V/s slope and 100 V amplitude is applied to the PSA in X- and Y-axis, respectively. As demonstrated in Fig. 6(a), the working range reaches up to $40.2 \times 42.9 \ \mu m^2$. The amplification ratios of the positioning stage are 5.14 in X-axis and 5.36 in Y-axis, respectively, which matches well with the analytic results. Meanwhile, the stage shows nonlinearity in both directions due to the hysteresis of PEA. The decoupling performance of the stage is also evaluated, as shown in Fig. 6(b). The output coupling ratios in X- and Y-axis are 0.6% and 0.63%, respectively, and the input coupling ratios are 3.51% and 3.47%, respectively. The coupling mainly results from machining error. The low coupling ratios indicate good decoupling capacity.

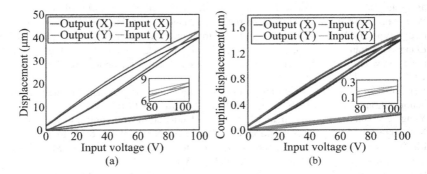

**Fig. 6.** (a) Stroke and (b) coupling evaluation of the stage

## 6   Conclusion

The modeling and testing of a novel XY flexure-based nano-positioning stage has been presented. A decoupling-guiding mechanism is designed for input decoupling and motion guiding. A bridge type amplifier is adopted to amplify the displacement of PEA and enhance the lateral stiffness, and symmetrical configuration is utilized to obtain decoupled motion. An analytical model is established and static simulation are carried out by finite element method. The prototype has been fabricated and experimental test of the stage has been carried out. The results show that the proposed stage has a working range of $40.2 \times 42.9 \ \mu m^2$. In addition, the output coupling ratios are around 0.6% and the input coupling ratios are about 3.5%, manifesting a good decoupling performance.

**Acknowledgments.** This research was supported by National Key R&D Program of China (nos. 2017YFB1104700, 2017YFE0112100, and 2016YFE0112100), National Natural Science Foundation of China (Grant nos. 51675376, 51675371 and 51675367), Science & Technology Commission of Tianjin Municipality (Grant no. 18PTZWHZ00160), China-EU H2020 MNR4SCell (no. 734174).

# References

1. Park, K., et al.: Measurement of adherent cell mass and growth. Proc. Natl. Acad. Sci. U.S. A. **107**(48), 20691–20696 (2010)
2. Efimov, A., et al.: A novel design of a scanning probe microscope integrated with an ultramicrotome for serial block-face nanotomography. Rev. Sci. Instrum. **88**(2), 023701 (2017)
3. Dai, G., Pohlenz, F., Danzebrink, H.: Metrological large range scanning probe microscope. Rev. Sci. Instrum. **75**(4), 962 (2004)
4. Guo, Z., et al.: Probe system design for three-dimensional micro/nano scratching machine. Microsyst. Technol. **23**(6), 2285–2295 (2017)
5. Tseng, A., Kuo, C., Jou, S.: Scratch direction and threshold force in nanoscale scratching using atomic force microscopes. Appl. Surf. Sci. **257**(22), 9243–9250 (2011)
6. Wang, F., et al.: A novel actuator-internal micro/nano positioning stage with an arch-shape bridge type amplifier. IEEE Trans. Ind. Electron. https://doi.org/10.1109/tie.2018.2885716
7. Liang, C., Wang, F., Tian, Y., Zhao, X., Zhang, D.: Development of a high speed and precision wire clamp with both position and force regulations. Robot. Com. Int. Manuf. **44**, 208–217 (2017)
8. Kenton, B., Leang, K.: Design and control of a three-axis serial-kinematic high-bandwidth nanopositioner. IEEE/ASME Trans. Mech. **17**(2), 356–369 (2012)
9. Yong, Y., Aphale, S., Moheimani, S.: Design, identification, and control of a flexure-based XY Stage for fast nanoscale positioning. IEEE Trans. Nanotechnol. **8**(1), 46–54 (2009)
10. Li, Y., Xu, Q.: Design and analysis of a totally decoupled flexure-based XY parallel micromanipulator. IEEE Trans. Robot. **25**(3), 645–657 (2009)
11. Wang, H., Zhang, X.: Input coupling analysis and optimal design of a 3-DOF compliant micro-positioning stage. Mech. Mach. Theory **43**(4), 400–410 (2008)
12. Wang, F., Liang, C., Tian, Y., Zhao, X., Zhang, D.: Design and control of a compliant microgripper with a large amplification ratio for high-speed micro manipulation. IEEE/ASME Trans. Mech. **21**(3), 262–1271 (2016)
13. Tian, Y., Shirinzadeh, B., Zhang, D., Alici, G.: Development and dynamic modelling of a flexure-based Scott-Russell mechanism for nano-manipulation. Mech. Syst. Signal Process. **23**(3), 957–978 (2009)
14. Wang, F., Liang, C., Tian, Y., Zhao, X., Zhang, D.: Design of a piezoelectric-actuated microgripper with a three-stage flexure-based amplification. IEEE/ASME Trans. Mech. **20**(5), 2205–2213 (2015)
15. Li, Y., Xu, Q.: A novel piezoactuated XY stage with parallel, decoupled, and stacked flexure structure for micro-/nanopositioning. IEEE Trans. Ind. Electron. **58**(8), 3601–3615 (2011)

# Effect of Damping Factor Variation on Eigenfrequency Drift for Ultrasonic Motors

Dawei An, Qingshuang Ning, Weiqing Huang$^{(\boxtimes)}$, Haodong Xue, and Jianhui Zhang

School of Mechanical and Electrical Engineering,
Guangzhou University, Guangzhou 510006, China
meehuangweiqing@gzhu.edu.cn

**Abstract.** Experimental studies reveal that the eigenfrequency of stator is increasing along with the growing preload. However, the inherent mechanism is obscure and the equivalent physical model is not investigated especially. By description variation of preload equivalently, the oscillatory differential equation at constrained boundary is established with the introduced parameters of damping factor and stiffness coefficient. With the characteristic parameters of piezoelectric vibrator measured by an impedance analyzer, mechanical quality factors are acquired and values of loss factor and stiffness coefficient are calculated. As the vibration mode of stator is high order, the finite element model is optimized to decrease the computational error. With loss factor and stiffness coefficient as the input parameters, the computed eigenfrequencies based on the equivalent physical model is sensitive to the variation of boundary conditions, which promotes the computational accuracy relating to the adjustable preload.

**Keywords:** Damping factor · Eigenfrequency drift · Ultrasonic motor

## 1 Introduction

Ultrasonic motors utilize the high frequency vibration of the stator particles to impel the rotor moving. The stator is composed of the elastic substrate and the piezoelectric ceramics. With the inverse piezoelectric effect, the electric energy stimulating the piezoelectric ceramics is transformed to the high frequency vibration of the elastomer particles. As the motion is dependent on the friction and the preload between the stator and the rotor, the ultrasonic motor has the unique characteristics of no electromagnetic interference, compact size, fast response and high power density [1–3]. The investigations of the physical models and structure modification are developed sustainably and the ultrasonic motors are utilized in different precision machinery such as space exploration, auto-focusing lens systems, laser systems, medical instruments [4–7]. Even though the principle is worked out gradually and the industrialization is implemented [8–10], some critical technical issues are still intractable and demanded to investigate deeply. The appropriate preload is one of the crucial parameters which define the output performance of the ultrasonic motor. While the preload is adjusted, the torque and the rotational speed are changing accordingly. However, the influence of the preload on the eigenfrequency is lacking of investigation. In the experimental

© Springer Nature Switzerland AG 2019
H. Yu et al. (Eds.): ICIRA 2019, LNAI 11741, pp. 285–291, 2019.
https://doi.org/10.1007/978-3-030-27532-7_26

studies, it is obvious that the driving frequency of the ultrasonic motor is deviated from the original eigenfrequency of the stator, which results in the difficulty of control and the instability of operation.

In this paper, the loss factor variation generated from the preload and the effect on the eigenfrequency drift is investigated. Impedance analyzer is used to measure the impedance characteristics of the stator at different prestress case. By deducing the analytic formula of the loss factor, the mechanism of action between eigenfrequency and preload is discussed.

## 2   Methods and Materials

The stator of ultrasonic motor is consisted of the elastomer and the piezoelectric ceramic wafer adhering the bottom, which is a typical piezoelectric vibrator device. The characteristic parameters of piezoelectric vibrator include eigenfrequency, electrome-chanical coupling coefficient, quality factor, etc. Experiments suggest that adjusting preload will cause the eigenfrequency drifting, resulting in the performance reduction and the operation instability. In order to explore the intrinsic mechanism of eigenfre-quency drift relating to the variable preload, the analysis scheme is designed as shown in Fig. 1. The characteristic parameters of the stator at different preload case are measured by impedance analyzer. Then, the equivalent physical model of stator is established to study the effect of the damping factor. Furthermore, the finite element model is optimized utilizing the loss factors or the damping factors as the input parameters. With concerning the effect of the variation of the preload, the eigenfre-quency of the stator at different constrained boundary is calculated accurately. The simulated results provide the more precise guidance for the design of ultrasonic motors.

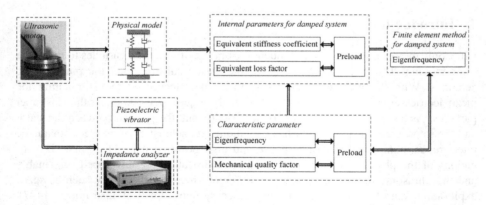

**Fig. 1.** Analysis scheme of the intrinsic mechanism of eigenfrequency drift.

Finite element analysis utilizing the mathematical approximation method to sim-ulate the real physical system, which is available and practical for the common fre-quency domain analysis. When the metal elastomer is constrained by the external force, the traditional finite element method is usually executed through two steps. Firstly, the steady-state analysis of the structure under the preload is carried out, and the stress changes and structural deformation under the preload are solved. Then, the frequency domain analysis of the structure is carried out taking into account the stiffness effects caused by the stress changes. This method is appropriate for solving low-order modes, which is widely adopted by majority of commercial finite element analysis software. However, the ultrasonic motor is operating within the supersonic frequency band and the vibration of the stator is at the high-order vibration mode. With the traditional finite element method, the calculated eigenfrequency is insensitive with the variation of the preload, bringing about nearly the same results in relation to the different boundary condition. The calculation is obviously inconsistent with the actual measurement. To decrease the calculation error and guide the design of ultrasonic motors, the damping factor of the stator is studied and the equivalent physical model is established. The schematic diagram of the preload exerting on the ultrasonic motor is described as Fig. 2 (a), and the equivalent physical model of the stator under external preload is described as Fig. 2(b).

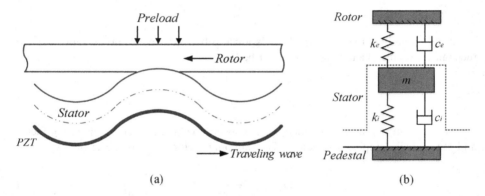

**Fig. 2.** (a) Schematic diagram of the preload exerting on ultrasonic motor. (b) Equivalent physical model of the stator under external preload.

As the ultrasonic motor is assembled and the preload is exerted, the upper surface of the stator is at constraint boundary and the preload is equivalent to external spring foundation and external damping. The corresponding oscillatory differential equation is described as:

$$m\ddot{x} + (c_i + c_e)\dot{x} + (k_i + k_e)x = 0 \qquad (1)$$

Where $c_i$ is internal damping factor, $c_e$ is external damping factor, $k_i$ is internal stiffness coefficient, $k_e$ is external stiffness coefficient. The total stiffness coefficient is equal to the sum of internal stiffness coefficient and external stiffness coefficient, which is described as:

$$k = k_i + k_e = \frac{(2\pi f_r)^2 m}{1 - \zeta^2} \tag{2}$$

Where $f_r$ is the eigenfrequency of the damped vibration system, $\zeta$ is the damping ratio of the stator. The stator of the ultrasonic motor is a piezoelectric vibrator, of which the mechanical loss is represented by the parameter of mechanical quality factor. The mechanical quality factor could be described as:

$$Q_m = \frac{f_r}{f_2 - f_1} \tag{3}$$

Where $f_1$ and $f_2$ are the half-power frequencies, $Q_m$ is mechanical quality factor and could be acquired from the impedance measurement. The damping ratio has the consistent relation with the eigenfrequency and the half-power frequencies. The damping ratio of the stator could be described as:

$$\zeta = \frac{f_2 - f_1}{2f_r} \tag{4}$$

Combining Eqs. (3) and (4), the relationship between the damping ratio and the mechanical quality factor could be described as

$$\zeta = \frac{1}{2Q_m} \tag{5}$$

The damping ratio is also defined as the specific value between the damping factor and the critical damping coefficient. The damping factor could be described as

$$c = \zeta \cdot c_c = 4\pi m f_r \frac{\zeta}{\sqrt{1 - \zeta^2}} = 4\pi m f_r \frac{\eta}{\sqrt{4 - \eta^2}} \tag{6}$$

Where $c$ is the damping factor, $c_c$ is the critical damping coefficient, $\eta$ is the loss factor. With the mechanical quality factor and the eigenfrequency measured by the impedance analyzer, the damping ratio and the loss factor is calculated.

## 3 Experiments and Results

For a traveling wave ultrasonic motor, it is annular structure that composed of a rigid stator and a flexible rotor with the diameters of 60 mm. when the preload is adjust from 0 N to 350 N with the step width of 25 N, the impedance parameters including mechanical quality factors and eigenfrequencies are measured by an impedance analyzer. The measured values of mechanical quality factors is shown as Fig. 3. When the preload is exerted on the ultrasonic motor, the mechanical quality factor is much less than the value at free boundary, which indicates that the consumptive energy used to counteract the internal friction is increased. However, when the preload is rising gradually, the variation of the mechanical quality factor is gentle. It is suggested that the energy loss caused by the internal friction is relatively stable under the constrained boundary.

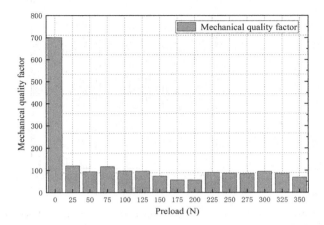

**Fig. 3.** Variation trend of mechanical quality factor versus preload.

According to the Eqs. 5 and 6, the damping ratio or loss factor could be deduced. The loss factor of the stator at different boundary conditions is varying as Fig. 4. When the stator is at free boundary, the preload is equal to zero and the loss factor is a fundamental quantity. As the preload is increasing, the loss factor is growing rapidly. The value at constrained boundary is about four to nine times higher than the value at free boundary. By adjusting the preload exerting on the ultrasonic motor, the variation of the loss factor is nonlinear but the order of magnitudes is maintained. On the basis of the values of loss factors and Eq. 2, the stiffness coefficient could be calculated and show as Fig. 5.

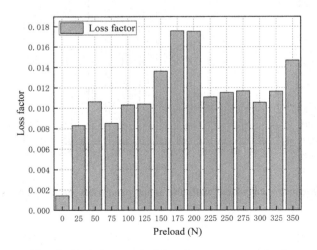

**Fig. 4.** Variation trend of loss factor versus preload.

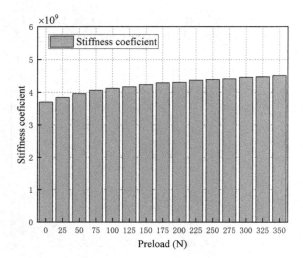

**Fig. 5.** The stiffness coefficient of the damped vibration system at different preload.

Adopting the stiffness coefficient and loss factor as the in-parameters of the finite element model of the stator, the frequency domain analysis is performed at different preload case. The eigenfrequencies are calculated with the values shown in Fig. 6. It is obvious that the growth of the eigenfrequency is consistent with the rise of the preload.

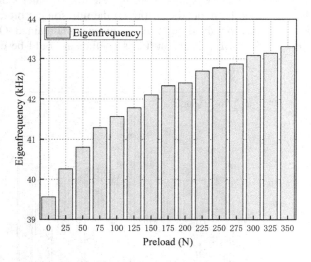

**Fig. 6.** Eigenfrequencies calculated with the input parameters of loss factors and stiffness coefficients.

# 4  Conclusions

The effect of damping factor variation on the eigenfrequency drift is investigated in this paper. With altering the preload exerting upon the ultrasonic motor, the characteristic parameters of the piezoelectric vibrator are measured by the impedance analyze. By establishing the equivalent physical model of the damped vibration system, the effect of the preload is equivalent to the introduced parameters of external stiffness coefficient and external damping factor, while the parameters of internal stiffness coefficient and internal damping factor represent the inherent attribute of the stator. With deducing the equations of the loss factor and stiffness coefficient, the relationship between preload and the introduced parameters are analyzed. Comparing to the stator at free boundary, the loss factor growing sharply at the onset of the preload infliction. However, when the preload is increasing sequentially, the growth of the loss factor is nonlinear and maintains the invariable order of magnitudes. Utilizing the loss factors and stiffness coefficients as the input parameters of the modified finite element model, the eigenfrequencies corresponding to the variable preload case are computed accurately, which is effective for the high-order vibration mode and sensitive to the adjustment of the boundary conditions.

# References

1. Pan, S., Zhang, J.-H., Huang, W.-Q.: Robust controller design of SGCMG driven by hollow USM. Microsyst. Technol. **22**(4), 741–746 (2016)
2. Peng, Y., Peng, Y., Gu, X., Wang, J., Yu, H.: A review of long range piezoelectric motors using frequency leveraged method. Sens. Actuators Phys. **235**, 240–255 (2015)
3. Isobe, H., Kyusojin, A.: Motion error correction for non-contact ultrasonic motor driven by multi-layered piezoelectric actuators. Microsyst. Technol. **11**(8–10), 970–973 (2005)
4. Cheng, L.P., Zhang, S.Y.: Parameter survey of the performance of a noncontact ultrasonic motor. J. Appl. Phys. **106**(7), 074506 (2009)
5. Lu, X., Hu, J., Yang, L., Zhao, C.: A novel dual stator-ring rotary ultrasonic motor. Sens. Actuators Phys. **189**, 504–511 (2013)
6. Cheon, S.-K., Jeong, S.-S., Ha, Y.-W., Lee, B.-H., Park, J.-K., Park, T.-G.: Driving characteristics of an ultrasonic rotary motor consisting of four line contact type stators. Ceram. Int. **41**, S618–S624 (2015)
7. Mohd Romlay, F.R., Wan Yusoff, W.A., Mat Piah, K.A.: Increasing the efficiency of traveling wave ultrasonic motor by modifying the stator geometry. Ultrasonics **64**, 177–185 (2016)
8. An, D., Yang, M., Zhuang, X., Yang, T., Meng, F., Dong, Z.: Dual traveling wave rotary ultrasonic motor with single active vibrator. Appl. Phys. Lett. **110**(14), 143507 (2017)
9. Lu, X., Hu, J., Zhao, C.: Analyses of the temperature field of traveling-wave rotary ultrasonic motors. IEEE Trans. Ultrason. Ferroelectr. Freq. Control **58**(12), 2708–2719 (2011)
10. Ou, W., Yang, M., Meng, F., Xu, Z., Zhuang, X., Li, S.: Continuous high-performance drive of rotary traveling-wave ultrasonic motor with water cooling. Sens. Actuators Phys. **222**, 220–227 (2015)

# Robot Vision and Scene Understanding

# Semantic Situation Extraction from Satellite Image Based on Neural Networks

Xutao Qu, Dongye Zhuang, and Haibin Xie[✉]

National University of Defense Technology, Changsha, China
quxutao10@nudt.edu.cn, xhb2575_sx@sina.com

**Abstract.** Satellite Image Situation Awareness (SISA) is a task that generates semantic situations from satellite images automatically. It requires not only the position and basic attributions (color, size, etc.) of targets but also the relationships (counting, relative position, existence, comparison, etc.) among them and realization of the situation analysis rules. We propose a novel framework which consists of the Background Process, Visual Question Answering (VQA), and Association Rules Set (ARS), in which, the Background Process deals with the situational map, the VQA and ARS identifies the relationships through answering a set of questions on SISA. To verify the performance of our method, we build the evaluation dataset based on CLEVR. Experiments demonstrate that our approach outperforms the traditional SISA systems on accuracy and automaticity. To the best of our knowledge, we are the first to solve SA problem using VQA method. The meaning of our research are: (1) We provide the possibility that SISA can be accomplished through VQA (without precise scene graph). (2) We broaden the application of VQA.

**Keywords:** Situation awareness · Visual question answering · Neural network

## 1 Introduction

Satellite Image Situation Awareness (SISA) is an Artificial General Intelligence (AGI) task that generates semantic situations from satellite images automatically. It requires not only the position and basic attributions (color, size, etc.) of targets but also the relationships (counting, relative position, existence, comparison, etc.) among them and realization of the situation analysis rules. Figure 1 provides an instance of Semantic Situation Extraction from satellite images, in which the vision-based target detection system labels the elements of the situation before Semantic Situation Extraction. These labels are abstract symbols and indicated by a group of geometric shapes in satellite images. After detection, we get a situation image in which the satellite image is the background and the geometric figures are foreground. The goal of SISA is to obtain semantic situations such as "which troop is getting the upper hand in the battle?". To answer such a question, the system needs to answer questions such as "Are there more

© Springer Nature Switzerland AG 2019
H. Yu et al. (Eds.): ICIRA 2019, LNAI 11741, pp. 295–307, 2019.
https://doi.org/10.1007/978-3-030-27532-7_27

artilleries of troop A than infantries of troop B?" and "What is the size of the occupation area of troop A lying east of troop B?". These questions involve the understanding of relative spatial relationships and interactions of attributions. Using the topologic structure faces the severe challenge that the interactions among objects are too complex to integrate into a scene graph [9,10,19]. With the development of Deep Neural Network, SISA receives benefits from the Visual Question Answering (VQA) task [5].

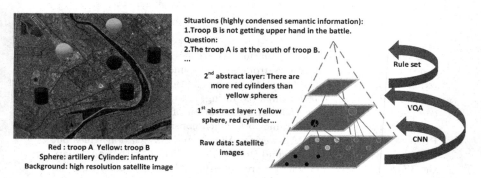

**Fig. 1.** Semantic Situation Extraction from satellite images. **Left:** A high-resolution satellite image from Digital Global (DG) [18]. DG is an American commercial vendor of space imagery and geospatial content, it serves many international corporations such as Google, governments, and presses. The 3D geometric figures on the satellite image are drawn manually to represent the result of target detection. **Right:** The information fusion layers of SISA. The raw data is satellite images. The output in the first layer is a situation map (labeled satellite image), showing the elements (objects positions and their attributions) of situation analysis. The output in the second layer is question-answer pairs on SISA, indicating the relative positions and relationships among attributes. The final output is the semantic situations about the satellite image.

VQA answers questions expressed in natural language about an image. Current VQA frameworks are learning-based [1–8]. A typical VQA framework consists of a CNN to extract the features of the image, and an RNN to transfer the natural language questions to sequential programs. A neural network executes the programs and outputs the answer in natural language. As shown in Fig. 1, the information provided by VQA is more abstract and condensed than the raw data and target detection. A VQA dataset is composed of images (without caption) and question-answer pairs. Besides images on the real-world scene, some researchers also develop synthetic images based on scene description. The synthetic images are able to represent elements of situation analysis, so we build our evaluation dataset based on CLEVR, a typical abstract diagnostic dataset for compositional language and elementary visual reasoning.

We build the evaluation dataset according to CLEVR, in which, we implement the Association Rules Set (as shown in Fig. 2) that the sphere represents artillery and cylinder for infantry, yellow for Troop A, red for troop B.

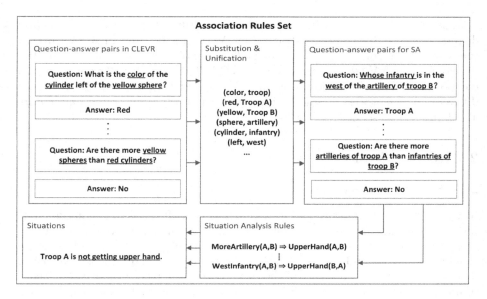

**Fig. 2.** The Association Rules Set to transfer SISA into VQA. **Step1:** Question-answer pairs in VQA are transferred into question-pairs in SA through substitution and unification. **Step2:** The semantic situations are generated based on situation analysis rules.

Through substitution and unification, the question "Are there more artilleries of troop A than infantries of troop B?" is transferred into "Are there more yellow spheres than red cylinders?". After VQA on the situation map, the system produces the answer "No". It indicates that the artilleries of Troop A are no more than infantries of Troop B". Based on such association rules, the semantic situation "The troop A is not getting the upper hand in the battle" is easily generated through situation analysis rules. Thus, the SISA problem is solved by VQA models trained on CLEVR.

In summary, our main contributions are three-fold:

- We propose a novel framework to automatically extract semantic situation from the satellite images without the Precise Scene Graph. This framework introduces neural networks in VQA, which output semantic situation (highly condensed information in natural language) instead of positions and basic attributions of objects.
- We build an Association Rules Set to transfer SISA into VQA. It inherits the high accuracy that VQA has already achieved.
- To verify the performance of our method, we build the situation map dataset based on CLEVR. It remains minimal bias with detailed annotations for each image, so it is accurate enough to estimate our framework through this ground-truth information. Experiments demonstrate that our approach outperforms the traditional SISA systems on accuracy and automaticity.

The paper is organized in the following structure: The section *Introduction* defines the task SISA and illustrates that VQA can be used in SISA through the Association Rules Set. The section *Related Works* separately summarizes the development in SA, Object Detection and VQA. The section *Method* explains the components of our framework. Section *Experiment* tests the framework under different image process methods. Finally, we put the *Conclusion and Future Work* in the last section.

## 2    Related Works

### 2.1    Situation Awareness

Situation Awareness has been studied for a long time. It refers to various domains including military, medical, aviation, emergency management, power system, etc. [20]. There is no standard definition of SA. Generally, SA involves obtaining a semantic status or tendency information from a situation map. Endsley, Wickens, etc. [9,20] present the influence of the concept on subsequent practice and theory of human factors, arguing that SA is a viable and important construct that still possesses some controversies over measurement issues. Kokara etc. [10] propose ontology method and provides a description of the classes and the properties in the ontology. Xu, Ning, etc. [19] study Scene Graph based method but it is still difficult to integrate a Scene Graph precisely [21].

### 2.2    Object Detection

Object Detection is a classical computer vision technique. It provides a foundation for SISA. Zhicheng Li etc. [11] explore an automatic approach to detect and classify targets in high-resolution broad-area satellite images, which relies on detecting statistical signatures of targets, in terms of a set of biologically-inspired low-level visual features. Hui Wu etc. [12] propose a new target detection framework based on Convolutional Neural Networks. Different from manually engineered features, CNN automatically learns the presentations from the massive image data and increases the computational efficiency of target detection. Besides, Object Detection for the satellite image is a typical small target detection problem. Corbane etc. [13] develop an operational ship detection algorithm which is based on statistical methods, mathematical morphology and other signal-processing techniques such as the wavelet analysis and Radon transform. Despite those target search methods can reliably and effectively detect highly variable target objects in large image datasets, it is still hard to sense the relative positions and relationships among the attributions.

### 2.3    Visual Question Answering

Visual Question Answering is a novel task in computer vision. Many researchers have developed various benchmarks for visual question answering. The visual data are about real-world scenes or synthetic shapes. For the real-world scenes, Antol, etc. [1] propose the task of free-form and open-ended VQA. Krishna etc. [2] collect dense annotations of objects, attributes, and relationships within each image. Zhu etc. [3] establish a semantic link between textual descriptions and image regions by object-level grounding. Tapaswi etc. [4] introduce the MovieQA dataset which aims to evaluate automatic story comprehension from both video and text. The visual data about the real-world scene inevitably lead to strong biases and difficulty for pinpointing model weakness [5,14]. To deal with such a problem, Johnson, etc. [5] present a diagnostic dataset called CLEVR that tests a range of visual reasoning abilities. Images in CLEVR are synthetic and have detailed annotations. Besides, the objects in CLEVR can be seen as labels on satellite images. Thus, our dataset derives from CLEVR. As for VQA models, current VQA models are learning-based. Andreas etc. [6] decompose questions into their linguistic substructures and uses these structures to dynamically instantiate modular networks. Johnson etc. [7] propose a model including a program generator that constructs an explicit representation of the reasoning process to be performed and an execution engine that executes the resulting program to produce an answer. Both the program generator and the execution engine are implemented by neural networks and are trained using a combination of backpropagation and REINFORCE [15].

## 3    Method

### 3.1    The Background Process

This component is designed for adaptation of various visual situation data. Our evaluation dataset is different from CLEVR mainly in the background, so it is necessary to apply the Background Process at the beginning of the framework. The background is the environment of situation analysis. There are not only important clues underlying the environment but also irrelevant distractions which will disturb the VQA component. In this paper, we study the relationship between the Background Process and the accuracy of the answers of VQA.

### 3.2    The VQA Models

**Formal Description.** The VQA process can be described as

$$a = \phi(x, q) \tag{1}$$

where $a \in A$ is an answer in natural language from a fixed set $A$ of possible answers, $x$ is the input image, $q$ is the input question, $\phi$ is the execution engine implemented using a Neural Module Network [6]. $x$ will be resized to $3 \times 224 \times 224$. Then after the process with ResNet-101 [17] pretrained on ImageNet [16] and two layers of ReLU, the extracted features of the image $x$ are represented as a $14 \times 14$ tensor. The residual learning framework eases the training of networks. The ReLU layers maintain the sparsity of the image. The question $q$ is converted by the encoder from a sequence of words to a fixed-length vector. Then the decoder receives this fixed-length vector as input and produces the predicted program as a sequence of functions $z$. The encoder and decoder do not share weights.

---

**Algorithm 1** Running VQA models on a single image

---

**Input:** The image, $I$; The question in natural language, $Q$;
**Output:** The answer, $A$;
 1: Build the $CNN$ to use for feature extraction;
 2: Load the image $I$ and preprocess it;
 3: Use $CNN$ to extract features $feats$ for the image $I$;
 4: Tokenize the question $Q$ into sequential numbers $Q_n$;
 5: Output the predicted program code $Program$ from $Q_n$;
 6: $Score = Execution(feats, Program)$;
 7: Output the answer $A$ according to the $Score$;
 8: **return** $A$;

---

The images and questions are processed separately into vectors: $feats$ and $Program$. With these two parameters settled, the execution engine output the predicted answer ID and then the answer $a$ in natural language. Any questions whether related to the image or not have an answer.

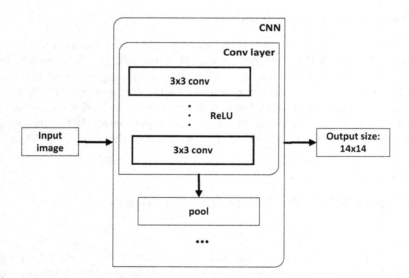

**Fig. 3.** The architecture of the CNN model used for feature extraction. The input image is resized to a fixed value. The convolution layer adopts ReLU as the activation function. The pooling layer significantly reduces the size of output.

**The Deep Residual Learning.** ResNet [17] is a Stochastic Gradient Descent (SGD) optimization method. It adds a residual layer to the previous CNN models as shown in Fig. 3, which helps training the deep network. Our model is pretrained on ImageNet.

### 3.3  The Association Rules Set

The Association Rules Set is represented by vectors and first-order logic as shown in Fig. 2. Here we provide 2 examples:

**The Association Rules Set for Battlefield.** { (color, troop), (object, type of camp), (red, Troop A), (yellow, Troop B), (gray, crowd), (sphere, artillery), (cylinder, infantry), (cube, depot)...}, {MoreArtillery(TroopA, TroopB) ⇒ UpperHand(TroopA, TroopB), West((Infantry ∧ TroopA), (Artillery ∧ TroopB)) ∨ East((Crowd ∧ TroopB), (Infantry ∧ TroopB)) ⇒ UpperHand(TroopB, TroopA)...}

**The Association Rules Set for UAV Detection.** { (color, status), (object, type of target), (red, hover), (yellow, circle), (gray, landing), (sphere, waters), (cylinder, trees), (cube, buildings)...}, {Hover(target) ⇒ Identify(target, quadrotor), Circle(target, waters) ∧ Landing(target, trees) ⇒ Identify(target, bird)...}

## 4  Experiment

The experiment aims at estimating the framework as shown in Fig. 4 with three components: Background Process, VQA, and Association Rules Set. The satellite image situation map dataset is based on CLEVR. The image feature extraction model is trained on ImageNet, and the program generator is trained with relatively 9k, 18k, 700k questions.

### 4.1  Dataset

Our evaluation dataset for SISA is shown in Fig. 5. The generation process is summarized as the following algorithm:

The generated dataset is largely according to CLEVR with a few important changes:

- The synthetic objects represent the attribution (position, status, identity, etc.) of targets in satellite images, but in CLEVR, the shapes are meaningless.
- The background is not simple for object detection due to the texture of the natural satellite images.

Our dataset inherits the advantages of CLEVR, especially the ground-truth scene description for each image and abundant question-answer pairs equipped with ground-truth programs. The way we test the model on our dataset is the same as on CLEVR.

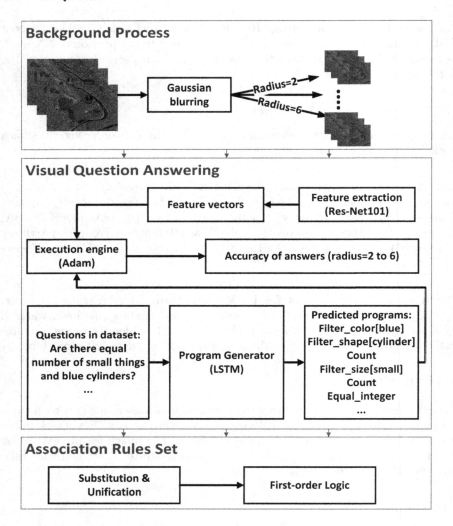

**Fig. 4.** The framework for SISA. **Background Process:** Offset the effect caused by the difference between our dataset and CLEVR. **VQA:** Answer the questions on situation elements. **Association Rules Set**: Generate semantic situations based on question-answer pairs from VQA.

## 4.2    The Background Process

We evaluate our framework on three types of test sets:

**CLEVR-Val:** This is the validation set of CLEVR, containing 15000 synthetic images and ground truth scene descriptions.

**SituationMap-Origin:** A situation map dataset without Background Process.

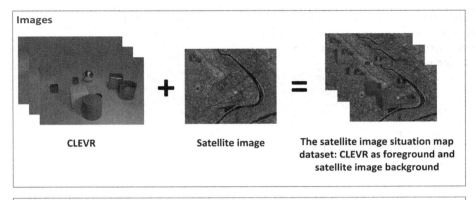

**Images**

CLEVR

Satellite image

The satellite image situation map dataset: CLEVR as foreground and satellite image background

**Questions**

Q: Are there equal number of small things and blue cylinders?
Q: What size if the sphere that is left of the yellow sphere and right of the blue cylinder?

**Fig. 5.** The satellite image situation map dataset. **Left:** Synthetic images in CLEVR. **Middle:** Satellite image from DG [18], a professional American satellite image vendor. **Right:** The background of images in CLEVR is changed from light gray to satellite images. Our dataset shares the question-answer pairs with CLEVR.

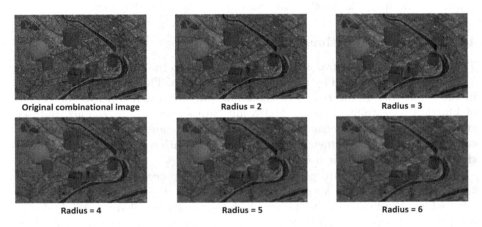

Original combinational image

Radius = 2

Radius = 3

Radius = 4

Radius = 5

Radius = 6

**Fig. 6.** Background Process Algorithm. As the radius of Gaussian blurring grows, the more details of background are discarded.

**SituationMap-2 to SituationMap-6:** The background(satellite images) is blurred with Gaussian blurring as shown in Fig. 6. The postfix number is the radius of Gaussian blurring, deciding the degree of blurring.

**Algorithm 2** Generating the evaluation datase: SituationMap

---

**Input:** The satellite image $SI$; A set of CLEVR $C$;
**Output:** The SituationMap dataset, $SM$;
1: **for** each *image* in $C$ **do**
2:     **for** each *pixel* in *image* **do**
3:         **if** *pixel* is light gray **then**
4:             $pixel = pixelinSI$
5:         **end if**
6:     **end for**
7:     save *image* as $SM_i$ in $SM$
8: **end for**
9: **return** $SM$;

---

### 4.3   The VQA Models

The VQA models include three Neural Networks: Feature Extraction, Program Generator, and Execution Engine. The Feature Extraction is ResNet-101 trained on ImageNeT. The Program Generator is LSTM trained with questions and ground-truth program codes. We use 9k, 18k, and 700k questions separately in the training period of the Program Generator. The Execution Engine is trained with Adam [22] with a learning rate of $1 \times 10^4$ and a batch size of 64. We train it for a maximum of 200,000 iterations and employ early stopping.

### 4.4   Performance Estimation

The performance of the framework is proportional to the accuracy of answers in VQA, which is influenced by the Background Process. The parameter we change in the framework is the radius of Gaussian blurring which controls the degree of blurring on satellite images. The results are shown in Fig. 7. Each dataset gets a relative accuracy answering. The training time and response time are not considered in our experiment, because the optimization of them is required in the realization for specific domain.

Images in CLEVR are generated using Blender according to the ground-truth description of the scene. As shown in Fig. 5, the background is almost pure white, the light gray parts are shadows caused by Blender. We first run pretrained models on CLEVR-val and SituationMap-origin. The result indicates that the Situation-origin cannot be directly received by VQA. It is because the SituationMap-origin is too different from the training set of CLEVR. To solve the problem, we implement Gaussian blurring on the images to eliminate the details brought by satellite images. Gaussian blur is a data smoothing method using Gaussian distribution. The two-dimension Gaussian function is

$$f(x,y) = Aexp(-\frac{(x - x_0^2) + (y - y_0^2)}{2\sigma^2}) \tag{2}$$

where $(x, y)$ is the relative coordinates of the pixels. The weights of each pixel are generated by this function. The radius $R$ and the standard deviation $\sigma$

decide the degree of blurring. We fix $\sigma$ and change $R$ from 2 to 6. We only blur the satellite image to make sure the irrelevant details are abandoned and the important information carried by objects are well maintained.

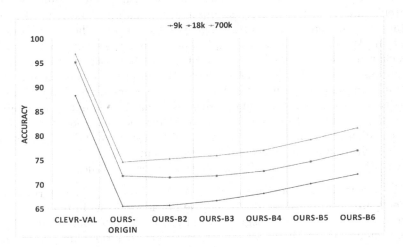

**Fig. 7.** Question answering accuracy on each dataset. We use three different Program Generator which is pretrained with 9k, 18k, and 700k questions. Each line shows how a complicated background and blurring process influence the accuracy of the answers.

Figure 7 shows that as the degree of blurring goes up, the accuracy of SituationMap increases. Because the pretrained models are overfitted, it owns poor generation ability on a much more complicated background image. If the high-frequency components are suppressed among the whole image, those valid features such as sharp edges will be discarded at the same time. Based on the experimental results, we make the following consequences:

- The ResNet-101 model which is used for Feature Extraction is sensitive to the complicated background. Gaussian blurring makes the value of each pixel more even through weights allocation and is proved to be an effective method to deduce the details of the background.
- The Program Generator and Feature Extraction are disentangled. Figure 7 shows that the rate of change is irrelevant to the quantity of pretrained questions. Generally, the more questions used for training the Program Generator, the more accurate VQA is.
- Compared to CLEVR-val, our datasets get lower accuracy but higher utility. Because images in CLEVR-val have no environment information, the seeming higher accuracy is obtained through severe loss of information. However, our datasets contain the environment information, and the performance is proved to be controllable. Besides, it is reliable in the emergency situation, because we have proved that the process on images significantly influences the performance.

# 5    Conclusion and Future Work

In this paper, we propose a novel approach to address the issue: extracting semantic situations from satellite images automatically. Our framework takes the satellite image situation map as input and semantic situations (describing the status or tendency in natural language) as output. The framework consists of the Background Process, VQA, and Association Rules Set, in which, the Background Process deals with the SituationMap dataset, VQA generates question-answer pairs for Association Rules Set to produce the semantic situation in natural language. Our situation map dataset remains minimal bias with detailed annotations for each image, so it is accurate enough to estimate our framework with ground-truth information. Experiments demonstrate that our approach inherits the high accuracy of the VQA system and outperforms the traditional SISA systems on accuracy and automaticity.

For further research, we will consider the following studies:

- Train a new VQA model using SituationMap dataset. The attributions of objects are customized to SISA, and the labels are icons in practice.
- Introduce image semantic segmentation algorithm into Background Process to distinguish the background and foreground in SituationMap more precisely.
- Customize the question set to SISA. Estimate the framework on different question types.
- Consider more variables related to performance such as the map scale, training time and response time.

# References

1. Antol, S., et al.: VQA: Visual Question Answering. In: International Conference on Computer Vision, pp. 2425–2433. IEEE Press (2015). https://doi.org/10.1109/ICCV.2015.279
2. Krishna, R., et al.: Visual genome: connecting language and vision using crowd-sourced dense image annotations. Int. J. Comput. Vision **123**(1), 32–73 (2017). https://doi.org/10.1007/s11263-016-0981-7
3. Zhu, Y., Groth, O., Bernstein, M.S., Feifei, L.: Visual7W: grounded question answering in images. In: Computer Vision and Pattern Recognition, pp. 4995–5004 (2016). https://doi.org/10.1109/CVPR.2016.540
4. Tapaswi, M., Zhu, Y., Stiefelhagen, R., Torralba, A., Urtasun, R., Fidler, S.: MovieQA: understanding stories in movies through question-answering. In: Computer Vision and Pattern Recognition, pp. 4631–4640 (2016). https://doi.org/10.1109/CVPR.2016.501
5. Johnson, J., Hariharan, B., van der Maaten, L., Feifei, L., Zitnick, C.L., Girshick, R.B.: CLEVR: a diagnostic dataset for compositional language and elementary visual reasoning. In: Computer Vision and Pattern Recognition, pp. 1988–1997 (2017)
6. Andreas, J., Rohrbach, M., Darrell, T., Klein, D.: Neural module networks. In: Computer Vision and Pattern Recognition, pp. 39–48 (2016)
7. Johnson, J., et al.: Inferring and executing programs for visual reasoning, pp. 3008–3017 (2017). https://doi.org/10.1109/ICCV.2017.325

8. He, K., Zhang, X., Ren, S., Sun, J.: Deep residual learning for image recognition. In: Computer Vision and Pattern Recognition, pp. 770–778 (2016). https://doi.org/10.1109/CVPR.2016.90

9. Wickens, C.D.: Situation awareness review of Mica Endsley's 1995 articles on situation awareness theory and measurement. Hum. Factors J. Hum. Factors Ergon. Soc. **50**(3), 397–403 (2008). https://doi.org/10.1518/001872008X288420

10. Kokara, M.M., Matheusb, C.J., Baclawskic, K.: Ontology-based situation awareness. Inf. Fusion **10**(1), 83–98 (2009)

11. Li, Z., Itti, L.: Saliency and gist features for target detection in satellite images. IEEE Trans. Image Process. **20**(7), 2017–2029 (2011). https://doi.org/10.1109/TIP.2010.2099128

12. Wu, H., Zhang, H., Zhang, J., Xu, F.: Typical target detection in satellite images based on convolutional neural networks, pp. 2956–2961 (2015). https://doi.org/10.1109/SMC.2015.514

13. Corbane, C., Najman, L., Pecoul, E., Demagistri, L., Petit, M.: A complete processing chain for ship detection using optical satellite imagery. Int. J. Remote Sensing **31**(22), 5837–5854 (2010). https://doi.org/10.1080/01431161.2010.512310

14. Agrawal, A., Batra, D., Parikh, D.: Analyzing the behavior of visual question answering models. In: Empirical Methods in Natural Language Processing, pp. 1955–1960 (2016)

15. Andreas, J., Rohrbach, M., Darrell, T., Klein, D.: Learning to compose neural networks for question answering. In: North American Chapter of the Association for Computational Linguistics, pp. 1545–1554 (2016)

16. Russakovsky, O., et al.: ImageNet large scale visual recognition challenge. Int. J. Comput. Vision **115**(3), 211–252 (2015)

17. He, K., et al.: Deep residual learning for image recognition. IEEE Press (2016). https://doi.org/10.1109/CVPR.2016.90

18. DigitalGlobe Company. https://www.digitalglobe.com

19. Xu, N., et al.: Scene graph captioner: image captioning based on structural visual representation. J. Vis. Commun. Image Represent. **58**, 477–485 (2019)

20. Endsley, M.R.: Situation awareness: operationally necessary and scientifically grounded. Cogn. Technol. Work **17**(2), 163–167 (2015)

21. Li, Y., Ouyang, W., Zhou, B., Wang, K., Wang, X.: Scene graph generation from objects, phrases and region captions. In: International Conference on Computer Vision, pp. 1270–1279 (2017). https://doi.org/10.1109/ICCV.2017.142

22. Kingma, D.P., Ba, J.: Adam: a method for stochastic optimization (2015)

# Efficient ConvNet for Surface Object Recognition

Wei Lin[1], Quan Chen[1], Xianzhi Qi[1], Bingli Wu[1], Xue Ke[1], Dezhao Yang[2],
Yongzhi Wang[2], and Jie Ma[1(✉)]

[1] National Key Laboratory of Science and Technology on Multispectral Information
Processing, School of Artificial Intelligence and Automation,
Huazhong University of Science and Technology, Wuhan 430074, Hubei, China
{wlin,chenquan,qxz_huster,wubingli,kexue0103,majie}@hust.edu.cn
[2] Shanghai Radio Equipment Research Institute, Shanghai 200090, China
yangdezhao1234@163.com, wyz_ht@163.com

**Abstract.** Surface object recognition plays an important role in surface
detection system. Comparing with feature-based classifier, deep neural
networks have evolved to the state-of-the-art technique for object recognition in complex background. However, excessive memory requirements,
expensive computational costs and overmuch energy consumption make
it difficult to deploy neural networks on embedded platform such as the
environment perception module of the Unmanned surface vessel (USV).
In this paper, we propose a dynamic-selecting criterion approach to prune
a trained Yolo-v2 model to deal with these drawbacks caused by redundant parameters in network and we can reduce inference costs for Yolo-v2
by up to 65% on it while regaining close to the original performance by
retraining the network. Moreover, we introduce a surface object dataset
for surface detection system.

**Keywords:** Surface object recognition · Model compression ·
Deep learning

## 1 Introduction

Computer vision technology is one of the most rapidly developing and mature
subfields in artificial intelligence. The task of surface object recognition moves
towards more complete image understanding. In this context, we need care not
only about classification images, but also about location of object contained
within the images. Vision based surface object detection technique has been
widely used in surface detection system such as the environment perception
module of the unmanned surface vessel (USV) and river ship monitor [1]. In the
above application scenarios, the sensors are always under working conditions,
which means that an efficient model is required to handle them.

However, automatically recognizing the surface object is demanding due to
the following issues. First, the color of some boats is similar to that of the rocks

H. Yu et al. (Eds.): ICIRA 2019, LNAI 11741, pp. 308–317, 2019.
https://doi.org/10.1007/978-3-030-27532-7_28

on the water. Second, the camera images are usually filled with light reflection and affected by waves; Third, the shape of boat is not always consistent, and is hard to define. Under such circumstances, traditional machine learning methods accompanied with hand-craft features often fail for the detection task on the sea-surface images.

As the rapid progress of deep learning, it has been a popular approach to many image classification and object detection task. In recent years, a breakthrough of image recognition has been made by deep convolution neural networks (CNNs) [2]. Deep CNN enforces end-to-end training, so that feature extraction and classification are intergrade in a single framework. Besides handing the case where only one conception is contained in an image [2–4], deep CNN has been extended for objects detection [5–8], where not only the objects contained in an image are recognized but their sites are marked by tight bounding boxes.

Nevertheless, comparing with traditional machine learning models, deep CNN models contain significant redundancy among different filters and feature channels [9], requiring plenty of space for models storage and a huge amount of computations for inference. Thus, compressing CNN models is necessary for computational efficiency improvement.

In this paper, we propose a novel filter pruning strategy to prune redundant parameters in Yolo-v2 model to reduce the storage and energy required to run inference on such large networks so they can be deployed on embedded platform. To achieve this goal, we evaluate the importance of filters by combining weights-based criteria with Taylor-based criteria by a dynamic scale factor, then prune filters which have less contributions to the output of networks, unlike [9,10] prune a filter in a prune iteration, we prune $N$ filters once an iteration to improve efficiency, and retrain networks to recover performance. Compared to pruning weights across the network, filter pruning is a naturally structured way of pruning without introducing sparsity and therefore does not require using sparse libraries or any specialized hardware [9]. The number of pruned filters correlates directly with acceleration by reducing the number of matrix multiplications, which is easy to tune for a target speedup.

## 2    Related Work

### 2.1    Object Detection

Object detection methods have been made great progress recently with the development of CNNs. In the past, researches focused on the design of useful hand-crafted features, such as HOG [11] and DPM [12]. But now, it shifts to the design of a good CNN architecture that can automatically capture high-level features for detection task.

To the best of our knowledge, DL-based detection approaches started with research [5] introduced by Christian et al., they presented a formulation a DNN-based regression which outputs a binary mask to predict object location. After that, two-stage architecture performed state-of-the-art in object detection task. Ross et al. [13] put forward R-CNN that adopts an additional selective search procedure. Later, this kind of method evolved to an approximate end-to-end model with using regional proposal network (RPN) in Faster R-CNN [6]. Many follow-up studies successively improve the performance such as R-FCN [14] and Mask R-CNN [15]. Moreover, some end-to-end model also achieve good performance in object detection such as SSD [7] and YOLO [8,16].

## 2.2  Model Compression

We can classify networks compression approach into four categories: low-rank factorization, quantization and binarization, knowledge distillation and parameter pruning [17]. Low-rank factorization based techniques use matrix/tensor decomposition to estimate the informative parameters of the deep CNNs. The works in [18,19] proposed used different tensor decomposition schemes, The low-rank approximation was done layer by layer. The parameters of one layer were fixed after it was done, and the layers above were fine tuned based on a reconstruction error criteria. Network quantization methods compress the original network by reducing the number of bits required to represent each weight and binarization is in the extreme case of 1-bit representation of each weight. The works [20,21] used 8-bit and 16-bit fixed-point respectively to represent weights, and they showed that this method significantly reduced memory usage and float point operations with little loss in classification accuracy. The knowledge distillation methods learn a distilled model and train a more compact neural network to reproduce the output of a larger network. The work in [22] introduced a KD compression framework, which eases the training of deep networks by following a student-teacher paradigm. Despite its simplicity, KD demonstrates promising results in various image classification tasks. The parameter pruning methods explore the redundancy in the model parameters with some criterion and try to remove the redundant and unuseful ones. Network pruning has been used both to reduce network complexity and to address the over-fitting issue. Some approaches [23,24] reduced the number of connections based on the Hessian of the loss function. And methods proposed in [25,26] was to prune non-informative parameters in a trained model. The above pruning schemes typically produce connections pruning in networks, which may not adequately reduce the computation costs in convolutional layers due to irregular sparsity [9]. Thus some works [9,10] prune unimportant filters based on different criterion to achieve both models storage compression and inference speedup.

## 3    Compressing CNN for Efficient Deployment

CNNs with large capacity usually have significant redundancy among different filters and feature channels. In this work, we focus on reducing the storage required and computation cost of well-trained CNNs by pruning filters. Our compression method involves a three-step process, as illustrated in Fig. 1. We evaluate which filters are important considering both weight-based criteria and Taylor-based criteria. The second step is to select $N$ filters by above two criterion separately by a dynamic scale factor across through the whole networks instead of a certain layer like [9]. The final step is to prune the filters in proposal filter set to reduce redundant parameters and retrain network to recover the performance of model.

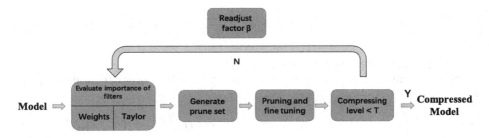

**Fig. 1.** Compressing procedure.

## 3.1   Weight-Based Criteria

The intention of selecting unimportant filters by weight-based criteria is that low-weight filters tend to make less impact to performance of network as compared to other filters [9]. We measure relative importance of a filter by calculate the average magnitude of its weight and the importance defined as follows:

$$s_i^{(j)} = \frac{1}{C_i} \sum_{j=1}^{C_i} \left| W_i^{(j)} \right| \quad W \in R^{k \times k} \tag{1}$$

Where $i$ denotes index of layer, $C_i$ denotes the number of channels in $i$-th layer, $W$ represents weight which size is $k \times k$ (e.g., $3 \times 3$).

In each iteration, we select $2N$ unimportant filters to generate a candidate set:

$$S_w = \{F_1^w, F_2^w, ..., F_{2N}^w\} \tag{2}$$

Where $w$ denotes the criteria is based on weight, $F$ denotes candidate filters and ascending sort by Eq. (1).

## 3.2   Taylor-Based Criteria

Considering that costs of network is determined by not only the weight of model, but also the task, i.e., the input data and the loss function of network, we evaluate importance of filters base on feature map and its grad computed by cost function with back propagation algorithm. we treat pruning as an optimization problem and take Taylor expansion [10] as criteria:

$$\left| \Delta C \left( z_i^{(j)} \right) \right| = \left| C \left( D, z_i^{(j)} \right) - C \left( D, z_i^{(j)} = 0 \right) \right| \tag{3}$$

Where $C(\cdot)$ denotes loss function, $z_i^{(j)}$ represents the feature map from $i$-th layer and $j$-th channel and $D$ is the data input.

Approximating $C(D, z_i^{(j)})$ with a first-order Taylor polynomial near $z_i^{(j)} = 0$, it can express as follows:

$$C\left(D, z_i^{(j)}\right) = C\left(D, z_i^{(j)} = 0\right) + \frac{\partial C}{\partial z_i^{(j)}} z_i^{(j)} + r_1\left(z_i^{(j)} = 0\right) \qquad (4)$$

Where $r_1(\cdot)$ is the first order remainder.

Substituting Eq. (4) to Eq. (3) and ignoring the first order remainder $r_1(\cdot)$, we have:

$$\left|\Delta C\left(z_i^{(j)}\right)\right| = \left|C\left(D, z_i^{(j)} = 0\right) + \frac{\partial C}{\partial z_i^{(j)}} z_i^{(j)} - C\left(D, z_i^{(j)} = 0\right)\right| = \left|\frac{\partial C}{\partial z_i^{(j)}} z_i^{(j)}\right| \qquad (5)$$

Equation (5) shows that we can approximate $|\Delta C(z_i^{(j)})|$ with the accumulation of the product of the activation and its gradient of the cost function, which can be easily computed in the process of back-propagation. Further, we define the importance of each feature map as follows:

$$s_i^{(j)} = \left|\frac{1}{M} \sum_{m=1}^{M} \frac{\partial C}{\partial z_{i,m}^{(j)}} z_{i,m}^{(j)}\right| \qquad (6)$$

Where $M$ is the number of samples in an epoch, the criteria is computed for each sample separately and averaged over $M$.

After computing the scores of each filter by its feature map and grad, we select $2N$ unimportant filters:

$$S_z = \{F_1^z, F_2^z, ..., F_{2N}^z\} \qquad (7)$$

Where $z$ denotes the criteria is based on Taylor expansion, $F$ denotes candidate filters and ascending sort by Eq. (6).

## 3.3   Filters Pruning and Retrain

The first criteria is weight based method which evaluates the importance of filters in model level, that is, the method is independent from data input and loss function. As complementary, the second criteria calculate by feature map and its grad, which takes data input and loss function into account. Intuitively, selecting filters from different criterion can reduce the dependence of filters on each other across through the whole network.

$S_w$ includes $2N$ filters selected by its criteria as well as $S_z$. In each pruning iteration, we pick $N$ filters to prune in following criteria: (1) if the number of filters in intersection of $S_w$ and $S_z$ is greater than $N$, we pick top $N$ filters from $S_w$ as the same from $S_z$. (2) if it is less than $N$, we pick all filters in the

---

**Algorithm 1.** Dynamic-selecting Criterion Pruning

---

**Input:** $\theta$: Trained model.

   $T$: Compressing level(total iteration).

**Output:** $\theta^-$: Compressed model.

1  **for** $t < T$ **do**

2  |  **Update** $\beta$: Readjust factor $\beta$ by Eq. (9)

3  |  **Filters proposal**: Select 2N filters based on two criteria separately by Eq. (1,6)

4  |  **Determining pruning set**: Pick $N$ filters to prune by Eq. (8)

5  |  **Pruning and retrain**: Pruning $N$ filters in each iteration and retrain to recovery performance.

6  |  $t = t + 1$.

7  **end**

---

intersection then we pick the rest in both $S_w$ and $S_z$ using adjustable ratio with parameter $\beta$. The present above can be formulated as:

$$S_p = \begin{cases} \Phi(N, S_w \cap S_z) & K \geq N \\ \Phi(K, S_w \cap S_z) \cup \Phi(\beta(N-K), S_w^-) \cup \Phi((1-\beta)(N-K), S_z^-) & K < N \end{cases} \quad (8)$$

Where $K$ is the number of filters in intersection, of $S_w$ and $S_z$, $\Phi(m, S)$ denotes the subset consist of top m elements in set $S$ and $S_w^-$ denotes the complementary set of $\Phi(K, S_w \cap S_z)$ as well as $S_z^-$, $\beta$ is a linear dynamic scale factor defined as follows:

$$\beta = \beta_0 - \frac{t}{T}(1 - \beta_0) \quad (9)$$

Where $\beta_0$ is initial value, $t$ is current iteration and $T$ is the total iteration. In our experiment $\beta_0 = 0.6$. Which means that we hope to prune min weights filters to handle overfitting at the beginning of pruning, but cost change need more consideration with the further pruning proceed.

## 4  Experiments

In this section, we apply our efficient model to surface object detection and present the result in some aspects.

### 4.1  Datasets and Experimental Settings

Our surface object dataset consists of 3219 images (2213 images for training and 1006 images for testing), which includes 5 kinds of common object on the water surface. Our experiments are implemented in NVIDIA GeForce GTX 1080 GPU and NVIDIA Jetson TX2 embedded platform. Moreover, we introduce focal loss [27] to address the unbalance between positive and negative samples during training stage. For a pruning-fine tuning iteration, we select 64 filters to prune, then fine tuning model with 15 epochs, after all pruning done, we fine tuning model with 10 epochs to recovery performance.

## 4.2 Experimental Results and Analysis

The result of several detection algorithm is shown in Table 1, we compare our Efficient YOLO with some well-known object detection models, including Faster-RCNN, SSD, and YOLOv2. Following other detection tasks, we use mean average precision (mAP) to evaluate performance of models. Moreover, storage requirement and inference time are also considered for efficiency of models. Our Efficient YOLO model can achieve almost the best performance at 76 FPS while require the smallest storage for weights.

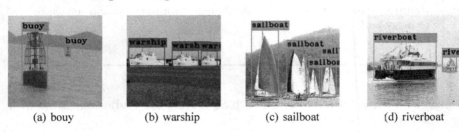

(a) bouy          (b) warship          (c) sailboat          (d) riverboat

**Fig. 2.** Some detection results in our datasets.

**Table 1.** Performance statistics for different models

| Algorithm | mAP (%) | Weights (MB) | FPS |
|-----------|---------|--------------|-----|
| Faster-RCNN | **87.1** | 518 | 8 |
| SSD512 | 84.5 | 104 | 23 |
| YOLOv2 | 86.3 | 280 | 42 |
| Efficient YOLO | 86.3 | **98** | **76** |

Compressing makes a lightweight model, which achieves significant speedup and energy efficiency improvement. We also compare original model and compressed model in two different hardware. For intuitive purpose, Table 2 presents multiple of improvement in the above aspects. We use *nvidia-smi* utility of GTX 1080 GPU and the *power-monitor-with-i2c* interface in TX2 embedded platform to observe the power consumption. Our Efficient YOLO model can reduce dependency on computational capacity and power supply to some extent, which is meaningful to device especially for embedded hardware.

**Table 2.** Efficiency improvement of compressed model

| Device | Speedup | Energy efficiency |
|--------|---------|-------------------|
| GTX 1080 | 1.8× | 2.4× |
| TX2 | 1.9× | 2.2× |

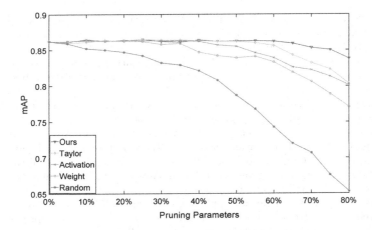

**Fig. 3.** Pruning of feature maps with different criterion.

Figure 3 shows pruning of darknet-19 with different criteria. Weight means filters with minimum weights would be prune. Activation and Taylor mean filters which corresponding to minimum score respectively would be pruned. We observed that performance of networks immune to a little pruning whichever criteria is used, but our strategy works well with the further pruning proceed.

## 5  Conclusion

In this paper, we present a method for fast and accurate detection of surface object with existing monitoring equipment. Focusing on the complex background of the surface object and the requirement of stability, accuracy, low storage and low power consumption in the application, this paper proposes an Efficient YOLO model. More specifically, we prune redundant convolution kernels by the combination of weights-based criteria and Taylor-based criteria, which takes into account both the effect of network itself and the effect of activation and its grads. The experimental results reveal that compared with some popular detection networks, our Efficient YOLO model can achieve almost the best performance at 76 FPS(GTX-1080)/15 FPS(TX2) while require the lower power consumption(GTX-1080 : 64W/TX2 : 2.9W) and the smaller storage for weights(98MB), which may lower the limitation in embedded system to run CNN models.

**Acknowledgments.** This work was supported by the Shanghai Aerospace Science and Technology Innovation Program under Grant sast2016063.

## References

1. Nanette, A.T., Olsen Richard, B., et al.: Literature review on vessel detection. Technical report (2004)

2. Krizhevsky, A., Sutskever, I., Hinton, G.E.: Imagenet classification with deep convolutional neural networks. In: Advances in Neural Information Processing Systems, pp. 1097–1105 (2012)
3. He, K., Zhang, X., Ren, S., Sun, J.: Deep residual learning for image recognition. In: Proceedings of the IEEE Conference on Computer Vision and Pattern Recognition, pp. 770–778 (2016)
4. Simonyan, K., Zisserman, A.: Very deep convolutional networks for large-scale image recognition. arXiv preprint arXiv:1409.1556 (2014)
5. Szegedy, C., Toshev, A., Erhan, D.: Deep neural networks for object detection. In: Advances in Neural Information Processing Systems, pp. 2553–2561 (2013)
6. Ren, S., He, K., Girshick, R., Sun, J.: Faster R-CNN: towards real-time object detection with region proposal networks. In: Advances in Neural Information Processing Systems, pp. 91–99 (2015)
7. Liu, W., et al.: SSD: single shot multibox detector. In: Leibe, B., Matas, J., Sebe, N., Welling, M. (eds.) ECCV 2016. LNCS, vol. 9905, pp. 21–37. Springer, Cham (2016). https://doi.org/10.1007/978-3-319-46448-0_2
8. Redmon, J., Farhadi, A.: Yolo9000: better, faster, stronger. In: Proceedings of the IEEE Conference on Computer Vision and Pattern Recognition, pp. 7263–7271 (2017)
9. Li, H., Kadav, A., Durdanovic, I., Samet, H., Graf, H.P.: Pruning filters for efficient convnets. arXiv preprint arXiv:1608.08710 (2016)
10. Molchanov, P., Tyree, S., Karras, T., Aila, T., Kautz, J.: Pruning convolutional neural networks for resource efficient transfer learning. arXiv preprint arXiv:1611.06440 (2016)
11. Dalal, N., Triggs, B.: Histograms of oriented gradients for human detection. In: international Conference on Computer Vision & Pattern Recognition (CVPR 2005), vol. 1, pp. 886–893. IEEE Computer Society (2005)
12. Felzenszwalb, P.F., Girshick, R.B., McAllester, D., Ramanan, D.: Object detection with discriminatively trained part-based models. IEEE Trans. Pattern Anal. Mach. Intell. 32(9), 1627–1645 (2010)
13. Girshick, R., Donahue, J., Darrell, T., Malik, J.: Region-based convolutional networks for accurate object detection and segmentation. IEEE Trans. Pattern Anal. Mach. Intell. 38(1), 142–158 (2016)
14. Dai, J., Li, Y., He, K., Sun, J.: R-FCN: object detection via region-based fully convolutional networks. In: Advances in Neural Information Processing Systems, pp. 379–387 (2016)
15. He, K., Gkioxari, G., Dollár, P., Girshick, R.: Mask R-CNN. In: Proceedings of the IEEE International Conference on Computer Vision, pp. 2961–2969 (2017)
16. Redmon, J., Divvala, S., Girshick, R., Farhadi, A.: You only look once: unified, real-time object detection. In: Proceedings of the IEEE Conference on Computer Vision and Pattern Recognition, pp. 779–788 (2016)
17. Cheng, Y., Wang, D., Zhou, P., Zhang, T.: A survey of model compression and acceleration for deep neural networks. arXiv preprint arXiv:1710.09282 (2017)
18. Denton, E.L., Zaremba, W., Bruna, J., LeCun, Y., Fergus, R.: Exploiting linear structure within convolutional networks for efficient evaluation. In: Advances in Neural Information Processing Systems, pp. 1269–1277 (2014)
19. Jaderberg, M., Vedaldi, A., Zisserman, A.: Speeding up convolutional neural networks with low rank expansions. arXiv preprint arXiv:1405.3866 (2014)
20. Vanhoucke, V., Senior, A., Mao, M.Z.: Improving the speed of neural networks on CPUs (2011)

21. Gupta, S., Agrawal, A., Gopalakrishnan, K., Narayanan, P.: Deep learning with limited numerical precision. In: International Conference on Machine Learning, pp. 1737–1746 (2015)
22. Hinton, G., Vinyals, O., Dean, J.: Distilling the knowledge in a neural network. arXiv preprint arXiv:1503.02531 (2015)
23. Xu, L., Jordan, M.I., Hinton, G.E.: An alternative model for mixtures of experts. In: Tesauro, G., Touretzky, D.S., Leen, T.K. (eds.) Advances in Neural Information Processing Systems 7, pp. 633–640. MIT Press (1995). http://papers.nips.cc/paper/906-an-alternative-model-for-mixtures-of-experts.pdf
24. Hassibi, B., Stork, D.G.: Second order derivatives for network pruning: optimal brain surgeon. In: Advances in Neural Information Processing Systems, vol. 5, pp. 164–171 (1993)
25. Han, S., Pool, J., Tran, J., Dally, W.: Learning both weights and connections for efficient neural network. In: Advances in Neural Information Processing Systems, pp. 1135–1143 (2015)
26. Chen, W., Wilson, J., Tyree, S., Weinberger, K., Chen, Y.: Compressing neural networks with the hashing trick. In: International Conference on Machine Learning, pp. 2285–2294 (2015)
27. Lin, T.-Y., Goyal, P., Girshick, R., He, K., Dollár, P.: Focal loss for dense object detection. In: Proceedings of the IEEE International Conference on Computer Vision, pp. 2980–2988 (2017)

# Deep Learning Based Fire Detection System for Surveillance Videos

Hao Wang[1(✉)], Zhiying Pan[1], Zhifei Zhang[1], Hongzhang Song[2],
Shaobo Zhang[3], and Jianhua Zhang[1]

[1] College of Computer Science and Technology,
Zhejiang University of Technology, Hangzhou, Zhejiang, China
375050581@qq.com
[2] High Dimension Vision Technology Co., Ltd.,
Hangzhou, Zhejiang Province, China
[3] Vision Entropy Technology Co., Ltd., Hangzhou, Zhejiang, China

**Abstract.** At present, the method of detecting fire by convolutional neural network only uses flame or smoke as an indicator of fire occurrence, and such a method is somewhat limited. This article also detects flames and smoke so that it can be alarmed only when smoke or flame is detected. When the smoke and flame are detected at the same time, the credibility of the alarm can be improved. Our experiments show that the proposed network achieves excellent accuracy and speed.

**Keywords:** Deep learning · Fire detection · Smoke detection · Surveillance videos

## 1 Introduction

Fire is one of the most probable disasters and poses a serious threat to the natural and social environment. According to data from the Ministry of Public Security of China, direct property damage caused by fire in 2016 reached RMB 3.72 billion, with 1,582 deaths. The timely discovery of fire points is extremely important for preventing widespread fire spread and fighting. In indoor environments, various sensors are mainly used as alarm devices, such as heat-sensitive detectors, light-sensitive detectors, and smoke-sensitive detectors. However, these sensors need to be installed near the fire point, so it is not suitable for a relatively open environment.

With the rapid spread of video surveillance systems, and the rapid development of image processing technology, applications that combine video surveillance systems and image processing are endless. Fire detection and alarm using computer vision technology are very promising topics in this regard. The fire detection technology based on digital image processing technology does not need to be close to the fire point in large rooms and open environments. It only needs to be modified with the existing video surveillance system to reduce the extra equipment installation and procurement, so it has the advantages of low cost and wide application. Therefore, fire detection technology based on video surveillance system has become a hot research target.

© Springer Nature Switzerland AG 2019
H. Yu et al. (Eds.): ICIRA 2019, LNAI 11741, pp. 318–328, 2019.
https://doi.org/10.1007/978-3-030-27532-7_29

Traditional image processing algorithms rely mainly on visual features such as motion, color, shape, transparency, and texture. Such as inter-frame difference method, optical flow method, background difference method. Chen et al. [1] studied the dynamic behavior and irregularities of flames in RGB and HSI color spaces. In order to predict fire and non-fire pixels, Marbach et al. [2] explored the combination of YUV color model and motion characteristics. Celik and Demirel [3] use YCbCr to separate the brilliance information from the brightness according to special rules, but only for close and large flames. Borges and Izquirdo [4] attempted to detect flames using a multi-model framework containing color, skewness, rough features, and Bayesian classifiers. Based on the work of Borges and Izquiredo, Rafiee [5] try to use a multi-resolution two-dimensional wavelet transform combined with energy and shape methods to reduce the error rate, but the effect is not obvious. Yusuf et al. [6] used SVM to detect flames, although it has good accuracy in close-range images, but performs poorly in images obtained from long distances.

Because deep learning can automatically learn image features from large quantities of data, there is no need to artificially design related feature extraction algorithms, and the information that can be extracted is more extensive, which is beneficial to image recognition and classification. Frizzi et al. used convolutional neural networks to detect smoke and flame in video. This paper uses a convolutional neural network structure similar to LeNet-5 structure, and as a classifier, the results show that it can achieve 97.9% accuracy [7, 8]. Tao et al. [9] used the AlexNet network structure to detect the flame. The model is capable of achieving 96.88% and 99.4% accuracy on large data sets and small data sets, respectively. Another article that also uses the AlexNet network structure, using images with artificial images as the background and artificially synthesized flames as training data, and then tested on actual images, showing high accuracy [10].

Although these algorithms have their own advantages, there is still room for improvement. In addition, the false positive rate is still high and needs to be further reduced. As can be seen from the above literature, the accuracy of fire detection is inversely related to the computational complexity. Therefore, it is necessary to develop a fire detection algorithm with low cost and low false alarm rate, and higher accuracy.

Therefore, this paper proposes a fire detection structure with double convolution structure. The two structures are the same. One is used to extract the characteristics of flame, the other is to extract the characteristics of smoke, and the confidence of the flame and the smoke are respectively output.

This article is organized as follows. Section 2 provides a brief introduction to convolutional neural networks. Section 3 introduce the proposed fire detection network. Section 4 discusses the results of the experiment and summarizes them.

## 2 Detection System Structure

In the past, most of the research on flame detection was based on traditional feature extraction methods. With the application of deep learning in the field of computer vision, algorithms have begun to detect fires based on deep learning. Deep learning originated from the study of artificial neural networks, and related concepts were proposed by Hinton et al. [11] in 2006. As one of the representative algorithms of deep learning, convolutional neural networks [12] are widely used in the field of computer vision.

An efficient target detection network is very important, and there are high requirements for the accuracy of detection in practical applications. According to this goal, we propose a fire detection system based on deep learning. The overall structure of the system is shown in Fig. 1.

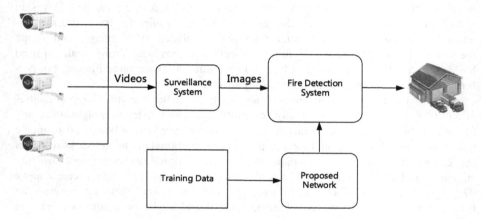

**Fig. 1.** Proposed fire detection framework

As a fire detection system based on video surveillance system, the first is the construction of video surveillance system. Under the multi-channel input video surveillance system, it mainly conducts fire and smoke detection for areas that need to be monitored, and is divided into indoor and outdoor scenarios. In the outdoor environment, the scene to be detected is particularly large, as shown in Fig. 2, which is a production environment where the system is applied, with a total area of about 45,000 square meters, and the red region is the part that the fire detection system needs to monitor. The monitoring of the outdoor part is a difficult point. The camera scans the entire area to be monitored by cruising, and needs to zoom to the local scene to ensure that the fire detection system has enough information to identify flame or smoke.

In the fire detection system, we need create threads as much as channels which need to be detected, so that the corresponding video images can be extracted from the monitoring system separately, and corresponding processing is performed according to actual needs for each channel of video, so as to improve detection accuracy.

## 3   The Proposed Network

This section mainly discusses the proposed network, it is benefited from [13], and its structure of detection and recognition will be discussed here, as shown in Fig. 3.

**Fig. 2.** The range needs to be detected in the outdoor scene, the red coil is the part of dump that needs to be monitored by the fire detection system. (Color figure online)

The detection part consists of two convolutional structures, the network structure of which is the same, except that the detection targets are different. It is a deep convolutional neural network consisting of ten layers of convolutional layers used to extract different features of the input image. We call this part the detection module. The detection module passes the feature maps extracted by the last convolutional layer to the three cascaded fully connected layers, and the fully connected layer finally outputs the bounding box prediction of the detected target. The recognition module uses the region of interest (ROI) pooling layer to extract the feature map of interest, and predicts whether there is flame or smoke in the input image through classifiers. The entire model is an end-to-end network for detecting fire.

Using a popular terminology 'attention' [14] in neural networks, the detection module serves as the 'attention' of this unified network. It tells the recognition module where to look. Then the recognition module extracts the ROI from shared feature maps and predicts whether flame or smoke. The proposed network, first sends the input image to the detection module, and extracts the feature maps through the convolution layer of the detection module. As the number of layers increases, the feature map of the output increases, but the size of the feature map gradually decreases. The feature map obtained from the last layer of convolution has higher level features of the input image, and it is more beneficial when detecting and locating. Suppose the center point x-coordinate, the center point y-coordinate, the width, and the height of the bounding box are $b_x, b_y, b_w, b_h$ respectively. Let W and H be the width and the height of the input image. The bounding box location $c_x, c_y, w, h$ satisfies:

$$cx = \frac{b_x}{W} \quad cy = \frac{b_y}{H} \quad w = \frac{b_w}{W} \quad h = \frac{b_h}{H}, 0 < cx, cy, w, h < 1 \quad (1)$$

Through experience, we know that the feature maps obtained by different layers in a network structure have different levels of features [15]. Moreover, previous work [16]

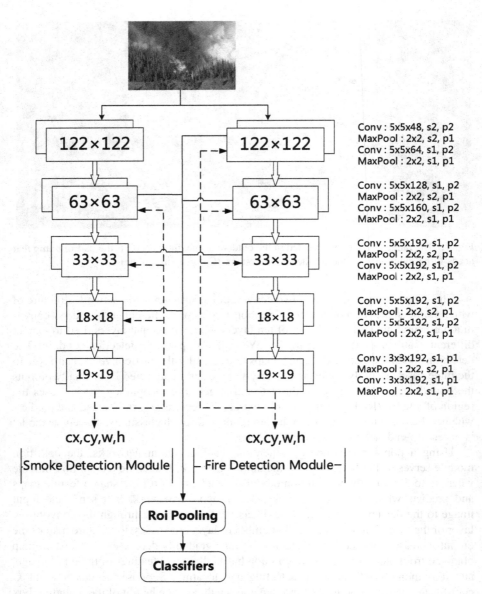

**Fig. 3.** The overall structure of our network. It is mainly divided into two parts: the detection module and the classification module. The detection module composed with smoke detection module and flame detection module, and output the bounding box prediction. The classification module using bounding box which comes from the detection module to extract feature maps from relating regions, then put them into ROI pooling layers, and feeds the combined feature maps to the subsequent Classifiers.

shows lower-level feature maps improve the quality of instance segmentation because the lower-level convolution layer preserves more detail of the input image. Therefore, we can use feature maps from lower-level convolution layer to recognize flame and smoke like semantic segmentation. At the same time, due to the difference between flame and smoke in the actual situation, that is, when the fire occurs, the size of the flame is smaller than the size of the smoke. After detection module compute all the feature maps, we can get a bounding box prediction of size $(m * h) * (n * w)$ with p channels from the full-connected layers. A feature map of the second, fourth, and sixth layer of convolutional layers used by the flame detection module. The smoke detection module uses the feature maps of the fourth, sixth and eighth convolution layers. And extracting the binding frame areas corresponding to the feature maps respectively. The sizes of extracted feature maps are $(122 * h) * (122 * w) * 64, (63 * h) * (63 * w) * 160,$ $(33 * h) * (33 * w) * 192$ both in fire detection module and smoke detection module. And then those feature maps will be converted by ROI Pooling layers into a feature maps with a fixed spatial extent of $P_H * P_W$ ($8 * 16$ in this paper). Afterwards, these six resized feature maps $2 * (8 * 16 * 64), 2 * (8 * 16 * 160)$ and $2 * (8 * 16 * 192)$ are concatenated to one feature map of size $8 * 16 * 832$ for classification.

## 4   Results and Analysis

The proposed network can be trained end-to-end and accomplishes flame or smoke bounding box detection and recognition. The training involves choosing suitable loss functions for detection performance and recognition performance, as well as pre-training the detection module before training the whole network end-to-end.

### 4.1   Datasets

For the research of fire detection, the acquisition of related datasets is very difficult. For example, the fire dataset of Korea's Keimyung University totals 2668 s, a total of 64,032 frames, but its background is relatively simple, and the pixel value is only $320 \times 240$ [17]. The dataset used in [18] contains 226 images. Although this dataset is relatively small, it contains a relatively large number of confusing images, such as the sun, a light similar to a flame, or an image of a sunset shining onto an object. As shown in Fig. 4.

In general, the relevant datasets are relatively few, and [19] demonstrates the reliability of using synthetic images as data sets. Therefore, this paper uses the combination of real image and synthetic image as the data set, the synthetic dataset and the real data set together, a total of 23,842 images, and divided 80% for the training set, 20% for the test set.

**Fig. 4.** The first row is an image similar to the flame, and the second row is an image with a real flame.

## 4.2   Training

The training of the whole model is divided into two parts, the detection module is trained first, and then the detection module is trained together with the recognition module. Therefore, the following explains how the loss function of these two modules is defined.

**Detection Module.** Before training the proposed network end-to-end, the recognition module needs bounding box $(cx, cy, w, h)$ as extract region. A reasonable prediction $(cx, cy, w, h)$ must meet $0 < cx, cy, w, h < 1$, and might try to meet $\frac{w}{2} \leq cx \leq 1 - \frac{w}{2}$, $\frac{h}{2} \leq cy \leq 1 - \frac{h}{2}$. Therefore, we need define the loss function of localization (loc). Let N be the size of a mini-batch in training. The localization loss (see Eq. (2)) is a Smooth L1 loss [20] between the predicted box ($pb$) and the ground truth box ($gb$).

$$L_{loc}(pb, gb) = \sum_{N} \sum_{m \in \{cx, cy, w, h\}} smooth_{L1}(pb^m - gb^m) \tag{2}$$

**Recognition Module.** The classification loss (cls) is defined as Eq. (3), It is a cross entropy loss. Let the ground-truth of flame and smoke be $gn_1$ and $gn_2$, $nc_1$ and $nc_2$ represent the possibility of belonging to each specific class. With the joint optimization of both localization and classification losses, the extracted features would have richer information about flame and smoke. Experiments show that both detection and recognition performance can be enhanced by jointly optimizing Eqs. (2) and (3).

$$L_{cls}(pn, gn) = \sum_N \sum_{i=1,2} \left\{ -pn_i[gn_i] + \log\left( \sum_{1 < j < (nc_1, nc_2)} \exp(pn_i[j]) \right) \right\} \quad (3)$$

$$L(pb, pn, gb, gn) = \frac{1}{N} (L_{loc}(pb, gb) + L_{cls}(pn, gn)) \quad (4)$$

### 4.3   Result and Analysis

Here we mainly compare the results with SSD [21], because the good performance of SSD makes it widely used in practice.

We follow the standard protocol in object detection Intersection-over-Union (IoU) [22]. The bounding box is considered to be correct if and only if its IoU with the ground-truth bounding box is more than 70% (IoU > 0.7).

The comparation result between SSD and proposed network is shown in Fig. 5. It shows whether the flame and smoke in dataset are correctly detected. True Positive Rate indicates the proportion of the fire correctly identified, False Positive Rate indicates the proportion of the fire that was incorrectly identified, and True Positive Rate indicates that it is correctly identified as the proportion of no fire, False Negative Rate indicates the proportion of misidentification as no fire. It can be seen from the figure that compared to SSD, the True Positive Rate increased from 82.2% to 94.4%, the False Positive Rate decreased from 17.8% to 5.6%, the True Negative Rate increased from 80.6% to 98.6%, and the False Negative Rate from 19.4% fell to 1.4%.

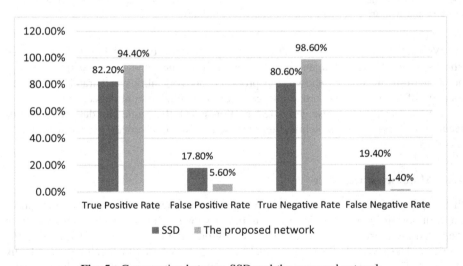

**Fig. 5.** Comparative between SSD and the proposed network

**Fig. 6.** The detection results of the proposed network, yellow box and text are detected smokes, red box and text are detected flames (Color figure online)

We show some detection result using the proposed network in Fig. 6. The original images have different sizes, and here they are reset to the same size for display. As can be seen from the images shown, the proposed network almost accurately marks the location of the flame and smoke and gives a fairly reliable confidence.

Another need to be presented is recognition speed, the single slot detector achieves recognition speed 36 fps, while the proposed network achieves higher recognition speed (51 fps).

## 4.4   Monitoring Interface

In this part, the proposed fire detection algorithm is integrated into the system, and a fire monitoring interface is designed, as Fig. 7 shows. This interface is separate from the video monitoring interface and shows only the monitoring screens that require fire detection. Here we only detect 6 channels as needed, each of which can be individually switched. The green box on the edge of each screen in the figure indicates that no alarm is currently occurring. If an alarm occurs, the green frame will change to a red box and flash. At the same time, an alarm box will pop up, showing the scene where the fire occurred, and the bounding box prediction output by the fire detection algorithm is marked in the figure.

**Fig. 7.** Fire detection and monitoring interface

## 5   Conclusion

Due to the challenges of fire detection in real environments, we propose a fire detection algorithm based on convolutional neural networks. It not only detects the flame, but also detects the smoke. It uses the small size of the flame in the case of long viewing distance, and the large size of the smoke increases the credibility of the alarm. The final experiment shows the accuracy. It reached 94.4%. However, the current algorithm still has certain limitations. At night, the video surveillance system automatically converts to the infrared mode, and the black and white image is obtained, which brings difficulty for detection. Therefore, there is still more work to be done.

**Acknowledgment.** This work was supported National Natural Science Foundation of China (61876167 and U1509207).

## References

1. Lin, M.X., Chen, W.L., Liu, B.S., et al.: An intelligent fire-detection method based on image processing. Adv. Eng. Forum **2–3**, 172–175 (2011)
2. Marbach, G., Loepfe, M., Brupbacher, T.: An image processing technique for fire detection in video images. Fire Saf. J. **41**(4), 285–289 (2006)
3. Çelik, T., Demirel, H.: Fire detection in video sequences using a generic color model. Fire Saf. J. **44**(2), 147–158 (2009)
4. Borges, P.V.K., Izquierdo, E.: A probabilistic approach for vision-based fire detection in videos. IEEE Trans. Circuits Syst. Video Technol. **20**(5), 721–731 (2010)

5. Rafiee, A., Tavakoli, R., Dianat, R., et al.: Fire and smoke detection using wavelet analysis and disorder characteristics. In: International Conference on Computer Research & Development, IEEE (2011)
6. Habiboğlu, Y.H., Günay, O., Çetin, A.E.: Covariance matrix-based fire and flame detection method in video. Mach. Vis. Appl. **23**(6), 1103–1113 (2012)
7. Frizzi, S., Kaabi, R., Bouchouicha, M., et al.: [IEEE IECON 2016 - 42nd Annual Conference of the IEEE Industrial Electronics Society - Florence, Italy (2016.10.23-2016.10.26)] IECON 2016 - 42nd Annual Conference of the IEEE Industrial Electronics Society - Convolutional neural network for video fire and smoke detection. In: Conference of the IEEE Industrial Electronics Society, IEEE, pp. 877–882 (2016)
8. Lecun, Y.L., Bottou, L., Bengio, Y., et al.: Gradient-based learning applied to document recognition. Proc. IEEE **86**(11), 2278–2324 (1998)
9. Tao, C., Zhang, J., Wang, P.: Smoke detection based on deep convolutional neural networks. In: International Conference on Industrial Informatics-computing Technology, IEEE (2017)
10. Tomas Polednik, Bc.: Detection of fire in images and video using CNN. Excel@FIT (2015)
11. Hinton, G.E., Salakhutdinov, R.R.: Reducing the dimensionality of data with neural networks. Science **313**(5786), 504–507 (2006)
12. Krizhevsky, A., Sutskever, I., Hinton, G.E.: Imagenet classification with deep convolutional neural networks. In: Advances in Neural Information Processing Systems, pp. 1097–1105 (2012)
13. Xu, Z., et al.: Towards End-to-end license plate detection and recognition: a large dataset and baseline. In: 15th European Conference, Munich, Germany, 8–14 September 2018, Proceedings, Part XIII (2018)
14. Chorowski, J.K., Bahdanau, D., Serdyuk, D., Cho, K., Bengio, Y.: Attention-based models for speech recognition. In: Advances in Neural Information Processing Systems, pp. 577–585 (2015)
15. Zhou, B., Khosla, A., Lapedriza, A., et al.: Object Detectors Emerge in Deep Scene CNNs. Computer Science (2014)
16. Long, J., Shelhamer, E., Darrell, T.: Fully convolutional networks for semantic segmentation. IEEE Trans. Pattern Anal. Mach. Intell. **39**(4), 640–651 (2014)
17. Simonyan, K., Zisserman, A.: Very deep convolutional networks for large-scale image recognition. arXiv preprint arXiv:1409.1556 (2014)
18. Li, B., Peng, X., Wang, Z., et al.: AOD-Net: all-in-one dehazing network. In: Proceedings of the IEEE International Conference on Computer Vision, pp. 4770–4778 (2017)
19. Ko, B.C., Ham, S.J., Nam, J.Y.: Modeling and formalization of fuzzy finite automata for detection of irregular fire flames. IEEE Trans. Circuits Syst. Video Technol. **21**(12), 1903–1912 (2011)
20. Girshick, R.: Fast R-CNN. Computer Science (2015)
21. Liu, W., Anguelov, D., Erhan, D., et al.: SSD: single shot multibox detector. In: European Conference on Computer Vision (2016)
22. Li, H., Wang, P., Shen, C.: Toward end-to-end car license plate detection and recognition with deep neural networks. IEEE Trans. Intell. Transp. Syst. **PP**(99) (2017)

# 3D Scanning and Multiple Point Cloud Registration with Active View Complementation for Panoramically Imaging Large-Scale Plants

Dajing Gu, Kai Zhu, Yuechen Shao, Wei Wu, Liang Gong$^{(\boxtimes)}$, and Chengliang Liu

Shanghai Jiao Tong University, Shanghai 200240, China
gongliang_mi@sjtu.edu.cn

**Abstract.** 3D scanning is a surface reconstruction and a data processing technique which has already been widely used in reverse engineering, agricultural identification and other fields. However, most of the Commercial Off-The-Shelf (COTS) 3D scanning instruments are now developed for small and medium-sized targets, and there lacks an effective means for large-scale objects. In this paper, a multi-scale 3D scanning scheme with active-recognition is presented, which can effectively realize 3D information reconstruction of large-scale targets and recognition. First, data collected by 3D scanners based on structured light technology, which are placed at multiple angles, can be aligned together to generate a complete point cloud. Second, in order to achieve the panoramic view of the target, a camera with higher precision is mounted on the robotic arm for close-up shooting of the areas that are not easy to accurately capture. Finally, multi-scale and multi-resolution target scanning are achieved through refined scanning and detail feature recognition. This method combines large-scale structured light scanning with close-range image acquisition, which has potentials in fruit picking positioning, flaw detection of large workpieces, and three-dimensional human body modeling.

**Keywords:** 3D scanning · Multi-scale · Target recognition · Point cloud registration

## 1 Introduction

With the renewal of agricultural production mode and the application of new technologies, the 21st century will be an important period for the intelligent development of agricultural machinery.

The research of agricultural picking robots has been 40 years, and the three-dimensional scanning reconstruction technology plays an important role in the development of the vision system, whose performance determines the picking efficiency, speed and quality of picking robots. Generally, the vision system consists of a camera, an image processing device, a distance measuring device and a computer. The fruit

© Springer Nature Switzerland AG 2019
H. Yu et al. (Eds.): ICIRA 2019, LNAI 11741, pp. 329–341, 2019.
https://doi.org/10.1007/978-3-030-27532-7_30

image is taken by the camera before picking, then the image is processed so that the fruit and the leaves can be identified, and the accurate spatial coordinates of the fruit can be finally determined.

The application of robotics technology to harvest fruits and vegetables was first proposed in 1968 by American scholars Schertz and Brown. A stereoscopic image method has been used by the University of Kyoto in Japan to identify the relative position of fruits in a watermelon harvesting robot named "STORK" [1]. Technologies like the near-infrared vision system (the Nether-lands Institute of Agricultural Environmental Engineering) [2], the intelligent color filtering algorithms and image morphology operations (Barry University of Technology in collaboration with Lecce University) [3], and the CCD camera and photoelectric sensor (Kyurgpook University) [4] have also been applied to the development of the agricultural robots.

Although 3D point cloud reconstruction technology is a high-tech which has been widely used in CT scanning [5] and in picking robots to improve efficiency. However, the scanning field of the 3D scanner is always too small to obtain the full three-dimensional information of large-scale targets, which limits the capabilities of the vision system. In order to realize the acquisition, this paper will present a large-scale target 3D scanning robot, which offers a surround scanning scheme for large-scale objects (in this scheme, two meters in diameter and two meters high): a complete point cloud can be obtained by aligning the scan results of multiple cameras (with each result of more than 10000+ vertices), and then corresponding point cloud processing is performed to identify the target for further refined identification.

The paper is structured as follows: Sect. 2 introduces the electromechanical control platform, in which the hardware and software framework design of the robot will be represented. Subsequently Sect. 3 analyzes the processing and registration methods of 3D point cloud. Section 4 introduces the recognition and positioning of key parts and the fine scanning of the manipulator after the point cloud processing. Then Sect. 5 shows the experiment results. Finally, Sect. 6 summarizes the work presented in this paper.

## 2    Electromechanical Control Platform

### 2.1    Hardware Framework

The design of the hardware system is mainly divided into three modules: a mobile platform, a robotic arm and a sensor, and an electric control cabinet to realize large-scale three-dimensional scanning.

The main mobile platform is a door structure. According to the location of the electric cabinet, it is divided into a near-door screw mechanism and a far-door screw mechanism. The top platform is connected in the middle, and a top screw mechanism is arranged in the middle. The screw adopts the Hiwin linear module set. A coded structured light sensor (consisting of a Logitech 1080P Full HD camera and an HP 1080p projector) is placed around the target at a fixed angle (30° here). A total of 12 sensors (360° totally) are placed, and the entire platform is driven by a stepper motor. The guide rail moves up and down, which enables the sensors to scan the target layer by layer. The image obtained by each sensor is reconstructed and aligned in three dimensions (Fig. 1).

**Fig. 1.** Mobile platform design drawings

In the top screw mechanism, the DoArm S6 6 DoF robotic arm is used to realize the further refined scanning. The DoArm S6 is a 6-DOF manipulator model. The WiFi control unit provides flexible control of the movement and grabbing of the robotic arm. The addition of a robotic arm can solve the blind corner of the surround scan, on which a camera can be installed to supplement the missing point cloud (Fig. 2).

**Fig. 2.** (a) Equipment diagram (b) Robotic arm diagram

## 2.2 Software Framework

The structured light three-dimensional vision measurement method can be divided into two types: monocular structured light and binocular structured light. The monocular system is used in this project because it is simpler, cheaper and more suitable for different scene applications. According to the principle of the monocular three-dimensional vision measurement system which is based on structured light and the software requirements of multi-device control, the following software modules are designed: multi-device control module, camera calibration module, projector calibration module and optical plane calibration module. Each module contains certain image processing algorithms and the relationship among the modules is shown in Fig. 3.

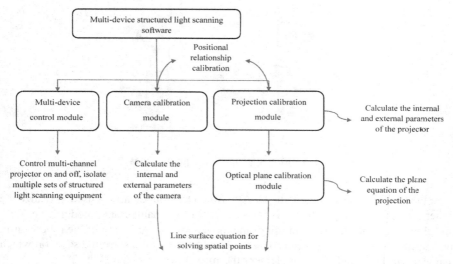

**Fig. 3.** Module diagram

## 3    Processing and Registration Methods of 3D Point Clouds

In this section, we detail the processing of the point cloud registration: from the device calibration to the point cloud processing after the point cloud acquisition, and to the point cloud registration. At the end of each part, the corresponding results will be represented.

### 3.1    Camera, Projector and System Calibration

There are many ways to calibrate the camera and the projector, the most common of which is Zhang's camera calibration algorithm [6]. It is a calibration method based on plane checkerboard and it is easy to manufacture since it requires only two-dimensional targets.

The main steps of this calibration method are as follows:

1. Get the two-dimensional chessboard for calibration
2. Obtain a series of photos with different checkerboard postures through rotation and translation
3. Get the checkerboard corner and find the sub-pixel corner
4. Estimate the internal and external parameter matrices assuming no distortion
5. Estimate the distortion matrix of the camera
6. Re-correct all parameters

System calibration is the geometric positional relationship between the camera and the projector. Now we define the world coordinate system (camera calibration plate coordinate system), camera coordinate system, and projector coordinate system.

The structure of the system and the relationship of each coordinate system can be simply represented as shown in Fig. 4:

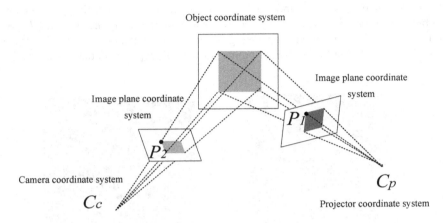

**Fig. 4.** System calibration schematic

According to the camera calibration method described above, the external parameters of the camera (i.e., the homogeneous transformation matrix of the camera coordinate system to the checkerboard coordinate system) and the external parameter matrix of the projector (i.e., the homogeneous transformation matrix of the projector coordinate system to the checkerboard coordinate system) are recorded as follows:

$$T_c = \begin{bmatrix} R_c & t_c \\ 0 & 1 \end{bmatrix}$$

$$T_p = \begin{bmatrix} R_p & t_p \\ 0 & 1 \end{bmatrix}$$

where $R$ represents a rotation transformation and $t$ represents a translation transformation. The homogeneous transformation matrix from the projector coordinate system to the transformation camera coordinate system can be obtained by spatial transformation of the coordinate system:

$$T = T_p T_c = \begin{bmatrix} R_p R_c & R_p t_c + t_p \\ 0 & 1 \end{bmatrix}$$

## 3.2    Point Cloud Data Preprocessing and Point Cloud Registration

**Point Cloud Data Preprocessing.** Due to the disorder of the point cloud data in the three-dimensional space which is shown in Fig. 5, the registration of the point cloud is interfered. Before splicing, filtering and noise reduction processing of the point cloud are required.

Sheng Yehua proposed a method for eliminating redundancies by using the K-nearest neighbor algorithm without reducing the original scanning sampling density [7]. Wu Yuquan proposed an improved denoising algorithm in which the noise removal is replaced by a small number of "center points" instead of all points in the space cells [8].

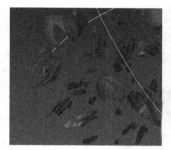

**Fig. 5.** Original point clouds          **Fig. 6.** Filtered point cloud

After filtering, the noise of the point cloud is removed and the data points are more concise, which is represented in Fig. 6. The number of vertices of scan results of one camera is reduced from 10000+ to 7000+ .

**Point Cloud Registration.** The robot described in this paper obtains point cloud data of all surfaces by multiple scans in different directions. In order to get a three-dimensional point cloud of the entire object, it is necessary to align the point clouds of

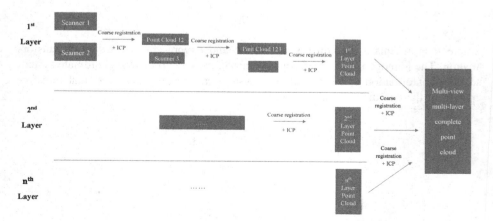

**Fig. 7.** Registration relationship diagram

each face together [9]. The method of coarse registration and the fine registration algorithm (ICP) is adopted and the method is shown in Fig. 7.

The ICP algorithm is the most widely used algorithm in the precise registration of point clouds [10]. The ICP algorithm is improved by the point set registration algorithm [11]. It calculates the distance from each point on the source point cloud to the target point cloud, matching it to the closest point of the target point cloud [12]. This allows the corresponding point set registration calculation to be performed, and then iteratively runs the above process and sets a threshold until the error is less than the threshold [13].

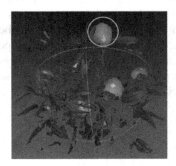

**Fig. 8.** Point clouds after coarse registration

In each layer, the coarse registration method is firstly used then the ICP algorithm is applied. After all the point cloud of each layer have been aligned, the point clouds will be spliced.

As is shown in Fig. 8, after rough calibration, the point clouds can be roughly spliced together, but there are still small gaps. However, the error can be effectively removed after accurate registration of ICP, which is presented in Fig. 9.

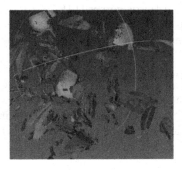

**Fig. 9.** Point clouds after fine registration of ICP.

# 4 Recognition and Positioning of Key Parts

## 4.1 Method of Recognition and Positioning

In order to reduce the amount of calculation and to better maintain the three-dimensional contour shape of the scene, we select the voxel center of gravity approximation method, by which we use the center of gravity of all points in each voxel grid to approximate all points in the voxel grid, thus reducing the number of points.

To get a more accurate description of the point cloud, we consider using both uniform sampling and Harris corner detection algorithms to detect key points. The uniform sampling method solely selects key points in space to ensure the number of key point sets. At the same time, in order to extract more discriminative feature points in complex locations, the Harris corner detection algorithm is used to supplement the points with larger autocorrelation functions in the point cloud, that is, the point where the point cloud density changes greatly. The autocorrelation function $E(x, y, z)$ at point $(x, y, z)$ can be expressed as:

$$E(x, y, z) = [\Delta x, \Delta y, \Delta z] M(x, y, z) \begin{bmatrix} \Delta x \\ \Delta y \\ \Delta z \end{bmatrix}$$

where $M$ is the covariance matrix:

$$M(x, y, z) = \sum_w \begin{bmatrix} I_x^2 & I_x I_y & I_x I_z \\ I_x I_y & I_y^2 & I_y I_z \\ I_x I_z & I_y I_z & I_z^2 \end{bmatrix}$$

where $w$ is the window centered on the point $(x, y, z)$, and $I_x, I_y, I_z$ are respectively the derivatives of the point cloud density function in the $x$, $y$, and $z$ directions. When the three eigenvalues of the matrix $M$ are all greater than the specified threshold, it is determined that this point is a Harris corner [14].

In order to fully reflect the shape characteristics of the point cloud, the union of uniform sampling and Harris corner detection results can be taken as a key point set.

## 4.2 Results of Recognition and Positioning

The peach tree is used as the scene point cloud, which is shown in Fig. 10. The peach is the model point cloud, the feature matching result is shown in Fig. 11, the green line is the matching result, the yellow part is the model point cloud, and the white part is the scene point cloud.

**Fig. 10.** Scene point cloud        **Fig. 11.** Feature    matching    result. (Color figure online)

The results of further target recognition are shown in Fig. 12, where the red part is the recognition result. It can be seen that most of the results are correctly identified. However, since the scene point cloud is derived from the ICP algorithm of multiple point clouds, there may be gaps between the point clouds, so multiple poses may be identified at the same target position.

**Fig. 12.** Target recognition result. (Color figure online)

To provide information to subsequent fine scans, camera capture point locations and viewpoint locations are offered based on the feature recognition results. The key point cloud with matching success is taken as input. The red point is uniformly sampled as the observation point, with a safe distance of 15 cm, and the distance from each observation point along its normal vector is taken as the camera shooting position, which is the blue point position in Fig. 13.

After the 3D scanning is completed, the robot processes and splices the scanned point cloud, identifies and targets the point cloud feature, obtains the target position, and expands it at a reasonable distance, thereby obtaining the camera position required for the fine scan. After obtaining the positioning information, based on the conversion matrix between the robotic arm base and the camera, the homogeneous matrix realizes the inverse kinematics equation and obtains the joint angle value, thus realizing the manipulator pose control.

**Fig. 13.** Camera shooting point selection (Color figure online)

## 4.3    Fine Scanning of the Manipulator

In this section, we introduce the kinematics modeling method of the robotic arm and how to perform hand-eye calibration.

**Robotic Arm Modeling.** To achieve kinematics, the robotic arm must be modeled. The modified D-H method (Modified Denavit-Hartenberg Matrix) is used to model the manipulator for kinematics. The D-H modeling method is a modeling method proposed by Denavit and Hartenberg which is mainly used in robot kinematics solution. The method establishes a coordinate system on each link, and realizes the transformation of coordinates on the two links by homogeneous coordinate transformation. In the system of multi-link series, The relationship between the first and last coordinate systems can be established by using the homogeneous coordinate transformation multiple times [15].

**Hand Eye Calibration.** Since the coordinate point of the re-scanning area is provided by the camera fixed to the circumferential scanning device, the calibration between the robotic arm base and the camera needs to be completed. The point in the camera coordinate system need to be converted into the robotic arm body coordinate system [16].

In the process of hand-eye calibration, four matrixes are mainly used:

A: The posture of the hand eye relation-ship robot TCP in the base coordinate system;
B: The posture of the camera in the TCP coordinate system at the end of the robot;
C: The posture of the calibration plate in the camera coordinate system;
D: The posture of the camera in the robot base coordinate system;

As shown in the matrix diagram of Fig. 14, the arm is moved to two different positions and we ensure that both positions allow the camera to see the calibration plate, so there are:

$$A_1 \cdot B \cdot C_1 = A_2 \cdot B \cdot C_2$$

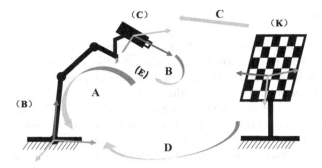

**Fig. 14.** Matrix diagram

After transformation:

$$\left(A_2^{-1} \cdot A_1\right) \cdot B = B \cdot \left(C_2 \cdot C_1^{-1}\right)$$

Then Calibration is performed by solving the AX = XB problem.

## 5   Experiment Results

With the software designed by ourselves, the point cloud scanned by each camera is filtered, and then aligned together. As shown in Fig. 15, a complete point cloud image is finally formed, which verifies the function of this large-scale three-dimensional scanning robot. The results of registration and recognition of large-scale objects are satisfactory.

**Fig. 15.** Final point clouds

# 6 Conclusion

In this paper, we presented a large-scale three-dimensional scanning robot which can effectively realize 3D information reconstruction of large-scale targets and recognition. The electromechanical control platform, the hardware and software framework design of the robot have been introduced. In addition, the processing and registration methods of 3D point cloud is analyzed. The recognition and positioning of key parts and the fine scanning of the manipulator after the point cloud processing are also presented. The experiment result has shown the effectiveness of this kind of scanning robot for large-scale targets in practical implement and its prospect in improving the efficiency of further agricultural picking robots.

**Acknowledgements.** This work was supported by a grant from the National Natural Science Foundation of China (No. 51775333) and Scientific Research Program of Shanghai Science and Technology Commission (No. 18391901000).

# References

1. Umeda, M., Kubota, S., Iida, M.: Development of "stork", a watermelon-harvesting robot. Artif. Life Robot. **3**(3), 143–147 (1999)
2. Ji, C., Zhang, J., Yuan, T.: Research on key technology of truss tomato harvesting robot in greenhouse. Appl. Mech. Mater. **442**, 480–486 (2013)
3. Foglia, M.M., Reina, G.: Agricultural robot for radicchio harvesting. J. Field Robot. **23**(6–7), 363–377 (2010)
4. Kondo, N., Ting, K.C.: Robotics for bioproduction systems. American Society of Agricultural Engineers (1998)
5. Kazuhiko, I., Kei, T., Yoshinori, O., Kazutoshi, M.: Development of three-dimensional facial approximation system using head CT scans of Japanese living individuals. J. Forensic Radiol. Imaging **17**, 36–45 (2019)
6. Zhengyou, Z.: Flexible camera calibration by viewing a plane from unknown orientations. In: Proceedings of the Seventh IEEE International Conference on Computer Vision, Kerkyra, Greece, vol. 1, pp. 666–673 (1999)
7. Sheng, Y., Kai, Z., Ka, Z.: Dissipative treatment of 3D laser scanning point cloud aftermultistation stitching. Bull. Surveying Mapp. **3**, 28–30 (2010)
8. Wu, Y., Li, P., Yang, Q.: Point cloud denoising algorithm based on neighborhood average method. J. Jiangxi Univ. Technol. **40**(01), 10–15 (2019)
9. Zhou, W., Ma, X., Zhang, L.: Three dimensional point cloud splicing of tree canopy based on multi-source camera. Acta Optica Sinica **34**(12), 185–192 (2014)
10. Rusinkiewicz, S.: Efficient variants of the ICP algorithm. In: Proceedings of the 3DIM (2001)
11. Chi, Y., Yu, X., Luo, Z.: 3D point cloud matching based on principal component analysis and iterative closest point algorithm. In: 2016 International Conference on Audio, Language and Image Processing (ICALIP), Shanghai, pp. 404–408 (2016)
12. Li, S., Wang, J., Liang, Z.: Tree point clouds registration using an improved ICP algorithm based on kd-tree. Geoscience & Remote Sensing Symposium. IEEE (2016)

13. Rui, Z., Li, G., Li, M.: Fusion of images and point clouds for the semantic segmentation of large-scale 3D scenes based on deep learning. ISPRS J. Photogram. Remote Sens. **143**, 85–96 (2018)
14. Harris, G., Stephens, M.: A combined corner and edge detector. In: Proceedings 4th Alvey Vision Conference, pp. 147–151 (1988). https://doi.org/10.5244/c.2.23
15. Tsai, C.Y., Lin, P.D.: The mathematical models of the basic entities of multi-axis serial orthogonal machine tools using a modified Denavit-Hartenberg notation. Int. J. Adv. Manuf. Technol. **42**(9–10), 1016–1024 (2009)
16. Tabb, A., Yousef, K.M.A.: Solving the robot-world hand-eye(s) calibration problem with iterative methods. Mach. Vis. Appl. **28**(5–6), 569 (2017)

# Industrial Robot Sorting System for Municipal Solid Waste

Zhifei Zhang[1(✉)], Hao Wang[1], Hongzhang Song[2], Shaobo Zhang[2],
and Jianhua Zhang[1]

[1] College of Computer Science and Technology,
Zhejiang University of Technology, Hangzhou, Zhejiang, China
zzf1623@gmail.com
[2] Hangzhou Visual Entropy Technology Co., Ltd., Hangzhou, China

**Abstract.** For the problem of low efficiency of industrial sorting robots that use traditional visual algorithms to identify and locate targets in complex environments. Our system introduces deep learning technology to detect and locate solid waste based on the existing algorithm. In this paper, the industrial robot sorting system platform is built by deep learning technology. Firstly, the visual area on the conveyor belt is captured by the depth camera. The computer uses a trained SSD model to recognize and locate the target, and obtain the information on the type and location of the solid waste. Then, based on the object detection, solid waste objects are segmented by three-dimensional background removal. Finally, the information of the geometric center coordinates and the angle of the long side of the target object are sent to the robot to complete the classification and grabbing of the solid waste. Simulation experiments show that the features learned by using SSD deep neural network have strong robustness and stability in complex environment, and can achieve the solid waste sorting efficiently.

**Keywords:** Complex background · Robotic grasping · Deep learning · Garbage sorting

## 1 Introduction

In recent years, with the development of computer vision technology, vision-based robotic grabbing research which is based on the premise stated earlier has become a key research direction in the field of robotics. However, in the actual industrial production, most robots use manual teaching method to plan the grasping action of the manipulator.

The grasping task will fail if the object position has changed, this method has great limitation and is difficult to popularize. In this article, we intend to apply computer vision technology to solve this problem. Firstly, we use camera to collect the image of the target object, then the computer uses image processing methods to analyze and process the image data, and obtains the effective information such as the spatial position and attitude of the solid waste. Finally, the control system of robotic arm accepts the information obtained to complete the capture of the solid waste.

This kind of vision-based robotic arm grabbing not only contains robotics, control theory, but also integrates computer vision theory, deep learning and artificial

© Springer Nature Switzerland AG 2019
H. Yu et al. (Eds.): ICIRA 2019, LNAI 11741, pp. 342–353, 2019.
https://doi.org/10.1007/978-3-030-27532-7_31

intelligence, and has important value to scientific research and application [1]. The target detection technology involved is also a research hotspot in the field of vision. [2–5] use traditional feature extraction methods to process image information. The feature extraction system based on vision has poor generalization ability and robustness, and it is susceptible to the shape, size, angle change and external illumination of the target object. It is usually necessary to propose an adaptive algorithm for each specific target [1], so it is difficult to adapt to new objects.

The grasping system in this paper refers to the technology of deep learning. Through the training of deep convolution neural network, the visual module can quickly identify solid waste. It needs to collect a large number of images to make a standard training set, the target recognition algorithm based on deep neural network is used to train the data offline, the obtained model is used for online recognition. R-CNN algorithm is the mainstream deep learning object detection algorithm for robot grasping, but it cannot meet the real-time requirement in terms of speed [6, 7]. In this paper, SSD object detection algorithm based on deep learning is applied to industrial robot sorting. The features learned by this method can adapt to new objects that have not appeared in the training set, and it can meet the requirements of real-time detection at the same time.

## 2  System Overview

In [8], after detecting the object, the grasping position is learned by using the method of manipulator grasping based on deep learning. Since the deep learning grab detection method does not require the center of gravity of the target object, so it will not be affected by the shape of the solid waste. However, the detection speed is significantly slower than the conventional position detection method, and it is not suitable for practical industrial production. [9] use the deep learning method to achieve the authenticity identification of target object in complex background by applying the Region Proposal Generation (RPN) and the VGG-16 model for object recognition and pose estimation.

In this paper, before calculating the grasping point of solid waste target, we need to segment the foreground of the target. [10] propose an efficient RGB-D based segmentation method for construction waste segmentation in harsh environment, an efficient background modeling strategy is designed to separate the solid waste regions from the cluttered background. [11] present a novel spatial adaptive projection method based on only one RGB-D sensor.

As shown in Fig. 1, based on RS050N of Kawasaki six-free-axis industrial robot, a sorting system platform of industrial robot based on deep learning is built in this paper. The main components of the industrial robot sorting system are: conveyor belt, robot bracket, six-free-axis industrial robot, ASUS depth camera, camera bracket, solid waste placement slot, etc.

Figure 2 shows the flow of the system in detail. Firstly, the camera collects the image of the solid waste that enter the working area on the conveyor belt, then the computer identifies and locates the solid waste on the image through the object detection algorithm. According to the transformation of the relationship between the

**Fig. 1.** Industrial sorting robot

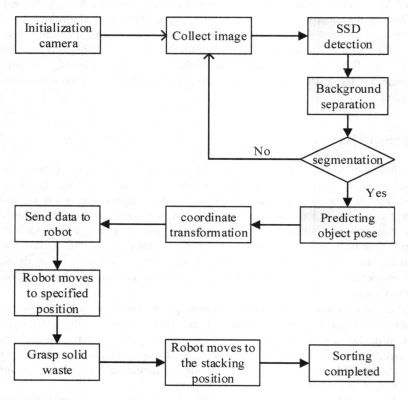

**Fig. 2.** Sorting process

target coordinate system and the robot coordinate system, the robot is guided to grab the target, and then different kinds of targets are placed in different slots.

## 3 Object Extraction

### 3.1 Camera Calibration

The purpose of camera calibration is to establish each relevant coordinate system and obtain the correspondence of spatial points between the image coordinate system and the spatial coordinate system [12]. Firstly, the corresponding coordinates of the pixel coordinates in the depth camera coordinate system should be calculated, the transformation relation is defined as:

$$
\begin{bmatrix} x_c \\ y_c \\ z_c \end{bmatrix} = Z_c M_{in}^{-1} \begin{bmatrix} u \\ v \\ 1 \end{bmatrix}, M_{in} = \begin{bmatrix} k_x & 0 & u_0 \\ 0 & k_y & v_0 \\ 0 & 0 & 1 \end{bmatrix} \tag{1}
$$

$M_{in}$ and $Z_c$ are the internal parameter of the depth camera and the depth values corresponding to the coordinate points, respectively. In order to complete the grasping, we must know the three-dimensional position information of the robot arm coordinate system corresponding to the target object, therefore it is necessary to convert the three-dimensional point in the camera coordinate system into a three-dimensional point in the robot arm coordinate system. That is to say, the conversion relationship coefficient between the camera coordinate system and the robot coordinate system should be obtained.

This paper uses the ASUS depth camera to capture images and uses the spatial 7-parameter method to couple the camera coordinate system with the robot coordinate system, which can obtain the coordinates in the robot coordinate system corresponding to the coordinates of the points in the image. According to the model of the seven-parameter space conversion, the seven parameters can be computed by

$$
\begin{bmatrix} X_2 \\ Y_2 \\ Z_2 \end{bmatrix} = (1+m) \begin{bmatrix} 1 & \epsilon_z & -\epsilon_y \\ -\epsilon_z & 1 & \epsilon_x \\ \epsilon_y & -\epsilon_x & 1 \end{bmatrix} \begin{bmatrix} X_1 \\ Y_1 \\ Z_1 \end{bmatrix} + \begin{bmatrix} \Delta X_0 \\ \Delta Y_0 \\ \Delta Z_0 \end{bmatrix} \tag{2}
$$

In engineering measure, the classical three-dimensional Hermitian method is the most rigorous conversion method from a mathematical point of view. Since up to seven conversion parameters can be obtained in the result, it is three translation parameters $(\Delta X_0, \Delta Y_0, \Delta Z_0)$, three rotation parameters $(\varepsilon_x, \varepsilon_y, \varepsilon_z)$, and a scale scaling factor 'm'. Therefore, this is often referred to as the seven-parameter method. If the seven parameter values can be solved, all coordinates to be converted can be obtained. However, the premise of calculating the seven conversion parameters is that at least three common points are needed for reference.

As shown in Fig. 3, There are nine pieces of paper on the belt, each piece of paper draws a circle and its center. First, we collect the image of the nine pieces of paper

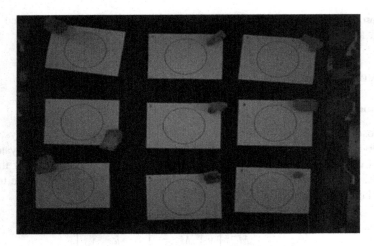

**Fig. 3.** Original image for camera calibration

through the camera to obtain the position coordinates of each center in the camera coordinate system. Then manipulating the robot arm so that the midpoint of the claw corresponds to the center of the circle on the paper. In this way we are able to record the coordinates of the robot coordinate system corresponding to the center of each circle on the teaching device.

After obtaining the coordinates of the points in the camera coordinate system and the robot coordinate system respectively, the conversion coefficient from the camera coordinate system to the robot coordinate system can be calculated by the Matlab algorithmic tool.

## 3.2   Object Detection

In this paper, the solid waste sorting system adopts Caffe-SSD deep learning framework. It is necessary to collect a large amount of solid waste images for classification and calibration, then making these pictures into data sets. The system can not only classify and locate solid waste accurately, but also recognize 50 images per second, which can fully meet the demand in the application. The SSD [13] detection flow chart is shown in Fig. 4.

## 3.3   Edge Detection

The classical edge detection operators include Sobel operator, Prewitt and Canny operator. However, canny operator has better signal-to-noise ratio, higher edge positioning performance and better detection effect under noisy environment, it is suitable for edge detection in different environments [14]. In this paper, the Canny edge detection operator is selected to obtain the edge of targets, it can help to calculate grasping posture.

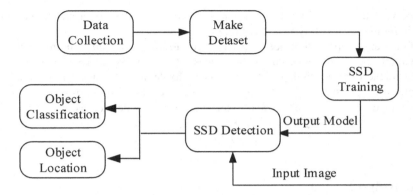

**Fig. 4.** The SSD detection flow chart

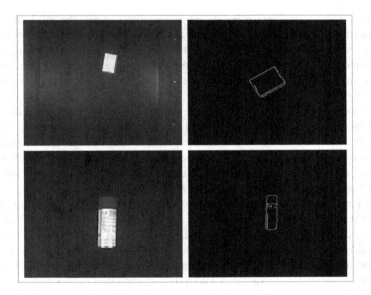

**Fig. 5.** Edge detection of solid waste

As shown in Fig. 5. Firstly, the first derivative of two-dimensional Gaussian function is used to smooth the image, then the gradient edge of the smoothed image is calculated. The two-dimensional Gaussian function and image convolution are defined as:

$$\begin{cases} G(x,y) = \frac{1}{2\pi\sigma^2} exp\left(-\frac{x^2+y^2}{2\sigma^2}\right) \\ I_G(x,y) = G(x,y) \cap I(x,y) \end{cases} \tag{3}$$

I (x, y) is the original image, σ is a scale factor. If σ is larger, it means that image noise is removed smoothly in a large range.

After Canny operator processing, in order to make the edge more visible for observation, binary image needs to be processed by expansion. Expansion is a processing method of morphology, it is necessary to define a "structural element", and performing a specific logical operation expansion on the area corresponding to the binary image at the position of each pixel, the formula is defined as follows:

$$I \cap S = \left\{ x \mid \widehat{S_{x,y}} \cap I \neq 0 \right\}$$ (4)

## 4    Grasping System

### 4.1    Grasping Posture

In order to get the proper grasp point and angle of the target, the minimum circumscribed rectangle of the object is one of the important parameters. The tangential rectangle of a geometric image contains all the points and lines on the figure, and each side of the rectangle contacts the figure. There are an infinite number of circumscribed rectangles for a graph, and the smallest area is called the Minimum Enclosing Rectangle (MER) [15].

Firstly, we use the camera to take pictures of the conveyor belt without objects, and use these pictures to build the background model with the Gaussian mixture model (GMM) [16]. Then the image object is segmented by the background model and the binary image containing the target information is obtained. The white part of the image is the target object, and the black part of the image is the background. Finally, the minimum bounding rectangle is calculated by the segmented image target.

In this paper, the search method for the main axes is used to determine the initial position of the horizontal and vertical main axes by the principle of center of gravity, and then the center of rotation and the initial circumscribed rectangle are determined in this way. In the sharp Angle region formed by the initial position of the horizontal spindle and the vertical spindle, the minimum external rectangle is found by rotating the initial external rectangle, and it is taken as the minimum external rectangle of the image target. Finally, the target is identified by the object detection algorithm of SSD, so, the location information of the target is obtained.

As shown in Fig. 6, there is a piece of wood on the belt, which is divided by a Gaussian mixture model to obtain its mask map, which makes it easier to calculate the target location information later.

As shown in Fig. 7, the largest blue box represents the detectable area, the yellow box is the detection result of SSD detection algorithm, the red box is the external rectangular box of the target contour. The red point is the central point of the contour. The green point in the figure is the particle of the contour, and we will use this point as the initial capture point. The final grasping coordinates of the target are calculated by the conversion coefficients between the camera coordinates and the robot coordinates. Then the angle between the external rectangle of the target contour and the x axis of the

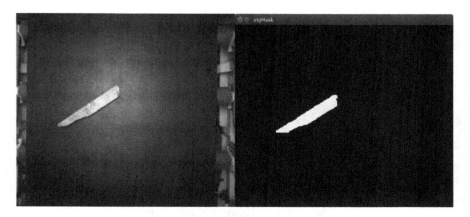

**Fig. 6.** Original image and mask map

**Fig. 7.** Algorithm detection

image is calculated, which is composed of a horizontal axis of rotated counterclockwise and the first side of the smallest circumscribed rectangle, and the range of angle is 0° to 180°. According to the relationship of angle conversion, computer will calculate the grasping angle of the robot and send it to the robot.

## 4.2 Obstacle Avoidance Control

After getting the grasping point and grasping angle, the system needs to make a judgment on the obstacle avoidance of robot. As shown in Fig. 8, there is a stone at the edge of the wood. If the center of object is selected as the grasping point, the claws of the robot and the object will collide on the belt, which will cause damage to the claw. In order to avoid collision, the system needs to determine whether there are some white pixels on the edge of the grasping point through the mask image. If some white pixels

**Fig. 8.** Original image and mask map

are detected around the target, which means the possibility of collision. The computer will calculate the coordinates of the three-quarter position near the edge by the circumscribed rectangle of the target object. Finally system modifies the grasping point to avoid collision immediately.

**Fig. 9.** Obstacle avoidance test

In Fig. 9, we can see that the grasping point on the wood block turns blue. After obstacle avoidance, the grasping point acquired by the robot completely avoids the position of the brick and can grasp the woods smoothly.

### 4.3 Communication Module

After obtaining the target information, the system needs to transmit the information to the controller, and then the controller controls the manipulator to complete the grasp. Firstly, the computer is connected to the controller through a network cable.

Secondly, When the target information is obtained, the system will determine whether the target is in the capture area. Computer will send the information of the target to the controller when the target enters the fetch area. If the target does not reach the grab area, the computer will calculate the waiting time and send it to controller. If the target exceeds the capture range, the system will get the next target information. Finally, the computer sends the target information to the controller in two steps, sends 'X, Z, A, L' to controller for the first time and 'Y, C' to controller for the second time. 'X, Z' are the x coordinate and y coordinate of the target grab point in the robot coordinate system respectively. 'A' is the grab angle, 'L' is the label, and the label indicates whether this information is valid. 'Y' is the y coordinate of the target grab point in the robot coordinate system, 'C' is the category information of the target.

## 5   Experiments and Results

Before object is identified and classified by SSD object detection algorithm, Caffe framework must be configured. Then algorithm will process the data from the ASUS depth camera. The algorithm will call the SSD network model to identify and locate the target in the image, and finally output the category and position of the object. The detection results are shown in the Fig. 10.

As shown in the Fig. 11, the robot captures the picture and grabs the target. On this platform, we have carried out many simulation capture experiments, the experimental results are shown in Table 1. It can also be detected when multiple targets appear in the

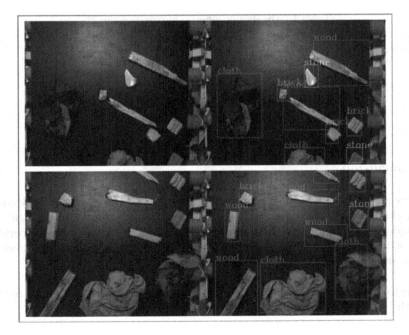

**Fig. 10.** The figure of object detection

visual area. Whether the target is at the center or at the edge of the region, the robot can almost grab it successfully. In general, the robot sorting system developed in this paper ensures a good accuracy of recognition and positioning, and achieves the goal of sorting workpieces. The number of category (NC), the number of successful detection (ND), the number of successful grasping (NG), the number of failure (NF).

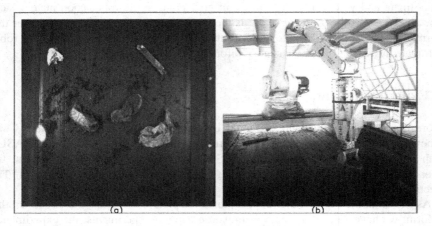

**Fig. 11.** (a) Picture captured. (b) Robot grasping solid waste

**Table 1.** The data of robotic grasping experiment

| Object | NC | ND | NG | NF |
|---|---|---|---|---|
| Wood | 50 | 50 | 49 | 1 |
| Cloth | 50 | 50 | 50 | 0 |
| Brick | 50 | 49 | 48 | 2 |
| Shoe | 50 | 50 | 50 | 0 |
| Beverage | 50 | 50 | 49 | 1 |

# 6  Conclusion

To sum up, this paper proposes a robotic grasping system based on deep learning, which elaborates the grasping process in detail and is capable of object detection, recognition and grasping with different poses. Finally, the results of sorting experiment show that the vision algorithm and the control method of the proposed system can achieve the solid waste sorting efficiently.

**Acknowledgments.** This work was supported National Natural Science Foundation of China (61876167 and U1509207).

# References

1. Haoyang, Y.U.: Reaerach on Montion Control of Servo Arm based on Binocular Vision. Dalian University of Technology, Dalian (2016). (in Chinese)
2. Maitin-Shepard, J., Cusumano-Towner, M., Lei, J., et al.: Cloth grasp point detection based on multiple-view geometric cues with application to robotic towel folding. In: IEEE International Conference on Robotics and Automation, Piscataway, pp. 2308–2315. IEEE, USA (2010)
3. Ramisa, A., Alenyà, G., Moreno-Noguer, F., et al.: Using depth and appearance features for informed robot grasping of highly wrinkled clothes. In: 2012 IEEE International Conference on Robotics and Automation. IEEE (2012)
4. Yun, J., Moseson, S., Saxena, A.: Efficient grasping from RGBD images: Learning using a new rectangle representation. In: IEEE International Conference on Robotics & Automation (2011)
5. Lin, Y., Sun, Y.: Robot grasp planning based on demonstrated grasp strategies. Int. J. Robot. Res. 34(1), 26–42 (2015)
6. Redmon, J., Divvala, S., Girshick, R., et al.: You only look once: unified, real-time object detection (2015)
7. Redmon, J., Farhadi, A.: YOLO9000: better, faster, stronger. In: 2017 IEEE Conference on Computer Vision and Pattern Recognition, Honolulu, 21–26 July 2017, pp. 6517–6525 (2016)
8. Zhe, Y., Xuedan, D., Miao, C., et al.: A method for robotic grasping position detection based on deep learning. Chinese High Technology Letters (2018)
9. Zhihong, C., Hebin, Z., Yanbo, W., et al.: A vision-based robotic grasping system using deep learning for garbage sorting. In: 2017 36th Chinese Control Conference (CCC). IEEE (2017)
10. Wang, C., Liu, S., Zhang, J., et al.: RGB-D based object segmentation in severe color degraded environment (2017)
11. Qiu, Y., Chen, J., Guo, J., et al.: Three dimensional object segmentation based on spatial adaptive projection for solid waste (2017)
12. Zhang, Z.: A flexible new technique for camera calibration. IEEE Trans. Pattern Anal. Mach. Intell. 22(11), 1330–1334 (2000)
13. Liu, W., et al.: SSD: single shot MultiBox detector. In: Leibe, B., Matas, J., Sebe, N., Welling, M. (eds.) ECCV 2016. LNCS, vol. 9905, pp. 21–37. Springer, Cham (2016). https://doi.org/10.1007/978-3-319-46448-0_2
14. Vasudevan, S.K., Dharmendra, T., Sivaraman, R., Karthick, S.: Automotive image processing technique using canny's edge detectior. Int. J. Eng. Sci. Technol. 2(7), 2632–2643 (2011)
15. Freeman, H., Shapira, R.: Determining the minimum-area encasing rectangle for an arbitrary closed curve. Commun. ACM 18(7), 409–413 (1975)
16. Stauffer, C., Grimson, W.E.L.: Learning patterns of activity using real-time tracking. Trans. Pami 22(8), 747–757 (2000)

# A Method Based on Data Fusion of Multiple Sensors to Evaluate Road Cleanliness

Xiang Yao[1,3], Wei Zhang[2], Wei Cui[1,3], Xu Zhang[1,3($\boxtimes$)], Ying Wang[1], and Jiale Xiong[1]

[1] School of Mechatronic Engineering and Automation, Shanghai University, No. 99 Shangda Road, Baoshan, Shanghai 200444, China
xuzhang@shu.edu.cn
[2] Juli Green Environmental Technology Research Center of Shanghai, Building 2, Lane 600, Tianshan Road, Changning, Shanghai 200444, China
[3] HUST-Wuxi Research Institute, No 329 YanXin Road, Huishan District, Wuxi 214100, China

**Abstract.** For the supervision and evaluation of the quality of garbage detection and sanitation cleaning of urban roads, it has been carried out on a road-by road inspection by manual means for a long time, and then the mobile phone is used to locate the garbage and quantify the score. However, there are many problems in manual supervision. Not only is the work efficiency very low, but also a lot of manpower and material resources are wasted. This has not been able to meet the current smart city governance needs. Therefore, we propose a method of integrating multi-sensor data to replace the manual detection and evaluation of road cleanliness automatically and intelligently, and design a complete system, which can be loaded on the car to work on the road efficiently and directly output the score. Experiments show that our method can replace manual well to realize the identification and classification of garbage on the road, the calculation of garbage area, and the calculation of the latitude and longitude of the garbage, then display the above information of garbage in real time on the web map side.

**Keywords:** Road sanitation assessment · Data fusion · Smart system

## 1 Introduction

With the marketization of sanitation cleaning, in most of China, the cleaning of urban roads is done by the cleaning service company that the government tendered for. Although the government has already recognized the importance of monitoring and evaluating the cleanness of the street. Many methods have been adopted, but the effect is not obvious, the reasons are as follows [1–3]: China's sanitation industry is low in information and intelligence, and the industry has low attention. For a long time, the garbage monitoring and cleanliness evaluation of urban pavements mainly relied on special personnel to inspect the streets one by one. When the inspector finds the garbage, first, they will take photos, record the location information, and measure the area, and then quantify the score, at last, notify the sanitation workers to clean up.

© Springer Nature Switzerland AG 2019
H. Yu et al. (Eds.): ICIRA 2019, LNAI 11741, pp. 354–367, 2019.
https://doi.org/10.1007/978-3-030-27532-7_32

This method of manual monitoring requires a lot of manpower and material resources, and the working environment of the workers is very bad. Whether it is severe cold or hot summer, it is necessary to conduct inspections on all roads in the jurisdiction, and the efficiency is very low. On the other hand, they will be lazy, it is difficult to supervision their work. In addition, there are too many subjective factors in the results of manual testing, which can not guarantee the fairness of the results.

The method of artificial supervision has exposed too many problems, it can not meet the current regulatory needs, and can not meet the current smart city governance needs. Therefore, we propose a new method of integrating multi-sensor data to identify and classify garbage on the road and calculate its area and latitude and longitude information. It can be a good substitute for manual work, and the machine and system will not be faked, nor will it be lazy, which can well solve the pain points of the sanitation evaluation industry.

For the supervision of urban road cleaning quality, it is mainly to detect the presence or absence of garbage on the road. If there is, it is necessary to distinguish whether it is household refuse, decorative garbage or large-sized garbage, then measure its area and record the latitude and longitude position information of the garbage.

The garbage in the city may appear in different scenes, and the complexity of the form of the garbage adds difficulty to the identification. Garbage is different from pedestrians, vehicles and other objects which have a relatively clear definition. The judgment of garbage has certain subjectivity. For the same object, there will be different judgment results in different scenarios. The traditional target recognition method can not overcome the morphological diversity of the target object, background diversity and other factors, the detection results are limited, and the accuracy is not ideal. Deep learning has a strong ability to extract and discriminate features. Using deep learning for garbage detection and discrimination has become a good choice. Mittal [4] opens up a method of deep learning garbage detection, which is embedded in the mobile phone through a deep convolution network to detect garbage on the road. However, due to the adoption of the network structure, the feature extraction capability is not too strong. The model's ability to detect garbage is relatively weak, and the detection accuracy remains at 87.9%. In addition, this method is based on the mobile phone APP to identify and locate and the field of view is very limited which means that it cannot meet the requirements of sanitation operations. Wei [5] proposed a garbage detection method with a high-speed regional convolutional neural network which is based on the idea of Faster RCNN [6]. The backbone of the model is ZF-Net [7], and it is a typical two-stage model. Generally speaking, two-stage network needs to perform two classification and regression operations which is slower, but the accuracy is higher. However, Wei uses ZF-Net rather than the ResNet [8] with strong feature extraction capability as the backbone which will cause a great loss of accuracy. And because of the two-stage approach, ZF-Net's speed advantage is also reduced. Therefore, this paper proposes a YOLOv3-darknet [9] garbage detection algorithm based on adaptive clustering anchor box to detect garbage on urban roads. The algorithm has strong real-time and generalization capabilities, and performs very well in terms of speed and accuracy.

For the calculation of the area, Qu [10, 11] proposed a method based on monocular vision, but for a slightly larger area, the calculation accuracy is very poor. You [12] proposed a method of measuring the area using binocular vision. Although the area can be effectively calculated, the binocular camera has a small field of view and is not suitable for calculating the area of an object at a long distance. Therefore, according to the characteristics of urban road garbage detection, this paper proposes a method of combining color camera and 3D Lidar to calculate the area of garbage. The algorithm combines the image information acquired by the camera with the point cloud information obtained by Lidar. Which can perform well in calculating garbage's area.

For the calculation of the garbage's location, since the latitude and longitude of the garbage cannot be directly obtained, it is necessary to convert through the relative relationship between the vehicle and the garbage and the latitude and longitude of the vehicle. Liu [13] deduced the problem of finding the distance of two points when knows their latitude and longitude and their relative declination. According to the actual working conditions, Li [14] gave a method and error analysis for calculating the distance between two known latitude and longitude. this paper simplifies the Gaussian projection model based on [15] and proposes a kind of way to calculate the location of the garbage based on the GPS information of the vehicle, the distance between the garbage and the vehicle acquired by Lidar, and the azimuth of the garbage relative to the direction of the vehicle, and visualize it in the map.

We integrated these algorithms into a system and mounted the system on a car for real-time road cleansing assessment. Through actual testing, the system can accomplish tasks well.

The innovation and contribution points of the method have the following aspects: (1) Adopting darknet53 with strong feature extraction ability as the back-bone of the network, discarding the RPN mode, the detection of single image can reach 60 ms; (2) Fusing the depth information acquired by Lidar with the 2D image information acquired by a color camera for distance measurement at a long distance. (3) Proposed an algorithm for calculating the latitude and longitude of another point based on a point latitude and longitude and a point and distance from the point in a short distance, and actually verified it.

## 2   Realization of the Function of Intelligent Sanitation System

### 2.1   Overall Framework of the System

The whole system involves multiple sensors. Different sensors acquire different data, then transmit the data to the on-board computer for data fusion, and finally analyze and output the results. As shown in Fig. 1, our method mainly uses the following hardware:

Among them, G-MOUSE satellite receiver is a GPS satellite positioning receiver with built-in satellite receiving antenna. It has a full range of high-precision positioning functions with a dynamic accuracy of less than 1 m. However, when GPS receivers are blocked by high-rise buildings, viaducts, tunnels, trees and so on, the signal will be lost. At this point, it can not provide positioning services for the user, for this reason, we add the IMU inertial sensor, which is mainly composed of inertial devices such as acceleration and angular velocity to output the most primitive data. The advantage is that you can get position without relying on the external environment. But the problem is that if you calculate for a long time, there is a cumulative error, and as time goes on,

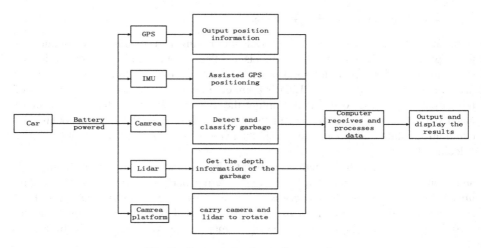

**Fig. 1.** System's hardware framework.

if there is no way to provide correction to it, the error will become larger and larger. Therefore, GPS and IMU can complement each other and form an inertial navigation system to provide accurate position information for the vehicle.

Color industrial cameras are mainly used to identify and classify garbage. Color images can provide us with rich texture information. We use deep learning object detection and segmentation methods to detect garbage. Lidar can sense three-dimensional spatial information. When the point cloud of the garbage is captured, the depth information of the garbage relative to the vehicle is obtained, and the pixel area information of the garbage acquired by the camera, we can fuse these data to calculate the actual area of the garbage.

The camera platform is used to keep the camera and Lidar rigidly connected and carry them for 360° rotation and ±90° pitch motion to detect garbage on the road around the vehicle with a better perspective. The two stepping motors inside the camera platform can also provide the current angle information of the camera and the Lidar, and then integrate the distance information provided by Lidar and the heading angle of the latitude and longitude of the vehicle provided by the GPS and the true north direction of the earth to calculate the garbage location. Then visualize them through the Baidu Maps API.

We loaded these devices with the top of the car, powered by a pair of 12 V 120AH lead battery packs placed in the trunk, and transmitted the data acquired by the sensor to the computer in the car through the interface such as USB for data processing, and finally the results are displayed on the screen in real time and sent to the sanitation regulator. Based on this information, they can dispatch personnel to clean up the garbage. Thereby achieving the function of road cleanliness supervision. By analyzing these data through big data technology, you can also find areas where pollution problems occur frequently and precise decisions can be made to solve it.

## 2.2 Area Calculation of the Garbage

According to the requirements of garbage monitoring and cleanliness evaluation of urban pavement, when the garbage's area is less than $0.3 \text{ m}^2$, it is called low pollution, $0.3–1 \text{ m}^2$ is medium pollution, and more than $1 \text{ m}^2$ is high pollution. Therefore, we used a color camera to integrate Lidar's point cloud information to calculate the area of the garbage. The color camera can capture the pixel area of the garbage in the image and its position in the image coordinate system, while the 3D Lidar can obtain the depth information of the point cloud, and the two sensors can complement each other to calculate the garbage.

First, we calibrate the camera according to the calibration algorithm of Zhang [16], and then calibrate Lidar and the camera's external parameters for data fusion. The image data captured by the camera is represented by (u, v), and the 3D point cloud captured by Lidar is represented by (x, y, z). Our goal is to create a transformation matrix M, which will be a 3D point (x, y, z) map to 2D points (u, v), which is:

$$
\begin{pmatrix} u \\ v \\ 1 \end{pmatrix} = \begin{pmatrix} f_u & 0 & u_0 & 0 \\ 0 & f_v & v_0 & 0 \\ 0 & 0 & 1 & 0 \end{pmatrix} \begin{pmatrix} R_{3 \times 3} & t_{3 \times 1} \\ 0 & 1 \end{pmatrix} \begin{pmatrix} x \\ y \\ z \\ 1 \end{pmatrix} = M \begin{pmatrix} x \\ y \\ z \\ 1 \end{pmatrix}
$$

$$
= \begin{pmatrix} m_{11} & m_{12} & m_{13} & m_{14} \\ m_{21} & m_{22} & m_{23} & m_{24} \\ m_{31} & m_{32} & m_{33} & m_{34} \end{pmatrix} \begin{pmatrix} x \\ y \\ z \\ 1 \end{pmatrix} \tag{1}
$$

$$
u = \frac{m_{11}x + m_{12}y + m_{13}z + m_4}{m_{31}x + m_{32}y + m_{33}z + m_{34}} \qquad v = \frac{m_{21}x + m_{22}y + m_{23}z + m_{24}}{m_{31}x + m_{32}y + m_{33}z + m_{34}} \tag{2}
$$

The matrix $(f_u, f_v, u_0, v_0)$ is the camera parameter, $f_u$ and $f_v$ are the scale factors (the effective focal length in the horizontal and vertical directions) of the X-axis and the Y-axis, $u_0, v_0$ is the center point of the image plane, also known as the principal point coordinates. R is the rotation matrix and t is the translation vector.

We built the calibration platform shown in Fig. 2. The camera and the Lidar are rigidly connected to be taken a photo of the calibration board simultaneously. The point cloud obtained by the Lidar is shown in Fig. 3. Next, we extract the point cloud part of the calibration plate by the filtering algorithm. Then, through the rectangular fitting, we find the three vertices of the rectangle and map their three-dimensional coordinates to the two-dimensional coordinates, as shown in Fig. 3. Therefore, according to the PNP algorithm [17], we can calculate the external parameters of the Lidar and camera.

After the calibration is completed, according to the external parameters, the three-dimensional points are projected onto the two-dimensional image plane. A picture of the fusion of Lidar and camera data is shown in Fig. 4. In this way, we can get the image information and depth information of the garbage. Then, according to the internal parameters of the camera, we can get the physical width and height of each pixel of the image on the CCD (Imaging component of the camera). And the depth

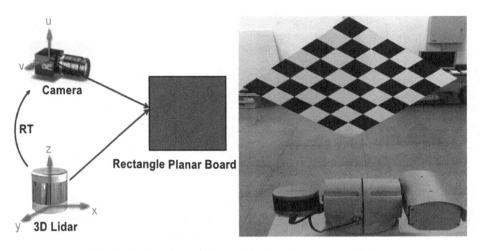

**Fig. 2.** External parameters calibration of camera and Lidar.

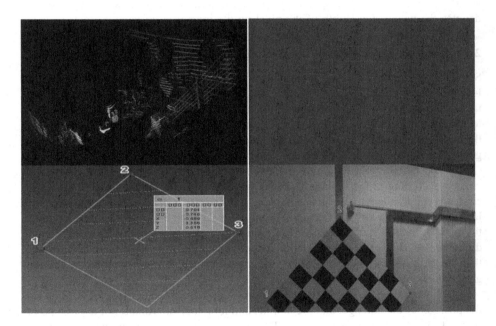

**Fig. 3.** Picture of calibration board taken by camera and Lidar.

between the garbage and the camera can be got by Lidar. Therefore, based on the pinhole imaging model, we can get the physical width and height of each pixel on the image, so as to calculate the area of each pixel, and then count the number of pixels of the garbage on the image, the area of the garbage can be calculated. Figure 5 can explain the above calculation principle very well. In the Fig. 5, f denotes the focal

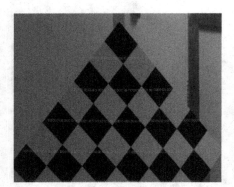

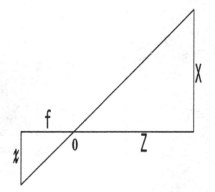

**Fig. 4.** Picture of data fusion with camera and Lidar.

**Fig. 5.** Picture of the principle of area calculation

length, x denotes the side length of the pixel on the CCD, Z denotes the depth, and X denotes the actual side length of the pixel on the image.

### 2.3 Location Calculation of the Garbage

Since the locator only gets the geographical location of the vehicle, what we need is the location of the garbage. And visualize on the map, which is convenient for the sanitation staff to quickly find the location of the garbage, and clean up in time. So we need to obtain the Euclidean distance and azimuth of the garbage relative to the vehicle through Lidar. Integrating the heading angle of the vehicle motion to calculate the geographical location of the garbage.

On the latitude and longitude map, the distance between two points can be calculated according to the latitude and longitude. Because all the longitude lines on the earth are equal in length, the actual arc length difference is about 111 km per degree of latitude. Since each latitude decreases from the equator to the two poles, the length on the 60° latitude is half of that on the equator, so the arc lengths with a longitude difference of one degree on each latitude are not equal. On the same latitude (assuming that the latitude of this latitude is $\alpha$), the actual arc length corresponding to the longitude is about 111cos$\alpha$km per degree.

As shown in Fig. 6, it is assumed that point A is the position of the vehicle, point B is the position of the garbage, and the latitude and longitude coordinates of the two points A and B are A (jA, wA) and B (jB, wB). Then the distance between the arcs AB is:

$$AB = R \arccos(\cos(wA)\cos(wB)\cos(jB - jA) + \sin(wA)\sin(wB) \qquad (3)$$

Due to the visible distance of the sensor, the distance between the garbage and the vehicle will not exceed 50 m, and the longitude range of China is 73°33′E–135°05′E; the latitude range of China is 3°51′N–53°. So we can use a simplified model to solve this problem, as shown in Fig. 7, we can directly convert the spherical coordinate system

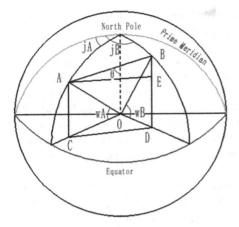

**Fig. 6.** Car and garbage in space geodetic coordinate system.

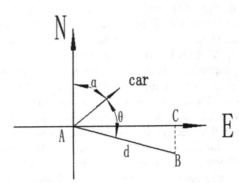

**Fig. 7.** Car and garbage in a plane rectangular coordinate system.

into a two-dimensional plane coordinate system. In Fig. 7, $\alpha$ is the heading angle of the vehicle's forward direction, which is rotated clockwise begin the north direction from 0 to 360°. It can be directly analyzed from the data obtained by the locator. $\theta$ is the angle between the garbage and the forward direction of the vehicle, which is rotated clockwise begin the forward direction of the vehicle from 0 to 360°. The data can be parsed from the head of the camera platform and the point cloud obtained by the Lidar. d is the distance between the car and the garbage, which can be parsed from the point cloud data obtained in Lidar. Considering that the relative position of garbage and vehicle is not fixed, it needs to be decomposed into four quadrants in the Cartesian coordinate system to solve the problem. After derivation, the solution formulas for different quadrants are the same. And the latitude and longitude of point B is:

$$jB = jA + d\sin(\theta + \partial)$$
$$wB = wA + d\cos(\theta + \partial)$$

(4)

## 2.4   Garbage Detection and Classification Based on Deep Learning

Garbage is an object with uncharacteristic features that can be clearly distinguished by the human eye, but it is difficult to define it for computers, while deep learning has a strong ability to extract and discriminate features. Using deep learning for detection and discrimination becomes a good choice.

Since the classification of garbage is more than just one label in the sanitation field. For example, domestic garbage may also be leaking garbage at the same time, so the original single label classification needs to be improved to multi-label classification when selecting category prediction. Therefore, our network structure replaces the softmax layer for single-label multi-classification with the logical regression layer for multilabel multi-classification. The logistic regression layer is mainly implemented by the sigmoid function, which can constrain the output to a range of 0 to 1. Therefore, when an image is subjected to feature extraction and a certain type of output is constrained by the sigmoid function. If the value is greater than 0.5, then it belongs to that class.

YOLOv3-darknet uses multi-scale prediction, and deep features are fused by up-sampling with shallow features to avoid loss of features. In addition, each grid cell corresponds to multiple anchor boxes. We cluster the training data to get a new anchor box. These sizes of boxes can reflect the distribution information of the actual garbage size. The anchor box method can adapt to different sizes of objects, and the detection of small target garbage is greatly improved.

On the GTX1080ti device, the detection speed of single-frame images is 60 ms, which can meet real-time detection, and the accuracy is also very high. Whether it is small paper scraps on the road, plastic bags or large pieces of garbage, it can be well recognized. Even under the dark yellow road lantern cover, there is no problem in identifying the garbage. The results of garbage detection and classification under different scales, non-categories and different scenarios are shown in Fig. 8.

**Fig. 8.** Detection results of different sizes of garbage in different scenarios. (Color figure online)

## 3 Experiment

In order to verify the correctness and feasibility of the proposed method, three types of experiments were designed to verify the calculation of the garbage's area, the calculation of the latitude and longitude position, and the identification and classification of the garbage. The platform built for the experiment is shown in Fig. 9. The camera and Lidar are fixed on the left and right sides of the camera platform. They are mounted on the roof of the car to rotate and pitch. The GPS locator is placed on the roof, and the computer, IMU, etc. are inside the car.

### 3.1   Experimental Verification of Garbage's Area Calculation

According to the experience of sanitation work, the area of common garbage on the road is 0.01 to 2 m². Therefore, we designed experiments to verify the correctness of our calculation method. According to the test on road, the distance between garbage and car is basically from 5 to15 m. Therefore, experiments are carried out in three groups. The relative distance between vehicles and garbage is 5 m, 10 m and 15 m respectively. Each group of experiments calculates the garbage's area $s_c$ of different sizes n times, and then compares with the real area s. The results are shown in Table 1.

$$\text{average error} = \frac{1}{n} \left( \sum_i^n \left( \frac{|s_i - s_{ci}|}{s_i} \right) \right) \tag{5}$$

The experimental results show that the farther the garbage is from the vehicle, the smaller the garbage, the less accurate the area calculation. This is because the 16-line laser radar we use cannot guarantee the depth information on the far and small garbage. This requires calculating the depth information of the garbage by searching for two adjacent lines. However, the accuracy requirement is not high, only a general range is needed, which is convenient for the supervisor to dispatch the appropriate number of personnel and the type of cleaning tools. Therefore, the garbage area calculated by the method can satisfy the application scenario of this paper.

**Fig. 9.** Intelligent sanitation system experimental platform.

**Table 1.** Average error of area's calculation

| Relative distance | 5 m | 10 m | 15 m |
| --- | --- | --- | --- |
| Average error of area | 10.5% | 13.3% | 19.8% |

## 3.2 Experimental Verification of Garbage's Latitude and Longitude Calculation

In order to verify the accuracy and reliability of the garbage latitude and longitude calculation method, we performed multiple verifications on the experimental platform of Fig. 9. Experiments were carried out in three groups, that is, the relative distance between the vehicle and the garbage was 5 m, 10 m, and 15 m, and then the vehicle heading angle, the pan-tilt deflection angle, and the relative positional relationship between the vehicle and the garbage were changed to ensure the inclusion of various relative positions that may occur in practice. Finally, we obtain the true latitude and longitude of the garbage through the locator, compare the difference between the calculated latitude and longitude of the garbage. The average value of the error are shown in Table 2:

**Table 2.** Average error of latitude and longitude in different situations.

| Relative distance | 5 m | 10 m | 15 m |
|---|---|---|---|
| Average error of latitude and longitude | (0.000028°, 0.000031°) | (0.000035°, 0.000030°) | (0.000021°, 0.000028°) |

The experimental results show that our simplified model calculates the latitude and longitude of another point is correct and reliable, and the error is small within a short distance, which can well meet the actual working conditions.

## 3.3 Experimental Verification of Garbage's Identification and Classification

We drove the car (Fig. 9) and traveled on a certain road in Shanghai for about 1.5 h, with an average speed of, a total of 269 pieces of garbage 30 km/h. A total of 14,835 pictures were taken. Through manual verification pictures were found. The specific results are shown in Tables 3 and 4.

**Table 3.** Correct detection rate of garbage detection.

| Total captured images | Images include garbage | Correctly detected images | Correct detection rate |
|---|---|---|---|
| 14835 | 269 | 251 | 93.31% |

**Table 4.** False detection rate of garbage detection.

| Total captured images | No garbage images | Incorrect detected images | False detection rate |
|---|---|---|---|
| 14835 | 14566 | 1225 | 8.41% |

Experiments show that our method has a high detection rate of garbage, and there is very little leakage detection. However, the main problem is a certain proportion of false detections. As shown in Fig. 10, one type of false detection, the white car was misidentified as garbage. The reason is that our tens of thousands of training sets has a lot of white plastic bags whose feature is similar to them. Subsequently, we added a large number of images include white car and labeled them as a separate category. Through probability comparison, the probability that the white car is recognized as car is much larger than that identified as a white plastic bag, thus achieving the purpose of eliminating misidentification. As shown in Fig. 11, the white car is correctly identified as car. In addition, there are other types of false detections, such as shoes on the feet of pedestrians, car lights, car tires, etc. We also use the same method to compete between classes to achieve the purpose of rejection. After using this method to optimize, our test results on the same pictures are shown in Table 5.

**Fig. 10.** The white car is misidentified as white trash.    **Fig. 11.** The white car is correctly identified as the car after optimized.

**Table 5.** False detection rate of garbage detection after optimizing.

| Total captured images | No garbage images | Incorrect detected images | False detection rate |
| --- | --- | --- | --- |
| 14835 | 14566 | 832 | 5.71% |

### 3.4 Experimental Verification of the Speed and Accuracy Among Different Model

We used 12,000 images for training and 8000 images for testing. Test images include 4,000 images with garbage and 4,000 images without garbage. In addition to YOLOv3 model, we conducted some comparative experiments. Including the comparison between two-stage and one-stage model. For the two-stage model, we chose Faster RCNN. For one-stage model, we selected three models which are RetinaNet, DSSD, and YOLOv3. Taking the accuracy and recall rate to evaluate the performance. More specifically, the models we have adopted have achieved the best speed and accuracy. The result is shown in Table 6.

**Table 6.** Speed and accuracy among different one-stage model.

| Model | Accuracy | Recall | Time (ms) |
|---|---|---|---|
| YOLOv3-darknet | 87.36% | 93.48% | 60 |
| RetinaNet-800 | 85.17% | 91.62% | 213 |
| DSSD513 | 83.47% | 89.33% | 164 |
| Faster RCNN | 79.54% | 85.57% | 500 |

### 3.5 Display of Data Fusion Results

As shown in the Fig. 12, this is the result of our system's test, which displays the garbage location information, the garbage category, the distance between the garbage and the vehicle, and the area of the garbage in real time on the image.

**Fig. 12.** The results of the calculation of garbage's location, category and area.

## 4    Conclusion

For the content of urban road garbage monitoring and cleanliness evaluation, the method proposed by us can judge the presence or absence of garbage and different garbage categories well, and can simultaneously calculate the area and latitude and longitude of the garbage, and realize the quantification result output of the cleanliness score, basically realized a fully automated and intelligent replacement of manual work. What's more, the system is gradually being applied to the sanitation industry in Shanghai.

**Acknowledgment.** This research was partially supported by the National Nature Science Foundation of China (Grant no. 51575332) and the key research project of Ministry of science and technology ((Grant no. 2017YFB1301503 and no. 2018YFB1306802).

# References

1. Zhuang, C.: Thoughts on the long-term supervision mechanism of sanitation and cleaning marketization. China Constr. Inf. **24**, 75–76 (2014)
2. Sun, J.: Problems and countermeasures of market operation supervision of sanitation roads. Big Technol. **3**(7), 308 (2016)
3. Wei, Z.: Discussion on the Market Supervision Mechanism of Environmental Sanitation Cleaning. Residential and Real Estate. **7**(3), 141,231 (2017)
4. Mittal, G., Yagnik, K.B., Garg, M., et al.: Spot Garbage: smart phone app to detect garbage using deep learning. In: ACM International Joint Conference on Pervasive and Ubiquitous Computing, pp. 940–945 (2016)
5. Wei, S., Cheng, Z.: Image-based automatic detection of urban scene garbage. Integr. Technol. **6**(01), 39–52 (2017)
6. Ren, S., He, K., Girshick, R., Sun, J.: Faster R-CNN: towards real-time object detection with region proposal networks. In: NIPS, pp. 91–99 (2015)
7. Zeiler, M.D., Fergus, R.: Visualizing and understanding convolutional networks (2013). arXiv:1311.2901,2013
8. He, K., Zhang, X., Ren, S., Sun, J.: Deep residual learning for image recognition. In: CVPR, pp. 1–8 (2016)
9. Redmon, J., Farhadi, A.: Yolov3: an incremental improvement (2018). arXiv:1804.02767,2018
10. Qu, S., et al.: Method for measuring height measurement area based on monocular vision ranging. Sci. Technol. Eng. **16**(02), 224–228 (2016)
11. Chen, Y.X., Das, M., Bajpai, D.: Vehicle tracking and distance estimation based on multiple image features. IEEE Computer and Robot Vision, pp. 371–378 (2007)
12. You, L., et al.: Application of USB camera parallel binocular vision system in area measurement. Appl. Technol. **02**, 1–5 (2008)
13. Liu, L., et al.: Derivation of calculation formula for conversion of GPS coordinates with direction and distance. Southern Agricultural Machinery (2018)
14. Li, Z., Li, J.: Fast calculation of distance between two points and measurement error based on latitude and longitude. Mapp. Spat. Geogr. Inf. **36**(11), 235–237 (2013)
15. Kong, X., et al.: Foundation of Geodesy, 2nd edn., pp. 158–179. WuHan University Press, Luojiashan (2005)
16. Zhang, Z.: A flexible new technique for camera calibration. Tpami **22**(11), 1330–1334 (2000)
17. Wu, Y., Hu, Z.: PnP problem revisited. J. Math. Imaging Vis. **24**(1), 131–141 (2006)

# Visual and Motional Learning in Robotics

# A Grid-Based Monte Carlo Localization with Hierarchical Free-Form Scan Matching

Mei Wu[1], Hongbin Ma[1(✉)], and Xinghong Zhang[2]

[1] School of Automation, Beijing Institute of Technology, Beijing 100081, China
mathmhb@bit.edu.cn
[2] Department of Automatic Control, Henan Institute of Technology,
Xinxiang 453000, China

**Abstract.** This paper is concerned with the localization problem of robot in unstable environment. To improve the accuracy of the localization result in the environment, a grid-based Monte Carlo localization algorithm with hierarchical free-form scan matching (MCL-HF) is proposed. In MCL-HF algorithm the distribution of the samples is adapted by the most recent observation. To simplify the process of the adaptation a feature-based scan-matching algorithm is adopted in the grid-based localization algorithm in a hierarchical free-form. The advantage of the proposed algorithm is demonstrated through the experiment results.

**Keywords:** Localization · Particle filter · Scan-matching

## 1 Introduction

With the vigorous development in robotics the uses of robots have become increasingly prevalent. The applications of robot are no longer restricted to traditional industry but also medical service, public security and business. To enable robots to fulfill the task assigned automatically the abilities to navigate and localize are important.

The research about localization has received significant attentions and various localization algorithms have been proposed, such as global positioning system (GPS) position estimation, WIFI position estimation and Monte Carlo localization (MCL). These methods have their own advantages and disadvantages. Although GPS provides reliable positioning services, the cost of equipping a robot with a GPS sensor with sufficient accuracy may be prohibitive. Other methods, such as WIFI are very useful, but the accuracy of these methods is not sufficient in many situations. To make a balance between cost and localization accuracy, this paper focuses on the issue of MCL algorithm with ranging sensors.

If a spatial model of the environment is available in the form of a map, it is possible for MCL algorithm to estimate the pose of a robot with better accuracy [16]. And it is not difficult to build a map manually with ranging

© Springer Nature Switzerland AG 2019
H. Yu et al. (Eds.): ICIRA 2019, LNAI 11741, pp. 371–380, 2019.
https://doi.org/10.1007/978-3-030-27532-7_33

sensors in a location where the environment is roughly flat, almost static and mostly structured. This mapping problem, which has been thoroughly studied since 1988, is also called simultaneous localization and mapping (SLAM). SLAM was first proposed by [1] and has since attracted the interests of many researchers. Many methods have been applied to solve this problem in [2,3], such as extended Kalman filter SLAM (EKF-SLAM) in [4], unscented Kalman filter SLAM (UKF-SLAM) in [5], particle filter SLAM (PF-SLAM) in [6], unscented particle filter SLAM (UPF-SLAM) in [7], FastSLAM in [8,9] and distributed particle filter SLAM in [10–13]. Some grid map-based SLAM algorithms were tested in [14]. The mapping capability of these algorithms is proved by the experimental results in this paper. And the map used in this paper is calculated by one of the most widely used mapping algorithm called Gmapping in [15].

Adaptive Monte carlo localization (AMCL) algorithm in [17], which adopts the idea of Kullback-Leibier distance (KLD) sampling, is a widely used MCL algorithm with known map. The key idea of KLD sampling is to adapt the number of the samples: when the probability density is concentrated on a small part of the state space, a smaller sample size is chosen, whereas higher uncertainty leads to a larger sample size. As a result, AMCL algorithm reduces the cost of computational resources.

However, the reduced sample size decreases the accuracy of the localization. Since the samples in AMCL algorithm are generated from the proposal distribution, the accuracy of AMCL algorithm is restricted to the accuracy of the proposal distribution, especially when the sample size is small. Thus, how to improve the accuracy of the estimation result remains an interesting topic. Although increase the number of samples in certain parts of the state space will increase the estimation accuracy [17] when highly accurate estimates are required, how to improve the estimation results without increasing the sample size is another interesting question.

Several works have reported solutions to this problem. In [15] the most recent observations of sensors is integrated to improve the proposal distribution. In [18] the observation data around these important spaces is recorded to improve the estimation results. However, the accuracy of these methods is unsatisfactory in unstable environments.

In this paper, we introduce a grid-based Monte Carlo localization algorithm with hierarchical free-form scan matching (MCL-HF). The purpose of this approach is to increase the accuracy of the localization result without increasing the sample size. To achieve this goal, we increase the density of the samples in the state space with high probability. In this approach, the features extracted from the observation are matched with the features extracted from the map. The difference between the matching pairs is utilized to adapt the proposal distribution of the samples. The advantages of the proposed algorithm are demonstrated through experiments. The remainder of the paper is organized as follows. We describe the idea and the algorithm of MCL-HF in Sect. 2. The experiment and results are introduced in Sect. 3. In the last section, we conclude this paper.

## 2  The Grid-Based Monte Carlo Localization with Hierarchical Free-Form Scan Matching

The aim of MCL-HF algorithm is to improve the estimation result when the accuracy of the motion model is limited. To achieve this goal, a hierarchical free-form map representation is adopted, in which a feature-based scan-matching process is embedded in the classic grid-based AMCL algorithm. The flowchart of this algorithm is shown in Fig. 1. As marked as red rectangles in Fig. 1, the line features in the grid map are extracted and matched with the line features in the data scanned by the laser sensor in a feature-based form. The rest of the procedure is conducted in a grid-based form. With a feature-based scan-matching procedure, we can improve the proposal distribution and enhance the accuracy of the localization result.

The basic steps of MCL-HF algorithm are shown in Algorithm 1.

---

**Algorithm 1.** Algorithm of MCL-HF $(X_{t-1}; u_t; z_t)$:

---

$X'_{t-1} = X_{t-1} = \emptyset$
$\hat{X}_t = \arg\max_X p(X|(\alpha,\phi)^T, z_t, \overline{X}_t)$
**if** $\hat{X}_t = failure$ **then**
    **for** $m = 1$ to $M$ **do**
        sample $x_t^{[m]} \sim p(X_t|u_t, X_{t-1}^{[M]})$
        $\omega_t^{[m]} = p(z_t|x_t^{[m]})$
        $X'_t = X'_t + < x_t^{[m]}, \omega_t^{[m]} >$
    **end for**
**else**
    **for** $m = 1$ to $M$ **do**
        sample $x_t^{[m]} \sim p(x_t|u_t, X_{t-1}^{[M]}, \phi_d)$
        $\omega_t^{[m]} = p(z_t|x_t^{[m]})$
        $X'_t = X'_t + < x_t^{[m]}, \omega_t^{[m]} >$
    **end for**
**end if**
**if** $x_t^{[m]}$ falls into empty bin b **then**
    $k = k + 1$
    $b = non - empty$
    **while** $n < \frac{1}{2\epsilon}\chi^2_{k-1,1-\delta}$ **do**
        $n = n + 1$
    **end while**
**end if**
**for** $m = 1$ to $M$ **do**
    draw $i$ with probability $\propto \omega_t^i$
    add $X_t^{[i]}$ to $X_t$
**end for**

---

The state vector $X_t$ of the robot is composed of the position $(x, y)$ and the orientation $\theta$. Here, the state denotes the state of the robot at time $t$. The motion model of the robot is shown below

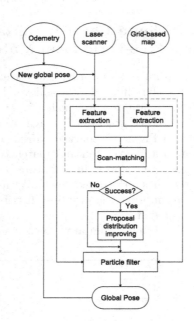

**Fig. 1.** Algorithm of MCL-HF. (Color figure online)

$$X_t = [x_t, y_t, \theta_t]^T \qquad (1)$$

$$\overline{X}_t = X_{t-1} + A_{t-1}u_{t-1} + w_{t-1} \qquad (2)$$

where $\overline{X}_t$ is the prior estimate of $X_t$ without the observations of time $t$, $A_{t-1}$ is the input matrix,

$$A_{t-1}X_{t-1} = \begin{pmatrix} cos(\theta_t + \frac{\omega_t}{2})\ 0 \\ sin(\theta_t + \frac{\omega_t}{2})\ 0 \\ 0 \qquad 1 \end{pmatrix} \qquad (3)$$

$w_{t-1}$ is the process state noise,

$$u_t = [\triangle_t, \omega_t] \qquad (4)$$

and $u_t$ is the input vector, which consists of the displacement and rotation of the robot.

The measurement model of the robot at time $t$ is given by

$$z_t = H_t(X_t) + q_t \qquad (5)$$

where $z_t$ is the observation information, $q_t$ is the measurement noise, $\gamma_{t,k}$ and $\varphi_{t,k}$ are the $k$th distance and angle gathered from the laser measurements at time $t$ respectively,

$$z_t = [\gamma_{t,k}, \varphi_{t,k}] \qquad (6)$$

$H_t$ is the measurement function,

$$H_t(x_t) = \begin{pmatrix} \sqrt{(m_y - y_t)^2 + (m_x - x_t)^2} \\ \arctan(m_y - y_t, m_x - x_t) - \theta_t \end{pmatrix} \tag{7}$$

$(m_x, m_y)^T$ represents the map of the environment.

The position of the object observed by the robot is calculated by Eq. (8).

$$\begin{pmatrix} \overline{m}_x \\ \overline{m}_y \end{pmatrix} = \begin{pmatrix} \overline{x}_t + \gamma_{t,k} cos(\overline{\theta}_t + \varphi_{t,k}) \\ \overline{y}_t + \gamma_{t,k} sin(\overline{\theta}_t + \varphi_{t,k}) \end{pmatrix} \tag{8}$$

If it is possible to find $\hat{X}_t$ by Eq. (9), it can be utilized to improve the proposal distribution for a better estimation result. However, as mentioned above, finding $\hat{x}_t$ by Eq. (9) directly is difficult; it is much easier to find $\hat{x}_t$ in the feature-based form such as Eq. (10). Here, the feature-based $(m_\alpha, m_\phi)^T$ and $(\overline{m}_\alpha, \overline{m}_\phi)^T$ can be calculated from the line extraction algorithm.

$$\hat{X}_t = \arg\max_X p(X|(m_x, m_y)^T, z_t, \overline{X}_t) \tag{9}$$

$$\hat{X}_t = \arg\max_X p(X|(m_\alpha, m_\phi)^T, z_t, \overline{X}_t) \tag{10}$$

Since there are some regular walls in the area we studied, we can extract wall features from the grid-based map $(m_x, m_y)^T$ by Hough transform via Eqs. (11) and (12).

$$(m_x, m_y)^T \Rightarrow (m_\alpha, m_\phi)^T \tag{11}$$

$$(\overline{m}_x, \overline{m}_y)^T \Rightarrow (\overline{m}_\alpha, \overline{m}_\phi)^T \tag{12}$$

where $(m_\alpha, m_\phi)^T$ denotes the line features extracted from the map. Grid-based maps are usually saved as a single picture with 3 colors: black white and gray. Obstacles, including walls, are usually shown as black pixels in the picture. Thus, the wall feature can be extracted by Hough transform from these pixels Fig. 2(a).

$(\overline{m}_\alpha, \overline{m}_\phi)^T$ represents the features extracted from the observation. The item being observed consists of a series of points reported from the laser sensor. With the Hough transform, $(\overline{m}_\alpha, \overline{m}_\phi)^T$ can be extracted from the observation.

Yet, as shown in Fig. 2(a), some bushes are also extracted as features. Selecting the line features $(\overline{m}_\alpha, \overline{m}_\phi)^T$ and $(m_\alpha, m_\phi)^T$ that are longer than the threshold, as shown in Fig. 2(b), can effectively eliminate these unreliable features.

An additional step is needed to remove the observation points of the bushes. Since the variance of the observation points is larger than the variance of the other observation points, deleting the observation point cloud with high variance in $(\overline{m}_\alpha, \overline{m}_\phi)^T$ and $(m_\alpha, m_\phi)^T$ can make the feature extraction more reliable.

$$(\overline{m}_x, \overline{m}_y)^T \Rightarrow (\overline{m}_\alpha, \overline{m}_\phi)^T \tag{13}$$

If the features $(\overline{m}_\alpha, \overline{m}_\phi)^T$ extracted from the laser scanner match the features $(m_\alpha, m_\phi)^T$ extracted from the map, it is feasible to improve the proposal distribution of the particles.

(a) Extracting the line in the grid-based map.

(b) Selecting the lines longer than the threshold.

**Fig. 2.** Line extracting.

However, sometimes there is only one line feature matching the feature map. Thus, the solution of Eq. (10) is infinite. Based on our experimental experience, the speed of error accumulation in orientation is much faster than that in position. Accordingly, the difference between the observation and the map in the matching pair calculated by Eq. (14) is utilized to improve the proposal distribution.

$$\phi_d = m_\phi - \overline{m}_\phi \tag{14}$$

$$x_t^{[m]} \sim p(x_t | u_t, x_{t-1}^{[M]}, \phi_d) \tag{15}$$

The main procedures of MCL-HF algorithm include:

I. Map feature extraction: extract the line in the grid-based-map, as shown Fig. 2(a), and select the lines longer than the threshold, as shown in Fig. 2(b).

II. Global transformation: transform the object observed by the robot from the robot frame to the global frame using Eq. (8).

III. Measurement extraction: extract the line feature from the measurement.

IV. Scan-matching: match the features from the map $(\alpha, \phi)^T$ and the features from the observation $(\overline{\alpha}, \overline{\phi})^T$.

V. Improving the proposal distribution: improve the proposal distribution with $\hat{x}_t$.

## 3    Experiment

To prove the effectiveness of MCL-HF algorithm, an experiment was performed in an outdoor area that is approximately 200 m long and 100 m wide. There are some brush woods at the south end of the factory as shown in Fig. 3(b). The computer in the robot runs Linux, and the code is written in C++. Before the experiment was performed, the robot was manually steered through the environment to build the map by GMapping. During the experiment the robot moves in the factory and localize itself with the localization algorithms introduced.

## 3.1 The Sensors and the Platform

The proposed localization approach runs on a 4-wheel differential platform equipped with a SICKLMS laser range finder, as shown in Fig. 3(a). The maximum range of this laser sensor is 200 m with measurement error less than 10 cm.

(a) The platform of the robot.           (b) The experiment environment.

**Fig. 3.** Experiment environment and the robot platform.

## 3.2 Results Analysis

The root mean square error (RMSE) criterion is employed to test the localization capability of MCL-HF algorithm and AMCL algorithm. The RMSE of the robot's position estimates by different localization methods are compared in Fig. 4.

The RMSE associated with these methods are distinguished by different colors. The vertical coordinate indicates the RMSE in the robot's position, and the horizontal coordinate indicates the time steps. The localization result obtained by the MCL-HF algorithm is better (in terms of localization accuracy) than that

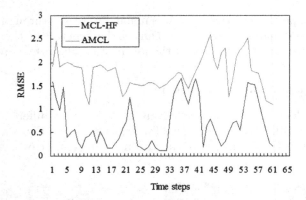

**Fig. 4.** The localization result.

of the AMCL algorithm overall, which shows that scan-matching can considerably improve the localization performance of robot.

The results shown in Table 1 give an intuitive comparison of the performance of the two methods. From the table, we can see that the average RMSE of the MCL-HF algorithm is less than the average RMSE of AMCL algorithm. The average RMSE of these 2 methods, that are shown in Fig. 5, are respectively, 0.693 dm and 1.772 dm.

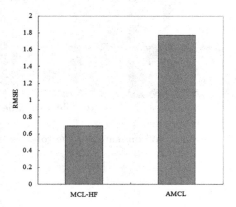

**Fig. 5.** The average localization result.

**Table 1.** The average RMSE.

| Method | Average RMSE (decimeter) |
| --- | --- |
| The MCL-HF algorithm | 0.693 |
| The AMCL algorithm | 1.772 |

We found that the accuracy of the localization result is related to the control input of the robot. In practice, the accuracy of the motion model decreases as the yaw rate of the robot increases. The proposal distribution may introduce bias because the original AMCL algorithm generated the proposal distribution with the motion model, so the proposal distribution is affected by the noise in the odometer measurement. Therefore, the proposal distribution is suboptimal, and the accuracy of the localization result is limited. To improve the accuracy of the estimation result, we integrate the most recent observation to generate the proposal distribution if the scan-matcher succeeds.

## 4   Conclusion

In this paper, MCL-HF algorithm, an algorithm for outdoor navigation in unstable environment is developed. In this algorithm, the proposal distribution of the samples is improved by integrating the most recent observation in a hierarchical free-form manner. Thus the density of the samples in the state space with high probability increases. And the localization accuracy of the MCL-HF algorithm is improved without the necessary to increase the number of the samples.

The proposed algorithm has been tested in experiment and the result is compared with the original algorithm. And the comparison results demonstrate the effectiveness and the advantage of the MCL-HF algorithm.

**Acknowledgement.** This work is partially supported by National Key Research and Development Program of China under Grant 2017YFF0205306, National Nature Science Foundation of China under Grant 91648117, and Beijing Natural Science Foundation under Grant 4172055.

## References

1. Smith, R., Cheeseman, P.: On the representation and estimation of spatial uncertainty. J. Robot. Res. **5**(4), 231–238 (1986). https://doi.org/10.1177/027836498600500404
2. Durrantwhyte, H.F., Bailey, T.: Simultaneous localization and mapping: part I. J. Robot. Autom. Mag. **13**(2), 99–110 (2006). https://doi.org/10.1109/MRA.2006.1638022
3. Bailey, T., Durrantwhyte, H.F.: Simultaneous localization and mapping (SLAM): part II. J. Robot. Autom. Mag. **13**(3), 108–117 (2006). https://doi.org/10.1109/MRA.2006.1678144
4. Huang, S., Dissanayake, G.: Convergence and consistency analysis for extended Kalman filter based SLAM. J. Robot. **23**, 1036–1049 (2007)
5. Wang, H., Fu, G., Li, J., et al.: An adaptive UKF based SLAM method for unmanned underwater vehicle. J. Control Decis. **2013**, 1–12 (2013). https://doi.org/10.1155/2013/605981
6. Montemerlo, M., Thrun, S., Roller, D., et al.: Fast SLAM 2.0: an improved particle filtering algorithm for simultaneous localization and mapping that provably converges. In: Proceedings of the 18th International Joint Conference on Artificial Intelligence, pp. 1151–1156 (2003)

7. Julier, S.J., Uhlmann, J.K.: Unscented filtering and nonlinear estimation. J. Proc. IEEE **92**(3), 401–422 (2004). https://doi.org/10.1109/JPROC.2003.823141
8. Garrido, S., Moreno, L., Blanco, D.: Exploration and mapping using the VFM motion planner. J. Instrum. Meas. **58**(8), 2880–2892 (2009). https://doi.org/10.1109/TIM.2009.2016372
9. Ma, Y., Ju, H., Cui, P.: Research on localization and mapping for lunar rover based on RBPF-SLAM, pp. 2880–2892 (2009). https://doi.org/10.1109/IHMSC.2009.200
10. Sheng, X., Hu, Y.H.: Distributed particle filters for wireless sensor network target tracking. In: IEEE International Conference on Acoustics, Speech, and Signal Processing, pp. 845–848 (2005). https://doi.org/10.1109/ICASSP.2005.1416141
11. Sheng, X., Hu, Y.-H., Ramanathan, P.: Distributed particle filter with GMM approximation for multiple targets localization and tracking in wireless sensor network. J. Inf. Process. Sensor Netw., 181–188 (2005). https://doi.org/10.1109/IPSN.2005.1440923
12. Zuo, L., Mehrotra, K.G., Varshney, P.K., et al.: Band width-efficient target tracking in distributed sensor networks using particle filters. In: International Conference on Information Fusion, pp. 1–4 (2006). https://doi.org/10.1007/s12243-010-0224-9
13. Gu, D., Sun, J., Hu, Z., et al.: Consensus based distributed particle filter in sensor networks. In: International Conference on Information and Automation, pp. 302–307 (2008). https://doi.org/10.1109/ICINFA.2008.4608015
14. Santos, J., Portugal, D., Rocha, R.P.: An evaluation of 2D SLAM techniques available in robot operating system. In: IEEE International Symposium on Safety, Security, and Rescue Robotics, pp. 1–6 (2013). https://doi.org/10.1109/SSRR.2013.6719348
15. Grisetti, G., Stachniss, C., Burgard, W.: Improved techniques for grid mapping with Rao-Blackwellized particle filters. J. IEEE Trans. Robot. **23**(1), 34–46 (2007). https://doi.org/10.1109/TRO.2006.889486
16. Thrun, S., Burgard, W., Fox, D.: Probabilistic Robotics. Intelligent Robotics and Autonomous Agents. MIT Press, Cambridge (2005)
17. Fox, D.: KLD-sampling: adaptive particle filters. J. Adv. Neural Inf. Process. Syst., 713–720 (2001)
18. Rowekamper, J., Sprunk, C., Tipaldi, G.D., et al.: On the position accuracy of mobile robot localization based on particle filters combined with scan matching. In: IEEE/RSJ International Conference on Intelligent Robots and Systems, pp. 3158–3164 (2012). https://doi.org/10.1109/IROS.2012.6385988

# A Method to Deal with Recognition Deviation Based on Trajectory Estimation in Real-Time Seam Tracking

Nianfeng Wang, Suifeng Yin[✉], Kaifan Zhong, and Xianmin Zhang

Guangdong Provincial Key Laboratory of Precision Equipment
and Manufacturing Technology, School of Mechanical and Automotive
Engineering, South China University of Technology, Guangzhou 510640, China
menfwang@scut.edu.cn, yin.suifeng@mail.scut.edu.cn

**Abstract.** In real time seam tracking process, recognition deviation is likely to occur due to various kinds of noise (e.g., reflection and scattering.......). In this paper, a method to correct deviation via replacing the deviation points with estimated points is proposed. Firstly, according to the characteristic of the real-time seam tracking process, standards for recognition deviation are developed to classify deviation points, and an abnormality judgment strategy is discussed. Then, a method of trajectory estimation is given and the detected trajectory of an abnormal deviation will be replaced with the estimated trajectory. Finally, experiments are conducted to prove the performance of the proposed method.

**Keywords:** Real-time seam tracking · Recognition deviation ·
Deviation judgment · Trajectory estimation

## 1 Introduction

At present, industrial welding robots have been widely used for various automatic manufacturing process. In the process of autonomous manufacturing, parts errors are unavoidable especially for some parts which are assembled manually. Since most of the welding robots work in the "teaching-and-playback" mode or off-line programming mode, it is difficult to adapt parts errors unless the robot is taught or programmed again. It will be time and labor consuming.

In order to adapt parts errors in autonomous manufacturing, seam tracking must be conducted in automatic welding process. Online correction method can be used to track the weld in real time. Firstly, current information of the workpiece should be obtained by sensor. Among a variety of sensors, vision sensors are widely used in robotic system due to its high precision, rich information and noncontact [1]. However, in the vision-based seam tracking system, interference such as arc, smoke, splashes and poor surface of the workpiece are nonnegligible. These interference may lead to recognition deviation during image processing. As a result, many researchers make an effort to avoid recognition deviation. By analyzing the MIG spectrum, G etc. provided guidance for designing optical filter system which can denoise the welding image [2]. Jia etc. used a cascade algorithm composed by medium value filter and homomorphic filter in welding

© Springer Nature Switzerland AG 2019
H. Yu et al. (Eds.): ICIRA 2019, LNAI 11741, pp. 381–391, 2019.
https://doi.org/10.1007/978-3-030-27532-7_34

image de-noising [3]. Under arc interference, Zhen etc. successfully extracted the centerline of weld seam in 8 steps: mean filter, edge detection by Sobel operator, dilation, erosion, area filter, seam-like edges search [4]. Nele etc. set up three templates and found the templates in the continuously captured images with welding noise during the welding process. Once the templates is found, the weld seam can be positioned with the help of the "pattern learning algorithm" [5]. Liu etc. proposed a new image analysis scheme based on active contour models to extract the edges of the seams under heavy spatter interference [6]. Because of good performance on weld seam feature acquisition and interference resistance, the structured-light vision sensor, which is classified into active vision sensor, has been widely used in seam tracking. Zou etc. designed a structured-light seam tracking system. Image processing method of this system was based on continuous convolution operator tracker (CCOT) object tracking algorithm which had good performance in interference resistance [7]. Based on a so call "Sequence Gravity Method", Li etc. extracted the centerline of laser stripe projected on the workpiece to cope with the interference during welding process [8]. Facing the noise in welding image, Liu etc. used the Radon transform method to transform the welding images and eliminated noise in the space of transformed images [9]. He etc. detected the laser stripe forming the weld seam profile by a visual attention model based on saliency even the molten pool and glare are within the same frame simultaneously [10]. Muhammad etc. proposed a sequential image processing and feature extraction algorithms to effectively extract the seam geometrical properties from a low quality laser image [11].

Most of the methods dealing with the interference during the welding process made an effort to avoid recognition deviation in image processing. However, the image processing can hardly be reliable at any time. Once the recognition deviation occurs, the welding torch will deviate from the weld seam and lead to welding deviation. To reduce the influence of the already happened recognition deviation, a method based on trajectory estimation is proposed in this paper.

## 2   Methodology of Abnormality Judgment

When recognition deviation occurs, end effector of the robot will be guided to a wrong position deviated from the weld seam. Therefore, the deviation points must be recognized. However, in a single captured image, recognition deviation is hard to be judged due to the lack of information except for grayscale distribution. As a result, it is reasonable to seek further information other than image grayscale distribution. In this section, methodology of the abnormality judgment will be discussed. Firstly, abnormality will be classified according to the statistical characteristic of detected points. Then, recognition deviation will be defined and quantified.

### 2.1   Classification of Abnormality

Recognition deviation of the visual system will occur momentarily during the real-time seam tracking process due to interference. In order to describe the recognition deviation, a set of detected points will be taken into consideration to find out the statistical characteristic.

Compared with normal detected points, spatial distribution of the detected points with deviation can be classified into three main forms as shown in Fig. 1. These three different forms of recognition deviation can lead to different levels of welding deviation. The large maximum recognition deviation and the overall recognition deviation may lead to serious welding deviation. What's more, since the vision sensor is mounted on the end effector of robot, once the end effector deviates from the weld seam seriously, seam tracking process may be disrupted for the reason that the weld seam may be out of view. Influenced by the large average recognition deviation, the trajectory of the end effector will be not smooth. As a result, appearance of the weld seam will be non-uniform. To describe the recognition deviation with different spatial distribution, definition and quantization of recognition deviation will be discussed in details in next section.

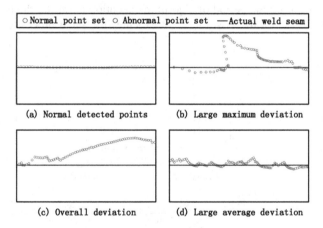

Fig. 1. Classification of abnormality

## 2.2 Abnormality Judgment

Since no more information can be obtained from the image except for grayscale distribution, it is hard to distinguish outliers from normal ones especially when the gray-value-based recognition method is out of work. Compared with the passive vision method, the structured-light vision method has stronger anti-interference ability and higher efficiency in image processing. However, some useful information such as trend of the weld seam and features of surfaces will lose. According to the characteristic of current seam tracking process, the obtained pre-taught trajectory, which gives out not only the initial position but also the shape and trend of the weld seam, can be used to make up for the shortcomings of structured-light vision. As a consequence, definition of recognition deviation is based on the pre-taught trajectory. Since the seam tracking is a real-time process and statistical characteristic of detected points has to be found out, segmentation strategy of the detected points should be discussed. Then, deviation quantification method based on the former segmentation strategy will be proposed.

**Trajectory Segmentation.** In order to recognize the outliers accurately and efficiently, we should adopt a reasonable strategy. If each detected points are taken to be processed, it will be time-consuming. Meanwhile, it is hard to extract useful features which can distinguish outliers and normal detected points significantly from a single detected point. As a result, it is necessary to divide the detected points into several segments so that we can deal with the segments one by one. The strategy is shown as Fig. 2. "Data 1" and "Data 2" are the detected points segments, while "Position 1" and "Position 2" are the location of detected points which are behind the "Data 1" and "Data 2" along "Working direction". The distance "d" can be set to an appropriate value. When the end effector of the robot reach to "Position 1", the detected points segment "Data 1" will be send to the processing algorithm. If "Data 1" contains outliers, the processing algorithm will give out the new data which has been eliminated outliers to replace "Data 1". Otherwise, the "Data 1" will not be replaced. It should be guaranteed that distance the end effector runs during the period of algorithm execution is shorter than "d" as shown in Fig. 2. When it comes to "Position 2", it executes the same process.

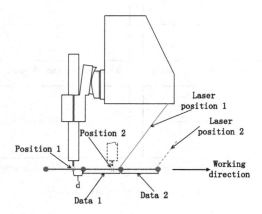

**Fig. 2.** Strategy of trajectory segmentation

**Deviation Quantification and Abnormality Judgment.** After segmenting the detected trajectory, recognition deviation can be quantified. As shown in Fig. 3, green points represent the points on one of the segments on the actual detected trajectory, while the red points represent the points on segments of the corresponding estimated trajectory. The strategy of obtaining the estimated trajectory will be discussed in next section. Point $P_1'$ and point $P_2'$ are two endpoints of the actual detected trajectory segment. By searching the nearest point on the estimated detected trajectory from two endpoints, point $P_1$ and point $P_2$ can be obtained. Then, line fitting using the least square method on two point sets will be carried out separately and line $l$, $l'$ can be obtained. Points $Q_1$, $Q_2$, $Q_1'$, $Q_2'$ are the corresponding foot points of points $P_1$, $P_2$, $P_1'$, $P_2'$ on two fitted lines as shown in Fig. 3. After obtaining two fitted line segments, the recognition deviation can be defined and quantified. In order to quantify three different forms of recognition deviation shown in Fig. 1, three evaluation indicators will be defined by Eqs. (1), (2) and (3).

$$I_1 = \left| \frac{\max(d_j)}{\max(d_i)} - 1 \right| \tag{1}$$

$$I_2 = \left| \frac{\sum\limits_{j=1}^{n} d_j/n}{\sum\limits_{i=1}^{m} d_i/m} - 1 \right| \tag{2}$$

$$\begin{cases} I_3 = S \\ I_4 = D \end{cases} \tag{3}$$

As shown in Fig. 3, $d_i$, $d_j$ represent the distance of points on estimated detected trajectory and actual detected trajectory to their corresponding fitted line (blue line and yellow line), while m, n represent the number of points on estimated detected trajectory and the actual one; S represents the area of quadrangle $\mathbf{Q_1Q_1'Q_2Q_2'}$, while D represents the distance between two non-uniplanar lines. $I_1$, $I_2$, $I_3$, $I_4$ are the self-defined evaluation indicators. Among these evaluation indicators, $I_1$ indicates the difference of maximum fluctuation between the actual detected trajectory and the estimated one, while $I_2$ indicates the difference of average fluctuation. Under normal circumstances, if no recognition deviation happens, fluctuation of the actual detected trajectory will be very similar to the estimated one and value of indicators $I_1$, $I_2$ will be closed to 0. When $I_1$ or $I_2$ is obviously greater than 0, it indicates that the fluctuation of the actual detected trajectory is very different from the estimated one and it is likely that a recognition deviation has occurred. When it comes to the indicators $I_3$, $I_4$, they are considered as a group and both of them can indicate the overall recognition deviation. If no overall recognition deviation happens, two fitted lines as shown in Fig. 3 are almost coincidental and indicators $I_3$, $I_4$ will be closed to 0. When the value of $I_3$, $I_4$ is obviously greater than 0, it is likely that the overall recognition has occurred. In short, the process of deviation quantification and abnormality judgment can be summarized in three steps:

- *Line fitting.* Fit the actual detected trajectory and the estimated one with linear model using least square method.
- *Indicators calculation.* Calculate the indicators which quantify the recognition deviation.
- *Abnormality judgment.* Compare the obtained value of the indicators with threshold and then the actual detected trajectory can be labeled as "Normal" or "Abnormal" according to the result of comparison.

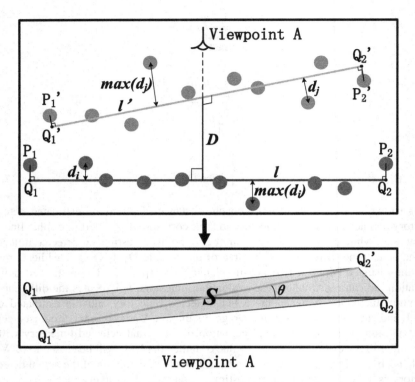

**Fig. 3.** Definition of deviation (Color figure online)

## 3    Estimation of Detected Path

In Sect. 2, judgment of recognition deviation has been discussed in details. During the process, the estimated trajectory plays an important role as the criterion of abnormality judgment. As a consequence, the estimated trajectory should be as close to the actual weld seam as possible. Since the previous actual detected trajectory and the pre-taught path have been obtained, current estimated trajectory can be obtained by the matching method. In this section, the process of obtaining the estimated trajectory will be discussed in details.

### 3.1    Principle of Matching Process

Matching is to calculate the rotation and translation matrix between two trajectories. In the field of point cloud matching, the most commonly used method is "Iterative closest point (ICP)". Iterative closest point (ICP) is an algorithm employed to minimize the difference between two clouds of points. Its main core is to minimize a target function shown as Eq. (4). The target function, whose independent variables are the rotation matrix $\mathbf{R}$ and the translation matrix $\mathbf{T}$, represents the quadratic sum of distance between two corresponding points. $\mathbf{D_i}$, $\mathbf{M_i}$ is a pair of corresponding points in two point sets, while $N_p$ represents the number of corresponding point pairs. Corresponding points can be searched by adopting different strategies. Taking a point on the source point set, the corresponding point of this point, which is belong to the target point set, can be the closest point, point in normal direction of source point set and point in self-defined projection direction as shown in Fig. 4. After searching the corresponding point pairs, the matrixes $\mathbf{R}$, $\mathbf{T}$ can be calculated using the least square method. Before Euclidean norm of the rotation matrix $\mathbf{R}$ is less than a threshold, the above process will be executed iteratively. In addition, to speed up the searching process of corresponding point pair, K-D tree is adopted.

$$f(R, T) = \frac{1}{N_P} \sum_{i=1}^{N_p} |D_i - R \cdot M_i - T|^2 \tag{4}$$

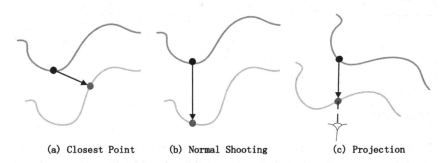

(a) Closest Point       (b) Normal Shooting           (c) Projection

**Fig. 4.** Method of searching corresponding point

## 3.2 Strategy of Detected Path Estimation

In Sect. 2.2, strategy of segmenting the actual detected path has been discussed in details (Fig. 2). According to the mentioned method of abnormality judgment in this section, each segments of actual detected points can be labeled as "Normal" or "Abnormal". Then, detected points on the segments which are labeled as "Normal" will be added to the target point set. Acting as the source point set, the pre-taught path will be transformed by the rotation matrix $\mathbf{R}$ and the translation matrix $\mathbf{T}$. The matrixes $\mathbf{R}$, $\mathbf{T}$ can be obtained from the matching process using the "Iterative closest point (ICP)" method mentioned above. At the same time, a new unlabeled segment of actual detected points has been generated. By searching the nearest point on the transformed pre-taught path from two endpoints of current detected point segment, segment of estimated trajectory can be obtained, and its endpoints are point $\mathbf{P_1}$ and point $\mathbf{P_2}$ as shown in Fig. 3. Finally, the overall process can be shown as Fig. 5.

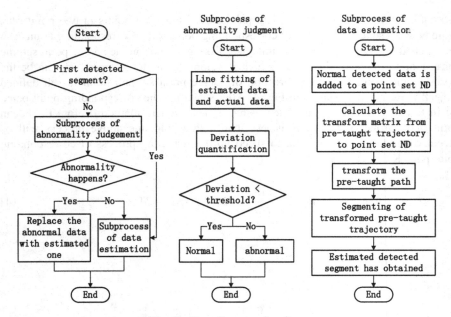

**Fig. 5.** Overall processing flow

## 4 Experiments

As shown in Fig. 6, experiments are conducted based on the robot structured-light vision system. The system consists of a robot welding system and a vision system. Arc welding robot, robot controller, electric welding machine and the welding gun belong to the robot welding system, while the vision system consists of a structured-light vision sensor mounted on the welding gun, an image capturing card and a PC used for image processing and communication with robot controller.

**Fig. 6.** Robot structured-light vision system

In order to demonstrate the effectiveness of the proposed method, experiments should be conducted. Before experiments, some preparation work is needed. Firstly, calibration for robot vision system is carried out. Then, as shown in Fig. 7, surface of the workpiece is partly polished artificially in order to form a surface that can cause recognition deviation of the vision sensor.

**Fig. 7.** The partly polished surface

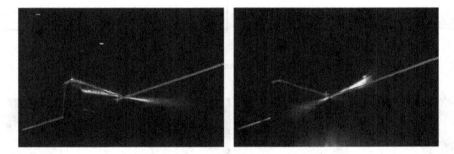

**Fig. 8.** Recognition deviation during welding process

After finishing the preparation work, the real-time seam tracking process can be executed. Welding mode is set to MIG welding, while the welding current is set to 150 A, welding voltage is set to 22 V and welding speed is set to 50 cm/min. During the process of seam tracking, the current detected point is ahead of the welding torch. As a result, when recognition deviation occurs as shown in Fig. 8, welding torch will not deviate from the weld seam immediately. However, according to the strategy of real-time seam tracking, if the deviation points are being searched and act as the target point, the welding torch will deviate from the weld seam. Only when the recognition deviation points can be eliminated and replaced with the points on the actual weld seam can welding deviation be avoided. As shown in Fig. 9, at the position where recognition deviation occurs, motion trajectory of the welding torch can transit to the estimated

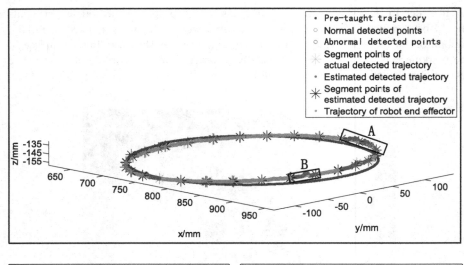

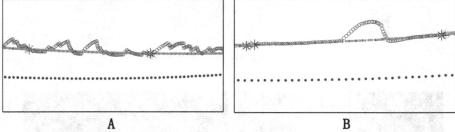

**Fig. 9.** Experiment data

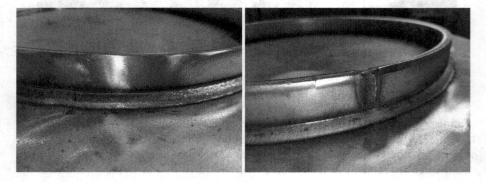

**Fig. 10.** Weld seam appearance

detected trajectory and reduce the influence of deviation points. Welding effect is shown as Fig. 10. Appearance of the weld seam is uniform and no welding deviation happens even in the partly polished area where recognition deviation happens. It proves that the proposed method is effective in dealing with recognition deviation and avoiding welding deviation in real-time seam tracking.

# 5 Conclusion

In this paper, a method for dealing with recognition deviation of structured-light vision system in real-time seam tracking process is proposed. According to the characteristic of current seam tracking process, a method based on segmenting the actual detected trajectory is presented. Then, the strategies of abnormality judgment, estimation of detected path and replacement of abnormal detected points are discussed in details. Finally, experiment is carried out and the proposed method is proved to be effective in dealing with recognition deviation and can correct welding deviation in real-time seam tracking.

**Acknowledgments.** The authors would like to gratefully acknowledge the reviewers' comments. This work is supported by National Natural Science Foundation of China (Grant Nos. U1713207), Science and Technology Planning Project of Guangdong Province (2017A010102005), Key Program of Guangzhou Technology Plan (Grant No. 201904020020).

# References

1. Rout, A., Deepak, B.B.V.L., Biswal, B.B.: Advances in weld seam tracking techniques for robotic welding: a review. Robot. Comput.-Integr. Manuf. **56**, 12–37 (2019)
2. Agapiou, G., Kasiouras, C., Serafetinides, A.A.: A detailed analysis of the MIG spectrum for the development of laser-based seam tracking sensors. Opt. Laser Technol. **31**, 157–161 (1999)
3. Jia, Q., Ma, G., Pei, L.: Image processing algorithm of weld seam based on crawling robot by binocular vision. In: Second International Conference on Mechanic Automation & Control Engineering (2011)
4. Ye, Z., Fang, G., Chen, S., Zou, J.J.: Passive vision based seam tracking system for pulse-MAG welding. Int. J. Adv. Manuf. Technol. **67**, 1987–1996 (2013)
5. Nele, L., Sarno, E., Keshari, A.: An image acquisition system for real-time seam tracking. Int. J. Adv. Manuf. Technol. **69**, 2099–2110 (2013)
6. Liu, J., Fan, Z., Olsen, S., Christensen, K., Kristensen, J.: Using active contour models for feature extraction in camera-based seam tracking of arc welding. In: IEEE/RSJ International Conference on Intelligent Robots & Systems (2009)
7. Zou, Y., Chen, T.: Laser vision seam tracking system based on image processing and continuous convolution operator tracker. Opt. Lasers Eng. **105**, 141–149 (2018)
8. Li, X., et al.: Robust welding seam tracking and recognition. IEEE Sens. J. **17**, 5609–5617 (2017)
9. Liu, X.: Image processing in weld seam tracking with laser vision based on radon transform and FCM clustering segmentation. In: International Conference on Intelligent Computation Technology & Automation (2010)
10. He, Y., Xu, Y., Chen, Y., Chen, H., Chen, S.: Weld seam profile detection and feature point extraction for multi-pass route planning based on visual attention model. Robot. Comput.-Integr. Manuf. **37**, 251–261 (2015)
11. Muhammad, J., Altun, H., Abo-Serie, E.: A robust butt welding seam finding technique for intelligent robotic welding system using active laser vision. Int. J. Adv. Manuf. Technol. **94**, 13–29 (2018)

# 3-D Dimension Measurement
# of Workpiece Based on Binocular Vision

Jiannan Wang, Hongbin Ma[✉], and Baokui Li

School of Automation, Beijing Institute of Technology,
Beijing 100081, People's Republic of China
mathmhb@bit.edu.cn
http://we-learn.net.cn/mathmhb

**Abstract.** In this paper, the three-dimensional measurement of workpiece is studied, and the left and right images of the target workpiece are captured by binocular camera. Firstly, the calibration principle and theoretical model of binocular camera are studied in detail, and the calibration of inside and outside parameters of left and right cameras is completed under the environment of Matlab. Secondly, Hough transform is used to detect the contour of the target workpiece after image processing such as filtering, graying and binarization, and to extract its two-dimensional feature point information. Then, on the basis of epipolar rectification, there is only lateral parallax between left and right images, and Block Matching (BM) algorithm is used for stereo matching of relative images. After that, the depth information of the pixels is extracted from the disparity map obtained by stereo matching, and the dimension of the workpiece is measured by combining the two-dimensional feature point information extracted by Hough transform and the three-dimensional Euclidean distance calculation formula. Finally, the experimental results show the validity of the proposed three-dimensional measurement results based on binocular vision.

**Keywords:** Binocular vision · Camera calibration · Stereo matching · Three-dimensional measurement

## 1 Introduction

With the gradual development of industrial automation, the requirement of workpiece geometric dimension measurement is getting higher and higher, and the requirement of detection accuracy and efficiency is getting stricter and stricter. On the contrary, the traditional contact manual detection is still the main means of workpiece dimension detection on production line. Therefore, only by constantly improving the detection methods and innovating the detection methods can the production quality of products be effectively improved. Traditional detection methods have the following shortcomings: high labor intensity, low work efficiency, measurement error, workpiece surface vulnerable to damage and other shortcomings. In contrast, the non-contact measurement method based on machine vision has won wide acclaim and has been widely used for its advantages of fast detection speed, high detection accuracy and wide application scenarios.

© Springer Nature Switzerland AG 2019
H. Yu et al. (Eds.): ICIRA 2019, LNAI 11741, pp. 392–404, 2019.
https://doi.org/10.1007/978-3-030-27532-7_35

Binocular stereo vision measurement technology is widely used in many fields, such as production monitoring, automatic classification of medical tablets, automatic mail sorting mechanism, performance analysis of chemical materials, license plate recognition [1] and so on. The application of this technology not only achieves the purpose of non-contact measurement which was difficult to achieve in the past, but also improves product quality and production efficiency, and saves human costs. This technology will produce tremendous economic value and have far-reaching significance and impact.

Consequently a lot of researches have been done for binocular stereo vision. Tokyo University of Japan has successfully developed a real-time walking robot navigation system by integrating the overall pose information of the robot and real-time binocular stereo vision system [2]. An augmented reality system based on binocular stereo vision has been developed by Nara University of Science and Technology in Japan [3]. The system improves the accuracy of the corrected feature points by means of dynamic correction. An adaptive binocular stereo vision servo system was developed by Osaka University in Japan [4]. With the joint development of Microsoft Group and Washington University, a wide-baseline stereo vision system was developed to support the Mars satellite [5]. This system enables the satellite to achieve high-precision navigation and positioning functions for different terrain over thousands of meters on Mars.

In addition, in the field of three-dimensional measurement, many scholars have put forward their own innovative methods. Abdelaziz and Karara [6] summarized a three-dimensional measurement method based on direct linear transformation (DLT) algorithm. Pollefeys et al. [7] can obtain the measurement and three-dimensional reconstruction of Euclidean geometry system by self-calibration under the assumption that the camera parameters are given certain. Faugeras et al. proposed a method to measure the shape of three-dimensional objects based on the information of external scenes. Sturm et al. [8] also applied a multi-image projection structure and motion algorithm based on factorization to three-dimensional measurement. Hartley et al. [9] developed a method of calculating the three-focus tensor based on the information of the line and point in three views, and then obtained the projection matrix by decomposition to achieve the purpose of three-dimensional measurement.

The remainder of this paper is organized as follows: Firstly, in Sect. 2, the principle of camera imaging and the related links of camera calibration are introduced. Secondly, Sect. 3, a series of image preprocessing methods are presented and a new method based on Hough transform is used to detect the contour of the target workpiece to extract its two-dimensional feature point information. Then, in Sect. 4, the epipolar rectification and stereo matching of binocular camera are introduced. The experimental result of measuring the dimensions of the workpiece is listed in Sect. 5. Finally, Sect. 6 concludes this paper by summarizing the work done.

# 2    Camera Calibration

## 2.1    Ideal Binocular Stereo Vision Model

The ideal binocular stereo vision model is a binocular stereo vision model with left and right cameras parallel to each other, as shown in Fig. 1.

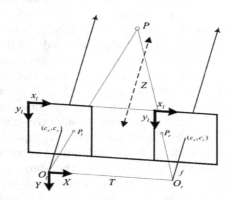

**Fig. 1.** Ideal binocular stereo vision model

In Fig. 1, $O_l$ and $O_r$ represent the position of the center of light of the left and right cameras, $T$ represents the distance between the two centers of light, the left and right imaging planes are located on the same plane, and the left and right optical axes formed by the connection of the center of light and the corresponding image principal points of the imaging plane are also parallel to each other.

Assuming that the coordinate system of the model is based on the left camera coordinate system, a point $P(X, Y, Z)$ in the real world is projected onto the imaging plane of the left and right cameras, respectively, point $p_l(x_l, y_l)$ and point $p_r(x_r, y_r)$. Because the model is based on the parallelism of left and right cameras, the left and right projection points of any world coordinate point in the imaging plane have the same longitudinal coordinate value, i.e. $y_l = y_r$. The only difference is in the abscissa, i.e. disparity $d = x_l - x_r$. Through the similar triangle theorem, the following deductions can be written as

$$\begin{cases} y_l = y_r. \\ \frac{Z}{T} = \frac{Z-f}{T-(x_l-x_r)}. \\ d = x_l - x_r. \end{cases} \tag{1}$$

The depth information obtained from the three equations in (1) is as follows.

$$Z = \frac{fT}{d} \tag{2}$$

From Fig. 1, the following relationships can be found.

$$\begin{cases} x_l - c_{xl} = f_{xl}\frac{X}{Z} \\ y_l - c_{yl} = f_{yl}\frac{Y}{Z} \end{cases} \tag{3}$$

Combining (1) and (3), we can obtain the actual three-dimensional coordinates of point $P$:

$$\begin{cases} X = \frac{Z(x_l - c_{xl})}{f_{xl}} \\ Y = \frac{Z(y_l - c_{yl})}{f_{yl}} \\ Z = \frac{f_{xl}T}{d} \end{cases} \tag{4}$$

## 2.2  Calibration Experiment

Based on Zhang's calibration algorithm [10], a calibration toolbox based on MATLAB and a checkerboard calibration board are used to calibrate binocular vision system. The interface of the calibration toolbox is shown in Fig. 2. The toolbox includes the following functions: reading the image with specified basic name and format into memory, extracting grid corners, calibrating internal parameters, displaying the relationship between camera and calibration board, error analysis of image space, distortion removal and stereo calibration, etc. It covers the whole process of single target calibration and binocular stereo calibration.

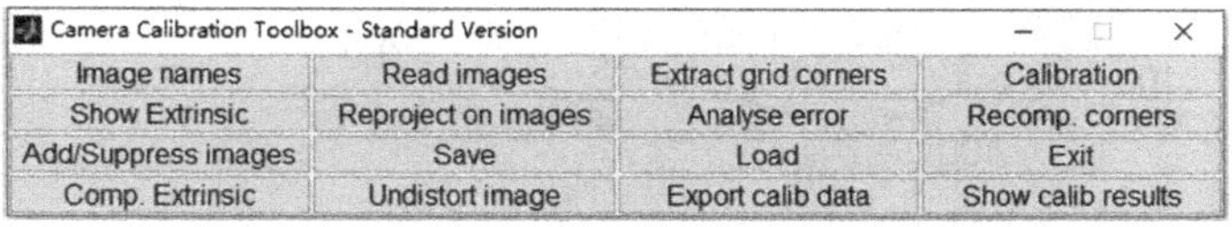

| Camera Calibration Toolbox - Standard Version | | | — ☐ ✕ |
|---|---|---|---|
| Image names | Read images | Extract grid corners | Calibration |
| Show Extrinsic | Reproject on images | Analyse error | Recomp. corners |
| Add/Suppress images | Save | Load | Exit |
| Comp. Extrinsic | Undistort image | Export calib data | Show calib results |

**Fig. 2.** Matlab camera calibration toolbox

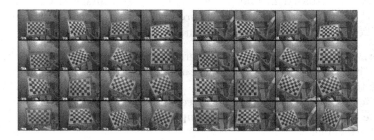

**Fig. 3.** Calibration board image imported by left and right cameras

The more pairs of images are imported into the Matlab camera calibration toolbox, the smaller the calibration error is. Therefore, 16 pairs of calibration plate images were selected to complete the calibration work. The imported calibration board image is shown in Fig. 3.

After a series of operations to obtain the internal and external parameters of the binocular camera, the final position relationship of the binocular camera is shown in Fig. 4.

## 3   Image Processing and Analysis

### 3.1   Image Preprocessing

After calibration, what we need to do is to process and transform the image appropriately to enhance the features, weaken the noise and optimize the quality of the image.

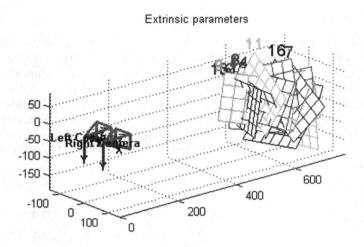

**Fig. 4.** Position relationship of binocular camera

Firstly, a sort-based median filter to process the image is chosen. Median filtering [11] can remove noise while preserving the original structure of the image. The specific operations of median filtering are as follows.

(1) All the pixels in the image are covered once by the center of the template.
(2) Get the gray value of each corresponding pixel under the template.
(3) Sort these gray values by size.
(4) Get a value in the middle from these values.
(5) Make the central position of the template pixel take its corresponding intermediate value.

Secondly, Because the camera captures the color image, and image processing on the gray image can reduce the amount of calculation, so we need to gray the image. Graying [12] is the process of transforming color image into gray image. Gray-level transformation usually takes the following way, giving each of the three color components R, G and B of the color image a certain weight coefficient, and getting the gray-level value of the transformed image by weighting calculation.

$$\begin{cases} V_{gray} = 0.30R + 0.59G + 0.11B \\ R = G = B = V_{gray} \end{cases} \tag{5}$$

Image binarization is the process of setting some pixels in gray image to 0 and remaining pixels to 1. Unlike gray images, which usually have 256 gray levels, binary images have only two levels of 0 and 1, namely black and white. The purpose of binarization [13] is to segment the image, make the target elements appear white and make some irrelevant elements into the background black.

## 3.2 Feature Points Extraction by a New Method Based on Hough Transform

The basic idea of Hough transform [14] is to make use of the duality of points and lines, that is, the parameters of all lines passing through a point $(x_0, y_0)$ will satisfy equation $b = -x_0 k + y_0$, that is, a point $(x_0, y_0)$ in image space corresponds to a line in parameter space k-b. For any point on a line $y = k_0 x + b_0$, its corresponding line in the parameter space will pass through the point $(k_0, b_0)$ in the parameter space, that is, a point $(k_0, b_0)$ in the parameter space corresponds to a line $y = k_0 x + b_0$ with slope $k_0$ and intercept $b_0$ in the image space (Fig. 5).

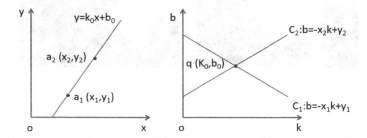

**Fig. 5.** One to one mapping relation between image space and parameter space

In order to avoid the problem of infinite slope of vertical line, polar coordinates $(\rho, \theta)$ are often used as transform space for the detection of straight line in any direction and position. The polar coordinate equation can be written as

$$\rho = x\cos\theta + y\sin\theta \tag{6}$$

The parameters $\rho$ and $\theta$ can uniquely determine a straight line. $\rho$ denotes the distance from the origin to the straight line, and $\theta$ is the angle between the normal of the straight line and the x-axis. For any point in $(x, y)$ space $(x_0, y_0)$, the polar coordinates $(\rho, \theta)$ are used as the parameter space, and the transformation equation can be written as

$$\rho = x_0\cos\theta + y_0\sin\theta \tag{7}$$

From (7), it can be seen that a point $(x_0, y_0)$ in the image space corresponds to a sinusoidal curve in the parameter space $(\rho, \theta)$.

The algorithm of Hough transform is described as follows.

(1) In the parameter space $(\rho, \theta)$, an accumulative array $A(\rho, \theta)$ is established, and the initial values of each element in the array A are set to zero. For each point $(x, y)$ represented by 1 in a binary image, let $\theta$ take all possible values on $\theta$ axis, and calculate corresponding $\rho$ according to (6). Then, according to the values of $\rho$ and $\theta$, the array is accumulated.

(2) By detecting the local peak value of array $A(\rho, \theta)$, the parameters $\rho$ and $\theta$ of the detected line are obtained.

Based on the above principle, the left and right images of the target workpiece after binarization are transformed by Hough transform respectively. Hough transform is used to extract the line where the edge is located, and the two-dimensional image coordinate information of its four vertices is obtained by the intersection of every two straight lines, which is as shown in Fig. 6.

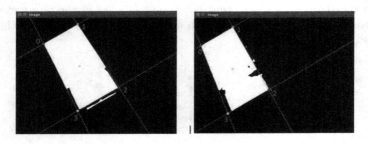

**Fig. 6.** Detection of left and right images by Hough transform

The coordinate table of four vertex pixels obtained by clockwise sorting of vertices 0 in the upper left corner is shown in Table 1.

**Table 1.** Pixel coordinates of workpiece vertices in left and right images

| Vertex coordinates | Left image | Right image |
| --- | --- | --- |
| 0 | (110.501, 107.699) | (27.2736, 117.082) |
| 1 | (245.068, 26.9594) | (154.384, 38.2336) |
| 2 | (408.472, 287.64) | (297.511, 299.888) |
| 3 | (245.98, 385.643) | (134.622, 396.858) |

## 4 The Epipolar Rectification and Stereo Matching of Binocular Camera

### 4.1 Epipolar Rectification

According to the binocular stereo vision model in reality, the geometric relationship between left and right cameras can be obtained, as shown in Fig. 7. If the projection points of a space point $A$ on the left and right image planes are $A_l$ and $A_r$ respectively, then $A_l$ and $A_r$ are a set of corresponding points.

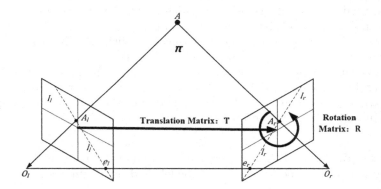

**Fig. 7.** Geometric relationship between left and right cameras

By determining the location of a point $A_l$ on the image plane $I_l$ and the corresponding point $A_r$ on the image plane $I_r$, we can obtain the three-dimensional coordinates of the spatial point A according to the principle of binocular vision. From the principle of epipolar geometry, we know that if the image point in one image plane is known, its position in another image plane is determined. As shown in Fig. 7, the corresponding point of point $A_l$ is located on a specific line in the plane $I_r$, which is called the corresponding polar line of point $A_l$ in the plane $I_l$.

The following are some concepts of polar geometry.

(1) Baseline: a line connecting the optical centers of the two cameras $O_l$ and $O_r$.
(2) Epipolar plane: any plane in which the baseline is included.
(3) Epipolar points: the two points $e_l$ and $e_r$ of the baseline $O_lO_r$ intersecting the two image planes.
(4) Epipolar lines: the intersecting lines $l_l$ and $l_r$ of the epipolar plane $\pi$ and two planes $I_l$ and $I_r$.

In Fig. 7, the polar plane $\pi$ includes a triangle composed of two camera optical centers $O_l$, $O_r$ and the spatial point $A$, and $A_l$ and $A_r$ are located on the epipolar lines $l_l$ and $l_r$, respectively. Since each point on the straight line $O_lA$ corresponds to the image point on the image plane $I_l$, which is $A_l$, analogous to the straight line $O_r A$, each point on the line corresponding to the image plane $I_r$ is $A_r$. Thus, for a certain point $A_l$ on the image plane $I_l$, it corresponds to a specific point $A_r$ on the image plane $I_r$, The specific position of $A_r$ is determined by the position of the spatial point $A$ on the straight line $O_l A$, that is, the distance of the spatial point $A$ from the optical center $O_l$, and thus the position of $A_r$ is constrained. The polar line reduces the search for the corresponding point from the 2D image to the one-dimensional line, narrows the search range, and improves the speed and accuracy, which plays a vital role.

There are many classical algorithms for epipolar rectification [15], including Hartley algorithm and Bouguet algorithm. Hartley algorithm is based on the corresponding point relationship between two images, so as to calculate the basic matrix. It can achieve epipolar rectification without calibration, but the proportion of images in the actual scene is not clear.

The principle of Bouguet algorithm is to minimize the number of reprojections of each image acquired by the left and right cameras, while ensuring the minimization of distortion and the maximization of the observed area. Specific work includes the following three links.

(1) By obtaining the parameter matrix of binocular camera after stereo calibration, the left and right cameras are rotated at a certain angle in a given direction, so that the orientation of the left and right cameras is roughly the same.
(2) Move the left and right cameras to the right position so that their optical axes are parallel to the x-axis.
(3) the rectification parameters are obtained by calculating the rectification image.

In this paper, Bouguet algorithm is used to rectify the original image in Ubuntu+OpenCV environment (Fig. 8).

**Fig. 8.** Left and right images after epipolar rectification

## 4.2 Stereo Matching

This paper uses BM algorithm [16] for stereo matching. The BM algorithm is a local stereo matching [17] algorithm based on the support window. It first assumes that the pixels in the support window have the same parallax, that is, define the window first, and then use the window to traverse the feature vector in the image to be matched. Then calculate and count the similarity between different windows and the window during the traversal process, and finally select the window with the highest similarity as the matching result. For the BM algorithm, it can both regard pixels as matching features and adaptively adjust windows according to image features. For searching optimal window, the principle of common optimal optimization algorithm is as follows: the first step is to calculate the matching cost of each pixel in different matching windows, and the second part is to find the window with the smallest matching cost, that is, the best matching window.

The matching cost is first calculated by BM algorithm, which represents the parallax $d \in (d_{min}, d_{max})$. The rectangular window is determined from the left and right images, and the center coordinates of the window are $p_1(x, y)$, $p_2(x + d, y)$, respectively. The similarity of the two rectangular windows can be calculated by matching cost function. Here, the matching cost functions mainly include SSD, SAD and ZSSD, which represent the sum of squares difference, absolute difference and normalized cross-correlation respectively. This topic chooses SAD window to find the best matching points in left and right images. In summary, the steps to implement BM algorithm are as follows.

(1) Normalize the brightness of left and right images and enhance the texture of images by pre-filtering.
(2) Use SAD window to search along the direction of the epipolar line.
(3) Re-filter, screen and remove mismatches.

The original left and right images of the workpiece are shown in Fig. 9, and the disparity map obtained by stereo matching is shown in Fig. 10.

**Fig. 9.** The original left and right images of the workpiece

**Fig. 10.** The disparity map obtained by stereo matching

## 5 The Experimental Result of Measuring the Dimensions of the Workpiece

According to the formulas of space three-dimensional coordinate points mentioned above, and combining with stereo matching technology, the disparity map of left and right images is obtained, thus the depth information of the image is obtained. The coordinates of two-dimensional feature points of left and right images are substituted and the three-dimensional coordinate information of space feature points is obtained through calculation, and finally the three-dimensional reconstruction link is completed. The three-dimensional coordinates of workpiece feature points are shown in Table 2.

**Table 2.** Three-dimensional coordinates of feature points of target workpiece

| Feature points number | Three-dimensional coordinates of feature points |
| --- | --- |
| 0 | (−12.775, 51.505, 280.016) |
| 1 | (72.962, 97.764, 292.997) |
| 2 | (173.763, −73.709, 279.497) |
| 3 | (88.026, −119.968, 266.516) |

After obtaining the three-dimensional coordinates of each feature point of the target workpiece, the dimension information of the workpiece can be calculated by using the Euclidean distance formula of two points in the three-dimensional space. Finally, the calculated value and the actual size of the workpiece are compared and analyzed, which are shown in Table 3.

**Table 3.** Actual length and calculated value of target workpiece (unit: mm)

| Side length | Actual length | Calculated value | Measurement error |
| --- | --- | --- | --- |
| Length | 198 | 199.364 | 0.69% |
| Width | 99 | 98.281 | −0.73% |

# 6  Concluding Remarks

A 3-D dimension measurement method of workpiece based on improved Hough transform is proposed in this paper. First, calibrate the inside and outside parameters of left and right cameras based on the Matlab camera calibration toolbox. Second, A series of image filtering, graying and binarization are processed to prepare for edge detection by Hough transform. Then a new method based on Hough transform is used in workpiece images to extract two-dimensional feature point information. Next is the epipolar rectification experiment, which weakens the image affected by the interference factors such as position, light and distortion. BM algorithm is selected to realize stereo matching model, and the stereo matching experiment of left and right images is carried out to obtain disparity map and three-dimensional coordinate information of space points. Finally, according to the three-dimensional coordinate information of the space point and the Euclidean distance formula of the three-dimensional space, the workpiece size can be calculated. The final experimental error is less than 1%, so the measurement method proposed in this paper has a good measurement effect.

**Acknowledgment.** This work is partially supported by National Key Research and Development Program of China under Grant 2017YFF0205306, National Nature Science Foundation of China under Grant 91648117, and Beijing Natural Science Foundation under Grant 4172055.

# References

1. Mantri, S., Bullock, D.: Analysis of feedforward-backpropagation neural networks used in vehicle detection. Transp. Res. Part C **3**(3), 161–174 (1995)
2. Okada, K., Inaba, M., Inoue, H.: Integration of real-time binocular stereo vision and whole body information for dynamic walking navigation of humanoid robot. In: IEEE International Conference on Multisensor Fusion and Integration for Intelligent Systems (2003)
3. Vallerand, S., Kanbara, M., Yokoya, N.: Binocular vision-based augmented reality system with an increased registration depth using dynamic correction of feature positions. In: Proceedings of the 2003 IEEE, Virtual Reality, pp. 271–272, 22–26 March 2003
4. Asada, M., Tanaka, T., Hosoda, K.: Visual tracking of unknown moving object by adaptive binocular visual servoing. In: Proceedings of the 1999 IEEE International Conference on Multisensor Fusion and Intelligent Systems (1999)
5. Olson, C.F., Abi-Rachedi, H., Ye, M., Hendrich, J.P.: Wide-baseline stereo vision for Mars rovers. In: Proceedings of the 2003 IEEE/RSJ International Conference on Intelligent Robots and Systems, October 2003
6. Abdelaziz, Y.I.: Photogrammetric potential of non-metric cameras. Thesis Illinois Univ. 74, 134 (2002)
7. Pollefeys, M., Koch, R., Gool, L.V.: Self-calibration and metric reconstruction inspite of varying and unknown intrinsic camera parameters. Int. J. Comput. Vision **32**(1), 7–25 (1999)

8. Sturm, P., Triggs, B.: A factorization based algorithm for multi-image projective structure and motion. In: Buxton, B., Cipolla, R. (eds.) ECCV 1996. LNCS, vol. 1065, pp. 709–720. Springer, Heidelberg (1996). https://doi.org/10.1007/3-540-61123-1_183

9. Hartley, R.: Lines and points in three views and the trifocal tensor. Int. J. Comput. Vision **22**(2), 125–140 (1997)

10. Zhu, Z., Wang, X., Liu, Q., Zhang, F.: Camera calibration method based on optimal polarization angle. Opt. Lasers Eng. **112**(SI), 128–135 (2019)

11. Tang, H., Ni, R., Zhao, Y., Li, X.: Median filtering detection of small-size image based on CNN. J. Vis. Commun. Image Represent. **51**, 162–168 (2018)

12. Zhang, X., Wang, X.: Novel survey on the color-image graying algorithm. In: IEEE International Conference on Computer and Information Technology, Helsinki, Finland, pp. 750–753, August 2017

13. Tung, C.H., Wu, Z.L.: Binarization of uneven-lighting image by maximizing boundary connectivity. J. Stat. Manag. Syst. **20**(2), 175–196 (2017)

14. Bachiller-Burgos, P., Manso, L.J., Bustos, P.: A variant of the Hough transform for the combined detection of corners, segments, and polylines. EURASIP J. Image Video Process. (1), 32 (2017)

15. Lin, G.-Y., Xu, C., Zhang, W.-G.: A robust epipolar rectification method of stereo pairs. In: 2010 International Conference on Measuring Technology and Mechatronics Automation, Changsha, China, pp. 322–326, March 2010

16. Liu, T., Shi, J.: Study on improvement of BM algorithm for intrusion detection. In: IEEE International Conference on Signal and Image Processing (2017)

17. Hu, T., Huang, M.: A new stereo matching algorithm for binocular vision. In: International Conference on Hybrid Information Technology, pp. 42–44 (2009)

# Co-simulation of Omnidirectional Mobile Platform Based on Fuzzy Control

Wenchao Zuo, Hongbin Ma$^{(\boxtimes)}$, Xin Wang, Cong Han, and Zhuang Li

School of Automation, Beijing Institute of Technology,
Beijing 100081, People's Republic of China
mathmhb@bit.edu.cn
http://we-learn.net.cn/mathmhb

**Abstract.** Slippage is inevitable when the mecanum wheel moves in a non-ideal environment which likes an uneven ground. Slippage is an important factor affecting the motion accuracy of the mecanum wheel. A novel six-input and five-output fuzzy controller is proposed to improve the motion accuracy of the mecanum wheel mobile platform (MWMP) in this paper. Firstly, the assembly model of the MWMP is designed by Solidworks software. The virtual prototype model can be obtained by Automatic Dynamic Analysis of Mechanical Systems (Adams) performing some parameter settings on the assembly model. Deviation data can be obtained easily and intuitively through ADAMS when the MWMP is moving. Co-simulation between Matlab and Adams is achieved through interface functions between them. Then, an ideal kinematics model is established in the global coordinate system. Finally, the thirteen fuzzy rules are designed based on the ten basic forms of motion of the MWMP. A fuzzy logic system (FLS) with adaptive function is established in Simulink. The experimental results indicate that the FLS can improve the robustness, adaptability and accuracy of the MWMP.

**Keywords:** FLS · Kinematics · Co-simulation · MWMP

## 1 Introduction

Recently, mobile robots play an increasingly important role in manufacturing, safety rescue and space exploration with the help of various sensors such as laser radar and camera [1]. The mecanum wheel mobile platform (MWMP) has two translational degrees of freedom and one degree of rotational freedom and can move in any direction in the plane [2]. The MWMP also has a high load capacity especially in small space such as prospect aircraft production plant and warehouse stacking [3]. The modeling analysis and motion control of the MWMP become a research focus in robotics field. The ideal kinematic analysis of the mecanum wheel has developed quite mature. Gfrerrer studied the geometry of rolls and the kinematics of a vehicle featured with mecanum wheels [4]. Tlale put forward the different motions of the MWMP achieved by a combination of

© Springer Nature Switzerland AG 2019
H. Yu et al. (Eds.): ICIRA 2019, LNAI 11741, pp. 405–416, 2019.
https://doi.org/10.1007/978-3-030-27532-7_36

different driven wheels and used the integrated motion sensor system to verify developed mathematical models [5]. There are many control strategies suitable for the motion control of the MWMP. Fuad found that model predictive control is more effective than traditional PID to velocity control for a heavy-duty MWMP [6]. Kuo et al. presented a trajectory tracking and heading adjustment system of a mecanum wheel robot with fuzzy logic controller to reduce the error caused by slippage in a non-ideal environment [7]. Tsai put forword an intelligent adaptive and sliding mode control approach to carry out formation control in presence of uncertainties by using the Lyapunov stability theory and online learning the system uncertainties via recurrent fuzzy wavelet neural networks [8]. Wen et al. used genetic algorithm to adjust the membership function of fuzzy subset and improved $A^*$ path planning algorithm to achieve a smooth motion for the robot [9]. Vlantis carried out an extensive experimental procedure using the omnidirectional KUKA youBot with the fault tolerant control problem which was efficiency in various faults [10]. Lu et al. used an adaptive sliding mode control scheme for the MWMP in presence of external disturbances and uncertainties. The simulation results showed that the sliding mode control method is more effective than PID control method [11]. It is difficult to establish the precise kinematics and dynamics model of the MWMP in the complex environment. Therefore, the dynamic simulation software is used to study the co-simulation and control algorithm of the MWMP. Jamali addressed a novel control system is designed using three separate fuzzy controllers in order to control the position and orientation of robot by Adams and Matlab [12]. Shahin et al. presented a co-simulation between Adams and Matlab to estimate the performance of the designed PID controller for synchronizing the motors of the MWMP and the experimental results showed that the performance of the designed PID controller was acceptable [13]. Ahmad Jamil et al. presented an intention method based on two inputs and three outputs self-tuning fuzzy PID controller, which has higher steady precision than the conventional PID controller [14]. In this paper, the three dimensional model of the MWMP is designed by Solidworks. The virtual prototype of the MWMP is obtained by setting some parameters of the entity model in Adams. Co-simulation is established based on the interface function provided with Matlab provided in Adams. The ideal kinematics model in the global coordinate system is established as a simplified mathematical model of the controlled object. The ten basic forms of motion of the MWMP are the basis for establishing fuzzy rules. A six-input and five-output fuzzy controller is built in Simulink to compensate the deviation of the MWMP during motion.

## 2    Modeling and Analysis

It is convenient to verify whether the design of the motion mechanism in the MWMP is reasonable by performing the dynamic simulation of the virtual prototype in Adams. Based on the assumption of no slippage, an accurate kinematics formula of the MWMP in the global coordinate system is derived.

## 2.1  Virtual Prototype Model of MWMP

The virtual prototype model of MWMP is shown as Fig. 1. The four mecanum wheels are arranged in rectangular pattern. The roller and the hub are connected by a rotary pair. Each mecanum wheel is equipped with a parallelogram and a spring-damped suspension structure, which ensures that the mecanum wheel can still have good vertical contact with the ground on uneven ground so that the mecanum wheels have enough effective driving force. The spring damping system in the independent suspension can reduce the influence of the vibration caused by the discontinuous contact between the roller and the ground to improve the positional accuracy in the height direction of the MWMP. The material of the roller and the ground in the MWMP is made of steel and rubber, respectively. Some important parameters need to be set for discontinuous contact between the roller and the ground as shown in Table 1. The dynamic analysis of the virtual prototype in Adams reveals that the slippage of the mecanum wheels causes a large error in the linear and angular displacement of the MWMP compared with the expected motion form.

**Fig. 1.** The virtual prototype model of the MWMP in Adams.

**Table 1.** The contact parameters between the roller and the ground

| Name | Numerical | Name | Numerical |
|------|-----------|------|-----------|
| Stiffness | 2855 | Force exponent | 2.2 |
| Damping | 0.57 | Penetration depth | 0.1 |
| Static coefficient | 0.3 | Dynamic coefficient | 0.25 |

## 2.2  Kinematic Analysis

It is assumed that there is no slippage when the mecanum wheel moves to simplify the kinematics analysis of the MWMP. In other words, the mecanum wheel moves at an ideal speed which including the magnitude and direction of the speed. The axis of the wheel is connected to the axis of the roller through the contact point of the roller with the ground [15]. The establishment of the kinematics model of the MWMP is so important that it is the basis for establishing

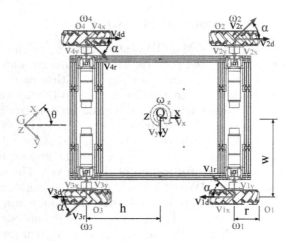

**Fig. 2.** The kinematics analysis of the MWMP.

a fuzzy control system. Figure 2 shows a bottom view of the MWMP which conveniently describes the speed of the rollers in contact with the ground. The motion of the mecanun wheel is derived by the speed of rollers in contact with the ground and the speed of the MWMP. Let $V_{id}$ and $V_{ir}$ represent the driving speed and free rolling velocity of the rollers of the $i$-th mecanum wheel, respectively. The range of $i$ is an integer from 1 to 4. Let $\omega_i$ represents the rotational velocity of the $i$-th mecanum wheel. Let $V_{ix}V_{iy}O_i$ represents the coordinate system of the $i$-th mecanum wheel and the positive direction of $V_{ix}$ is the same direction of $V_{id}$. The $\alpha$ represents an angle of 45° between $V_{id}$ and $V_{ir}$. Let $V_x$, $V_y$ and $\omega_z$ represent the moving velocity of the MWMP in the x, y direction and the rotational velocity around the Z axis, respectively. Let $\omega_z$ is positive when the MWMP rotates counterclockwise. Let $xyz - O$ and $xyz - G$ represent the MWMP coordinate system and the global coordinate system, respectively, which belong to the right hand coordinate system. Let $\theta$ represents the deflection angle of $xyz - O$ with respect to $xyz - G$. Let $h$ and $w$ represent the distance between the contact point of the roller in contact with the ground and the center of the moving platform in the x direction and the y direction, respectively. Let $r$ represents the wheel radius. Here $w$ is equal to 275 mm, $h$ is equal to 225 mm, $r$ is equal to 76.2 mm.

$$v_{id} = \omega_i r \tag{1}$$

$$v_{ix} = v_{id} + e_{i1}v_{ir}\cos\alpha = v_x + e_{i3}\omega_z w \tag{2}$$

$$v_{iy} = e_{i2}v_{ir}\sin\alpha = v_y + e_{i4}\omega_z h \tag{3}$$

$$\omega_i = J_i \dot{q}_O \tag{4}$$

Formula (4) can be obtained by the formulas (1), (2) and (3). The $J_i$ and $\dot{q}_O$ denote $\left[\frac{1}{r} - \frac{e_n}{e_{i2}r\tan\alpha} \quad \frac{e_{i2}e_{i3}w\tan\alpha - e_{i1}e_{i4}h}{e_{i2}r\tan\alpha}\right]$ and $[v_x v_y \omega_z]^T$, respectively.

The transformation matrix of $\dot{q}_O$ to $\begin{bmatrix} \omega_1 & \omega_2 & \omega_3 & \omega_4 \end{bmatrix}^T$ can be expressed as Eq. (5).

$$J_O = \begin{bmatrix} \frac{1}{r} & -\frac{1}{r} & -\frac{h+w}{r} \\ \frac{1}{r} & \frac{1}{r} & \frac{h+w}{r} \\ \frac{1}{r} & \frac{1}{r} & -\frac{h+w}{r} \\ \frac{1}{r} & -\frac{1}{r} & \frac{h+w}{r} \end{bmatrix} \tag{5}$$

$$J_O^+ = \begin{bmatrix} \frac{r}{4} & \frac{r}{4} & \frac{r}{4} & \frac{r}{4} \\ -\frac{r}{4} & \frac{r}{4} & \frac{r}{4} & -\frac{r}{4} \\ -\frac{r}{4(h+w)} & \frac{r}{4(h+w)} & -\frac{r}{4(h+w)} & \frac{r}{4(h+w)} \end{bmatrix} \tag{6}$$

$$P_{GO} = \begin{bmatrix} \cos\theta & -\sin\theta & 0 & x_0 \\ \sin\theta & \cos\theta & 0 & y_0 \\ 0 & 0 & 1 & z_0 \\ 0 & 0 & 0 & 1 \end{bmatrix} \tag{7}$$

Let $\begin{bmatrix} \omega_1 & \omega_2 & \omega_3 & \omega_4 \end{bmatrix}^T$ be denoted as $\omega_O$. The inverse kinematics model of the MWMP can be expressed as $\omega_O = J_O\dot{q}_O$. The forward kinematics model of the MWMP can be expressed as equation $\dot{q}_0 = J_O^+\omega_O$. The transformation matrix $J_O^+$ of the MWMP forward kinematics can be obtained from the pseudo inverse of $J_O$. Let $P_{GO}$ denotes a pose transformation matrix of the MWMP coordinate system with respect to the global coordinate system. The $x_0$, $y_0$ and $z_0$ represent the displacement offsets of the MWMP coordinate system relative to the global coordinate system, respectively. Equation (8) is the forward kinematics model of the MWMP in global coordinate system.

$$q_G = P_{GO} \int_0^t q_o dt \tag{8}$$

## 3   Fuzzy Control System

Since the MWMP is a nonlinear and strongly coupled motion system, which is difficult to establish a complete and accurate mathematical model through idealized kinematic analysis. Fuzzy control is an intelligent control method that does not need for an accurate mathematical model of the controlled object.

### 3.1   The Structure of FLS

The error of linear displacement and angular displacement of the MWMP and error rate are easily obtained by the co-simulation of Adams and Matlab. The six-input and five-output fuzzy controller is proposed and its structure is shown as Fig. 3. The product of $k_i$ and $ASF$ is used as the speed compensation amount of the $i$-$th$ mecanum wheel. $e_x$ and $e_y$ represent the error between the theoretical linear displacement and the actual linear displacement of the MWMP in the x and y directions, respectively. Their ranges are $[-5, 5]$ mm. $e_z$ represents the error between the theoretical angular displacement and the actual angular displacement when the MWMP is rotated about the z-axis. Its range is $[-5, 5]°$. The range of error rate of linear displacement is $[-100, 100]$ mm/s. The range of error rate of angular displacement is $[-5, 5]°/s$. Let $de_x/dt$, $de_y/dt$ and $de_z/dt$ represent the rate of change of $e_x$, $e_y$ and $e_z$, respectively. The rate of change of the error and error are used as the input to the fuzzy controller. Let $QF$ stands for quantitative factor, which is represented by a saturation function. Let $D$ stands for database, which includes a library of membership functions and a library of clarity methods. Let $R$ stands for Rule Base, which stores conditional statements and approximate reasoning algorithms for approximate reasoning. Let $D/F$ indicates the fuzzy process. Let $A^* \circ R$ indicates the fuzzy inference process. The $A^*$ consists of the rate of error. Let $F/D$ indicates the clarification process. Let $ASF$ stands for adaptive scale factor and its range is $[0\ 6]$. The $k_{1\sim4}$ represent the speed compensation coefficients of each mecanum wheel and their ranges are $[-1\ 1]$. The centroid method is used as a defuzzification algorithm for the fuzzy controller in this paper. The subset selection of fuzzy inputs takes the triangle membership function. The subset of the speed compensation coefficient selects the triangle membership function and the trapezoid membership function. The subset of the $ASF$ selects the triangle membership function. The input and output variables of the fuzzy controller are composed of three fuzzy subsets respectively, which are negative $(N)$, zero $(Z)$ and positive $(P)$.

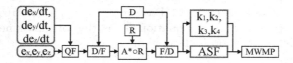

**Fig. 3.** The structure of the six-input and five-output fuzzy controller.

## 3.2   Fuzzy Rules

Due to the slippage, the actual speed of each mecanum wheel does not equal the desired speed which ultimately causes the MWMP to deviate from the desired motion state. According to the dynamic simulation of the virtual prototype in Adams, it can be found that the smaller the distance of the MWMP and the higher the accuracy of the motion obtained. The correspondence between the velocity of the mecanum wheel and the motion form of the MWMP is shown in Table 2. The $\omega$ is the velocity of the mecanum wheel. The symbols $+$ and $-$ represent the positive and negative directions of the velocity of the mecanum wheel, respectively. The front and the left respectively represent the positive direction of x and the positive direction of y in the coordinate system of the MWMP. Thirteen fuzzy rules in the form of IF-THEN based on the ten basic motion forms of the MWMP as shown in Table 3. Each of these rules has a weight of 1. The $ec_x$, $ec_y$, and $ec_z$ represent the rate of error. Let $k_k$ represents ASF. The fuzzy controller outputs a corresponding $k_i$ factor according to the error magnitude of the MWMP. The fuzzy controller outputs a corresponding

*ASF* according to the error rate of the MWMP. The velocity operation conforms to the parallelogram rule. Therefore, the MWMP can compensate the speed of the mecanum wheel in real time through the superposition of the basic motion forms.

**Table 2.** The corresponding relationship between the ten basic motion forms of the MWMP and the speed of the mecanum wheels.

| $(\omega_1, \omega_2, \omega_3, \omega_4)$ | Direction of motion | $(\omega_1, \omega_2, \omega_3, \omega_4)$ | Direction of motion |
|---|---|---|---|
| $(+\omega, +\omega, +\omega, +\omega)$ | front | $(+\omega, 0, 0, +\omega)$ | right-front |
| $(-\omega, -\omega, -\omega, -\omega)$ | behind | $(0, -\omega, -\omega, 0)$ | right-behind |
| $(+\omega, -\omega, -\omega, +\omega)$ | right | $(-\omega, 0, 0, -\omega)$ | left-behind |
| $(-\omega, +\omega, +\omega, -\omega)$ | left | $(+\omega, -\omega, +\omega, -\omega)$ | clockwise |
| $(0, +\omega, +\omega, 0)$ | left-front | $(-\omega, +\omega, -\omega, +\omega)$ | counterclockwise |

**Table 3.** The Fuzzy rules based on ten basic motion forms.

| No. | Detailed rules |
|---|---|
| 1 | If $(ec_x$ is N) or $(ec_y$ is N) or $(ec_z$ is N) then $(k_k$ is N) (1) |
| 2 | If $(ec_x$ is Z) or $(ec_y$ is Z) or $(ec_z$ is Z) then $(k_k$ is Z) (1) |
| 3 | If $(ec_x$ is P) or $(ec_y$ is P) or $(ec_z$ is P) then $(k_k$ is P) (1) |
| 4 | If $(e_x$ is N) and $(e_y$ is N) and $(e_z$ is Z) then $(k_2$ is N) $(k_3$ is N) (1) |
| 5 | If $(e_x$ is N) and $(e_y$ is Z) and $(e_z$ is Z) then $(k_1$ is N) $(k_2$ is N) $(k_3$ is N) $(k_4$ is N) (1) |
| 6 | If $(e_x$ is N) and $(e_y$ is P) and $(e_z$ is Z) then $(k_1$ is N) $(k_4$ is N) (1) |
| 7 | If $(e_x$ is Z) and $(e_y$ is N) and $(e_z$ is Z) then $(k_1$ is P) $(k_2$ is N) $(k_3$ is N) $(k_4$ is P) (1) |
| 8 | If $(e_x$ is Z) and $(e_y$ is Z) and $(e_z$ is N) then $(k_1$ is P) $(k_2$ is N) $(k_3$ is P) $(k_4$ is N) (1) |
| 9 | If $(e_x$ is Z) and $(e_y$ is P) and $(e_z$ is Z) then $(k_1$ is N) $(k_2$ is P) $(k_3$ is P) $(k_4$ is N) (1) |
| 10 | If $(e_x$ is Z) and $(e_y$ is Z) and $(e_z$ is P) then $(k_1$ is N) $(k_2$ is P) $(k_3$ is N) $(k_4$ is P) (1) |
| 11 | If $(e_x$ is P) and $(e_y$ is N) and $(e_z$ is Z) then $(k_1$ is P) $(k_4$ is P) (1) |
| 12 | If $(e_x$ is P) and $(e_y$ is Z) and $(e_z$ is Z) then $(k_1$ is P) $(k_2$ is P) $(k_3$ is P) $(k_4$ is P) (1) |
| 13 | If $(e_x$ is P) and $(e_y$ is P) and $(e_z$ is Z) then $(k_2$ is P) $(k_3$ is P) (1) |

The error between the actual output of the MWMP and the desired input and the rate of the error are used as input to the fuzzy control system. The sum of the output of the fuzzy system and the theoretical output obtained by the inverse kinematics of the MWMP is used as a new input to the MWMP. The negative feedback control of the MWMP is realized through co-simulation. The co-simulation of the fuzzy control system of the MWMP is shown in Fig. 4. Out1, Out2 and Out3 represent the desired linear displacement in the x-axis direction, the desired linear displacement in the axial direction, and the desired angular displacement in the z-axis rotation, respectively. The desired linear speed and angular velocity can be obtained by differential operation. The desired velocity of each mecanum wheel of the MWMP is obtained by the inverse kinematics analysis of the MWMP. The final input speed of each mecanum wheel can be obtained by summing the ideal speed of each mecanum wheel with the corresponding speed compensation amount.

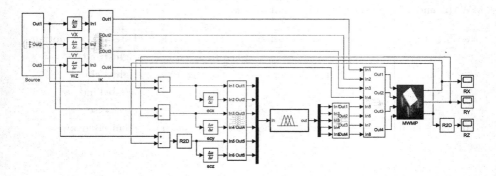

**Fig. 4.** The co-simulation diagram of MWMP based on fuzzy control system.

## 4    Experiments

The MWMP has three degrees of freedom that can be expressed primarily as the ten basic forms of motion in Table 2. Any complex motion trajectory can be obtained from a combination of these ten basic motion forms. Therefore, to improve the motion accuracy of the basic motion form of the MWMP is a prerequisite for improving the accuracy of complex trajectory tracking. The origin of the coordinate system of the MWMP is used as the starting and ending point of the trajectory.

### 4.1    Square Trajectory

The MWMP moves 10 s in each direction, which contains the positive direction of the x-axis, the positive direction of the y-axis, the negative direction of the x-axis and the negative direction of the y-axis. The rotational velocity of each mecanum wheel is 1 r/s. The trajectory of the square is completed by the above process. It is apparent that the free state MWMP fails to eventually return to the end point from Fig. 5(a). The linear displacement errors in the x-axis and y-axis directions are about −50 mm and −100 mm respectively and the angular displacement error around the z-axis is about 0.12° from Fig. 5(b–d). The MWMP with fuzzy control system can return to the end point more accurately. The linear displacement error is about 150 mm and the angular displacement error is about 0.2° are generated during the lateral motion and longitudinal motion transition as a result of the inertia of the MWMP from Fig. 5(b–d). It can be seen that the movement state of the free state MWMP is relatively large and the maximum is close to 180 mm. The MWMP with a fuzzy control system can quickly adjust for errors due to inertia. It reduces the linear displacement error of approximately 100 mm and the angular displacement error of approximately 0.1° to expected state, which takes about 1 s.

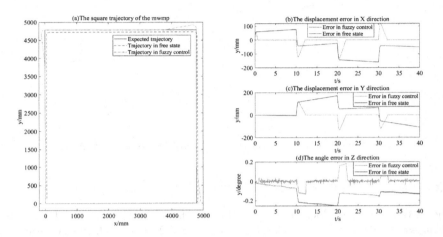

**Fig. 5.** The square trajectory and error curve of the MWMP.

## 4.2 Diamond Trajectory

The MWMP moves 10 s in each direction, which contains the right-front, the right-behind, the left-behind and the left-front. The rotational velocity of each mecanum wheel is 1 r/s. The trajectory of the diamond is completed by the above process. It is apparent that the free state MWMP fails to eventually return to the end point from Fig. 6(a). The linear displacement errors in the x-axis and y-axis directions are about −40 mm and 40 mm respectively and the angular displacement error around the z-axis is about 1.4° from Fig. 6(b–d). The MWMP with fuzzy control system can return to the end point more accurately. The linear displacement error of approximately 60 mm and an displacement error of approximately 0.5° are generated during changing the form of motion because of the inertia of the MWMP from Fig. 6(b–d). The error of the maximum linear displacement of the MWMP in the free state is close to 60 mm. The error of the maximum angular displacement is close to 1.5°. The MWMP with fuzzy control system can have a good rapidity for the displacement error caused by the inertia action. The fuzzy control system takes about 1 s to complete the adjustment of the linear displacement and angular displacement errors to the ideal state.

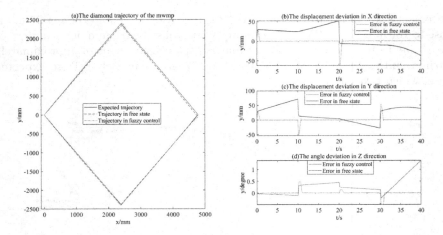

**Fig. 6.** The diamond trajectory and error curve of the MWMP.

## 4.3 Arc-Shaped Trajectory

The MWMP moves clockwise along the arc-shaped trajectory for 10 s, counterclockwise along the arc-shaped trajectory for 20 s and clockwise along the arc-shaped trajectory for 10 s. The velocity of the MWMP in the x and y directions vary according to the laws of sine and cosine, respectively. The maximum velocity of the mecanum wheel is 1 r/s. The circular trajectory is completed following the above process. It is obvious that the trajectory of the MWMP in the free state has a larger error than the ideal trajectory from Fig. 7(a–d). The circular trajectory of the MWMP with fuzzy control system is basically

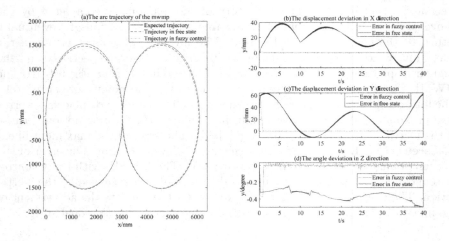

**Fig. 7.** The Arc-shaped trajectory and error curve of the MWMP.

consistent with the ideal trajectory. The linear displacement error of approximately 60 mm and an angular displacement error of approximately 0.4° are generated during changing the form of motion because of the inertia of the MWMP from Fig. 7(b–d). The error of the maximum linear displacement of the MWMP in the free state is close to 60 mm. The error of the maximum angular displacement is close to 0.5°. The MWMP with fuzzy control system can have a good rapidity for the displacement deviation caused by the inertia action. It takes about 1 s to adjust the linear displacement error of 60 mm and the angle displacement error of 0.4° to be close to the ideal situation at the beginning of the experiment. The pose error of the MWMP is substantially zero during the movement of 1 to 40 s. It shows that the fuzzy controller has strong robustness and adaptability.

## 5    Conclusion

A original multi-input and multi-output fuzzy control system is designed for the situation of positional error during the movement of MWMP. A six-input and five-output fuzzy controller with ASF is designed in Matlab. Thirteen fuzzy rules are established based on the ten basic motion patterns of the MWMP. The experimental results show that the fuzzy controller has stronger robustness, adaptability and rapidity than the free state of the MWMP and decreases the error of the pose to improve the motion accuracy. The fuzzy logic system can effectively reduce the adverse effects of the slippage on the motion accuracy of the MWMP.

**Acknowledgment.** This work is partially supported by National Key Research and Development Program of China under Grant 2017YFF0205306, National Nature Science Foundation of China under Grant 91648117, and Beijing Natural Science Foundation under Grant 4172055.

## References

1. Hu, M., Chen, J., Shi, C.: Three-dimensional mapping based on SIFT and RANSAC for mobile robot. In: 2015 IEEE International Conference on Cyber Technology in Automation, Control, and Intelligent Systems (CYBER), pp. 139–144. IEEE (2015)
2. Alakshendra, V., Chiddarwar, S.S.: A robust adaptive control of Mecanum wheel mobile robot: simulation and experimental validation. In: 2016 IEEE/RSJ International Conference on Intelligent Robots and Systems (IROS), pp. 5606–5611. IEEE (2016)
3. Xie, L., Herberger, W., Xu, W., Stol, K.A.: Experimental validation of energy consumption model for the four-wheeled omnidirectional Mecanum robots for energy-optimal motion control. In: 2016 IEEE 14th International Workshop on Advanced Motion Control (AMC), pp. 565–572. IEEE (2016)
4. Gfrerrer, A.: Geometry and kinematics of the Mecanum wheel. Comput. Aided Geom. Des. **25**(9), 784–791 (2008)

5. Tlale, N., de Villiers, M.: Kinematics and dynamics modelling of a Mecanum wheeled mobile platform. In: 2008 15th International Conference on Mechatronics and Machine Vision in Practice, pp. 657–662. IEEE (2008)
6. Fuad, A., et al.: Modeling and simulation for heavy-duty Mecanum wheel platform using model predictive control. In: IOP Conference Series: Materials Science and Engineering, vol. 184, p. 012050. IOP Publishing (2017)
7. Kuo, C.-H., et al.: Trajectory and heading tracking of a Mecanum wheeled robot using fuzzy logic control. In: 2016 International Conference on Instrumentation, Control and Automation (ICA), pp. 54–59. IEEE (2016)
8. Tsai, C.-C., Wu, H.-L., Tai, F.-C.: Intelligent sliding-mode formation control for uncertain networked heterogeneous Mecanum-wheeled omnidirectional platforms. In: 2016 IEEE International Conference on Systems, Man, and Cybernetics (SMC), pp. 000539–000544. IEEE (2016)
9. Wen, R., Tong, M.: Mecanum wheels with Astar algorithm and fuzzy PID algorithm based on genetic algorithm. In: 2017 International Conference on Robotics and Automation Sciences (ICRAS), pp. 114–118. IEEE (2017)
10. Vlantis, P., Bechlioulis, C.P., Karras, G., Fourlas, G., Kyriakopoulos, K.J.: Fault tolerant control for omni-directional mobile platforms with 4 Mecanum wheels. In: 2016 IEEE International Conference on Robotics and Automation (ICRA), pp. 2395–2400. IEEE (2016)
11. Lu, X., Zhang, X., Zhang, G., Jia, S.: Design of adaptive sliding mode controller for four-Mecanum wheel mobile robot. In: 2018 37th Chinese Control Conference (CCC), pp. 3983–3987. IEEE (2018)
12. Jamali, P., Tabatabaei, S.M., Sohrabi, O., Seifipour, N.: Software based modeling, simulation and fuzzy control of a Mecanum wheeled mobile robot. In: 2013 First RSI/ISM International Conference on Robotics and Mechatronics (ICRoM), pp. 200–204. IEEE (2013)
13. Shahin, S., Sadeghian, R., Sedigh, P., Masouleh, M.T.: Simulation, control and construction of a four Mecanum-wheeled robot. In: 2017 IEEE 4th International Conference on Knowledge-Based Engineering and Innovation (KBEI), pp. 0315–0319. IEEE (2017)
14. Ahmad Jamil, A.-F., Omar, R., Yaacob, S., Mokhtar, M.: Development of fuzzy PID controller for Mecanum wheel robot. Int. J. Appl. Eng. Res. **12**, 14478–14483 (2017)
15. Adamov, B.I.: A study of the controlled motion of a four-wheeled Mecanum platform. Nelin. Dinam. **14**(2), 265–290 (2018)

# Static Hand Gesture Recognition for Human Robot Interaction

Josiane Uwineza$^{(\boxtimes)}$, Hongbin Ma, Baokui Li, and Ying Jin

School of Automation, Beijing Institute of Technology,
Beijing 100081, People's Republic of China
inezajoyorange@gmail.com, mathmhb@bit.edu.cn
http://we-learn.net.cn/mathmhb

**Abstract.** Human-robot interaction is making a robot understanding human action, working and sharing the same space with the human. To achieve this, the communication between human and robot must be effective. The most used ways in this communication are the vocal and the body gestures such as full body actions, hand and arm gestures or head and facial gestures. Hand gestures are used as a natural and effective way of communicating between human and robot. The difference in hand size and posture, light variation and background complexity makes the hand gesture recognition to be a challenging issue. Different algorithms have been proposed and they gave better results. Yet, some problems such as poor computational scalability, trivial human intervenes and slow speed learning are still appearing in this field. In this paper, these issues are solved using a combination of three features extraction methods: Haralick texture, Hu moments, and color histogram and extreme learning machine (ELM) method for classification. The ELM results were compared to that of K-Nearest Neighbors, Random Forest Classifier, Linear Discriminant Analysis, Convolution Neural Networks and these experiment was evaluated on National University of Singapore (NUS) dataset II. ELM performed better than any of the above algorithms with an accuracy of 98.7% and time used of 109.7 s which is the proof of the satisfactory of the model.

**Keywords:** Human robot interaction · Hu moments ·
Color histogram · Haralick texture · Extreme Learning Machine

## 1 Introduction

With advanced technology, the use of robots in our daily live is increasing. Nowadays, it can be seen that the robots are being applied in various domains such as military battle, scientific exploration, entertainment, hospital care, social activities and so on. Due to that, human robot interaction attracts the attention of many researchers. Human robot interaction is defined as studying, understanding, designing, and evaluating robot's systems used by or work with humans. The interaction between human and robot requires effective communication between

© Springer Nature Switzerland AG 2019
H. Yu et al. (Eds.): ICIRA 2019, LNAI 11741, pp. 417–430, 2019.
https://doi.org/10.1007/978-3-030-27532-7_37

them and its' efficiency will determine the behavior of the robot. The most used ways in this communication are the vocal and body gestures. By definition, human gestures are nonverbal content which may be used with or without verbal communication in order to express intention (willful) of the speech [1]. The human gestures may be body gestures (fully body actions), hand and arm gestures or head and facial gestures [2]. Hand gestures are very important way of communication between humans during face to face communication, especially when they are doing discussions, they emphasize points and really show the enthusiasm of speaker. The hand gestures being an easy way of communication between humans, they can also be used by humans during their interaction with robots and they provide intelligent, natural and convenient way of communication.

The mathematical model interpretation of human hands' activity or motions using a computing device is known as hand gesture recognition. In computer vision, there are two main techniques for recognizing hand gestures which are: data glove and vision based techniques. In data glove technique, the user wears the glove which is connected to the mechanical or optical sensors for converting the hand orientation, finger motion, and flexions into electrical signals which are used in recognizing the hand gesture performed. The drawbacks of this technique are the lack of naturalness as the user must carry the heavy cables connected to the computer, requires experienced people for the operation and also requires expensive devices [3]. The vision based technique requires only one or more cameras for accumulating hands movement for hand gestures recognition without the use of any wearable device, so it achieves natural interaction between human and robot. The vision based technique is broadly classified into two methods which are appearance and 3D model based methods [4]. The appearance based uses the features of training images to model the visual appearance and compare these features with the features of the test image. 3D model based methods rely on the 3D kinematic model by estimating the angular and linear parameters of the model. Due to that, 3D model based are quite complex, which leads the 2D model based to be the mostly used for hand gesture recognition [5].

Hand gesture being an efficient and natural way of communication between human and robot or computer, several pieces of research has been conducted on hand gesture recognition (HGR), however, it is more challenging due to that hands structure are complex, hands have different size, hand gestures are performed differently, light variation, and complex background [6].

## 1.1    Related Works

Even if hand gesture recognition is a challenging field, yet, several researches has been conducted where different methods have been employed. Meenakshi in his paper for recognizing hand gestures, he converted input RGB images into YCbCr in the preprocessing step, then after, using K-means clustering, separated foreground image from the background image and the four types of features which are centroid, thumb detection, finger detection, and Euclidian distance were computed. Based on these features, a five-bit binary sequence was utilized for hand gesture classification [7].

Haria, Subramanian, Asokkuma, Poddar and Nayak in the designing a robust marker-less hand gesture recognition system followed these steps: converted input RGB images into grayscale images, used filter to remove noises in the input images, converted the images into binary images using Otsu and inverted binary thresholding, used contour, convex hull, and convexity defect methods for extracting features and used haar cascade classifier for classification [8].

For recognizing static hand gesture Jambhale and Khaparde in [5] converted RGB images into grayscale image, using Otsu thresholding algorithm the grayscale images were segmented and counter extraction was applied to get the feature descriptors and time dynamic wrapping and piecewise dynamic time wrapping was used for classification of feature descriptors.

In real-time Indian sign language (ISL) recognition Shenoy, Dastane, Rao and Vyavaharkar in [9] used the skin color segmentation for separating foreground from the background images and for noise removal, morphology operation was performed. To get feature descriptors grid-based fragmentation technique was used and finally the classification was done using hidden markov model (HMM).

In [10] support vector machine (SVM) was used in the classification of feature descriptors of the hand gestures which were obtained using the histogram of gradient, the researchers used the bound box for separating foreground from the background and canny' edge detection for resizing the images. Gao et al. applied parallel CNN (RGB-CNN and Depth-CNN) for hand gesture recognition [11].

Most of the methods which have been used in hand gesture recognition such as SVM, CNN and so on, gave better accuracy. However, both SVM and ANN encounter some difficulties such as poor computational scalability, trivial human intervenes and slow speed learning. Using a combination of Hu moments, Haralick texture and color histogram for feature extraction and extreme learning machine method for gestures classification conquered some of these challenges. The rest of this paper is organized as follows: Sect. 2, presents the detail of the proposed model, Sect. 3, shows experiment, results, and discussions, finally Sect. 4 concludes the paper.

## 2   Proposed Method

The gesture recognition is mainly done in four stages which are: image preprocessing, segmentation, feature extraction, and image classification. Each one of them contribute to the accuracy of recognition of the system. Figure 1 shows the procedures that we followed this paper.

### 2.1   Preprocessing and Image Segmentation

Image segmentation is a technique for breaking up an image into parts called segments. The aim of this process is to represent an image in a meaningful and easily analyzable way. In this paper, the method used for image segmentation

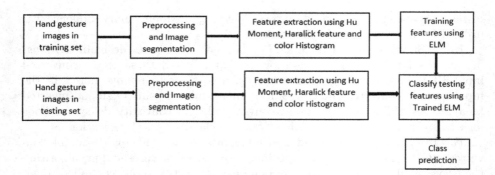

**Fig. 1.** A block diagram.

is called the GrabCut method. GrabCut is done in the following steps: In the first step, the background, foreground and unknown part of the image which can be either foreground or background is identified. Here a rectangle around the region of interest (ROI) in an image is chosen and the region inside the rectangle is considered as unknown and the pixel outside the rectangle is considered as background. In the second step, the computer starts the image segmentation and the unknown pixels are considered as foreground and all known pixels are considered as background. In the third step, the Gaussian mixture model is utilized to model the foreground and the background of an image. In the fourth step, The Gaussian component in the foreground GMMs are mostly selected from the pixel in the foreground while the pixels in the background have high probability be assigned as Gaussian components in background GMMs. In the fifth step, After forming the new pixel sets as shown in the previous step, learn the new GMMs, in the sixth step, build a graph and after use graph cut to obtain a new classification of foreground and background pixels. Then repeat the 4–6 step till the desired result is obtained [12]. After separating the foreground from the background the obtained image is converted into grayscale and then the gaussian filter is applied to remove the noise.

## 2.2   Image Features Extraction

The image features are measurements which specify some quantifiable property of an image. The process of obtaining the set of features from the image is known as feature extraction and its main objective is to get relevant information from the image. The better choice of feature extraction method leads to an accurate recognition system. The image features are classified as the low-level features which are directly extracted from the image and based on these, high-level features like shape, texture, and color are obtained. In this paper, three different techniques of features extraction were combined: Haralick texture which extracts texture features, Hu moments which extracts shape features, and color histogram color histogram which extracts color features. By combining these three methods, the feature vectors which are relevant were obtained as each one of them contains three different characteristics of the image that it is representing. Also, these feature vectors are invariant to the scale, translation and rotation which contribute to the accuracy of the system.

**Haralick Texture Image Feature Extraction.** This method of feature extraction was introduced by Haralick in 1973 and he extracted the texture features from the images [13]. Haralick texture feature extraction is done in two steps: the first step is the computation of Gray Level Co-occurrence Matrix (GLCM) and the second step, is to compute haralick texture features based on GLCM. The GLCM is generated from the grayscale image and shows how often a pixel with gray-level value $i$ occurs either vertically, horizontally, or diagonally to adjacent pixels with the value $j$. Figure 2 shows how the GLMc matrix is computed.

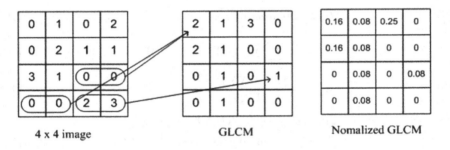

Fig. 2. Gray level co-occurence matrix example.

Using this GLMC, 13 equations of haralick texture features: Angular second moments ($f_1$), contrast ($f_2$), correlation ($f_3$), variance ($f_4$), inverse difference moment ($f_5$), sum average ($f_6$), sum variance ($f_7$), sum entropy ($f_8$), difference variance ($f_{10}$), entropy ($f_9$), difference entropy ($f_{11}$), information measure of correlation ($f_{12}$ and $f_{13}$) and maximal correlation coefficient ($f_{14}$ are computed as it is shown in the Eqs. (1) to (14).

$$f_1 = \sum_i^{N_g} \sum_j^{N_g} (\frac{P(i,j)}{R})^2) = \sum_i \sum_j (p(i,j)^2) \tag{1}$$

$$f_2 = \sum_{k=0}^{N_g-1} k^2 \left\{ \sum_i^{N_g} \sum_j^{N_g} \delta_{i+j,k} p(i,j) \right\} = \sum_{k=0}^{N_g-1} k^2 p_{x-y}(k) \tag{2}$$

$$f_3 = \frac{\sum_{i=1}^{N_g} \sum_{j=1}^{N_g} (i,j)p(i,j) - \mu_x \mu_y}{\sigma_x \sigma_y} \tag{3}$$

$$f_4 = \sum_{i=1}^{N_g} \sum_1^{N_g} (i - \mu)^2 p(i,j) \tag{4}$$

$$f_5 = \sum_{i=1}^{N_g} \sum_{1}^{N_g} \frac{1}{1+(i-j)^2} p(i,j) \tag{5}$$

$$f_6 = \sum_{i=1}^{2N_g} i p_{x+y}(i) \tag{6}$$

$$f_7 = \sum_{i=2}^{2N_g} (i - f_8)^2 p_{x+y}(i) \tag{7}$$

$$f_8 = -\sum_{i=2}^{2N_g} p_{x+y}(i) \log(p_{x+y}(i)) \tag{8}$$

$$f_9 = -\sum_{i=1}^{N_g} \sum_{J=1}^{N_g} p(i,j) \log(p(i,j)) \tag{9}$$

$$f_{10} = variance\, of\, p_{x-y} \tag{10}$$

$$f_{11} = -\sum_{i=1}^{N_g-1} p_{x-y}(i) log(p_{x-y}(i)) \tag{11}$$

$$f_{12} = \frac{f_9 - HXY1}{max(HX, HY)} \tag{12}$$

$$f_{13} = [1 - exp(-2(HXY2 - f_9))]^{\frac{1}{2}} \tag{13}$$

$$f_{14} = (second\, largest\, eigenvalue\, of\, Q)^{\frac{1}{2}} \tag{14}$$

$$Q(i,j) = \sum_k \frac{p(i,k)p(j,k)}{p_x(i)p_y(k)} \tag{15}$$

$$HX = -\sum_i p_x(i) \log(p_x(i)) \tag{16}$$

$$HY = -\sum_j p_y(i) \log(p_y(i)) \tag{17}$$

$$HXY1 = -\sum_i \sum_j p(i,j) \log(p_x(i)p_y(j)) \tag{18}$$

$$HXY2 = -\sum_i \sum_j p_x(i)p_y(j) \log(p_x(j)p_y(j)) \tag{19}$$

$$p(i,j) = \frac{P(i,j)}{\sum_{i=1}^{N_g} \sum_{j=1}^{N_g} P(i,j)} \tag{20}$$

**Hu Moments Image Feature Extraction.** This method extracts feaures from the image based on its shape and the features are obtained by combining the moments of different order of the image [14]. Here the image must be converted in binary format and the relative moments of the image is calculated as follows:

$$\mu_{m,n} = \sum_{x=0}^{M-1} \sum_{y=0}^{N-1} (x - x_c)^m (y - y_c)^n f(x, y) \tag{21}$$

where: $x_c = \frac{\mu_{10}}{\mu_{00}}$, $y_c = \frac{\mu_{01}}{\mu_{00}}$ and $(x_c, y_c)$ is the centroid of the image.

Based on normalized central moments, Hu introduced seven invariant moments which are invariant to scale, rotation and translation. The invariant moments are the follows:

$$h_1 = \mu_{20} + \mu_{02} \tag{22}$$

$$h_2 = (\mu_{20} - \mu_{02})^2 + 4\mu_{11} \tag{23}$$

$$h_3 = (\mu_{30} - 3\mu_{12})^2 + (3\mu_{21} - \mu_{30})^2 \tag{24}$$

$$h_4 = (\mu_{30} + \mu_{12})^2 + (\mu_{21} + \mu_{03})^2 \tag{25}$$

$$h_5 = (\mu_{30} - 3\mu_{12})(\mu_{30} + \mu_{12})((\mu_{30} + \mu_{12})^2 - 3(\mu_{21} + \mu_{03})^2)$$
$$+ (3\mu_{21} - \mu_{03})(\mu_{21} + \mu_{03})(3(\mu_{30} - \mu_{12})^2 - (\mu_{21} + \mu_{03})^2) \tag{26}$$

$$h_6 = (\mu_{20} - \mu_{02})((\mu_{30} - \mu_{12})^2 - (\mu_{21} - \mu_{03})^2)$$
$$4\mu_{11}(\mu_{30} + 3\mu_{12})(\mu_{21} + \mu_{03}) \tag{27}$$

$$h_7 = (3\mu_{21} - \mu_{30})(\mu_{30} + \mu_{12})((\mu_{30} + \mu_{12})^2 - 3(\mu_{21} + \mu_{03})^2)$$
$$- (\mu_{30} - 3\mu_{12})(\mu_{21} + \mu_{03})(3(\mu_{30} + \mu_{12})^2 - (\mu_{21} + \mu_{03})^2) \tag{28}$$

**Color Histogram Image Feature Extraction.** The color features are the crucial features for finding an image from a group of images. These color features are easy to be analyzed and they are invariant to the change of scale and orientation of an image [15]. Histogram method, statistical method, and color model method are methods which can be used for extracting color features from an image. In this paper, color histogram was used, been it is simple and is often used in color features extraction. The color histogram is defined as the representation of the distribution of the composition of color in the image. It shows different types of colors appeared in the image and their corresponding number of pixels. During color histogram features extraction, these steps were followed: Subdividing of color space into cells, associating each cell to a histogram bin, and computing the pixel of each cell and keeping their count in the perspective corresponding to histogram bin.

## 2.3   Classification Using Extreme Learning Machine

Feedforward neural network is an artificial neural network where the information moves in one direction, i.e from the input layer, pass through hidden layer then to the output layer. The feedforward neural networks are of two types: single layer perceptron and multi-layer perceptron. Single layer perceptron is made by input layer and output layer only, while multi-layer perceptron is made by input layer, one or more hidden layer(s), and the output layer. Multi-layer perceptron which has one hidden layer is called single layer feedforward neural network (SLFNs). It has been proved that the working of SLFNs is not inferior to that multi-layer feedforward neural network and due to its simplicity and responding speed, it attracted the attention of many researchers and has been applied extensively.

To acquire the desired performance, the parameters of SLFNs must be adjusted in this way the weights adapt correspondingly with the error correction, this process is known as training. The gradient-based, optimization learning, and least square algorithms are the three most used techniques for training SLFNs. Although all those training methods require the parameters to be tuned. Due to that their learning speed of SLFNs are slow, they may easily stack into a local minimum. In 2004 Huang [16] proposed a new algorithm which is a special type of single hidden layer feedforward neural network where input weights and hidden layer biases are randomly generated and do not need to be adjusted and the output weights are determined analytically, this is called extreme learning machine (ELM). As the parameters of ELM do not need to be adjusted, it provides the best generalization performance at very high speed which can be even thousands of times faster than the traditional feedforward neural network learning algorithms like backpropagation. In [17] Bartlett stated that as the network tends to have smaller weights, the better generalization performance it will have. Huang, Zhu and Siew in [16] showed that ELM does not only reach the smallest squared error on training examples but also reaches the smallest weights which imply that ELM has better generalization performance. In additional, ELM has a unified framework for classification, regression, semi-supervised, supervised and unsupervised tasks [18]. Based on these advantages, in this paper, ELM was used in classifying the data and its mathematical model is shown below: Having N distinct arbitrary samples $(x_i, t_i)$ where $x_i = [x_{i1}, x_{i2}, \ldots x_{in}]^T \in R^n$ and $t_i = [t_{i1}, t_{i2}, \ldots t_{im}]^T \in R^m$ where $t_i$ is the target and Having L hidden neurons and activation function g(x), ELM is mathematically modeled as:

$\sum_{i=1}^{L} \beta_i g(w_i x_j + b_j) = o_j$

where: $w_i = [w_{i1}, w_{i2}, \ldots w_{in}]^T$: it is input weight vector

$B_i = [\beta_{i1}, \beta_{i2}, \ldots \beta_{in}]^T$: output weight

$o_j = \{o_{j1}, o_{j2}, \ldots, o_{jn}\}$: output vector of the network

For standard SLFNs, $\exists \{\beta_i, w_i, b_j\}$ such that $\sum_{i=1}^{L} \|o_j - t_j\| = 0$ and in this case: $\sum_{i=1}^{L} \beta_i g(w_i x_j + b_j) = t_j$ and this can be simply written as $H\beta = T$ where:

$$H([w_1, w_2, \ldots w_L, b_1, b_2, \ldots b_L, x_1, x_2, \ldots x_N]) =$$

$$\begin{bmatrix} g(w_1 x_1 + b_1) & \cdots & g(w_L x_j + b_L) \\ \vdots & \ddots & \vdots \\ g(w_1 x_N + b_1) & \cdots & g(w_L x_N + b_L) \end{bmatrix}_{N \times L}$$

$$\beta = \begin{bmatrix} \beta_1^T \\ \vdots \\ \beta_L^T \end{bmatrix}_{N \times L} \quad \text{and} \quad T = \begin{bmatrix} T_1^T \\ \vdots \\ T_N^T \end{bmatrix}_{N \times m}$$

ELM model may be overdetermined $(N > L)$, determined $(N = L)$or under-determined $(N < L)$ [19]. But in most case, the number of the input nodes are not equal to the number of hidden nodes and in this case, H is not invertible. So when computing the output weight $\beta$, Moore-Penrose generalized inverse $H^+$ of H is used [20]. Then $\beta = H^+ T$ and $H^+ = (H^T H)^{-1} H^T$.

To increase the capability of extreme learning machine a non-linear activation function is used in the hidden layer such as sigmoid function, Gaussian function, hard limit function, radial biases function and multi- quadratic function [21]. The main aim of extreme learning machine is to reach better generalization performance with small training error and small norm weights, which is witten mathematically as: minimize $\sum_{i=1}^{N} \|\beta h(x_i) - t_i\| = 0$ and minimize: $\|\beta\|$ [22] and this is equivalent to this proposed constrained-optimization- based ELM [23].

Minimize: $L_p = \frac{1}{2} \|\beta\|^2 + C\frac{1}{2} \sum_{i=1}^{N} \zeta_i^2$ Subject to: $h(x_i)\beta = t_i - \zeta_i$, where $i = 1, 2, 3, \cdots, N$ According to the Karush-Kuhn-Tucker (KKT) theorem [24], solving the above equation is the same as solving the following dual optimization problem:
$L_D = \frac{1}{2} \|\beta\|^2 + C\frac{1}{2} \sum_{i=1}^{N} \zeta_i^2 - \sum_{i=1}^{N} \alpha_i(h(x_i)\beta - t_i + \zeta_i)$ where $\alpha_i$ is the Lagrange multiplier

The optimum condition for KKT is this:

$\frac{\partial L_D}{\partial \beta} = 0 \rightarrow \beta = \alpha_i h(x_i)^T = H^T \alpha$
$\frac{\partial L_D}{\partial \zeta_i} = 0 \rightarrow \alpha_i = C\zeta_i, i = 1, 2, \cdots, N$
$\frac{\partial L_D}{\partial \alpha_i} = 0 \rightarrow h(x_i)\beta - t_i \zeta_i, i = 1, 2, \cdots, N$ where $\alpha = [\alpha_i, \cdots, \alpha_T]^T$

By using the above two equations into the third one, we get:
$(\frac{I}{C} + HH^T)\alpha = T$ and finally $\beta = H^T(\frac{I}{C} + HH^T)^{-1})T$
Therefore the output of ELM can be written as:
$f(x) = h(x)\beta = h(x)H^T(\frac{I}{C} + HH^T)^{-1}T$
The above process is the $L_2$ regularization and it will prevent the extreme learning machine model to be over-fitted.

## 3 Experiment, Result, and Discussions

In this paper, hand gesture recognition experiment is conducted on PC with Intel Core i7 2.5 GHz, with Processor of 8 GB RAM under Python2.7. combined with Open Source Computer Vision (OpenCV) library and is evaluated on NUS hand posture dataset II, which was created by Pramod Kumar, Prahlad Vadakkepat, and Loh Ai Poh. The researcher use 9 classes among the 10 classes created. This dataset was taken in complex backgrounds and the postures have various shapes and sizes. In this paper, the GrabCut method was used to separate foreground from the background and data augmentation was done to increase data from 200 images for each class to 1500 images. As the RGB images are very sensitive to light variation, they were converted into grayscale images and Gaussian filter was used to remove noises in the grayscale images. The result of this process is shown in Fig. 3.

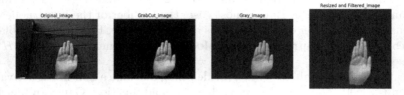

**Fig. 3.** An image preprocessed.

Using Hu moments, Haralick texture and color histogram feature extraction methods we got $13500 \times 532$ feature descriptors. 75% of these feature descriptors are used for training while other 25% are used for testing. We used extreme learning machine for classification and we compare its accuracy and time used to that of K-nearest neighbor (KNN), linear discriminant analysis (LDA), decision Tree (CART), random forest classifier (RF) and convolution neural networks (CNN). The results of these models are shown in the Table 1. And their errors are shown in Fig. 4.

**Table 1.** Table of models accuracy and time taken

| Name of classifier | Accuracy (%) | Time used/seconds |
|---|---|---|
| Decision Tree (CART) | 65.97 | 17.63 |
| Linear Discriminant Analysis (LDA) | 68.5 | 25.79 |
| K Nearest Neighbor (KNN) | 78.27 | 68.18 |
| Random Forest (RF) | 91.79 | 61.36 s |
| Convolution Neural Networks (CNN) | 95.26 | 548 |
| Extreme Learning Machine (ELM) | 98.7 | 109.7 |

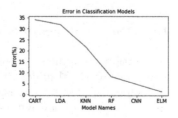

**Fig. 4.** Error in classification.

The result shows that classification using extreme learning machine provides highest accuracy at higher learning speed. In extreme learning machine classification, 4000 hidden neurons for sigmoid activation function and 532 hidden neurons for linear activation function were used. ($L_1$) regularization is used as pruning method and ($L_2$) regularization is used to avoid ELM model to be overfitted. The confusion matrix which shows the visualization of the performance of an algorithm is shown in Fig. 5. In this matrix all correct classified data are appeared in the diagonal of the confusion matrix and off diagonal data are incorrect classified data.

The result analysis of confusion matrix is shown in the Fig. 6.

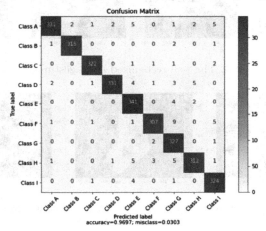

**Fig. 5.** A confusion matrix.

|  | precision | recall | f1-score | support |
|---|---|---|---|---|
| 0 | 0.99 | 0.95 | 0.97 | 349 |
| 1 | 0.99 | 0.99 | 0.99 | 319 |
| 2 | 0.99 | 0.98 | 0.99 | 327 |
| 3 | 0.99 | 0.95 | 0.97 | 347 |
| 4 | 0.94 | 0.98 | 0.96 | 347 |
| 5 | 0.98 | 0.95 | 0.96 | 324 |
| 6 | 0.93 | 0.99 | 0.96 | 330 |
| 7 | 0.97 | 0.95 | 0.96 | 328 |
| 8 | 0.96 | 0.98 | 0.97 | 330 |
| | | | | |
| micro avg | 0.97 | 0.97 | 0.97 | 3001 |
| macro avg | 0.97 | 0.97 | 0.97 | 3001 |
| weighted avg | 0.97 | 0.97 | 0.97 | 3001 |

**Fig. 6.** Analysis of confusion matrix.

Figures 7, 8 and 9 show the recognized hand gestures. The first word that appears on these images is the label given by the model. The percentage that appears on them is the recognition rate. The correct word appears on these images when the model finds that the label to be given to the image is similar to its' name on the disk where it is saved; otherwise incorrect word appears on it.

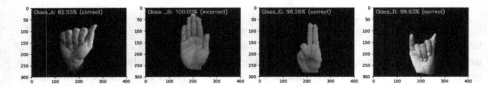

**Fig. 7.** The well recognized hand gestures-1.

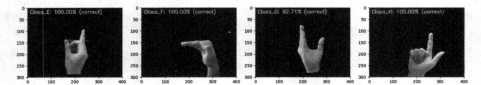

**Fig. 8.** The well recognized hand gestures-2.

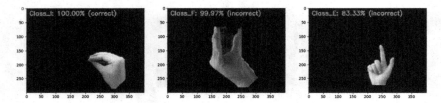

**Fig. 9.** The first is well classified and 2 last are misclassified hand gestures.

## 4    Conclusions

A hand gesture recognition system necessitates robustness, accuracy and efficiency. In this paper, we proposed hand gesture recognition using combined feature extraction methods which are Hu Moments, Haralick texture, and color histogram, and Extreme Learning Machine for classification. Using CART, KNN, LDA and RF classification models we got better accuracy at high learning speed but this accuracy is lower than the one of ELM. Using CNN, we got high accuracy but still lower than the one of ELM and learns at lower speed than the one of ELM. Based on the result obtained, our proposed model is faster, accurate and robust to the translation, rotation and scale. The accuracy of 98.7% was obtained which is a better accuracy and proves that ELM model can be applied in Human-Robot interaction.

**Acknowledgment.** This work is partially supported by National Key Research and Development Program of China under Grant 2017YFF0205306, National Nature Science Foundation of China under Grant 91648117, and Beijing Natural Science Foundation under Grant 4172055.

# References

1. Zafar, Z., Berns, K.: Recognizing hand gestures for human-robot interaction. In: Proceedings of the 9th International Conference on Advances in Computer-Human Interactions (ACHI), pp. 333–338 (2016)
2. Mitra, S., Acharya, T.: Gesture recognition: a survey. IEEE Trans. Syst. Man Cybern. Part C (Appl. Rev.) **37**(3), 311–324 (2007)
3. Prakash, R.M., Deepa, T., Gunasundari, T., Kasthuri, N.: Gesture recognition and finger tip detection for human computer interaction. In: 2017 International Conference on Innovations in Information, Embedded and Communication Systems (ICIIECS), pp. 1–4. IEEE (2017)
4. Pisharady, P.K., Saerbeck, M.: Recent methods and databases in vision-based hand gesture recognition: a review. Comput. Vis. Image Underst. **141**, 152–165 (2015)
5. Jambhale, S.S., Khaparde, A.: Gesture recognition using DTW & piecewise DTW. In: 2014 International Conference on Electronics and Communication Systems (ICECS), pp. 1–5. IEEE (2014)
6. Islam, M.R., Mitu, U.K., Bhuiyan, R.A., Shin, J.: Hand gesture feature extraction using deep convolutional neural network for recognizing American sign language. In: 2018 4th International Conference on Frontiers of Signal Processing (ICFSP), pp. 115–119. IEEE (2018)
7. Panwar, M.: Hand gesture recognition based on shape parameters. In: 2012 International Conference on Computing, Communication and Applications, pp. 1–6. IEEE (2012)
8. Haria, A., Subramanian, A., Asokkumar, N., Poddar, S., Nayak, J.S.: Hand gesture recognition for human computer interaction. Procedia Comput. Sci. **115**, 367–374 (2017)
9. Shenoy, K., Dastane, T., Rao, V., Vyavaharkar, D.: Real-time Indian sign language (ISL) recognition. In: 2018 9th International Conference on Computing, Communication and Networking Technologies (ICCCNT), pp. 1–9. IEEE (2018)
10. Nagashree, R., Michahial, S., Aishwarya, G., Azeez, B.H., Jayalakshmi, M., Rani, R.K.: Hand gesture recognition using support vector machine. Int. J. Eng. Sci. **4**(6), 42–46 (2005)
11. Gao, Q., Liu, J., Ju, Z., Li, Y., Zhang, T., Zhang, L.: Static hand gesture recognition with parallel CNNs for space human-robot interaction. In: Huang, Y.A., Wu, H., Liu, H., Yin, Z. (eds.) ICIRA 2017. LNCS (LNAI), vol. 10462, pp. 462–473. Springer, Cham (2017). https://doi.org/10.1007/978-3-319-65289-4_44
12. Basavaprasad, B., Hegadi, R.S.: Improved grabcut technique for segmentation of color image. Int. J. Comput. Appl. **975**, 8887 (2014)
13. Haralick, R.M., Shanmugam, K., et al.: Textural features for image classification. IEEE Trans. Syst. Man Cybern. **6**, 610–621 (1973)
14. Huang, Z., Leng, J.: Analysis of Hu's moment invariants on image scaling and rotation. In: 2010 2nd International Conference on Computer Engineering and Technology, vol. 7, pp. V7–476. IEEE (2010)
15. Munje, P.N., Kapgate, D., Golai, S.: Novel techniques for color and texture feature extraction. Int. J. Comput. Sci. Mob. Comput. **3**(2), 497–507 (2014)
16. Huang, G.-B., Zhu, Q.-Y., Siew, C.-K., et al.: Extreme learning machine: a new learning scheme of feedforward neural networks. Neural Netw. **2**, 985–990 (2004)
17. Bartlett, P.L.: The sample complexity of pattern classification with neural networks: the size of the weights is more important than the size of the network. IEEE Trans. Inf. Theory **44**(2), 525–536 (1998)

18. Huang, G., Song, S., Gupta, J.N., Wu, C.: Semi-supervised and unsupervised extreme learning machines. IEEE Trans. Cybern. **44**(12), 2405–2417 (2014)
19. Akusok, A., Björk, K.-M., Miche, Y., Lendasse, A.: High-performance extreme learning machines: a complete toolbox for big data applications. IEEE Access **3**, 1011–1025 (2015)
20. Chen, X., Koskela, M.: Using appearance-based hand features for dynamic RGB-d gesture recognition. In: 2014 22nd International Conference on Pattern Recognition, pp. 411–416. IEEE (2014)
21. Anam, K., Al-Jumaily, A.: Evaluation of extreme learning machine for classification of individual and combined finger movements using electromyography on amputees and non-amputees. Neural Netw. **85**, 51–68 (2017)
22. Ding, X.-J., Lei, M.: Optimization elm based on rough set for predicting the label of military simulation data. Math. Prob. Eng. **2014**, 8 (2014)
23. Huang, G.-B., Zhou, H., Ding, X., Zhang, R.: Extreme learning machine for regression and multiclass classification. IEEE Trans. Syst. Man Cybern. Part B (Cybern.) **42**(2), 513–529 (2012)
24. Leng, Q., Qi, H., Miao, J., Zhu, W., Su, G.: One-class classification with extreme learning machine. Math. Probl. Eng. **2015**, 11 (2015)

# Multi-sensor Based Human Balance Analysis

Haichuan Ren, Zongxiao Yue, and Yanhong Liu[✉]

School of Electrical Engineering,
Zhengzhou University, Zhengzhou, Henan, China
liuyh@zzu.edu.cn

**Abstract.** The human balance ability is investigated using a multi-sensor human balance assessment system. Based on the pressure sensor, the gyroscope, the accelerometer and the magnetometer, the quantitative perception of human balance under different postures is realized. The characteristics of human balance ability are extracted through time domain methods and a new hybrid feature extraction. The results demonstrate that the hybrid feature extraction method with the support vector machine method can effectively classify and evaluate the human balance ability under different postures.

**Keywords:** Human balance · Multi-sensor · Hybrid feature extraction · Support Vector Machine

## 1 Introduction

Balance is an essential physiological function for the human body. The regulation of the human balance is a comprehensive process of human activities with respect to nerves and muscles [1]. Fine balance ability is an important guarantee for the human body to complete various daily activities [2]. Therefore, the evaluation of the human balance ability is greatly significant in medical care and life.

In general, three evaluation methods for the human balance ability are applied in clinics, including the observation method, the scale method and the balance meter test method [3]. The observation method and the scale method are commonly used in the initial examination of the patient balance ability. But both methods are strongly dependent of the doctor experiences through subjective observations, and are lack of objective quantization standard [4]. For the balance meter test method, the signal of the human balance through various test instruments and equipment are acquired and processed by the signal processing methods, for example time-frequency domain methods [5]. The commonly used balance meters map the gravity of the human body to the foot, and the variations of the foot pressure center reflects the relevant characteristics of the human balance ability [6]. Rocchi and Ji et al. found that the maintenance of the human balance is a dynamic adjustment procedure with respect to the hip joint motions and the ankle joint motions. Rocchi and Ji et al. found that the process of

Research supported by the National Natural Science Foundation of China (61473265,61803344), the Post-doctoral Funding in Henan province (001703041) and the Innovation Research Team of Science & Technology of Henan Province (17IRTSTHN013).

H. Yu et al. (Eds.): ICIRA 2019, LNAI 11741, pp. 431–438, 2019.
https://doi.org/10.1007/978-3-030-27532-7_38

maintaining the human balance is implemented through the dynamic adjustment of hip and ankle movements, while the dynamic adjustment of upper body is realized through hip movements [7]. Hence, the position information of the human body pressure center is not sufficient to evaluate the human balance ability by the center of gravity projection method. With large variations of the human body pressure center in the unit time, the assessment result of the human balance ability is short of objectivity.

With the rapid development of electronic technologies, the inertial measurement unit (IMU) is recently used to acquire the human motions in different areas. In the paper, a new set of human body balance assessment system based on IMU is introduced in details. In order to better access the human balance ability by the multi-sensor system, the characteristics of the human balance is exacted from multi-model data by the feature extraction method. Furthermore, the classification of the human balance ability is elaborately studied through tests.

## 2  System Design

The human balance is the dynamical adjustment procedure of the human body with non-stop swinging. When the human balance is lost, the body can adjust the position variation of its gravity and the foot pressure center through collaborative motions of hip joints and ankle joints, and maintenance the human balance [8].

The pressure center (COP) directly reflects the projection variation of the human gravity on the earth as well as the adjustment motion of the ankle joint during the processing of balance maintenance. The variation of the pressure center position resulting in the ankle joint is acquired by the pressure sensor when the human maintains the balance. Generally, the process of maintaining the human balance can be regarded as an inverted pendulum model. Even if the position of the pressure center is the same the acceleration and angular velocity of the human posture information may be still different. The acceleration and angular velocity demonstrate the swing speed of the human body when maintaining balance and the angle shows the tilt angle information. Therefore, the change procedure of the human gravity modulated by the hip is obtained by triaxial accelerations, gyroscopes, and magnetometers.

A multi-sensor human balance assessment system is designed to assess and evaluate the balance of the human body. The designed system structure includes multiple sensors, the data transmission module and the terminal equipped with the data processing software, as shown in Fig. 1. The signals of the human balance are acquired by multi-sensors, and transmitted by data transmission module with wireless Bluetooth communication to the terminal. Then these acquired human balance data are handled and displayed on the terminal by the data processing software. The resolution of each pressure sensor is $0.02\%F \cdot S$ and its measurement range is 200 kg. The applied type of posture sensor is MPU9250 with a three-axis accelerometer, a three-axis gyroscope and a three-axis magnetometer. The accelerometer range of the MPU9250 is $\pm 2$ g, and the angle measurement range of gyroscope is $\pm 2000°/s$ with the accuracy scale of $0.05°$.

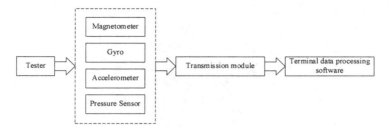

**Fig. 1.** Diagram of the human balance assessment system

# 3   Feature Extraction Method

The quantitative evaluation of the human balance ability is mainly based on the feature extraction for multi-sensor data, when the testers complete the specified action tasks. Herein, the time domain feature extraction method and a new mixed feature extraction method will be elaborately introduced as follows.

## 3.1   Time Domain Feature

Human balance is the ability to maintain a relatively stable state through active adaption of the body. At present, the swing of the human body is generally measured by the balance instruments, in order to evaluate the human balance ability. The characteristics of the body swing obtained by the time domain method better describes the nature of the human body swing objectively, quantitatively and meticulously, and also provides the effective and accurate criteria of the human balance evaluation for users. The time domain indicators used in this paper are the trajectory length of the pressure center swing, its envelope area of the pressure center trajectories as well as its offset, the triaxial acceleration variation, the angular velocity variation and the angular variation of IMU.

In Fig. 2, $(x_{COP_i}, y_{COP_i})$ shows the COP coordinates at a certain time $i$. The Area of all sectors is the COP envelope area. The offset coordinate of each COP trajectories in the original sector coordinate is $(X_{COP_i}, Y_{COP_i})$, R is the radius of the fan shape from COP. A total of $n$ COP points is acquired during the test time, and the calculation formula of the COP envelope Area is:

$$Area = \sum_{i=1}^{n-1} \frac{1}{2}R\sqrt{\left(X_{\text{cop}_{i+1}} - X_{\text{cop}_i}\right)^2 + \left(Y_{\text{cop}_{i+1}} - Y_{\text{cop}_i}\right)} \tag{1}$$

*Lng* denotes the total movement path length of COP during the test, which reflecting the frequency of the COP oscillation. The calculation of the COP trajectory length during the test for $n$ points is expressed as the following equation

$$Lng = \sum_{i=1}^{n-1} \sqrt{\left(x_{\text{cop}_{i+1}} - x_{\text{cop}_i}\right)^2 + \left(y_{\text{cop}_{i+1}} - y_{\text{cop}_i}\right)^2} \tag{2}$$

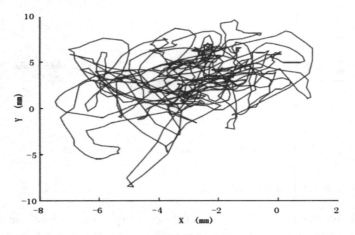

**Fig. 2.** The COP trajectories

The offset of COP in the paper is the maximum swing range during the process of maintaining the human balance. It is comprised of the left and right offset, the front and back offset, and the maximum offset of the COP trajectories, respectively representing the maximum swing range between the left and the right, between the front and the back, and among track points during tests.

Left and right offset:

$$D_{lr} = x_{\text{cop}_{\max}} - x_{\text{cop}_{\min}} \tag{3}$$

Front and back offset:

$$D_{fb} = y_{\text{cop}_{\max}} - y_{\text{cop}_{\min}} \tag{4}$$

Maximum offset:

$$D = \sqrt{\left(x_{\text{cop}_i} - x_{\text{cop}_j}\right)^2 + \left(y_{\text{cop}_i} - y_{\text{cop}_j}\right)^2}_{\max} \quad i, j \in n, i \neq j \tag{5}$$

The roll angle variation of the rotation around the X axis and the yaw angle variation around the Z axis are selected as the time-domain index of the human balance based on IMU. The variation of the acceleration and the angular velocity variation in the X-axis and Z-axis directions is used to respectively demonstrate the adjustment intensity for the front and back balance and the left and right balance.

## 3.2   Hybrid Feature

The multi-sensor data of human balance is a kind of non-stationary time series data. The processing method of non-stationary time series data is mostly based on Fourier transform [9], but this method of Fourier transform is only applied for linear systems.

Victoria [10] pointed out that human balance is a complex control process, and the output signal of the human balance should be seen to be non-linear. The Lyapunov exponent is an important parameter on describing nonlinear time series data.

The calculation formula of the Lyapunov exponent is:

$$s(r, m, \tau) = \left\langle \ln\left(\frac{1}{|u_n|}\right) \sum_{x_{n'} \in u_n}^{n} |x_{n+\tau} - x_{n'+\tau}| \right\rangle \tag{6}$$

$\tau$ is the delay time, $m$ is the embedding dimension, $u_n$ is an r adjacent correlation coefficient of $x_n$, and $s(r, m, \tau)$ shows a linear increase of the same slope within the reasonable variation range $r$, and the slope can be equal to the estimate of the largest Lyapunov exponent.

The Lyapunov exponent denotes the variation index of the phase space trajectory by phase space reconstruction, and the divergence degree of the trajectory in the phase space is better described by the maximum Lyapunov exponent. Both the Lyapunov exponent and the maximum Lyapunov exponent cannot demonstrate the relationship between the channels, therefore multivariate multi-scale entropy in the paper is herein used to study the relationship between the channels [11].

Multivariate multi-scale entropy is an effective method to evaluate the complexities among various channels of signals. Different scales have been widely applied in biologics and physiologies. There are two important processes for the computing of multivariate multi-scale entropy. The core section is the coarse-grained calculation. For a time series $(x_1, x_2, \cdots, x_N)$ with a sequence length of $N$, a new time series is obtained after coarse graining:

$$y_j^{(\tau)} = \frac{1}{\tau} \sum_{i=(j-1)\tau+1}^{j\tau} x_i \tag{7}$$

Where $1 \leq j \leq N/\tau$, $\{y(\tau)\}$ represents the time series of continuous coarse granulation at time scale factor $\tau$.

According to the multi-embedded theories, a multi-variable compound delay vector $x_m$ is generated for p time series $\{x_{k,i}\}_{i=1}^{n}$, $k = 1, 2, \cdots, p$:

$$x_m(i) = [x_{1,i}, x_{1,i+\tau_1}, \cdots, x_{1,i+(m_1-1)\tau_1}, x_{2,i}, x_{2,i+\tau_1}, \\ \cdots, x_{2,i+(m_1-1)\tau_1}, \cdots, x_{p,i}, x_{p,i+\tau_1}, \cdots, x_{p,i+(m_1-1)\tau_1}] \tag{8}$$

The multivariate multi-scale entropy is expressed as the following equation

$$MMSE = -\ln\left[\frac{P^{m+1}(r)}{P^m(r)}\right] \tag{9}$$

$P^m(r)$ and $P^{m+1}(r)$ respectively represent the conditional probabilities of any two vector similarities in $m$ and $m+1$ respectively dimension.

The maximum Lyapunov exponent denotes the orbital motion spread degree of the phase space for the whole system. The multivariate multi-scale entropy embodies the complexity between multi-channel time series. The human balance can be integrated into the multi-sensor signal maximum Lyapunov exponent (LLE) and the multivariate multi-scale entropy (MMSE). Considering the phase space motion characteristics and complex features of the human balance, the LLE and the MMSE are combined to obtain the mixed eigen-values reflecting the human balance ability. The calculation process of the hybrid feature is shown in Fig. 3.

$$LMMSE = \frac{SLLE}{MMSE} = \sum_{l=1}^{p} y_l \Big/ MMSE \tag{10}$$

$\sum_{l=1}^{p} y_l$ denotes the sum of Lyapunov exponents for all channels, and $MMSE$ denotes the multivariate multiscale entropy for all channels.

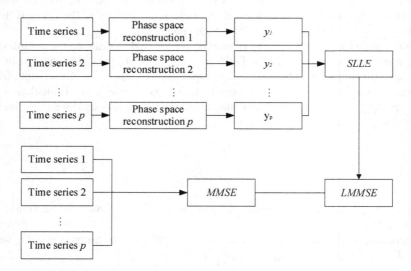

**Fig. 3.** The calculation procedure of the hybrid feature

## 4    Results and Discussion

In this experiment, the subjects were asked to complete three movements. The movement 1 is to open eyes without supports, the movement 2 is to close eyes without support and the movement 3 is to upright with one leg. Each movement data is collected three times, and the duration for each data acquisition is 20 s, the data sampling frequency of the sensor is 100 Hz. After each acquisition, the software will automatically save the collected data.

Through the multi-sensor human balance assessment system, the human balance ability is classified to three levels which are strong balance ability, general balance ability and poor balance ability. Support Vector Machine (SVM) is a supervised classification algorithm for predictive learning and statistical problems with smaller samples. Hence, the SVM with the hybrid feature is used to classify the human balance ability.

In each test, 540 sets of feature vectors were obtained, and three kinds of 540 sets of feature vectors were obtained using 270 sets of training samples by a one-to-one SVM classifier method, and three classifiers were obtained by using the trained classifiers. The remaining 270 sets of feature vectors are used to validate the classifier. The recognition accuracy rate for remaining 270 sets of eigenvectors is as shown in Table 1.

From Table 1, the recognition accuracy rate under different human motions based on SVM classifier is up to 89.25%. The average recognition accuracy rate of three different patterns reaches 86.11%. The test results demonstrate that the hybrid feature extraction method with the support vector machine method can effectively classify and evaluate the human balance ability under different postures.

**Table 1.** Recognition results for different motions

| Motion type | Recognition accuracy rate |
| --- | --- |
| Movement 1 | 89.25% |
| Movement 2 | 85.18% |
| Movement 3 | 85.55% |

# 5  Conclusion

Human balance evaluation have the broad prospects in the fields of disability assistances, health monitoring and auxiliary medical cares. In this paper, pressure sensors, accelerometers, gyroscopes and magnetometer are used to acquire the multi-sensor information of human body under different postures. The feature of the human balance is extracted through the time-domain index and hybrid index of using multi-sensors. The SVM is used to analyze and evaluate the balance ability of human body. The results show that the method can effectively classify the balance ability of human body's different posture modes. Future work will focus on the classification and evaluation of human balance ability in complex modes such as when the human body is subjected to external forces and after intensity training.

# References

1. Nashner, L.M., Shupert, C.L., Horak, F.B.: Head-trunk movement coordination in the standing posture. Prog. Brain Res. **76**(3), 243–251 (1988)
2. Barton, J.E., Roy, A., Sorkin, J.D., et al.: An engineering model of human balance control—part I: biomechanical model. J. Biomech. Eng. **138**(1), 1–11 (2016)

3. Terekhov, Y.: Stabilometry as a diagnostic tool in clinical medicine. Can. Med. Assoc. J. **115**(7), 631–633 (1976)
4. Lord, S.R., Clark, R.D., Webster, I.W.: Postural stability and associated physiological factors in a population of aged persons. J. Gerontol. **46**(3), 69–76 (1991)
5. Toro, B., Nester, C., Farren, P.: A review of observational gait assessment in clinical practice. Physiother. Theory Pract. **19**(3), 137–149 (2003)
6. Molnar, C.A., Zelei, A., Insperger, T.: Human balancing on rolling balance board in the frontal plane. IFAC-PapersOnLine **51**(14), 300–305 (2018)
7. Pereira, L.M., Marcucci, F.C.I., Menacho, M.D.O., et al.: Electromyographic activity of selected trunk muscles in subjects with and without hemiparesis during therapeutic exercise. J. Electromyogr. Kinesiol. **21**(2), 327–332 (2011)
8. Horak, F.B.: Postural orientation and equilibrium: what do we need to know about neural control of balance to prevent falls? Age Ageing **35**(2), 7–11 (2006)
9. Wang, D.Q., Wang, F.F., Zhu, W.C., et al.: Prediction for non-stationary non-linear time series based on empirical mode decomposition. Syst. Eng. **32**(5), 138–142 (2014)
10. Wu, N., Jiang, H., Yang, G.: Emotion recognition based on physiological signals. In: Zhang, H., Hussain, A., Liu, D., Wang, Z. (eds.) BICS 2012. LNCS (LNAI), vol. 7366, pp. 311–320. Springer, Heidelberg (2012). https://doi.org/10.1007/978-3-642-31561-9_35
11. Liu, K., Wang, H., Xiao, J.Z., et al.: Analysis of human standing balance by largest Lyapunov exponent. Comput. Intell. Neurosci. **2015**(2), 151–154 (2015)

# Wrist Motor Function Rehabilitation Training and Evaluation System Based on Human-Computer Interaction

Haichuan Ren, Qi Song, and Yanhong Liu[✉]

School of Electrical Engineering, Zhengzhou University,
Zhengzhou, Henan, China
liuyh@zzu.edu.cn

**Abstract.** Based on human-computer interaction, a wrist motor function rehabilitation training and evaluation system is developed for the treatment or improvement of wrist motor dysfunction. Specifically, the joint angle sensor and the MYO wristband are used to realize the perception of the wrist motion on the ROS, the wrist motor function rehabilitation training game with information feedback is designed, and the quantitative evaluation on the wrist motor function is realized. The experimental results demonstrate that in the rehabilitation training session, the online accuracy of wrist motion recognition is 95.2%, and in the evaluation session, the root mean square error of the measured and actual values of the wrist joint angle is less than 5°. The paper works provide the basis for further clinical experiments of the wrist motor function rehabilitation training and evaluation.

**Keywords:** Human-computer interaction · ROS ·
Wrist motor function evaluation · Rehabilitation training

## 1 Introduction

As an important part of hand function, wrist motor function is the basis of human life activities. The wrist is highly flexible, delicate and complex, and is also extremely vulnerable to injury. Stroke and external injury are the main causes of motor dysfunction for the wrist [1]. Studies have shown that rehabilitation training can well treat wrist motor dysfunction and improve the motor function of the wrist joint [2, 3]. At the same time, the evaluation of wrist motor function plays a guiding role in rehabilitation medicine, which can evaluate the effect of rehabilitation training and make further rehabilitation trainings more targeted [4]. The traditional evaluation of wrist motor

Research supported by the National Natural Science Foundation of China (61473265, 61803344), the Post-doctoral Funding in Henan province (001703041) and the Innovation Research Team of Science & Technology of Henan Province (17IRTSTHN013).

© Springer Nature Switzerland AG 2019
H. Yu et al. (Eds.): ICIRA 2019, LNAI 11741, pp. 439–446, 2019.
https://doi.org/10.1007/978-3-030-27532-7_39

function is dependent of the subjective experience of physicians, and it is unable to quantitatively evaluate the loss of motor function rehabilitation training with the disadvantages of single training method and low patient cooperation, resulting in the unsatisfaction of rehabilitation training effects [5].

Human-computer interaction is a process of information exchange between a person and a computer, using a certain dialogue language between a person and a computer in a certain interactive manner. Using a computer-generated graphical interface and virtual environment to immerse users, it is a computer simulation system that can create and experience virtual worlds [6]. Virtual reality technology can give users a strong immersion due to its characteristics of interaction and imagination, which is helpful to enhance the user concentration [7]. The application of human-computer interaction technology in the field of the wrist motor function rehabilitation training and evaluation attracts more attention from scholars in the recent years.

At present, the investigation on the rehabilitation and evaluation of wrist motor function based on human-computer interaction still has the following main problems:

(1) Most of the research is focused on the rehabilitation training of wrist motor function, and there are few studies on the quantitative evaluation of wrist motor function involving human-computer interaction, and the evaluation results are lack of the support to rehabilitation medical standards [8]. (2) The evaluation results cannot fully reflect the real state of the wrist motor function [9]. (3) Not focusing on the transmission of rehabilitation training and evaluation information, ignoring the communication and guidance between doctors and patients online or offline. (4) The portability of the system is poor, and is still more developed on Windows systems, and few attempts to research on Linux, OS, Android and other platforms.

Based on the sensor technology, the signal processing technology and the human-computer interaction technology, we design and implement a human-computer interaction wrist motor function rehabilitation training and evaluation system on the platform of ROS in terms of data processing and 3D simulation performance. The joint angle sensor and MYO wristband are used to acquire wrist motion data, and complete the processing of data, the development of interactive interface and the design of rehabilitation training game in ROS. The system realizes six types of wrist motion rehabilitation training, including the flexion of the radiocarpal joint, the extension of the radiocarpal joint, the radial deviation, the ulnar deviation, the pronation of the radio-ulnar joints and the supination of the radio-ulnar joints, as shown in Fig. 1. The wrist motor function can be comprehensively, objectively and quantitatively evaluated, in light of wrist rehabilitation medicine.

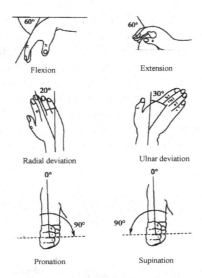

**Fig. 1.** Six types of wrist motion normal angle

## 2   System Design

The wrist motor function evaluation and rehabilitation training system based on ROS includes the hardware layer, the software layer and the application layer. The hardware layer consists of a joint angle sensor, a MYO wristband, a development board of NVIDIA Jetson TX2 and a touch screen monitor. The joint angle sensor acquires the angle value of the wrist; the MYO wristband acquires the original surface electromyographic signals (sEMG) generated by the forearm muscles when the wrist performs six movements including the flexion of the radiocarpal joint, the extension of the radiocarpal joint, radial deviation, the ulnar deviation, the pronation of the radio-ulnar joints and the supination of the radio-ulnar joints; the NVIDIA Jetson TX2 development board is the hardware foundation for data processing; the touch screen monitor is both an input device and an output display device, which is a medium between users and system. The system software layer includes an information acquisition module, an information processing module, a human-computer interaction module and a rehabilitation game module. The information acquisition module senses wrist motions based on the joint angle sensor and the MYO wristband; the information processing module is used to realize the equivalent calculation of joint angle, and the wrist motion recognition based on sEMG signals, which is the foundation for the implement of system functions; the human-computer interaction module is used to establish the bridge among users, systems and functions, and facilitate the information exchange between users and systems; The rehabilitation game module is a guarantee for the rehabilitation training of the wrist motor function. The application layer consists of several user-oriented application services, where most important parts are the wrist motor function rehabilitation training and the wrist motor function evaluation.

The designed system in this paper has two core functions, including the wrist motor function rehabilitation training with VR and the wrist motor function quantitative evaluation. The system schematic diagram is shown in Fig. 2. Rehabilitation training is implemented for the flexion of the radiocarpal joint, the extension of the radiocarpal joint, the radial deviation, the ulnar deviation, the pronation of the radio-ulnar joints and the supination of the radio-ulnar joints, meeting daily needs of the user. At the same time, the joint angle is used as an quantitative index, to achieve the real-time evaluation for wrist motor function. Meanwhile, the system can record historical data of evaluation results and rehabilitation training effects, which is convenient for users to query and track them.

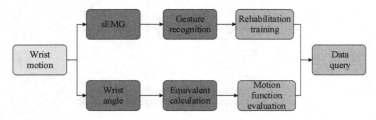

**Fig. 2.** System schematics

# 3   Rehabilitation Training and Evaluation Method

## 3.1   Wrist Motor Function Rehabilitation Training

Based on the 3D physics simulation by ROS Gazebo, virtual reality environments and games of the wrist motor function rehabilitation training are designed. For example, the box game shown in Fig. 3, the movement of the car in the virtual environment is controlled using six types of wrist motions. The box can also be moved by the car motion. Until the box is in order arrival into different yellow square areas, the rehabilitation training task is judged to be completed at last. Therefore, patients can do their wrist motor function trainings in pleasant rehabilitation sensorics.

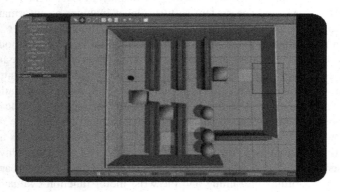

**Fig. 3.** Rehabilitation training game interface (Color figure online)

When the flexion of the radiocarpal joint (expressed by "F"), the extension of the radiocarpal joint (expressed by "E"), the radial deviation (expressed by "R"), the ulnar deviation (expressed by "U"), the pronation of the radio-ulnar joints (expressed by "P") and the supination of the radio-ulnar joints (expressed by "S") is detected, the car in the virtual reality environment of the box game can be correspondingly controlled to move up and down, stop, accelerate, left and right, as shown in Table 1. When the designed system detects a certain wrist motion, the car will continue to keep the corresponding state. Until the next wrist motion is detected, the car will stop the previous state of movement and go into the next state of movement corresponding to the wrist motion at this moment.

**Table 1.** Different wrist motions corresponding to the state of the car

| Wrist motion | Car state |
|---|---|
| F | Up |
| E | Down |
| R | Stop |
| U | Acceleration |
| P | Left |
| S | Right |

## 3.2   Wrist Motor Function Rehabilitation Evaluation

After the patient finished a period of wrist motor function rehabilitation training, it is necessary to quantitatively evaluate the effect of rehabilitation training, and the evaluation results will provide some guidance for the implement of future rehabilitation training.

Referring to the wrist motor function assessment standard introduced by the International Hand Surgery Society, the loss assessment of wrist motor function is subdivided into six types of the flexion of the radiocarpal joint, the extension of the radiocarpal joint, the radial deviation, the ulnar deviation, the pronation of the radio-ulnar joints and the supination of the radio-ulnar joints. The wrist joint angle value is used as a quantitative feature, to comprehensively and systematically evaluate the wrist motor function. When the joint angle of the wrist reaches the standard range of angle as shown in Table 2, the wrist joint motion function can be judged to be normal.

**Table 2.** Standard angle range for six types of wrist motion

| Wrist motion | Standard angle range |
|---|---|
| F | 50°–70° |
| E | 50°–70° |
| R | 15°–25° |
| U | 25°–35° |
| P | 80°–90° |
| S | 80°–90° |

# 4  Test Results and Discussion

In this paper, 20 volunteers with different ages and genders were selected in the experiments, including 12 young persons at the age from fifteen years old to thirty-five years old, 6 middle-aged persons at the age from thirty-six years old to filthy-nine years old, and 2 elderly persons at the age of sixty years old or older. During the test, these selected volunteers meets the experimental needs of comprehensiveness and representativeness.

## 4.1  Wrist Motion Recognition Accuracy

For the wrist motor function rehabilitation training, the aforementioned six types of wrist motions can be successfully recognized and classified through the BP neural network algorithm in terms of sEMG signals. Each volunteer performs six types of wrist motion twice for the left hand and the right hand. The recognition results and accuracies for total performances of the wrist motion were recorded and shown in Table 3.

**Table 3.** Results and accuracy of wrist motion recognition

|   | F | E | R | U | P | S | Accuracy |
|---|---|---|---|---|---|---|----------|
| F | 74 | 0 | 6 | 0 | 0 | 0 | 92.5% |
| E | 0 | 75 | 2 | 3 | 0 | 0 | 93.8% |
| R | 5 | 0 | 75 | 0 | 0 | 0 | 93.8% |
| U | 2 | 5 | 0 | 73 | 0 | 0 | 91.3% |
| P | 0 | 0 | 0 | 0 | 80 | 0 | 100% |
| S | 0 | 0 | 0 | 0 | 0 | 80 | 100% |

In summary, the average recognition accuracy of the system for six types of wrist motion are up to 95.2%. The ulnar motion is easily misclassified from the extension of the radiocarpal joint, because the force position of the forearm muscle is similar to that of the radiocarpal joint extension, but the recognition accuracy can still up to 91.3%.

## 4.2  Evaluation Accuracy

The joint angle is used as the basis quantitative feature for the evaluation of the wrist motor function. Hence, the reliability of the evaluation results is dependent of the measuring accuracy of the wrist joint angle. In the paper, the actual value of the joint angle is measured by the protractor, the measured value of the joint angle is acquired by the designed system.

For example, the left wrist of the sample number 1 completes the flexion of the radiocarpal joint, the extension of the radiocarpal joint, the radial deviation, the ulnar deviation, the pronation of the radio-ulnar joints and the supination of the radio-ulnar joints once, the actual and measured values of the joint angle for six types of wrist motions are recorded and shown in Table 4.

**Table 4.** Wrist motion values from the protractor and designed system.

| Wrist motion | Actual values | Measured values |
| --- | --- | --- |
| F | 60.0° | 60.8° |
| E | −60.0° | −61.3° |
| R | 30.0° | 30.8° |
| U | −20.0° | 18.6° |
| P | 90.0° | 88.2° |
| S | −88.0° | −90.3° |

Based on the calculation of the root mean square, total errors between measured and actual values for 20 volunteers are shown in Table 5. Total results show that the root mean square error of the measured value and the actual value of joint angle is less than 5°. Hence, the designed system can provide the basis for further clinical experiment of the wrist motor function quantitative evaluation.

**Table 5.** Errors between measured and actual values

| Wrist motion | Error |
| --- | --- |
| F | 2.53° |
| E | 3.72° |
| R | 4.87° |
| U | 3.13° |
| P | 1.86° |
| S | 1.52° |

## 5  Conclusion

In view of wrist motor dysfunction caused by stroke or external injury, this paper based on human-computer interaction technology, to design wrist motor function rehabilitation training and evaluation system in ROS. The wrist motion information perception is constructed using joint angle sensor and MYO wristband, and the wrist motor function feedback rehabilitation training and quantitative evaluation was realized through human-computer interaction. Preliminary experimental results show that in the rehabilitation training session, the accuracy of online recognition of six wrist motions is 95.2%. In the evaluation session, the root mean square error of the measured and actual values of the wrist joint angle is less than 5°. The paper works provide the basis for further clinical experiments of the wrist motor function rehabilitation training and evaluation.

# References

1. Pandian, S., Arya, K.N., Davidson, E.W.R.: Comparison of Brunnstrom movement therapy and motor relearning program in rehabilitation of post-stroke hemiparetic hand: a randomized trial. J. Bodywork Mov. Ther. **16**(03), 330–337 (2012)
2. Serrien, D.J., Strens, L.H., Cassidy, M.J., et al.: Functional significance of the ipsilateral hemisphere during movement of the affected hand after stroke. Exp. Neurol. **190**(02), 425–432 (2004)
3. Tsoupikova, D., Stoykov, N.S., Corrigan, M., et al.: Virtual immersion for post-stroke hand rehabilitation therapy. Ann. Biomed. Eng. **43**(02), 467–477 (2015)
4. Hasani, F.N., MacDermid, J.C., Tang, A., Kho, M.E.: Cross-cultural adaptation and psychometric testing of the Arabic version of the Patient-Rated Wrist Hand Evaluation (PRWHE-A) in Saudi Arabia. J. Hand Ther. **28**(4), 412–420 (2015)
5. Kennedy, S.A., Stoll, L.E., Lauder, A.S.: Human and other mammalian bite injuries of the hand: evaluation and management. J. Am. Acad. Orthop. Surg. **23**(1), 47–57 (2015)
6. Thielbar, K.O., Lord, T.J., Fischer, H.C., et al.: Training finger individuation with a mechatronic-virtual reality system leads to improved fine motor control post-stroke. J. Neuroengineering Rehabil. **11**(01), 171 (2014)
7. Rivas, J.J., Heyer, P., et al.: Towards incorporating affective computing to virtual rehabilitation; surrogating attributed attention from posture for boosting therapy adaptation. In: International Symposium on Medical Information Processing and Analysis, vol. 92(87), 58–63 (2015)
8. Heuser, A., Kourtev, H., Hentz, V., et al.: Tele-rehabilitation using the Rutgers Master II glove following Carpal Tunnel Release surgery. In: International Workshop on Virtual Rehabilitation, vol. 15(01), pp. 88–93 (2007)
9. Sucar, L.E., Orihuela, E.F., Velazquez, R.L., et al.: Gesture therapy: an upper limb virtual reality-based motor rehabilitation platform. IEEE Trans. Neural Syst. Rehabil. Eng. **22**(03), 634–643 (2014)

# Signal Processing and Underwater Bionic Robots

# Novel Spread Spectrum Based Underwater Acoustic Communication Technology for Low Signal-to-Noise Ratio Environments

Feng Zhou[1,2,3], Wenbo Zhang[1,2,3], Gang Qiao[1,2,3],
Zongxin Sun[1,2,3(✉)], Bing Liu[1,2,3], Wenting Zheng[1,2,3], and Liang Li[4]

[1] Acoustic Science and Technology Laboratory, Harbin Engineering University,
Harbin 150001, China
sunzongxin@hrbeu.edu.cn
[2] Key Laboratory of Marine Information Acquisition and Security,
(Harbin Engineering University), Ministry of Industry and Information
Technology, Harbin 150001, China
[3] College of Underwater Acoustic Engineering,
Harbin Engineering University, Harbin 150001, China
[4] Systems Engineering Research Institute of China State Shipbuilding
Corporation, Beijing 100036, China

**Abstract.** Underwater acoustic channels are unstable and acoustic waves when propagating in the ocean are subjected to variety of interference, such as noise, reflections, scattering and so on. To cope with this severe interference, spread spectrum communication technology is used. The traditional spread spectrum communication technology can communicate reliably in a lower signal-to-noise ratio environment, but at the cost of lower data rate. This paper thus proposes an underwater acoustic spread spectrum communication technology, which combines direct sequence spread spectrum and cyclic shift keying modulation to improve the data rate. Besides, a time-frequency two-dimensional search algorithm is used to realize the synchronization of this system. In order to reduce the bit error rate, the hybrid system is improved by adjusting power allocation of the transmitted signal. The performance of the proposed system is analyzed by the simulation and is verified by the experiment.

**Keywords:** Underwater acoustic communication ·
Spread spectrum communication · Hybrid spread spectrum

## 1 Introduction

So far, underwater acoustic (UWA) communication is the only available medium to communicate over long distances in water. However, it offers more challenges than the conventional terrestrial wireless communications. The complicated marine environment causes various kinds of interference in UWA channels [1]. For lower frequencies, noise in the seawater is random, inconsistent and frequency varying while for high frequencies, the waves suffer high attenuation, thus leaving only a limited band of frequencies for UWA communication [2]. Besides, the acoustic signal reaches the

© Springer Nature Switzerland AG 2019
H. Yu et al. (Eds.): ICIRA 2019, LNAI 11741, pp. 449–460, 2019.
https://doi.org/10.1007/978-3-030-27532-7_40

receiver along different paths due to interface, reflections, refractions, random scattering, etc. [3]. These factors lead to distortion of the received signal and degradation of the performance of an UWA communication system.

To cope with this challenging UWA channel, researchers have proposed several algorithms and communication techniques [4]. For multipath interference and low signal-to- noise ratio (SNR), a commonly used technique is spread spectrum communication [5, 6]. Spread spectrum method is a type of transmission, in which the bandwidth occupied by the signal exceeds the minimum bandwidth required to transmit information [7]. DSSS communication technology promises high reliability but at the cost of lower communication rate, for it uses one pseudo-random noise (PN) sequence to spread one bit of information. In order to improve the performance of the DSSS system, a new hybrid spread spectrum system is thus proposed, which can not only guarantee high reliability, but can also improve the communication rate to a significant extent.

Hybrid system proposed in this paper is based on the combination of DSSS and cyclic shift keying (CSK) utilizing orthogonal dual-modulation [8]. In-phase branch is used to carry DSSS signal and quadrature branch is used to carry CSK signal [9]. Compared with traditional DSSS communications, parallel transmission through two orthogonal branches with different spread modulation, on the one hand can guarantee the reliability, and on the other hand can improve the communication rate of the system without interfering with each other [10]. Simulations and pool tests are performed to show the better performance of the proposed system. Furthermore, it has also been shown that tradeoff between reliability and data rate can be resolved by adjusting the signal power of two branches.

This paper is organized as follows. The DSSS technology is introduced in Sect. 2, and the CSK technology is introduced in Sect. 3. Section 4 explains the hybrid spread spectrum communication system in detail. In Sect. 5, the simulation results are presented and analyzed. Finally, the conclusion of this paper is summarized.

## 2  Direct Sequence Spread Spectrum Technology

The DSSS technology expands the spectrum of the transmitted signal directly with a high-speed spread spectrum sequence, and then despreads the received signal with the same spread spectrum sequence at the receiver [11]. The schematic diagram of the DSSS communication system is shown in Fig. 1.

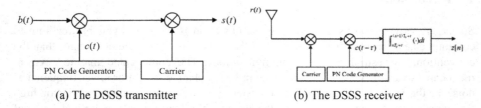

(a) The DSSS transmitter                    (b) The DSSS receiver

**Fig. 1.**  Schematic diagram of the DSSS system

At the transmitter side, the original signal $b(t)$ is multiplied by a PN code, to expand the spectrum of the original signal. If the symbol interval of the original information is denoted by $T_s$, and the chip interval of the PN sequence is denoted by $T_c$, the relationship between $T_s$ and $T_c$ can be shown as follows

$$T_S = NT_c \tag{1}$$

where $N$ denotes the length of the PN sequence. The DSSS transmitted signal can be described as

$$s(t) = \sqrt{2P}b(t)c(t)\cos(2\pi f_c t + \varphi) \tag{2}$$

where $P$, $f_c$ and $\varphi$ represent the power of transmitted signal, the carrier frequency and initial phase of the signal respectively.

Assuming that the transmitted signal reaches the receiver after passing an UWA channel, the received signal can be expressed as

$$
\begin{aligned}
r(t) &= \sum_{i=0}^{L-1} A_i b(t - \tau_i)c(t - \tau_i)\cos(2\pi f_c t + \varphi_i) + n(t) \\
&= A_0 b(t - \tau_0)c(t - \tau_0)\cos(2\pi f_c t + \varphi_0) + \\
&\quad \sum_{i=1}^{L-1} A_i b(t - \tau_i)c(t - \tau_i)\cos(2\pi f_c t + \varphi_i) + n(t)
\end{aligned} \tag{3}
$$

where $L$ is the number of multipath signals, $A_i$ is the multipath signal amplitude. The phase $\varphi_i$ can be written as

$$\varphi_i = \varphi - 2\pi f_c \tau_i \tag{4}$$

At the receiver, the signal is first demodulated to recover the baseband signal. The receiver also generates a local reference carrier for synchronization. The signal which has been demodulated is send to a low-pass filter to remove the residual high-frequency. Therefore, the signal can be deduced as

$$
\begin{aligned}
r_L(t) &= LPF(\mathrm{r(t)}(\cos(2\pi f_c) + \phi_0)) \\
&= LPF \left(
\begin{array}{l}
A_0 b(t - \tau_0)c(t - \tau_0)[\frac{1}{2} + \frac{1}{2}\cos(4\pi f_c t + 2\phi_0)] + \\
\sum_{i=1}^{L-1} A_i b(t - \tau_i)c(t - \tau_i)[\frac{1}{2}\cos(\phi_0 - \phi_i) + \frac{1}{2}\cos(4\pi f_c t + \phi_0 + \phi_i)] + n'(t)
\end{array}
\right) \\
&= \frac{1}{2}A_0 b(t - \tau_0)c(t - \tau_0) + \frac{1}{2}\sum_{i=1}^{L-1} A_i b(t - \tau_i)c(t - \tau_i)\cos(\phi_0 - \phi_i) + n'(t)
\end{aligned} \tag{5}
$$

Then, the baseband signal is despread by the same PN sequence used at the transmitter. According to the character of PN code, the original signal can be obtained by

$$
\begin{aligned}
z[n] &= \int_{nT_b + t}^{(n+1)T_b + \tau} \left( \begin{array}{l} \frac{1}{2}A_0 b(t - \tau_0)c(t - \tau_0) + \\ \frac{1}{2}\sum_{i=1}^{L-1} A_i b(t - \tau_i)c(t - \tau_i)\cos(\phi_0 - \phi_i) \end{array} \right) c(t - \tau_0)dt \\
&= \int_{nT_b + t}^{(n+1)T_b + \tau} \frac{1}{2}A_0 b(t - \tau_0)c(t - \tau_0)c(t - \tau_0)dt \\
&= \frac{1}{2}T_b b[n]
\end{aligned}
\tag{6}
$$

where $n$ is the number of the original information symbols. This process is called correlation de-spreading. In addition, matched filters can be used to detect DSSS signals.

## 3   Cyclic Shift Keying Technology

The CSK technology uses the phase of spread spectrum sequences to transmit information. The amount of information contained in each cyclic shift sequence depends on the length of the spread spectrum sequence [12]. If the spread spectrum sequence is the m sequence and the order of the sequence is $r$, the maximum amount of information carried by a cyclic shift sequence is $r - 1$ bits. The modulated sequence by CSK can be expressed as follows

$$
c^k(t) = \begin{cases} c(t + k\Delta\tau) & (0 \leq t \leq T_s - k\Delta\tau) \\ c(t - T_s + k\Delta\tau) & (T_s - k\Delta\tau < t \leq T_s) \end{cases}
\tag{7}
$$

where $k$ represents the information modulated by CSK and $c(t)$ is the spread spectrum code.

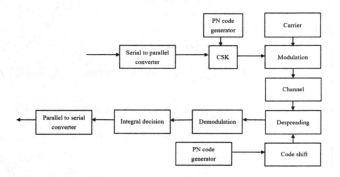

**Fig. 2.**  Schematic diagram of the CSK spread spectrum system

The schematic diagram of the CSK spread spectrum system shown in Fig. 2 is similar to the DSSS system. The difference is that the transmitted signal is modulated by CSK instead of DSSS. At the receiver, the same cyclic shift sequence is used to despread the signal again. The advantage of CSK is to increase the communication rate for each spread spectrum sequence by carrying $r - 1$ bits information instead of 1 bit as in DSSS. There is however a small tradeoff with the bit error rate (BER) performance over DSSS because of the cross-correlation of PN sequence interference [13].

## 4  Hybrid Spread Spectrum Communication System

The schematic diagram of the hybrid spread spectrum communication system is shown in Fig. 3. The original data is first converted into a low-speed parallel sub-data stream by series-to-parallel conversion. The DSSS modulation carries 1 bit in each PN sequence and the CSK modulation carries $k_0$ bits. The two branches are orthogonal to each other with one branch is DSSS modulated while the other branch is CSK modulated.

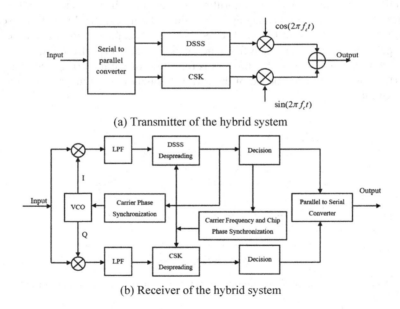

(a) Transmitter of the hybrid system

(b) Receiver of the hybrid system

**Fig. 3.** Schematic diagram of the hybrid spread spectrum system

Because two branches are used to transmit data at the same time, the bandwidth utilization of this system is $\frac{1+k_0}{2N}$, and the communication rate is increased to $\frac{1+k_0}{T_s}$. The transmitted signal of the system can be expressed as

$$s(t) = \sqrt{2P}[b_0(t)c(t)\cos(2\pi f_c) + c^{(b_1(t))}(t)\sin(2\pi f_c t)] \tag{8}$$

where $b_0(t)$ represents the information carried by DSSS modulation, and $b_1(t)$ represents the information carried by CSK modulation. $c^{(b_1(t))}$ is the cyclic shift spread spectrum sequence modulated by $b_1(t)$. In this model, the initial phase of two orthogonal carriers is assumed to be 0.

If the transmitted signal passes through the additive white Gaussian noise (AWGN) channel, it can be expressed as

$$r(t) = \sqrt{2P} \begin{bmatrix} b_0(t - \tau)c(t - \tau)\cos(2\pi(f_c + f_d)t + \varphi) + \\ c^{(b_1(t))}(t - \tau)\sin(2\pi(f_c + f_d)t + \varphi) \end{bmatrix} + n(t) \qquad (9)$$

where $f_d$ is the Doppler shift, which is caused by the relative motion between the transmitter and receiver [14]. $\varphi$ is the difference between the transmitter phase and the receiver phase. Besides, $n(t)$ represents AWGN with zero mean and double-sided power spectral density of $\frac{N_0}{2}$.

In the receiver, the received signal needs to be synchronized in both time and frequency domain [15]. For this purpose, the proposed hybrid system uses a time-frequency two-dimensional search algorithm (the detail has been discussed in literature [2]). The frequency range that may appear in this scheme can be divided into several frequency bands as shown in Fig. 4. The receiver searches for the possible phase of all spread spectrum sequences in each frequency band. If spread spectrum sequence is not found in this frequency band, this process is repeated for the next frequency band and so on. The search unit is composed of the carrier frequency offset interval and the code phase interval.

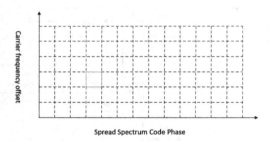

Fig. 4. Visual map of the time-frequency two-dimensional search algorithm

Figure 5 shows the schematic diagram of the two-dimensional time-frequency search algorithm. Firstly, the received signal is demodulated by the two orthogonal carriers. Both the orthogonal carriers are in a specific frequency search band. Then, the two signals separately pass through low-pass filters, and are despread by the spread spectrum sequences with different phases or shifts. After all decision values are obtained and the search frequency is updated. The whole process is repeated until the maximum of these decisions reaches an already set threshold. Therefore, the carrier frequency and the phase or shift of the spread spectrum sequence required for the signal demodulation are obtained.

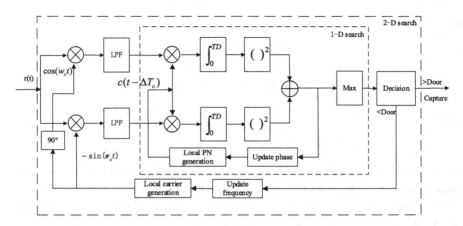

**Fig. 5.** Schematic diagram of the time-frequency two-dimensional search algorithm

Coherent demodulation will cause the phase ambiguity when the phase of the local reference carrier is offset. Therefore, it is necessary to estimate the phase of the carrier. Assuming that the carrier frequency and symbol phase synchronization are realized at the receiver. After orthogonal down-conversion, demodulation and low-pass filtering, the two signals of different branches can be written as

$$I(t) = LPF(r(t)\cos(2\pi(f_c + f_d)(t - \tau)))$$
$$= b_0(t)c(t)\cos(\varphi_0) - c^{(b_1(t))}(t)\sin(\varphi_0) + n'_I(t) \tag{10}$$

and

$$Q(t) = LPF(r(t)\sin(2\pi(f_c + f_d)(t - \tau)))$$
$$= -b_0(t)c(t)\sin(\varphi_0) + c^{(b_1(t))}(t)\cos(\varphi_0) + n'_Q(t) \tag{11}$$

where $n'_I(t)$ and $n'_Q(t)$ are the noise.

If the signals of both branches are multiplied by $c(t)$, they can be expressed as

$$I' = \frac{1}{T_s}\int_0^{T_s} I(t)c(t)dt$$
$$= b_0\cos(\varphi_0)\frac{1}{T_s}\int_0^{T_s} c(t)c(t)dt$$
$$- \sin(\varphi_0)\frac{1}{T_s}\int_0^{T_s} c^{(b_1(t))}(t)c(t)dt$$
$$+ \frac{1}{T_s}\int_0^{T_s} n'_I(t)c(t)dt$$
$$= b_0\cos(\varphi_0) - \sin(\varphi_0)R(c, c^{(b_1)}) + n'_I$$
$$= b_0\cos(\varphi_0) + n''_I \tag{12}$$

and

$$
\begin{aligned}
Q' &= \tfrac{1}{T_s} \int_0^{T_s} Q(t)c(t)dt \\
&= -b_0 \sin(\varphi_0) \tfrac{1}{T_s} \int_0^{T_s} c(t)c(t)dt \\
&\quad + \cos(\varphi_0) \tfrac{1}{T_s} \int_0^{T_s} c^{(b_1(t))}(t)c(t)dt \\
&\quad + \tfrac{1}{T_s} \int_0^{T_s} n_Q'(t)c(t)dt \\
&= -b_0 \cos(\varphi_0) + \sin(\varphi_0)R(c, c^{(b_1)}) + n_I' \\
&= -b_0 \cos(\varphi_0) + n_Q''
\end{aligned}
\tag{13}
$$

In these two expressions, $R(c, c^{(b_1)})$ is the cross correlation of $c(t)$ and $c^{(b_1(t_i))}(t)$. As the spread spectrum sequence has good correlation characteristics, the value of $R(c, c^{(b_1)})$ can be seen as zero. $n_I''(t)$ and $n_Q''(t)$ are caused by the noise, and they can be ignored. It can be deduced that the estimated carrier phase is

$$
\varphi_0' = -\tan^{-1}\left(\frac{Q'}{I'}\right)
\tag{14}
$$

## 5   Simulation and Experiment Results

### 5.1   Simulation Results

In this section, the performance of the hybrid system is analyzed with the help of simulation, and compared with that of the traditional DSSS system and the CSK system. For the proposed hybrid system, the m sequence with the length of 63 is used in both branches. The simulation parameters are displayed in Table 1. It is known that the theoretical value of the communication rate of this system is 190.5 bps.

**Table 1.** Simulation Parameter

| Parameter name | Value and unit |
| --- | --- |
| Sample rate | 48 kHz |
| Carrier frequency | 10 kHz |
| Communication bandwidth | 4 kHz |
| The information quantity of DSSS modulation | 1 bit |
| The information quantity of CSK modulation | 5 bits |

It is shown in Table 1 that the CSK signal carries more information than the DSSS signal. The hybrid system's average BER performance for different SNR in the AWGN channel is plotted in Fig. 6. It can be seen that there is a clear gap in the anti-noise performance between the DSSS branch and the CSK branch. Compared to the CSK signal, the DSSS signal has a higher reliability. The BER of the CSK branch is closed to the mixed signal. When the SNR is more than -7 dB, the curves of the CSK and mixed signals are closer and overlap each other.

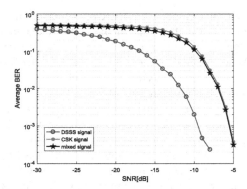

**Fig. 6.** The average BER curve of the hybrid system in the AWGN channel

The hybrid system is also simulated and analyzed in the multipath channel. The channel parameters used in the simulation is shown in Table 2. The rest of the parameters are the same as given in Table 1.

**Table 2.** Multipath parameter

| Path number | Amplitude | Time delay |
|---|---|---|
| 1 | 1 | 0 ms |
| 2 | 0.4 | 3.1 ms |
| 3 | 0.3 | 8.3 ms |
| 4 | 0.2 | 14.6 ms |
| 5 | 0.15 | 18.7 ms |

The BER of the DSSS signal, the CSK signal and the mixed signal are again compared, and the simulation results are shown in the Fig. 7.

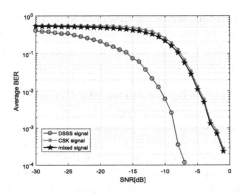

**Fig. 7.** The average BER curve of the hybrid system in the multipath channel

Due to the multipath interferences, the BER performance of the hybrid system in the multipath channel is worse than that in the AWGN channel. Since the spread spectrum technology can resist multipath interferences, the performance of this hybrid system is still stable. When the SNR is more than −5 dB, the BER of both branches are lower than $10^{-2}$. The experiment shows that the hybrid system is suitable for the UWA communication with multipath interferences.

As can be seen from Figs. 6 and 7, the difference of BER between the two branches is obvious. In order to improve the performance of the hybrid system, the power distribution of the two branches can be adjusted appropriately. The total power of the transmitted signal is kept unchanged, the amplitude of the DSSS signal is reduced to 60% of the original signal, and the transmitting power of the CSK modulated signal is increased accordingly. It can thus be seen from the Fig. 8 that the BER performance of the two power-adjusted signals is close to each other. After power adjustment, the BER of the mixed signal is lower than before. With similar BER conditions, the performance of the power-adjusted hybrid system is improved about 2 dB.

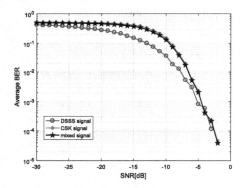

**Fig. 8.** The average BER curve after the transmitted power is adjusted

## 5.2    Experiment Results

In order to verify the performance of the proposed hybrid system, a pool experiment was also carried out in January 2018 in the channel pool of Harbin Engineering University. The pool is 45 m long, 6 m wide and 5 m deep. It is surrounded by silent wedges and has a sandy bottom. The transmitting transducer and receiving hydrophone used in the experiment are omni-directional. They are placed 2 m below the water surface, and the horizontal distance is 10 m. The UWA channel impulse response (CIR) output by simulation is showed in Fig. 9.

The experimental parameters are kept same as the simulation parameters. The frequency band of the selected transducer is 8 kHz–16 kHz. First, the original binary data is modulated and spread by the transmitter of the hybrid communication system and converted into the acoustic signal. It is sent out by the speaker of a notebook computer. After passing through the UWA channel, the signal is received by the receiving hydrophone, and transmitted back to the computer by the signal transfer box.

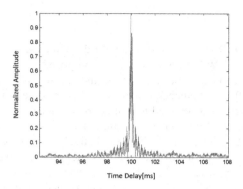

**Fig. 9.** Simulation using CIR

In order to display the BER performance more intuitively, the experiment transmits a binary black-and-white picture, which are four black characters on the white background. The amount of information in this picture shown in Fig. 10 is 16384 bits.

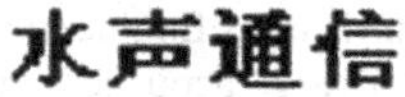

水声通信

(a) The original picture

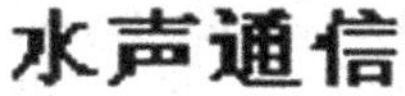

水声通信

(b) The received picture (without power adjustment)

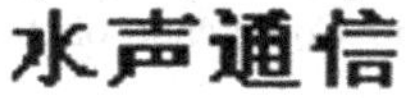

水声通信

(c) The received picture (after power adjustment)

**Fig. 10.** The transmitting and receiving images

When the transmitting power of the DSSS signal and the CSK signal is not adjusted, the received SNR is 5.8 dB and the BER is 0. When the amplitude of the DSSS signal decreases to 60% of the original signal, and the power of the CSK signal is increased accordingly under the condition that the total power of the transmitted signal is kept unchanged, the received SNR is 5.2 dB. Besides, the receiver of the hybrid spread spectrum system can correctly recover the original transmitted picture.

In another experiment, the hybrid system is compared with the DSSS system in the same experimental environment. The DSSS system uses a m sequence with the length of 63 as the spread spectrum sequence. Under the same experimental conditions, the received SNR of the hybrid system after adjusting the signal power is close to that of the DSSS system. However, the transmission time of the DSSS system is 8.60 min, while that of the hybrid system is 1.43 min. It therefore confirms that the hybrid communication system can effectively improve the communication rate, while ensuring the reliability of transmission.

## 6 Conclusions

Based on the traditional DSSS technology, a hybrid spread spectrum system modulated by DSSS and CSK for UWA communication is proposed in this paper. In this communication scheme, two orthogonal carriers are used to modulate the original data by DSSS and CSK in different branches respectively. Meanwhile, a time-frequency two-dimensional search method is adopted to realize the carrier frequency synchronization and the spread spectrum phase synchronization. Under the premise of ensuring the reliable transmission of signals, this scheme effectively improves the communication rate. Furthermore, the reliability of the hybrid system is improved by adjusting the power of two signals in different branches. The proposed system can be applied to UWA communications in low SNR environment. Besides, we will consider how to further improve the anti-jamming ability of this system in the future.

## References

1. Catipovic, J.A.: Performance limitations in underwater acoustic telemetry. IEEE J. Oceanic Eng. **15**(3), 205–216 (1990)
2. Zhou, F.: The study of the key technologies for underwater acoustic spread-spectrum communication. Ph.D. Dissertation, Harbin Engineering University, Harbin, China (2011)
3. Stojanovic, M., Preisig, J.: Underwater acoustic communication channels: propagation models and statistical characterization. IEEE Commun. Mag. **47**(1), 84–89 (2009)
4. Chitre, M., Shahabudeen, S., Freitag, L.: Recent advances in underwater acoustic communications & networking. In: Oceans. IEEE (2008)
5. Rice, J., Green, D.: Underwater acoustic communications and networks for the US Navy's SeaWeb program. In: International Conference on Sensor Technologies & Applications. IEEE (2008)
6. Loubet, G.; Capellano, V.; Filipiak, R.: Underwater spread-spectrum communications. In: Oceans. IEEE (1997)
7. Pickholtz, R., Schilling, D., Milstein, L.: Theory of spread-spectrum communications - a tutorial. IEEE Trans. Commun. **30**(5), 855–884 (1982)
8. Yin, Y., Zhou, F., Qiao, G., Liu, S., Yu, Y.: Burst mode hybrid spread spectrum technology for covert acoustic communication. In: Oceans. IEEE (2014)
9. Morgera, S.: Multiple terminal acoustic communications system design. IEEE J. Oceanic Eng. **5**(3), 199–204 (1980)
10. Walree, V.P.A.: Comparison between direct-sequence and multicarrier spread-spectrum acoustic communications in time-varying channels. J. Acoust. Soc. Am. **128**(6), 3525 (2010)
11. Deshmukh, S., Bhosle, U.: Performance evaluation of spread spectrum system using different modulation schemes. Proc. Comput. Sci. **85**, 176–182 (2016)
12. Yin, Y., Zhou, F., Qiao, G., Liu, S.: Orthogonal multicarrier M-ary cycle shift keying spread spectrum underwater acoustic communication. Acta Physica Sinica **62**(22), 224302 (2013)
13. Fengzhong, Q., Liuqing Y., Yang, T.C.: High reliability direct-sequence spread spectrum for underwater acoustic communications. In: Oceans (2009)
14. Zhou, F., Wang, Q., Nie, D., Qiao, G.: DE-Sync: a doppler-enhanced time synchronization for mobile underwater sensor networks. Sensors **18**, 1710 (2018)
15. Ravi, K.V., Ormondroyd, R.F.: Simulation performance of a quantized log-likelihood sequential detector for PN code acquisition in the presence of data modulation and Doppler shift. In: IEEE Military Communications Conference (1991)

# Application of PMN-PT Piezoelectric Monocrystal in Wideband Transducer with Composite Rod Matching Layer

Feng-hua Tian[1,2(✉)], Jun Li[2], Yi-ming Liu[1], Zhuo Xu[3], and Yun-chuan Yang[1]

[1] The 705 Institute of China Shipbuilding Industry Corporation, Xi'an 710077, China
tfh2000526@163.com
[2] School of Mechanical Engineering, Xi'an Jiaotong University, Xi'an 710049, China
[3] School of Electronic and Information Engineering, Xi'an Jiaotong University, Xi'an 710049, China

**Abstract.** In view of the characteristics of high energy density, high piezoelectric constant, low frequency constant and good low frequency performance of PMN-PT piezoelectric monocrystal material, this paper studies the corresponding technology from the perspective of engineering application. Aiming at the weakness of PMN-PT piezoelectric monocrystalline material, such as low phase transition temperature, low coercivity field and fragile, and combining with specific application background and demand, the solution is given. A batch of PMN-PT piezoelectric monocrystal transducers were developed and tested for its voltage-resistance, temperature stability and acoustic performance. The results show that the PMN-PT piezoelectric monocrystalline material has obvious advantages of acoustic performance of transmission and reception, it also reflects good low-frequency broadband characteristics and can be used in the high-power composite rod matching layer broadband transducer. The research results can be used to guide the application of PMN-PT piezoelectric monocrystal in sonar.

**Keywords:** PMN-PT piezoelectric monocrystal · Matching layer · Broad band · Acoustic transducer

## 1 Introduction

With the rapid development of modern underwater sound and signal processing technology, it is necessary to obtain more underwater information in order to improve the detection ability. As a result, the acoustic performance, working bandwidth, low-frequency performance, volume, size, weight and environmental adaptability of underwater acoustic transducer are also put forward higher requirements.

At present, the hydroacoustic transducer using PZT4 and its modified piezoelectric ceramics as the driving element has reached the bottleneck stage of development. It is difficult to improve its comprehensive performance by changing the structural design

© Springer Nature Switzerland AG 2019
H. Yu et al. (Eds.): ICIRA 2019, LNAI 11741, pp. 461–471, 2019.
https://doi.org/10.1007/978-3-030-27532-7_41

and processing technology. Therefore, it is necessary to find piezoelectric materials with superior performance to solve this problem.

Compared with the traditional series of PZT ceramic in energy density, the piezoelectric constant, frequency constant, low frequency performance and so on, PMN-PT piezoelectric crystal materials has manifested the better superiority and has been used in the field of underwater acoustic for a longer time. Meyer et al., also carried out a series of research work [1–4], mainly including PMN-PT longitudinal transducers in mode 32 and mode 33, as well as the comparative study with piezoelectric ceramics. With the appearance of ternary PB-MG-PT and Mn-doped single crystal (Mn: PINPMN-PT), the phase transition temperature of relaxation ferroelectric single crystal is obviously increased, and the loss factor is greatly reduced [5] as well: phase transition temperature from 95 °C to 125 °C, the loss factor from 0.26 to 0.15, the loss factor is usually only 1/2 of PZT piezoelectric ceramics series. The longitudinal transducer was made of modified piezoelectric single crystal. The results show that the new formula single crystal material is more suitable for high-power and large duty ratio. Compared with PZT4 series piezoelectric ceramics, resonant frequency transducer improves sound source level by 5 dB. Under the condition that the sound source level and power capacity at the resonant frequency are basically equivalent, the working bandwidth is doubled, and the maximum sound source level beyond the resonant frequency is increased by about 6 dB. In addition, due to the low frequency characteristics of PMN-PT piezoelectric monocrystal material, compared with PZT4 series piezoelectric ceramics, the volume and weight of PMN-PT piezoelectric monocrystal transducer will be greatly reduced under the same frequency band. For the engineering application of PMN-PT piezoelectric monocrystalline materials, the research conditions are relatively mature. Combining different application background and demand, this paper overcomes such weaknesses as poor batch consistency of PMN-PT piezoelectric single crystal material, low phase transition temperature [9], weak coercivity field and low thermal stability [10] from theoretical analysis, structural design [6–8], process implementation and other aspects. This paper focuses on the study of the PMN-PT piezoelectric single crystal transducer used by sonar receiver and transmitter to solve the problem of high-power transmission.

## 2   Theoretical Design of PMN-PT Piezoelectric Single Crystal Transducer

Due to the low coerce-field (600 V/mm) of PMN-PT piezoelectric monocrystal material, in order to avoid breakdown or depolarization under the condition of high-power emission, the thickness of the chip selected in this paper is 6 mm and 8 mm respectively. The allowable voltage is $v_{p-p} = 3600$ V and $v_{p-p} = 4800$ V respectively.

$$SVL = 170.8 + 10\log(P * \eta) + DI \tag{1}$$

$$SVL = TVR + 20 * LOG(V) \tag{2}$$

# 3  Simulation Design of PMN-PT Piezoelectric Single Crystal Transducer

In this paper, PMN-PT piezoelectric monocrystal material provided by Xi'an jiaotong university was used and its density is 8141 kg/m$^3$. Material parameters of z-direction polarization are shown in Tables 1, 2 and 3 respectively:

**Table 1.** Relative dielectric constant matrix $(\varepsilon_{ij}/\varepsilon_0)$

| Const E | $\varepsilon_{11}^s$ | $\varepsilon_{22}^s$ | $\varepsilon_{33}^s$ | Const T | $\varepsilon_{11}^T$ | $\varepsilon_{22}^T$ | $\varepsilon_{33}^T$ |
|---|---|---|---|---|---|---|---|
| | 1509 | 1509 | 905 | | 1666 | 1666 | 4532 |

**Table 2.** Piezoelectric stress constant matrix e(N/V.m)

| $e_{15}$ | $e_{24}$ | $e_{31}$ | $e_{32}$ | $e_{33}$ |
|---|---|---|---|---|
| 9.48 | 9.48 | −4.81 | −4.81 | 19.31 |

**Table 3.** Elastic constant matrix C

| 1. const E($10^{10}$N/m$^2$) | | | | | | | | |
|---|---|---|---|---|---|---|---|---|
| $C_{11}$ | $C_{12}$ | $C_{13}$ | $C_{22}$ | $C_{23}$ | $C_{33}$ | $C_{44}$ | $C_{55}$ | $C_{66}$ |
| 11.57 | 10.03 | 10.15 | 11.57 | 10.15 | 11.32 | 6.45 | 6.45 | 5.44 |
| 2. const D($10^{10}$N/m$^2$) | | | | | | | | |
| $C_{11}$ | $C_{12}$ | $C_{13}$ | $C_{22}$ | $C_{23}$ | $C_{33}$ | $C_{44}$ | $C_{55}$ | $C_{66}$ |
| 11.86 | 10.32 | 8.99 | 11.86 | 8.99 | 15.97 | 7.12 | 7.12 | 5.44 |

By using the finite element software and the above material parameters, the PMN-PT piezoelectric single crystal transducer is simulated. The finite element model is shown in Fig. 1, and the AC voltage of Rms which is 1 V is added to the transducer electrode. The calculation results are shown in Figs. 2, 3, 4 and 5.

**Fig. 1.** Finite element model of PMN-PT piezoelectric single crystal transducer

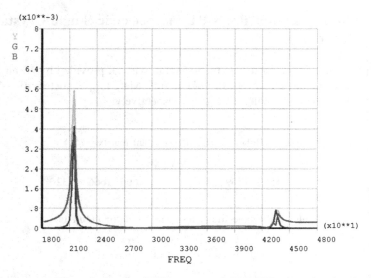

**Fig. 2.** Frequency (f) ~ admittance (GBY) curve of PMN-PT piezoelectric single crystal transducer

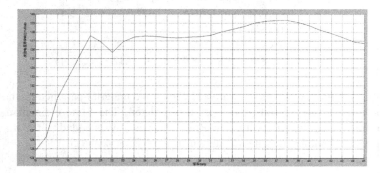

**Fig. 3.** Frequency (f) ~ transmission (TVR/dB) curve of PMN-PT piezoelectric single crystal transducer

The simulation results show that the first resonant frequency of the transducer is 21.3 kHz and the second resonant frequency is 43.4 kHz. In the frequency band of 19 kHz–45 kHz, the transmitted voltage response is greater than 135 dB, fluctuation is less than 4 dB, free field voltage receiving sensitivity is −166 db, fluctuation is less than 5 dB. At f = 25 kHz, −3 db beam width is 101°.

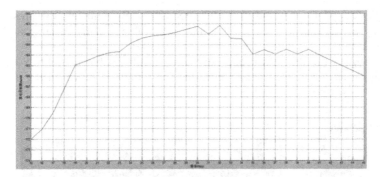

**Fig. 4.** Frequency (f) ~ receiving (Me/dB) curve of PMN-PT piezoelectric single crystal transducer

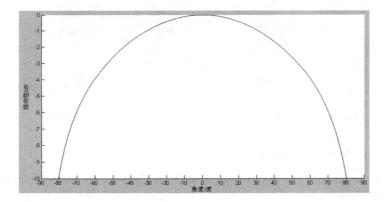

**Fig. 5.** Directivity curve of PMN-PT piezoelectric single crystal transducer f = 25 kHz

# 4  Test of PMN-PT Piezoelectric Single Crystal Transducer

## 4.1  Fabrication of Array Elements

In order to solve the problem of poor toughness of PMN-PT piezoelectric monocrystal material, the static pressure test of 20 MPa was carried out on piezoelectric monocrystal wafer before making the transducer. The results show that the PMN-PT piezoelectric wafer has strong static pressure resistance and poor shear resistance, that is, it cannot be applied with large torque. When the prestress is applied to the transducer, only the axial force is applied to avoid the tangential force. In order to circumvent the PMN - PT piezoelectric single crystal material's problem of low phase transition temperature and temperature stability, the ladder slowly rise and cooling method was adopted in the process of production of transducer, and the maximum temperature of 80 °C, and time aging was carried on. In order to reduce the influence of poor consistency of PMN-PT piezoelectric single wafer on the consistency of acoustic transducers, the adhesion process was optimized. The sample of transducers was viscose prestressed for 2 h and then measured again. By adjusting the prestress, the consistency of transducers was close to the ideal value. Finally, heating and curing were carried out.

According to the theoretical and simulation results, a batch of PMN-PT piezo-electric single-crystal transducers were made. The sample is shown in Fig. 6.

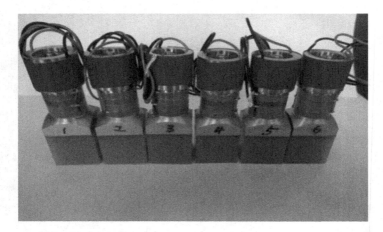

**Fig. 6.** Sample of PMN-PT piezoelectric single crystal transducer

## 4.2    Test of Array Elements

In order to summarize the rule, the application of PMN-PT piezoelectric monocrys-talline materials in high-power sonar is studied in depth. This section uses 4294 impedance analyzer, voltage withstand tester, PCB394c06 standard exciter, oscillo-scope and other basic instruments to test the pressure resistance, acceleration sensitivity and acoustic performance of the developed PMN-PT piezoelectric single crystal transducer in the air medium. The results are shown in Figs. 7, 8, 9 and Table 4.

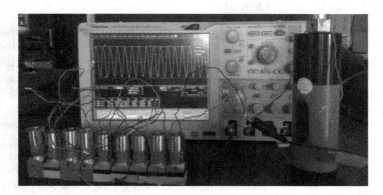

**Fig. 7.** Acceleration sensitivity test diagram of PMN-PT piezoelectric single crystal transducer

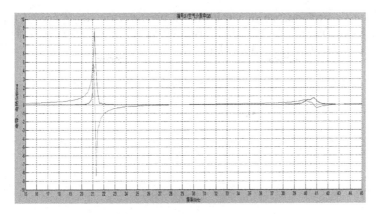

**Fig. 8.** Frequency f(kHz) ∼ admittance GB (ms) curve of PMN-PT piezoelectric single crystal transducer

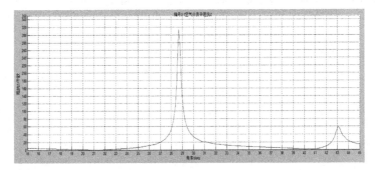

**Fig. 9.** Frequency f(kHz) ∼ impedance (ms) curve of PMN-PT piezoelectric single crystal transducer

**Table 4.** Acceleration sensitivity of PMN-PT piezoelectric single crystal transducer

| Serial number | Acceleration sensitivity (v/g) |
|---|---|
| 1 | 0.427 |
| 2 | 0.418 |
| 3 | 0.415 |
| 4 | 0.42 |

At room temperature and pressure, the piezoelectric single-crystal PMN-PT transducer sample was tested for its voltage resistance. The results show that the transducer can withstand 1500 V/min dc high voltage, and the peak current is above 1.0 A.

It can be seen from the above results that the first resonant frequency of the PMN-PT piezoelectric monocrystal transducer manufactured in the air medium is 21.1 kHz, the second resonant frequency is 40.8 kHz, and the acceleration sensitivity is less than 0.45 v/g.

The acoustic performance of the PMN-PT piezoelectric single crystal transducer was tested by means of an automatic measuring system in a silencer tank. The results are shown in Figs. 10, 11, 12, 13 and 14.

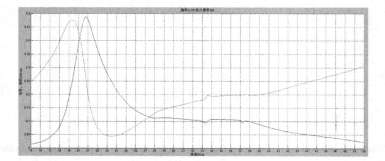

**Fig. 10.** PMN-PT piezoelectric single crystal transducer frequency f(kHz) ~ admittance GB (ms) curve

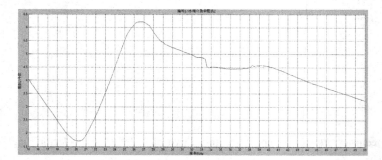

**Fig. 11.** Frequency f(kHz) ~ impedance (kΩ) ms curve of PMN-PT piezoelectric single crystal transducer

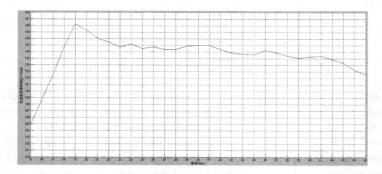

**Fig. 12.** PMN-PT piezoelectric single crystal transducer f(kHz) ~ TVR (dB) curve

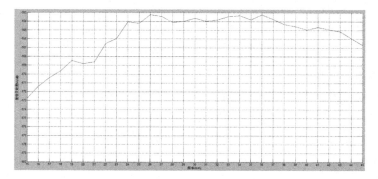

**Fig. 13.** PMN-PT piezoelectric single crystal transducer f(kHz) ~ Me (dB) curve

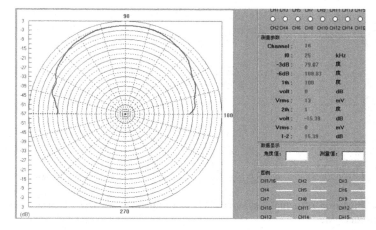

**Fig. 14.** Directivity of PMN-PT piezoelectric single crystal transducer f = 25 kHz

It can be seen from the above results that, in the frequency band of 19 kHz–41 kHz, the transmission voltage response of the PMN-PT piezoelectric monocrystal transducer manufactured is greater than 135 dB, fluctuation is less than 6 dB, free field voltage receiving sensitivity is −169 db, fluctuation is less than 6 dB. At f = 25 kHz, −3 db beam width is 79.

## 4.3  Comparative Analysis of Test Results

In order to verify the reliability of PMN-PT piezoelectric single crystal material parameters and the matching degree with the corresponding transducer structure, the theoretical design results and the measured results are compared and analyzed in this paper, as shown in Figs. 15 and 16.

As can be seen from Figs. 15 and 16, the theoretical design value is slightly higher than the measured value. For the transmission performance, the high frequency band decreases rapidly, while for the receiver, the low frequency band differs greatly, which

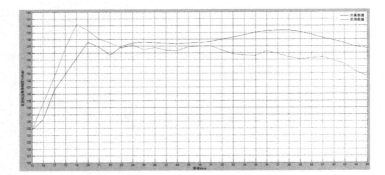

**Fig. 15.** Comparison of TVR measurement and simulation of PMN-PT piezoelectric single crystal transducer

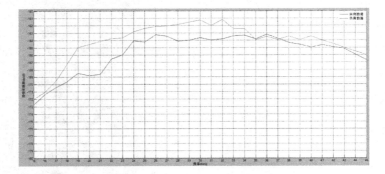

**Fig. 16.** Comparison of actual measurement and simulation of PMN-PT piezoelectric single crystal transducer Me

is caused by the small clamping force of the radiation head and the small thickness of the matching layer. Over all, the theoretical design results are in good agreement with the measured results.

## 5   Conclusion

In this paper, the advantages of PMN-PT piezoelectric monocrystal materials are fully utilized to develop a batch of high-power transmission and receiving broadband transducers. In the process of design and fabrication, the weakness of PMN-PT piezoelectric single crystal material is fully considered. The frequency band width of the PMN-PT piezoelectric transducer exceeds one octave range. In the entire frequency band, the frequency response of the transmitted voltage is greater than 135 dB, and the receiving sensitivity of the free field voltage is greater than −170 db. The transducer has passed the voltage withstand test, fully reflecting the advantages of PMN-PT piezoelectric single crystal material. The results show that the piezoelectric single crystal can be used in high power transmitter under the condition of satisfying the key index of PMN-PT piezoelectric single crystal material. The transmission and reception performance can be improved greatly at the same time. Combined with different application backgrounds and requirements, it is necessary to carry out subsequent studies on the power aging, vibration impact resistance and corresponding environmental adaptability of PMN-PT piezoelectric single crystal transducers.

# References

1. Meyer, R.J., Montgomery, T.C., Hughes, W.J., et al.: Tonpilz transducers designed using single crystal piezoelectrics. In: OCEANS 02 MTS/IEEEE, vol. 4, pp. 2328–2333. IEEE (2002)
2. Snook, K.A., Rehrig, P.W, et al.: Advanced piezoelectric single crystal based transducers for naval sonar applications. In: 2005 IEEE Ultrasonics symposium, vol. 2, pp. 1065–1068. IEEE (2005)
3. Rehrig, P.W., Hackenberger, W.S., Jing, X.N., et al.: Naval device applications of relaxor piezoelectric single crystals. In: 2002 IEEE Ultrasonics Symposium, vol. 1, pp. 733–737. IEEE (2002)
4. Rehrig, P.W., Snook, K.A., Hackenberger, W.S., et al.: Tailored single crystal orientations for improved tonpilz transducer performance. In: 2006 IEEE Ultrasonics Symposium, pp. 359–362. IEEE (2006)
5. Sherlock, N.P., Meyer, R.J.: Modified single crystals for high-power under water projectors. IEEE Trans. Ultrason. Ferroelectr. Freq. Control **59**(6), 1285–1291 (2012)
6. Tang, Y., Yu, H., Wen, N., Li, J.: Effect of changing the transducer impedance on the matching layer parameter. Appl. Acoust. **21**(6), 36–39 (2002)
7. Chen, H., Zhang, M., Li, Z.: Design of wide-band longitudinal mode piezoelectric transducers with impedance matching layers. Appl. Acoust. **20**(2), 31–34 (2001)
8. Rajapan, D.: Performance of a low-frequency, multi-resonant broadband tonpilz transducer. Acoust. Soc. Am. **111**, 1692–1694 (2002)
9. Peng, J., Luo, H., He, T., Xu, H., Lin, D.: Elastic, dielectric, and piezoelectric characterization of $0.70Pb(Mg_{1/3}Nb_{2/3})O_3$-$0.30PbTiO_3$ single crystals. Mater. Lett. **59**, 640–643 (2005)
10. Meng, H., Yu, H., Luo, H., et al.: Using PMNT in underwater acoustic transducers. Acoust. Electron. Eng. **73**(1), 22–26 (2004)

# Optimal Anti-submarine Search Path for UUV via an Adaptive Mutation Genetic Algorithm

Wenjun Ding[1,2(✉)], Hui Cao[1], Hao Wu[3], and Zhaoyong Mao[2]

[1] State Key Laboratory of Electrical Insulation and Power Equipment,
School of Electrical Engineering,
Xi'an Jiaotong University, Xi'an 710049, China
dingwj.nwpu@gmail.com, huicao@mail.xjtu.edu.cn
[2] Key Laboratory of Unmanned Underwater Vehicle Ministry of Industry
and Information Technology, School of Marine Science and Technology,
Northwestern Polytechnical University, Xi'an 710072, China
maozhaoyong@nwpu.edu.cn
[3] Department of Naval Architecture, Dalian University of Technology,
Dalian 116023, China
wuhao@mail.dlut.edu.cn

**Abstract.** Unmanned underwater vehicle (UUV) is significant equipment for underwater anti-submarine operation. In this paper, the optimal anti-submarine search path for UUV is investigated through an adaptive mutation genetic algorithm (AMGA). The AMGA utilizes three control factors to dominate the direction and amplitude of mutation adaptively and to improve the convergence speed. The mathematical programming model for UUV optimal search is established by maximizing cumulative detection probability (CDP). The enemy submarine is described as Markovian target, and the search radius and search width of the UUV are considered. Reasonable and efficient search paths are obtained under different conditions. The results indicate that the optimal path for UUV is effective and suggestive for anti-submarine search.

**Keywords:** Unmanned underwater vehicle (UUV) · Anti-submarine search · Optimal path · Adaptive mutation genetic algorithm (AMGA)

## 1 Introduction

Unmanned underwater vehicle (UUV) is a type of particular underwater robots [1], which is released by submarines, naval vessels or unmanned latent platforms. UUV can be operated with autonomous navigation, long operative time and large voyage. Moreover, UUV can perform military and civil tasks such as intelligence collection, underwater and aquatic surveillance, combat and strike, and logistics support [2, 3].

Anti-submarine search is a significant military mission for UUV. When an enemy submarine is discovered by detection devices via submarines, sonobuoys, naval vessels or underwater latent platforms, a UUV can be released to search the enemy submarine in the discovered zone automatically [4–6]. The enemy submarine usually continues to maintain its original motion without perceiving its exposure.

© Springer Nature Switzerland AG 2019
H. Yu et al. (Eds.): ICIRA 2019, LNAI 11741, pp. 472–479, 2019.
https://doi.org/10.1007/978-3-030-27532-7_42

The endurance of the UUV is inevitable limited by its carried lithium batteries. Thus, it is meaningful that intelligent computing and modern search theory should be applied for UUV anti-marine search path planning [7].

Kierstead [8] proposed a genetic algorithm (GA) to settle the optimal search path planning problem. The GA was put forward based on path geometry for optimal search in complex detection environment, and a satisfactory search scheme was achieved. Cho [9] presented an adaptive GA with high mutation rate based on searcher's direction coding. And the search problem of stationary target and simple directional moving target were analyzed. However, these two models assumed that the target was stationary or simple uniform motion, which is not conducive for practical application [10, 11]. In this paper, the Markovian enemy submarine is investigated.

## 2 UUV Moving Model

During search operation, the UUV's motion with stable direction and velocity is regarded as a search step. A UUV search path contains the following elements: the searcher's start node $SS$, the search time $T_S$, the stage duration $Step_S$, the direction $\theta_S$, and the velocity $V_S$ (subscript S indicates the searcher), where $\theta_S \in [0, 2\pi)$, $V_S$ keeps constant. Figure 1 presents a sample search path. In this paper, the time spending and path deviation in direction adjustment of each stage are ignored. Only the moving direction $\theta_S$ is considered as the decision variable.

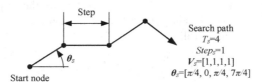

**Fig. 1.** Sample path model.

## 3 UUV Detection Model

UUV utilizes the underwater sonar to detect the enemy submarine. The UUV's detection capability is depended on the effective search width $w$ of the sonar ($w = 2 \cdot r \cdot \sin\beta$, $r$ is the maximum detection distance and $\beta$ is the single-side effective search sector angle), as shown in Fig. 2. The UUV detects submarines through underwater sonar with interval time $\Delta t_D$.

In this paper, the detection model is simplified. The detection probability is considered as 1 if the submarine is within the sonar detection sector. Otherwise, it is considered as 0. When the enemy submarine is detected by the UUV, the position relationship between the UUV $(X_i, Y_i)$ and the submarine $(X, Y)$ can be expressed as follows.

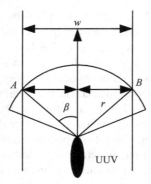

**Fig. 2.** Detection model with effective width

$$\begin{cases} \sqrt{(X_i - X)^2 + (Y_i - Y)^2} \le r \\ \arccos \dfrac{r^2 + (X_i-X)^2 + (Y_i-Y)^2 - (X_i + r\cos\theta_{si}-X)^2 - (Y_i + r\sin\theta_{si}-Y)^2}{2r\sqrt{(X_i + r\cos\theta_{si}-X)^2 + (Y_i + r\sin\theta_{si}-Y)^2}} \le \beta \end{cases} \tag{1}$$

## 4  Optimal Search Path Planning Model

### 4.1  Objective Function

The cumulative detection probability (CDP) is selected as the objective function to evaluate the UUV's search efficiency in each path through the Monte Carlo method. The CDP can be expressed as follows.

$$F_{CDP}(t) = \frac{N_D(t)}{N_T} \times 100\%, t \in [0, T_S] \tag{2}$$

Where: $N_T$ is the total number of simulations through Monte Carlo Method; $N_D(t)$ is the number of the submarine is detected.

### 4.2  Planning Model

The optimal search path planning model for UUV is established as follows:

$$\text{Max } F_{\text{CDP}}(X, t), \text{ s.t.} \begin{cases} X \in \Psi \\ t \in [0, T_s] \end{cases} \tag{3}$$

Where, the decision variable $X = (x_1, x_2, \ldots, x_N)^{\mathrm{T}}$ is a search path planning scheme. $N$ is the total number of search steps. $(x_1, x_2, \ldots, x_N)^{\mathrm{T}}$ is the direction $\theta_s$ of the UUV at each search step. $F_{\text{CDP}}(X, t)$ is the CDP of a search path $X$ at $t$ moment. The constraint condition of the decision variable is $\Psi = \{X | x_i \in [a_i, b_i]\}, a_i < b_i$, real constant, $i = 1, 2, \ldots, N$. In practical operation, $\Psi = \{X | x_i \in [0, 2\pi]\}, i = 1, 2, \ldots, N$.

# 5  Adaptive Mutation Genetic Algorithm

## 5.1  Coding Strategy

An adaptive mutation genetic algorithm (AMGA) is put forward for UUV optimal anti-submarine search. Three adaptive factors are introduced to improve the mutation operation. The genetic population is denoted as $Pop(k) = \left\{ C_1^k, C_2^k, \cdots C_j^k, \cdots C_M^k \right\}$, each chromosome $\mathbf{C}_j^k$ can be expressed as follows:

$$\mathbf{C}_j^k = \left[ \theta_{j1}^k, \theta_{j2}^k, \cdots \theta_{ji}^k, \cdots \theta_{jN}^k \right] \tag{4}$$

$$i = 1, 2, \cdots, N; \quad j = 1, 2, \cdots, M; \quad k = 1, 2, \cdots, G_{\max} \tag{5}$$

Where: $k$ is the $k$th evolutionary generation. $\mathbf{C}_j^k$ is the $j$th chromosome (a search path of the UUV with each step's direction) in the $k$th evolutionary generation. $\theta$ is the coding gene of the direction. $G_{\max}$ is the maximum number of evolutionary generations. $j$ is the $j$th chromosome. $i$ is the $i$th position in a chromosome (the $i$th step's direction). $M$ is the population size. $N$ is the length of each chromosome (the number of the total search steps).

## 5.2  Genetic Manipulation

AMGA employs improved crossover and mutation operators to guide population evolution. The elite parents are selected with ratio $P_E$, the crossover is performed with ratio $P_C$, and the mutation is operated with ratio $P_M$. In this paper, $P_E = 0.01$, $P_C = 0.24$, $P_M = 0.75$ ($P_E + P_C + P_M = 1$). Then, the descendant population is generated.

In order to improve the mutation efficiency and accelerate the algorithm's convergence, an adaptive mutation strategy is employed as follows [10, 11].

$$\theta_{ji}^k = \theta_{ji}^{k-1} + D \cdot Sgn(\theta_{ji}^{k-1}) \cdot \eta(i) \cdot \gamma(k) \cdot R \tag{6}$$

$$i = 1, 2, \cdots, N; j = 1, 2, \cdots, M; k = 2, \cdots, G_{\max} \tag{7}$$

Where, $\theta_{ji}^k$ is the $k$th gene in a population (the $k$th step's direction). $Sgn(\cdot)$ is a control factor for the mutation direction. $\eta(i)$ is a control factor for the gene position. $\gamma(k)$ is a control factor for evolution. $R$ is a random number in the range of $[0,1]$ with uniform distribution. $D$ is a constant number in the range of $[0, b_i - a_i]$. If $\theta_{ji}^k$ obtained after the mutation through Eq. (6) is out of the feasible space $\boldsymbol{\Psi}$, it should be adjusted by Eq. (8).

$$\theta' = \begin{cases} \theta - 2\pi, \theta > 2\pi \\ \theta + 2\pi, \theta < 0 \\ \theta \end{cases} \tag{8}$$

In this paper, constant number $D$, control factor $\eta(i)$ and control factor $\gamma(k)$ are obtained through Eq. (9). Comparing a large number of simulations, the AMGA can perform satisfactorily and get stable results under these selected parameters.

$$\begin{cases} D = \frac{1}{2} \cdot (2\pi - 0) = \pi \\ \eta(i) = \frac{i}{N} \\ \gamma(k) = \exp[-2.7 \cdot (\frac{k}{G_{\max}})] \end{cases} \tag{9}$$

The control factor of mutation direction $Sgn(\cdot)$ can guide the operated individual to mutate toward the optimal direction. The parent individual is denoted as $C_{Best}^{k-1} = [\theta_{B1}^{k-1}, \theta_{B2}^{k-1}, \cdots, \theta_{Bi}^{k-1}, \cdots, \theta_{BN}^{k-1}]$, then this control factor $Sgn(\cdot)$ can be determined by the following expressions.

$$Sgn(\theta_{ji}^{k-1}) = \begin{cases} \frac{\sin(\theta_{Bi}^{k-1} - \theta_{ji}^{k-1})}{|\sin(\theta_{Bi}^{k-1} - \theta_{ji}^{k-1})|}, & \theta_{ji}^{k-1} \neq \theta_{Bi}^{k-1} \\ \pm 1 \end{cases} \tag{10}$$

As aforementioned, the AMGA algorithm induces three control factors: $Sgn$, $\eta$ and $\gamma$ for adaptive mutation strategy. The mutation direction is controlled by factor $Sgn$. The mutation amplitude is controlled by constant number $D$, random number $R$, and factor $\eta$ and factor $\gamma$, simultaneously.

## 6    UUV Anti-submarine Search Analysis

### 6.1    Target with Unknown Direction

In this example, an enemy submarine is assumed to be discovered by an underwater latent platform at $T = 0$ h in point $TS$ near the sea surface, then it submerges into underwater. A UUV for anti-submarine search is released by the underwater latent platform immediately. The enemy submarine's motion is described as follows: start node $TS$ = (50 n mile, 50 n mile), velocity $V_T$ with normal distribution ($\mu_{vT} = 3$ kn, $\sigma_{vT} = 0.5$ kn), direction $\theta_T$ with uniform distribution in [0 rad, $2\pi$ rad], and time step $Step_T$ (subscript T represents the enemy target). The distributions of the target at $T = 3$ h and $T = 10$ h simulated by Monte Carlo method are as shown in Fig. 3 (simulation times $N_T = 1000$).

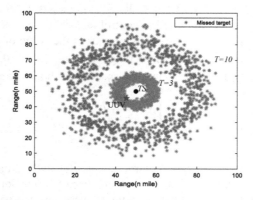

**Fig. 3.** Distribution of missed submarine with unknown direction at $T = 3$ h and $T = 10$ h

The UUV's anti-submarine search operation is started at $T = 0$ h from start node $SS = (45$ n mile, 45 n mile), search velocity $V_s = 5$ kn. The total search time is set as $T_s = 10$ h, and the time of each search step is set as *Stepts* = 0.5 h. Thus, the total number of search steps is $N_{Step} = 20$. The decision variable, the moving direction $\theta_S$ is in the range of [0 rad, $2\pi$rad), the number of the decision variables is 20 (equal to $N_{Step} = 20$). The interval detection time is $\Delta tD = 0.1$ h. Thus, the UUV detects 5 times during a search step, and 100 times during the anti-submarine search operation. The cumulative detection probability of each path is calculated through Monte Carlo method based Eqs. (1) and (2).

In this paper, the provided AMGA is employed to analyze the optimal search path. Some parameters are set as follows, the population size $M = 100$, the length of each chromosome $N = 20$, the maximum number of evolutionary generations $G_{max} = 100$, the elite ratio $P_E = 0.01$, the crossover ratio $P_C = 0.24$, and the mutation ratio $P_M = 0.75$.

As shown in Fig. 4, the AMGA presents the optimal search path for the UUV after 100 independent simulations. The CDP can reach to $F_{CDP}(10) = 82\%$. The optimal search path for UUV anti-submarine search is similar to the logarithmic spiral search curve, which is a suitable search method for searcher with constant search velocity to search escaping target with constant speed [10]. The logarithmic spiral curve is expressed as follows.

$$r(\varphi) = r_0 \exp[k(\varphi - \varphi_0)] \tag{11}$$

Where, $r$ is the diameter of the logarithmic spiral curve. $\varphi$ is the polar angle. $(r_0, \varphi_0)$ is the initial diameter and polar angle at start point. Coefficient $k = \tan[arcsin(V_T/V_S)]$, $V_T$ is the target's velocity, $V_S$ is the UUV's velocity.

The similarity indicates that the AMGA is effective for UUV's anti-submarine search path planning. The following sector will present the influence analysis of different parameters on CDP during UUV's anti-submarine search operation.

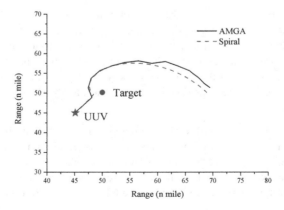

**Fig. 4.** Optimal search path from AMGA and logarithmic spiral search path

## 6.2   Target with Known Direction

In this section, the target's direction is known and assumed to be distributed normally ($\mu_{\theta T} = \pi/4$, $\sigma_{\theta T} = \pi/10$). Other parameters are as the same as the aforementioned section. The distributions of the target at $T = 3$ h and $T = 10$ h are presented in Fig. 5 (simulation time $N_T = 1000$).

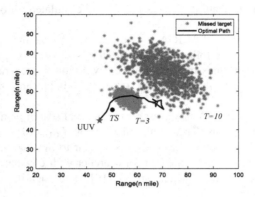

**Fig. 5.** Distribution of missed submarine with known direction and optimal anti-submarine search path of UUV

The CDP for enemy submarine with known direction can reach to $F_{CDP}(10) = 95\%$. Hence, in order to improve the CDP prominently, some measures can be utilized to estimate the target's direction for increasing the CDP during anti-submarine search operation.

## 7   Conclusions

In this paper, the optimal anti-submarine search path planning for UUV is presented based on an adaptive mutation genetic algorithm (AMGA). The developed algorithm uses cumulative detection probability (CDP) as the objective function. As a gene in the evolution process, the gene represents the moving direction of the UUV at a search step. The enemy submarine is described as Markovian target, and the search radius and search width of the UUV are considered. In simulation analysis, some conclusions are drawn as follows:

(1) For target with unknown direction, an approximate logarithmic spiral path is found through AMGA, which indicates that the optimal path of UUV via AGMA is effective and suggestive for anti-submarine search.
(2) For target with known direction, the CDP is enhanced greatly. It is suggested that target direction estimation can improve the CDP for UUV optimal anti-submarine search.

**Acknowledgements.** This research was partially supported by the National Natural Science Foundation of China (Grant Nos 61375055), the scholarship from China Scholarship Council (Grant No. 201506290080), the China Postdoctoral Science Foundation (Grant No. 2019M653652) and the Fundamental Research Funds for the Central Universities.

# References

1. Verfuss, U.K., Aniceto, A.S., Harris, D.V., et al.: A review of unmanned vehicles for the detection and monitoring of marine fauna. Mar. Pollut. Bull. **140**, 17–29 (2019)
2. Qian, D., Zhao, J., Yang, Y.: Development trend of military UUV (II): a review of US military unmanned system development plan. J. Unmanned Undersea Syst. **25**(3), 107–150 (2017)
3. Kumar, A., Kurmi, J.: A review on unmanned water surface vehicle. Int. J. Adv. Res. Comput. Sci. **9**(2), 95 (2018)
4. Chen, P., Wu, X.: Optimal extended position call-search method for UUVs' formation. Syst. Eng. Electron. **35**(5), 987–992 (2013)
5. Chen, P., Wu, X.-F., Chen, Y.: Method of call-search for Markovian motion targets using UUV cooperation. Syst. Eng. Electron. **34**(8), 1630–1634 (2012)
6. Li, B., Chiong, R., Gong, L.-G.: Search-evasion path planning for submarines using the artificial bee colony algorithm. In: 2014 IEEE Congress on Evolutionary Computation (CEC), pp. 528–535 (2014)
7. Chen, J., Chen, C., Sun, M.: Optimization calculation of continuous search path. Syst. Eng. Electron. **40**(5), 1155–1159 (2018)
8. Kierstead, D.P., Delbalzo, D.R.: A genetic algorithm applied to planning search paths in complicated environments. Mil. Oper. Res. **8**(2), 45–59 (2003)
9. Cho, J.-H., Kim, J.S., Lim, J.-S., et al.: Optimal acoustic search path planning for sonar system based on genetic algorithm. Int. J. Offshore Polar Eng. **17**(03), 218–222 (2007)
10. Zhang, X., Ren, Y., Wang, R.: Research on optimal search path programming in continuous time and space based on an adaptive genetic algorithm. Acta Armamentarii **36**(12), 2386–2395 (2015)
11. Zhang, X., Ren, Y.-F., Shen, J.: Improved double chains genetic algorithm for optimal searcher path problem in continuous time and space. Syst. Eng. Electron. **37**(5), 1092–1098 (2015)

# An Improved Genetic Algorithm for Optimal Search Path of Unmanned Underwater Vehicles

Zhaoyong Mao, Peiliang Liu$^{(\boxtimes)}$, Wenjun Ding, and Guo Hui

Key Laboratory of Unmanned Underwater Vehicle Ministry of Industry and
Information Technology, School of Marine Science and Technology,
Northwestern Polytechnical University, Xi'an 710072, China
maozhaoyong@nwpu.edu.cn, 1063134777@qq.com,
dingwj.nwpu@gmail.com, guohui_nwpu@qq.com

**Abstract.** To solve path planning problem of continuous space-time Markov moving targets for UUV search, an optimal path planning model is established. The search direction of the UUV is set as decision variables. An improved genetic algorithm is adopted to pursue an optimal path for underwater anti-submarine search. The algorithm utilizes an improved real number encoding method to describe the path. The target's motion is assumed as uniform distribution in direction and normal distribution in velocity around an initial speed. The results show that the search path planning is more reasonable through a certain number of genetic and cross mutation operations. The proposed method has the advantages of high search efficiency, good stability and short reaction period, and is suitable for solving underwater path-searching problems.

**Keywords:** Optimal search path problem (OSPP) ·
Unmanned underwater vehicle (UUV) · Markov moving target ·
Improved genetic algorithm

## 1 Introduction

Search theory originated from a series of research work on German submarines conducted by the scientists of the United States during World War II. It is mainly to utilize optimization theories and methods to find specified targets. From 1956 to 1980, through many researchers' efforts [1–3], a number of theoretical achievements were mainly obtained for optimal search resource allocation for stationary targets and moving targets, which contributed to the theoretical foundation of search theory. However, such problems require the search resources to be arbitrarily subdivided within discrete or continuous time and space. The searcher's maneuver ability is not constrained, and the search resources can be arbitrarily transferred and allocated within the search space.

Optimal search path problem (OSPP) of UUV is a kind of complex optimization problem in which the searcher's motion is constrained. It requires the searcher to construct a search path and to maximize the search benefit under the limited resources. In 1986, Trummel [4] already proved that OSPP is an NP completeness problem.

H. Yu et al. (Eds.): ICIRA 2019, LNAI 11741, pp. 480–488, 2019.
https://doi.org/10.1007/978-3-030-27532-7_43

Cutting plane method [8], branch and bound method [5–7], heuristic algorithm [9, 10] and greedy algorithm [11] were adopted to solve the problem. These methods require the search space to be discretized into many cells. The target is restricted in the cells, and most of their motions are assumed as stationary or discrete state Markov motion. Due to the complexity of the problem, the design of these algorithms often compromised between the optimization effect and the calculation time. At present, a general effective algorithm is still not been found to solve this problem [12].

In order to make the model closer to reality, some papers studied complex continuous space-time OSPP. Some researchers [13, 14] utilized the optimal control theory. However, this method required that the target and the searcher's motion should satisfy the strict differential equation. In Kierstead's research [15], a genetic algorithm (GA) was applied to solve continuous time-space OSPP, and some significant results were achieved. The investigation indicated that the GA has its advantages for solving complex path planning. Then, Cho [16] proposed a GA with high variability rate in searcher's direction. The search problem with stationary targets and simple directional moving targets were discussed. The results indicate that the improved algorithm is suitable for solving OSPP.

In this paper, a Markov target is considered for solving the OSPP within continuous space and time. Firstly, the motion models of target and searcher are established, respectively. Then, an improved genetic algorithm is presented. The searcher's direction is chosen as decision variables, and an adaptive control method for crossover and mutation is proposed. Finally, the algorithm is applied to some simulations. The simulation results can show that the improved genetic algorithm has the advantages of good stability and strong searching ability, and is suitable for solving the underwater search path problem. The research results have certain application value for solving OSPP.

## 2 Motion Model

In continuous time and space, a complex Markov moving target is considered in this paper. The target is hypothesized as a two-dimensional Markov process $\{X(t), t \geq 0\}$ with a state of $R^2$ and a time set of $[0, +\infty]$. It means that the position of the target has no aftereffect. If the state of the target is known at time $t'$, then the probability distribution of the position of the target at future time $t$ $(t > t')$ is only related to the present position, regardless of the past position of the target. The analytical expressions of the transition probability distribution function for general Markov moving targets is difficult to achieved, but it can be approximately calculated by Monte Carlo method, or probability statistics approximation.

The search problem discussed in this paper belongs to the unidirectional search category in search theory, that is, the target does not respond to the searcher's behavior, and its motion is not affected by the searcher strategy. Meanwhile, the depth effect is not taken into consideration in this paper. The searcher and target are assumed to move in a 2-dimensional space.

# 3  Expression of Search Path

During practical operation, targets and searchers usually maintain a stable direction and speed for a certain period, and adjust intermittently according to the situation.

The motion process with stable direction and speed is regarded as a 'step', consisting of the following elements: start node (*SS*), search time ($T_{search}$), stage duration (*Step$_s$*), direction ($\theta_s$) and velocity ($V_s$). $V_s \in [V_{min}, V_{max}]$ and $\theta_s \in [0, 2\pi]$. In this paper, the direction $\theta_s$ is chosen as decision variable to make the model more generally.

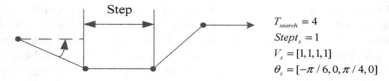

$$T_{search} = 4$$
$$Step_s = 1$$
$$V_s = [1, 1, 1, 1]$$
$$\theta_s = [-\pi/6, 0, \pi/4, 0]$$

**Fig. 1.**  Search path model

Figure 1 shows a simple search model that is divided into four steps. The speed of the search in each step is constant. The directions of four search steps are presented as $[-\pi/6, 0, \pi/4, 0]$, the speeds are given as $[1, 1, 1, 1]$. The issues discussed in this paper are based on this two-dimensional model, regardless of the influence of depth.

# 4  Planning Model Description of the Search Path

## 4.1  Objective Function

Cumulative detection probability (CDP) is employed as the objective function for search path planning to evaluate search efficiency. When $0 \leqslant t \leqslant T$, the CDP at time t is denoted as $F_{cdp}(t)$, which is defined as the probability of the target is detected at least one more times in the time period [0,T]. Thus, the CDP can be expressed as $F_{cdp}(t) = P$ {the target is detected at least once before time $t$}. In practical operation, it is very difficult to obtain accurate $F_{cdp}(t)$ by analytical method. The Monte Carlo method is usually adopted to approximately calculate $F_{cdp}(t)$. In this paper, the detection model is assumed in the ideal situation. When the target enters the sonar detection range, the probability of detecting the target is 1, otherwise it is 0.

$$F_{CDP}(t) = \frac{N_D(t)}{N_T} \times 100\%, t \in [0, T_S] \tag{1}$$

Where: $N_T$ is the total number of simulations through Monte Carlo Method; $N_D(t)$ is the number of the submarine is detected.

## 4.2    Planning Model

$$\max F_{CDP}(X, t) \quad s.t. \begin{cases} t \in [0, T_{search}] \\ X \in \varphi \end{cases} \tag{2}$$

Where, the decision variable $X$ represents a search path plan. $N$ represents the total number of search path steps. $X = (x_1, x_2, \cdots, x_N)^T$ is the direction of each stage of the search path. $F_{CDP}(X, t)$ represents the cumulative probability of detection along the search path $X$ at time $t$. Thus, $F_{CDP}(X, t)$ is a monotonically increasing function of $t$.

# 5    Improved Genetic Algorithm

## 5.1    Individual Coding Scheme

IGA uses a single-chain real number coding scheme: each chromosome represents a search path consisting of direction code. The genetic population is set as .., One of the chromosomes $C_j^k$ is represented as:

$$C_j^k = \left[ \left| \theta_{j1}^k \right| \cdots \left| \theta_{ji}^k \right| \cdots \left| \theta_{jN}^k \right| \right], \quad i = 1, 2, \cdots, N; \; j = 1, 2, \cdots M; \; k = 1, 2, \cdots, G_{max}; \tag{3}$$

Where $k$ represents generation; $C_j^k$ represents chromosome, i.e. a search path; $\theta$, $v$ represent the direction and velocity of the coding gene; $G_{max}$ represents the largest generation; $j$ represents the $j$ th individual of the population; $i$ represents the genetic position, i.e. search The $i$ th stage of the path; $M$ represents the population size; $N$ represents the total number of stages of the path.

During the evolution process, the variables $\theta$ in the search phase is used for genetic operations.

## 5.2    Genetic Algorithm Strategy

IGA uses improved crossover and mutation operators to guide population evolution. In genetic iteration, the progeny consists of three parts: the elite individual in the parent, the progeny population after the crossover operation, and the progeny population after the mutation operation. In each generation, two genetic operations (crossover and mutation) are performed independently, and the resulting two groups of new individuals and parent elites form a descendant population. The proportion of the elite elites in the population is called the elite individual ratio $P_E$, and the proportion of the two groups of new individuals in the offspring population is called the crossover probability and the mutation probability, which are recorded as $P_C$ and $P_M$ ($P_E + P_C + P_M = 1$). The definitions of crossover probability and mutation probability are not the same as those in other GAs. Through many experiments and parameter comparisons, this paper selects $P_E = 0.01$, $P_C = 0.24$, $P_M = 0.75$.

In order to improve the mutation efficiency and accelerate the algorithm's convergence, this paper improves the mutation operation and proposes the following adaptive mutation strategy:

$$\theta_{ji}^{k} = \theta_{ji}^{k-1} + A \cdot D \cdot \lambda(i) \cdot \delta(k) \cdot Rand, \ i = 1, 2, \cdots, N; \ j = 1, 2, \cdots, M; \ k = 2, \cdots, G_{max} \quad (4)$$

Where: $\theta_{ji}^{k}$, $v_{j(i+N)}^{k}$ are the kth generation gene; $D$ is the variation direction control factor; $\lambda(i)$ is the gene position control factor; $\delta(k)$ is the evolutionary generation control factor; Rand is the rand number between [0,1]; $A$ is a constant. If the gene value obtained after the mutation of (4) is out of the feasible range, it is adjusted by (5).

$$\theta' = \begin{cases} \theta - 2\pi, \theta > 2\pi \\ \theta + 2\pi, \theta < 0 \\ \theta \end{cases} \quad (5)$$

Through a large number of experiments and parameter comparisons, the constant values and control factors selected in this paper are given by (6) to (7). Under these parameters, the algorithm can achieve the best optimization performance and obtain stable operation results.

$$\begin{cases} A = \pi \\ \lambda(i) = \frac{i}{N} \\ \delta(k) = \exp[-2.7 \cdot (\frac{k}{G_{max}})] \end{cases} \quad (6)$$

In the design of the mutation direction control factor $D$, acting the guiding role of the optimal individual of the father, make the offspring mutate toward the optimal individual. The father's optimal individual is recorded as $C_{B}^{k-1} = [|\theta_{B1}^{k-1}| \cdots |\theta_{Bi}^{k-1}| \cdots |\theta_{BN}^{k-1}|]$. The directional control factors $D$ are determined by (7):

$$D_1 = \begin{cases} 1, \theta_{ji}^{k-1} < \theta_{Bi}^{k-1} \\ -1, \theta_{ji}^{k-1} > \theta_{Bi}^{k-1} \end{cases} \quad (7)$$

The adaptive mutation direction of the gene obtained by $D$ can make the operated search path continue to approach the optimal path of the parent (Fig. 2).

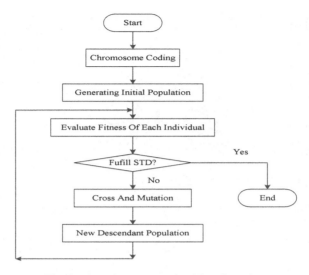

**Fig. 2.** Genetic operator algorithm flow chart

## 6  Simulation and Analysis

At $T = 0$ h, the enemy submarine target emerges in a certain sea area at the $TS$ point and is discovered by detection equipment, then the submarine submerges into the water and escapes from the water surface quickly. The UUV is immediately released by some platform with the detection information, which rushes to the certain sea area and operates the anti-submarine search. Based on this background, The submarine's and UUV's information is described as follows: target coordinates ($TS$ = [120 n mile, 120 n mile]), direction of submarine (uniform distribution in $[-\pi/3, \pi/3]$), velocity of submarine (normal distribution $\mu_{vT} = 4$ kn, $\sigma_{vT} = 0.5$ kn), UUV coordinates ($SS$ = [100 n mile, 100 n mile]), velocity of UUV ($V_s = 5$ kn), search time ($T = 10$ h), single-stage search duration ($T_{step} = 0.5$ h). The distributions of the submarine at $T = 3$ h and $T = 10$ h simulated by Monte Carlo method are as shown in Fig. 3 (simulation times $N_T = 1000$).

In this paper, the provided IGA is employed to analyze the optimal search path. Some parameters are set as follows, the population size $M = 100$, the length of each chromosome $N = 20$, the maximum number of evolutionary generations $G_{max} = 100$, the elite ratio $P_E = 0.01$, the crossover ratio $P_C = 0.24$, and the mutation ratio $P_M = 0.75$.

Figure 4 shows the optimal path search paths with the highest CDP for selected generations (1th, 25th, 55th and 100th generation). The CDP of the presented optimal search path for the UUV anti-submarine search can reach to $F_{CDP}(10) = 43.72\%$. Moreover, the evolutional process indicates that the IGA performs effectively to increasing the CDP.

Figure 5 shows five search paths of high cumulative detection probability. Their average cumulative detection probability is 37.31% (presented in Table 1), which is only 5% less than the optimal search path, indicating that the IGA has good stability and the resulting path is similarly high, which can be regarded as convergence.

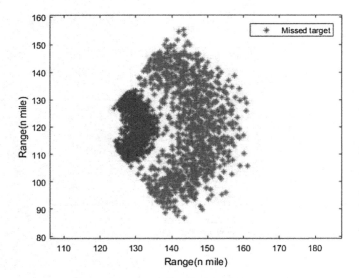

**Fig. 3.** Target distribution at T = 4 h and T = 10 h

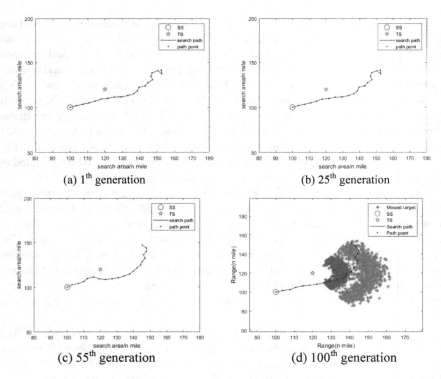

(a) 1ᵗʰ generation

(b) 25ᵗʰ generation

(c) 55ᵗʰ generation

(d) 100ᵗʰ generation

**Fig. 4.** Optimal search path of selected generation

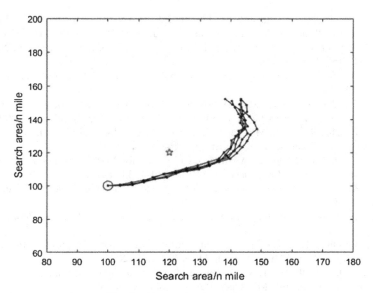

**Fig. 5.** Five optimal search paths

**Table 1.** Results of five optimal search paths

| Population size | Number of evolutions | Optimal $F_{CDP}$ (%) | Lowest $F_{CDP}$ (%) | Average $F_{CDP}$ (%) |
|---|---|---|---|---|
| 100 | 100 | 43.72 | 27.35 | 37.31 |

## 7 Conclusion

In order to solve the path planning problem of searching target for UUV, this paper proposes an improved genetic algorithm. The simulation and comparison prove that this method can solve the path planning problem of searching targets under certain conditions, which has positive significance for optimal path planning of UUV.

## References

1. Koopman, B.O.: The theory of search. Oper. Res. **4**(3), 324–346 (1956)
2. Stone, L.D.: Theory of Optimal Search. Academic Press, New York (1975)
3. Brown, S.S.: Optimal search for moving target in discrete time and space. Oper. Res. **28**(6), 1275–1289 (1980)
4. Trummel, K.E., Weisinger, J.R.: The complexity of the optimal searcher path problem. Oper. Res. **34**(2), 324–327 (1986)
5. Eagle, J.N., Yee, J.R.: An optimal branch - and - bound procedure for the constrained path, moving target search problem. Oper. Res. **38**(1), 110–114 (1990)

6. Lau, H., Huang, S., Dissanayake, G.: Discounted MEAN bound for the optimal searcher path problem with non-uniform travel times. Eur. J. Oper. Res. **190**(2), 383–397 (2008)
7. Sato, H., Royset, J.O.: Path optimization for the resource - constrained searcher. Nav. Res. Logistics **57**(5), 422–440 (2010)
8. Royset, J.O., Sato, H.: Route optimization for multiple searchers. Nav. Res. Logistics **57**(8), 701–717 (2010)
9. Hong, S.P., Cho, S.J., Park, M.J.: A pseudo - polynomial heuristic for path - constrained discrete - time Markovian - target search. Eur. J. Oper. Res. **193**(2), 351–364 (2009)
10. Hong, S.P., Cho, S.J., Park, M.J., et al.: Optimal search – relocation trade-off in Markovian - target searching. Comput. Oper. Res. **36**(6), 2097–2104 (2009)
11. Chen, P., Wu, X.F., Chen, Y.: Method of call search for Markovian motion targets using UUV cooperation. Syst. Eng. Electron. **34**(8), 1630–1634 (2012)
12. Zhu, Q.X.: Optimal Search Theory in Discrete and Continuous Spaces. Science Press, Beijing (2005)
13. Ohsumi, A.: Optimal searching for a Markovian - target. Nav. Res. Logistics **38**(4), 531–554 (1991)
14. Zhu, Q.X., Qing, L., Peng, B.: Optimal control model of search problem for randomly traveling targets. Control Theor. Appl. **24**(5), 841–845 (2007)
15. Kierstead, D.P., DelBalzo, D.R.: A genetic algorithm applied to planning search paths in complicated environments. Mil. Oper. Res. **8**(2), 45–59 (2003)
16. Cho, J.H., Kim, J.S., Lim, J.S., et al.: Optimal acoustic search path planning for sonar system based on genetic algorithm. Int. J. Offshore Polar Eng. **17**(3), 218–224 (2007)

# An Efficient Turning Control Method Based on Coordinating Driving for an Underwater Snake-Like Robot with a Propeller

Shan Li[1], Xian Guo[2(✉)], Junfang Zhou[1], Chao Ren[1], and Shugen Ma[1]

[1] The School of Electrical and Information Engineering,
Tianjin University, Tianjin 300072, China
[2] The Institute of Robotics and Automatic Information Systems,
Nankai University, Tianjin 300071, China
guoxian@nankai.edu.cn

**Abstract.** In this paper, the dynamics of a multi-link underwater snake-like robot with a propeller is modeled by recursive Newton-Euler algorithm. In order to improve the turning performance during the locomotion, a coordinated driving turning control method is proposed. The idea of this method is to use the center of mass of whole snake-like robot as a reference target. By judging whether the propulsion is consistent with the direction of turning gait locomotion, the timing of propulsion generated by the propeller is selected to match the turning gait locomotion. The simulation results demonstrate that the method can not only coordinate the forward gait to accomplish the corresponding movement, but also improve the maneuverability of the turning gait process.

**Keywords:** Underwater snake-like robot · Propeller ·
Coordinated driving · Maneuverability

## 1 Introduction

By bending their elongated and slender bodies in several special ways, snakes generate thrust from the interaction between the movements of their bodies and the environment, which is considerably superior to the mobility of conventional wheeled and tracked vehicles [1]. Inspired by the astonishing abilities of snakes, many researchers set out to research on the design and movements of snake-like robots. Since Hirose had developed the first machine snake ACM-III of the world in 1972 [2], many research laboratories had started research on machine snakes. Many prototypes, like Discoverer II, PIKo and AmphiBot series, have been designed one after another. Cheng [3] proposed to optimize tail fin propulsion structure of robot fish to improve the propulsion efficiency. This means that research in a underwater snake-like robots with a propeller is also of great significance for improving motion performance.

© Springer Nature Switzerland AG 2019
H. Yu et al. (Eds.): ICIRA 2019, LNAI 11741, pp. 489–500, 2019.
https://doi.org/10.1007/978-3-030-27532-7_44

In order to research motion-related performance of snake-like robots more convenient, it is necessary to establish a precise and practical model. Kelasidi proposed a kinematics and dynamics model of a planar underwater snake-like robot based on Newton-Euler analytical method [4]. Anfan [5] novelly defined a non-inertial system that is consistent with the direction of snake-like robots motion, and established an analytical two-dimensional underwater snake-like robots' dynamics model under this non-inertial system. The above modeling methods are based on the analysis of Newton-Euler method, and the established models are highly nonlinear and coupled. In order to facilitate the numerical simulation analysis, this paper establishes the dynamic model of underwater snake-like robot with a propeller based on recursive Newton-Euler algorithm.

This paper introduces an efficient turning control method based on coordinating driving for an underwater snake-like robot with a propeller designed by our laboratory. It is characterized by installing a propeller in the last joint of snake-like robot. The propeller can continuously or intermittently generate a forward propulsion to promote snake-like robot to accomplish turning action efficiently and quickly. The idea of this method is to use the center of mass of whole snake-like robot as a reference target. By judging whether the propulsion is consistent with the direction of the turning gait movement, the timing of propulsion generated by the propeller is selected to match the turning gait movement. Finally, the feasibility of the proposed method is demonstrated by some comparative simulations of the coordinating driving in different gaits.

The contributions of this paper include establishing Newton-Euler equation of an underwater snake-like robot with a propeller, proposing a coordinating driving method of gait and propeller and completing some simulations of a propeller coordinating driving in different gaits. The remainder of this paper is organized as follows. In Sect. 2, a model of underwater snake-like robots with a propeller is derived. The turning control method based on coordinating driving is presented in Sect. 3. In Sect. 4, simulation results and discussions of the proposed coordinating driving method are presented. Finally, conclusions are drawn in Sect. 5.

## 2    Model of the Snake-Like Robots with a Propeller

### 2.1    A Snake-Like Robot with a Propeller

The biological snakes realize wriggle movement by swinging their bodies. The research of bionic machine science makes snake-like robot prototypes have many specific gaits. When given a turning gait, a snake-like robot can complete a turning motion. In nature, aquatic organisms have caudal fins. They can quickly change their movement state by swinging caudal fins. Inspired by this, our laboratory has designed a new amphibious snake-like robot with a propeller, as shown in Fig. 1. The amphibious snake-like robot features a driver module mounted on the tail joint, and the driver module is shown in Fig. 2. The propeller has a DC brushless motor that generates force to push the liquid in the tail and liquid in return pushes snake-like robot forward. Currently the direction of propulsion generated by the propeller is consistent with the direction of the snake-like robots tail. Later we will add vector propulsion that the direction propulsion can be controlled to improve propulsion efficiency.

**Fig. 1.** The snake-like robot with a propeller

**Fig. 2.** Drive module

## 2.2   Hydrodynamic Modeling

This section is aimed at modeling hydrodynamic of underwater snake-like robots. Although there are many methods of hydrodynamic modeling, the main hydrodynamic modeling methods are the resistance theory proposed by Taylor and the slender body theory proposed by Lighthill [6]. Considering that the swimming environment of the snake-like robot is in the water and belongs to the medium Reynolds coefficient, the slender body theory suitable for the larger Reynolds coefficient is chosen here.

The hydrodynamic forces of a underwater snake-like robot include additional mass and water resistance [6]. Assuming the robot's buoyancy and gravity balance, the cross section is a cylinder with a radius $r$ and the length of a single module is $l$. The additional quality of snake-like robot under water is:

$$m_a = C_a \rho \pi r^2 l. \tag{1}$$

The additional inertia is:

$$I_a = \frac{1}{12} C_a \rho \pi r^2 l^3, \tag{2}$$

where $C_a$ is the additional quality factor. According to the slender body theory, the additional mass force of the body direction of the snake-like robot is 0, the additional mass force is:

$$M_a = \begin{bmatrix} 0 & 0 & 0 \\ 0 & m_a & 0 \\ 0 & 0 & m_a \end{bmatrix}. \tag{3}$$

The additional inertia matrix is:

$$I_a = \begin{bmatrix} 0 & 0 & 0 \\ 0 & I_a & 0 \\ 0 & 0 & I_a \end{bmatrix}. \tag{4}$$

The corresponding coefficient of shape resistance and viscous drag is:

$$C_d = \begin{bmatrix} 0.5\rho\pi C_f r l & 0 & 0 \\ 0 & \rho\pi C_D r l & 0 \\ 0 & 0 & \rho\pi C_D r l \end{bmatrix}, \tag{5}$$

where $C_d$ is the resistance correlation coefficient matrix in the fluid coordinate frame, $\rho$ is the fluid density, and $C_f$ and $C_D$ represent the tangential and normal resistance coefficients, respectively. The linear resistance and nonlinear resistance applied to the link $i$ under the respective coordinate frame $i$ are obtained:

$$_i^i f_{drag} = C_d(_i^i v + _i^i v \left| _i^i v \right|), \tag{6}$$

where $_i^i v$ represents the linear velocity of the coordinate frame $i$. Under the respective coordinate frame $i$, the additional mass force applied to link $i$ represents:

$$_i^i f_{added} = M_a {}_i^i \hat{w} {}_i^i \hat{w} S_i, \tag{7}$$

where $_i^i \hat{w}$ is the oblique symmetric matrix of the vector $_i^i w$, and $S_i$ represents the vector of the $i - th$ joint to the centroid of the $i - th$ link.

The linear resistance torque and the nonlinear resistance torque applying to the link $i$ is expressed as:

$$_i^i N_{drag} = \int_{-\frac{l}{2}}^{\frac{l}{2}} s d f = \int_{-\frac{l}{2}}^{\frac{l}{2}} \rho r l C_D(_i^i w s + _i^i w \left| _i^i w \right| s) ds = \lambda_2 {}_i^i w + \lambda_3 {}_i^i w, \tag{8}$$

where $\lambda_2 = \begin{bmatrix} 0 & 0 & 0 \\ 0 & \frac{4}{3} C_D \rho r(\frac{1}{2}l)^4 & 0 \\ 0 & 0 & \frac{4}{3} C_D \rho r(\frac{1}{2}l)^4 \end{bmatrix}$, $\lambda_3 = \begin{bmatrix} 0 & 0 & 0 \\ 0 & C_D \rho r(\frac{1}{2}l)^5 & 0 \\ 0 & 0 & C_D \rho r(\frac{1}{2}l)^5 \end{bmatrix}$.

The additional mass torque applying to the $i - th$ link is expressed as:

$$_i^i N_{added} = \frac{4}{3} \hat{S}_i M_a {}_i^i \hat{w} {}_i^i \hat{w} S_i, \tag{9}$$

where $\hat{S}_i$ is the oblique symmetric matrix of the vector $S_i$.

Therefore, the total hydrodynamic force received by the $i - th$ link is:

$$_i^i \mathbf{f_{ei}} = \begin{bmatrix} _i^i f_{ei} \\ _i^i N_{ei} \end{bmatrix} = \begin{bmatrix} _i^i f_{drag} \\ _i^i N_{drag} \end{bmatrix} + \begin{bmatrix} _i^i f_{added} \\ _i^i N_{added} \end{bmatrix}. \tag{10}$$

## 2.3    Recursive Newton-Euler Algorithm

This section is to use the recursive Newton-Euler algorithm [7] to model the inverse dynamics of 3D snake robot. Although the analytical model [4] and the model [8,9] that facilitates the design of the controller have been established, the recursive Newton-Euler method is easy to implement and to simulate whatever the number of degrees of freedom of the robot. The algorithm can be divided into reverse kinetics and direct kinetics. The following is a detailed description of the modeling of inverse dynamics.

**Kinematics Modeling of the Structure.** The object studied in this paper is a squid snake-like robot. It consists of $N+1$ links and $N$ joints. Here, the link of the head is marked as the $0-th$ link, which is sequentially followed by the mark to the link $N$ of the snake robot.

The transformation matrix from frame $\sum i-1$ to frame $\sum i$ can be represented by a function of the following parameters:

$\alpha_i$: The angle between the $z_{i-1}$ axis and the $z_i$ axis about the $x_{i-1}$;

$d_i$: The distance between the $z_{i-1}$ axis and the $z_i$ axis about the $x_{i-1}$;

$\theta_i$: The angle between the $x_{i-1}$ axis and the $x_i$ axis about the $z_{i-1}$;

$r_i$: The distance between the $x_{i-1}$ axis and the $x_i$ axis about the $z_{i-1}$.

Defining the homogeneous transformation matrix from the two adjacent coordinate frame $\sum i$ to the coordinate frame $\sum i-1$ is:

$$
{}^{i-1}_{i}T = \begin{bmatrix} C\theta_i & -S\theta_i & 0 & d_i \\ C\alpha_i S\theta_i & C\alpha_i C\theta_i & -S\alpha_i & -r_i S\alpha_i \\ S\alpha_i S\theta_i & S\alpha_i C\theta_i & C\alpha_i & r_i C\alpha_i \\ 0 & 0 & 0 & 1 \end{bmatrix}, \tag{11}
$$

where $S*$ and $C*$ are logograms for $\sin *$ and $\cos *$, respectively. Here, the matrix $(3 \times 3)$ on the left of ${}^{i-1}_{i}T$ and the coordinate frame $\sum i$ to the coordinate frame $\sum i-1$ represents rotation operator ${}^{i-1}_{i}R$. Correspondingly, the matrix $(3 \times 1)$ on the right side of ${}^{i-1}_{i}T$ and the coordinate frame $\sum i$ to the coordinate frame $\sum i-1$ represents translation operator ${}^{i-1}_{i}P$.

Defining the transformation matrix from the world coordinate frame $\sum 0$ to the head coordinate frame $\sum w$ is ${}^{w}_{0}T$. This matrix is known when $t=0$, and it will be updated by integrating the head acceleration.

As shown in Fig. 3, the position of the centroid of the entire snake robot is defined as:

$$
\mathbf{p} = \begin{bmatrix} p_x \\ p_y \\ p_z \end{bmatrix} = \begin{bmatrix} \frac{1}{N+1} \sum_{k=0}^{N} x_k \\ \frac{1}{N+1} \sum_{k=0}^{N} y_k \\ \frac{1}{N+1} \sum_{k=0}^{N} z_k \end{bmatrix} = \frac{1}{N+1} \begin{bmatrix} e^T X \\ e^T Y \\ e^T Z \end{bmatrix}, \tag{12}
$$

where $e = \begin{bmatrix} 1 \dots 1 \end{bmatrix}^T \in R^{N+1}$, $X = \begin{bmatrix} x_1 \dots x_{N+1} \end{bmatrix}^T \in R^{N+1}$, $Y = \begin{bmatrix} y_1 \dots y_{N+1} \end{bmatrix}^T \in R^{N+1}$, $Y = \begin{bmatrix} z_1 \dots z_{N+1} \end{bmatrix}^T \in R^{N+1}$. The direction of the $i-th$ link in the world coordinate frame is defined as:

$$
\theta_i = \theta_0 + \varphi_i, \tag{13}
$$

where $\theta_0$ represents the direction of the head link in the world coordinate frame, and $\varphi_i$ represents the relative angle between the $(i-1)-h$ link and the $i-th$ link, namely the angle of the servo output. The direction angle of the entire snake robot is defined as:

$$
\bar{\theta} = \frac{1}{N+1} \sum_{i=0}^{N} \theta_i. \tag{14}
$$

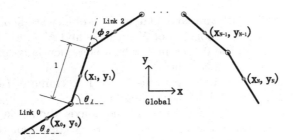

**Fig. 3.** The joint-link skeleton model of a snake robot

**Dynamics Modeling.** Since the inverse iterative Newton-Euler algorithm is forward iterative for velocity and acceleration, the definition of the spin transformation matrix is:

$$
{}^i_{i-1}T = \begin{bmatrix} {}^i_{i-1}R & -{}^i_{i-1}R_i^{i-1}\hat{P} \\ 0_{3\times3} & {}^i_{i-1}R \end{bmatrix}.
\tag{15}
$$

The speed of the coordinate frame $\sum i - 1$ determined by the adjacent joint $i-1$ transmitted to the coordinate frame $\sum i$ can be expressed as:

$$
{}^i_iV = {}^i_{i-1}T{}^{i-1}_iV + \dot{q}_i{}^i_ia,
\tag{16}
$$

where $\dot{q}_i$ represents the angular velocity under the coordinate frame $\sum i$, ${}^i_ia = \begin{bmatrix} 0_{3\times1} \\ {}^i_ik \end{bmatrix}$. ${}^i_iV = \begin{bmatrix} {}^i_iv^T & {}^i_iw^T \end{bmatrix}^T$ is a $6 \times 1$ Cartesian velocity.

The acceleration of the coordinate frame $\sum i - 1$ determined by the adjacent joint $i - 1$ transmitted to the coordinate frame $\sum i$ can be expressed as:

$$
{}^i_i\dot{V} = {}^i_{i-1}T{}^{i-1}_i\dot{V} + {}^i_i\gamma,
\tag{17}
$$

where ${}^i_i\gamma = \begin{bmatrix} {}^i_{i-1}R[{}^{i-1}_{i-1}w \times ({}^{i-1}_{i-1}w \times {}^{i-1}_i p))] \\ {}^i_{i-1}R^{i-1}_iw \times \dot{q}_i{}^i_ia \end{bmatrix} + \ddot{q}_i{}^i_ia$.

Basing on the equation of motion given above, and Cartesian velocity and acceleration of connecting link, the total external force of the $i - th$ joint is obtained according to Newton Euler equation:

$$
{}^i_iF = {}^i_iJ{}^i_i\dot{V} + \begin{bmatrix} {}^i_iw \times ({}^i_iw \times M_iS_i) \\ {}^i_iw \times ({}^i_iJ{}^i_iw) \end{bmatrix},
\tag{18}
$$

where ${}^i_iF = \begin{bmatrix} {}^i_i\mathbf{F^T} & {}^i_i\mathbf{N^T} \end{bmatrix}^T$, ${}^i_i\mathbf{F}$ represents the total external force on the link $i$, ${}^i_i\mathbf{N}$ represents the total torque of the link $i$ around the coordinate origin $O_i$. ${}^i_iJ$ is the inertia matrix($6 \times 6$) of the link $i$, ${}^i_iJ = \begin{bmatrix} \mathbf{M_i}I_3 & -M_i\hat{S}_i \\ M_i\hat{S}_i & {}^i_i\mathbf{J} \end{bmatrix}$, $I_3$ is a unit matrix($3 \times 3$), $\mathbf{M_i}$ is the mass of the $i - th$ link, and $M_iS_i$ is the first-order inertia of the link $i$ with respect to the frame $\sum i$.

As shown in Fig. 4, the equilibrium equation for the force is:

$$
{}^i_if = {}^i_iF + {}^{i+1}_iT{}^{i+1}_{i+1}f + {}^i_if_e,
\tag{19}
$$

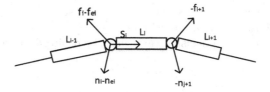

**Fig. 4.** Forces and torque on link $i$

where $_i^i f$ is the internal force rotation of the link $i - 1$ to the link $i$, and $_i^i f_e$ represents the external force rotation. The external force rotation of the last connecting link is:

$$_n^n f_e = {}_\mathbf{n}^\mathbf{n}\mathbf{f_{ei}} + {}_\mathbf{n}^\mathbf{n}\mathbf{F_p}, \tag{20}$$

where ${}_\mathbf{n}^\mathbf{n}\mathbf{F_p} = \begin{bmatrix} {}_n^n F_p\, 0\, 0\, 0\, 0\, 0 \end{bmatrix}$.

The inverse dynamics calculation process is divided into three iterative processes:

Step1: Forward iteration. Use (15)–(18) to calculate the speed, acceleration, and external force of each joint.

$$_i^i \beta = {}_i^i f_e + \begin{bmatrix} {}_i^i w \times ({}_i^i w \times M_i S_i) \\ {}_i^i w \times ({}_i^i J_i^i w) \end{bmatrix}. \tag{21}$$

Step2: Backward iteration. This process is to get the head acceleration. Bring (19) into (18) to get:

$$_i^i f = {}_i^i J_i^i \dot{V} + {}_i^i \beta + {}_i^{i+1} T^T {}_{i+1}^{i+1} f. \tag{22}$$

Establishing the relationship between Eqs. (17) and (21), we obtain:

$$_i^i f = {}_i^i J^{c\,i} \dot{V} + {}_i^i \beta^c, \tag{23}$$

where $_i^i J^c = {}_i^i J + {}_i^{i+1} T^T {}_{i+1}^{i+1} J^{c\,i+1} T$, $_i^i \beta^c = {}_i^i \beta + {}_i^{i+1} T^T {}_{i+1}^{i+1} \beta^c + {}_i^{i+1} T^T {}_{i+1}^{i+1} J^{c\,i+1} \gamma$. Let $_n^n J^c = {}_n^n J, {}_n^n \beta^c = {}_n^n \beta$, the head acceleration is:

$$_0^0 \dot{V} = -({}_0^0 J^c)^{-1}{}_0^0 \beta^c. \tag{24}$$

Step3: Forward iteration. We can get each joint acceleration and joint torque.

# 3   Turning Control Method Based on Coordinating Driving

## 3.1   Turning Based on Pure Swimming Gait

Any closed curve can represent a gait in the gait plan [10], and the turning gait is generated by requiring that the integral in the closed curve is not zero [11]. According to this method, a variety of different gaits can be obtained. A survey of existing two-dimensional gaits reveals that sinusoidal gait and anguilliform gait are the two most commonly used gait.

To reduce the number of decision variables, the basic gait is defined as follows:

$$\varphi_i = \alpha g(n, i) \sin(wt + (i - 1)\beta) + \gamma, \tag{25}$$

where $\alpha$ is the gait amplitude, $g(n, i)$ is the body amplitude as a function of body length, $w$ is the gait angular frequency, $\beta$ is the phase offset, and $\gamma$ is the angular offset. The difference in $g(n, i)$ means that the gait mode is different, and the $\gamma$ angle offset is used to control the steering.

Sinusoidal gait is the most commonly used gait in various literatures, $g(n, i) = 1$. The gait is more commonly used in amphibious snake-like robots considered to have high propulsion efficiency. Anguilliform gait is inspired by the swimming of the biological eel, $g(n, i) = \frac{i}{n+1}$. This gait is characterized by a small head amplitude and a large tail amplitude.

## 3.2   Coordinating Driving

As is shown in Fig. 5, assuming that the snake-like robot maintains a certain position, only the propulsion generated by the propeller is considered, and it is analyzed as a whole. The model combining gait with the propulsion generated by the propeller is described in the Sect. 2. Taking the centroid position of the snake-like robot as the research target, the torque of the thrust in the world coordinate frame can be obtained as:

$$\tau = \mathbf{r} \times \mathbf{F}, \tag{26}$$

where $\mathbf{r}$ represents the vector of the snake-like robot centroid $p$ to the tail position, and $\mathbf{F}$ represents the vector in world coordinate frame.

Since the centroid position of snake-like robot and the propulsion direction generated by the propeller are constantly changing, the torque generated by the propeller will periodically change as shown in Fig. 6 in swimming gait. The torque will partially promote the turning process, but the other part impedes turning process. Taking into account the above situation, selecting the propulsion that promotes its turning during the whole movement can not only improve the turning performance, but also reduce the energy consumption and improve its movement efficiency. Taking the torque obtained from the front as a reference, the propulsion coordinated control method is obtained:

$$F_p = F_p sign(\tau), \tag{27}$$

where $\text{sign}(\tau) = \begin{cases} 1, \tau > 0 \\ 0, others \end{cases}$.

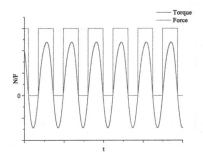

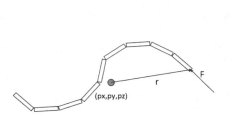

**Fig. 5.** The torque generated by a propeller

**Fig. 6.** The relationship between the coordinating driving propulsion output and the torque

## 4    Numerical Simulations

This section is the content of the simulation. The simulation includes coordinating driving between forward gait and propulsion, a contrast experiment of different ways of applying propulsion in the same turning gait and a contrast experiment of different turning gaits in the same mode of applying propulsion.

The following table gives the relevant physical parameter values referred to [4] during the simulation process (Table 1).

**Table 1.** Related physical parameters

| Name and symbol of parameter | Parameters values |
| --- | --- |
| Length of a single link $l$ | 0.18 m |
| Number of joints $n$ | 8 |
| Mass of a single module $m$ | 0.816 kg |
| Density of fluid environment $\rho$ | 1000 kg/m$^3$ |
| Single model cross section radius $r$ | 0.0375 m |
| Additional quality factor $C_a$ | 1 |
| Tangential drag coefficient $C_f$ | 0.03 |
| Normal resistance coefficient $C_D$ | 2 |

### 4.1    Coordinating Driving Between Forward Gait and Propulsion

We choose sinusoidal forward gait: $\alpha = 0.6$, $\beta = -\frac{\pi}{4}$, $\gamma = 0, w = 2$. Propeller model 1: propulsion $F = 5N$ is always applied, propeller model 2: propulsion $F = 5N$ is periodically applied by the coordinated control method.

As can be seen from Fig. 7, when the input is forward gait, if the propeller always generates propulsion, the effect of the propulsion and forward gait is that the snake-like robot is still in forward motion, but can accelerate its motion

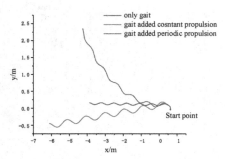
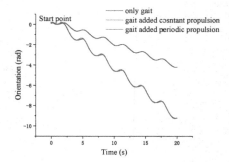

**Fig. 7.** The centroid trajectory of the snake-like robot when no propulsion applied and the propeller model applied

**Fig. 8.** The orientation of the snake-like robot when no propulsion applied and the propeller model applied

speed; if the propeller adopts the propulsion obtained by the coordinated control method, the change of the direction angle of the snake-like robot in a single motion cycle is $-0.1651$ rad (here, the counterclockwise rotation is positive), that is, when the snake-like robot applied by the above propulsion, turning can be achieved in the forward motion gait.

## 4.2 Coordination Driving Between Turning Gait and Propulsion

In order to quantitatively compare the maneuverability of the snake-like robot under different driving modes, the turning efficiency evaluation index is defined here:

$$\eta_T = \frac{\theta}{T} \tag{28}$$

where $\theta$ represents the change in orientation angle during a single motion cycle, $T$ represents the ratio of the time that thrust F acts in a single cycle to the total cycle time.

**Different Driving Propulsion on the Same Turning Gait.** We choose sinusoidal forward gait: $\alpha = 0.6$, $\beta = -\frac{\pi}{4}$, $\gamma = 0.1$, $w = 2$. Propeller model 1: propulsion $F = 5N$ is always applied, propeller model 2: propulsion $F = 5N$ is periodically applied by the coordinated control method.

It can be seen from Fig. 8 that under the same turning gait, the propulsion can greatly improve the turning orientation of the snake-like robot; although the time for periodically applying propulsion is shorter than the time for constantly applying propulsion, the orientation angle changes almost. In order to better explain the performance of the turning, taking working time of the propeller into account, use the indicator of turning efficiency to describe the effect of constantly applying propulsion and the periodically applying propulsion on turning performance.

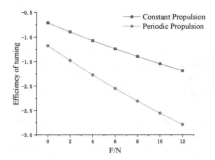

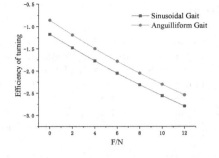

**Fig. 9.** The change in turning efficiency of the snake-like robot when the propulsion applied constantly and the propulsion applied periodically

**Fig. 10.** The relationship between propulsion and the turning efficiency of sinusoidal gait and anguilliform gait in the same way of driving propulsion

As can be seen from Fig. 9, supposing that turning gait is the same and the propulsion are equal, the turning efficiency generated by the propulsion applied periodically is higher than the turning efficiency generated by the propulsion applied constantly.

**Different Turning Gait on the Same Driving Propulsion.** We choose sinusoidal forward gait: $\alpha = 0.6$, $\beta = -\frac{\pi}{4}$, $\gamma = 0.1$, $w = 2$, anguilliform turning gait: $\alpha = 0.6, \beta = -\frac{\pi}{4}, \gamma = 0.1, w = 2$. The propulsion of the propeller is obtained by above coordinated control method.

As can be seen from Fig. 10, when the propulsion is both applied by the coordinated control method and is equal, the turning efficiency produced in sinusoidal turning gait is higher than anguilliform turning gait's. It's accidental that the efficiency curves are parallel in the two gaits.

## 5   Conclusion

Based on recursive Newton-Euler method, a model of the underwater snake-like robot with a propeller is established in this paper. Then a way of generating propulsion by the propeller is proposed to match better turning gait. Based on above work, some numerical simulations are conducted. It is showed that coordinating driving can not only match forward gait to accomplish the corresponding movement, but also promote snake-like robots in turning gait to finish turning process.

**Acknowledgement.** This work was supported in part by the National Natural Science Foundation of China under Grant 61603200.

# References

1. Ouyang, W., Liang, W., Li, C., et al.: Steering motion control of a snake robot via a biomimetic approach. Front. Inf. Technol. Electron. Eng. **20**, 32–44 (2019)
2. Takaoka, S., Yamada, H., Hirose, S.: Snake-like active wheel robot ACM-R4.1 with joint torque sensor and limiter. In: International Conference on Intelligent Robots and Systems (2011)
3. Cheng, Y., Chang-geng, S.: Kinematic analysis and simulation of the one-link and fin-driven robot fish. J. Ocean Technol. (2018)
4. Kelasidi, E., Pettersen, K.Y., Gravdahl, J.T.: Modeling of underwater snake robots. In: 2014 IEEE International Conference on Robotics and Automation (2014)
5. Anfan, Z., Bin, L., Minghui, W.: Modeling and simulation of eel robots in nonlinertial frame. Mech. Sci. Technol. Aerosp. Eng. (2019)
6. Khalil, W., Gallot, G., Boyer, F., et al.: Dynamic modeling and simulation of a 3-D serial eel-like robot. IEEE Trans. Syst. Man Cybern. Part C (Appl. Rev.) **37**, 1259–1268 (2007)
7. Khalil, W., Gallot, G., Ibrahim, O.: Dynamic modeling of a 3-D serial eel-like robot. In: IEEE International Conference on Robotics and Automation (2006)
8. Pettersen, K.Y., Gravdahl, J.T.A.: Control oriented model of underwater snake robots. In: 2014 IEEE International Conference on Robotics and Biomimetics (2014)
9. Kohl, A.M., Pettersen, K.Y., Kelasidi, E., Gravdahl, J.T.: Analysis of underwater snake robot locomotion based on a control-oriented model. In: 2015 IEEE International Conference on Robotics and Biomimetics (2015)
10. Xian, G., Shugen, M., Bin, L.: Modeling and optimal torque control of a snake-like robot based on the fiber bundle theory. Sci. China Inf. Sci. **58**, 1–13 (2015)
11. Tytell, E.D., Lauder, G.V.: The hydrodynamics of eel swimming. J. Exp. Biol. **207**, 1825–1841 (2004)

# A Review of Biomimetic Artificial Lateral Line Detection Technology for Unmanned Underwater Vehicles

Qiao Hu [1,2,3(✉)], Chang Wei[1], Yu Liu[1], and Zhenyi Zhao[1]

[1] School of Mechanical Engineering,
Xi'an Jiaotong University, Xi'an 710049, China
hqxjtu@mail.xjtu.edu.cn
[2] State Key Laboratory of Manufacturing Systems Engineering,
Xi'an Jiaotong University, Xi'an 710049, China
[3] Shaanxi Key Laboratory of Intelligent Robots, Xi'an Jiaotong University,
Xi'an 710049, China

**Abstract.** Due to the disturbance of complex underwater environment in the existing acoustic and optical detection systems, it is difficult for the acoustic or optical detection system to obtain accurate near-field sensing information for unmanned underwater vehicles (UUVS). This paper discusses the characteristics and difficulties of the detection technology for UUVS, and reviews the research advances with respect to the artificial lateral line (ALL) array and the signal processing. The key problems existing in the current researches are pointed out, including perception principle, layout and micro-process of ALL, and application of artificial intelligence algorithm and the approaches for solving these problems are discussed. After the above problems are solved, the ALL detection technology will have broad application prospects and application value in intelligent swarm detection for UUVS.

**Keywords:** Underwater swarm vehicles · Biomimetic detection · Artificial lateral line (ALL) · Signal processing

## 1 Introduction

Due to the significant changes in the international strategic situation and the surrounding security environment, the development of the oceans and the protection of maritime rights and interests will be one of the most important strategic goals of countries in recent years and for a long time to come. To build a maritime power, it is necessary to enhance the international competitiveness of marine equipment and related technologies. Future underwater combat will change the traditional submarine warfare mode, and make underwater operations shift to close monitoring, rapid response,

This work was supported by Key R&D Program Projects in Shaanxi Province (No. 2018ZDXM-GY-111); Equipment Pre-research Foundation Project (No. 61404160503); the Fundamental Research Funds for the Central Universities (No. xjjgf2018005); Major Program of National Natural Science Foundation of China (No. 61890961).

© Springer Nature Switzerland AG 2019
H. Yu et al. (Eds.): ICIRA 2019, LNAI 11741, pp. 501–516, 2019.
https://doi.org/10.1007/978-3-030-27532-7_45

precision strike and networked mode. Through the space-based platform, distributed underwater sensors and other early-warning detection methods, the clearer battlefield situation map and the precise target position are equipped with weapons for underwater attack using the unmanned underwater vehicle (UUVS) of high cost performance and concealment. The new generation of underwater swarm combat system is composed of a large number of multi-platform swarm UUVSs such as torpedoes and bionic robotic fishes, which is built on the single platform combat capability and supported by the synergistic interaction between platforms. And a new underwater attack and defense combat system is constructed with invulnerability, low cost, functional distribution and group intelligence. At present, research on underwater swarm combat equipment is receiving wide attention from various military powers in the world [1]. Among them, underwater detection technology is a prerequisite and technical guarantee for underwater swarm equipment research, which is also a technical difficulty and research hotspot.

Unmanned vehicles such as torpedoes and UUVSs typically use acoustic and optical systems as the information interaction approach for underwater information perception. For optical sensing, the pre-processing of acquired underwater image data is required before image processing to reduce the amount of noise, correct attenuation and geometric distortion, and the swarm UUVSs perception abilities are realized through the cumbersome observation and recognition techniques. However, the optical perception ability is limited in a turbid dark underwater environment [2]. As a window for information acquisition, the sonar system can perform effective underwater detection. When the spatial structure of the underwater swarm equipment working environment is complex, the sound waves will return to the transducer through multiple channels (multipath effect), where the multiple active sonar signals emitted by the swarm UUVSs will affect the other sonars, and the swarm UUVSs detection system are unable to accurately perceive the surrounding near-field environment [3]. And at the same time, the navigation interference and each environmental interference noise between the swarm equipment can also greatly reduce the sonar perception performance. In summary, the existing underwater optical and acoustic information perception technology is difficult to provide the high-sensitivity and high-precision near-field sensing information for the swarm UUVSs, which also restricts the application and development of underwater detection technology, and becomes a technical bottlenecks. Therefore, it is necessary to explore a new high-sensitivity and high-precision detection technology suitable for the swarm UUVSs.

The underwater fish group can achieve rapid and efficient movement, such as avoiding hunt and group migration, which mainly depends on the ability of the lateral line system to sense the changes of the surrounding environment. Reference to the lateral line perception of fish, the researchers designed an artificial lateral line (ALL) system, which provides a new idea for the detection method of the swarm UUVSs. This paper reviews and analyzes the research status and progress of ALL detection technology for the swarm UUVSs. The key problems with the ALL system design and related information processing methods are revealed, and the solutions of these key problems have been suggested.

# 2 Characteristics and Difficulties of Target Detection for the Swarm UUVSs

The core advantages of underwater swarm equipment are low-cost, large number of groups, and high group intelligence. The benefits can be maximized by using low-cost UUV swarms to combat high-cost ships. Compared with single platform, it has larger detection range and stronger survivability, so it has higher application value to use underwater swarms equipment for underwater detection and combat. UUVS detection technology is one of the most critical technologies of the swarm system. Because of the importance of data, there are many ways to detect air targets and obtain stable information. At present, the research on Unmanned Aerial Vehicle (UAV) swarm equipment is relatively early and mature at home and abroad. In contrast, due to the complexity of the underwater physics and working environment, the research on underwater swarm equipment has just started. The corresponding underwater detection problems also have their own characteristics and difficulties. They are shown as following.

(1) Due to the communication distance and formation requirements of underwater swarm equipment, the distance between individuals is relatively close, which is a near-field detection problem. The simultaneous movement and operation of multiple UUVSs in underwater swarm equipment lead to an extremely complex underwater detection problem. When multiple UUVS swarms work, the interference factors such as radiated noise and target intensity will greatly affect the sonar detection performance. They will also disturb the water and increase the turbidity of the water, thus affecting the optical detection performance. Traditional sonar and optical detection methods will fails in the UUVS swarm working state to accurately capture the surrounding environment and target information.

(2) The underwater acoustic detection system, which is often used in underwater swarm equipment, is vulnerable to human or environmental interference. The underwater swarm equipment detection system is also vulnerable to the suppression of underwater acoustic interference devices, such as underwater acoustic jammer, gas veil bubbler, underwater acoustic decoys, etc. It is also susceptible to multipath effects and acoustic propagation characteristics caused by interface reflection. These problems greatly increases the difficulty of underwater acoustic target detection.

(3) The underwater sonar detection and optical detection system used in underwater swarm equipment detection is the large size and high energy consumption. The array and matching network in sonar detection system, as well as the hardware system such as laser or imaging system in optical detection system, make it difficult to miniaturize the detection system. They take a lot of energy to work. Therefore, these underwater detection methods cannot be used in miniaturized swarm equipment such as bionic robotic fish.

In view of the characteristics of the above underwater swarm equipment and many difficulties in the detection, the existing underwater detection technology is difficult to meet the urgent demands for accurate acquisition of underwater swarm equipment information and environmental adaptability of underwater equipment.

# 3   Research Progress of ALL

Research on underwater swarm equipment started shortly. In recent years, researchers from the Massachusetts institute of technology made use of the mobile sensor network. The sensor network composed of multiple underwater robots equipped with different types of sensors to try to collaborate and conduct marine surveys in specific sea area [4, 5]. Princeton University research team attempted to establish an autonomous ocean sampling system to observe the ecological environment of Monterey Bay through observation and analysis of fish population behavior [6–8]. Researchers at the University of Porto, Portugal, constructed a marine data collection system to perform tasks such as marine ecological environment survey. The modularization system that was inexpensive and advanced consisted of multiple underwater vehicles [9]. The UK Nekton Research Institute developed an underwater multi-agent platform for multiple underwater applications. Their research was related to some key problems such as robot distributed search algorithm, formation control, and marine stereo survey [10, 11]. Aquabotix company of the United States tested a self-propelled underwater vehicle Swarm-Diver that was capable of mimicking population behavior in 2018. It was equipped with sensors for defense, research and surveillance, driven by propellers. The advanced sensors make it possible for underwater vehicles to realize autonomous navigation and swarm cooperative detection.

Comparatively speaking, the research on underwater cluster equipment started late in China. Based on the research of micro-miniature bionic robotic fish, the intelligent control laboratory of Peking University School of Engineering established a multi-bionic robotic fish collaboration system. The system was based on global vision, which achieved some representative cooperative tasks, such as multiple robotic fish cooperative transportation, cooperative blasting, group cruise and so on. The collaborative tasks solved the problem of collision avoidance between robotic fish and dynamic obstacles [12, 13]; Zou et al. [14] combined neural network and sliding mode control method to realize trajectory tracking of multiple bionic robotic fish. Shao et al. [15] used the fuzzy reinforcement learning method to realize the robot fish cooperative heading task under the counter environment. The Ocean Engineering Center of Harbin Engineering University focuses on the architecture problems, coordination problems of multi-underwater robot systems, and multi-platform data fusion problems in the aspects of ocean exploration. They also studied the coordinated autonomous operation for multi-intelligent underwater robot systems [16].

Aiming at the theory and technology of bionic detection represented by artificial lateral line (ALL), domestic and foreign scholars have carried out related research from bionic artificial lateral line array and signal processing. They also obtained certain research results.

## 3.1   Bionic ALL Array

Biological studies have found that fish use a large number of receptors distributed on the surface of the body for environmental detection. These receptors can help fish identify changes in water pressure around the water. They also can help fish to avoid obstacles, prey and track [17, 18]. Studies on fish lateral lines [19] have shown that the information obtained by the lateral line system plays an important guiding role in the behavior of fish populations. The receptors of fish are divided into two types: mechanoreceptors and electroreceptors. Among them, mechanoreceptors are divided into two types: ductal nerve mounds and epidermal nerve mounds, which are the main sensory organs of fish for underwater activities (see Fig. 1). Because of the mechanoreceptors in lateral system, fish can sense water pressure, water flow and other information through the lateral system to improve motion perception. When the fish and the surrounding water flow move with each other, the velocity and pressure of the water will cause the ciliary tilt of the fish's body surface, which causes the sensory nerve under the cilia to generate nerve signals. In this way, it is used for peer inter-action, preying and avoiding predators. These functions of lateral line organs, such as surface nerve mounds and ductal nerve hills, allow fish to navigate, locate and communicate in extreme environments [20, 21].

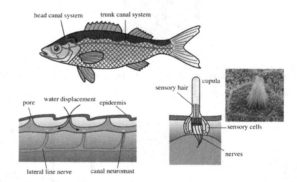

**Fig. 1.** Lateral line system of a fish [55].

At present, based on the theory of bionics, scholars have conducted many researches on the field of ALL. As shown in Fig. 2, Nelson et al. [22] designed a modular ALL system based on a pressure sensor array. Liu et al. [23] designed an ALL array of micro-pressure sensors to achieve turbulence velocity estimation and obstacle avoidance. In mathematical model research, the biomechanical model of the duct nerve hill consists of a frictionless plate and a rigid hemisphere. The surface neural hill model is composed of multiple connected flexible beams, which can reveal the perception of the mound and its mechanism of interaction with fluids [24]. In the actual biomimetic device, one approach is to use the pressure sensors to directly build an array, and the other is based on a plastic deformation magnetic assembly technology and a micro-electro-mechanical system (MEMS) manufacturing technology to make a miniature sense array, as shown in Fig. 3. According to the sensing principle of the sensors, they can be divided into piezoresistive ALL, capacitive ALL, piezoelectric ALL, optical ALL and hot wire ALL (see Fig. 4).

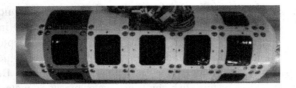

**Fig. 2.** Modular lateral line system

**Fig. 3.** Pressure sensors array of micro-electro-mechanical system (MEMS)

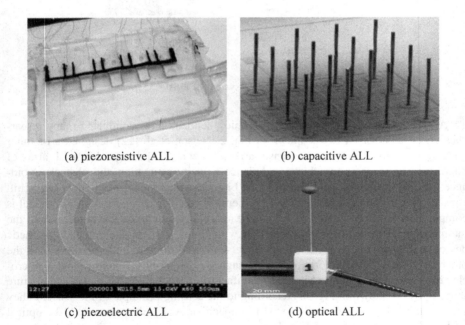

(a) piezoresistive ALL          (b) capacitive ALL

(c) piezoelectric ALL          (d) optical ALL

**Fig. 4.** Different ALL array

Piezoresistive ALL: Piezoresistive ALL is the most widely studied category. Usually, the material is stretched or compressed under external mechanical action, and its own resistance changes. The external deformation or pressure can be measured by detecting the resistance. It is usually used to measure small motion. But the DC output of Piezoresistive ALL is very poor and an external power supply is required. According to the specific structure, piezoresistive ALL can also be subdivided into two categories: one is the vertical hair cell structure simulating the lateral line. The vertical structure is fabricated by plastic deformation magnetic assembly (PDMA) technology and MEMS technology. It mainly simulates the surface neural crest to detect the flow velocity. In the typical study, most of the silicon matrix materials are used, and a small amount of nickel-chromium alloy is used. Fan et al. [25] produced the first piezoresistive ALL, fabricated by PDMA technology. The unit's planar size is 100 μm × 180 μm and the sensitivity to speed is 0.1 m/s. Yang et al. [26] used PDMA technology to fabricate piezoresistive ALL. The unit has a planar size of 100 μm × 40 μm and sensitivity of 0.1 mm/s. McConney et al. [27] used the photo-polymerization process to fabricate piezoresistive ALL. The unit has a planar size of 550 μm × 100 μm and sensitivity of 75 μm/s. The other category is to directly measure the pressure using a flat-structured sensor, which primarily simulates the direct sensing of pressure in the tube's neural mound. The unit of pressure array manufactured by Izadi et al. [28] has a perceptual sensitivity of 1 μV/Pa (10 V) and a pressure resolution of 1 Pa. The pressure sensing unit made by Kottapalli et al. [29] has a pressure perceptual sensitivity of 14.3 μV/Pa, a velocity perceptual sensitivity of 90.5 mV/ms$^{-1}$, and a resolution of fluid velocity of 25 mm/s. The pressure resolution of the flexible perception unit made by Yaul et al. [30] is 1.5 Pa.

Piezoelectric ALL: Piezo ALL is based on the principle that piezoelectric materials can directly generate electrical response under pressure to detect flow field information. The main researches are as follows: Asadnia et al. [31] fabricated a pressure sensing array based on Pb(Zr0.52Ti0.48)O$_3$ film with a perceived resolution of 3 mm/s. Asadnia et al. [32] produced a cilia-type piezoelectric ALL based on Si60 with a sensitivity of 22 mV/ms$^{-1}$.

Capacitive ALL: Capacitive ALL is based on external mechanics to change the relative position of the capacitor plates, thereby changing the size of the capacitors. It can measure the mechanical effects by detecting changes in capacitance. The measurement method has the characteristics of high precision and low power consumption. Izadi et al. [33] developed capacitive ALL based on SU-8 technology. The thickness of the thin plate is 500–800 nm and the capacitor adopts parallel plate capacitor structure. Krijnen et al. [34] fabricated a capacitive ciliary array made of sacrificial polysilicon technology and SU-8 polymer technology with a cilia length of 1 mm. A similar structure was developed by Stocking et al. [35]. Numerical simulations show that the capacitance change is 1 pF when the velocity of the structure changes from 0 to 1.0 m/s. A similar structure was also developed by Baar et al. [36].

Optical ALL: The optical method to measure displacement and mechanical quantities is also a common approach and can therefore be used to fabricate ALL. Literature [37] proposed two kinds of optical ALL. Although the optical measurement has the advantage of high precision, the ALL structure based on the method is complex to be miniaturized and integrated, and only stays in the design stage [38].

Hot wire ALL: The principle is that the resistance and temperature of the metal have a linear relationship when the fluid flows through the heated metal to cool down. Therefore, the resistance of the metal is proportional to the flow velocity, and the temperature is measured to obtain the flow velocity. Dagamseh et al. [39] developed a surface microstructure with a feature size ranging from 50 μm to 2 mm. Chen et al. [40] developed a similar hotline ALL to simulate a ductal nerve hill. Liu et al. [41] reported a thermal film ALL sensing array.

From the view of ALL sensing technology, the current perceptual performance is far from the performance of biological lateral organs. In recent years, a new type of flexible mechanical sensing material, ionic polymer, has been discovered with the development of materials technology. It can sense pressure [42] and tangential force [43]. It is an important opportunity for the ALL organ. For example, it is found that the pressure difference of bending electrical response is caused by the normal stress gradient of bending deformation [42]. Tan et al. [44] developed a new ALL (see Fig. 5) based on ionic polymer-metal composites (IPMC). The ALL positioning accuracy is a body length of the target position, and it has been confirmed that the ionic polymer can be applied to ALL. Liu et al. have conducted a detailed and profound comparative study on the different principles, advantages and disadvantages, and applicable situations of a variety of ALL [21].

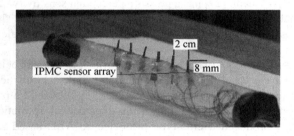

**Fig. 5.** Ionic polymer-metal composites (IPMC) sensor array for artificial lateral line (ALL)

In fact, the electrical response of the ionic polymer is very similar to the bioelectrical formation mechanism of the skin. When an external force is sensed, the ion channel on the tactile receptor is opened. The ions inside and outside the cell membrane are redistributed, resulting a haptic voltage in an average of 90–130 mV [45]. Obviously, both of these electrical responses are based on ion-based migration redistribution. The signals array are detected by the artificial lateral line sensor array composed of pressure/velocity sensor. The signals are processed to obtain the flow field information around the underwater vehicle, which is especially suitable for the dark and complex sea bottom topography. Due to the differences in the track characteristics aroused by the different underwater vehicles during the navigation, ALL is expected to achieve collaborative communication and identification between underwater vehicles indirectly through flow field perception [46].

## 3.2   Signal Processing

In the aspect of intellisense and array signal processing of underwater targets, early echo direction estimation methods include maximum likelihood spectrum estimation method based on statistical analysis, maximum entropy spectrum estimation method, auto regression moving average (ARMA), spectral analysis methods [47], multiple signal classification (MUSIC) algorithm [48], and coherent array signal processing [49, 50], etc. However, the computational complexity of these methods is generally high, and they cannot completely match the requirements in practical applications.

For the ALL system, the signal sensed by the ALL array is transformed into the flow field and the target information, which has certain similarities with the working principle of the sonar array. The difference is that the signal sensed by the ALL array is the mechanical fluctuation signal. The technology of the sonar array sensing information processing can be applied to ALL sensing information processing. Among them, the array beamforming algorithm is widely used and has a certain universality to different sensor arrays. The team of Professor Tan of Michigan State University [51] uses a three-layer neural network and ALL to locate underwater vibration sources. Wu et al. [52] of Shanghai Jiaotong University used linear discriminant analysis (LDA) and support vector machine (SVM) to identify the flow pattern of water flow. The test results are shown in Table 1. In 2017, Boulogne et al. [53] of the University of Groningen used multi-layer perceptrons and ALL systems to detect underwater targets.

**Table 1.** Measurement of water flow based on artificial lateral line

| Flow direction | Angle/(°) | | | | | |
|---|---|---|---|---|---|---|
| | 135 | 270 | 0 | 45 | 90 | 180 |
| Actual flow velocity/m·s$^{-1}$ | 1.8 | 1.6 | 1.8 | 1.0 | 1.6 | 2.5 |
| Test result/m·s$^{-1}$ | 1.818 | 1.257 | 1.181 | 0.888 | 1.323 | 2.630 |

In the study of ALL array data processing, most scholars handle the information of each channel obtained by the lateral line array. They do not make full use of the body lateral line organs to obtain comprehensive information like fish. In recent years, some scholars have analyzed the correlation between lateral line array signals and flow field mechanical models to achieve the positioning and identification of moving targets, such as Dagamseh et al. [54, 55] of Twente University. They used the ALL system and beamforming techniques for dipole sources to explore near-field imaging. However, these studies only consider typical fluid models and linear array conditions. It is difficult to apply the technology to complex and strong interference working environments such as underwater multi-motion target coupling and underwater space stereoscopic bionic lateral line arrays.

The identification of underwater targets has always been one of the problems that need to be overcome in the field of underwater detection. In recent years, in view of the unprecedented application prospects of deep learning in many fields, many scholars have introduced it into underwater target recognition research. Kamal et al. [56] used deep belief networks (DBN) to identify and classify hydroacoustic data of underwater targets acquired by sonar, achieving 90.23% accuracy on a test set of 40 classes of 1000 instances. Cao et al. [57] of Northwestern Polytechnical University used a sparse autoencoder (SAE) to identify and classify underwater target spectrum information. After whitening preprocessing, they compared it with SVM and probabilistic neural network (PNN). The results show that deep learning has higher recognition classification accuracy. In 2017, Chen et al. [58] of the National Key Laboratory of Applied Acoustics Technology used sonar to obtain underwater target acoustic information. At the same time, they used DBN and stacked denoising auto encoder (SDAE) for identification and classification. Traditional machine learning SVM, PNN, and general regression neural network (GRNN) methods are compared. The results show that deep learning has better performance. In 2017, Zhu et al. [59] of Cornell University in the United States used convolutional neural networks (CNN) to identify and classify sonar images with an accuracy of 95.88%. In 2018, Liu et al. [60] of Ocean University of China used the artificial neural network (AN) based on ALL systems to identify the frequency and amplitude of the underwater vibration source, and the accuracy rate reached 93%. Hu et al. of Xi'an Jiaotong University applied the support vector machines (SVMs) to the ALL detection. The testing results show that the proposed method has better detection performance than the traditional method, such as FFT and neural network. Their experiments provide a new way for the collaboration robotic fish [61] (see Fig. 6). At present, there are few studies on combining artificial intelligence algorithms into ALL array signal processing. The methods used are limited to traditional shallow structures such as perceptrons and SVMs. Moreover, most of the underwater target recognition technologies focus on the target discovery and location, without further identification of the detected target information and features.

**Fig. 6.** The experiment equipment and environment

### 3.3   Research Progress Analysis

Combined with the above research progress at home and abroad, it can be seen that some scientific research institutes and universities have been committed to the research of new bionic detection methods and underwater target sensing methods for many years. Some of the research institutes have achieved certain research results in the mechanism research and manufacturing process of artificial lateral lines through long-term research accumulation and repeated experiments. Compared with other detection methods, ALL system mainly play a role in the accurate detection in the close range. When they are applied to the equipment of underwater swarms, they have little interference with each other, which is more suitable for the near-field detection of underwater swarms. Combined with the research on ionic polymer bionic lateral line, more and more ALL systems can be developed.

In recent years, more researchers have realized that artificial intelligence methods could bring new opportunities and challenges to underwater target perception with different from traditional underwater detection methods. Therefore, it opens up a new situation in the research of bionic detection technology for underwater swarm equipment from the aspects of basic theory research and new methods.

Nevertheless, there are still the following key problems to be solved in the current research.

# 4   Key Issues and Solutions

## 4.1   Key Issues

Through a comprehensive analysis of existing literature and research progress at home and abroad, it is found that the main direction of ALL's current research is to simulate lateral line sensing neural colliculus of fish to detect the velocity and pressure. The main problems are as follows:

(1) ALL sensing principle: From the comparative study of existing sensor components, it can be found that the most widely studied is the piezoresistive ALL, but the piezoresistive ALL is sensitive to temperature and requires very precise temperature compensation measures. Although the capacitive ALL has higher precision and lower power consumption, the water has an impact on the insulation performance of electrodes.

(2) The layout of ALL: The number of ALL units in most existing studies is no more than 12, which is very small compared with the lateral line organs of fish. So it is difficult to achieve the fish's perception performance. Most studies are either simulating surface nerve hills or simulating ductal nerve hills. Few studies have been able to simulate the lateral line organs of fish comprehensively, so usually it cannot fully perceive the fluid dynamics characteristics. In addition, due to the small number of sensor units, there is little in-depth study of the layout of sensor units.

(3) Micro-Process of ALL: From the research of piezoresistive ALL, most of them use PDMA and MEMS processes to process sensing arrays. The research on the adaptability of the sensing structure of this process to the environment is not enough. The comprehensive research on the micromachining process and the material sensing principle is lacking.

(4) There are few studies on the combination of artificial intelligence algorithms into ALL array signal processing. The methods adopted are only limited to the traditional perceptron, such as SVM and other shallow structures. Moreover, most of

the underwater target identification technologies are still in the stage of target discovery and location, without further identification of the detected target information.

## 4.2  Solutions

In view of the characteristics and difficulties of the bionic detection technology and the key problems existing in the current research, the author believes that some research of underwater ALL bionic detection should be carried out in the following aspects to make up for the deficiency of existing theory and technology. As is shown in Fig. 7. They provide a reliable theoretical basis and effective technical means for bionic detection of underwater swarm equipment.

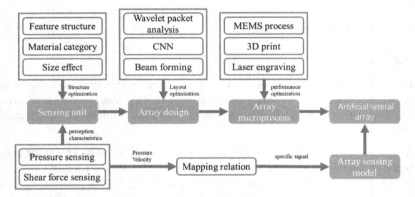

**Fig. 7.** Artificial lateral line detection research technology route

(1) The new intelligent material represented by ionic polymer has the characteristics of simultaneous perception of pressure and tangential forces, matching well with underwater environment and advanced processing technology. Therefore, it is the main goal to imitate the channel colliculus (fluid pressure) and the surface colliculus (fluid velocity). The influence rules of structural characteristics and size effect on sensor perception performance should be studied in depth to obtain the design criteria of high-performance ALL perception units. The mapping relationship should be established between fluid field information and sensing units. At the same time, the perceptual characteristics of the sensing unit to the distance, frequency and intensity of the vibration source should be studied. The mapping relationship between the structural unit and the characteristics of the vibration source should be established.

(2) The studies should focus on the comprehensive perception for the ALL array. Only by combining the velocity and pressure distribution of the flow field, can the system fully perceive the characteristics of fluid dynamics. On the basis of the research on optimizing the single pressure/flow velocity sensing unit, several

bionic layouts of surface array and pipeline array ALL should be optimized and designed. In order to improve the perception sensitivity and resolution, it is an effective approach to miniaturize and array real fish lateral line organs. At the same time, the perception characteristics of ALL array layout parameters on target distance, size and orientation should be studied. The underwater target perception model of ALL need to be established.

(3) Based on the perception principle of materials, the adaptability of the sensing structure to the environment should be studied in depth. The processing properties of materials and specific micro-processing technology should be further improved.

(4) New theories and methods for further identification of detected target information should be studied in depth. Simulating the central nervous system of fish, the deep learning method that proves to have better performance than traditional or shallow learning method should be widely used for underwater target perception in the bionic lateral line system. The deep learning method is also needed to intelligently identify the parameters of underwater multi-moving target, such as category, speed, position, distance and size, etc.

## 5  Summary

The characteristics and difficulties of bionic detection in underwater swarm equipment are describes in this paper. The research status of domestic and overseas are analyzed. The key problems in current research are revealed.

At the same time, the way to solve the problem is given (Fig. 7). To improve existing bionic detection technology for underwater swarm equipment, it is necessary to study new theory and new methods in the perception of the ALL sensor unit, the sensing characteristics of the ALL array, and the fabrication process of the ALL array.

## References

1. Pham, L.V., Dickerson, B., Sanders, J., et al.: UAV swarm attack: protection system alternatives for destroyers. Systems Engineering Project Report. Naval Postgraduate School, California (2012)
2. Tyo, J.S.: Hyperspectral measurement of the scattering of polarized light by skin. In: Proceedings of SPIE, vol. 8160, no. 22, p. 31 (2011)
3. Sun, R.-G., Shu, X.-L., Qu, D.-W.: Multipath effect of sonar pulse waveforms in shallow water. J. Ordnance Equipment Eng. 34(12), 56–59 (2013)
4. Zhang, Y., Streitlien, K., Bellingham, J.G., et al.: Acoustic doppler velocimeter flow measurement from an autonomous underwater vehicle with applications to deep ocean convection. J. Atmos. Oceanic Technol. 18(12), 2038–2051 (2000)
5. Willcox, J.S., Bellingham, J.G., Zhang, Y., et al.: Performance metrics for oceanographic surveys with autonomous underwater vehicles. IEEE J. Oceanic Eng. 26(4), 711–725 (2001)
6. Liu, Y., Passino, K.M.: Stability analysis of swarms in a noisy environment. In: 42nd IEEE International Conference on Decision and Control. IEEE, Maui (2003)

7. Leonard, N.E., Fiorelli, E.: Virtual leaders, artificial potentials and coordinated control of groups. In: Proceedings of the 40th IEEE Conference on Decision and Control. IEEE, Orlando (2001)
8. Gallowaykevin, C., Beckerkaitlyn, P., Phillips, B., et al.: Soft robotic grippers for biological sampling on deep reefs. Soft Robot. **3**(1), 23–33 (2016)
9. Yoon, S., Qiao, C.: Cooperative search and survey using autonomous underwater vehicles (AUVs). IEEE Trans. Parallel Distrib. Syst. **22**(3), 364–379 (2011)
10. Byrne, R.H., Savage, E.L.: Algorithms and analysis for underwater vehicle plume tracing. Sandia National Laboratories, United States (2003)
11. Schulz, B., Hobson, B., Kemp, M., et al.: Field results of multi-UUVS missions using ranger micro-UUVSs. In: Oceans 2003. IEEE, San Diego, pp. 956–961 (2003)
12. Chen, J., Sun, D., Yang, J., et al.: Leader-follower formation control of multiple non-holonomic mobile robots in-corporating a receding-horizon scheme. Int. J. Robot. Res. **29** (6), 727–747 (2010)
13. Zhao, W., Hu, Y., Wang, L.: Construction and central pattern generator-based control of a flipper-actuated turtle-like underwater robot. Adv. Robot. **23**(1–2), 19–43 (2009)
14. Zou, K., Wang, C., Xie, G., et al.: Cooperative control for trajectory tracking of robotic fish. In: 2009 American Control Conference, pp. 5504–5509. IEEE, St. Louis (2009)
15. Shao, J., Yu, J., Wang, L.: Formation control of multiple biomimetic robotic fish. In: 2006 IEEE/RSJ International Conference on Intelligent Robots and Systems, pp. 2503–2508. IEEE, Beijing (2007)
16. Qiao, G., Gan, S., Liu, S., et al.: Digital self-interference cancellation for asynchronous in-band full-duplex underwater acoustic communication. Sensors **18**(6), 1700 (2018)
17. Voronina, E.P., Hughes, D.R.: Lateral line scale types and review of their taxonomic distribution. Acta Zoologica **99**(1), 65–86 (2017)
18. Bleckmann, H., Zelick, R.: Lateral line system of fish. Integr. Zool. **25**(1), 411–453 (2006)
19. Mekdara, P.J., Schwalbe, M., Coughlin, L.L., et al.: The effects of lateral line ablation and regeneration in schooling giant danios. J. Exp. Biol. **221**(Pt 8), jeb.175166 (2018)
20. Rizzi, F., Qualtieri, A., Dattoma, T., et al.: Biomimetics of underwater hair cell sensing. Microelectron. Eng. **132**, 90–97 (2015)
21. Liu, G., Wang, A., Wang, X., et al.: A review of artificial lateral line in sensor fabrication and bionic applications for robotic fish. Appl. Bionics Biomech. **2016**(5), 1–15 (2016)
22. Nelson, K., Mohseni, K.: Design of a 3-D printed, modular lateral line sensory system for hydrodynamic force estimation. Mar. Technol. Soc. J. **51**(5), 103–115 (2017)
23. Liu, G., Wang, M., Wang, A., et al.: Research on flow field perception based on artificial lateral line sensor system. Sensors **18**(3), 838 (2018)
24. Tan, S.: Underwater artificial lateral line flow sensors. Microsyst. Technol. **20**(12), 2123–2136 (2014)
25. Fan, Z., Chen, J., Zou, J., et al.: Design and fabrication of artificial lateral line flow sensors. J. Micromech. Microeng. **12**(5), 655 (2002)
26. Yang, Y., Nguyen, N., Chen, N., et al.: Artificial lateral line with biomimetic neuromasts to emulate fish sensing. Bioinspiration Biomimetics **5**(1), 16001 (2010)
27. Mcconney, M.E., Chen, N., Lu, D., et al.: Biologically inspired design of hydrogel-capped hair sensors for enhanced underwater flow detection. Soft Matter **5**(2), 292–295 (2009)
28. Izadi, N., Krijnen, G.J.M.: Design and fabrication process for artificial lateral line sensors. In: Frontiers in Sensing, pp. 405–421. Springer, Vienna (2012). https://doi.org/10.1007/978-3-211-99749-9_28
29. Kottapalli, A.G.P., Asadnia, M., Miao, J.M., et al.: A flexible liquid crystal polymer MEMS pressure sensor array for fish-like underwater sensing. Smart Mater. Struct. **21**(11), 115030 (2012)

30. Yaul, F.M., Bulovic, V., Lang, J.H.: A flexible underwater pressure sensor array using a conductive elastomer strain gauge. J. Microelectromech. Syst. 21(4), 897–907 (2012)
31. Asadnia, M., Kottapalli, A.G.P., Shen, Z., et al.: Flexible and surface-mountable piezoelectric sensor arrays for underwater sensing in marine vehicles. IEEE Sens. J. 13 (10), 3918–3925 (2013)
32. Asadnia, M., Kottapalli, A.G., Miao, J., et al.: Artificial fish skin of self-powered micro-electromechanical systems hair cells for sensing hydrodynamic flow phenomena. J. R. Soc. Interface 12(111), 20150322 (2015)
33. Izadi, N., De Boer, M.J., Berenschot, J.W., et al.: Fabrication of superficial neuromast inspired capacitive flow sensors. J. Micromech. Microeng. 20(8), 085041 (2010)
34. Krijnen, G., Lammerink, T., Wiegerink, R., et al.: Cricket in-spired flow-sensor arrays. In: Sensors 2007, pp. 539–546. IEEE, Atlanta (2007)
35. Stocking, J.B., Eberhardt, W.C., Shakhsheer, Y.A., et al.: A capacitance-based whisker-like artificial sensor for fluid motion sensing. In: Sensors 2010, pp. 2224–2229. IEEE, Kona (2010)
36. Baar, J.J.V., Dijkstra, M., Wiegerink, R.J., et al.: Fabrication of arrays of artificial hairs for complex flow pattern recognition. In: Sensors 2003, pp. 332–336. IEEE, Toronto (2004)
37. Klein, A., Bleckmann, H.: Determination of object position, vortex shedding frequency and flow velocity using artificial lateral line canals. Beilstein J. Nanotechnol. 2(1), 276–283 (2011)
38. Herzog, H., Steltenkamp, S., Klein, A., et al.: Micro-machined flow sensors mimicking lateral line canal neuro-masts. Micromachines 6, 1189–1212 (2015)
39. Dagamseh, A.M.K., Lammerink, T.S.J., Kolster, M.L., et al.: Dipole-source localization using biomimetic flow - sensor arrays positioned as lateral-line system. Sens. Actuators, A 162(2), 355–360 (2010)
40. Chen, J., Engel, J., Chen, N., et al.: Artificial lateral line and hydrodynamic object tracking. In: IEEE International Conference on MICRO Electro Mechanical Systems MEMS 2006, pp. 694–697. IEEE, Istanbul (2006)
41. Liu, P., Zhu, R., Que, R.: A flexible flow sensor system and its characteristics for fluid mechanics measurements. Sensors 9(12), 9533–9543 (2009)
42. Zhu, Z., Horiuchi, T., Kruusamäe, K., et al.: Influence of ambient humidity on the voltage response of ionic polymer-metal composite sensor. J. Phys. Chem. B 120(12), 3215–3225 (2016)
43. Kocer, B., Zangrilli, U., Akle, B., et al.: Experimental and theoretical investigation of ionic polymer transducers in shear sensing. J. Intell. Mater. Syst. Struct. 14, 1–13 (2014)
44. Ahrari, A., Lei, H., Deb, K., et al.: Robust Design Optimization of Artificial Lateral Line System [EB/OL]. http://pdfs.semanticscholar.org/85ab/9776ef0d412bed74811c9c9528d77 1561743.pdf. Accessed 06 May 2018
45. Zhong, K.: Design and environmental perception of artificial lateral line system for robotic fish. East China Jiaotong university, Nanchang (2014)
46. Zheng, X., Wang, C., Fan, R., et al.: Artificial lateral line based local sensing between two adjacent robotic fish. Bioinspiration Biomimetics 13(1), 016002 (2017)
47. Hu, B., Hua, C., Chen, C., et al.: MUBFP: multi-user beam-forming and partitioning for sum capacity maximization in MIMO systems. IEEE Veh. Technol. Soc. 66(1), 233–245 (2016)
48. Lin, X., Tao, M., Xu, Y., et al.: Outage probability and finite-SNR diversity-multiplexing tradeoff for two-way relay fading channels. IEEE Trans. Veh. Technol. 62(7), 3123–3136 (2013)
49. Vaidyanathan, P.P., Pal, P.: Sparse sensing with co-prime samplers and arrays. IEEE Trans. Sig. Process. 59(2), 573–586 (2011)

50. Vaidyanathan, P.P.: Theory of sparse coprime sensing in multiple dimensions. IEEE Trans. Sig. Process. **59**(8), 3592–3608 (2011)
51. Abdulsadda, A.T., Tan, X.B.: Underwater source localization using an IPMC-based artificial lateral line. In: IEEE International Conference on Robotics and Automation, pp. 2719–2724. IEEE, Shanghai (2011)
52. Wu, N.L., Wu, C., Tong, G.E., et al.: Flow recognition of underwater vehicle based on the perception mechanism of lateral line. J. Mech. Eng. **52**(13), 54–59 (2016)
53. Boulogne, L.H., Wolf, B.J., Wiering, M.A., et al.: Performance of neural networks for localizing moving objects with an artificial lateral line. Bioinspiration Biomimetics **12**(5), 056009 (2017)
54. Dagamseh, A., Wiegerink, R., Lammerink, T., et al.: Artificial lateral-line system for imaging dipole sources using beamforming techniques. Procedia Eng. **25**(35), 779–782 (2011)
55. Dagamseh, A., Wiegerink, R., Lammerink, T., et al.: Imaging dipole flow sources using an artificial lateral-line system made of biomimetic hair flow sensors. J. R. Soc. Interface **10** (83), 20130162 (2013)
56. Kamal, S., Mohammed, S.K., Pillai, P.R.S., et al.: Deep learning architectures for underwater target recognition. In: 2013 Ocean Electronics, pp. 48–54. IEEE, Kochi (2013)
57. Cao, X., Zhang, X., Yu, Y., et al.: Deep learning-based recognition of underwater target. In: 2016 IEEE International Conference on Digital Signal Processing, pp. 89–93. IEEE, Beijing (2016)
58. Chen, Y., Xu, X.: The research of underwater target recognition method based on deep learning. In: IEEE International Conference on Signal Processing, Communications and Computing, pp. 1–5. IEEE, Xiamen (2017)
59. Zhu, P., Isaacs, J., Fu, B., et al.: Deep learning feature extraction for target recognition and classification in underwater sonar images. In: IEEE Conference on Decision and Control, pp. 2724–2731. IEEE, Melbourne, Australia (2017)
60. Liu, G., Gao, S., Sarkodie, G., et al.: A novel biomimetic sensor system for vibration source perception of autonomous underwater vehicles based on artificial lateral lines. Measur. Sci. Technol. **29**, 125102 (2018)
61. Hu, Q., Liu, Y., Zhao, Z.Y.: Intelligent detection for artificial lateral line of bio-inspired robotic fish using EMD and SVMs. In: 2018 IEEE International Conference on Robotics and Biomimetics (ROBIO), Kuala Lumpur, Malaysia, pp. 106–111 (2018)

# Soft Locomotion Robot

# Design and Experimental Study of a New Flexible Driven Parallel Soft Massage Robot

Yanzhi Zhao[1]($\boxtimes$), Hang Wei[1], Pengbo Li[1], Guoqing Li[1], Lizhe Qi[2], and Hongnian Yu[3]

[1] College of Mechanical Engineering,
Yanshan University, Qinhuangdao 066000, China
yzzhao@ysu.edu.cn
[2] Academy for Engineering and Technology,
Fudan University, Shanghai 200000, China
[3] Fuaculty of Science and Technology, Bournemouth University, Poole, UK

**Abstract.** In recent years, the demand for massage robots has increased dramatically in the field of Medical care. Traditional massage robots are mostly rigid robots. Compared with rigid robots, soft robots are more suitable for massage because of their softness and safety. However, the existing soft robots can not provide much output force for massage. In this paper, a flexible-driven multi-parallel soft massage robot with large output force is designed, which can realize two massage techniques, palm-pressing and palm-kneading. The robot is composed of three groups of flexible driving elements in parallel. It has strong adaptability and flexibility in the environment. It can solve the problems of difficult motion control and low output force of traditional soft robots. The kinematics and mechanics of the robot are modeled and analyzed, and the finite element simulation analysis is carried out by using ABAQUS software. The prototype is made and the experimental test platform is set up for experimental verification.

**Keywords:** Flexible drive · Soft · Massage robot · Finite element simulation

## 1 Introduction

Massage robot is an important field of medical care robots, and many countries have carried out relevant research in this field. Toyohashi University in Japan successfully developed a humanoid multi-finger massage robot [1] in 2006. This massage robot has four massage fingers and can learn sensors at the end of its fingers. In 2007, Waseda University and Asahi University in Japan cooperated to develop a facial massage robot [2], which has the same 6-DOF manipulator on both sides. At present, massage robots are generally rigid robots composed of rigid components, but the contact between rigid components and human body is easy to cause harm to human body, which has a certain danger. As a result, more and more scholars pay attention to flexible actuators in recent years. Among all kinds of flexible actuators, pneumatic drive is particularly prominent. More and more scholars at home and abroad have studied it. Zhigang Zhao team of Lanzhou Jiaotong University proposed a three-degree-of-freedom flexible pneumatic

© Springer Nature Switzerland AG 2019
H. Yu et al. (Eds.): ICIRA 2019, LNAI 11741, pp. 519–530, 2019.
https://doi.org/10.1007/978-3-030-27532-7_46

continuous robot joint [3], which was driven by pneumatic artificial muscle and cable, and carried out kinematics analysis. Qinghua Yang team of Zhejiang University of Technology proposed a new type of flexible pneumatic actuator (FPA) [4, 5]. Based on this, the flexible pneumatic bending joints, spherical joints and torsion joints, and flexible pneumatic finger were developed [6, 7]. Compared with traditional rigid robots, soft robots have good environmental adaptability and safety. Shixin Mao designed a flexible starfish-like soft robot [8] based on the structural characteristics of starfish, which has a remarkable symmetrical structure and a soft inner skeleton. Michael T. Tolley's team proposed an unconstrained soft robot [9], which can achieve directional jumping. Onal and others designed a soft rolling robot [10, 11], and proposed a modular method to enhance the safety and adaptability of the soft robot.

In the research of flexible-driven soft robots, the existing research focuses on how to improve the environmental adaptability and flexibility of the soft robots, but there are few studies on how to achieve flexible driving while having larger output force. In this paper, a new flexible-driven parallel soft massage robot is proposed, which not only has the flexible deformation characteristics of the soft robots, but also can meet the needs of massage.

## 2   Introduction to the Function of Massage Robot

### 2.1   Massage Manipulation

According to the characteristics and advantages of the flexible soft robot, a kind of flexible soft massage robot is proposed, which can realize the palm-pressing and palm-kneading. The palm-pressing method is a method of gradually pressing the massaged part or acupoint with the palm root from light to heavy, and then from heavy to light [12]. Its essence is that the palm exerts force downward in the vertical direction of the massaged part or acupoint of the human body as shown in Fig. 1. Palm-kneading is a method of circular or spiral kneading with the root of the palm focused on the massaged part or acupoint [13]. Its essence is that the palm exerts force downward in the vertical direction of the massaged part or acupoint and 360° around the massaged part or acupoint as shown in Fig. 2. The completion of this manipulation requires a vertical degree of freedom of movement along the human body parts or acupoints and two degrees of freedom of rotation.

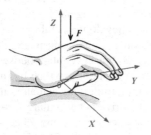

**Fig. 1.** Palm-pressing method

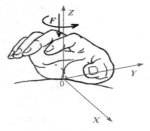

**Fig. 2.** Palm-kneading method.

## 2.2    Structural Design of Massage Robot

In order to meet the needs of palm-pressing and palm-kneading, flexible-driven multi-parallel soft massage robot needs the ability of linear elongation and omni-directional bending. The robot consists of two moving platforms and three groups of flexible driving elements as shown in Fig. 3. Because of the good compressibility of air, air pressure is adopted as a flexible driving, and its power density is high. Traditional flexible actuators adopt a cylindrical structure with radial ripple, which can achieve axial elongation and bending motion. However, when they are subjected to pressure loads and bending moments, the output force of flexible actuators is small because of their low stiffness and easy to break or torsion deformation. In this paper, the flexible driving elements are divided into multi-layer structures by means of multi-layer splitting and parallel connection. When the flexible driving elements are subjected to pressure loads under bending conditions, the pressure loads can be transferred by layer-by-layer adjustment to avoid the breaking or torsional deformation of the flexible driving elements, so that the output force of the robot is large, the motion control is simple and the adjustable range of motion is large.

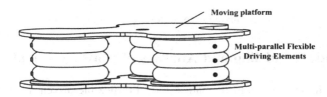

**Fig. 3.**    Flexible driven multi-parallel soft massage robot.

## 2.3    Structural Characteristics of Single-Layer Flexible Driving Unit

Each group of flexible driving elements is composed of multi-layer driving units in parallel. The internal structure of single-layer driving units is shown in Fig. 4. The thin-walled areas at the upper and lower ends are elongated deformation areas, and the thickness of the radial side edge is large. At the same time, rigid rings are embedded inside, which can effectively prevent the radial expansion of flexible driving units during the expansion deformation.

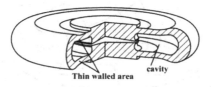

**Fig. 4.**    Internal structure of single-layer driving unit.

## 2.4    Structural Characteristics of a Single Group of Flexible Driving Elements

Multilayer flexible driving units are combined into flexible driving elements by parallel connection as shown in Fig. 5. The thin-walled deformable area of each driving unit can be independently deformed and the internal pressure can be independently controlled, which makes it possible for the bending deformation of the robot, enlarges the adjustable range of motion and enhances the flexibility. Because the adjacent two-layer driving units are connected as a whole, the stiffness of flexible driving elements is enhanced, and they can withstand larger tangential forces under bending conditions, so they can output larger driving forces under various deformation conditions.

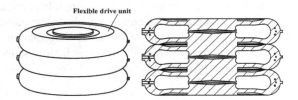

**Fig. 5.** A single group of flexible driving elements.

## 3    Kinematics Modeling and Analysis of Massage Robot

In this paper, the kinematics mathematical model of flexible-driven multi-parallel soft massage robot under ideal bending is solved by using homogeneous coordinates and homogeneous transformation.

A fixed coordinate systems $O$-$XYZ$ and dynamic coordinate systems $O_1$-$X_1Y_1Z_1$ are established respectively on the fixed platform and the moving platform of parallel massage robot. The length and bending angle of the axis of the parallel soft massage robot are $L$ and $\alpha$. $OO_1$ is connected to the center of the fixed platform and the moving

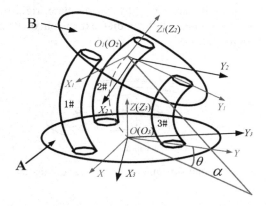

**Fig. 6.** Simplified model of massage robot.

platform of the parallel soft massage robot and projected into the $OXY$ plane. The projection line segment will form an angle of $\theta$ with the $OY$ axis.

According to Fig. 6, the derivation process of homogeneous coordinate transformation from $O_1$-$X_1Y_1Z_1$ to $O$-$XYZ$ is divided into three steps.

In the first step, the moving coordinate system $O_1$-$X_1Y_1Z_1$ is rotated around the axis $O_1 Z_1$ by an Angle $\theta$ to the intermediate coordinate system $O_2$-$X_2Y_2Z_2$. The second step is to rotate the intermediate coordinate system $O_2$-$X_2Y_2Z_2$ around the axis $O_2X_2$ by an Angle $\alpha$, and then shift the coordinate system $O_2$-$X_2Y_2Z_2$ along the axis $O_2 O_3$ to the intermediate transitional coordinate system $O_3$-$X_3Y_3Z_3$. The third step is to transform the intermediate transition coordinate system $O_3$-$X_3Y_3Z_3$ around the axis $O_3 Z_3$ by an Angle $-\theta$ to the fixed coordinate system $O$-$XYZ$. The corresponding homogeneous transformation matrices ${}_1^0T$, ${}_2^1T$, ${}_3^2T$ can be obtained by analysis.

By matrix multiplication ${}_3^0T = {}_1^0T{}_2^1T{}_3^2T$. The homogeneous transformation matrix of the three-step transformation coordinates is synthesized, and the homogeneous transformation matrix ${}_3^0T$ between the fixed platform and the moving platform of the flexible-driven parallel robot is obtained.

When $\alpha \neq 0$ the transformation matrix ${}_3^0T$ is:

$$
{}_3^0T = \begin{bmatrix} c^2\theta + s^2c\alpha & -c\theta s\theta + c\theta s\theta c\alpha & s\theta s\alpha & s\theta \dfrac{L}{a}(1-c\alpha) \\[2mm] -c\theta s\theta + c\theta s\theta c\alpha & s^2\theta + c^2\theta c\alpha & c\theta s\alpha & c\theta \dfrac{L}{\alpha}(1-c\alpha) \\[2mm] -s\theta s\alpha & -s\alpha c\theta & c\alpha & \dfrac{L}{a}s\alpha \\[2mm] 0 & 0 & 0 & 1 \end{bmatrix} \tag{1}
$$

According to formula (1), the coordinates of the origin $O_1$ of the coordinate system $O_1$-$X_1Y_1Z_1$ in the fixed coordinate system $O$-$XYZ$ can be obtained as follows:

$$
\begin{bmatrix} x & y & z \end{bmatrix}^{\mathrm{T}} = \begin{cases} \left[ s\theta \frac{L}{\alpha}(1-c\alpha) & c\theta \frac{L}{\alpha}(1-c\alpha) & \frac{L}{\alpha}s\alpha \right]^T (\alpha \neq 0) \\ \begin{bmatrix} 0 & 0 & L \end{bmatrix}^T (\alpha = 0) \end{cases} \tag{2}
$$

The inverse solution of formula (2) is obtained.

$$
\begin{cases} \theta = atan2(x,y) \\ \alpha = cos^{-1} \frac{z^2-x^2-y^2}{x^2+y^2+z^2} \\ L = \begin{cases} \frac{z\alpha}{sin\alpha} (\alpha \neq 0) \\ z(\alpha = 0) \end{cases} \end{cases} \tag{3}
$$

Through the above kinematics modeling and analysis, the relationship between the state parameters of the parallel massage robot and the position and posture of the moving platform, as well as the relationship between the state parameters and the length of three groups of flexible driving units are obtained.

## 4  Mechanical Modeling and Analysis of Massage Robot

### 4.1  Output Force Under Vertical Elongation

The internal force analysis of the single-layer flexible driving unit is carried out as shown in Fig. 7. Fixed one end of the driving unit, the pressure of the internal cavity is $P$, and the other end of the driving unit will be subjected to a pressure $F_{load}$ Considering it as a flexible spring, a simplified model can be obtained as shown in Fig. 8. The relationship between the spring stiffness and the extension of the driving unit is assumed by the experimental method. The resilient force produced by the flexible driving unit is $f(x)$. The relationship between the three forces can be obtained from the force balance condition as follows:

$$F_{load} + f(x) = F_P \tag{4}$$

Among them, $F_P$ is the acting force produced by the pressure inside the driving unit, and its value is $P * A$, and $A$ is $\pi/4D^2$. The above formula can be rewritten as follows:

$$F_{load} = \frac{P}{4}\pi D^2 - f(x) \tag{5}$$

The output force of the parallel robot in the vertical direction can be calculated by formula (5) with known pressure $P$.

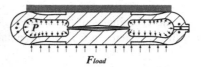

**Fig. 7.**  Internal force analysis.

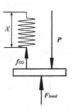

**Fig. 8.**  Force analysis sketch.

## 4.2  Output Force Under Bending Condition

When one end of the driving element is fixed and the other end is subjected to tangential force $F_t$ and bending moment, the driving element will bend as shown in Fig. 9, and at the same time it will be subjected to an external load pressure $F_{load1}$. Through the method of layer by layer analysis, a single group of driving elements is divided, and a layer of driving elements is selected to simplify the force analysis.

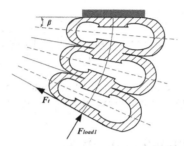

**Fig. 9.** Force analysis under bending conditions.

The first layer driving unit has a reaction force $F_0$, bending moment $M_0$ and tangential force $F_{t0}$ on the fixed platform as shown in Fig. 10. $F_1$ and $F_{t1}$ are the load and the tangential reaction force produced by the next driving unit. $F_{P10}$ and $F_{P20}$ are the resultant forces of air pressure in the direction away from bending and bending respectively.

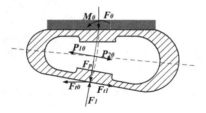

**Fig. 10.** Analysis of single layer force.

According to the principle of static equilibrium, it can be concluded that:

$$F_1 = F_0 \cos 2\beta + F_{t0} \sin 2\beta - \left(F_{p10} - F_{p20}\right) \sin \beta + F_P \tag{6}$$

$$F_{t1} = F_{t0} \cos 2\beta - F_0 \sin 2\beta - \left(F_{p10} - F_{p20}\right) \cos \beta \tag{7}$$

According to the force transfer relationship between multi-layer flexible driving units, $F_n$ and $F_{tm}$ are the forces perpendicular to the lower end surface and tangential to the upper driving unit of the next layer. According to the force balance in these two directions, we can get the force analysis of the n-layer flexible driving unit as follows:

$$F_n = F_{n-1}\cos(2\beta_{n-1}) + F_{m-1}\sin 2\beta_{n-1} - (F_{p10} - F_{p20})\sin\beta_{n-1} + F_P \quad (8)$$

$$F_{tn} = F_{m-1}\cos 2\beta_{n-1} - F_{n-1}\sin 2\beta_{n-1} - (F_{p10} - F_{p20})\sin\beta_{n-1} \quad (9)$$

From this, it can be concluded that:

$$\begin{bmatrix} F_n \\ F_{tn} \\ 1 \end{bmatrix} = A_{n-1}\cdots A_1 A_0 \begin{bmatrix} F_0 \\ F_{t0} \\ 1 \end{bmatrix} = \prod_{i=0}^{n} A_i \begin{bmatrix} F_0 \\ F_{t0} \\ 1 \end{bmatrix} \quad (10)$$

Through formula (10), the driving force of a single group of flexible driving elements can be obtained under the condition of known pressure and curvature.

## 5  Finite Element Simulation Analysis

In this paper, rubber is chosen as flexible material, which has the characteristics of large non-linear deformation. First, the silicone rubber material is defined as hyperelastic body. Second-order Yeoh model is adopted. Then one end of the driving unit is fixed. Finally, air pressure load is added to simulate the parallel soft massage robot by finite element method.

a) Before deformation    b) After deformation

**Fig. 11.**  Deformation of single-layer flexible driving unit.

**Fig. 12.**  Motion of parallel soft massage robot.

Firstly, the single-layer driving unit model is modeled and adjusted by ABAQUS soft. The single-layer driving unit model is loaded uniformly on all surfaces of the cavity with a single step of 5 kPa. When the pressure is gradually applied to the surface of the cavity to 45 kPa, its deformation is shown in Fig. 11. From the figure, it can be seen that the deformation of the single-layer driving unit is basically consistent with the expected structure design, and its radial deformation is small, but the deformation effect of thin-walled deformation area is obvious.

In the same way, the flexible-driven multi-parallel soft massage robot is simulated and analyzed. One of the platforms is set as a fixed platform, and three groups of flexible driving elements are respectively fed into different air pressure values. The simulation results are shown in Fig. 12. It is shown that when the air pressure inside the flexible driving unit is changed, the moving platform of the parallel soft massage robot will deflect at different angles.

## 6   Experimental Verification

The flexible driving unit in the prototype of flexible-driven multi-parallel soft massage robot is made of silica gel. As shown in the left figure of Fig. 13, the die is made by 3D printing technology and the prototype is made by investment casting method. Finally, the prototype shown in the right figure of Fig. 13 is obtained. The platform on the robot is fixed as shown in Fig. 14a, and the pneumatic control measuring platform is built as shown in Fig. 14b.

**Fig. 13.**  Manufacture of prototype.

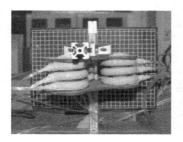

a) Prototype fixing.          b) Measurement and control platform.

**Fig. 14.**  Composition of experimental system.

When the pressure in the cavity increases, the flexible driving unit deforms and extends along the axial direction. With a single step size of 5 kPa, the air pressure is increased to 45 kPa, and the deformation of flexible driving unit under different cavity pressure is measured. The relationship between the deformation elongation of a groups of flexible driving elements and the pressure in the cavity under no load condition is obtained. The simulation results are compared with those in Fig. 15.

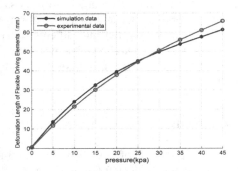

**Fig. 15.** Relationship between pressure and deformation of flexible components.

A group of flexible driving elements or two groups of flexible driving elements are selected arbitrarily and inflated into the cavity. The bending deformation of the prototype is shown in Fig. 16a. The bending deflection angles of the prototype under different pressures are measured. The experimental results are shown in Fig. 16b.

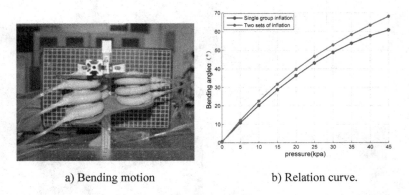

a) Bending motion                    b) Relation curve.

**Fig. 16.** Motion of parallel soft massage robot.

# 7 Conclusion

1. In this paper, a new flexible-driven parallel soft massage robot is designed. The kinematics analysis of the parallel robot is carried out by establishing coordinate system and using homogeneous coordinate transformation method. The relationship between the length of three groups of flexible elements $L_1$, $L_2$, $L_3$ and the state parameters $L$, $\alpha$, $\theta$, and the coordinates of the origin of the moving coordinate system in the fixed coordinate system are obtained. Through mechanics modeling analysis, the force analysis of parallel soft robot under various states is carried out.
2. Finite element simulation analysis was carried out to verify the rationality of the deformation of flexible driving unit, and the deformation nephogram of parallel robot under different pressure conditions was obtained.
3. Through the prototype experiment, it is verified that the massage robot can achieve the massage action of palm-pressing and palm-kneading, and the experimental results are analyzed. The relationship between the pressure and the bending angle of parallel soft massage robot is obtained, and the relationship between the pressure and the elongation of flexible driving unit is obtained.

**Acknowledgement.** This work was supported in part by the National Key Research and Development Program under Grant 2017YFE0112200, in part by the Natural Science Foundation of Hebei Province under Grant E2018203436, in part by the Science Technology Research of Higher Education of Hebei Province under Grant ZD2018024, and Guangdong Province Jihua Laboratory under Grant Y80311W180.

# References

1. Terashima, K., Kitagawa, H., Miyoshi, T., et al.: Modeling and massage control of human skin muscle by using multi-fingered robot hand. Integr. Comput.-Aided Eng. **13**(3), 233–248 (2006)
2. Solis, J., Obokawa, Y., Ishii, H., et al.: Development of oral rehabilitation robot WAO-1R designed to provide various massage techniques. In: IEEE International Conference on Rehabilitation Robotics, pp. 23–26. IEEE, Kyoto (2009)
3. Zhao, Z., Chen, Z.: Joint structure design and kinematics analysis of flexible pneumatic continuum robot. Mech. Sci. Technol. **34**(02), 184–187 (2015)
4. Yang, Q.: Pneumatic flexible joint based on pneumatic flexible actuator and its application. Zhejiang University of Technology (2005)
5. Yang, Q., Bao, G., Zhang, L., et al.: Analysis and simulation of dynamic characteristics of flexible pneumatic actuator FPA. In: International Conference on Mechatronics and Automation, pp. 25–28. IEEE, Luoyang (2006)
6. Shao, T.: Research on pneumatic flexible elephant nose continuous robot. Zhejiang University of Technology (2014)
7. Zhang, J., Yang, Q., Shao, T., et al.: Simulation of flexible and flexible finger bending. Electromech. Eng. **31**(2), 1001–4551 (2014)
8. Mao, S., Dong, E., Jin, H., et al.: Gait study and pattern generation of a starfish-like soft robot with flexible rays actuated by SMAs. J. Bionic Eng. **11**(3), 400–411 (2014)

9. Tolley, M.T., Shepherd, R.F., et al.: An untethered jumping soft robot. In: IEEE/RSJ International Conference on Intelligent Robots and Systems, pp. 14–18. IEEE, Chicago (2014)

10. Onal, C.D., Rus, D.: A modular approach to soft robots. In: IEEE Ras and Embs International Conference on Biomedical Robotics and Biomechatronics, pp. 24–27. IEEE, Rome (2012)

11. Marchese, A.D., Onal, C.D., Rus, D.L.: Soft robot actuators using energy-efficient valves controlled by electropermanent magnets. In: IEEE/RSJ International Conference on Intelligent Robots and Systems, pp. 25–30. IEEE, San Francisco (2011)

12. Gao, F., Yang, Y.: Application of relaxation massage in physical education. New Technol. Prod. China (13), 234 (2009)

13. A brief introduction of massage manipulation-rubbing manipulation. Mod. Dist. Educ. Chin. Tradit. Med. 11(10), 87 (2013)

# A Vacuum-Powered Soft Linear Actuator Strengthened by Granular Jamming

Yangqiao Lin, Jun Zou[(✉)], and Huayong Yang

State Key Laboratory of Fluid Power and Mechatronic Systems,
Zhejiang University, Hangzhou 310027, China
junzou@zju.edu.cn

**Abstract.** Vacuum-powered soft pneumatic actuators (V-SPAs) are considered to be fail-safe, because their maximum forces and displacements are restricted by environmental pressure from actuating. However, their performances are significantly influenced by the selection of materials. V-SPAs fabricated by materials with low modulus of elasticity might fall short of output forces for many tasks. This article proposes a novel approach aiming to improve the performance of V-SPAs. Based on our previously developed vacuum-powered soft linear actuators (called as "VSLA"), a new vacuum-powered soft linear actuator strengthened by granular jamming (called as "J-VSLAs") is proposed to achieve higher actuation stress without sacrificing compliance. The new J-VSLA changes the stiffness partially and it can lift about four times of weight (at 20% of strains) compared to its no-granule version. In addition, the mechanical efficiencies of the J-VSLAs is increased by about 10%. Our results highlight the effectiveness of J-VSLAs for improving the mechanical properties of soft actuators and reducing the material selection constraints on the performance of V-SPAs.

**Keywords:** Soft robotics · Granular jamming · Vacuum-powered soft actuator

## 1 Introduction

Soft robots possess the potential to operate in highly variable environments or in close cooperation with humans, as they take the advantage of a materials-based approach to create compliant systems. Compared to using impedance control methods to achieve compliance of robots [1, 2], the materials-based approach alleviates the difficulty of control, which is recognized to be useful in designing robots that work in unstructured environments [3]. Recent years, inherently compliant and flexible materials such as silicone rubber are used to fabricate various soft actuators [4–11]. In this domain, soft pneumatic actuators (SPAs), which are powered by pneumatic pressure to stretch or bend through inflation or deformation of elastic chambers to produce useful mechanical work, are widely used. A variety of SPA-driven systems show the abilities, such as delicate handing [7], rough terrain locomotion [12] and human interaction tasks [13].

Negative pressure systems have been investigated recently as an alternative approach in soft actuators. Yang et al. introduced a series of vacuum-powered soft pneumatic actuators (V-SPAs), including the rotary actuators [14], the vacuum-actuated muscle-inspired pneumatic structures (VAMPs) [15] and the shear-vacuum-actuated

© Springer Nature Switzerland AG 2019
H. Yu et al. (Eds.): ICIRA 2019, LNAI 11741, pp. 531–543, 2019.
https://doi.org/10.1007/978-3-030-27532-7_47

machines (shear-VAMs) [16]. Robertson and Paik introduced a multifunctional vacuum-power system which can be combined with different vacuum-powered modules to achieve a variety of tasks including multimodal locomotion, object manipulation, and stiffness tuning [17]. Li et al. proposed fluid-driven origami-inspired artificial muscles (FOAMs) which can generate stresses of about 600 kPa, and produce peak power densities over 2 kW/kg [18]. Compared to the traditional soft pneumatic system which is driven by a positive pressure, these V-SPAs are fail-safe because they would not burst like other soft actuators that operate under high positive pressure (e.g., McKibben actuators [19]). The maximum forces and displacements of these V-SPAs are limited by the environmental pressure from actuating. Contrary to expanding motion based on a positive pressure, V-SPAs produce contractile motion and do not expand in the cross-sectional area during an actuation, which allows them to operate in space-constrained environments.

In our previous study [20], a vacuum-powered soft linear actuator (abbreviated as VSLA) was proposed which contract under negative pressure and recover when the negative pressure is turned off (see Fig. 1A). It was verified by experiments that through this combination of linear motion actuators, different forms of soft robots could be build, such as a tube-crawling robot, a reconfigurable omnidirectional motion robots (see Fig. 1B, C). However, the maximum actuation stresses of current vacuum-powered soft linear actuators depend on their materials (see Table 1). Actuators made by softer materials generate smaller stress than those made by stiffer materials. This means we must choose between the output power and material flexibility, either using large elastic modulus materials to increase output power and sacrifice flexibility, or using small elastic modulus materials to retain flexibility and sacrifice output power.

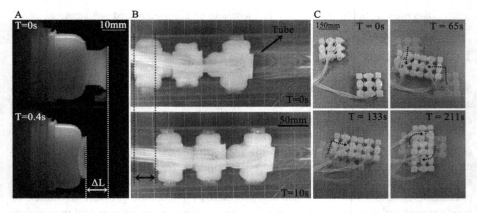

**Fig. 1.** Our previous work [20]. (A) Vacuum-powered soft cylinder. (B) A Tube-crawling robot actuated by soft cylinder. (C) Two Omnidirectional crawling robot actuated by soft cylinder. These robots are capable of three degrees of freedom, and the two robots can be automatically assembled into a larger robot.

**Table 1.** Comparison of vacuum-powered soft linear actuator

| Vacuum-powered soft linear actuator | Maximum actuation strain | Maximum actuation stress | Maximum modulus of elasticity of the major part (kPa) | Materials of the major part |
|---|---|---|---|---|
| J-VSLA | ~45% | 12.8 kPa | 43 kPa | Ecoflex 00-30 |
| Zou et al. [20] | ~45% | 1.4 kPa | 43 kPa | Ecoflex 00-30 |
| Yang et al. [15] | ~45% | 1.0 kPa | 43 kPa | Ecoflex 00-30 |
| | ~45% | 10.0 kPa | 520 kPa | Elastosil M4601 |
| | ~22% | 65.0 kPa | 2500 kPa | Stratasys PolyJet |
| Li et al. [19] | ~50% | 285.0 kPa | 25000 kPa | Thermoplastic polyurethane (TPU) |
| | ~31% | 582.0 kPa | 460000 kPa | TPU-coated nylon fabric |

We consider stiffness tuning as an effective way to achieve a balance between the compliance and high performance of V-SPAs. Stiffness tuning is an important strategy for soft structures, both natural and artificial, to effectively interact with the environment. We demonstrate a jamming-strengthened vacuum-powered soft linear actuators (J-VSLA). Compared with the few existing examples of vacuum-powered actuators [14–17], this new soft actuator is able to output higher force and remain compliant without inducing rigid structures, because the granular jamming-based system is capable of enabling a reversible transition between a fluid-like and a solid-like material [21, 22]. When the granular material is not subjected to external pressure, the granular material exhibit a loose state, similar to a fluid-like state. When a negative pressure is applied to the granular media, the granular material is tightly bound to form a complex network of force chains. These force chains allow the system to withstand a certain yield pressure, similar to a solid-like state. The two different states of the particles effectively change the stiffness of the side walls and allow the actuators to output higher forces at jamming state and remain compliant at unjamming state. Increased stiffness enhances the output force of a J-VSLA. Experimental results show that a J-VSLA can lift about four times of weight (at 20% of strains) compared to its original version (VSLA). In addition, the added granular jamming system can use the same vacuum source to trigger the jamming state, and only some pipes and regulators shall be added. The granular jamming-system can be integrated with the vacuum-powered actuator cost-effectively and seamlessly.

## 2    Methods and Materials

### 2.1    J-VSLA Concept: VSLA Strengthened by Granular Jamming

This study focuses on the performance of a vacuum-powered soft linear actuator (VSLA) and its enhanced version (J-VSLA) as shown in Fig. 2A, B. The working principle of both versions is that, the deflation of the inner chamber results in a displacement as a vacuum source is applied to it. $\Delta P_i$ is defined as difference of the pressure between that of atmosphere external to the actuator ($P_{ext}$), and that of the partial vacuum inside the inner chamber ($P_{int}$) (as defined in Eq. 1). The difference between a J-VSLA and a VSLA is that, a side chamber is added into the sidewalls of the J-VSLA and particles (alumina particles with an average diameter of 0.83 mm) are added into the side chamber. When a J-VSLA operates, a vacuum source is applied to the side chamber of the J-VSLA, and trigger the granular jamming to increase the stiffness of the sidewalls. The vacuum degree of the side chamber is denoted as $\Delta P_g$ (as defined in Eq. 2).

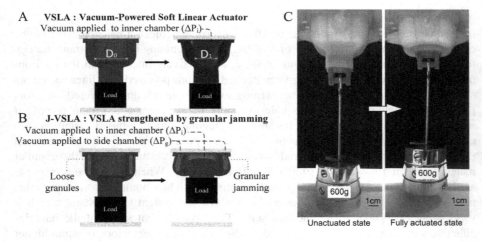

**Fig. 2.** Schematic description of the J-VSLA and the VLSA. (A) The VSLA (blue portions) is fabricated by Ecoflex 00-30 and fixed on a wall. It is supposed to shrink as in (B) under small load conditions when a vacuum is applied to its inner chamber. However, when the load is large enough, a greater vacuum degree would make the side wall inwardly concaved ($D0 > D1$) which reduces the pulling force and the actuator falls short of force to pull up the load. (B) The J-VSLA is an improved version of the VSLA. Granules (red portions) are embedded in the chamber of the side walls. (C) Images of a J-VSLA lifting a load ($m = 600$ g) when actuated by applying vacuum to the inner chamber ($\Delta P_i = 80$ kPa) and granules ($\Delta P_g = 75$ kPa). (Color figure online)

$$\Delta P_i = P_{ext} - P_{int} \tag{1}$$

$$\Delta P_g = P_{ext} - P_{granule} \tag{2}$$

A J-VSLA or a VSLA is similar to a pneumatic or hydraulic piston, in that it works by converting an applied pneumatic pressure to an output force $F$. We define $A_i$ as the initial cross-sectional area of the actuator, and define $A_e$ as the equivalent cross-sectional area when the vacuum is applied to the inner chamber. $F$ is the product of $\Delta P_i$ and $A_e$ at zero displacement (as defined in Eq. 3).

$$F = \Delta P_i A_e \tag{3}$$

For both versions, a larger $\Delta P_i$ gives a larger output force $F$, however, the J-VSLA can lift more weight due to the increment of the stiffness of the side walls. For a VSLA, as show in Fig. 2A, when the load is large enough, a constantly increasing $\Delta P_i$ may cause the buckling of the side walls, which results in a constantly reduction of the equivalent cross-sectional area $A_e$, so the output force $F$ would not increase after reaching the critical point. For a J-VSLA, the increment of the stiffness of the side walls limits the change in $A_e$ and provides a larger implementing force (see Fig. 2B). Figure 2C shows that a J-VSLA lift a load of 600 g when it is actuated by applying vacuum to the inner chamber ($\Delta P_i = 80$ kPa) and granules ($\Delta P_g = 75$ kPa).

## 2.2 Design and Fabrication of J-VSLAs

The diagram of a J-VSLA is illustrated in Fig. 3. A 3D printed hook (red part) was fixed on the top, which was used to hang the loads in the experiments. The elastomeric parts of a J-VSLA were fabricated using the mold and casting approach. The molds required were designed by computer-aided design (Solidworks) and made of ABS thermoplastics using a 3D printer (Makerbot replicator Z18) with a resolution of 0.1 mm. Curing a silicone-based elastomer (Ecoflex 00-30) against the molds at room temperature for 4 h produced the parts required to assemble a J-VSLA. There were some ribs inside the side chamber, which were used to ensure that the structure can maintain its shape after the addition of particles. We used a puncher to make three holes (1 mm in diameter) in each of the ribs to ensure that the air could flow throughout the chamber. Four connectors, conically shaped piece of the elastomer, were symmetrically bonded to the side of the actuators to provide additional material that allowed tubing to be securely attached to the structure. Two of the tubes were connected to the side chamber (purple portions) and the other two were connected to the inner chamber (green portions). Alumina particles (black dots) with an average diameter of 0.83 mm were then added into the side chamber before a sheet (1 mm in thickness) was bonded to the bottom of the actuator and sealed the chambers. These elastomeric parts were aligned and bonded together by applying uncured elastomer at their interfaces, prior to placing them in an oven and curing at 65 °C for 10 min. The detailed production process is demonstrated in Fig. 4. Physical properties of J-VSLAs are given in Table 2.

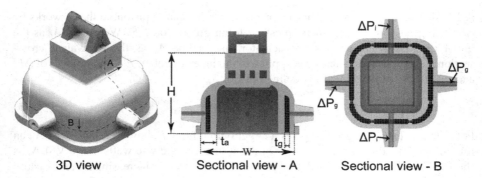

**3D view**              **Sectional view - A**              **Sectional view - B**

**Fig. 3.** Diagrams of a J-VSLA. Four connectors are symmetrically distributed on the sides of the J-VSLA. Two of the connectors allow tubing to the inner chamber (*green portions*) and the other two allowed tubing to the side chamber (*purple portions*), in which the vacuum degrees were denoted as $\Delta P_i$ and $\Delta P_g$, respectively. The black dots represent granules which are placed in the side chamber. The red part is a 3D printed hook used to hang the load. Parameters are given in Table 2. (Color figure online)

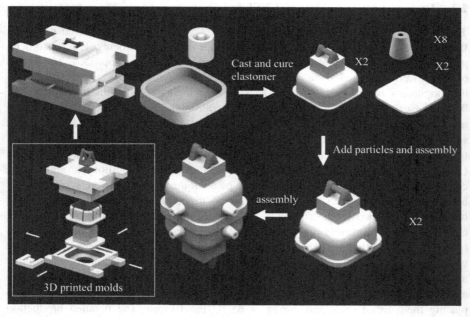

**Fig. 4.** Steps involved in the fabrication of J-VSLAs. Two J-VSLAs are aligned and bonded together by applying uncured elastomer at their interfaces and they can produce a muscle-like contraction.

**Table 2.** Physical properties of J-VSLAs

| Parameters | Description | Value |
|---|---|---|
| H | Height of the actuator (without hook) | 51 mm |
| W | Width of the actuator | 58 mm |
| $t_a$ | Side wall thickness | 10 mm |
| $t_g$ | Granular layer thickness | 3 mm |
| $A_i$ | Initial cross-sectional area of the internal chamber | 14.1 cm$^2$ |
| $R_g$ | Average diameter of the granules | 0.83 mm |
| $\varepsilon_{max}$ | Maximum strain rate | ~45% |
| M | Mass of the actuator | ~110 g |
| $M_g$ | Mass of the granules | ~30 g |

# 3  Results

## 3.1  Step Response Characterizations of J-VSLAs and VSLAs

The step response characterizations of J-VSLAs and VSLAs were measured. Experimental setup is shown in Fig. 5A. The actuators were glued onto a stiff board with Sil-Poxy silicone rubber adhesive (Smooth on Inc.) and clamped on a fixed bracket. $\Delta P_i$ was fixed at 80 kPa which was sufficient to collapse the inner chamber completely. A high-speed camera was used to record the rising height ($\Delta h$) of different loads. Data shown are mean ± S.D. for 15 tests (5 tests for each of three actuators).

The average step responses of $\Delta h$ under different $\Delta P_g$ and different loads are shown in Fig. 5B. We focus on the ability of the actuators to lift the load and the response speed. To characterize the step responses, we define two variables, $H$ and $Tr$, labeled in Fig. 5B. H is defined as the maximum height at which the step response reaches a steady state, and Tr is defined as the time elapsed from the beginning of the response to the steady state. The responding speed is defined as $v = H/Tr$. The changes in $H$ and $v$ reflect the changes in the load capacity and response speed of the actuators.

It can be seen from Fig. 5C and D that the load capacity $H$ and the response speed $v$ of J-VSLAs are increased after a certain negative pressure $\Delta P_g$ was applied to the side chamber. As the load increased, both $H$ and $v$ for all J-VSLAs and VSLAs showed decreasing trends. The difference is that they had different loading values for a significant drop. For a J-VSLA with $\Delta P_g = 0$ kPa, in which the side wall is softer than a VSLA, a rapid decrease appeared from the very beginning. After that, VSLAs showed a significant downward trend at $m = 200$ g. The significant drop of $H$ and $v$ of J-VSLAs was postponed with the increase of $\Delta P_g$, and J-VSLAs which strengthened by the biggest vacuum degree ($\Delta P_g = 75$ kPa) showed the best performance. $H$ and $v$ still maintained more than half the maximum value ($m = 0$ g) when the load reached $m = 1400$ g.

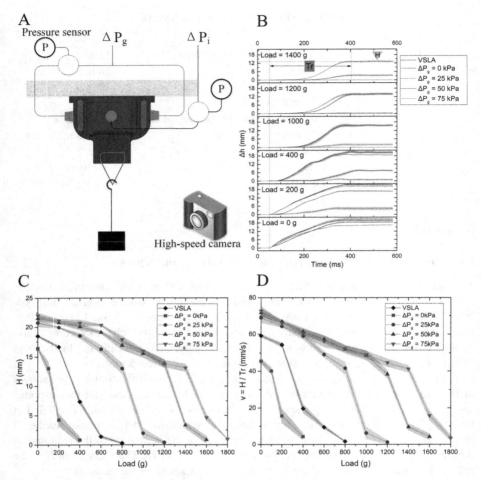

**Fig. 5.** Step response characterizations of J-VSLAs and VSLAs. (A) Experimental setup for measuring the step response characterizations of J-VSLAs and VSLAs. (B) The average step responses under different $\Delta P_g$ and different loads. (C) The relationship between $H$ and the force of actuation of J-VSLAs and VSLAs under different $\Delta P_g$ and different loads. (D) The relationship between the responding speed (defined as $v = H/Tr$) of J-VSLAs and VSLAs under varying $\Delta P_g$ and varying loads.

## 3.2    Measurements of the Thermodynamic Efficiency and the Loss of Efficiency

Pressure-volume hysteresis curves of J-VSLAs and VSLAs were observed in quasi-static measurements by pumping water in and out of the actuators with a slow flow rate at 2 ml/min. Experimental setup is shown in Fig. 6A. The actuators were glued onto a stiff board with Sil-Poxy silicone rubber adhesive (Smooth on Inc.) and clamped in a glass tank. We recorded the change in pressure in the internal chamber during the deflation and inflation cycle. Figure 6B shows the pressure-volume hysteresis curves of a VSLA lifting a weight ($m = 200$ g).

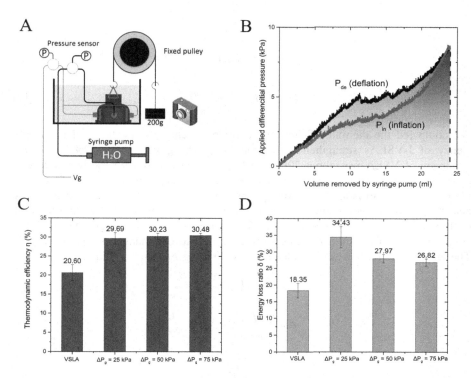

**Fig. 6.** Measurements of the thermodynamic efficiency and the loss of efficiency. (a) Schematics of the experimental setup. (b) Pressure-volume curves of a VSLA lifting a 200 g weight. The actuation curve is marked in black and the return curve is marked in red. The shaded area represents the fluidic energy input via the syringe pump. (c) The thermodynamic efficiency $\eta$ of VSLAs and J-VSLAs (with different levels of $\Delta P_g$) lifting a 200 g weight. (d) The energy loss ratio $\delta$ of operation (active and return) of VSLAs and J-VSLAs. (Color figure online)

During a deflation and inflation cycle, a weight ($m = 200$ g) was lifted up and put down. A high-speed camera was placed perpendicular to the direction of motion. Since water is effectively incompressible, the volume decrease/increase of fluid in the syringe is equal to that of the increase/decrease in the inner chamber of the actuators. Within each test, the process was switched from deflation to inflation when we removed $V_0 = 24$ ml of water (about 60% of the volume of the inner chamber). We calculated the thermodynamic efficiency $\eta$ by dividing $W$ which is defined as the energy converted into effective work to $E_{de}$ which is defined as the energy input to the actuator from the syringe pump in the deflation process (Eq. 4). $W$ was obtained by calculating the potential energy gain of lifting the weight ($g$ is the gravitational constant) (Eq. 5).

$E_{de}$ was obtained by integrating the differential pressure of the inflation process with respect to the change in volume (Eq. 6).

$$\eta = \frac{W}{E_{de}} \tag{4}$$

$$W = mg\Delta h \tag{5}$$

$$E_{de} = \int_0^{V_0} P_{de}(V)dV \tag{6}$$

We compared the thermal efficiencies of different actuators and found that the efficiency of J-VSLAs strengthened by granular jamming was about 30%, while the efficiency of VSLA was about 20% (see Fig. 6C). The reason for the increased efficiency is that the energy stored in actuators as elastic energy is reduced. In fact, since the granular system is an energy dissipating system, more energy was converted into heat for J-VSLAs. We define $E_{loss}$ as the energy loss during a deflation and inflation cycle which can be calculated from Eq. 7. $E_{in}$ was obtained by integrating the differential pressure of the inflation process with respect to the change in volume (Eq. 8). The energy loss ratio $\delta$ can be calculated by dividing $E_{loss}$ to $E_{de}$ (Eq. 9).

$$E_{loss} = E_{de} - E_{in} \tag{7}$$

$$E_{in} = \int_0^{V_0} P_{in}(V)dV \tag{8}$$

$$\delta = \frac{E_{loss}}{E_{de}} \tag{9}$$

For VSLAs, the energy loss ratio of one cycle was $\delta = 18.35 \pm 2.18$ (%) while that of J-VSLAs was $\delta = 34.42 \pm 3.15$ (%) for $\Delta P_g = 25$ kPa, $\delta = 27.97 \pm 1.27$ (%) for $\Delta P_g = 50$ kPa and $\delta = 26.81 \pm 1.08$ (%) for $\Delta P_g = 75$ kPa (see Fig. 6D). Data shown are mean $\pm$ S.D. for 5 tests. The granular system induces more thermal energy loss, but increasing the vacuum degree which intensifies the granular jamming would reduce loss of energy in granular particle collisions. For $\Delta P_g = 25$ kPa, the side walls of the actuator were still inwardly concaved, resulting in more loss of energy. For $\Delta P_g = 50$ kPa and $\Delta P_g = 75$ kPa, the deformation of the side wall of the actuator before lifting was limited, but the shrinking process of the actuator will still cause mutual friction between the particles. Using particles with smoother surface can also reduce the energy loss in granular particle friction of J-VSLAs further.

### 3.3   Using J-VSLAs in Robots that Locomote

Two J-VSLAs were aligned and bonded together by applying uncured elastomer at their interfaces and they could produce a muscle-like contraction (see Fig. 7A). This linear contraction could be used in different applications. We designed a four-wheeled "walker" which is capable of a unidirectional movement (see Fig. 7B). Eight one-way bearings were mounted on the "walker". The movement of the "walker" consisted of two steps in one cycle, the first step was the contraction of the actuators by applying vacuum to the inner chamber, the second step was the elongation of the actuator by connecting the internal chamber to the atmosphere. In the contraction process, the two brackets had a tendency to move close to each other (compression). The rear wheel roll forward while the front wheel was unable to roll back due to the one-way bearing, providing forward friction to the "walker". In the elongation process, the two brackets move away from each other. The front wheels roll forward and the rear wheels provide forward friction to the entire "walker". Repeating this cycle, the "walker" would be able to move forward (see Fig. 7C). The vacuum degree of the inner chamber was set to $\Delta P_i = 50$ kPa while the vacuum degree of side chamber was set to $\Delta P_g = 70$ kPa for the actuators to generate enough forces to actuate the "walker".

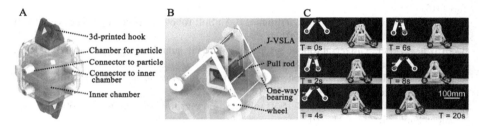

**Fig. 7.** A soft robotic walker actuated by J-VSLAs. (A) Two J-VSLAs were aligned and bonded together to build an artificial muscle. (B) Schematics of the walker. (C) Frames from a movie of the soft robotic walker moving on a level surface.

## 4   Conclusions

We propose a new method to enhance vacuum-powered soft pneumatic actuators by granular jamming and demonstrate an empowered vacuum-powered soft linear actuator using this method. The proposed actuator has a significant performance improvement compared to its no-granule version. This method can also be applied to other V-SPAs effectively, since there is no specific requirement of inducing a new vacuum source. This is very useful for some applications, such as man-machine interaction, where the maximum output force could be limited to a certain level to ensure safety.

This work concludes that the use of granular jamming can effectively enhance the actuator performance. But it is found that the equivalent cross-sectional area reduces with the increasing of pressure. Optimizing the structure and using other different particles with larger surface friction coefficients can make better results. It was noticed that a portion of the input energy was consumed by the granular system and lost as heat. A larger vacuum or an optimized particles choice can decrease the energy dissipation.

**Acknowledgments.** This work was supported by the National Natural Science Foundation (Nos. 51875507).

# References

1. Ikeura, R., Inooka, H.: Variable impedance control of a robot for cooperation with a human. In: Proceedings of 1995 IEEE International Conference on Robotics and Automation, pp. 3097–3102. IEEE, Nagoya (1995)
2. Calanca, A., Muradore, R., Fiorini, P.: Impedance control of series elastic actuators using acceleration feedback. In: González-Vargas, J., et al. (eds.) Wearable Robotics: Challenges and Trends, pp. 33–37. Springer, Cham (2017). https://doi.org/10.1007/978-3-319-46532-6_6
3. Kemp, C., Edsinger, A., Torres-Jara, E.: Challenges for robot manipulation in human environments. IEEE Robot. Autom. Mag. **14**, 20–29 (2007)
4. Rus, D., Tolley, M.T.: Design, fabrication and control of soft robots. Nature **521**, 467–475 (2015)
5. Farm, J., Lin, H.-T., Leisk, G.G., Trimmer, B.A.: Soft robots in space: a perspective for soft robotics. Acta Futur. **6**, 69–79 (2013)
6. Brown, E., et al.: Universal robotic gripper based on the jamming of granular material. Proc. Natl. Acad. Sci. **107**, 18809–18814 (2010)
7. Ilievski, F., Mazzeo, A.D., Shepherd, R.F., Chen, X., Whitesides, G.M.: Soft robotics for chemists. Angew. Chemie Int. Ed. **50**, 1890–1895 (2011)
8. Kim, S., Laschi, C., Trimmer, B.: Soft robotics: a bioinspired evolution in robotics. Trends Biotechnol. **31**, 287–294 (2013)
9. Suzumori, K., Iikura, S., Tanaka, H.: Development of flexible microactuator and its applications to robotic mechanisms. In: Proceedings of the 1991 IEEE International Conference on Robotics and Automation, pp. 1622–1627. IEEE Compute Society Press, Sacramento (1991)
10. Martinez, R.V., et al.: Robotic tentacles with three-dimensional mobility based on flexible elastomers. Adv. Mater. **25**, 205–212 (2013)
11. Mosadegh, B., et al.: Pneumatic networks for soft robotics that actuate rapidly. Adv. Funct. Mater. **24**, 2163–2170 (2014)
12. Tolley, M.T., et al.: A resilient, untethered soft robot. Soft Robot. **1**, 213–223 (2014)
13. Polygerinos, P., et al.: Towards a soft pneumatic glove for hand rehabilitation. In: IEEE International Conference on Intelligent Robots and Systems, Tokyo, Japan, pp. 1512–1517 (2013)
14. Yang, D., et al.: Buckling of elastomeric beams enables actuation of soft machines. Adv. Mater. **27**, 6323–6327 (2015)
15. Yang, D., et al.: Buckling pneumatic linear actuators inspired by muscle. Adv. Mater. Technol. **1**, 1600055 (2016)
16. Yang, D., Verma, M.S., Lossner, E., Stothers, D., Whitesides, G.M.: Negative-pressure soft linear actuator with a mechanical advantage. Adv. Mater. Technol. **2**, 1600164 (2017)
17. Robertson, M.A., Paik, J.: New soft robots really suck: vacuum-powered systems empower diverse capabilities. Sci. Robot. **2**, eaan6357 (2017)
18. Li, S., Vogt, D.M., Rus, D., Wood, R.J.: Fluid-driven origami-inspired artificial muscles. Proc. Natl. Acad. Sci. **114**, 13132–13137 (2017)
19. Daerden, F., Lefeber, D., Daerden, F., Lefeber, D.: Pneumatic artificial muscles: actuators for robotics and automation. Eur. J. Mech. Environ. Eng. **47**, 11–21 (2002)

20. Zou, J., Lin, Y., Ji, C., Yang, H.: A reconfigurable omnidirectional soft robot based on caterpillar locomotion. Soft Robot. **5**, 164–174 (2018)
21. Cates, M.E., Wittmer, J.P., Bouchaud, J.-P., Claudin, P.: Jamming, force chains, and fragile matter. Phys. Rev. Lett. **81**, 1841–1844 (1998)
22. Liu, A.J., Nagel, S.R.: Jamming is not just cool any more. Nature **396**, 21–22 (1998)

# A Soft Robot for Ground Crawling: Design and Analysis

Yuxuan Lu[1,2] , Fengyu Xu[1,2(✉)] , Yudong Yang[1,2] ,
and Fanchang Meng[1,2]

[1] College of Automation, Nanjing University of Posts
and Telecommunications, Nanjing, China
xufengyu598@163.com
[2] Jiangsu Engineering Lab for IOT Intelligent Robots
(IOTRobot), Nanjing, China

**Abstract.** This paper presents the concept and design of a rolling soft crawling robot, which is made of natural soft or extensible material. Capabilities of squeezing, crawling, and morphing would rarely possible with a method based only on rigid links. In this article, the flexibility of soft robot is applied to crawling ground, which largely enhances the stability of machine and anti-interference. The idea is to apply the principle of the stiffness gradient layer on soft actuator, which can have the structure of 3 different stiffness layers. Based on establishing the mechanical model of soft crawling robot, the analysis of mechanical characteristics of robots, surface traction on the new soft climbing robot is provided. On this basis, finite element analysis and experiment are given to verify the robot actual crawling and expanding ability. This paper intends to provide a type of analysis of soft crawling robot and compare analysis with experiment to verify the robot's crawling ability and stability. Potential problems and future are discussed.

**Keywords:** Soft robot · Gradient stiffness layer ·
Viscous mechanical properties

## 1 Introduction

Conventionally, engineers have employed rigid crawling robots instead of manual work, which has obvious advantages in safety, stability and accuracy. Rigid materials are traditionally made up to create precise and predictable system [1]. However, rigid robots have low compatibility with environments in some cases, which can hardly apply in dynamic, unknown, unstructured systems. Through increasing the degree of freedom, the flexibility of robots can be largely improved. Therefore, more degrees of freedom have been added to the rigid robot to make it have a certain continuous deformation ability, forming a hyper-redundant robot. But it still has deficiency in contacting with environment. So an increasing number of researchers pay attention on soft crawling robots.

Rigid crawling robots have been employed in various aspects such as detection, exploration and so on. University of Illinois Urbana-Champaign developed a crawling

© Springer Nature Switzerland AG 2019
H. Yu et al. (Eds.): ICIRA 2019, LNAI 11741, pp. 544–555, 2019.
https://doi.org/10.1007/978-3-030-27532-7_48

robot driven by multi-stable origami [2]. University of Southern Denmark and Nanjing University of Aeronautics and Astronautics designed a bio-inspired Crawling Robot [3]. Swiss scientist Gehring C, Bellicoso C D, Coros S, et al presented Dynamic trotting on Slopes for Quadrupedal Robots [4]. University of Electro-Communications, Tokyo presented a mobile robot for Climbing Steep Stairs [5], for climbing steep stairs.

Locomotion is a key requirement in a robot designed for crawling, which means ability to move without being hindered and interconnect safely with environment is vital. While these are largely successful [2–5], they cannot apply in where space in constraint. So soft robots with a better flexibility and lightweight which are highly dexterous in avoiding obstacle and high flexibility, can adequately apply in ground crawling. Numerous devises have been developed and put into experiments. University of Bristol, Digumarti K M, Cao C, Guo J, et al. designed Multi-directional crawling robot that combines soft electroactive polymer actuators with compliant electro adhesive feet [6]. Harvard University presented a soft multigait soft robot [7], which is composed exclusively soft materials. Case Western Reserve University developed a Worm-like robots [8], rely on mechanical actuation and require large complex structures to accommodate large actuators. Barry A. Trimmer research team of Tufts University developed the GoQBot robot [9], based on curved reptiles and driven by shape memory alloy (SMA). The robot uses a retractable pneumatic soft actuator that can crawling ground in a constraint place.

From the above article, the situation of soft ground crawling robot has been detailed. The soft crawling robots generally use Flexible Fluidic Actuator, a new low-power soft actuator with high ductility and adaptability. This paper intends to apply the idea of high softness to solve the key problems of stability and obstacle performance of crawling robot. This article analyzes mechanical characteristics based on a new soft ground crawling robot and verifies the robot's actual crawling ability and stability. The structure and concept of the soft crawling robot is described in Sect. 2, while Sect. 3 analyze all characterization of robot, their surface traction and crawling force. Fabrication, tests and performance assessment are detailed in Sect. 4. All work were summarized and future work discussed in Sect. 5.

## 2    Structure and Concept of Soft Crawling Robot

As shown in Fig. 1, the design of soft actuator adopts the principle of the stiffness gradient layer, body of the actuator is layered with different stiffness materials, as so to have various stiffness characteristics. The stiffness of the deformed layer, the support layer and the constraint layer gradually increases. The deformation layer region is made of soft silicone material. When the cavity is pressurized, the deformation layer region can generate a large range of deformation, and can form a driving force for the robot movement by interaction with the hard surface; the support layer, made of medium hardness silicone material, plays the role of supporting the whole mechanism of the robot. Under the action of air pressure, it can only be compressed to produce a small range of deformation, and cannot occur in a wide range of deformation. The design of the support layer is beneficial to improve the whole stability of the mechanism, and to play the role of compliant obstacle function; the application of the constrained layer area has a relatively rigid material design (but not a rigid material), it is basically not deform under a certain pressure. This layer can support the entire drive mechanism and, where needed, can carry equipment such as batteries, boards and inspection equipment.

As shown in Fig. 2, when the cavity is pressurized, the deformation layer will have a lager deformation owing to stiffness. With the help of clamping force to overcome the robot's own gravity, we inflate the first cavity. When the deformed layer is deformed enough to squeeze the hard surface to make the actuator move, the next cavity will be inflated. At the same time, the first cavity will be deflated. Repeat this process, the robot will crawl the slope and go forward. The sequence of inflating cavities satisfies the following: $1 \rightarrow (1\&2) \rightarrow 2 \rightarrow (2\&3) \rightarrow 3 \rightarrow (3\&4) \rightarrow \cdots \rightarrow (6\&1) \rightarrow 1$ (Fig. 2).

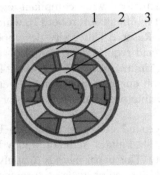

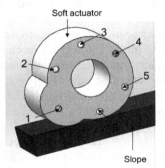

**Fig. 1.** Stiffness gradient design and construct of soft actuator. (layer 1 is deformation layer, layer 2 is the support layer, layer 3 is the constraint layer)

**Fig. 2.** The crawling diagram of soft actuator.

## 3    Crawl Analysis and Analysis of Surface Traction

### 3.1    Crawling Analysis

As shown in Fig. 3, the mechanical model of the soft actuator has been established. With the clamping force $Q$ under the action of the clamping mechanism, the robot contact with the surface of the ground. Since the robot and the surface are not smooth, the frictional force that hinders the crawling will be affected during the process of crawling. Assuming that the clamping force have overcame the gravity of the robot $m_r$, the ground and the robot are arranged as shown in Fig. 3. Assuming that the initial contact point between the actuator and the contact surface is $I$. And contact point between the deformed layer of the cavity and the hard surface after deformation is $J$, as the deformation increases, the deformed layer and the contact surface form an extrusion. And $F$ is combined force of the hard surface which will give the robot a reaction force $N = F$ (to the right of the common normal line along the contact surface of the ground and the deformation layer, called the driving force). $l$ is arm length from $N$ to $I$. With the influence of the couple of clamping force and driving force, the robot will rotate counterclockwise. Because the robot and the ground surface are not rigid, they will be deformed. There will be a contact surface, which will generate rolling friction when the robot rolls. In the end, the robot must overcome the rolling friction resistance moment $M_g$ (its direction is opposite to the rolling tendency). When the driving force increases to a certain value, the actuator is in a critical state of being moved.

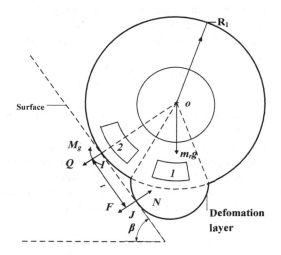

**Fig. 3.** The simplified model of mechanics for crawling the slope.

When the soft actuator is placed on the slope plane as shown in Fig. 3, it is only subjected to gravity. When the actuator can scroll down under gravity, the force balance equation is satisfied:

$$m_r g R_1 \sin \beta - \delta(m_r g \cos \beta) \geq 0 \tag{1}$$

Here, $m_r$ is the mass of the actuator, $g$ is gravitational acceleration, $R_1$ is the radius of the actuator, $\beta$ is the angle of the slope, and $\delta$ is rolling friction coefficient. Assuming that the soft actuator does not slip with the slope, the robot will roll at a constant speed during the movement, and the moment balance will satisfied:

$$\beta \geq \arctan \frac{\delta}{R_1} \tag{2}$$

According to the physical model produced by the laboratory, give the parameters of the system: $m_r = 0.2\,\text{kg}$, $R_1 = 0.02\,\text{m}$, $\delta = 0.2 \times 10^{-2}\,\text{m}$. The slope used in the experiment is cardboard, and the friction between the silicone rubber and the cardboard is relatively large, taking the rolling friction coefficient between the two $\delta = 0.2 \times 10^{-2}$m. By calculating, it will not roll down the slope under the force of gravity until the angle of slope is $\beta \geq 5.7°$.

In order for the actuator to roll up the slope, the driving torque needs to satisfy the following moment balance equation:

$$Nl - m_r g R_1 \sin \beta - \delta(m_r g \cos \beta + Q) \geq 0 \tag{3}$$

Here, N is the driving force, $l$ is the arm of force, $m_r$ is the mass of the actuator, $g$ is gravitational acceleration, $R_1$ is the radius of the actuator, $\beta$ is the angle of the slope, $\delta$ is rolling friction coefficient, and $Q$ is clamping force.

To calculate theoretical ability of crawling slope, it can be obtained by Eq. (3):

$$R_1 \sin \beta + \delta \cos \beta = \frac{Nl - \delta Q}{m_r g} \tag{4}$$

According to the above analysis, take simulation of the the motion capability of the soft actuator. Give the parameters of the system from the physical model produced in the laboratory: $m_r = 0.2$ kg, $R_1 = 0.02$ m, $\delta = 0.2 \times 10^{-2}$ m. Assuming that no clamping force is applied to actuator ($Q = 0$), the driving force provide by deformation of actuator is $N = 1.3$ N. As shown in Fig. 4, calculate the relationship between parameters. According to simulation, we can obtain that the theoretical climbing angle is 35°. While it is difficult to achieve due to the actual soft actuator is not perfect.

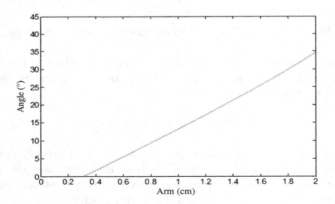

**Fig. 4.** Relationship between arm and climbing angle

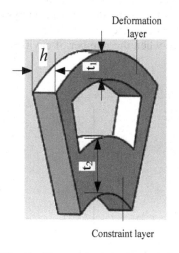

Fig. 5. 3D model of single module.

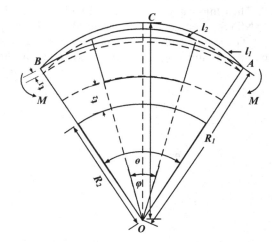

Fig. 6. Analysis of single module.

## 3.2 Analysis of the Deformation Layering Analysis

Establish the mechanical model of the soft actuator in Fig. 6. Applying the principle of minimum potential energy, we can obtain the relation between bending rigidity D and pressure P, volume V and pressure P. Because the direction and size of the curve exhibited by the deformation layer are determined by the pressure P and bending rigidity D, the relationship between the pressure V and the crawling force will be provided. Assuming that the deformation layer equation is $f(x)$. According to application of the principle of minimum potential energy, we can yield [10].

$$k_p = \frac{6pl_2\left[R_1^2 - (R_2 + t_2)^2\right]}{Et_1^3 l_1} \tag{5}$$

$$D = \lim_{M \to 0} \frac{M}{k - k_p} = \frac{Eht_1^3\left\{6^4 l_2\left[R_1^2 - (R_2 + t_2)^2\right]^{1/2}P + Et_1^3 l_1\right\}}{12\left\{3l_2\left[R_1^2 - (R_2 + t_2)^2\right]^{1/2}P + Et_1^3 l_1\right\}} \tag{6}$$

Here, in Fig. 6, $D = \frac{Ewt_1^3}{12}$, E is elastic modulus, the thickness of the module taken is $h$ (Fig. 5) and $t_1$, $t_2$ is thickness of the deformation layer and the constraint layer respectively, length of the whole deformation layer module is $l_1$, the length of the outer wall of the cavity is $l_2 = R_1 \varphi$.

In summary, bending rigidity D and volume V have affine dependences on pressure P. Then this paper analyzed and verified the relationship by Finite element analysis (ANSYS). Applying super-elastic Monny-Riviling two parameter model [11].

The relationship between deformation and pressure when the number of cavities is 6 and only inflating one cavity, was shown in Fig. 7.

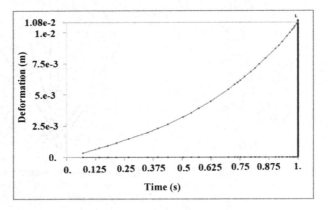

**Fig. 7.**  Deformation-pressure of one cavity

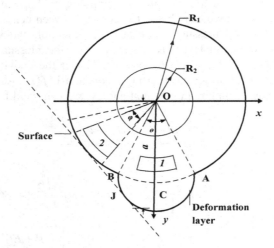

**Fig. 8.**  Analysis of the deformation layer

Since the nonlinear equation of the elastic body is very complicated, the deformation of 3D cavity module can be simplified into a 2D curve (shown in Fig. 8) by using the plane strain theory of elastic mechanics. According to the previous analysis, as shown in Fig. 7. In the support layer, the support layer only undergoes a small deformation during the inflation, so it is assumed that two points (A and B) are unchanged after the inflation deformation. Using the center of the circular actuator as the coordinate origin O, establish a Cartesian coordinate system as shown in Fig. 8. Where A is $(R_1 \sin, (\frac{\theta}{2}), R_1 \cos(\frac{\theta}{2}))$, distance from point O to point C is $a$. So C is $(0, a)$. The plane AB equation according to the plane strain theory of elastic mechanics is approximated as:

$$f(x) = a^2 \sqrt{1 - \frac{a^2 - \left(R_1 \cos \frac{\theta}{2}\right)^2}{\left(R_1 \sin \frac{\theta}{2}\right)^2 a^2} x^2} \tag{7}$$

The curvature of the deformed layer:

$$k(x) = \frac{|f(x)|}{\left(1 + f'(x)^2\right)^{3/2}} \tag{8}$$

Combine (7) and (8), yield:

$$k(x) = \frac{\dfrac{a^2 R_1 \sin \frac{\theta}{2}}{\sqrt{a^2 - \left(R_1 \cos \frac{\theta}{2}\right)^2}}}{\left[\left(\dfrac{a^2 - \left(R_1 \cos \frac{\theta}{2}\right)}{R_1 \sin \frac{\theta}{2}} - 1\right) x^2 + \dfrac{\left(R_1 \sin \frac{\theta}{2}\right)^2}{a^2 - \left(R_1 \cos \frac{\theta}{2}\right)^2}\right]^{3/2}} \tag{9}$$

The equation of the line between the actuator and the ground surface is:

$$f_1(x) = (\tan \theta)x + \frac{R_1}{\cos \theta} \tag{10}$$

Substituting (7) into Eq. (10) yields

$$a^2 \sqrt{1 - \frac{a^2 - \left(R_1 \cos \frac{\theta}{2}\right)^2}{\left(R_1 \sin \frac{\theta}{2}\right)^2 a^2} x^2} = (\tan \theta)x + \frac{R_1}{\cos \theta} \tag{11}$$

When Eq. (12) have a solution, taking $R_1 = 2$ cm, $R_2 = 0.8$ cm respectively. When the number of cavities is 5, 6, the relationship between the distance from the C to the circular O and the abscissa of the contact point on the deformation layer are obtained by Matlab simulation (Fig. 9).

The horizontal ordinate represents the distance C from the point O on the deformed layer to the origin of the coordinate (ie, the length of $a$), and the ordinate represents the intersection of the deformed layer and the ground surface (i.e., the contact point). The deformed layer is just in contact with the cable surface. When the number of cavities is 5, $a \approx 4.4$ cm, and the number is 6, $a \approx 3.1$ cm. Assuming $R_1 = 2$ cm and the number of cavities is 5, the theoretical demand deformation is about 2.4 cm; the number is 6, the theoretical demand deformation is about 1.1 cm.

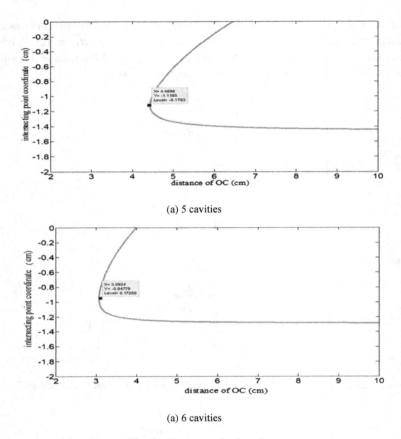

(a) 5 cavities

(a) 6 cavities

**Fig. 9.** Contact point location.

# 4   Soft Robot Fabrication and Experiments

## 4.1   Fabrication of Silicone

In the Sect. 2, structure of robot is detailed. The robot needs 3 different stiffness materials. As shown in Table 1, prepare three kinds of silicone, Ecoflex-0030, Ecoflex-0050, Dragon skin-10. Ecoflex-0030 can be used to make deformation layer due to its high flexibility. Ecoflex-0050 can be used to make support layer because it has a greater hardness than Ecoflex-0030. Dragon skin-10 can be used to make the constraining layer due to its highest hardness.

Firstly, the silicone used is divided into two parts, A and B, which needs to be arranged in proportion to 1:1.

Next, stir several times and place the cup in a vacuum degasser for several minutes until there is no bubble. Then it can be used after standing for a few minutes.

**Table 1.** Main parameters of the material.

| Material type | Parameters | |
|---|---|---|
| Ecoflex 0030 Silicone | Shore hardness: 00–30 | Tensile strength: 200 psi |
| Ecoflex 0050 Silicone | Shore hardness: 00–50 | Tensile strength: 315 psi |
| Dragon Skin 10 Silicone | Shore hardness: 10 A | Tensile strength: 102 pli |

## 4.2    Fabrication of the Soft Actuator

Soft robots are generally made of soft materials, so that they mostly can only be made by casting, lamination and bonding and 3D print [12]. The soft robot in the paper designed in the basic structure of the stiffness gradient layer. According to this concept, this paper took the method of layer casting, which accelerate thermoforming by digital display hot plates and use glue to strengthen the tightness of the joint. The specific process is given below:

Firstly, apply the Vaseline to the printed mold (shown in Fig. 10) surface to prevent the silicone from being absorbed on the mold.

The mold is assembled and the method of solidification by layer casting is adopted. (first Dragon skin-10 to make constraining layer, second Ecoflex-0050 to make support layer, last Ecoflex-0030 to make deformation layer). Finally, remove the shell mold, base, intermediate fan cavity, etc. and add a base for the finished part.

(a) Shell        (b)Cavity      (c)Base ring   (d)Constraint ring

(e)Cap-A                (f)Cap-B

**Fig. 10.** Mold of soft robot

The thickness of the upper and lower bottoms is about 1 cm, one end is closed, and the other end is reserved for the air inlet. The total length of the actuator is about 18 cm, the outer radius is about 2 cm, the outer thickness of the sector cavity is 0.1 cm, the radius of the large circular cavity is 9 mm, and the radius of the hose used is 1.5 mm.

### 4.3  Experiment

To analyze the mechanical characterization of robot, this paper used the ways that make robot crawled on plane and bevel with a certain angle and measured slope and material of ground that exactly make robot crawl successfully. As shown in Fig. 8, this paper measured the minimum and maximum slope that the robot can crawl without clamping force. First, this paper make the experiment that drive the robot crawl in the plane without any slope (Figs. 11 and 12). The robot can overcome the friction and route forward. Then increasing the slop, the maximum slope without clamping machine was measured (20°).

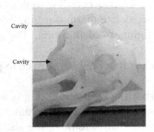

Fig. 11.  Plane (0°).

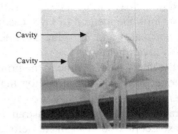

Fig. 12.  Plane (20°)

## 5  Conclusion

This paper has presented a rolling soft ground crawling robot based on stiffness gradient layer and flexible actuator. The fabrication and basic structure has been detailed, and the crawling characterizations of its performance have been provided. Through the analysis of the mechanical characteristics of the soft robot, we can come to the conclusion that the deformation of deformable layer has a affine dependency on pressure. Finite element analysis further verify the relationship between deformation we need and pressure. Furthermore, with the support of the clamping force, the squeezing force and reaction force will provide the robot with the crawling force. By experiment, the maximum slop and the material that make robot crawl successfully was given and the deformation size was measured.

Subsequent work will include accurately measuring the robot's crawling ability, exploring whether it can crawl the cable which has a certain curvature and an extensive study of the kinematics and dynamics of the robot. Finally, a entire robot will be provide, combined with clamping device to verify the robot's capability of crawling.

**Acknowledgment.** This research is supported by National Natural Science Foundation of China (51775284), Primary Research & Developement Plan of Jiangsu Province (BE2018734), Joint Research Fund for Overseas Chinese, Hong Kong and Macao Young Scholars (61728302), and Postgraduate Research &Practice Innovation Program of Jiangsu Province (SJCX18_0299).

# References

1. Laschi, C., Mazzolai, B., Cianchetti, M.: Soft robotics: technologies and systems pushing the boundaries of robot abilities. Sci. Robot. **1**, eaah3690 (2016)
2. Pagano, A., Yan, T., Chien, B., Wissa, A., Tawfick, S.: A crawling robot driven by multistable origami. Smart Mater. Struct. **26**(9), 094007 (2017)
3. Ji, A., Zhao, Z., Manoonpong, P., et al.: A bio-inspired climbing robot with flexible pads and claws. J. Bionic Eng. **25**(2), 368–378 (2018)
4. Gehring, C., Bellicoso, C.D., Coros, S., et al.: Dynamic trotting on slopes for quadrupedal robots. In: 2015 IEEE/RSJ International Conference on Intelligent Robots and Systems (IROS). IEEE (2015)
5. Tanaka, M., Nakajima, M., Suzuki, Y., et al.: Development and control of articulated mobile robot for climbing steep stairs. In: 2018 IEEE/ASME Transactions on Mechatronics, p. 1 (2018)
6. Digumarti, K.M., Cao, C., Guo, J., et al.: Multi-directional crawling robot with soft actuators and electroadhesive grippers. In: IEEE 2018 IEEE International Conference on Soft Robotics (RoboSoft) - Livorno, Italy, 24–28 April 2018, pp. 303–308 (2018)
7. Shepherd, R.F., et al.: Multigait soft robot. Proc. Natl. Acad. Sci. U.S.A. **108**, 20400–20403 (2011)
8. Horchler, A.D., et al.: Worm-like robotic locomotion with a compliant modular mesh. In: Wilson, Stuart P., Verschure, Paul F.M.J., Mura, A., Prescott, Tony J. (eds.) LIVINGMACHINES 2015. LNCS (LNAI), vol. 9222, pp. 26–37. Springer, Cham (2015). https://doi.org/10.1007/978-3-319-22979-9_3
9. Lin, H.T., Leisk, G.G., Trimmer, B.: GoQBot: a caterpillar-inspired soft-bodied rolling robot. Bioinspiration Biomim. **6**(2), 026007 (2016)
10. Carmel, M., et al.: Influence of surface traction on soft robot undulation. Int. J. Robot. Res. **32**(13), 1577–1584 (2013)
11. Wang, J.: Exact solution of the Mooney-Rivilin compression rod model and its dynamics. J. Yuxi Teachers Coll. **33**(284), 9–24 (2017)
12. Gul, J.Z., Sajid, M., Rehman, M.M., et al.: 3D printing for soft robotics – a review. Sci. Technol. Adv. Mater. **19**(1), 243–262 (2018)

# An Active Steering Soft Robot for Small-Bore T-Branch Pipeline

Tianbo Li, Yang Yang, Yonggan Liu, Yongjian Zhao,
Yan Peng, Jun Ke[✉], and Yuyi Zhai

Shanghai University, Shanghai 200444, China
sus_ke@shu.edu.cn

**Abstract.** The existing small-bore in-pipe robots are difficult to pass through complicated pipelines such as T-branch pipeline. Aiming at the challenge, this study designs an active steering robot with better flexibility and over-bending capability, which is suitable for small pipelines inspection. It is made of compliant silica gel and 3D printed mold and consists mainly of three parts, wherein the middle axial actuator has three uniform fan-shaped cavities through special design. The air pressure of the three cavities can be adjusted according to different turning requirements to realize active turning in the pipeline. In addition, the kinematics model of the in-pipe robot is established, and the relationship between the center position of the robot head and the air pressure of the three cavities is deduced, which provides theoretical support for the motion control of the robot. Finally, the accuracy of the model and the performance of the robot are verified by the experiments.

**Keywords:** In-pipe robot · Active steering · Silica gel · Fiber reinforcement

## 1 Introduction

As a carrier of transportation medium, pipelines are widely used to transport gas, liquid and solid devices. Among them, the one-inch pipelines are especially popular for transporting water or gas in houses and factories. However, it is difficult for the robots to inspect such small-diameter pipelines, which has the risk being stuck. Generally, the pipelines need to be sawed in sections for inspection, but this inspection method will cause irreversible damage to the pipelines.

In recent years, a variety of robots have been developed for pipelines inspection, which can be divided into wheel type, caterpillar type and snake-like in-pipe robots. While the wheeled robot is convenient to application and control, it is difficult to realize miniaturization limited by the complex structure. Okada and Sanemor [1] have developed a robot named MOGRER, whose driving wheel is passively pressed against the pipeline wall through springs and connecting rods. It is mainly used for monitoring tasks in pipelines with diameters of more than ten to twenty centimeter. Hirose et al. [2] proposed the These series wheeled in-pipe robots that are suitable for medium and small pipeline diameters. The applicable pipeline diameters for this series of pipeline inspection vehicles ranged from 25 mm to 150 mm. However, with the passive over-bending form, they can only pass through the large turning radius of pipelines. Roh and

Choi [3] developed a micro differential drive chassis in-pipe robot with wheels to inspect city gas pipelines with an inner diameter of 4 inches. In the past few decades, the snake-like robots have been introduced into pipeline detection due to their high adaptability to complex environments. MAKRO [4] project carried out by Rainer Hitzel GmbH Research Center in Germany has developed a multi-stage cableless robot platform with main wheels, which can bypass obstacles and is mainly used for sewer inspection with a diameter larger than 300 mm. The MRINSPECT [5] robot can move in horizontal and vertical pipelines for leak inspection of natural gas pipelines. Moreover, many researches have been done for the modeling of snake-like robot [6–8]. Limited by the existence of rigid elements such as motors and gears, the rigid robots are difficult to enter pipelines with diameters less than 150 mm or pipelines with varying structural sizes, and the higher requirements are put forward in the aspects of dustproof and waterproof. In addition, most of them cannot pass through right-angle bends at pipeline joints or do not have the capability of actively selecting directions of T-branch pipeline.

To overcome the miniaturization and compliance limitation of the rigid in-pipe robots, researchers focused on the development of the new soft robots. Among them, peristaltic in-pipe robots imitate inchworm peristalsis to creep forward in small-diameter pipelines. Fukuda et al. [9] developed a self-driven rubber actuator for testing small and medium-sized pipelines. Bertetto and Ruggiu [10] developed a peristaltic compliant robot for pipe inspection, and established a dynamic model considering compliance, damping and friction. Martinez et al. [11] designed a serrated soft actuator that can actively bend and twist. Heunget et al. [12] have developed a earthworm-like robot for intestinal tract, that can bend and move forward actively. Ariel et al. [13] have designed and manufactured a multi-actuator soft peristaltic robot by using a new method. The peristaltic robot can move forward in a small space and generate sufficient force to ensure stable movement when rubbing against the pipe wall. However, it can only passively turn according to the shape of the pipe, and cannot actively select the direction, thus they are difficult to be used for T-branch pipeline. In addition, the poor control precision and modeling accuracy still limit the application of the soft robotics.

Based on 3D printing technology, solidified silica gel [14] and fiber reinforcement [15, 16], a soft in-pipe robot for one-inch pipelines inspection is fabricated in this paper, as shown in Fig. 1. The robot can actively select the turning direction and pass through complex pipelines such as T-branch pipelines. In addition, the flexibility of the soft robot makes it have good adaptability to the structural size of the pipeline, and the ability to resist impact and deformation. The paper is organized as follows. In Sect. 2, the principle and manufacturing process of the robot is introduced. Section 3 describes the gait of the in-pipe robot in the T-branch pipeline. The Sect. 4 establishes the kinematic model of the in-pipe robot. In Sect. 5, several groups of tests are performed to evaluate the expected performance of the in-pipe robot. The conclusion and future works are given in Sect. 6.

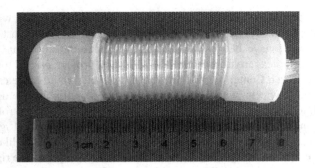

**Fig. 1.** The prototype of the proposed in-pipe robot.

## 2  Concept and Mechanism

From the perspective of biological inspiration engineering, the structure of in-pipe robot replicates some functions of earthworm body to some extent. The earthworms move forward peristaltically by fixing the surrounding soil with bristles on the surface of the body through the alternating expansion and contraction of the ring muscle and the longitudinal muscle [17].

As shown in Fig. 2, the pneumatic in-pipe robot introduced in this paper consists of three parts: rear radial actuator, intermediate axial actuator and front radial actuator. All parts of the robot share a common air pump source, and each independent cavity is respectively controlled by an electromagnetic valve (CKD Company, MEVT series) connected with an air pipeline (polyurethane PU hose with inner diameter of 1 mm and outer diameter of 2 mm). The rear radial actuator and the front radial actuator are fabricated to a cavity with a diameter of 20 mm, a length of 10 mm, and a thickness of 2 mm. The radial actuator anchors the inner wall of the pipeline after expansion, providing enough friction for the in-pipe robot. The intermediate axial actuator is a cylinder with a diameter of 16 mm and a length of 30 mm. There are three independent and uniform distribution fan-shaped cavities in the middle, and the overall thickness is uniform 2 mm. The external surface of the axial actuator is wrapped with cross-fibre reinforcement to limit its radial expansion and enlarge its axial elongation [18].

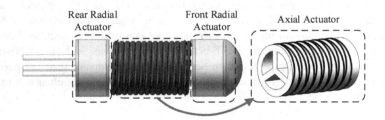

**Fig. 2.** Structure diagram of in-pipe robot.

The front steering head unit is specially designed and made by 3D printing, and can carry various sensors. The radian head improved the fault-tolerant ability of the in-pipe robot and ensures that the robot can pass through the bend pipeline smoothly. A 3D printed annular support unit is attached to the surface of each silicone unit to limit the expansion and extension of the silicone unit on the end surface, and to enhance the strength of the whole structure. It is noticed that the air pipeline of the front radial actuator is helical and evenly wound around the outer side of the axial actuator to supply air to the front radial actuator without affecting the over-bending of the robot.

Ecoflex platinum catalyzed silicone rubber is used to manufacture silicone rubber driving unit, and the rigid mold is made of PLA material by 3D printing technology. In order to facilitate injection molding and demolding, the mold is designed into multiple parts. After assembly, the mold is injected, and after molding, the silica gel unit can be obtained after demolding.

## 3   Gait for T-Branch Pipeline

When the robot encounters T-branch pipeline, the electromagnetic valve needs to be controlled according to the specific pipeline environment to change the air pressure in the three chambers. The air pressure difference between the three chambers is utilized to enable the robot to generate deflection angle and elongation required by over-bending, and front and rear radial actuators are matched to alternately anchor the pipeline wall to realize the turning of the in-pipe robot.

As shown in Fig. 3, the gait sequence of the pneumatic in-pipe robot for passing through the T-branch pipeline bend is as follows.

1. The rear radial actuator expands to anchor to the pipeline;
2. According to the position in the pipeline, the robot determine the elongation and angle of the required turning, and control the electromagnetic valve to generate air pressure difference of three cavities of the axial actuator to make turning action;
3. The front radial actuator expands and anchors the pipeline;
4. The intermediate axial actuator and the rear radial actuator contract together to drive the robot forward;
5. The rear radial actuator and the front radial actuator expand to anchor the pipeline together;
6. Repeat steps 1–5 until the whole robot passes through the T-branch pipeline;

The six steps form a turning process of the robot. After the sixth step, the robot's gait is converted into its walking gait in the straight pipeline, and the action is repeated until the next turning. Figure 3b shows a control sequence for controlling the robot to move forward one stride in the T-branch pipeline, wherein orange lines and purple lines indicate that the electromagnetic valve corresponding to the actuator is in an intermediate state of full opening and full closing.

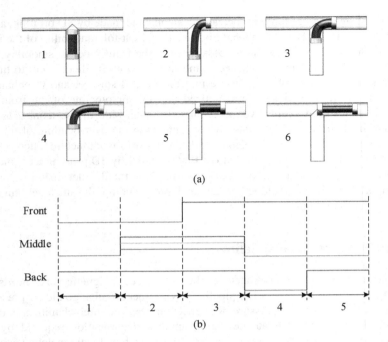

(a)

(b)

**Fig. 3.** The motion sequence of in-pipe robot for passing through T-branch pipeline: (a) the gait in the T-branch pipeline, (b) the control sequence of the controller.

## 4  Kinematics Modeling

The steering motion of the developed robot is completed by the cooperation of the three cavities of the axial actuator. Although the three cavities are independently driven, the extension of each cavity will be constrained by the other two cavities, thus causing the complicated coupling influence. In this study, the three fan-shaped cavities of the axial actuator are simplified into three arcs of constant curvature [19], and the forward kinematics model is established by combining the robot size and geometric analysis. Then, the relationship between the end position of the in-pipe robot and the air pressure of the three cavities is obtained.

### 4.1  Modeling of Air Pressure-Cavity Length

The intermediate axial actuator can be divided into three fan-shaped parts with the same shape, structure and size. Thus, the axial actuator is divided into the same three parts for analysis, and the structural performance of each part is considered to be exactly the same.

The relationship between the length of a single chamber and the pressure of a sector chamber is obtained through experiments. In the initial state, the pressure of the cavity is 0 kPa, and then the pressure inside the cavity is changed by an increment of 10 kPa until the pressure is increased to 50 kPa. Based on the length of the robot multiple measured manually, the relationship shown in Fig. 4 can be obtained by least squares.

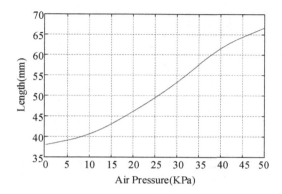

**Fig. 4.** The cavity length under various air pressure.

### 4.2    Forward Kinematics

Based on the above analysis, the corresponding length $l_1$, $l_2$, $l_3$ can be obtained from the air pressure of each sector cavity. The following analysis simplifies the three sector cavity parts of the axial actuator into three arcs of constant curvature, and the end position of the axial actuator can be determined through the center lines of the three arcs:

$$l = \frac{1}{3}(l_1 + l_2 + l_3)$$

(1)

where $l$ is the length of the axial actuator centerline. Assuming that the relationship between the air pressures of the three chambers is $P_1 > P_2 = P_3 > 0$ when the in-pipe robot turns in the T-branch pipeline. As shown in Fig. 5, the following equations can be obtained through geometric analysis.

$$(R + \delta)\theta = l_1$$

(2)

$$(R - \frac{1}{2}\delta)\theta = l_2 = l_3$$

(3)

where $\delta$ is the distance between the center of the sector area and the center of the axial actuator and $R$ is the radius of curvature of the center of the axial actuator. According to (2) and (3), (4) can be obtained.

$$R = \frac{(l_1 + \frac{1}{2}l_2)\delta}{l_1 - l_2}, \theta = \frac{l(l_1 - l_2)}{(l_2 + \frac{1}{2}l_1)\delta}$$

(4)

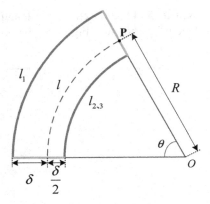

**Fig. 5.** Robot over-bend diagram.

Figure 6 shows the process of the robot as passing through the T-branch pipeline. For the convenience of analysis, it is considered that the plane of the robot and the plane of the pipeline are parallel.

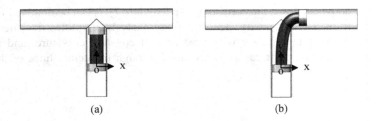

(a)                                      (b)

**Fig. 6.** Process of the robot as passing through T-branch pipeline.

The coordinate system $Oxy$ is established at the center of the rear radial actuator of the in-pipe robot. In which, the center coordinate $(x_0, y_0)$ of the front radial actuator in the initial state is as follows.

$$\begin{pmatrix} x_0 \\ y_0 \end{pmatrix} = \begin{pmatrix} 0 \\ l_0 + h \end{pmatrix} \tag{5}$$

The center coordinates $(x, y)$ of the front radial actuator of the inflated in-pipe robot can be obtained by combining the above formula as follows.

$$\begin{pmatrix} x \\ y \end{pmatrix} = \begin{pmatrix} R - R\cos\theta + \frac{h}{2}\sin\theta \\ \frac{h}{2} + R\sin\theta + \frac{h}{2}\cos\theta \end{pmatrix} == \begin{pmatrix} \frac{(l_1+\frac{1}{2}l_2)\delta}{l_1-l_2}\left(1 - \cos\frac{l(l_1-l_2)}{(l_2+\frac{1}{2}l_1)\delta}\right) + \frac{h}{2}\sin\frac{l(l_1-l_2)}{(l_2+\frac{1}{2}l_1)\delta} \\ \frac{(l_1+\frac{1}{2}l_2)\delta}{l_1-l_2}\sin\frac{l(l_1-l_2)}{(l_2+\frac{1}{2}l_1)\delta} + \frac{h}{2}\left(1 + \cos\frac{l(l_1-l_2)}{(l_2+\frac{1}{2}l_1)\delta}\right) \end{pmatrix} \tag{6}$$

# 5 Experiments and Discussions

## 5.1 Experimental Setup

To verify the validity of the proposed model and evaluate the robot's motion performance, the following two groups of tests were performed.

(1) The model is verified by braking one cavity of the intermediate axial actuator. The pressure is gradually pressurized from 0 kPa to 50 kPa for a single cavity. The position of the robot is manually measured during the process, and the experimental measurement is repeated five times to obtain the desired motion trajectory.
(2) To test the motion performance of the robot, it was driven to pass through a T-branch pipeline with an inner diameter of 25 mm, and the bending situation was recorded.

## 5.2 Testbed

The motion ability of pneumatic in-pipe robot in various kinds of pipelines was tested. The experimental device includes the designed in-pipe robot, Ardunio control board, air valve (integrated MEVT-500), air compressor, precision pneumatic regulator, air pipe and PVC transparent pipeline. The system platform is shown in Fig. 7.

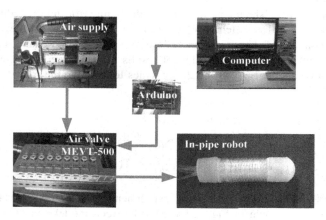

**Fig. 7.** Flow chart of in-pipe robot control.

## 5.3 Experimental Results

**Model Accuracy**

To verify the validity of the theoretical model established in this study, the single-cavity actuator was used to test the movement position of the center point of the front radial actuator of the in-pipe robot in the $XOY$ plane. $X$ and $Y$ respectively represent the movement displacement point of the center point of the front radial actuator along the $X$-axis and the $Y$-axis, and Fig. 8 is the movement diagram of the end position. It can be seen that the experimental results and the predict results have the similar trend. However, there is a certain error, and the maximum coordinate deviation is about 10 mm. It is attributed to axial tracheal lateral trachea, approximate kinematic modeling, measurement error, etc.

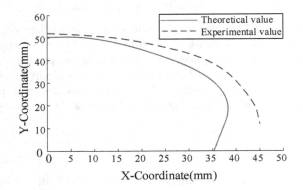

**Fig. 8.** Comparison of the theoretical value and experimental value for robot end position.

**Modified Model**

Through the above analysis, it can be seen that the main error in the model introduced from the influence on the stretching of the other two cavities when the single cavity system is not considered. These influences lead to certain regular changes in the errors of the experimental results and theoretical results. Thus, correction coefficients are introduced to the lengths $l_2$, $l_3$ of the 2, 3 cavities to improve the model accuracy.

$$\begin{pmatrix} x \\ y \end{pmatrix} = \begin{pmatrix} R - R\cos\theta + \frac{h}{2}\sin\theta \\ \frac{h}{2} + R\sin\theta + \frac{h}{2}\cos\theta \end{pmatrix}$$
$$= \begin{pmatrix} \frac{(l_1 + \frac{1}{2}Cl_2)\delta}{l_1 - Cl_2}\left(1 - \cos\frac{l(l_1 - Cl_2)}{(Cl_2 + \frac{1}{2}l_1)\delta}\right) + \frac{h}{2}\sin\frac{l(l_1 - Cl_2)}{(Cl_2 + \frac{1}{2}l_1)\delta} \\ \frac{(l_1 + \frac{1}{2}Cl_2)\delta}{l_1 - Cl_2}\sin\frac{l(l_1 - Cl_2)}{(Cl_2 + \frac{1}{2}l_1)\delta} + \frac{h}{2}\left(1 + \cos\frac{l(l_1 - Cl_2)}{(Cl_2 + \frac{1}{2}l_1)\delta}\right) \end{pmatrix} \quad (7)$$

The correction coefficient is calculated experimentally, which is a variable value in this model [20]. As shown in Fig. 9, the error between model and the experimental results is greatly reduced. The new model is suitable for single-chamber actuating and the new model will be used in subsequent trials and work.

### 5.4    T-Branch Pipeline Test

The motion performance of the robot was test in a T-branch pipeline, which is generally located at the joint of the pipeline and belongs to a complex environment in the pipeline. As shown in Fig. 10, it is confirmed that although there are many alternative routes, the robot can actively select one of the routes according to requirements, and complete turning through the T-branch pipeline with inner diameter of 25 mm.

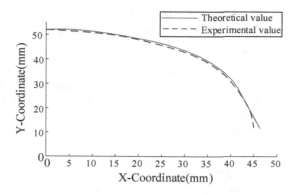

**Fig. 9.** Motion position of robot end considering correction coefficient.

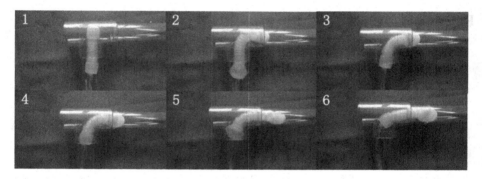

**Fig. 10.** One-inch T-branch pipeline test.

## 6 Conclusion

In this paper, an in-pipe robot for thin pipelines inspection was designed and manufactured by using silica gel and 3D printing, which consists of two radial actuators and one axial actuator. The axial actuator with three uniform cavities ensures that the robot can actively bend in the pipeline, and fiber reinforcement is adopted to limit the radial expansion and maximize the axial expansion.

(1) The soft in-pipe robot can smoothly adapt to the changes of internal dimensions of pipelines. Axial actuators evenly distributed with three cavities enable the in-pipe robot to bend in any direction, thus can complete turning in complicated pipelines. In addition, the kinematics model is established, and the relationship between the center point of the front radial actuator and the air pressure of the three chambers is deduced, which provides a theoretical basis for the motion control of the robot.

(2) The in-pipe robot has universal applicability. It can be applied to pipelines with various sizes and types, such as straight pipes, tee pipes or vertical pipes.

(3) Comparing with rigid robots, the pure soft in-pipe robots have more possibilities, such as traveling in pipelines filled with liquid without considering factors such as dustproof and waterproof.

This design has verified the feasibility and universal applicability of the in-pipe robot by several groups of experiments. It can actively choose the direction and pass through complicated pipelines such as T-branch pipeline, which significantly expand the application fields. In the future, sensors will be integrated to the robot to make it more intelligent and to improve control accuracy.

**Acknowledgment.** This study was supported by National Natural Science Foundation of China (Grant No.61773254), Shanghai Sailing Program (Grant No. 17YF1406200), Shanghai Y-oung Eastern Scholar Program (Grant No. QD2016029), and Shanghai civil-military integration program (Grant No. JMRH-2018-1043).

# References

1. Okada, T., Sanemori, T.: MOGRER: a vehicle study and realization for in-pipe inspection tasks. IEEE J. Robot. & Autom. **3**(6), 573–582 (1987)
2. Hirose, S., Ohno, H., Mitsue, T.: Design of in-pipe inspection vehicles for Φ25, Φ50, Φ150 pipes. In: Proceedings of IEEE International Conference of Robotics and Automation, pp. 2309–2314 (1999)
3. Roh, S.G., Choi, H.R.: Differential-drive in-pipe robot for moving inside urban gas pipelines. IEEE Trans. Rob. **21**(1), 1–17 (2005)
4. Rome, E., Hertzberg, J., Kirchner, F.: Towards autonomous sewer robots: the MAKRO project. Urban Water **1**(1), 57–70 (1999)
5. Roh, S.G., Ryew, S.M., Yang, J.H.: Actively steerable in-pipe inspection robots for underground urban gas pipelines. In: Proceedings 2001 ICRA IEEE International Conference on Robotics and Automation (Cat. No. 01CH37164), vol. 1, pp. 761–766. IEEE (2001)
6. Transeth, A.A., Leine, R.I., Glocker, C.: Snake robot obstacle-aided locomotion: modeling, simulations, and experiments. IEEE Trans. Rob. **24**(1), 88–104 (2008)
7. Liljebäck, P., Pettersen, K.Y., Stavdahl, Ø.: A review on modelling, implementation, and control of snake robots. Robot. Autom. Syst. **60**(1), 29–40 (2012)
8. Transeth, A.: 3-D snake robot motion: nonsmooth modeling, simulations, and experiments. IEEE Trans. Rob. **24**(2), 361–376 (2008)
9. Fukuda, T.: Rubber gas actuator driven by hydrogen storage alloy for in-pipe inspection mobile robot with flexible structure. In: IEEE International Conference on Robotics & Automation. IEEE (1989)
10. Bertetto, A.M., Ruggiu, M.: In-pipe inch-worm pneumatic flexible robot. In: 2001 IEEE ASME International Conference on Advanced Intelligent Mechatronics. Proceedings (Cat. No. 01TH8556), vol. 2, pp. 1226–1231. IEEE (2001)
11. Martinez, R.V., Branch, J.L., Fish, C.R.: Robotic tentacles with three-dimensional mobility based on flexible elastomers. Adv. Mater. **25**(2), 205–212 (2013)
12. Heung, H.L., Chiu, P.W.Y., Li, Z.: Design and prototyping of a soft earthworm-like robot targeted for GI tract inspection. In: 2016 IEEE International Conference on Robotics and Biomimetics (ROBIO), pp. 497–502. IEEE (2016)

13. Calderón, A.A., Ugalde, J.C., Zagal, J.C.: Design, fabrication and control of a multi-material-multi-actuator soft robot inspired by burrowing worms. In: 2016 IEEE International Conference on Robotics and Biomimetics (ROBIO), pp. 31–38. IEEE (2016)
14. Suzumori, K., Endo, S., Kanda, T.: A bending pneumatic rubber actuator realizing soft-bodied manta swimming robot. In: Proceedings 2007 IEEE International Conference on Robotics and Automation, pp. 4975–4980. IEEE (2007)
15. Galloway, K.C., Polygerinos, P., Walsh, C.J.: Mechanically programmable bend radius for fiber-reinforced soft actuators. In: 2013 16th International Conference on Advanced Robotics (ICAR), pp. 1–6. IEEE (2013)
16. Galloway, K.C., Becker, K.P., Phillips, B.: Soft robotic grippers for biological sampling on deep reefs. Soft Robot. 3(1), 23–33 (2016)
17. Schulke, M., Hartmann, L., Behn, C.: Worm-like locomotion systems: development of drives and selective anisotropic friction structures. Universitätsbibliothek Ilmenau (2011)
18. Polygerinos, P., Wang, Z., Galloway, K.: Soft robotic glove for combined assistance and at-home rehabilitation. Robot. Autom. Syst. 73, 135–143 (2014)
19. Webster, R.J., Jones, B.A.: Design and kinematic modeling of constant curvature continuum robots: a review. Int. J. Robot. Res. 29(13), 1661–1683 (2010)
20. Giannaccini, M.E., Xiang, C., Atyabi, A.: Novel design of a soft lightweight pneumatic continuum robot arm with decoupled variable stiffness and positioning. Soft Robot. 5(1), 54–70 (2018)

# Analysis and Application of the Bending Actuators Used in Soft Robotics

Wen Zhou[1,2], Jiahuan Chen[1,2], Xudong Wang[1,2], Jiadong Hu[1,2], and Yiqing Li[3(✉)]

[1] School of Mechanical Engineering,
Xi'an Jiaotong University, Xi'an 710049, China
[2] State Key Laboratory for Manufacturing and Systems Engineering,
Xi'an 710049, China
[3] School of Mechatronic Engineering, Xi'an Technological University,
Xi'an 710021, China
yi@dr.yitsi.org

**Abstract.** Two types of soft bending actuators with the rib structure and the pleated structure are introduced in this study. We illustrate the advantages of the two types of actuators, as well as their applicability to different tasks. We build a finite element model to simulate the deformation of the two actuators under the internal pressure. The simulation result shows a visible difference between the responses of the two actuators to the same internal pressure. We qualitatively explain the reason for these differences based on the simulation result. The two actuators are made using the same process, which is briefly described in the work. We establish two prototypes of soft robots, a robotic gripper and a robotic fishtail, which are used to verify the applicability of the actuator with pleated structure and actuator with rib structure respectively.

**Keywords:** Soft bending actuator · Rib structure · Pleated structure · Robotic gripper · Robotic fishtail

## 1 Introduction

Compared with traditional robots, software robots, made from hyperelastic material, have many advantages, such as lightweight, compliance, flexible design, and adaption to the unstructured environment [1–7]. These advantages make them very suitable for soft interactions. In recent years, software robots have gradually been used in industrial, medical, and biomimetic fields, etc. [8–16].

The soft bending actuator is one type of the most widely used actuators in the soft robotics. This type of actuators is usually composed of two parts, a softer one that is highly stretchable, and a harder one that is negatively stretchable [16, 17]. The softer part contains several chambers, into which, gas or liquid is filled to inflate it. When the softer part stretches, the harder part remains inextensible, which induces a moment in the actuator. The soft bending actuator is mostly used in grasping robots like bionic hand [3, 6, 10] and locomotion robots like bionic fish [14, 18] and bionic snake [19]. Most bending actuators have the same characteristic in general, but there is some

© Springer Nature Switzerland AG 2019
H. Yu et al. (Eds.): ICIRA 2019, LNAI 11741, pp. 568–575, 2019.
https://doi.org/10.1007/978-3-030-27532-7_50

difference in structure. Marchese and colleagues developed a symmetrically structured bending actuator segment, which has four tubular air chambers around the central harder tuber [20]. The actuator can bend to any direction via controlling the pressure in the four tubular air chambers. The actuator is modularly designed to make it easy to assemble into a manipulator. Correll and colleagues [8] presented a uni-directional bending soft actuator with rib air chambers. Katzschmann and colleagues [3] also presented a uni-directional bending actuator with a pleated shape. Compared with Correll's actuator, this type of actuator has gaps between every two air chambers, which make it able to bend in a large degree. It is very suitable for the soft grasping robot. Polygerinos modeled a fiber-reinforced actuator with a slender outline [21]. The actuator has just one chamber. The outside of the actuator is wrapped with fiber, which significantly reduces the balloon effect. Meanwhile, the fiber wrapped around the actuator greatly enhances its stiffness, so this type of actuator can be used for soft locomotion robot as legs. Katzschmann proposed a bending actuator used for bionic fish [22]. The actuator is composed of two rubber blocks laterally attached on an inextensible constraint layer. The symmetrical structure makes it able to bend bi-directionally. There are air chambers in the rubber blocks. Different from actuators with pleated structure, there is no gap in this type of actuator between the chambers, which induces a relatively small bending angle. However, the actuator has a good frequency response characteristic, which makes it quite applicable to the swimming task.

In this work, we introduced two different soft bending actuators with rib structure and pleated structure, compared the deformation responses of the two actuators under the same pressure by finite element simulation. The comparison mainly focused on the difference between the bending angle of the two types of actuators at the same pressure. We further discussed the reasons for this difference. We also established a robotic gripper and robotic fishtail to verify the applicability of the two types of actuators for robotic gripper and robotic fishtail respectively.

## 2 Structure and Fabricating

### 2.1 Structure of the Actuator

The soft bending actuators are usually composed of two parts, a softer one that is highly stretchable, and a harder one that is negatively stretchable. The softer part contains several chambers, into which, gas or liquid is filled to inflate it. When the softer part stretches, the harder part remains inextensible, which induces a moment in the actuator.

Figure 1 shows two different structures for bending actuators, the rib structure and the pleated structure. Actuators with the rib structure have better dynamic response characteristics because of their higher stiffness. Therefore, they are more suitable for oscillating robots like bionic fish, snake, etc. Although actuators with pleated structure have lower stiffness, they are capable to achieve larger bending angle and curvature, which are important for robotic grippers.

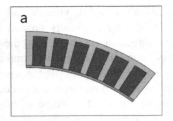
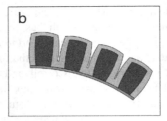

**Fig. 1.** Actuators with different structures. (a) Rib structure. (b) Pleated structure.

## 2.2 Material

Silicon rubber is a usual material for pneumatic/hydraulic actuators for its following advantages:

1. Silicon rubber is easy to fabricate, which is liquid and able to be transferred into solid by means of chemical reaction under room temperature.
2. Silicon rubber has a relatively good high and low-temperature resistance.
3. Silicon rubber is anti-aging.

The silicon rubber Ecoflex0030 from Smooth-on co. Ltd., which has been widely applied in soft robots, was utilized in our research. The uniaxial tensile test was conducted to gain its mechanical characteristics. Figure 2 shows the specimen and equipment used in the material testing.

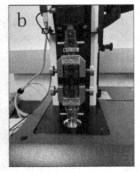

**Fig. 2.** Matiral testing. (a) Ecoflex0030 silicon rubber specimen for the uniaxial tensile test. (b) Small force material testing equipment

The Force-Displacement curve measured from the tensile test is shown in Fig. 3. It is indicated that the relationship between stress and strain is obviously nonlinear. The Force-Displacement curve can be converted into the stress-strain curve, which will be used in the deforming analysis of the actuators.

The other material used in soft actuators should be unstretchable, which can limit the deformation of silicon rubber and produce bending motion. The other material in the actuators is ABS, with Young's modulus of 2 GPa and Poisson's ratio of 0.39.

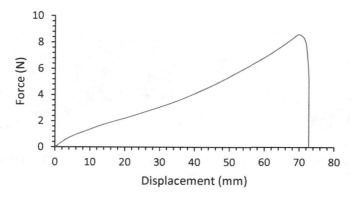

**Fig. 3.** Force-displacement curve of Ecoflex0030

## 3 Analysis

Modeling is an important part of the research on soft robots. We hope that we can express the deformation of soft actuators by an analytical formula but it is Unrealistic. Too many details increased not only the difficulty of modeling but also the difficulty of the model-based control strategy. On the contrary, by means of the finite element method, we can capture all the details of the deformation of actuators. For example, we can easily find the positions where strain and stress increase rapidly while conducting structural optimization.

We used FEM to model a robot finger actuator with the pleated structure and a robot fish actuator with the rib structure respectively and to learn their responses to the internal pressure. The two FE models have similar boundary conditions. One of the end faces is fixed. The internal pressure applies on the chamber surfaces directly as a force boundary condition. The rubber blocks are laterally glued to the ABS neutral layer with a "Tie" type constraint. The material property of the Ecoflex0030 is transferred from the material test to the FE model directly. The rubber block is modeled using the solid hexahedral linear hybrid element and the ABS plank is modeled using solid hexahedral linear element.

Compared with the rib structure, the pleated structure has weaker constraints in the length direction, which induces a more uniform strain distribution (see Fig. 4(a)). On the contrary, the strain in the rib structure mainly distributes in the ribs along the height direction, which is relatively not favorable for the actuator to bend (see Fig. 4(b)). As a result, the robotic finger in the pleated structure can bend a larger angle (see Fig. 5). However, an almost unidirectional and very concentrate strain distribution means the actuator with pleated structure overcomes less material stickiness during the deforming and recovering phases. Therefore, this type of actuators has better frequency response characteristics. That why we tend to apply such actuators to swimming task.

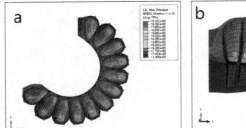
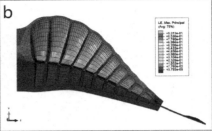

**Fig. 4.** The result of the FE analysis under internal pressure of 20 kPa. (a) The FEM result of the robotic finger. (b) The FEM result of the robotic fish.

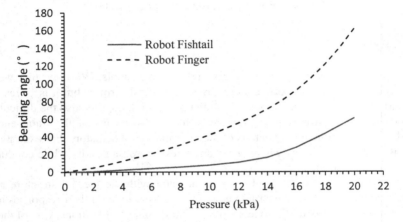

**Fig. 5.** Fishtail and finger

## 4 Application

We made two actuators that used for robotic gripper and robotic fishtail respectively, as examples to show the application of the soft actuators.

### 4.1 Fabrication of the Actuator

The two actuators are fabricated in the same way. The fabricating approach can be divided into three steps. Figure 6 shows the three steps to make a robot fish tail. Step 1: Make the half bodies of the fishtail. The fully mixed liquid silicone rubber was poured into a casting mold made by 3D printing, and released from the mold after cooling to get the half fishtail. Vaseline was smeared on the inner surface of the mold to make it easy to release the cured silicon rubber. Step 2: Make the center constraint layer. The center constraint layer is made via cutting an ABS plank into the shape of fish. Step 3: Glue the fish tails and the center constraint layer together. Then two half fishtails were later-ally glued to the ABS plate with 780-silicone adhesive. The bonding surfaces of the half fishtails were brushed with 770-primer before gluing to improve its adhesiveness.

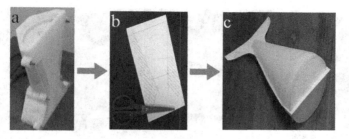

**Fig. 6.** Three steps of fabricating a soft actuator by pasting diagrams. (a) Fabricating half tails. (b) Cutting out center constraint. (c) Pasting them together.

## 4.2 Soft Gripper

Three independent bending actuators and a rigid base construct the soft gripper. In all parts, the soft actuator is manufactured by silicon rubber through the casting process as same as the robot fishtail. And the base is made of PLA plastic by 3D printing. Three soft actuators are uniform distribution on the base and supplied by an air pump. Two solenoid valves are connected in the air path to control the air passage. Figure 7 shows the soft gripper that is holding a cup. Thanks to the softness of the soft material, the soft gripper can easily grab objects of different shapes without pinching them.

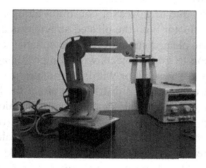

**Fig. 7.** Actuated gripper holding a cup.

## 4.3 Robotic Fishtail

We also established a robotic fishtail to verify the applicability of the actuator with the rib structure to be used for robotic fish. Unlike the soft gripper, we built a hydraulic power system to drive the robotic fishtail. A gear pump is used to provide the power system with a hydraulic source and control the fluid path. The power system is quite simple. It does not require a fluid supply and reversing valves neither, which allows it to be fully integrated into the robotic fish. Figure 8 show the prototype of the robotic fishtail. The robotic fishtail can swing regularly as respected. The robotic fish that can swim automatically will be implemented in further work.

**Fig. 8.** Bionic fish

## 5 Conclusion

In this work, we introduced two types of bending actuators with different structures, pleated structure, and rib structure. The responses of the two bending actuators to their internal pressure are studied through a finite element model. The result of the finite element analysis shows significate differences between the deformation of the two actuators. The actuator with pleated structure can bend to a larger angle than the actuator with rib structure, due to a weaker constraint along its length direction. The strain distribution in the actuator with the pleated structure is also more uniform. As a result, the actuator with the pleated structure is quite suitable for grasping tasks, which require a large deformation to grasp objects with complex shape.

In contrast, the strain in the actuator with rib structure mainly concentrates in the ribs, and almost shows a unidirectional distribution along the height direction. So the deformation of this type of actuator along the length direction is very small which results in a litter bending angle. However, the actuator with rib structure has a good frequency response characteristic due to the strong constraint along its length direction. This type of actuator is relatively suitable for swimming tasks.

To verify the applicability of the two actuators for grasping task and swimming tasks, we established a robotic gripper and a robotic fishtail. The robotic gripper works well in grasping. The robotic fishtail can swing regularly in water. In our further work, a robotic fish with the capability of automatically swimming will be implemented.

## References

1. Paez, L., Agarwal, G., Paik, J.: Design and analysis of a soft pneumatic actuator with origami shell reinforcement. Soft Robot. **3**(3), 109–119 (2016)
2. Sedal, A., Bruder, D., Bishop-Moser, J., Vasudevan, R., Kota, S.: A continuum model for fiber-reinforced soft robot actuators. J. Mech. Robot. **10**(2), 024501–024509 (2018)
3. Katzschmann, R.K., Marchese, A.D., Rus, D.: Autonomous object manipulation using a soft planar grasping manipulator. Soft Robot. **2**(4), 155–164 (2015)

4. Marchese, A.D., Komorowski, K., Onal, C.D., Rus, D.: Design and control of a soft and continuously deformable 2D robotic manipulation system. In: Proceedings - IEEE International Conference on Robotics and Automation, pp. 2189–2196 (2014)

5. Shepherd, R.F., et al.: Multigait soft robot. PNAS **108**(51), 20400–20403 (2011)

6. Hughes, J., Culha, U., Giardina, F., Guenther, F., Rosendo, A., Iida, F.: Soft manipulators and grippers: a review. Front. Robot. AI **3**, 1–12 (2016)

7. Wu, P., Jiangbei, W., Yanqiong, F.: The structure, design, and closed-loop motion control of a differential drive soft robot. Soft Robot. **5**(1), 71–80 (2018)

8. Correll, N., Önal, Ç.D., Liang, H., Schoenfeld, E., Rus, D.: Soft autonomous materials-using active elasticity and embedded distributed computation. In: Khatib, O., Kumar, V., Sukhatme, G. (eds.) Experimental Robotics. Springer Tracts in Advanced Robotics, vol. 79. Springer, Heidelberg (2014). https://doi.org/10.1007/978-3-642-28572-1_16

9. Abidi, H., et al.: Highly dexterous 2-module soft robot for intra-organ navigation in minimally invasive surgery. Int. J. Med. Robot. Comput. Assist. Surg. **14**(1), 1–9 (2018)

10. Manti, M., Hassan, T., Passetti, G., D'Elia, N., Laschi, C., Cianchetti, M.: A bioinspired soft robotic gripper for adaptable and effective grasping. Soft Robot. **2**(3), 107–116 (2015)

11. Jusufi, A., Vogt, D.M., Wood, R.J., Lauder, G.V.: Undulatory swimming performance and body stiffness modulation in a soft robotic fish-inspired physical model. Soft Robot. **4**(3), 202–210 (2017)

12. Ilievski, F., Mazzeo, A.D., Shepherd, R.F., Chen, X., Whitesides, G.M.: Soft robotics for chemists. Angew. Chem. **123**(8), 1930–1935 (2011)

13. Renda, F., Giorgio-Serchi, F., Boyer, F., Laschi, C., Dias, J., Seneviratne, L.: A unified multi-soft-body dynamic model for underwater soft robots. Int. J. Robot. Res. **37**(6), 648–666 (2018)

14. Marchese, A.D., Onal, C.D., Rus, D.: Autonomous soft robotic fish capable of escape maneuvers using fluidic elastomer actuators. Soft Robot. **1**(1), 75–87 (2014)

15. Marchese, A.D., Katzschmann, R.K., Rus, D.: Whole arm planning for a soft and highly compliant 2D robotic manipulator. In: IEEE International Conference on Intelligent Robots and Systems, pp. 554–560 (2014)

16. Onal, C.D., Chen, X., Whitesides, G.M., Rus, D.: Soft mobile robots with on-board chemical pressure generation. In: Christensen, H.I., Khatib, O. (eds.) Robotics Research. STAR, vol. 100, pp. 525–540. Springer, Cham (2017). https://doi.org/10.1007/978-3-319-29363-9_30

17. Alici, G., Canty, T., Mutlu, R., Hu, W., Sencadas, V.: Modeling and experimental evaluation of bending behavior of soft pneumatic actuators made of discrete actuation chambers. Soft Robot. **5**(1), 24–35 (2018)

18. Zhang, Z., Philen, M., Neu, W.: A biologically inspired artificial fish using flexible matrix composite actuators: analysis and experiment. Smart Mater. Struct. **19**(9), 094017 (2010)

19. Luo, M., Agheli, M., Onal, C.D.: Theoretical modeling and experimental analysis of a pressure-operated soft robotic snake. Soft Robot. **1**(2), 136–146 (2014)

20. Marchese, A.D., Rus, D.: Design, kinematics, and control of a soft spatial fluidic elastomer manipulator. Int. J. Robot. Res. **35**(7), 840–869 (2016)

21. Polygerinos, P., et al.: Modeling of soft fiber-reinforced bending actuators. IEEE Trans. Rob. **31**(3), 778–789 (2015)

22. Katzschmann, R.K., Marchese, A.D., Rus, D.: Hydraulic autonomous soft robotic fish for 3D swimming. In: Hsieh, M.Ani, Khatib, O., Kumar, V. (eds.) Experimental Robotics. STAR, vol. 109, pp. 405–420. Springer, Cham (2016). https://doi.org/10.1007/978-3-319-23778-7_27

# Teleoperation Robot

# A Control System Framework Model for Cloud Robots Based on Service-Oriented Architecture

Kui Qian[1]([✉]), Yiting Liu[1], Aiguo Song[2], and Jialu Li[3]

[1] School of Automation, Nanjing Institute of Technology, Nanjing, China
kuiqian@njit.edu.cn
[2] Key Lab of Remote Measurement and Control Technology in Jiangsu Province,
Southeast University, Nanjing, China
a.g.song@seu.edu.cn
[3] The 28th Research Institute of China Electronics Technology Group Corporation,
Nanjing, China
lijialu0108@126.com

**Abstract.** Aiming at the problems of robot ontology resource limitation and task simplification, a control system framework model for cloud robots based on service-oriented architecture is proposed. By introducing a hierarchical service model idea, a cloud robot control system architecture is established. Then it divides the service into task service, entity service and utility service. The cloud robots dynamically invoke services on demand through service-oriented architecture(SOA) mechanism. Under the control of the intelligent service engine, cloud robots could obtain sufficient flexible resources to complete advanced tasks such as deep learning, voice interaction, and knowledge sharing. Experimental results show that this method could effectively improve the efficiency of cloud robot task combination, and support for highly complex systems with fine-grained services.

**Keywords:** Cloud robots · Control system framework ·
Service-oriented architecture · Task combination

## 1 Introduction

Robots are complex mechatronic devices with functions such as sensing, transmission, calculation, decision making, and control. In order to understand and respond to the real world and accurately complete operational tasks, robots often need to carry a large amount of hardware and software resources to enhance the perception, calculation and control capabilities. The robot control system is complex and the execution task is single.

With the rapid development of new generation information technologies such as cloud computing, big data, artificial intelligence, cloud robots that combine next-generation information technology with traditional robots have been hot

© Springer Nature Switzerland AG 2019
H. Yu et al. (Eds.): ICIRA 2019, LNAI 11741, pp. 579–588, 2019.
https://doi.org/10.1007/978-3-030-27532-7_51

research topics in recent years. Cloud computing allows centralized data storage and online access to computer services or resources with large groups of remote servers. Robots can benefit from the powerful computational and storage resources in the cloud.

Kuffner [1] proposed "cloud robotics" concept, causing extensive discussion at the Humanoids 2010 conference. Unload most of the complex computing and storage tasks into the cloud without enhancing the capabilities of the cloud robot itself. At the same time, cloud computing makes each robot individual no longer isolated from each other, but could learn and cooperate with each other. Du [2] proposed a "robot cloud" structure to bridge the power of robots and cloud computing. The system had both the advantages of the two, that the robots in the system could communicate with each other and exchange data with the remote cloud server. The RoboEarth [3,4] program was launched by a number of scientists from leading schools and companies around the world to build robotic databases and the Internet.

For massive data and service resources, how cloud robots call resources on demand is a key issue. Deng [5] introduced a new type of cloud robotics of ROSClone that was promoted to solve remote monitoring robotics and multi-robot information sharing in the clouds through the internet. In order to make the distribution of robot resources more balanced, a service framework for ROS-based cloud robot was proposed by Chen [6]. The framework uses open-source robot operating system ROS as the basis for running the robot, enhancing its portability to different hardware and software environment.

Loosing cloud robot control and service would solve problems such as high local computing cost and scarcity of service applications, and it could also quickly respond to the changing complex tasks. The innovation of this paper is to propose a cloud service framework including edge computing, and to refine the service model. Specifically, a control system framework model for cloud robots based on service-oriented architecture is proposed. Based on hierarchical service model idea, a cloud robot control system architecture is established. Then it divides the service into task service, entity service and utility service. Under the control of the intelligent service engine, the cloud robots dynamically invoke services on demand through SOA mechanism [8], and obtain sufficient flexible resources to complete advanced tasks such as deep learning, voice interaction, knowledge sharing and so on. Robot advanced complex applications would be implemented through service combination invokes.

## 2    Control System Framework Model

### 2.1    The Composition of Cloud Robot

In general, the transmission of robots and remote cloud data and applications needs to be done over the WAN. On the one hand, it will lead to excessive occupation of network resources, resulting in data accumulation, causing long network delays. On the other hand, some special robots do not have Internet connectivity, only LAN or data transmission.

Deploy cloud computing resources based on the principle of proximity to improve resource utilization. For the deficiency of cloud computing environment, fog calculation is introduced to improve the interactivity and real-time of the system [7]. The overall composition of the cloud robot system is shown in Fig. 1. The system mainly includes cloud computing services, fog computing services, communication transmission services and robot ontology.

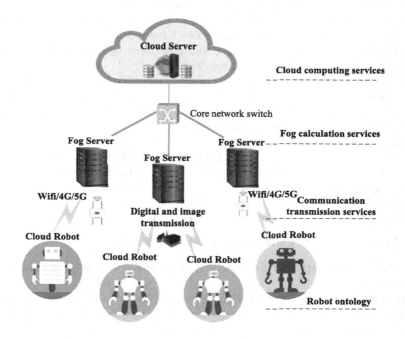

**Fig. 1.** Cloud robot structure

Cloud computing services realize unified management, dynamic allocation and flexible expansion of the resources, and provide massive computing resources and data resources for data analysis, learning, and action planning in robot control task [9].

Fog calculation services can be regarded as a cloud computing mode in which cloud data centers are close to terminal devices such as robots. Deploying a fog server node near the cloud robot, the data that originally need to be processed on the remote cloud can be run on the local fog server node. Fog calculation can greatly improve the real-time performance of data processing and meet the real-time requirements of robot tasks.

Communication transmission services includes Wifi, 4G, 5G and digital radio, image transmission, etc. Among them, digital and image transmission are mainly used for robot control in special environments [10].

Cloud robot ontology senses the surrounding environment and target information through the sensors carried by the robot. The sensor information is transmitted to the fog service node, and after the service share is called, the robot receives the analysis result and the control information.

## 2.2   Design Principles of Service Architecture

For the combined environment of cloud computing and robots, the cloud robot service architecture should follow the following main principles.

Loose coupling. Cloud robots are not required to be coupled by services. The robots produced by various companies have different hardware standards and operating environments. The decoupling between cloud robots and services ensures the consistency of access to services.

Scalability. Robots need to constantly update services to perform more tasks, so cloud robots must have high scalability. New executable services can be quickly deployed in the cloud for cloud robots to call, resulting in cloud robots gaining new capabilities through service combinations.

Real-time performance. Unlike other traditional cloud computing scenes, the data generated by the robot has a higher real-time performance. The sensor data is continuously sent to the control system. Through real-time stream processing, the message queue in cloud can always get the latest sensor data, so the real-time performance of the data is also guaranteed.

## 2.3   Architecture of Control Framework Model

The cloud robot control framework model consists of a layered architecture shown as Fig. 2.

The bottom part is the robot control center, called as the "cloud". The robot control center provides infrastructure resource, including network resources, computing resources and storage resources. Based on resource virtualization, the infrastructure resource layer realizes on-demand acquisition and flexible allocation of all resources.

The layers above the infrastructure resource can be regarded service layers, composed of big data storage and analysis service, deep learning service, and robot as a service (RaaS).

Big data storage and analysis service can provide a large number of resources in the cloud infrastructure layer for cloud robot systems. These resources include storage data resources such as images, videos, maps, sensor networks, and parallel computing resources. Based on the support of big data storage and analysis services, some applications of cloud robots could be implemented using the shared big data.

Deep learning service provides deep learning algorithm library, development tools and GPU acceleration to develop machine learning models and applications. With deep learning service, the cloud robot could use advanced algorithms [11–14] such as convolutional neural networks (CNN), long short-term memory (LSTM), generative adversarial networks (GAN) and graph neural networks (GNN).

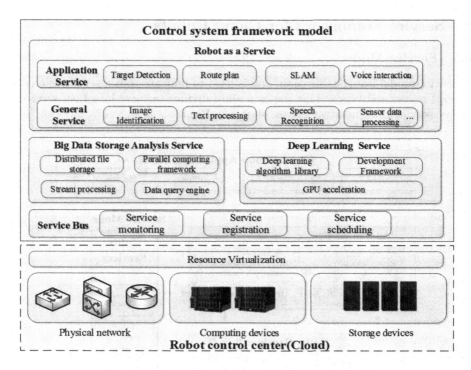

**Fig. 2.** Architecture of Control Framework model

RaaS is a cloud computing unit that facilitates the seamless integration of robot and embedded devices into Web and cloud computing environment. It contains basic services and application services. Basic services provide general-purpose and fine-grained services used in robot work. For basic services, image processing, text processing, speech processing and sensor data processing are shared. While application services are task-oriented. Cloud robot could obtain capabilities of route plan, object detection, SLAM and voice interaction.

All the above services are managed and scheduled through the service bus [15]. A service registration management system is designed in the cloud or fog, so that service providers can quickly deploy and update services according to certain rules. In particular, application services are formed by a combination of basic services. Under the support of the service bus, different basic services are combined to form specific application services. For example, voice interaction would use the speech recognition and text processing services, route plan would utilize sensor data processing and video processing service.

# 3   Service Framework for Cloud Robots

## 3.1   Service Mode

A service model is a classification, and is used to indicate that a service is one of several predefined types. This paper mainly divides services into task services, entity services and utility services, shown as Fig. 3.

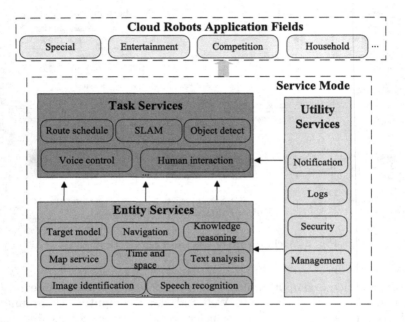

**Fig. 3.** Service mode

Task services correspond to application service in cloud robot control system framework model. They are usually a combination of entity services and provide application support for cloud robots to perform different tasks. Task services mainly include path planning, navigation control, object detect, and human-computer interaction, etc.

Entity services are reusable services that are associated with robots task entities. Service providers provide executable services for cloud robots in cloud computing environment, such as image identification, speech recognition, navigation, text analysis and knowledge reasoning, etc. The robots do not need to deploy any positioning and navigation resources locally, and obtain any required data and services through the cloud server or fog server.

Utility services are application-independent functional service, which encapsulates the low-level, technology-centric features functions, including service logs, service notifications, and service security.

## 3.2   Service Framework

As the core part of the entire system framework, the cloud service layer provides the necessary services for the robot, which is the guarantee for the cloud robot to successfully complete the task. As shown in Fig. 4, the service layer follows the SOA mechanism, and all services are loosely decoupled components. Services can be developed independently and combined through standard information exchange protocols. They also can be updated and replaced without affecting robot operation.

Service providers use cloud data and resources to develop a variety of services for robots. It involves various aspects such as sensor data processing, environmental target model, human-computer interaction and motion control. These developed services are aggregated into the service framework in the cloud through service registration.

The service framework provides a range of service support functions, including service catalogs, service monitoring, protocol conversion, and service log management. When the robots need to invoke the services, firstly discover the services through the service directory information, and then accesses the registered service instance according to the protocol type specified. The cloud service is managed and controlled by the service management system. The cloud robot does not need to know the parameters required for the cloud service to run.

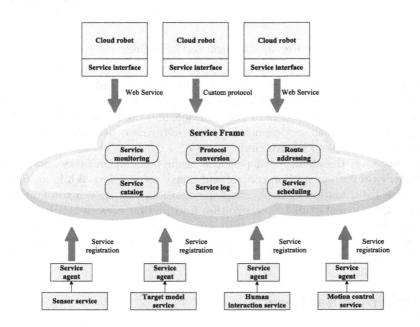

**Fig. 4.** Cloud Robots service framework

### 3.3   Intelligent Service Engine

Decompose the robot application into service-oriented logic units and reassemble these units into new applications. While greatly improving software reusability, it also enhances the robot's flexible response capabilities and expands new capabilities.

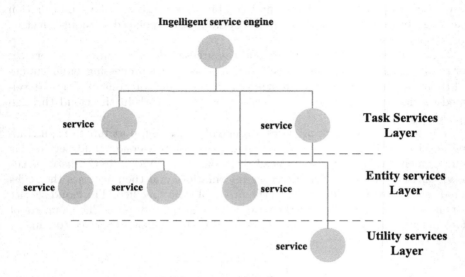

**Fig. 5.** Intelligent service engine

The intelligent service engine located above service members flexibly invokes service members based on robot tasks (see Fig. 5). The engine knows the robot task logic, the context of the individual service, and the transaction control context. Additionally, each service member can also invoke other services, ultimately resulting in a complete service chain.

For instance, the cloud robot performs scene recognition tasks and needs to invoke services such as motion control and image recognition. While in the voice navigation task, motion control, image recognition, and speech recognition are invoked. Consequently, image recognition and motion control can be regarded as entity services. Based on the service engine, the robot would invoke the corresponding service on demand when performing different tasks. The robot does not need to be reprogrammed, and there is no need to carry a lot of computing resources locally.

## 4   Experimental Results

The cloud robot control framework model proposed in this paper can provide a wide range of expansion capabilities for robots. The cloud robot realizes multi-task switching based on shared data and shared services in the cloud environment.

In order to verify the feasibility of the cloud robot service framework, the experimental platform constructed by public cloud is used for deploying service. The cloud environment has four servers with i7 eight-core CPU and 64G memory. The cloud robot uses a regular laptop as the core of the operation.

Take the execution of text sentiment recognition task as an example. Text sentiment recognition can be seen as a task service, which includes three entity services: segmentation service, word vector representation and sentiment classification, and one utility service: response service.

Table 1 shows the comparison of two task modes. Cloud service mode calculation time is much smaller than local mode. The most important thing is that the cloud service model can form a new service through service combination. New services can serve as a foundational service to support more advanced tasks. In the more advanced speech emotion analysis tasks, the combined sentiment recognition service will be used.

**Table 1.** The comparison of two task modes

| Time of task(s) | Local mode | Cloud service mode |
|---|---|---|
| Segmentation service | 2.1 | 0.2 |
| Word vector representation | 21.77 | 1.8 |
| Sentiment classification | 0.6 | 0.3 |
| Response service | - | 0.09 |
| Total time | 24.53 | 2.39 |

In addition, when the cloud robots do not carry the network communication device with WLAN/LAN, it can be connected to the fog server through a digital transmission station. After the service framework deployed on the fog server resolves the service request, it obtains the required resources and services from the cloud center, and finally feeds back the calculation result to the cloud robot.

## 5   Conclusion

Due to the problems of computing cost of robots and scarcity of service applications, a control system framework model for cloud robots based on service-oriented architecture is proposed. By introducing a hierarchical service model idea, a cloud robot control system architecture is established. Then it divides the service into task service, entity service and utility service, and the cloud robots dynamically invoke services on demand through SOA mechanism. Under the control of the intelligent service engine, cloud robots could obtain sufficient flexible resources to complete advanced tasks such as deep learning, voice interaction, and knowledge sharing. Experimental results show that this method could effectively improve the efficiency of cloud robot task combination, and support for highly complex systems with fine-grained services. On the one hand, cloud robots can be operated lightly with fast response; On the other hand, service combinations can be performed on demand, with more complex application functions.

Especially after the combination of robots and Internet of Things, cloud robots will have a broader application space with sharing the data and information of the Internet of Everything. In the future work, more tasks under more challenging environments will be considered.

**Acknowledgment.** This paper is supported by the Open Foundation of key Lab of Remote Measurement and Control Technology in Jiangsu Province (2242019k30036), Science Foundation for Young Scientists of Jiangsu (BK20181017) and Institute Research Foundation (YKJ201822, JCYJ201820).

# References

1. Kuffner James, J.: Cloud-enabled humanoid robots. In: IEEE-RAS International Conference on Humanoid Robotics (2010)
2. Du, Z., He, L., Chen, Y., et al.: Robot cloud: bridging the power of robotics and cloud computing. Future Gener. Comput. Syst. **21**(4), 301–312 (2016)
3. Zweigle, O., van de Molengraft, R., D'Andrea, R., et al.: RoboEarth: connecting robots worldwide. In: International Conference on Interaction Sciences: Information Technology. ACM (2009)
4. Waibel, M.: RoboEarth-a world wide web for robots. IEEE Robot. Autom. Mag. **18**(2), 69–82 (2011)
5. Chang, D.: Design and implementation of cloud robotics based on robot operating system. J. Shanghai Univ. Eng. Sci. **32**(4), 319–323 (2018)
6. Chen, X., Wu, Y.J.: Service framework for ROS-based cloud robot. Comput. Syst. Appl. **25**(10), 73–80 (2016)
7. Anton, F., Borangiu, Th., Morariu, O., et al.: Decentralizing cloud robot services through edge computing. Mech. Mach. Sci. **67**, 618–626 (2019)
8. Spiess, P., Karnouskos, S., Guinard, D., et al.: SOA-based integration of the Internet of Things in enterprise services. In: IEEE International Conference on Web Services (2009)
9. Kar, A., Dutta, A.K., Debnath, S.K.: Task management of robot using cloud computing. In: 2016 International Conference on Computer, Electrical and Communication Engineering, Kolkata, pp. 1–6 (2016)
10. Qian, K., Song, A.G., Bao, J.T., et al.: Small teleoperated robot for nuclear radiation and chemical leak detection. Int. J. Adv. Robot. Syst. (IJARS) **9**, 1–9, 19 September 2012
11. Hinton, G.E., Salakhutdinov, R.R.: Reducing the dimensionality of data with neural networks. Science **313**(5786), 504–7 (2006)
12. Goodfellow, I., Pouget-Abadie, J., Mirza, M., et al: Generative adversarial nets. In: Advances in Neural Information Processing Systems, pp. 2672–2680 (2014)
13. Gers, F.A., Schmidhuber, J., Cummins, F.: Learning to forget: continual prediction with LSTM. Neural Comput. **12**(10), 2451–2471 (2000)
14. Scarselli, F., Gori, M., Tsoi, A.C., et al.: Computational capabilities of graph neural networks. IEEE Trans. Neural Netw. **20**(1), 81–102 (2009)
15. Sah, A., Dumka, A., Rawat, S.: Web technology systems integration using SOA and web services. In: Handbook of Research on Contemporary Perspectives on Web-Based Systems, pp. 24–45 (2018)

# A Novel Method for Finger Vein Segmentation

Junying Zeng[✉], Fan Wang, Chuanbo Qin, Junying Gan, Yikui Zhai,
and Boyuan Zhu

Faculty of Intelligent Manufacturing, Wuyi University,
Jiangmen 529020, Guangdong, China
zengjunying@126.com, victorwfl219@163.com,
tenround@163.com, junyinggan@163.com,
yikuizhai@163.com, zhuboyuan586@163.com

**Abstract.** In terms of such problems as the traditional finger vein segmentation algorithm cannot achieve good segmentation effect, the public finger vein dataset is small, and there is no suitable reference standard for neural network training, this paper proposes a finger vein segmentation algorithm based on LadderNet. Based on the conventional U-Net structure, we simplify the network and reduce the parameters in view of the characteristic of the finger vein dataset, and U-Net network is taken as part of the LadderNet. By splicing the feature channels of expanding path and contracting path in the network, the semantic information of the image can be obtained as more as possible on the basis of good venous details. With the increase of transmission paths, more complex venous characteristics can be captured. In the process of neural network training, we randomly select the center of each image to obtain sub-blocks for data augmentation; on the other hand, the patterns extracted by detecting the local maximum curvature in cross-sectional of a vein image method are taken as the gold standard, which can extract the centerlines of the veins consistently without being affected by the fluctuations in vein width and brightness, so its pattern matching is highly accurate. We tested this method on two benchmark datasets such as SDU-FV and MMCBNU_6000, the experimental results show that LadderNet-based finger vein segmentation algorithm has achieved superior performance with an AUC of 91.56%, 92.91% and an accuracy of 92.44%, 93.93% respectively over methods in the literature.

**Keywords:** Finger vein segmentation · LadderNet · U-Net ·
Data augmentation · Gold standard

## 1 Introduction

In recent years, with the increasing demand for the safety and accuracy of biometric systems, biometric recognition technology has received more and more attention. Finger vein recognition, as one of many biometric recognition technologies, has

This work is supported by NNSF (No. 61771347), Characteristic Innovation Project of Guangdong Province (No. 2017KTSCX181), Young innovative talents project of Guangdong Province (2017KQNCX206), Jiangmen science and technology project ([2017] No. 268), Youth Foundation of Wuyi University (No. 2015zk11).

© Springer Nature Switzerland AG 2019
H. Yu et al. (Eds.): ICIRA 2019, LNAI 11741, pp. 589–600, 2019.
https://doi.org/10.1007/978-3-030-27532-7_52

become a hot spot of current research due to its advantages of non-contact collection, biopsy detection, hardly forged and low cost [1]. Vessel segmentation of finger vein image is a key step in vein recognition technology. The quality of segmentation directly affects the precision and accuracy of subsequent recognition.

In practical applications, the image captured contains not only vein patterns, but also irregular noise, shadows caused by different thicknesses of finger bones and muscles [2]. In addition, finger veins vary with temperature or physical conditions, so it is difficult to accurately extract the details of veins. Traditional image segmentation algorithms, such as Otsu algorithm [3], Entropy algorithm [4], K-means algorithm [5], and Fuzzy C-means algorithm [6], cannot achieve good segmentation results because of the need for more thresholds for low-quality finger vein images.

In order to accurately segment the blood vessels in finger vein images, many solutions are proposed. Miura et al. [7] randomly initialize a batch of points in the finger vein image, and then obtain finger vein patterns in the whole image by repetitive line tracking. This method can obtain the skeleton of finger vein patterns more accurately, but the algorithm itself needs repeated iterations, which is time-consuming. Liu et al. [8] improved the original method of repeat line tracking, which improved the robustness and efficiency of the original method. Qin et al. [9] used region growing operator to obtain finger vein patterns, which had better effect, but had lower efficiency. Yang et al. [10] first used the eight-direction Gabor filter to obtain the finger vein pattern information, and then used the reconstruction algorithm to fuse and derive the finger vein pattern image. Zhang et al. [11] used curve wave to enhance the original finger vein image at multi-scale, and then designed a neural network with local interconnection structure to extract finger vein patterns.

The main disadvantage of the above methods is that vein patterns are marked based on various thresholds, such as tracking times threshold, the number of specific adjacent points threshold, etc. In fact, the selection of these thresholds is very difficult. If the thresholds are too large, vein patterns will be lost, and if the thresholds are too small, the noise points will be regarded as vein points.

Although deep learning-based semantics segmentation has been successfully applied to image classification, segmentation and detection tasks, and has achieved superior performance [12], such as FCN [13], SegNet [14], DeepLab [15], RefineNet [16], PSPNet [17], U-Net [18], etc., few methods have been applied to finger vein segmentation. The main problem is that the public finger vein dataset is small, and there is no suitable gold standard for training vein images of neural networks. In this paper, a finger vein segmentation algorithm based on LadderNet [19] is proposed. By consulting the literature, it is known that there is no such network applied in this field. LadderNet network is an improvement of traditional U-Net network, which can fuse multi-path transmission information, so it can capture more complex vein features and obtain higher accuracy. In order to make full use of the limited dataset, we cut and partition the random selection center of each image to perform data augmentation, so that it can support the training of deep neural network. In addition, we use the vein patterns extracted by the local maximum curvature detection method as the gold standard for the training of neural network, which has strong robustness to the fluctuation of pulse width and brightness.

## 2 Background Knowledge

### 2.1 Gold Standard

Because the images often contain shadows of different thicknesses of finger bones and muscles, and finger veins vary with temperature or physical conditions, there is no suitable gold standard for training neural networks. In this paper, the vein patterns extracted by detecting the local maximum curvature are regarded as our gold standard (label). This method can extract the central line of vein without the influence of pulse width and brightness fluctuation, and has high matching accuracy.

Because the vein is darker than the surrounding area, the cross-sectional contour of the vein is composed of many concave curves, and these concave curves have larger curvature, so the central position of the vein can be obtained by calculating the local maximum curvature of the cross-sectional contour. The curvature at the cross section is defined as:

$$\kappa(z) = \frac{d^2 P_f(z)/dz^2}{(1 + (dP_f(z)/d(z))^2)^{3/2}} \tag{1}$$

$z$ is the position of the contour, $P_f(z)$ is the cross-sectional contour obtained in any direction and position.

Then check the intensity relationship between the two adjacent pixels on the right side and the two adjacent pixels on the left side of the pixel $(x, y)$. If the pixel intensity $v(x, y)$ at the pixel $(x, y)$ has a large pixel value and the pixel values on both sides are very small, then it should be noise at the $(x, y)$ side. At this time, the value should be reduced to eliminate the noise. This process is given by formula (2) and then connected to the central position of the vein.

$$C_{d1}(x, y) = \min\{\max(v(x+1, y), v(x+2, y)), \max(v(x-1, y), v(x-2, y))\} \tag{2}$$

Finally, by using thresholds to binarize, the pixels whose values are less than or equal to the thresholds are marked as part of the image background, and the pixels whose values are greater than or equal to the thresholds are marked as part of the vein region.

### 2.2 Network Architecture

Inspired by the traditional U-Net network, the neural network architecture used in this paper is deduced and used as a benchmark to construct the LadderNet network with multiple information transmission paths.

Different from the traditional U-Net network, which takes an entire image as input and uses elastic deformation to perform data augmentation, we randomly select the center of each finger vein image to obtain sub-blocks for data augmentation, and use them as our network input. Compared with the features of the whole image, the vein features in sub-blocks will be greatly reduced, so we freeze the two-layer duplicate structure of the traditional U-Net network, reduce the parameters and simplify the calculation on the basis of fully learning the characteristics of veins.

The network consists of a contracting path and an expanding path. Contracting path follows the typical repetitive structure of convolution networks. There are two convolution layers and one pooling layer in each repetition. After each down-sampling, we double the number of feature channels. Through two max pooling operations, the image resolution becomes 1/4 of the original image, so that the final output unit corresponds to a larger receptive field area, which can capture more abundant global vein information. In the expanding path, two deconvolutions are used to recover the original resolution by up-sampling the convolution core obtained by learning. Each time deconvolution is used, the number of feature channels is halved, and the result of deconvolution is joined with the corresponding feature map of the same number of channels in the contracting path. This can get as strong image semantic information as possible on the basis of good vein details.

In LadderNet network, by adding the characteristics of coding and decoding branches, the two U-Nets are connected. The information transmission paths increase exponentially with the number of coding and decoding pairs and the number of different spatial scales. Therefore, more complex vein features can be captured and higher accuracy can be obtained.

## 2.3    Finger Vein Segmentation Algorithm Based on LadderNet

Figure 1 shows the flow chart of the finger vein segmentation algorithm based on LadderNet. Firstly, the images of two datasets are divided into three types (index finger, middle finger and ring finger). Each type of image is preprocessed by ROI extraction, normalization, contrast-limited adaptive histogram equalization and gamma adjustment, with the aim of highlighting areas rich in vein patterns, reduce processing time and increase accuracy; then we use the local maximum curvature method to extract the central line of vein without the influence of pulse width and brightness fluctuation, and connect the central position of vein as a gold standard for network training. Then we randomly select the center of the preprocessed image to obtain sub-blocks for data augmentation, and take each sub-block as the input of the neural network. On the one hand, the introduction of sub-blocks can enlarge the details of veins in network training, on the other hand, it can support the training process of LadderNet network. Finally, inspired by the traditional U-Net network structure, compared with the whole image, the vein features of the block image obtained are greatly reduced. So freezing the two-layer repetitive structure simplifies the network and reduces the parameters on the basis of guaranteeing good vein details, and use this as a benchmark to splicing two U-Net networks to get the LadderNet network we use. By integrating the expanding path with the contracting path feature channel, the network can obtain as strong image semantic information as possible on the basis of getting good vein details. With the increase of transmission paths, more complex vein features can be captured. In the test, we extract multiple successive overlapping blocks at a fixed step. By averaging the probability of all prediction blocks covering the pixel, we obtain the probability that the pixel is a venous vessel.

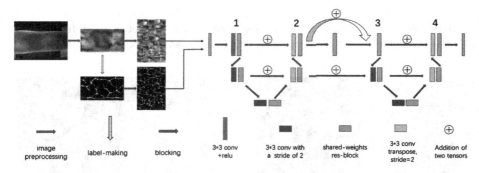

**Fig. 1.** Flow diagram of finger vein segmentation based on LadderNet

# 3 Experiment

## 3.1 Datasets

The datasets used in this paper is SDU-FV dataset created by MLA Laboratory of Shandong University [20] and MMCBNU_6000 dataset created by National University of North Korea [21]. There were 106 subjects in the SDU-FV dataset, and the finger vein images of the index finger, middle finger and ring finger of each person's left and right hands were collected, and 6 images were taken from each finger. So there are 636 classes (106 persons × 6 fingers) and 3816 images (106 persons × 6 fingers × 6 samples) in the dataset. The MMCBNU_6000 dataset contains 100 subjects, and the finger vein images of the index finger, middle finger and ring finger of each person's left and right hands were collected, and 10 images were taken from each finger. So there are 600 classes (100 persons × 6 fingers) and 6000 images (100 persons × 6 fingers × 10 samples) in the dataset.

For finger vein image segmentation, it will no longer be our research focus to determine whether two images are the same finger of the same person. We only care about the final image segmentation results and the impact on subsequent recognition. This is a binary classification task. Neural network will predict whether each pixel in finger vein image is a blood vessel.

## 3.2 Training and Testing

Before training, we first classify the dataset into three types: index finger, middle finger and ring finger, each of which randomly selects 20 images for training and 20 for testing. Then we preprocess all finger vein images for training and testing, including ROI extraction, normalization, contrast-limited adaptive histogram equalization and gamma adjustment. The size of the image is uniformly adjusted to 270 × 150.

We set the size of the sub-blocks to 48 × 48, and randomly select 10,000 sub-blocks for each image. A total of 200,000 sub-blocks for 20 training images are used as training datasets. Figure 2 shows examples and labels of blocks for training on two datasets. For convenience, we show only 40 randomly extracted blocks. Although there may be overlaps between blocks, unlike traditional U-Net networks, we will not perform further data augmentation. The first 90% of the dataset is used for training (180,000 sub-blocks) and the remaining 10% (20,000 sub-blocks) for validation.

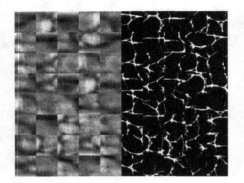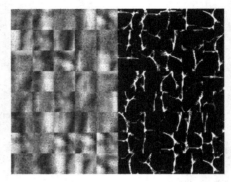

**Fig. 2.** Block (left) and label (right) of neural network training on two datasets

U-Net network is optimized by stochastic gradient descent method, LadderNet network is optimized by Adam method, both methods adopt default parameter index, and we choose a drop-out rate of 0.2 and 0.25 respectively between two continuous convolution layers. Experiments show that for SDU-FV dataset, the U-Net network obtains the minimum validation loss of index finger, middle finger and ring finger after 184, 155 and 167 iterations respectively, and LadderNet obtains the minimum validation loss of index finger, middle finger and ring finger after 114, 182 and 113 iterations respectively. For MMCBNU_6000 dataset, the U-Net network obtains the minimum validation loss of index finger, middle finger and ring finger after 165, 161 and 169 iterations respectively. LadderNet obtains the minimum validation loss of index finger, middle finger and ring finger after 230, 272 and 192 iterations respectively.

For the test image, the block size is still 48 × 48. We extract several continuous overlapping blocks for each test image with five steps in width and height. Because the uniform size of the image used to predict in our input network is 270 × 150, 22 blocks are extracted in height, 46 blocks in width, 1012 blocks were extracted from each image, and 20 test images totaled 20240 blocks. Then, for each pixel of 810,000 (20 images × 270 wide × 150 high) pixels, the probability that the pixel is a venous vessel is obtained by averaging the probability of all prediction blocks covering the pixels.

# 4   Experimental Results and Analysis

## 4.1   Experimental Results on SDU-FV Dataset

We use the following indicators to evaluate the performance of the model, including Accuracy (AC), Precision (PR), Sensitivity (SE), Specificity (SP), F1-score and Jaccard similarity, in addition to the ROC curve and the area under the curve AUC.

Figure 3 shows some experimental prediction segmentation results on SDU-FV dataset. Examples of finger vein segmentation from left to right are index finger, middle finger and ring finger respectively. From top to bottom are original ROI images, labels and prediction segmentation results. Visually, the predicted segmentation results are very close to the labels. In fact, most predicted segmentation maps give more "accurate" segmentation results than labels. The reason is that the label we use is a binary image, and the value higher than the threshold is marked as part of the finger vein. The vein patterns extracted by detecting the local maximum curvature are robust to the fluctuation of pulse width and brightness. In practice, because of the influence of temperature and physical conditions, the width of the collected finger veins will change. LadderNet network can learn this change by fusing the transmission information of multiple contracting paths and expanding paths, and even capture more complex features that cannot be observed by the naked eye. Therefore, the predicted segmentation results are more in line with the actual situation, and the individual differences of finger vein patterns are more obvious. It will be more promising to use the predicted segmentation results for subsequent finger vein recognition.

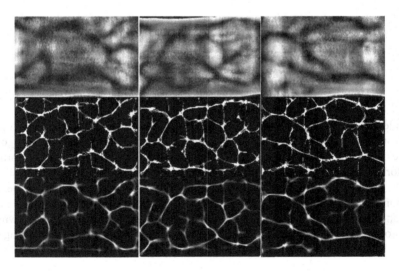

**Fig. 3.** Example of predictive segmentation results on SDU-FV dataset

Figure 4 shows the ROC curves of the current mainstream methods and the average area under the curves (average the segmentation results of three types of fingers: index finger, middle finger and ring finger). For the sake of unification, the two traditional methods we reproduced are also based on the vein patterns extracted by the local maximum curvature detection method as a gold standard. Miura et al.'s repeat line tracking method largely depends on the selection of tracking times threshold, which is very difficult, so the effect is the worst. The area under ROC curve is 81.49%. Yang et al.'s eight-direction Gabor filter, because the self-built finger vein image in the original paper is similar to SDU-FV dataset, makes the fusion result of reconstruction algorithm better than that of repeat line tracking. The area under the ROC curve is 83.11%; the U-Net network splices the contracting path that captures the context information in the image with the expanding path that precisely locates the part to be segmented in the image, so that the image semantic information can be obtained as strong as possible on the basis of good vein details, and the average area under the curve reaches 89.82%; By splicing two U-Net networks, LadderNet network can increase the number of information transmission paths, so it can capture more complex features. The average area under ROC curve is the highest, reaching 91.56%.

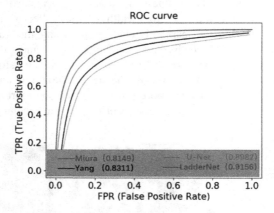

**Fig. 4.** ROC curve and area under the curve

Table 1 shows the quantitative performance indicators of several methods. It can be seen from the table that the LadderNet-based finger vein segmentation algorithm achieves the best results, and achieves 92.44% accuracy. In fact, the performance indicators based on U-Net and LadderNet only represent the learning ability of the network. If the influence of pulse width, noise or other physical conditions in the actual operation process is considered, these indicators will be improved. Because the finger vein pattern is extracted by detecting the local maximum curvature method, which is robust to the pulse width and brightness. The idea of dividing the whole image into blocks also enables the network to learn more detailed vein details.

### 4.2    Experimental Results on MCBNU_6000 Dataset

Figure 5 shows some experimental prediction segmentation results on MMCBNU_6000 dataset. Examples of finger vein segmentation from left to right are index finger, middle finger and ring finger respectively. From top to bottom are original ROI image, label and prediction segmentation results. Compared with SDU-FV dataset, the dataset has more low-contrast images. However, due to histogram equalization and other image enhancement methods, the final predictive segmentation results are very close to the label visually, and the network also learns the influence of venous width or other physical conditions in the actual operation process. It can be used for further finger vein recognition to achieve better classification results.

Figure 6 shows the ROC curves of the current mainstream methods and the average area under the curves. Consistent with the SDU-FV dataset, the other two traditional methods are also based on the vein patterns extracted by detecting the local maximum curvature. Because MMCBNU_6000 dataset has more low contrast vein images than SDU-FV dataset, the ROC curve area of both traditional methods has decreased. Yang et al.'s eight-direction Gabor filter method has the worst effect, because the contrast of vein image in the original self-built dataset is lower than that of the low-contrast vein image in the MMCBNU_6000 dataset, which makes the vein patterns derived from the fusion of the reconstruction algorithm more missing. But after dividing the image into several sub-blocks, the details of veins are enlarged. Because the sub-blocks are randomly selected from the center, there will be overlap between the blocks, which enables the network to integrate the details of veins learned each time. In addition, the labels produced are not affected by the fluctuation of pulse width and brightness, so the low contrast vein image has little influence on them. Therefore, the effect of finger vein segmentation based on U-Net network and LadderNet network is not very different. On the contrary, due to the lack of physical conditions of low contrast image quality and other practical operation process, the venous details are not as good as SDU-FV dataset, and the network also learns this, so the two network performance indicators have slightly increased. The finger vein segmentation based on LadderNet network achieves the best performance because of the fusion of multi-path transmission information. The area under the curve reaches 92.91%.

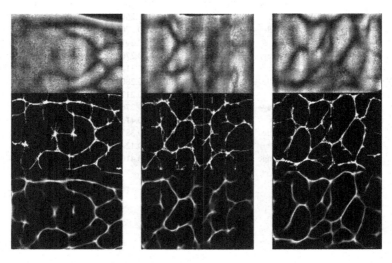

**Fig. 5.** Example of predictive segmentation results on MMCBNU_6000 dataset

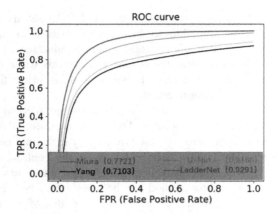

**Fig. 6.** ROC curve and area under the curve

Table 2 gives more detailed performance indicators of several methods. The finger vein segmentation method based on LadderNet network achieves the best experimental results with 93.93% accuracy by data augmentation, gold standards with strong robustness to pulse width and brightness fluctuations, and transmission information of multi-path fusion.

**Table 1.** Performance index of methods on SDU-FV dataset

| Dataset | Method | Types | AUC | AC | PR | SE | SP | F1-score | Jaccard similarity |
|---------|--------|-------|-----|-----|-----|-----|-----|----------|-------------------|
| SDU-FV | Repeat line tracking [7] | Index | 0.8129 | 0.8272 | 0.4728 | 0.2117 | 0.8331 | 0.2925 | 0.8272 |
| | | Middle | 0.8163 | 0.8303 | 0.4752 | 0.2104 | 0.8412 | 0.2917 | 0.8303 |
| | | Ring | 0.8154 | 0.8231 | 0.4839 | 0.2073 | 0.8443 | 0.2903 | 0.8231 |
| | | Average | 0.8149 | 0.8269 | 0.4773 | 0.2098 | 0.8395 | 0.2915 | 0.8269 |
| | Eight-direction Gabor filter [10] | Index | 0.8340 | 0.8442 | 0.4928 | 0.2506 | 0.8752 | 0.3322 | 0.8442 |
| | | Middle | 0.8376 | 0.8472 | 0.5013 | 0.2708 | 0.8854 | 0.3516 | 0.8472 |
| | | Ring | 0.8217 | 0.8490 | 0.5231 | 0.2910 | 0.8966 | 0.3740 | 0.8490 |
| | | Average | 0.8311 | 0.8468 | 0.5057 | 0.2708 | 0.8857 | 0.3526 | 0.8468 |
| | U-Net [23] | Index | 0.8920 | 0.9135 | 0.5776 | 0.3123 | 0.9762 | 0.4054 | 0.9135 |
| | | Middle | 0.9048 | 0.9189 | 0.6385 | 0.2809 | 0.9838 | 0.3901 | 0.9189 |
| | | Ring | 0.8979 | 0.9158 | 0.6734 | 0.2171 | 0.9890 | 0.3284 | 0.9158 |
| | | Average | 0.8982 | 0.9161 | 0.6298 | 0.2701 | 0.9830 | 0.3746 | 0.9161 |
| | LadderNet [24] | Index | 0.9161 | 0.9231 | 0.6425 | 0.4185 | 0.9757 | 0.5069 | 0.9231 |
| | | Middle | 0.9108 | 0.9240 | 0.6472 | 0.3876 | 0.9785 | 0.4848 | 0.9240 |
| | | Ring | 0.9199 | 0.9260 | 0.6741 | 0.4247 | 0.9785 | 0.5211 | 0.9260 |
| | | Average | **0.9156** | **0.9244** | **0.6546** | **0.4103** | **0.9776** | **0.5043** | **0.9244** |

**Table 2.** Performance index of methods on MMCBNU_6000 dataset

| Dataset | Method | Types | AUC | AC | PR | SE | SP | F1-score | Jaccard similarity |
|---|---|---|---|---|---|---|---|---|---|
| MMCBNU_6000 | Repeat line tracking [7] | Index | 0.7671 | 0.7682 | 0.4527 | 0.2102 | 0.8231 | 0.2870 | 0.7682 |
| | | Middle | 0.7646 | 0.7702 | 0.4629 | 0.2110 | 0.8344 | 0.2899 | 0.7702 |
| | | Ring | 0.7826 | 0.7314 | 0.4622 | 0.2139 | 0.8351 | 0.2925 | 0.7314 |
| | | Average | 0.7721 | 0.7566 | 0.4593 | 0.2117 | 0.8309 | 0.2898 | 0.7566 |
| | Eight-direction Gabor filter [10] | Index | 0.7081 | 0.7024 | 0.4438 | 0.2029 | 0.8104 | 0.2785 | 0.7024 |
| | | Middle | 0.7177 | 0.7100 | 0.4476 | 0.2051 | 0.8167 | 0.2813 | 0.7100 |
| | | Ring | 0.7052 | 0.7054 | 0.4358 | 0.2082 | 0.8244 | 0.2819 | 0.7054 |
| | | Average | 0.7103 | 0.7059 | 0.4424 | 0.2054 | 0.8172 | 0.2805 | 0.7059 |
| | U-Net [23] | Index | 0.9188 | 0.9319 | 0.5595 | 0.4105 | 0.9740 | 0.4735 | 0.9319 |
| | | Middle | 0.9154 | 0.9269 | 0.5277 | 0.4100 | 0.9696 | 0.4615 | 0.9269 |
| | | Ring | 0.9163 | 0.9301 | 0.5533 | 0.4062 | 0.9731 | 0.4685 | 0.9301 |
| | | Average | 0.9168 | 0.9296 | 0.5468 | 0.4089 | 0.9722 | 0.4678 | 0.9296 |
| | LadderNet [24] | Index | 0.9267 | 0.9406 | 0.6550 | 0.4297 | 0.9818 | 0.5189 | 0.9406 |
| | | Middle | 0.9367 | 0.9422 | 0.6749 | 0.4710 | 0.9812 | 0.5548 | 0.9422 |
| | | Ring | 0.9238 | 0.9350 | 0.6003 | 0.4260 | 0.9767 | 0.4984 | 0.9350 |
| | | Average | **0.9291** | **0.9393** | **0.6434** | **0.4422** | **0.9799** | **0.5240** | **0.9393** |

## 5 Conclusion

In this paper, a finger vein segmentation algorithm based on LadderNet network is proposed. Firstly, the gold standard for training the neural network is obtained by detecting the local maximum curvature of finger vein image. This method has strong robustness to the fluctuation of image pulse width and brightness. There is no quantitative index for vein label itself, so we may consider the advantages of fusing various methods to extract vein patterns, and integrate a gold standard closer to the original image. Then the whole image is divided into blocks to support the training of deep neural network. In the experiment, 20 images are randomly selected for training and testing for each type of finger. To a certain extent, the generality will not be lost. In the future, we consider adjusting the network to support the processing of massive data. Finally, based on the conventional U-Net structure, we simplify the network and reduce the parameters in view of the characteristic of the finger vein dataset, and U-Net network is taken as part of the LadderNet. By fusing multi-path transmission information, more complex vein features can be captured. The experimental prediction results are very close to the label visually. Quantitative experimental indicators also obtain the best segmentation performance on both datasets. In fact, LadderNet network not only learns the vein patterns in the label, but also learns the variation of pulse width caused by the actual operation process in the original image. Therefore, the performance indicators only represent the learning ability of the network. It will be more promising to use the predictive segmentation map for finger vein recognition.

# References

1. Yang, J., Shi, Y.: Finger–vein ROI localization and vein ridge enhancement. Pattern Recogn. Lett. **33**(12), 1569–1579 (2012)
2. Miura, N., Nagasaka, A., Miyatake, T.: Extraction of finger-vein patterns using maximum curvature points in image profiles. IEICE Trans. Inf. Syst. **90**(8), 1185–1194 (2007)
3. Otsu, N.: A threshold selection method from gray-level histograms. IEEE Trans. Syst. Man Cybern. **9**(1), 62–66 (2007)
4. Chen, W.T., Wen, C.H., Yang, C.W.: A fast two-dimensional entropic thresholding algorithm. Proc. SPIE Int. Soc. Opt. Eng. **27**(7), 885–893 (1994)
5. Mignotte, M.: A de-texturing and spatially constrained K-means approach for image segmentation. Pattern Recogn. Lett. **32**, 359–367 (2011)
6. Ji, Z., Sun, Q.S., Xia, D.S.: RETRACTED: a framework with modified fast FCM for brain MR images segmentation. Pattern Recogn. **44**(5), 999–1013 (2011)
7. Miura, N., Nagasaka, A., Miyatake, T.: Feature extraction of finger-vein patterns based on iterative line tracking and its application to personal identification. Mach. Vis. Appl. **15**(4), 194–203 (2004)
8. Liu, T., Xie, J.B., Yan, W., et al.: An algorithm for finger-vein segmentation based on modified repeated line tracking. Imaging Sci. J. **61**(6), 491–502 (2013)
9. Qin, H., Qin, L., Yu, C.: Region growth–based feature extraction method for finger-vein recognition. Opt. Eng. **50**(5), 572081–572088 (2011)
10. Yang, J., Yang, J., Shi, Y.: Finger-vein segmentation based on multi-channel even-symmetric Gabor filters. In: IEEE International Conference on Intelligent Computing and Intelligent Systems, pp. 500–503 (2009)
11. Zhang, Z., Ma, S., Han, X.: Multiscale feature extraction of finger-vein patterns based on curvelets and local interconnection structure neural network. In: International Conference on Pattern Recognition, pp. 145–148 (2006)
12. Hu, H.: Research of Finger Vein Authentication Based on Convolutional Neural Network. South China University of Technology, Guangzhou (2018)
13. Long, J., Shelhamer, E., Darrell, T.: Fully convolutional networks for semantic segmentation. IEEE Trans. Pattern Anal. Mach. Intell. **39**(4), 640–651 (2014)
14. Badrinarayanan, V., Kendall, A., Cipolla, R.: SegNet: a deep convolutional encoder-decoder architecture for image segmentation (2015)
15. Chen, L.C., Papandreou, G., Schroff, F., et al.: Rethinking atrous convolution for semantic image segmentation (2017)
16. Lin, G., Milan, A., Shen, C., et al.: RefineNet: multi-path refinement networks for high-resolution semantic segmentation (2016)
17. Zhao, H., Shi, J., Qi, X., et al.: Pyramid scene parsing network (2016)
18. Ronneberger, O., Fischer, P., Brox, T.: U-Net: convolutional networks for biomedical image segmentation (2015)
19. Zhuang, J.: LadderNet: Multi-path networks based on U-Net for medical image segmentation (2018)
20. Yin, Y., Liu, L., Sun, X.: SDUMLA-HMT: a multimodal biometric database. In: Chinese Conference on Biometric Recognition (2011)
21. Lu, Y., Xie, S.J., Yoon, S., et al.: An available database for the research of finger vein recognition. In: International Congress on Image & Signal Processing. IEEE (2014)

# WSMR Dynamics Based DWA for Leader-Follower Formation Control

Yun Ling[1($\boxtimes$)], Jian Wu[1], Zhenxing Zhang[1], and Changcheng Wu[2]

[1] Robot Lab, Nanjing Research Institute of Simulation Technology,
Nanjing, China
lingrobot@seu.edu.cn
[2] College of Automation Engineering,
Nanjing University of Aeronautics and Astronautics, Nanjing, China

**Abstract.** One of the critical problems in multi-robots formation is motion control. To achieve the fast formation in the leader-follower formation control, the paper proposes an improved dynamic window approach (DWA) to control the followers moving towards the virtual goals which are generated by the distance-orientation method. The proposed DWA is based on the dynamic model of the wheeled skid-steer mobile robot (WSMR) instead of the conventional kinematics model. First of all, the kinematic model and dynamic model of the WSMR are analyzed and built. After that, the DWA is introduced to achieve the faster following control by using the WSMR dynamics to predict the trajectories of the followers. Then, the motor-wheel model is described by an empirical model and a velocity mapping model of the robot is deduced to map the linear and angular velocities to the rotation speeds of the wheels. Finally, the experiments are carried out to verify the feasibility of the proposed method, especially in the forming stage of the formation control. The comparison of the experimental results between the conventional DWA and the dynamics based DWA show that the latter is faster and more stable in the forming stage of the formation control.

**Keywords:** WSMR · Formation · DWA · Kinematics · Dynamics · Target mobile robot

## 1 Introduction

In the recent years, with the urgent requirements of the high-level training in the military and the steadily worsened situation of anti-terrorists in the society, the intelligent target mobile robots are employed in the training systems and shooting ranges in order to better simulate the combat situations [1]. Instead of the fixed target, the target mobile robot can move freely to simulate a walking enemy or a terrorist. Among these robots, a typical one is the wheeled skid-steer mobile robot (WSMR). For many cooperative training subjects, the formation control is adopted to simulate the enemies' patrol and team combat [2].

© Springer Nature Switzerland AG 2019
H. Yu et al. (Eds.): ICIRA 2019, LNAI 11741, pp. 601–612, 2019.
https://doi.org/10.1007/978-3-030-27532-7_53

## 1.1    Related Works and Motivations

Generally, there are two types of formation control which have been developed: the centralized methods which adopt a center unit to monitor and control the whole team of the robots [3]; and the distributed methods which allow each robot to make decision by their own observations [4]. From the aspect of control methods, the formation control can be summarized into five types, i.e., the behavior based methods [5–7], the artificial field methods [8, 9], the leader-follower methods [10–12], the virtual structure methods [13, 14] and the graph theory methods [15]. Among these methods, the last two belong to the centralized methods and the former three belong to the distributed methods [16].

Based on the leader-follower formation control, the distance-orientation method is applied to generate the dynamic virtual goals for the followers. The tracking of these goals at the beginning leads to the forming control [17]. The goals for the followers are virtual points that the followers should reach and stay. Thus, the formation forming and keeping can be handled as the point tracking problem by reducing the distance deviation and orientation error. According to the Lyapunov theory, the control law is designed to control the followers [18]. However, for more practical applications, the direct tracking control methods are adopted such as the conventional motion control [4], the artificial potential field method [19] and the model predictive control [20]. For the control methods above, the planning is not used to evaluate the control outputs.

## 1.2    Main Contribution

By considering the advantages and disadvantages of the control methods mentioned in Subsect. 1.1, the paper introduced an improved dynamic window approach (DWA) into the formation control. The DWA can dynamically evaluate the potential control outputs by scoring the corresponding trajectories [21]. Compared with the traditional DWA, the paper proposes a dynamics based DWA for the followers.

This paper is organized into five sections. Section 2 builds the kinematic model, dynamic model and the motor-wheel model of the target mobile robot. The former is used to obtain the global pose of the robot. In addition, the velocity mapping model is built to map the control outputs of the linear velocity and the angular velocity to the actual control velocities of left wheels and right wheels. Section 3 introduces the distance-orientation method to generate the virtual goals and the DWA that is based on the dynamic model and constructs the cost function of the DWA. Section 4 demonstrates the implementation of the proposed control method in formation by practical tests. Section 5 draws the conclusions and the future work.

## 2    Prediction Model of the WSMR

The prediction model for the DWA is composed of four parts: the WSMR kinematic model, the motor-wheel model and the velocity mapping model. The outputs of the prediction model are used by the DWA evaluator to compute the optimal control voltages of the left-side motors and the right-side motors, as shown in Fig. 1.

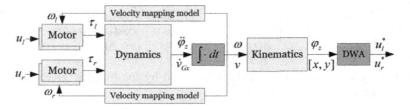

**Fig. 1.** Prediction model diagram.

The motor-wheel model generates the drive torque according to the inputs of voltage and the current rotate speed, whose output is taken as the input of the dynamic model. The outputs of the dynamic model, i.e., the angular acceleration $\ddot{\varphi}_z$ and the linear acceleration $\dot{v}_{Gx}$, are integrated to get the angular velocity $\omega$ and the linear velocity $v$, respectively. They are used to obtain the wheels' velocities through the velocity mapping model. In the mean time, the kinematic model is used to transfer $\omega$ and $v$ to the global pose of the robot, a series of which are used by the DWA to find the best trajectories.

## 2.1    Kinematics Modeling

The kinematic model of the WSMR is built based on the linear velocity and the angular velocity. Let $x(t)$ and $y(t)$ denote the robot's coordinate at time $t$ in the global coordinate system, and let the robot's orientation be described by $\varphi(t)$, as shown in Fig. 2.

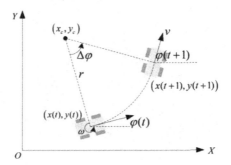

**Fig. 2.** Illustration of velocity based kinematic model of the robot.

The matrix $[x(t), y(t), \varphi(t)]^{\mathrm{T}}$ describes the pose of the robot whose motion is constrained in a way such that the linear velocity $v$ always leads in the steering direction $\varphi$. Namely it is in a non-holonomic constraint [22]. The time interval between $t$ and $t+1$ is indicated by $\Delta t$. Then the pose of the robot at time $t+1$ can be expressed as a function given as follows:

$$\begin{pmatrix} x(t+\Delta t) \\ y(t+\Delta t) \\ \varphi(t+\Delta t) \end{pmatrix} = \begin{pmatrix} x(t) \\ y(t) \\ \varphi(t) \end{pmatrix} + \frac{v}{\omega} \cdot \begin{pmatrix} -\sin\varphi + \sin(\varphi + \omega \cdot \Delta t) \\ \cos\varphi - \cos(\varphi + \omega \cdot \Delta t) \\ \omega^2 \cdot \Delta t / v \end{pmatrix} \tag{1}$$

Alternatively, the kinematic model is replaced by the function given as follows when the angular velocity $\omega$ is zero:

$$\begin{pmatrix} x(t+\Delta t) \\ y(t+\Delta t) \\ \varphi(t+\Delta t) \end{pmatrix} = \begin{pmatrix} x(t) \\ y(t) \\ \varphi(t) \end{pmatrix} + v \cdot \Delta t \cdot \begin{pmatrix} \cos\varphi \\ \sin\varphi \\ 0 \end{pmatrix} \tag{2}$$

## 2.2   Simplified Dynamics Modeling

Considering the balance between the motion features of the WSMR and the embedded computation consumption, the simplified dynamic model is built by assuming that the influence of the wind field and the ground slope is ignorable. In addition, the force analysis of the tires is not performed, neither. Thus, the dynamic model of the target mobile robot can be illustrated like Fig. 3.

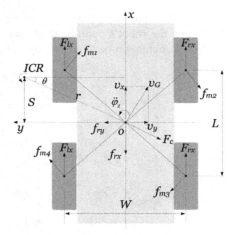

**Fig. 3.** Dynamic model of the WSMR.

The drive forces of the wheels are generated by the torques of the motors, which is denoted by $F_{lx}$ and $F_{rx}$ respectively. Let $f_{rx}$ denotes the force of rolling friction whose direction is just opposite to the local $x$-axis and $f_{ry}$ denotes the force of sliding friction whose direction is always the same to the local $y$-axis. Let $f_{mi}$ ($i$ = 1, 2, 3, 4) indicates the resistance force of friction when the robot is rotating. We have:

$$\begin{cases} m(\dot{v}_x + \dot{v}_y \dot{\varphi}_z) = 2(F_{Lx} + F_{Rx}) - F_c \sin\theta - f_{rx} \\ m(\dot{v}_y - \dot{v}_x \dot{\varphi}_z) = F_c \cos\theta - f_{ry} \\ J\ddot{\varphi}_z = W(F_{Rx} - F_{Lx}) - \frac{1}{4}\sqrt{W^2 + L^2} \cdot \sum_{i=1}^{4} f_{mi} \end{cases} \quad (3)$$

where:

$$f_{rx} = u_r mg \cdot \text{sgn}(v_x) \quad (4)$$

$$f_{ry} = u_s mg \cdot \text{sgn}(v_y) \quad (5)$$

$$f_{mi} = \frac{1}{4}\mu_a mg \quad (6)$$

$$F_c = m\frac{v_G^2}{r} = mv_G\dot{\varphi}_z \quad (7)$$

$$\tan\theta = \frac{v_y}{v_x} \quad (8)$$

$$J = \frac{m}{12}(L^2 + W^2) \quad (9)$$

where $u_r$ and $u_s$ denote the rolling friction coefficient and the sliding friction coefficient. The character $m$ is the mass of the robot. The symbol $u_a$ indicates the actual friction coefficient of the movement which combines rolling and sliding. In an approximating modeling way, the actual friction coefficient $u_a$ can be fitted by a non-linear function with regard to three static parameters: the linear velocity of the robot, the angular velocity and the slippage ratio of the robot. In addition, the dynamic variables, i.e., the angular velocity and linear velocity, should be counted in. Thus, the function can be approximately fitted to an empirical formula as follows:

$$\mu_a = \left\{ \left[ (1 - \frac{1}{\lambda})\mu_s + \frac{1}{\lambda}\mu_r \right] - \mu_r \right\} \cdot \frac{2}{\pi}\arctan(5 \cdot \left| \frac{\dot{\varphi}}{V_x} \right|) \quad (10)$$

Note that $\lambda$ denotes the slippage rate of the robot, which is the function of the ratio of $L$ and $W$.

## 2.3   Motor-Wheel System Modeling

The torque of the in-wheel motor is related to the input voltage $u$ and the rotation speed of the motor $\omega_m$ [23]. The in-wheel motors that the target mobile robot adopts can be modeled as an empirical formula as follows:

$$\tau(t) = (-0.07\omega_m(t) + 1) \cdot (\tau_{max} + 20) \cdot \frac{2}{\pi}\arctan(\frac{u(t)}{10}) \quad (11)$$

where $\tau_{max}$ indicates the maximum torque that the motor can output.

## 2.4   Velocity Mapping Model

The rotation speeds of the motors must be obtained such that the torques of the motors can be generated by the empirical formula. The linear velocity and the angular velocity generated by the dynamic model must be converted to the rotation velocities of the left and right wheels. We assume that the robot is strictly symmetric and the speeds of both wheels on the same side are exactly the same. The kinematic model of the WSMR can be equivalent to a differential drive model according to [24], as shown in Fig. 4.

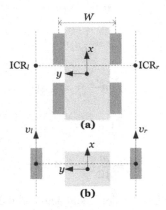

**Fig. 4.**  Equivalent model (a) WSMR (b) differential drive model

The instantaneous center of rotation (ICR) of wheels can be equivalent to the contact points of wheels of an equivalent differential drive robot. Thus, the inverse kinematic model can be written as follows:

$$\begin{cases} v_l = v_{set} + x_{ICRl} \cdot \omega \\ v_r = v_{set} + x_{ICRr} \cdot \omega \end{cases} \tag{12}$$

We assume that the ICRs of two-side wheels are symmetrical with respect to the local $y$-axis, a steering efficiency index $\chi$ can be defined as follows:

$$\chi = \frac{W}{x_{ICRr} - x_{ICRl}} = \frac{W}{2 \cdot x_{ICRr}}, \chi \in (0, 1] \tag{13}$$

When applying an equal opposite velocities, i.e., $v_l = -v_r$, within a certain period of time, the robot will reach an approximately pure rotation about the local $z$-axis. The ICRs of wheels can be estimated in this situation. Let $\phi$ indicates the steering angle, we have:

$$\chi = \frac{W\phi}{\int v_r dt - \int v_l dt} \tag{14}$$

The relationship between the linear/angular velocity $v$, $\omega$ and the left/right wheel velocities can be deduced by substituting Eq. (13) into Eq. (12):

$$
\begin{cases}
v_l = v - \dfrac{W}{2\chi} \cdot \omega \\[2mm]
v_r = v + \dfrac{W}{2\chi} \cdot \omega
\end{cases}
\tag{15}
$$

## 3    Dynamics Based DWA in Formation Control

### 3.1    Virtual Goals of Followers

Considering the limits of the communication in practical formation and the feasibility of engineering applications, the leader-follower method is adopted in the military combat situation and the anti-terrorist scene simulation. By using the distance-orientation method, the dynamic virtual goals are computed in real time by the followers according to the off-line calculation of the team shape table with regard to the pose of the leader, as shown in Fig. 5. The formation effects mostly depend on the tracking control of the followers.

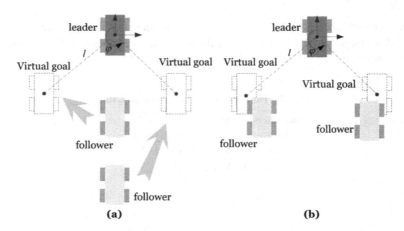

**Fig. 5.** Virtual goals in leader-follower control (a) formation changing (b) formation maintenance

### 3.2    DWA for the Control of Followers

According to the control inputs of the prediction model, as shown in Fig. 1, a series of input voltages are generated within a certain range. The future poses and velocities of the robot can be computed by the WSMR dynamics based prediction model. Each pair of control inputs generates a predictive trajectory which will be evaluated by the cost function. Every single node (pose of the robot) in the trajectory is scored by the following aspects: (1) the distance deviation between the virtual goal and the node predicted by the DWA; (2) the error between the orientation of the leader and that of each node; (3) the amplitude variation of $v$ and $\omega$ compared to the current $v_0$ and $\omega_0$ of the robot; (4) the velocity error between the leader's velocity and the velocity of the node. Let $P_i$ and $\alpha_i$ denote the position and the orientation of the robot; $P_g$ and $\alpha_g$ denotes the position and the orientation of the virtual goal. Thus, the cost function can be designed as follows:

$$
\begin{aligned}
c_i = w_1 \cdot \frac{\|P_i - P_g\|_{L2}}{\max\{\|P_i - P_g\|_{L2}\}} + w_2 \cdot \frac{|\alpha_i - \alpha_g|}{\max\{|\alpha_i - \alpha_g|\}} \\
+ w_3 \cdot \frac{|(\omega_i - \omega_0) \cdot (v_i - v_0)|}{\max\{|(\omega_i - \omega_0) \cdot (v_i - v_0)|\}} + w_4 \cdot \frac{|v_i - v_g|}{\max\{|v_i - v_g|\}}
\end{aligned}
\tag{16}
$$

where $w_i$ ($i = 1, 2, 3, 4$) denotes the weight values for each item that has been normalized. $\omega_i$ and $v_i$ indicate the angular velocity and the linear velocity computed by the WSMR dynamics. Note that $\omega_0$ is always set to zero to prefer stable motion without big turn. $v_g$ is the aim speed of the virtual goal, which is equal to the speed of the leader.

# 4   Experiments

The experiments are carried out in an open area such that the positioning can be supported by the GPS. The parameters of the target mobile robot and the experimental setup are listed in Table 1.

**Table 1.** Parameters and experimental setup.

| Parameters of dynamics | | Parameters of DWA | |
|---|---|---|---|
| $m$ | 80 kg | Formation speed | 2 m/s |
| W | 0.45 m | Predict time | 3 s |
| L | 0.40 m | $w_1$ | 0.35 |
| $u_r$ | 0.03 | $w_2$ | 0.25 |
| $u_s$ | 0.35 | $w_3$ | 0.10 |
| $\lambda$ | 2 | $w_4$ | 0.30 |
| $\chi$ | 0.86 | $v_0$ | 2 m/s |
| $\tau_{max}$ | 8 Nm | $\omega_0$ | 0 rad/s |

The trajectories predicted by using the DWA and the best trajectories are illustrated in Fig. 6. The predicted trajectories and the best trajectories when the robot is at the middle course based on Fig. 6(a) are illustrated in Fig. 6(d). At every single pose, the DWA evaluates each trajectory and find the trajectory with the lowest score, which means the corresponding control action is the optimal choice currently. In this way, the global optimal action during the formation control process can be deduced via establishing every single optimal action since the formation control can be considered as a Markov Decision Process (MDP). The best actions related to the lowest-score trajectories in Fig. 6(a) and (d) are shown in Fig. 6(b) and (c), respectively.

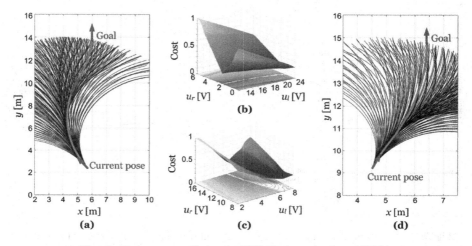

**Fig. 6.** Trajectory prediction by WSMR dynamics based DWA

The errors, control outputs and the actual trajectories are shown in Fig. 7. Compare with the conventional kinematics based DWA, the proposed dynamics based DWA can make the reduction of distance errors faster, as seen in Fig. 7(a), whereas the differences of orientation errors are not obvious between these two methods, as seen in Fig. 7(b). The control voltage of two-side motors and the control velocity of two-side wheels are shown in Fig. 7(c) and (d), respectively. The trajectories of three robots when they are in a triangle shape formation by using the conventional DWA and the proposed dynamics based DWA are illustrated in Fig. 7(e) and (f) respectively. The former goes further in $y$-axis direction because of the slower reduction of errors which results in a long process of adjusting the whole team.

The pictures of the target robots' mobile platforms are taken in the process of formation control. The linear, triangle and square formation are achieved by the proposed control method, as shown in Fig. 8.

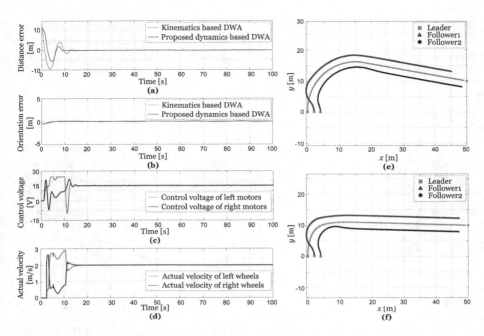

**Fig. 7.** Comparison of kinematics based DWA and dynamics based DWA in formation

**Fig. 8.** Pictures of target mobile robots in formation experiments.

# 5   Conclusions

This paper introduced the formation application in the anti-terrorist training. First, the prediction model based on the WSMR was built, which includes the kinematic model, the simplified dynamic model, the motor-wheel model and the velocity mapping model. Second, the dynamic virtual goal was illustrated in the leader-follower formation control and the principle of the DWA was described by the cost function. Finally, the experiments were carried out to verify the feasibility of the proposed dynamics based DWA. It shows that the proposed method has a better performance in the distance error convergence in the forming stage compared with the conventional kinematics based DWA.

As for future work, the emphasis will be put on the studies and tests of more robots, e.g. six target robots will be employed in the formation control to test the performance of the proposed method. Furthermore, considering that the proposed control algorithm cannot void the collision, the motion attributes of other robots and obstacles will be added in detection and communication such that the potential collision of robots can be realized in the algorithm.

**Acknowledgement.** This work was partially supported by the National Science Foundation of China under Grant (No. 61803201) and Jiangsu Natural Science Foundation under Grant (No. BK20170803).

# References

1. National research council of the national academies: Technology development for army unmanned ground vehicles. National Defense Industry Press, Beijing (2009)
2. Voth, D.: A new generation of military robots. IEEE Intell. Syst. **19**(4), 2–3 (2004)
3. Farinelli, A., Iocchi, L., Nardi, D.: Multi robot systems: a classification focused on coordination. IEEE Trans. Syst. Man Cybern. B Cybern. **34**(5), 2015–2028 (2014)
4. Yang, T.T., Liu, Z.Y., Chen, H., Pei, R.: Formation control of mobile robots: state and open problems. CAAI Trans. Intell. Syst. **2**(4), 21–27 (2007)
5. Liang, H.Z., Sun, Z.W., Wang, J.Y.: Finite-time attitude synchronization controllers design for spacecraft formations via behavior-based approach. Proc. Inst. Mech. Eng. Part G-J. Aerosp. Eng. **227**(11), 1737–1753 (2013)
6. Cristoforis, P.D., Pedre, S., Nische, M.A.: Behavior-based approach for educational robotics activities. IEEE Trans. Educ. **56**(1), 61–70 (2013)
7. Balch, T., Arkin, R.C.: Behavior-based formation control for multi-robot teams. IEEE Trans. Robot. Autom. **14**(6), 926–939 (1998)
8. Khatib, O.: Real-time obstacle avoidance for manipulators and mobile robots. Int. J. Robot. Res. **5**(1), 290–298 (1986)
9. Zhu, Y., Zhang, T., Song, J.Y.: Artificial field path planning for non-holonomic mobile robots. Control Theory Appl. **27**(2), 152–158 (2010)
10. Defoort, M., Floquet, T., Kokosy, A.: Sliding-mode formation control for cooperative autonomous mobile robots. IEEE Trans. Industr. Electron. **22**(11), 3944–3953 (2008)
11. Gao, Y., Zhang, H.F.: Leader-follower method and galactic dynamics based formation control for multi-robots. J. Xiamen Univ. **52**(1), 14–18 (2013)

12. Biglarbegian, M.: A novel robust leader-following control design for mobile robots. J. Intell. Rob. Syst. **71**(3), 391–402 (2013)
13. Lewis, M.A., Tan, K.H.: High precision formation control of mobile robots using virtual structure. Auton. Robot. **1**(4), 387–403 (1997)
14. Sadowska, A., Broek, T., Huijberts, H., Wouw, N.A.: Virtual structure approach to formation control of unicycle mobile robots using mutual coupling. Int. J. Control **84**(11), 1886–1902 (2011)
15. Yang, A.L., Naeem, W., Irwin, G.W., Li, K.: Stability analysis and implementation of a decentralized formation control strategy for unmanned vehicles. IEEE Trans. Control Syst. Technol. **22**(2), 706–720 (2014)
16. Liu, J.M., Wu, J.B.: Multi-agent Robotic Systems. CRC Press, Boca Raton (2001)
17. Zhang, R.L., Li, S., Chen, Q.W.: Formation control for a kind of nonholonomic mobile robots. Control Decis. **28**(11), 1751–1755 (2013)
18. Zhang, R.L., Li, S., Chen, Q.W., Yang, C.: Formation control for multi-robot system in complex terrain. Control Theory Appl. **31**(4), 531–537 (2014)
19. Jia, Q.L., Yan, J.G., Wang, X.M.: Formation control of multiple robot system based on potential function. Robot **28**(2), 111–114 (2006)
20. Gu, D.B., Hu, H.S.: A model predictive controller for robots to follow a virtual leader. Robotica **27**(6), 905–913 (2009)
21. Fox, D., Burgard, W., Thrun, S.: The dynamic window approach to collision avoidance. IEEE Robot. Autom. Mag. **4**(10), 23–33 (1997)
22. Courbon, J., Nezouar, Y., Martinet, P.: Indoor navigation of a non-holonomic mobile robot using a visual memory. Auton. Robot. **25**(3), 253–266 (2008)
23. Watts, A., Callance, A., Whitehead, A.: The technology and economics of in-wheel motors. SAE Int. J. Passeng. Cars Electron. Electr. Syst. **3**(2), 37–54 (2010)
24. Martinez, J.L., Mandow, A., Morales, J., Pedraza, S., Garcia-Cerezo, A.: Approximating kinematics for tracked mobile robots. Int. J. Robot. Res. **24**(10), 867–878 (2005)

# Adaptive Position and Force Tracking Control in Teleoperation System with Time-Varying Delays

Haochen Zhang[1,2], Aiguo Song[1(⊠)], and Huijun Li[1]

[1] State Key Laboratory of Bioelectronics,
Jiangsu Key Lab of Remote Measurement and Control,
School of Instrument Science and Engineering, Southeast University,
Nanjing 210096, People's Republic of China
lut_zhc@163.com, {a.g.song,lihuijun}@seu.edu.cn
[2] College of Electrical and Information Engineering,
Lanzhou University of Technology, Lanzhou 730050, People's Republic of China

**Abstract.** In this work, a novel position and force tracking control scheme are proposed in teleoperation system under time-varying delay and uncertain dynamics. First, two new auxiliary variables are designed for the master controller and slave controller. Second, the adaptive control laws based on Radial Basis Function (RBF) neural network are proposed. Then, the Lyapunov theory is used to verify the stability of the closed-loop teleoperation system. The main contribution of this work is the position error, position error integral, and force error are introduced into the auxiliary variable for the controller design to obtain the better position and force tracking effect. Finally, the system with the proposed control method is simulated to show effectiveness.

**Keywords:** Teleoperation system · Time-varying delay ·
RBF neural network · Adaptive control · Position-force tracking

## 1 Introduction

Teleoperation system can help human working in an unknown and dangerous environment, which has been widely applied in space operation, underwater exploration, medical rehabilitation, and so on [1–3]. A teleoperation system consists of the master robot, human operator, slave robot, task environment, and communication channel. The operator can remotely control the slave robot to perform work and feel the environment information with the master robot and signals in the communication channel. Therefore, stability and transparency are introduced into the bilateral teleoperation system to evaluate the system performance [4]. The stability means that the closed-loop teleoperation system can be stable under time-varying delays and other conditions. The transparency indicates that the teleoperation system can achieve position tracking and force tracking between the master and slave sides [5].

© Springer Nature Switzerland AG 2019
H. Yu et al. (Eds.): ICIRA 2019, LNAI 11741, pp. 613–624, 2019.
https://doi.org/10.1007/978-3-030-27532-7_54

In practical application of the teleoperation system, nonlinear dynamics, unknown model parameters, and communication time delays are all inevitable problems for controller design. Many control methods have been proposed to overcome these problems and make the teleoperation system has a better performance. The passivity theory is first developed for stability analysis of the teleoperation system. The scattering method [6,7] and wave-variable with 2-port network structure [8,9] are proposed to deal with time delays. In [10] PD control is investigated for position tracking of the teleoperation system with constant and variable communication delay. In [11] the linear parameterizable method is introduced to deal with uncertainty dynamics and novel control laws are designed for bilateral control in teleoperation system. In [12,13] the neural networks are used to estimate the unknown dynamics and adaptive controllers are designed. In [14] and our work in [15] the finite-time control methods with non-singular terminal sliding mode are applied in teleoperation controller design for the fast convergence speed. However, position tracking is mainly addressed in the above works, and the force feedback tracking is not considered.

In [16] a novel control scheme with PD position control and torque error at the master side is proposed to achieve position and force tracking. In [17] a nonlinear-proportional plus nonlinear damping controller is investigated to guarantee position and force tracking in teleoperation system with time-varying delays. In [18–20] the external force estimation method are applied to estimate the human and environment force, and control laws are designed for position and force tracking. But in these works, the force estimation method is based on dynamic models of the robot, the dynamic uncertainty is not considered. In [21] a new adaptive bilateral control scheme is proposed, the forgetting factor recursive least squares method is applied to estimate the environment force and the neural network is used to eliminate the uncertainties. But the time-varying communication delay is not mentioned.

In this paper, we design the new auxiliary variable, introduce the position-force bilateral teleoperation architecture and proposed the novel adaptive control laws based on Radial Basis Function (RBF) neural network for master and slave robot. Different from the method proposed above, we design a force filter and introduce the position error, position error integral, and force tracking error into the auxiliary variable at the master side. Moreover, the inaccurate dynamic models are considered in this work, the RBF neural network is applied to deal with these problems. The remainder of this paper is organized as follows. The system dynamics are described in Sect. 2. The control laws are designed in Sect. 3. In Sect. 4, the stability of the closed-loop teleoperation system is analyzed. In Sect. 5 the simulation results and analysis are shown. Finally, this work is concluded in Sect. 6.

## 2   Problem Formulation

The master and slave robot studied in this work are both $n$ degree-of-freedom (DOF) manipulator with revolute joints. The dynamic models of master and slave manipulators can be given as

$$\begin{cases} \boldsymbol{M}_m(\boldsymbol{q}_m)\ddot{\boldsymbol{q}}_m + \boldsymbol{C}_m(\boldsymbol{q}_m, \dot{\boldsymbol{q}}_m)\dot{\boldsymbol{q}}_m + \boldsymbol{G}_m(\boldsymbol{q}_m) + \boldsymbol{B}_m(\dot{\boldsymbol{q}}_m) = \boldsymbol{\tau}_m + \boldsymbol{F}_h, \\ \boldsymbol{M}_s(\boldsymbol{q}_s)\ddot{\boldsymbol{q}}_s + \boldsymbol{C}_s(\boldsymbol{q}_s, \dot{\boldsymbol{q}}_s)\dot{\boldsymbol{q}}_s + \boldsymbol{G}_s(\boldsymbol{q}_s) + \boldsymbol{B}_s(\dot{\boldsymbol{q}}_s) = \boldsymbol{\tau}_s - \boldsymbol{F}_e. \end{cases} \quad (1)$$

where for $j = m, s$, $\boldsymbol{q}_j \in \mathcal{R}^n$, $\dot{\boldsymbol{q}}_j \in \mathcal{R}^n$, and $\ddot{\boldsymbol{q}}_j \in \mathcal{R}^n$ are the vectors of joint position, joint velocity, and joint acceleration respectively. $\boldsymbol{M}_j(\boldsymbol{q}_j) \in \mathcal{R}^{n \times n}$ is the inertia matrix. $\boldsymbol{C}_j(\boldsymbol{q}_j, \dot{\boldsymbol{q}}_j) \in \mathcal{R}^{n \times n}$ is the centripetal and Coriolis torques matrix. $\boldsymbol{G}_j(\boldsymbol{q}_j) \in \mathcal{R}^n$ is the gravitational torque. $\boldsymbol{B}_j(\dot{\boldsymbol{q}}_j) \in \mathcal{R}^n$ is the friction torque. $\boldsymbol{\tau}_j \in \mathcal{R}^n$ is the control torque. $\boldsymbol{F}_h \in \mathcal{R}^n$ and $\boldsymbol{F}_e \in \mathcal{R}^n$ are the human operator and environment torques respectively.

It is impossible to obtain the exact dynamic in engineering application. Therefore, we introduce the uncertain and nominal dynamic parts to describe the inaccurate dynamics as

$$\begin{cases} \boldsymbol{M}_j(\boldsymbol{q}_j) = \boldsymbol{M}_{jo}(\boldsymbol{q}_j) + \Delta \boldsymbol{M}_j(\boldsymbol{q}_j), \\ \boldsymbol{C}_j(\boldsymbol{q}_j, \dot{\boldsymbol{q}}_j) = \boldsymbol{C}_{jo}(\boldsymbol{q}_j, \dot{\boldsymbol{q}}_j) + \Delta \boldsymbol{C}_j(\boldsymbol{q}_j, \dot{\boldsymbol{q}}_j), \\ \boldsymbol{G}_j(\boldsymbol{q}_j) = \boldsymbol{G}_{jo}(\boldsymbol{q}_j) + \Delta \boldsymbol{G}_j(\boldsymbol{q}_j). \end{cases} \quad (2)$$

In addition, there are some well-known properties in (1) are given as

**Property 1:** $\boldsymbol{M}_{qj}(\boldsymbol{q}_j)$ is the positive-definite, symmetric, and bounded matrix, for $j = m, s$.

**Property 2:** $\dot{\boldsymbol{M}}_{qj}(\boldsymbol{q}_j) - 2\boldsymbol{C}_{qj}(\boldsymbol{q}_j, \dot{\boldsymbol{q}}_j)$ is the skew symmetric matrix, and for any vector $\boldsymbol{x} \in \mathcal{R}^n$ the equation $\boldsymbol{x}^T[\dot{\boldsymbol{M}}_{qj}(\boldsymbol{q}_j) - 2\boldsymbol{C}_{qj}(\boldsymbol{q}_j, \dot{\boldsymbol{q}}_j)]\boldsymbol{x} = 0$ is always held.

**Assumption 1:** $d_m(t)$ is represented as the varying-time delay from the master to slave side; $d_s(t)$ is represented as the varying-time delay from the slave to master side. For $j = m, s$, $d_j(t)$ and the change rate $\dot{d}_j(t)$ are assumed to be bounded as: $0 \le d_j(t) \le \bar{d}_j$, $|\dot{d}_j(t)| \le D_j$.

Based on [17] the human and environment torques $\boldsymbol{F}_h$ and $\boldsymbol{F}_e$ can be modeled as the spring-damper structure as

$$\begin{cases} \boldsymbol{F}_h = -\boldsymbol{f}_h - \boldsymbol{D}_h \dot{\boldsymbol{q}}_m - \boldsymbol{S}_h \boldsymbol{q}_m, \\ \boldsymbol{F}_e = \boldsymbol{D}_e \dot{\boldsymbol{q}}_m + \boldsymbol{S}_e \boldsymbol{q}_m. \end{cases} \quad (3)$$

Therefore, for $j = m, s$ the dynamics of teleoperation in (1) can be rewritten as:

$$\boldsymbol{M}_{jo}(\boldsymbol{q}_j)\ddot{\boldsymbol{q}}_j + \boldsymbol{C}_{jo}(\boldsymbol{q}_j, \dot{\boldsymbol{q}}_j)\dot{\boldsymbol{q}}_j + \boldsymbol{G}_{jo}(\boldsymbol{q}_j) = \boldsymbol{\tau}_j + \boldsymbol{P}_j. \quad (4)$$

where $\boldsymbol{P}_m = -\Delta \boldsymbol{M}_m(\boldsymbol{q}_m)\ddot{\boldsymbol{q}}_m - [\Delta \boldsymbol{C}_m(\boldsymbol{q}_m, \dot{\boldsymbol{q}}_m) + \boldsymbol{D}_h]\dot{\boldsymbol{q}}_m - \boldsymbol{S}_h \boldsymbol{q}_m - \Delta \boldsymbol{G}_m(\boldsymbol{q}_m) - \boldsymbol{B}_m(\dot{\boldsymbol{q}}_m) - \boldsymbol{f}_h$, $\boldsymbol{P}_s = -\Delta \boldsymbol{M}_s(\boldsymbol{q}_s)\ddot{\boldsymbol{q}}_s - [\Delta \boldsymbol{C}_s(\boldsymbol{q}_s, \dot{\boldsymbol{q}}_s) + \boldsymbol{D}_e]\dot{\boldsymbol{q}}_s - \boldsymbol{S}_e \boldsymbol{q}_s - \Delta \boldsymbol{G}_s(\boldsymbol{q}_s) - \boldsymbol{B}_s(\dot{\boldsymbol{q}}_s)$.

In our work, the RBF neural network is applied to estimated the $\boldsymbol{P}_j$ as

$$\boldsymbol{P}_j = \boldsymbol{\theta}_j^T \boldsymbol{Y}_j(\boldsymbol{Z}_j) + \boldsymbol{\varepsilon}_j. \quad (5)$$

where $\boldsymbol{Z}_j = \left[ \boldsymbol{q}_j^T, \dot{\boldsymbol{q}}_j^T, \ddot{\boldsymbol{q}}_j^T \right]$; $\boldsymbol{\theta}_j \in \mathcal{R}^{k \times n}$ is the matrix of idea parameters, $\boldsymbol{\varepsilon}_j \in \mathcal{R}^n$ is the approximation error; $\boldsymbol{Y}_j(\boldsymbol{Z}_j) \in \mathcal{R}^{k \times 1}$ is the known Gaussian basis function vector and $\boldsymbol{Y}_j(\boldsymbol{Z}_j) = [Y_{j1}, Y_{j2}, \ldots, Y_{jk}]$ can be obtained as

$$Y_{ji} = e^{-\frac{(\boldsymbol{z}_j - \boldsymbol{c}_j)^T (\boldsymbol{z}_j - \boldsymbol{c}_j)}{2b_j^2}}, i = 1, 2, \ldots k. \tag{6}$$

# 3    Controller Design

This section investigates the controller design for the teleoperation system.

First we define the joint tracking error $\boldsymbol{e}_m$ and $\boldsymbol{e}_s$ as

$$\begin{aligned} \boldsymbol{e}_m &= \boldsymbol{q}_m(t) - \boldsymbol{q}_s(t - d_s(t)), \\ \boldsymbol{e}_s &= \boldsymbol{q}_s(t) - \boldsymbol{q}_m(t - d_m(t)). \end{aligned} \tag{7}$$

The change rates of position error are $\dot{\boldsymbol{e}}_m = \dot{\boldsymbol{q}}_m(t) - \dot{\boldsymbol{q}}_s(t - d_s(t)) + \dot{\boldsymbol{q}}_s(t - d_s(t))\dot{d}_s$ and $\dot{\boldsymbol{e}}_s = \dot{\boldsymbol{q}}_s(t) - \dot{\boldsymbol{q}}_m(t - d_m(t)) + \dot{\boldsymbol{q}}_m(t - d_m(t))\dot{d}_m$. It is obvious that the $d_m$ and $d_s$ are difficult to obtain in practical application. To simplify the expression, we define $\dot{\boldsymbol{e}}_{mv}$, $\dot{\boldsymbol{e}}_{sv}$, $\ddot{\boldsymbol{e}}_{mv}$, and $\ddot{\boldsymbol{e}}_{sv}$ for controller design, which they are described as

$$\begin{aligned} \dot{\boldsymbol{e}}_{mv} &= \dot{\boldsymbol{q}}_m(t) - \dot{\boldsymbol{q}}_s(t - d_s(t)), \\ \ddot{\boldsymbol{e}}_{mv} &= \ddot{\boldsymbol{q}}_m(t) - \ddot{\boldsymbol{q}}_s(t - d_s(t)), \\ \dot{\boldsymbol{e}}_{sv} &= \dot{\boldsymbol{q}}_s(t) - \dot{\boldsymbol{q}}_m(t - d_m(t)), \\ \ddot{\boldsymbol{e}}_{sv} &= \ddot{\boldsymbol{q}}_s(t) - \ddot{\boldsymbol{q}}_m(t - d_m(t)). \end{aligned} \tag{8}$$

The torque tracking error at the master side is defined as

$$\Delta \boldsymbol{F}_m = \boldsymbol{F}_h - \boldsymbol{F}_e(t - d_s(t)). \tag{9}$$

Second, the auxiliary variable $\boldsymbol{s}_m$ and $\boldsymbol{s}_s$ for the controller are designed as

$$\begin{aligned} \boldsymbol{s}_m &= \dot{\boldsymbol{e}}_{mv} + \boldsymbol{\lambda}_{m1}\boldsymbol{e}_m + \boldsymbol{\lambda}_{m2}\int_0^t \boldsymbol{e}_m d\tau + \boldsymbol{\alpha}_m, \\ \boldsymbol{s}_s &= \dot{\boldsymbol{e}}_{sv} + \boldsymbol{\lambda}_{s1}\boldsymbol{e}_s + \boldsymbol{\lambda}_{s2}\int_0^t \boldsymbol{e}_s d\tau. \end{aligned} \tag{10}$$

where for $i = m, s$, $\boldsymbol{\lambda}_{j1}$ and $\boldsymbol{\lambda}_{j2}$ are the positive definite diagonal matrix. $\boldsymbol{\alpha}_m$ is the output of the torque error filter and is described as

$$\dot{\boldsymbol{\alpha}}_m = -L_{m1}\boldsymbol{\alpha}_m + L_{m2}\Delta \boldsymbol{F}_m. \tag{11}$$

where $L_{m1}$ and $L_{m2}$ are all positive constants.

Therefore, with (4) (8), (10), and (11), we can get

$$\begin{cases} \boldsymbol{M}_{mo}\dot{\boldsymbol{s}}_m = \boldsymbol{\tau}_m + \boldsymbol{P}_m - \boldsymbol{M}_{mo}\left[\ddot{\boldsymbol{q}}_s(t - d_s(t)) - \boldsymbol{\lambda}_{m1}\dot{\boldsymbol{e}}_{mv} - \boldsymbol{\lambda}_{m2}\boldsymbol{e}_m - \boldsymbol{\alpha}_m\right] \\ \qquad - \boldsymbol{C}_{mo}\dot{\boldsymbol{q}}_m - \boldsymbol{G}_{mo} + \boldsymbol{z}_m\dot{d}_s, \\ \boldsymbol{M}_{so}\dot{\boldsymbol{s}}_s = \boldsymbol{\tau}_s + \boldsymbol{P}_s - \boldsymbol{M}_{so}\left[\ddot{\boldsymbol{q}}_m(t - d_m(t)) - \boldsymbol{\lambda}_{s1}\dot{\boldsymbol{e}}_{sv} - \boldsymbol{\lambda}_{s2}\boldsymbol{e}_s\right] \\ \qquad - \boldsymbol{C}_{so}\dot{\boldsymbol{q}}_s - \boldsymbol{G}_{so} + \boldsymbol{z}_s\dot{d}_m. \end{cases} \tag{12}$$

where $z_m = M_{mo}[\ddot{q}_s(t - d_s(t)) + \dot{q}_s(t - d_s(t))]$ and $z_s = M_{so}[\ddot{q}_m(t - d_m(t)) + \dot{q}_m(t - d_m(t))]$.

Then the control laws for master and slave robot can be designed as

$$
\begin{cases}
\boldsymbol{\tau}_m = \boldsymbol{\tau}_{m1} + \boldsymbol{\tau}_{m2}, \\
\boldsymbol{\tau}_{m1} = M_{mo}[\ddot{q}_s(t - d_s(t)) - \lambda_{m1}\dot{e}_{mv} - \lambda_{m2}e_m + L_{m1}\alpha_m - L_{m2}\Delta F_m] \\
\qquad + C_{mo}\dot{q}_m + G_{mo} - K_{m1}s_m, \\
\boldsymbol{\tau}_{m2} = -\hat{\boldsymbol{\theta}}_m Y_m - \dfrac{s_m}{2a_{m1}}\hat{\eta}_m - \dfrac{z_m z_m^T s_m}{2a_{m2}}\hat{D}_m.
\end{cases}
\tag{13}
$$

$$
\begin{cases}
\boldsymbol{\tau}_s = \boldsymbol{\tau}_{s1} + \boldsymbol{\tau}_{s2}, \\
\boldsymbol{\tau}_{s1} = M_{so}[\ddot{q}_m(t - d_m(t)) - \lambda_{s1}\dot{e}_{sv} - \lambda_{s2}e_s] + C_{so}\dot{q}_s + G_{so} - K_{s1}s_s, \\
\boldsymbol{\tau}_{s2} = -\hat{\boldsymbol{\theta}}_s Y_s - \dfrac{s_s}{2a_{s1}}\hat{\eta}_s - \dfrac{z_s z_s^T s_s}{2a_{s2}}\hat{D}_s.
\end{cases}
\tag{14}
$$

where for $j = m, s$, $K_{j1} \in \mathcal{R}^n$ is the positive diagonal matrix. $a_{j1}$ and $a_{j2}$ are positive constants.

The adaptive laws can be described as

$$
\begin{cases}
\dot{\hat{\boldsymbol{\theta}}}_j = \Gamma_{j1} Y_m s_m^T - \hat{\boldsymbol{\theta}}_j, \\
\dot{\hat{\eta}}_j = \dfrac{\Gamma_{j2} s_j^T s_j}{2a_{j1}} - \hat{\eta}_j, \\
\dot{\hat{D}}_j = \dfrac{\Gamma_{j3} s_j^T z_j z_j^T s_j}{2a_{j2}} - \hat{D}_j.
\end{cases}
\tag{15}
$$

where $\Gamma_{j1}$, $\Gamma_{j2}$, and $\Gamma_{j3}$ are all positive constants.

Consequently, the closed-loop system is composed of dynamic (4), auxiliary variable (10), torque error filter (11), control laws (13), (14), and adaptive laws (15).

## 4   Stability Analysis

This section gives the stability proof process of closed-loop teleoperation system.

**Theorem 1.** *Consider the teleoperation system in (4) with time delays and dynamic uncertainties, with the Assumption 1, then the closed-loop teleoperation system is stable and all signals in system are uniformly ultimately bounded (UUB), if the control laws (13), (14), and adaptive laws (15) are adopted, and the parameters in control and adaptive laws satisfy that $K_{j1}$ is positive-definite diagonal matrix, $L_{j1}$, $L_{j2}$, $\Gamma_{j1}$, $\Gamma_{j2}$, and $\Gamma_{j3}$ are all positive constants.*

*Proof.* Let consider the following Lyapunov candidate function as $V = V_1 + V_2$

$$V_1 = \sum_{j=m,s} \frac{1}{2} \boldsymbol{s}_j^T \boldsymbol{M}_{jo} \boldsymbol{s}_j,$$

$$V_2 = \sum_{j=m,s} \left[ \frac{1}{2} \mathrm{tr} \left( \tilde{\boldsymbol{\theta}}_j^T \Gamma_{j1}^{-1} \tilde{\boldsymbol{\theta}}_j \right) + \frac{\Gamma_{j2}^{-1}}{2} \tilde{\eta}_j^2 + \frac{\Gamma_{j3}^{-1}}{2} \tilde{D}_j^2 \right].$$

where $\tilde{\boldsymbol{\theta}}_j = \boldsymbol{\theta}_j - \hat{\boldsymbol{\theta}}_j$, $\tilde{\eta}_j = \eta_j - \hat{\eta}_j$, and $\tilde{D}_j = D_j - \hat{D}_j$.
The differential of $V_1$ is

$$\dot{V}_1 = \sum_{j=m,s} \left[ \boldsymbol{s}_j^T \boldsymbol{M}_{jo} \dot{\boldsymbol{s}}_j + \frac{1}{2} \boldsymbol{s}_j^T \dot{\boldsymbol{M}}_{jo} \boldsymbol{s}_j - \boldsymbol{s}_j^T \boldsymbol{C}_{jo} \boldsymbol{s}_j + \boldsymbol{s}_j^T \boldsymbol{C}_{jo} \boldsymbol{s}_j \right].$$

With the Property 1 and 2, we have

$$\dot{V}_1 = \sum_{j=m,s} \left[ \boldsymbol{s}_j^T \boldsymbol{M}_{jo} \dot{\boldsymbol{s}}_j + \boldsymbol{s}_j^T \boldsymbol{C}_{jo} \boldsymbol{s}_j \right].$$

Based on (12), the $\dot{V}_1$ can be rewritten as

$$\dot{V}_1 = \boldsymbol{s}_m^T \left\{ \boldsymbol{\tau}_m + \boldsymbol{P}_m - \boldsymbol{M}_{mo} \left[ \ddot{\boldsymbol{q}}_s(t - d_s(t)) - \boldsymbol{\lambda}_{m1} \dot{\boldsymbol{e}}_{mv} - \boldsymbol{\lambda}_{m2} \boldsymbol{e}_m - \boldsymbol{\alpha}_m \right] \right.$$
$$\left. - \boldsymbol{C}_{mo} \left( \dot{\boldsymbol{q}}_m - \boldsymbol{s}_m \right) - \boldsymbol{G}_{mo} + \boldsymbol{z}_m \dot{d}_s \right\}$$
$$+ \boldsymbol{s}_s^T \left\{ \boldsymbol{\tau}_s + \boldsymbol{P}_s - \boldsymbol{M}_{so} \left[ \ddot{\boldsymbol{q}}_m(t - d_m(t)) - \boldsymbol{\lambda}_{s1} \dot{\boldsymbol{e}}_{sv} - \boldsymbol{\lambda}_{s2} \boldsymbol{e}_s \right] \right.$$
$$\left. - \boldsymbol{C}_{so} \left( \dot{\boldsymbol{q}}_s - \boldsymbol{s}_s \right) - \boldsymbol{G}_{so} + \boldsymbol{z}_s \dot{d}_m \right\}.$$

With (5) and control laws (13), (14), based on Young's inequality, there has

$$\dot{V}_1 = \sum_{j=m,s} \boldsymbol{s}_j^T \left[ -\boldsymbol{K}_{j1} \boldsymbol{s}_j - \hat{\boldsymbol{\theta}}_j \boldsymbol{Y}_j(\boldsymbol{Z}_j) - \frac{\boldsymbol{s}_j}{2a_{j1}} \hat{\eta}_j - \frac{\boldsymbol{z}_j \boldsymbol{z}_j^T \boldsymbol{s}_j}{2a_{j2}} \hat{D}_j \right.$$
$$\left. + \boldsymbol{\theta}_j^T \boldsymbol{Y}_j(\boldsymbol{Z}_j) + \boldsymbol{\varepsilon}_j + \boldsymbol{z}_j \dot{d}_{j'} \right]$$
$$\leq \sum_{j=m,s} - \boldsymbol{s}_j^T \boldsymbol{K}_{j1} \boldsymbol{s}_j + \boldsymbol{s}_j^T \tilde{\boldsymbol{\theta}}_j^T \boldsymbol{Y}_j(\boldsymbol{Z}_j) + \frac{\boldsymbol{s}_j^T \boldsymbol{s}_j}{2a_{j1}} \tilde{\eta}_j + \frac{\boldsymbol{s}_j^T \boldsymbol{z}_j \boldsymbol{z}_j^T \boldsymbol{s}_j}{2a_{j2}} \tilde{D}_{j'} + \frac{a_{j1} + a_{j2}}{2}.$$

where for $j = m, s$, $j' = s, m$. Based on the RBF neural network property, the approximation error $\boldsymbol{\varepsilon}_j$ is bounded. Therefore, we define $\| \boldsymbol{\varepsilon}_j^T \boldsymbol{\varepsilon}_j \| \leq \eta_j$. Based on Assumption 1, $|d_{j'}| \leq D_{j'}$.
The differential of $V_2$ is

$$\dot{V}_2 = \sum_{j=m,s} \left[ \mathrm{tr} \left( \tilde{\boldsymbol{\theta}}_j^T \Gamma_{j1}^{-1} \dot{\tilde{\boldsymbol{\theta}}}_j \right) + \Gamma_{j2}^{-1} \tilde{\eta}_j \dot{\tilde{\eta}}_j + \Gamma_{j3}^{-1} \tilde{D}_j \dot{\tilde{D}}_j \right]$$
$$= \sum_{j=m,s} \left[ -\mathrm{tr} \left( \tilde{\boldsymbol{\theta}}_j^T \Gamma_{j1}^{-1} \dot{\hat{\boldsymbol{\theta}}}_j \right) - \Gamma_{j2}^{-1} \tilde{\eta}_j \dot{\hat{\eta}}_j - \Gamma_{j3}^{-1} \tilde{D}_j \dot{\hat{D}}_j \right]$$

For tr $\left(\tilde{\boldsymbol{\theta}}_j^T \Gamma_{j1}^{-1} \hat{\boldsymbol{\theta}}_j\right)$, $\Gamma_{j2}^{-1} \tilde{\eta}_j \hat{\eta}_j$, and $\Gamma_{j3}^{-1} \tilde{D}_j \hat{D}_j$, there has

$$\text{tr}\left(\tilde{\boldsymbol{\theta}}_j^T \Gamma_{j1}^{-1} \hat{\boldsymbol{\theta}}_j\right) \leq -\frac{1}{2}\text{tr}\left(\tilde{\boldsymbol{\theta}}_j^T \Gamma_{j1}^{-1} \tilde{\boldsymbol{\theta}}_j\right) + \frac{1}{2}\text{tr}\left(\boldsymbol{\theta}_j^T \Gamma_{j1}^{-1} \boldsymbol{\theta}_j\right)$$

$$\Gamma_{j2}^{-1} \tilde{\eta}_j \hat{\eta}_j \leq -\frac{\Gamma_{j2}^{-1}}{2}\tilde{\eta}_j^2 + \frac{\Gamma_{j2}^{-1}}{2}\eta_j^2$$

$$\Gamma_{j3}^{-1} \tilde{D}_j \hat{D}_j \leq -\frac{\Gamma_{j3}^{-1}}{2}\tilde{D}_j^2 + \frac{\Gamma_{j3}^{-1}}{2}D_j^2.$$

With the adaptive laws (15), the $V_2$ can be rewritten as

$$\dot{V}_2 \leq \sum_{j=m,s}\left[\boldsymbol{s}_j^T \tilde{\boldsymbol{\theta}}_j^T \boldsymbol{Y}_j(\boldsymbol{Z}_j) + \frac{\boldsymbol{s}_j^T \boldsymbol{s}_j}{2a_{j1}}\tilde{\eta}_j + \frac{\boldsymbol{s}_j^T \boldsymbol{z}_j \boldsymbol{z}_j^T \boldsymbol{s}_j}{2a_{j2}}\tilde{D}_{j'}\right.$$
$$-\frac{1}{2}\text{tr}\left(\tilde{\boldsymbol{\theta}}_j^T \Gamma_{j1}^{-1} \tilde{\boldsymbol{\theta}}_j\right) - \frac{\Gamma_{j2}^{-1}}{2}\tilde{\eta}_j^2 - \frac{\Gamma_{j3}^{-1}}{2}\tilde{D}_j^2$$
$$\left.+\frac{1}{2}\text{tr}\left(\boldsymbol{\theta}_j^T \Gamma_{j1}^{-1} \boldsymbol{\theta}_j\right) + \frac{\Gamma_{j2}^{-1}}{2}\eta_j^2 + \frac{\Gamma_{j3}^{-1}}{2}D_j^2\right].$$

Then jointing $\dot{V}_1$ and $\dot{V}_2$ above, $\dot{V}$ is obtained as

$$\dot{V} \leq \sum_{j=m,s}\left[-\boldsymbol{s}_j^T \boldsymbol{K}_{j1} \boldsymbol{s}_j - \frac{1}{2}\text{tr}\left(\tilde{\boldsymbol{\theta}}_j^T \Gamma_{j1}^{-1} \tilde{\boldsymbol{\theta}}_j\right) - \frac{\Gamma_{j2}^{-1}}{2}\tilde{\eta}_j^2 - \frac{\Gamma_{j3}^{-1}}{2}\tilde{D}_j^2\right.$$
$$\left.+\frac{1}{2}\text{tr}\left(\boldsymbol{\theta}_j^T \Gamma_{j1}^{-1} \boldsymbol{\theta}_j\right) + \frac{\Gamma_{j2}^{-1}}{2}\eta_j^2 + \frac{\Gamma_{j3}^{-1}}{2}D_j^2 + \frac{a_{j1}+a_{j2}}{2}\right].$$

Define $o_j = \frac{1}{2}\text{tr}\left(\boldsymbol{\theta}_j^T \Gamma_{j1}^{-1} \boldsymbol{\theta}_j\right) + \frac{\Gamma_{j2}^{-1}}{2}\eta_j^2 + \frac{\Gamma_{j3}^{-1}}{2}D_j^2 + \frac{a_{j1}+a_{j2}}{2}$, $o_{ms} = o_m + o_s$ is the positive constant. Let $k = \min\{\frac{2\lambda_{min}(\boldsymbol{K}_{j1})}{\lambda_{min}(\boldsymbol{M}_{jo})}, 1\}$, we can get that

$$\dot{V} \leq -kV + o_{ms}.$$

Based on the boundedness theory of Khalil in [22], the closed-loop teleoperation system is stable and the signals are UUB. Then the proof is completed.

## 5    Simulation Results

In this section, the simulation is implemented and the simulation results are shown to illustrate the effect of the proposed control method. The master and slave robot in the simulation are considered as 2-dof manipulator with revolute joint respectively. The dynamic models are described as

$$\boldsymbol{M}_j = \begin{bmatrix} (m_{j1} + m_{j2})\, l_{j1}^2 + m_{j2}l_{j2}\,(l_{j2} + 2l_{j1}\cos q_{j2})\,, & m_{j2}l_{j2}\,(l_{j2} + l_{j1}\cos q_{j2}) \\ m_{j2}l_{j2}\,(l_{j2} + l_{j1}\cos q_{j2})\,, & m_{j2}l_{j2}^2 \end{bmatrix}$$

$$C_j = \begin{bmatrix} -m_{j2}l_{j1}l_{j2}\dot{q}_{j2}\text{sin}q_{j2}, & -m_{j2}l_{j1}l_{j2}\left(\dot{q}_{j1}+\dot{q}_{j2}\right)\text{sin}q_{j2} \\ m_{j2}l_{j1}l_{j2}\dot{q}_{j1}\text{sin}q_{j2}, & 0 \end{bmatrix},$$

$$G_j = \begin{bmatrix} \left(m_{j1}+m_{j2}\right)l_{j1}g\text{cos}q_{j1}+m_{j2}l_{j2}g\text{cos}\left(q_{j1}+q_{j2}\right) \\ m_{j2}l_{j2}g\text{cos}\left(q_{j1}+q_{j2}\right) \end{bmatrix},$$

$$F_j = \begin{bmatrix} f_{j1}\dot{q}_{j1}+f_{j2}\text{sign}\left(\dot{q}_{j1}\right) \\ f_{j3}\dot{q}_{j1}+f_{j4}\text{sign}\left(\dot{q}_{j2}\right) \end{bmatrix}.$$

The actual parameters of master and slave manipulators are chosen as $m_{j1} = 3.5$kg, $m_{j2} = 2.5$ kg, $l_{j1} = 0.3$ m, $l_{j2} = 0.35$ m, $f_{m1} = f_{m3} = 0.5$, $f_{m2} = f_{m4} = 0.2$, $f_{s1} = f_{s3} = 0.3$, $f_{s2} = f_{s4} = 0.3$, $g = 9.8$ m/s$^2$. $D_h = \text{diag}(0.3, 0.3)$, $D_e = \text{diag}(0.1, 0.1)$, $S_h = \text{diag}(6, 6)$, $S_e = \text{diag}(6, 6)$. The $M_j$, $C_j$, $G_j$, and $B_j$ can be calculated. Considering the perturbation of the dynamic models, the final dynamics of teleoperation system used for simulation is defined as $M_j = M_{jo} + 0.01\sin(2t)M_{jo}$, $C_j = C_{jo} + 0.01\sin(2t)C_{jo}$, and $G_j = G_{jo} + 0.01\sin(2t)G_{jo}$.

The controller parameters are given as $m_{jo1} = 2.0$ kg, $m_{jo2} = 2.0$ kg, $l_{jo1} = 0.3$ m, $l_{jo2} = 0.3$ m. Where $m_{jo1}$, $m_{jo2}$, $l_{jo1}$, and $l_{jo2}$ are the nominal parameters of $m_{j1}$, $m_{j2}$, $l_{j1}$, and $l_{j2}$ respectively. Then the nominal dynamic of $M_{jo}$, $C_{jo}$, and $G_{jo}$ can also be obtained. $\lambda_{m1} = \lambda_{s1} = \text{diag}(2.6, 2.5)$, $L_{m1} = L_{m2} = 1$, $K_{m1} = K_{s1} = \text{diag}(10.0, 6.0)$, $a_{j1} = a_{j2} = 15$, $\Gamma_{j1} = \Gamma_{j2} = \Gamma_{j3} = 0.6$. For the RBF neural network, the number of node is $k = 5$, the center of the Gaussian matrix is $c_j = 5 \times [cc_j, cc_j, cc_j, cc_j, cc_j, cc_j]^T$, $cc_j = [-1, -0.5, 0, 0.5, 1]^T$, the width of the Gaussian function is $b_j = 5$. The vary-time delays $d_m(t)$ and $d_s(t)$ are shown in Fig. 1.

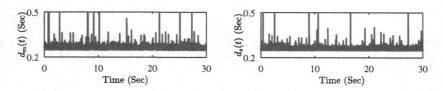

**Fig. 1.** Actual communication delays $d_m(t)$ and $d_s(t)$ used for simulation.

Two parts of the simulation have been achieved to show the performance of the designed controller.

## 5.1   Simulation in Free Motion

In free motion, the slave robot does not contact the environment. Therefore, the torque of the environment is zero. The simulation results are shown in Figs. 2, 3, 4 and 5. The joint positions $q_m$ and $q_s$ are shown in Fig. 2. The position tracking performance is shown in Fig. 3. The adaptive parameters $\hat{\eta}_m$, $\hat{\eta}_s$, $\hat{D}_m$, and $\hat{D}_s$ are shown in Fig. 4. The adaptive parameters of RBF neural network $\hat{\theta}_m$ and $\hat{\theta}_s$ are shown in Fig. 5.

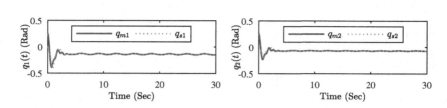

**Fig. 2.** Joint positions of master and slave robot in free motion.

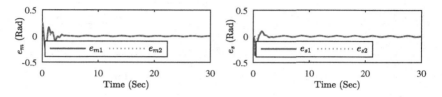

**Fig. 3.** Joint tracking errors of master and slave side in free motion.

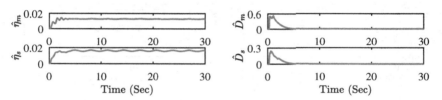

**Fig. 4.** Adaptive parameters $\hat{\eta}_m$, $\hat{\eta}_s$, $\hat{D}_m$, and $\hat{D}_s$ in free motion.

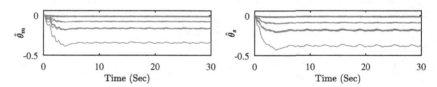

**Fig. 5.** Adaptive parameters $\hat{\theta}_m$ and $\hat{\theta}_s$ in free motion.

## 5.2 Simulation in Contact Motion

In this subsection, the slave robot contacts the environment and the operator exogenous torque is also applied. The operator exogenous torque in x-direction $f_{hx}$ is shown in Fig. 6 and in y-direction $f_{hy} = 0$.

The joint positions $q_m$ and $q_s$ with contact motion are shown in Fig. 7. The position tracking errors $e_m$ and $e_s$ are shown in Fig. 8. The torque error at master side $\Delta f$ is shown in Fig. 9.

It is clear that the performance of the teleoperation system in free and contact motion is achieved by the proposed control method.

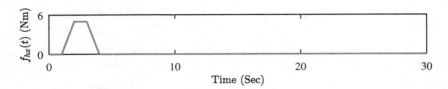

**Fig. 6.** Operator exogenous torque in x-direction $f_{hx}$.

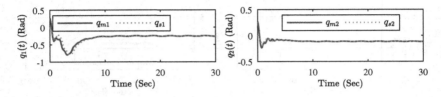

**Fig. 7.** The joint positions $q_m$ and $q_s$ with contact motion.

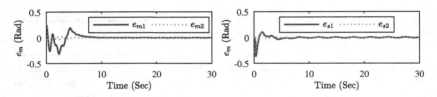

**Fig. 8.** The joint errors $e_m$ and $e_s$ with contact motion.

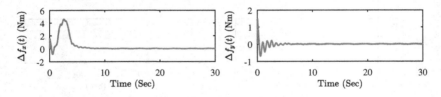

**Fig. 9.** The torque error $\Delta f$ with contact motion.

## 6    Conclusion

This work presents a novel position-force tracking control method for n-dof nonlinear teleoperation system with variable time-delay and uncertain dynamics. In order to achieve position and force tracking, a new auxiliary variable which contains position error integral and force error is designed. Control and adaptive laws are presented. The stability of the closed-loop system is also proven based on Lyapunov theory. The simulation based on a pair of 2-dof robots is performed to verify the effectiveness of proposed control methods. Frankly speaking, the experiment is not concerned in our work, and this problem will be considered in our follow-up work.

**Acknowledgments.** This work is supported in part by the National Key Research and Development Program of China under Grant No.2016YFB1001301, in part by the National Natural Science Foundation of China under Grant No.91648206 and No. U1713210.

# References

1. Imaida, T., Yokokohji, Y., Doi, T., Oda, M., Yoshikwa, T.: Ground space bilateral teleoperation of ETS-VII robot arm by direct bilateral coupling under 7-s time delay condition. IEEE Trans. Robot. Autom. **147**(3), 499–511 (2004). https://doi.org/10.1109/TRA.2004.825271

2. Haddadi, A., Razi, K., Hashtrudi-Zaad, K.: Operator dynamics consideration for less conservative coupled stability condition in bilateral teleoperation. IEEE/ASME Trans. Mechatron. **20**(5), 2463–2475 (2015). https://doi.org/10.1109/TMECH.2014.2385637

3. Xiong, P.W., Zhu, X.D., Song, A.G., Hu, L.Y., Liu, X.P.P., Feng, L.H.: A target grabbing strategy for telerobot based on improved stiffness display device. IEEE-CAA J. Autom. Sinica. **4**(4), 661–667 (2016). https://doi.org/10.1109/JAS.2016.7510256

4. Chan, L.P., Naghdy, F., Stirling, D.: Application of adaptive controllers in teleoperation systems: a survey. IEEE Trans. Hum.-Mach. Syst. **44**(3), 337–352 (2014). https://doi.org/10.1109/THMS.2014.2303983

5. Lu, Z., Huang, P., Liu, Z.: Predictive approach for sensorless bimanual teleoperation under random time delays with adaptive fuzzy control. Trans. Ind. Electron. **65**(3), 2439–2448 (2018). https://doi.org/10.1109/TIE.2017.2745445

6. Anderson, R., Spong, M.W.: Bilateral control of teleoperators with time delay. IEEE Trans. Autom. Control. **34**(5), 494–501 (1989). https://doi.org/10.1109/9.24201

7. Anderson, R.J., Spong, M.W.: Asymptotic stability for force reflecting teleoperators with time delay. Int. J. Robot. Res. **11**(2), 135–149 (1992). https://doi.org/10.1177/027836499201100204

8. Sun, D., Naghdy, F., Du, H.: Application of wave-variable control to bilateral teleoperation systems: a survey. Ann. Rev. Control **38**(1), 12–31 (2014). https://doi.org/10.1016/j.arcontrol.2014.03.002

9. Yang, C.G., Wang, X.J., Li, Z.J., Li, Y.A., Sun, C.Y.: Teleoperation control based on combination of wave variable and neural networks. IEEE Trans. Syst. Man Cybern. Syst. **47**(8), 2125–2136 (2017). https://doi.org/10.1109/TSMC.2016.2615061

10. Lee, D., Spong, M.W.: Passive bilateral teleoperation with constant time delay. IEEE Trans. Robot. **22**(2), 269–281 (2006). https://doi.org/10.1109/TRO.2005.862037

11. Liu, Y.C., Khong, M.H.: Adaptive control for nonlinear teleoperators with uncertain kinematics and dynamics. IEEE-ASME Trans. Mechatron. **20**(5), 2550–2562 (2015). https://doi.org/10.1109/TMECH.2015.2388555

12. Xie, X.L., Hou, Z.G., Cheng, L., Ji, C., Tan, M., Yu, H.: Adaptive neural network tracking control of robot manipulators with prescribed performance. Proc. Inst. Mech. Eng. Part I-J. Syst. Control Eng. **225**(16), 790–797 (2010). https://doi.org/10.1177/0959651811398853

13. Yang, Y.N., Ge, C., Wang, H., Li, X.Y., Hua, C.C.: Adaptive neural network based prescribed performance control for teleoperation system under input saturation. J. Franklin Inst. Eng. Appl. Math. **352**(2), 1850–1866 (2015). https://doi.org/10.1016/j.jfranklin.2015.01.032
14. Wang, Z.W., Chen, Z., Liang, B., Zhang, B.: A novel adaptive finite time controller for bilateral teleoperation system. Acta Astronaut. **144**, 263–270 (2018). https://doi.org/10.1016/j.actaastro.2017.12.046
15. Zhang, H.C., Song, A.G., Shen, S.B.: Adaptive finite-time synchronization control for teleoperation system with varying time delays. IEEE Access **6**, 40940–40949 (2018). https://doi.org/10.1109/ACCESS.2018.2857802
16. Hashemzadeh, F., Tavakoli, M.: Position and force tracking in nonlinear teleoperation systems under varying delays. Robotica **33**(4), 1003–1016 (2015). https://doi.org/10.1017/S026357471400068X
17. Ganjefar, S., Rezaei, S., Hashemzadeh, F.: Position and force tracking in nonlinear teleoperation systems with sandwich linearity in actuators and time-varying delay. Mech. Syst. Signal Process. **86**, 308–324 (2017). https://doi.org/10.1016/j.ymssp.2016.09.023
18. Amini, H., Rezaei, S.M., Zareinejad, M., Ghafarirad, H.: Enhanced time delayed linear bilateral teleoperation system by external force estimation. Trans. Inst. Measure. Control **35**(5), 637–647 (2013). https://doi.org/10.1177/0142331212464643
19. Chan, L.P., Naghdy, F., Stirling, D.: Position and force tracking for non-linear haptic telemanipulator under varying delays with an improved extended active observer. Robot. Auton. Syst. **75**, 145–160 (2016). https://doi.org/10.1016/j.robot.2015.10.007
20. Azimifar, F., Abrishamkar, M., Farzaneh, B., Sarhan, A.A.D., Amini, H.: Improving teleoperation system performance in the presence of estimated external force. Robot. Comput.-Integr. Manuf. **46**, 86–93 (2017). https://doi.org/10.1016/j.rcim.2016.12.004
21. Adel, O., Farid, F, Toumi, R.: Bilateral control of nonlinear teleoperation system using parallel force/position control approach and online environment estimation. In: 21st International Conference on Methods and Models in Automation and Robotics, pp. 1110–1115. IEEE Press (2017)
22. Khalil, H.K.: Nonlinear Systems, 3rd edn. Prentice-Hall, New York (2002)

# Designer of a Multi-DOF Adaptive Finger for Prosthetic Hand

Changcheng Wu[1,3]([✉]), Qingqing Cao[2], Yuchao Yan[1], Fei Fei[1],
Dehua Yang[1], Baoguo Xu[3], Hong Zeng[3], and Aiguo Song[3]

[1] College of Automation Engineering,
Nanjing University of Aeronautics and Astronautics, Nanjing, China
changchengwu@nuaa.edu.cn
[2] School of Aviation Engineering,
Nanjing Institute of Industry Technology, Nanjing, China
[3] School of Instrument Science and Engineering,
Southeast University, Nanjing, China

**Abstract.** To realize the adaptive grasping of different objects and capture the joint angles of the finger, this paper presents a multi degree of freedom (DOF) adaptive finger. There are three joints in the designed finger. The maximum rotation angle of the finger joints are 90°. And the bending angles of the finger joints can be captured. First, the mechanism design and analysis of the measurement theory are described in detail. Then, we introduce the measurement circuit and analyze the measurement error. Joint angle testing and object grasping experiments are conducted to verify the validity of the designed finger. The experimental result shows that the root-mean-square (RMS) of the finger joint angle measurement error is 0.79°. The designed finger can realize the adaptive grasping of the objects with different shape.

**Keywords:** Prosthetic hand · Joint angle measurement · Adaptive grasping

## 1 Introduction

Robot hand is with widely use. There are many kinds of robot hands, such as Schunk hand, HERI II hand, Sensor Hand, MPH-II hand, iLimb and etc. [1–5]. Some of them are used are assembled to the robots, some of them are used installed on human's body to replace the amputees' missing limbs.

The research of robot hand includes structure design, information perception, motion control and so on. In terms of structural design, Zhang presented a hand named HIT hand. The hand has five fingers and each finger has 2 DOFs and two joints [6]. Li proposed a 3D-printed robot hand with three linkage-driven underactuated fingers [7]. Liu developed an underactuated, two-finger, motor-driven compliant gripper for grasping size-varied unknown objects [8].

In terms of information perception, most scholars focus on the measurement of force/tactile information such as grip strength and slip sensation. Wu designed a mechanical-sensor integrated finger for one DOF prosthetic hand which can realize the measurement of grab force and the contact position between the object and the finger

H. Yu et al. (Eds.): ICIRA 2019, LNAI 11741, pp. 625–636, 2019.
https://doi.org/10.1007/978-3-030-27532-7_55

[9]. To realize the monitoring slip in the robotic grasping, Venter offered a design and prototype technology of a tactile sensor based on the principle of surface texture recognition [10]. Luberto presented an approach to achieve adaptive grasp of unknown objects whose position is only approximately known via point-cloud data [11]. Wookeun investigated a finger motion measurement system based on soft sensor. The performance of the proposed system was verified by a camera based motion capture system [12]. Othman proposed an adjustable angle sensor based on rotary poten-tiometer for measuring and monitoring finger flexion [13].

For the hands based on rigid linkage, the angle of each joint can be easily calculated by the relation of the linkage. Therefore, there is no need to set up joint sensors. But for multi degree of freedom adaptive hand, the joint sensors play an important role, especially in the dexterous control of hands. Due to volume limitations, most prosthetic hands do not have the finger joints sensor.

In this work, we investigate a multi-DOF adaptive finger for prosthetic hand, which can realize the adaptive grasping according to the shape of object and can realize the capture of the angles of the finger joints.

The rest paper is organized as follows. Section 2 describes the design of the finger in detail. The experiments are performed in Sect. 3, and the conclusions of the paper are in Sect. 4.

## 2   Finger Design

The following section describes the design of the multi-DOF adaptive finger.

### 2.1   Mechanism Design

As shown in Fig. 1, the designed finger consists of a distal phalange, an intermediate phalange, a proximal phalange, a metacarpal and etc. There are three rotatable joints in the designed finger. The movement of each phalange is pulled by a wire rope. In this paper, the phalanges are made by 3D printing.

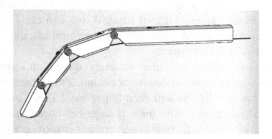

**Fig. 1.** The model of the designed finger

Under the condition that finger does not contact with object, the three phalanges move synchronously under the traction of wire rope. In the procedure of object grasping, some phalanges of finger will contact with the object. The movement of the phalange which contacts with the object is restrained. And the phalanges which are at the front of the restrain phalange and does not contact with object will remain unchanged.

To realize the accurate measurement of the bending angle of each joint, a mechanical-sensor integrated finger joint is designed in this paper. Figure 2 shows a designed finger joint. The rotatable joint is consisted of a roller, a torsion spring, and four bearings. The roller runs through the four bearings and the torsion spring. One leg of the torsion spring is fixed inside the proximal phalange, the other leg is pressed by a small aluminum plate. And the aluminum plate is fixed on the metacarpal by two screws.

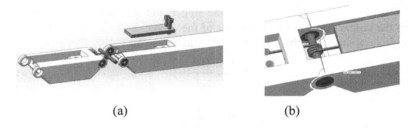

(a)                              (b)

**Fig. 2.** Assembly drawing of the finger joint

In this structure, the finger is straight under the condition that there is no drive force on the wire rope. The finger will bend under the drive of wire rope. And after the driving force disappears, the finger will remain straight again.

Taking the joint between proximal phalange and metacarpal as an example. Torsion spring will output a torque, when there is a angle between proximal phalange and metacarpal. Because one leg of the torsion spring is restricted by the torsion spring, the torque output from the spring will transfer to force and apply to aluminum plate.

Within the limit of the spring, torsion springs obey an angular form of Hooke's law as following.

$$M = k\theta \tag{1}$$

where $M$ is the torque exerted by the spring, $\theta$ is the angle of twist, and $k$ is the spring's torsion coefficient.

The force applied on the aluminum plate is as following

$$F = kl_s\theta \tag{2}$$

where $l_s$ is the length of the torque arm.

Since one side of the aluminum plate is fixed on the metacarpal, the aluminum plate can be regarded as a cantilever beam. Figure 3 shows the simplified assembly drawing of the aluminum plate and the torsion spring.

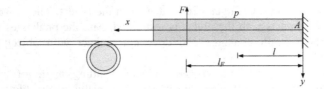

**Fig. 3.** The assembly drawing of the aluminum plate and the torsion spring.

When a finger bends, the moment of the cross section of the cantilever beam is as following

$$M(x) = -F(l_F - x) \tag{3}$$

where $F$ is the contact force between the finger and the object, $l_F$ is the distance between the contact position and the root of the finger.

The flexural stress on the cross section is as following

$$\sigma_x = \frac{M(x)y}{I_z} \tag{4}$$

$$I_z = \int_A y^2 \, dA = \int_{-\frac{h}{2}}^{\frac{h}{2}} y^2 \, dy = \frac{bh^3}{12} \tag{5}$$

where $b$ and $h$ are the width and thickness of the cantilever beam respectively.

The axial strain of any point on the cross section is as following

$$\varepsilon_x = \frac{\sigma_x}{E} = \frac{12F}{Ebh^3}(l_F - x)y, y \in [-\frac{h}{2}, \frac{h}{2}] \tag{6}$$

where $E$ is the Young's modulus of the material.

According to the formula (6), the axial strain at the point $p$ is as following:

$$\varepsilon_p = \frac{6F}{Ebh^2}(l_F - l) \tag{7}$$

where $l$ is the distance between point $p$ and the root of the aluminum plate.

Combining formula (2) and (7), we can get

$$F = \frac{\varepsilon_p Ebh^2}{6(l_F - l)} \tag{8}$$

Combining formula (2) and (8), we can get the relationship between finger joint angle ($\theta$) and axial strain on the surface of the aluminum plate ($\varepsilon_P$) as following

$$\theta = \varepsilon_p \frac{Ebh^2}{6(l_F - l)kl_s} \tag{9}$$

Within the recoverable deformation range of the aluminum plate, the relationship between $\theta$ *and* $\varepsilon_P$ is linear. That is to say, once we get $\varepsilon_P$, we can get the finger joint angle $(\theta)$ by simple calculation.

## 2.2  Signal Measurement Circuit Design

In this paper, strain gauge is adopted to measure the axial strain on the surface of the aluminum plate. Within the limit of the strain gauge, the relationship between the variation of the resistance and the axial strain is linear.

The maximum bending angle of the designed finger in this paper is 90°. Therefore, the maximum axial strain on the surface of the aluminum plate is as following.

$$\varepsilon_{P\_\text{max}} = \frac{kl_s\theta_\text{max}6(l_F - l)}{bh^2E}$$
$$= \frac{540kl_s(l_F - l)}{bh^2E} \tag{10}$$

According to the analysis above, the strain gauges with the parameters as shown in Table 1 is employed to realize the measurement of the axial strain on the surface of the aluminum plate.

**Table 1.** Parameters of the strain gauge

| Parameter | Value |
| --- | --- |
| Length (mm) | 3.6 mm |
| Width (mm) | 3.1 mm |
| Resistance ($\Omega$) | 350 |
| Sensitivity factor | 2 |

As shown in Fig. 4, four strain gauges are pasted on the upper and lower surface of the aluminum plate. Two of them, sg2 and sg3, are pasted on the upper surface of the aluminum plate, and the other two, sg1 and sg4, are on the lower surface. When finger bending, the force applied on the aluminum plate by the torsion spring will lead to the deformation of the aluminum plate. And the deformation of the aluminum plate causes the same deformation of the strain gauge. Since the extensional deformation and compressive deformation lead to the increasing and decreasing of the resistance of strain gauge respectively, the bending of the finger leads to the resistance increasing of sg1 and sg4, and leads to the decreasing of sg2 and sg3. And since $sg_2$, $sg_3$ and $sg_1$, $sg_4$ are symmetrically distributed, the resistance variations of $sg_1$, $sg_2$, $sg_3$ and $sg_4$ are the same.

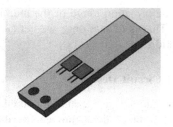

**Fig. 4.** Stick diagram of strain gauges

As shown in Fig. 5, the strain gauges, $sg_1$, $sg_2$, $sg_3$ and $sg_4$, are plugged into the circuit. Then we can get the output of the circuit:

$$U_g = \frac{(R_4 + \Delta R_4) \times E_p}{(R_2 - \Delta R_2) \times E_p + (R_4 + \Delta R_4)} - \frac{(R_3 - \Delta R_3) \times E_p}{(R_1 - \Delta R_1) + (R_3 - \Delta R_3)} \quad (11)$$

where $E_P$ is the value of the supply power, $\Delta R_1$, $\Delta R_2$, $\Delta R_3$ and $\Delta R_4$ are resistance variation of the four strain gauges.

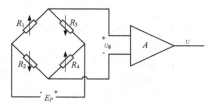

**Fig. 5.** Measurement circuit of the strain gauges

Under the assumption that $sg_1$ and $sg_3$ are pasted on the surface of the cantilevered beam symmetrically and $R_1 = R_2 = R_3 = R_4$, the formula (8) can be simplified as follows:

$$U_g = \frac{\Delta R_1}{R_1} E_P \quad (12)$$

In the practical measurement, the output voltage of the Wheatstone bridge should be amplified for the signal is weak. So, the measured voltage is as following.

$$U = AU_g = \frac{AE_P \Delta R_1}{R_1} \quad (13)$$

where $A$ is the amplification. In this paper, amplifiers are designed based on AD620.

The relationship between strain and relative variation of the resistance is linear within a large range.

$$\frac{\Delta R}{R} = K\varepsilon \qquad (14)$$

where $R$ is the initial value of the resistance, $\Delta R$ is the variation of the resistance, $K$ is the sensitivity factor of the strain gauge.

The relationship between the circuit output and the strain of the strain gauge can be expressed as following.

$$U = AU_g = \frac{AE_p \Delta R_1}{R_1} = AE_p \Delta R\varepsilon \qquad (15)$$

That is

$$\varepsilon = \frac{U}{AE_p K} \qquad (16)$$

Combining formula (9) and (16), we can get:

$$\theta = \frac{F}{kl_s} = \frac{Ebh^2}{6(l_F - l)AE_P K \, kl_s} U \qquad (17)$$

According to the formula (17), the stability of the supply power will affect the accuracy of the joint angle measurement. And the deviation of the locations which the strain gauges are pasted on is also a factor affecting the measurement accuracy.

There are three finger joints with the same structure in the designed finger. Therefore, three measurement circuits as shown in Fig. 5 are designed.

Figure 6 shows the aluminum plate with strain gauges and the phalanges equipped with aluminum plates.

**Fig. 6.** Aluminum plate with strain gauges and phalanges equipped with aluminum plates

# 3  Experiment and Results

To verify the designed finger, Joint angle measurement experiment and the grasping experiment are conducted.

## 3.1  Data Collection

Figure 7 shows the data collection system. A data acquisition card (USB5936) is employed in the experiments. Signals output from the measurement circuits are digitalized by USB5936. And the digitalized signals are sent to computer via USB. Computer software based on MFC framework is developed to display the signals and record the data.

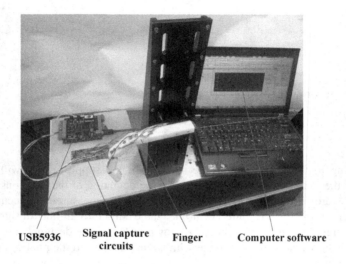

USB5936      Signal capture      Finger      Computer software
                    circuits

**Fig. 7.**  Data collection system

## 3.2  Joint Angle Measurement Experiment

As shown in Fig. 8, there are two vertical brackets on the platform. The assembly of the proximal phalange and metacarpal is held horizontally on a vertical bracket. The other bracket is fixed with the steering gear. One side of the wire rope is fixed on the end of the proximal phalange, the other side of the wire rope is fixed to the swing arm of the steering gear after passing through the finger. The bending of the fingers can be realized by controlling the swinging of the steering gear.

**Fig. 8.** Joint angle measurement experiment

In this paper, a six axis gyroscope based on MPU6050 is employed to measure the finger joint angle. The gyroscope is pasted on the lower surface of the proximal phalange. The gyroscope outputs the rotation angle of the proximal phalange in real time at a speed of 100 Hz. The dynamic measurement precision is 0.1°. Figure 9 shows the finger assembly with the gyroscope.

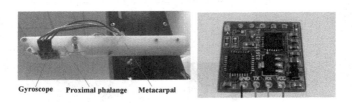

Gyroscope    Proximal phalange    Metacarpal

**Fig. 9.** Finger assembly with the gyroscope.

In the procedure of the joint angle measurement experiment, the steering gear is turned so that the proximal phalange gradually bends from 0 to 90°, and then gradually recovers from 90 to 0°. At the same time, the signals output from the gyroscope and the strain gauge measurement circuit are recorded synchronously. Figure 10 shows the joint angle measurement experiment results. The mean error, mean absolute error and the root mean square error of the joint angle measurement are 0.19°, 0.51° and 0.79° respectively.

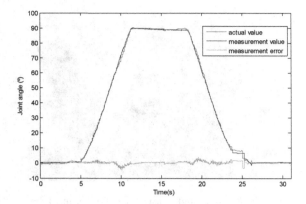

**Fig. 10.** The results of the finger joint angle measurement experiment

## 3.3   Grasping Experiment

Four objects with different shape are selected in this experiment. Figure 11 shows the grasping scene. Objects with different shape can be held by the designed finger. Figure 12 shows the angle curves of the three finger joint in the procedure of holding a rubber balloon. A1, A2 and A3 are the angles between distal phalange and intermediate phalange, intermediate phalange and proximal phalange, proximal phalange and metacarpal respectively.

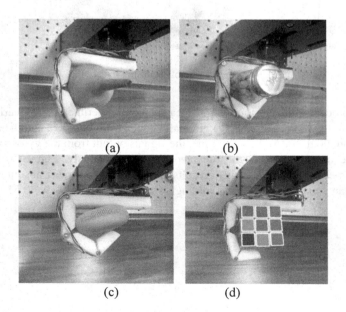

**Fig. 11.** Different objects grasping scene by the designed finger

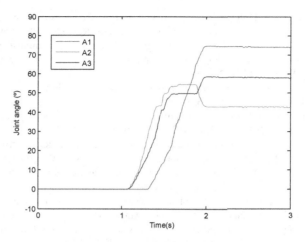

**Fig. 12.** The results of grasping experiments

# 4 Conclusion

For the purpose of dexterous manipulation of a robotic hand, this paper proposes an adaptive finger with the ability to joint angle measurement. The proposed finger has three joints. The mechanism design, analysis, signals measurement, joint angle testing and grasping experiments are conducted. The experimental results show that the designed finger can realize the measurement of finger joint angle.

For the further work, we will research the control strategy for the designed finger and design a hand with the fingers proposed in this paper.

**Acknowledgement.** This paper is supported by the National Science Foundation of China under Grant No. 61803201, 91648206. Jiangsu Natural Science Foundation under Grant No. BK20170 803. Young Teacher Startup Foundation of Nanjing University of Aeronautics and Astronautics under Grant No. 56YAH17027. The Fundamental Research Funds for the Central Universities, No. NS2018023.

# References

1. Ren, Z.: HERI II: a robust and flexible robotic hand based on modular finger design and under actuation principles. In: 2018 IEEE/RSJ International Conference on Intelligent Robots and Systems (IROS). IEEE (2018)
2. Wu, C., Song, A., Zhang, H., et al.: A backstepping control strategy for prosthetic hand based on fuzzy observation of stiffness. Robot **35**(6), 686 (2013)
3. Van, D., Bongers, R., Sluis, C.: Functionality of i-LIMB and i-LIMB pulse hands: case report. J. Rehabil. Res. Dev. **50**(8), 1123 (2013)
4. Dang, L., Song, J., Wei, Y., et al.: COSA-LET finger: a novel coupled and self-adaptive robot finger with a linear empty-trip transmission. In: International Conference on Advanced Robotics & Mechatronics. IEEE (2018)

5. Belter, J., Segil, J., Dollar, A.: Mechanical design and performance specifications of anthropomorphic prosthetic hands: a review. J. Rehabil. Res. Dev **50**(5), 599 (2013)
6. Zhang, T., Fan, S., Jiang, L., et al.: Design and control of a multisensory five-finger prosthetic hand. In: Proceedings of the World Congress on Intelligent Control and Automation (WCICA) (2015)
7. Li, X., Wu, L., Lan, T.: A 3D-printed robot hand with three linkage-driven underactuated fingers. Int. J. Autom. Comput. **15**(5), 593–602 (2018)
8. Liu, C., Chen, T., Chiu, C., et al.: Optimal design of a soft robotic gripper for grasping unknown objects. Soft Robot. **5**(4), 452–465 (2018)
9. Wu, C., Fei, F., Xie, M., et al.: Mechanical-sensor integrated finger for prosthetic hand. In: IEEE International Conference on Robotics and Biomimetics (2018, In press)
10. Venter, J., Mazid, A.: Tactile sensor based intelligent grasping system. In: IEEE International Conference on Mechatronics (2017)
11. Luberto, E., Wu, Y., Santaera, G., et al.: Enhancing adaptive grasping through a simple sensor-based reflex mechanism. IEEE Robot. Autom. Lett. **2**(3), 1664–1671 (2017)
12. Wookeun, P., Kyongkwan, R., Suin, K., et al.: A soft sensor-based three-dimensional (3-D) finger motion measurement system. Sensors **17**(2), 420 (2017)
13. Othman, A., Hamzah, N., Hussain, Z., et al.: Design and development of an adjustable angle sensor based on rotary potentiometer for measuring finger flexion. In: IEEE International Conference on Control System. IEEE (2017)

# Fuzzy Sliding Mode Control Based on RBF Neural Network for AUV Path Tracking

Xiang Wang, Yonglin Zhang[✉], and Zhouzhou Xue

School of Electronics and Information, Jiangsu University
of Science and Technology, Zhenjiang 212003, Jiangsu, China
zhangyonglin@just.edu.cn

**Abstract.** Aiming at the path tracking problem of AUV (autonomous under-water vehicle) in the process of docking, a fuzzy sliding mode control algorithm based on RBF (radial basis function) neural network is proposed. Firstly, the sliding mode control is used to track the trajectory, the fuzzy control is used to continuously correct the parameters of the exponential reaching rate in the sliding mode control to alleviate the shaking problem. Then the RBF neural network is used to compensate uncertainty in the AUV motion model and the external unknown interference. Finally, the stability of the control system is proved by Lyapunov stability theory. The simulation result shows that the designed control algorithm can track the trajectory of AUV effectively. By comparing tracking effects with traditional sliding mode control and fuzzy sliding mode control, it is proved that the proposed control method has faster tracking speed, better stability and better tracking performance.

**Keywords:** Autonomous underwater vehicle · Path tracking control · RBF neural network · Fuzzy control · Sliding mode control

## 1 Introduction

With the continuous development and utilization of marine resources by human beings, autonomous underwater vehicle has become an important carrier for exploring the ocean. The accurate path tracking capability of autonomous underwater vehicle is one of the technical guarantees for underwater operations [1–4]. The marine environment is extremely complex and full of uncertainties. In actual operation, due to strong non-linearity, uncertainty, and multi-coupling characteristic of AUV, the hydrodynamic, inertial force, and Coriolis centripetal force that AUV received will change when the operating speed and operating environment change, and it is difficult to establish a precise dynamics model to track its trajectory [5–8].

At present, fuzzy control, adaptive robust control, neural network and various combined forms of these control algorithms are used for the motion control of AUV [9–13]. Literature [14] designs a depth control algorithm for autonomous underwater vehicle based on the command filtered backstepping method to solve the trajectory tracking control problem of the horizontal plane of discrete autonomous underwater vehicle. Literature [15] proposes a depth control strategy which combines backstepping method and sliding mode control to suppress the problem of attitude imbalance.

© Springer Nature Switzerland AG 2019
H. Yu et al. (Eds.): ICIRA 2019, LNAI 11741, pp. 637–648, 2019.
https://doi.org/10.1007/978-3-030-27532-7_56

In [16], a depth control algorithm based on the fuzzy sliding mode is presented, which effectively suppresses the shaking problem in traditional sliding mode control. In [17], for deep tracking of AUV, the pitch attitude control algorithm is designed based on neural network. At present, the research on AUV trajectory tracking problem is still one of the hotspots in the field of AUV research.

This paper proposes a fuzzy sliding mode control algorithm based on RBF neural network. On the premise of using sliding mode control to track the trajectory of an AUV, fuzzy control is used to adjust the parameters of the exponential reaching law in sliding mode control to alleviate the jitter problem and a RBF neural network is used to compensate the uncertainty in the AUV dynamics model and the external unknown interference. The stability of the system is proved by a Lyapunov function. Compared the tracking effects with traditional sliding mode control proposed in [11] and fuzzy sliding mode control proposed in [16], the control method adopted in this paper can effectively compensate the uncertainty of the system and external interference, and has faster tracking time and better tracking performance.

## 2   AUV Mathematical Model

The motion of the AUV is related to two right-handed coordinate systems: the static coordinate system $E - \xi\eta\zeta$ (the geodetic coordinate system) and the motion coordinate system $o - xyz$ (the carrier coordinate system), as shown in Fig. 1:

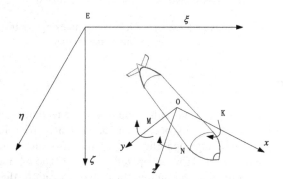

**Fig. 1.** AUV motion coordinate system

The six-degree-of-freedom dynamics model of AUV can be described as a vector form in motion coordinate system:

$$M\dot{v} + C(v)v + D(v)v + g(\eta) = B\tau \tag{1}$$

$$\dot{\eta} = J(\eta)v \tag{2}$$

Where, $\eta = [x \quad y \quad z \quad \varphi \quad \theta \quad \psi]$ indicates the position and attitude vector of the system in the inertial coordinate system; $v = [u \quad v \quad w \quad p \quad q \quad r]^T$ indicates the linear velocity and angular velocity of the system in the motion coordinate system $M$ is the inertia matrix associated with the rigid body and the additional mass; $C(v)$ is the matrix of centripetal force and Coriolis force caused by the rigid body and the additional mass. $D(v)$ is the hydrodynamic matrix; $J(\eta)$ is the transformation matrix; $g(\eta)$ is the gravity and buoyancy vector; $\tau$ is the generalized force vector.

Suppose $x = [x, y, z, \varphi, \theta, \psi]^T$ is the position and attitude vector of AUV in the static coordinate system, according to the dynamics model shown in Eqs. (1) and (2), it can be converted to yield a nonlinear uncertain system in the form of a state equation as shown in Eqs. (3), (4) and (5):

$$\dot{x}_1(t) = x_2(t) \tag{3}$$

$$\dot{x}_2(t) = f(\dot{x}, t) + \Delta f(\dot{x}, t) + Bu + d(t) \tag{4}$$

$$y = x_1(t) \tag{5}$$

Where, $x_1(t)$ and $x_2(t)$ denote the state vector of the system; $u = M^{-1}\tau$ is the control vector of the system; $f(\dot{x}, t) = -M^{-1}(C(v)v + D(v)v + g(\eta))$ is the nonlinear term of the system; $y$ is the output vector; B is the control coefficient; $\Delta f(\dot{x}, t)$ is the uncertainty of the nonlinear system; $d(t)$ is the external random interference of the system, Suppose it satisfies the condition of $\|d(t)\| \leq D$, $D$ is the upper bound of the interference.

## 3 Fuzzy Sliding Mode Control Based on RBF Neural Network

In order to solve the influence of the uncertainty in the AUV motion model and the external unknown interference, and eliminate the jitter problem of the traditional sliding mode, this paper studies a fuzzy sliding mode control algorithm based on RBF neural network. Its structure is shown in Fig. 2.

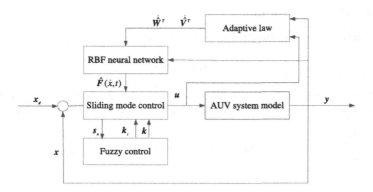

**Fig. 2.** Control system structure

## 3.1 Sliding Mode Control

Suppose $x$ is the actual motion trajectory of AUV, $x_d$ is the desired motion trajectory. Then the tracking error is $e = x_d - x$.

The switching function is $s = \lambda e + \dot{e}$, where, $\lambda = diag(\lambda_1, \lambda_2, \lambda_3 \ldots \lambda_n)$ is a positive definite diagonal matrix; $s$ is the sliding surface. According to Eq. (4):

$$\dot{s} = \lambda\dot{e} + \ddot{e} = \lambda\dot{e} + \ddot{x}_d - \ddot{x} = \lambda\dot{e} + \ddot{x}_d - (f(\dot{x},t) + \Delta f(\dot{x},t) + Bu + d(t)) \qquad (6)$$

In the sliding mode control, reaching law is generally used to improve the dynamic quality in the process of approaching motion. The principle of designing the reaching law is: when moving away from the switching surface, the speed at which the moving point tends to the switching surface is high, The speed decreases toward zero as it approaches the switching surface.

Therefore, this paper takes the reaching law is the exponential reaching law:

$$\dot{s} = -k_c \, \mathrm{sgn}\, s - ks \qquad (7)$$

For the system with model uncertainty and external interference, the designed control law is:

$$u = B^{-1}(\lambda\dot{e} + \ddot{x}_d - f(\dot{x},t) - \Delta f(\dot{x},t) - d(t) + ks + k_c \, \mathrm{sgn}(s)) \qquad (8)$$

The rapidity and the stability of the system are usually achieved by selecting appropriate parameters $k_c$ and $k$. Choosing a small $k_c$ can effectively suppress high frequency vibration, However, a small value of $k_c$ will increase the time to enter a stable sliding mode, it weakens the dynamic quality of the system. Increasing $k$ will speed up the process of approaching, however, the control strength will be increased. Decreasing $k$ will reduce the approaching speed, but increase the approaching time.

In order to solve the contradiction of reaching law in sliding mode control, in this paper, fuzzy logic is used to adjust the $k_c$ and $k$ in the reaching law to improve the quality of the arrival phase of the system and alleviate the shaking of the system.

## 3.2 Fuzzy Control Algorithm

The fuzzy form of the exponential reaching law is:

$$\dot{s} = \alpha_1 k_c - \alpha_2 ks \qquad (9)$$

Select a positive constant $\alpha$, make $s_n = \alpha s$ as the input to the fuzzy controller, $k_c$ and $k$ as outputs. The design of fuzzy controller can be divided into the following steps:

(1) Defining fuzzy collection
    Define the fuzzy set of input as $A_i$ and output as $B_j, C_l$, then:

$$A_i = \{NB, NM, NS, Z, PS, PM, PB\}$$

$$B_J = \{NB, NM, NS, Z, PS, PM, PB\}$$

$$C_l = \{PS, PM, PB\}$$

(2)  Membership function

The input of each controller is $s_n$, the outputs are $k_c$ and $k$. Transform the input and output into the discrete domain of [0, 1]. Their membership functions are trigonometric functions, as shown in Fig. 3.

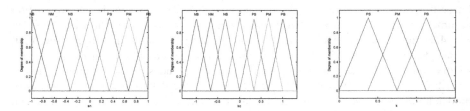

**Fig. 3** The membership functions of $s_n$, $k_c$, $k$

(3)  Fuzzy rule

In order to solve the motion coupling between the each degree of freedom and achieve decentralized decoupling, this paper designs single input multiple output sub-fuzzy controller and uses a decentralized switching mode. Therefore, each subsystem is controlled separately. The parameters $k_c$ and $k$ are adjusted dynamically by designing separate fuzzy controller for each degree of freedom. Each degree of freedom is controlled by the same control rules, Fuzzy rules are defined as shown in Table 1.

**Table 1.**  Fuzzy control rule table

| $s_n$ | NB | NM | NS | Z | PS | PM | PB |
|---|---|---|---|---|---|---|---|
| $k_c$ | PB | PM | PS | Z | PS | NM | NB |
| $k$ | PB | PB | PS | PM | PS | PS | PS |

(4)  Defuzzification

Defuzzification is the conversion of the amount of ambiguity inferred from the fuzzy controller into an exact amount. The commonly used methods are the maximum membership method, the median method, and the center of gravity method. This paper uses the center of gravity method in Eqs. (10) and (11) to solve the model. $\mu$ the analytic expression of membership function.

$$k_c = \sum_{j=1}^{n} \mu_B(B_j)B_j / \sum_{j=1}^{n} \mu_B(B_j) \tag{10}$$

$$k = \sum_{l=1}^{n} \mu_C(C_l)C_l / \sum_{j=1}^{n} \mu_C(C_l) \tag{11}$$

### 3.3   Fuzzy Sliding Mode Control Based on RBF Neural Network

The RBF neural network has a strong learning ability and can approximate any non-linear function to a certain extent. The learning speed is fast and the approximation accuracy is high. The RBF network is a three-layer network structure as shown in Fig. 4, which includes an input layer, a hidden layer and an output layer. The input signal of the input layer is $x = [e \quad \dot{e}]$, Where $e$ is the error between the actual trajectory and the expected trajectory. The hidden layer includes a series of implicit nodes. The structure and complexity of the neural network are determined by the number of hidden nodes. Each neuron in the hidden layer acts through a radial basis function, and maps to the output layer. Due to uncertainties in the underwater environment, when the operating speed and operating environment change, the hydrodynamic force, inertial force, and Coriolis centripetal force of the AUV will change with them. It is difficult to establish a precise dynamics model to track its trajectory. Therefore, a RBF neural network is used to approximate the uncertainty of motion model and the external unknown interference. To some extent, it reduces the impact of unknowns, at the same time it increases the stability of the system and improves tracking accuracy.

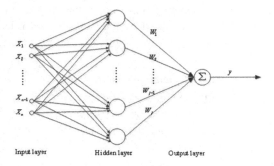

**Fig. 4.** RBF neural network topology

The neural network is used to approximate the uncertainty of motion model and the external unknown interference since it has universal approximation. Model uncertainty in the motion model can be combined with the external unknown interference into uncertainties $\Delta F(\dot{x}, t) = \Delta f(\dot{x}, t) + d(t)$, a RBF neural network algorithm is used to approach $\Delta F(\dot{x}, t)$, the algorithm is:

$$h_j = \exp\left(\frac{\|x - c_j\|^2}{2b_j^2}\right) \tag{12}$$

$$\Delta F(\dot{x}, t) = W^{*T}h(x) + V^{*T}h(x) + \varepsilon \tag{13}$$

Where $x$ is the input of the network, $j$ is the $j$th node of the network hidden layer, $h = [h_j]^T$ is the output of the Gaussian function, $b_j$ is the base width parameter, $c_j$ is the center vector, $W^*$, $V^*$ are ideal weight of the network, and $\varepsilon$ is the approximation error of the network, $\varepsilon \leq \varepsilon_N$.

If the input of network is $x = [e \quad \dot{e}]$, the output is $\hat{F}(\dot{x}, t)$.

$$\hat{F}(\dot{x}, t) = \hat{W}^T h(x) + \hat{V}^T h(x) \tag{14}$$

$\tilde{F}(\dot{x}, t) = \Delta F(\dot{x}, t) - \hat{F}(\dot{x}, t)$, and the uncertainties are approximated online by the RBF neural network, their approximation effect is:

$$\begin{aligned}
\Delta F(\dot{x}, t) - \hat{F}(\dot{x}, t) &= W^{*T}h(x) + V^{*T}h(x) + \varepsilon - \hat{W}^T h(x) - \hat{V}^T h(x) \\
&= \tilde{W}^T h(x) + \tilde{V}^T h(x) + \varepsilon
\end{aligned} \tag{15}$$

Define the Lyapunov function as:

$$V = \frac{1}{2}s^T s + \frac{1}{2\gamma_1}\tilde{W}^T \tilde{W} + \frac{1}{2\gamma_2}\tilde{V}^T \tilde{V} \tag{16}$$

where, $\tilde{W} = W^* - \hat{W}$, $\tilde{V} = V^* - \hat{V}$, $\gamma > 0$

Designed control law is:

$$u = B^{-1}(\lambda\dot{e} + \ddot{x}_d - f(\dot{x}, t) - \hat{F}(\dot{x}, t) + ks + k_c\text{sgn}(s)) \tag{17}$$

Then:

$$\begin{aligned}
\dot{s} &= \lambda\dot{e} + \ddot{x}_d - f(\dot{x}, t) - \Delta F(\dot{x}, t) - Bu \\
&= \lambda\dot{e} + \ddot{x}_d - f(\dot{x}, t) - \Delta F(\dot{x}, t) - (\lambda\dot{e} + \ddot{x}_d - f(\dot{x}, t) - \hat{F}(\dot{x}, t) \\
&\quad + k_c\text{sgn}(s) + ks) \\
&= -\tilde{F}(\dot{x}, t) - k_c\text{sgn}(s) - ks
\end{aligned} \tag{18}$$

Take the adaptive law as: $\dot{\hat{W}} = \gamma_1 sh(x)$, $\dot{\hat{V}} = \gamma_2 sh(x)$, $k_c > |\varepsilon_N|$

And then:

$$
\begin{aligned}
\dot{V} &= s^T \dot{s} + \frac{1}{\gamma_1} \tilde{W}^T \dot{\tilde{W}} + \frac{1}{\gamma_2} \tilde{V}^T \dot{\tilde{V}} \\
&= s^T(-\tilde{F}(\dot{x}, t) - k_c \, \text{sgn}(s) - ks) - \frac{1}{\gamma_1} \tilde{W}^T \dot{\tilde{W}} - \frac{1}{\gamma_2} \tilde{V}^T \dot{\tilde{V}} \\
&= s^T(-\tilde{W}^T h(x) - \tilde{V}^T h(x) - \varepsilon - k_c \, \text{sgn}(s) - ks) - \frac{1}{\gamma_1} \tilde{W}^T \dot{\tilde{W}} - \frac{1}{\gamma_2} \tilde{V}^T \dot{\tilde{V}} \quad (19) \\
&\leq -s^T \varepsilon - |s^T| k_c - s^T ks \\
&\leq -s^T ks \\
&\leq 0
\end{aligned}
$$

It is known from Eq. (19) that the designed control law satisfies the requirement of Lyapunov stability.

## 4  Simulation Analysis

MATLAB is used to simulate the tracking trajectory to verify the validity and reliability of the proposed control method. During the movement of the AUV, the influence of the roll direction is small. Therefore, this paper only considers the movements of five degrees of freedom in surge, sway, heave, pitch and yaw.

The path tracking simulation is performed by a six-degree-of-freedom AUV, which quality is m = 42.5 kg and the model moment of inertia are: $I_{xx} = 0.3$ kg m$^2$ $I_{yy} = 19.3$ kg m$^2$, $I_{zz} = 19.3$ kg m$^2$. In fuzzy control, coefficients of exponential reaching law are $\alpha_1 = 0.75$, $\alpha_2 = 10$, and $\alpha = diag(10, 10, 10, 10)$. In sliding mode switching function: $\lambda = diag(10.86, 10.86, 10.8, 20.86)$. The number of RBF neural network nodes is 14, $c_j$ is uniformly distributed in the interval [−1.5, 1.5], $b_j$ takes 3.0, $\gamma_1$ takes 1.5, $\gamma_2$ takes 10, The model uncertainty for each degree of freedom is 10sin (0.1t) and the external unknown interference is 10cos(0.1t).

The desired trajectory of the surge and sway directions is 0.05 m/s, the desired trajectory of the heave direction is kept at 10 m. The trajectory in the pitch direction is cos(0.25t), and the trajectory in the yaw direction is sin(0.25t). The initial state of the AUV is $x_0 = [0.2; 0.18; 9.8; 0.06]$, Fig. 5 is the speed tracking situation under the control method proposed in this paper. Figures 6, 7, and 8 are the tracking trajectories of AUV in each degree of freedom under different control methods, where the dotted line is the desired trajectory and the solid line is the actual tracking trajectory.

Figure 5 shows the speed tracking situation of AUV in each degree of freedom under the control method proposed in this paper. It can be seen from the figure that each direction can quickly track to the desired speed after a slight shaking.

It can be seen from the simulation result that all three control methods can track the path of the AUV. Figure 6 shows the path tracking under the traditional sliding mode control proposed in [11]. Although path tracking can be performed, due to the uncertainties and the chattering problem in sliding mode control itself, the chattering of

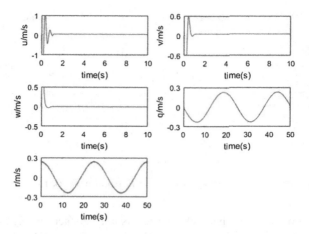

**Fig. 5.** The speed tracking situation in all directions

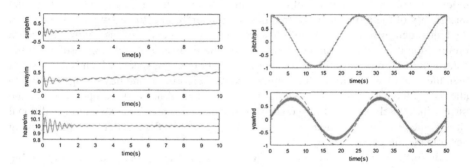

**Fig. 6.** Traditional sliding mode control for AUV path tracking

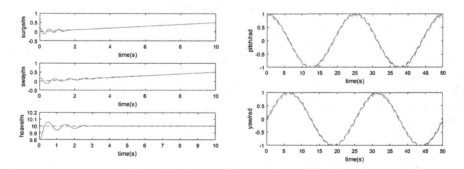

**Fig. 7.** Fuzzy sliding mode control for AUV path tracking

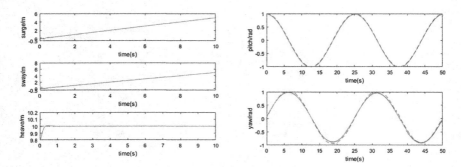

**Fig. 8.** Fuzzy sliding mode control based on RBF neural network for AUV path tracking

tracking path is obvious, and the tracking effect is not satisfactory. Figure 7 is the path tracking curve under fuzzy sliding mode control proposed in [16], this control algorithm adjusts the exponential reaching rate with fuzzy control on traditional sliding mode control, it has a good effect in eliminating chattering, however, due to the uncertainty of the model and external unknown interference, the early jitter is large and the adjustment time is long. Figure 8 shows the tracking curve of the control algorithm proposed in this paper. It can be seen from the comparison of simulation results that the control algorithm proposed in this paper has higher tracking speed, which is $2\sim 3$ s less than the convergence time of the common control algorithm, and has stronger ability to alleviate jitter with almost no shaking point. The neural network compensates for the uncertainties well, and the fuzzy control adjusts the jitter problem existing in traditional sliding mode control, which make the overall control effect better and the tracking performance is good.

For further analysis, the data in Figs. 6, 7 and 8 are processed. The processing results are shown in Table 2:

**Table 2.** Comparison of tracking data of different control methods

|  | Mean square error (m) | Average absolute tracking error (m) | Shaking situation |
|---|---|---|---|
| Method proposed in this paper | 0.016 | 0.003 | None |
| Sliding mode control | 0.029 | 0.008 | Obvious |
| Fuzzy sliding mode control | 0.018 | 0.004 | Weak |

It can be seen from Table 2 that the control method proposed in this paper compared with the traditional sliding mode control proposed in [11], the mean square error of tracking error reduces by 45%, and the average absolute tracking error reduces by 62.5%. Compared with the tracking effect of fuzzy sliding mode control proposed in [16], the mean square error of tracking error reduces by 11%, and the average absolute tracking error reduces by 25%. Therefore, the proposed control method in this paper is superior to traditional sliding mode control and fuzzy sliding mode control, and has practical value.

## 5 Conclusion

Aiming at the accurate path tracking problem of AUV, this paper proposes a fuzzy sliding mode control algorithm based on RBF neural network. In the proposed control method, sliding mode control is the main path tracking control method. The RBF neural network is used to compensate the uncertainty in the AUV dynamics model and the external unknown interference. Fuzzy control is used to continuously correct the parameters of the exponential reaching rate in sliding mode control to alleviate the jitter problem in sliding mode control. The stability of the proposed control algorithm is proved by Lyapunov's theorem. At the same time, by comparing path tracking effects under different control methods, it is concluded that under the same conditions, the fuzzy sliding mode control algorithm based on RBF neural network proposed in this paper has faster convergence and better tracking performance, which is more suitable for practical applications.

**Acknowledgements.** This work was supported by Jiangsu International Science and Technology Cooperation Project (No. BZ2016031), and Jiangsu University of Science and Technology Ph.D. Fund Project, which are greatly appreciated your review.

## References

1. Monroy, J.A., Campos, E., Tomes, J.A.: Attitude control of a micro AUV through an embedded system. IEEE Lat. Am. Trans. **15**(4), 603–612 (2017)
2. Heidemann, J., Stojanovic, M., Zorzi, M.: Underwater sensor networks: advances and challenges. Philos. Trans. R. Soc.-Ser. A-Math. Phys. Eng. Sci. **370**(1958), 158–175 (2012)
3. Avila, J.P.J., Donha, D.C., Adamowski, J.C.: Experimental model identification of open-frame underwater vehicles. Ocean Eng. **60**, 81–94 (2013)
4. Marani, G., Choi, S.K., Yuh, J.: Underwater autonomous manipulation for intervention missions AUVs. Ocean Eng. **36**(1), 16–23P (2009)
5. Marani, G., Choi, S.K., Yuh, J.J.: Underwater autonomous manipulation for intervention missions AUVs. Ocean Eng. **36**(1), 15–23 (2009)
6. Maki, T., et al.: Deployment of a hovering type AUV based on a seafloor station. In: The Proceedings of JSME Annual Conference on Robotics and Mechatronics (Robomec) (2016)
7. Kiyotaka, T., Hiroshi, Y., Shojiro, I., Yutaka, O., Fan, F., Makoto, S.: Development of autonomous underwater vehicle "Otohime" and underwater recharging system. In: The Proceedings of JSME Annual Conference on Robotics and Mechatronics (Robomec) (2016)
8. Gianluca, A.: Adaptive/integral actions for 6-DOF control of AUVs. In: Proceedings 2006 IEEE International Conference, pp. 3214–3219 (2006)
9. Park, R.E., Hwang, E.-J., Lee, H., Park, M.: Motion control of an AUV (Autonomous Underwater Vehicle) using fuzzy gain scheduling. J. Inst. Control Robot. Syst. **16**(6), 592–600 (2010)

10. Liu, Y., Wan, H., Song, J.: Sliding mode control under wave disturbances for an AUV using nonlinear observer method. In: Proceedings of 2018 2nd International Conference on Electrical Engineering and Automation (ICEEA2018). Advanced Science and Industry Research Center, Science and Engineering Research Center, 5 (2018)
11. Khan, I., Bhatti, A.I., Khan, Q., Ahmad, Q.: Sliding mode control of lateral dynamics of an AUV. In: 2012 9th International Bhurban Conference on Applied Sciences and Technology (IBCAST) (2012)
12. Londhe, P.S., Santhakumar, M., Patre, B.M., et al.: Task space control of an autonomous underwater vehicle manipulator system by robust single-input fuzzy logic control scheme. IEEE J. Oceanic Eng. **42**(1), 13–28 (2017)
13. Gao, F., Pan, C., Han, Y.: Design and analysis of a new AUV's sliding control system based on dynamic boundary layer. Chin. J. Mech. Eng. **26**(01), 35–45 (2013)
14. Yang, C., Yao, F., Zhang, M.J.: Adaptive backstepping terminal sliding mode control method based on recurrent neural networks for autonomous underwater vehicle. Chin. J. Mech. Eng. **31**(06), 228–243 (2018)
15. Liang, X., Wan, L., Blake, J., et al.: Path following of an under actuated AUV based on fuzzy back-stepping sliding mode control. Int. J. Adv. Robot. Syst. **13**(122), 1–11 (2016)
16. Lakhekar, G., Deshpande, R.: Diving control of autonomous underwater vehicles via fuzzy sliding mode technique. In: International Conference on Circuit Power and Computing Technologies (2015)
17. Yan, Z.P., Yu, H.M., Hou, S.P.: Diving control of under actuated unmanned undersea vehicle using integral-fast terminal sliding mode control. J. Central South Univ. **23**(5), 1085–1094 (2016)

# Design of Control System and Human-Robot-Interaction System of Teleoperation Underwater Robot

Pengcheng Xu[✉], Qingjun Zeng, Guangyi Zhang,
Chunlei Zhu, and Zhiyu Zhu

Jiangsu University of Science and Technology, Zhenjiang, China
just_xpc@163.com

**Abstract.** In order to meet the urgent need of underwater safety inspection and operating and solve the key problem of difficult control of teleoperation underwater robot, this paper proposes a Human-Robot-Interaction scheme for the independently developed teleoperation underwater robot, and successfully develops this underwater robot and Human-Robot-Interaction system. This paper introduces the general composition, key parameters, control system structure and control algorithm of the robot. And expounds the Human-Robot-Interaction system of the robot which includes three parts: visual interaction, data interaction and manipulator interaction. The visual interaction consists of an onshore monitor and an underwater camera. The data interaction is the premise of the normal operation of the robot. The manipulator interaction is designed to realizing underwater grapping and cutting. The system debugging is normal, and the underwater tests carried out in the pool and Qiandao Lake proved that the entire set of stability, reliability, real-time performance of control system and Human-Robot-Interaction system can achieve the design effect to meet the requirements of teleoperation underwater safety inspection and operating.

**Keywords:** Control system · Human-Robot-Interaction · Teleoperation · ROV · Underwater · Manipulator

## 1 Introduction

With the continuous development of marine undertakings, the exploration and maintenance of deep-sea resources and structural safety have become more and more indispensable. However, due to the poor underwater environment, the limited depth of human diving, underwater robots are needed to be submerged for underwater safety inspection and operating.

Underwater robots are divided into three categories: Human Occupied Vehicle (HOV), Autonomous Underwater Vehicle (AUV), Remotely Operated Vehicle

This work is supported by The National Natural Science Foundation of China (11574120); Natural Science Foundation of Jiangsu Province funded projects (BK20160564); Key Research and Development Project of Jiangsu Province (BE2018103).

H. Yu et al. (Eds.): ICIRA 2019, LNAI 11741, pp. 649–660, 2019.
https://doi.org/10.1007/978-3-030-27532-7_57

(ROV) [1]. With the advantages of deep working depth, sufficient power and adaptability to the harsh underwater environment [2], the remotely operated vehicle are widely used in different industries such as the inspection of marine pipelines, the maintenance of offshore platforms, the inspection of underwater dams, and aquaculture [3]. The umbilical cord serves as a safety guard against robot loss while providing power and data communication, which greatly improves its safety performance, but the fly in the ointment is that the umbilical cord limited ROV's range of motion [4]. Many domestic scholars have done plenty of researches on robot development. Literature [5] introduced the system composition of a ROV and its characteristics, and discussed the application and development trend of ROV, illustrating the great role of underwater robots; Literature [6] introduced a "conch type" ROV's control system structure and directional control technology, this robot can dive to a depth of 100 m without a manipulator for underwater operating; An ROV relying on manipulator operating was developed in [7], which is mainly through the abdominal operating mechanism to complete the docking and recovery.

Since the birth of "Hailong" ROV and "Haima" ROV, domestic companies have paid more and more attention to the ROV industry, and gradually some civilian-grade ROV appeared, such as "Trident" ROV launched by OpenROV company [8].

In this paper, an independent development teleoperation underwater robot, "METI-01", which is equipped with independently developed Human-Robot-Interaction system is presented.

## 2   General Design of "METI-01"

The independently developed ROV, "METI-01", is mainly composed of four parts: onshore console, power cabinet, umbilical cable and ROV body. The ROV system is shown in Fig. 1.

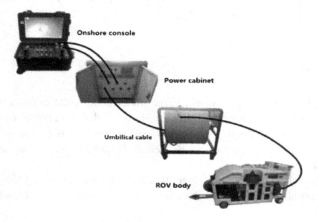

**Fig. 1.** ROV system

ROV body consists of nine parts as shown in Fig. 2: 1. Floating body; 2. Open frame; 3. Thruster; 4. PTZ camera; 5. Manipulator; 6. Underwater lights; 7. Wheelset module; 8. Electronic pressure tank; 9. Hydrofoil balancing module.

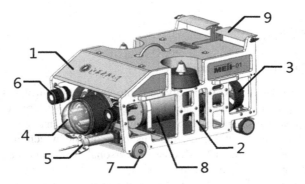

**Fig. 2.** ROV body

The onshore console sends control command to control ROV body. Data traffic between onshore console and ROV body are transmitted through a twisted pair in the umbilical cable. On the one hand, the power cabinet supplies power to the onshore console; on the other hand, it converts alternating current into high-voltage direct current to supply power to the underwater robot body. High-voltage direct current is conducive to reducing the cable diameter and power loss on the transmission line. The umbilical cord contains two pairs of twisted-pair cables and a pair of power cords for power transmission, a pair of twisted-pair cables for data communication, and another pair for video signal transmission. This ROV body can dive to a depth of 300 m, the specific technical parameters are shown in Table 1. This ROV is equipped with an underwater camera to take underwater images and videos to realize the function of inspecting underwater structures. When the ROV carried out the underwater operating,

**Table 1.** Key parameters of ROV

| Object | Index |
|---|---|
| Structure type | Open frame |
| Size | 600 × 500 × 400 (mm) |
| Working depth | 300 m |
| Speed | 1.5 m/s |
| Weight in the air | 50 kg |
| Power supply | 400VDC |
| Propeller | Vertical-2; Lateral-2; Longitudinal-2 |
| Operating equipment | Console |
| Assisting equipment | Manipulator |
| Sensor | Depth; Inertial navigation; Water leak inspection |
| Visual lighting | CCD camera; PTZ; Underwater lights |

ROV's motion and manipulator movements are realized through the joystick and the control buttons on the onshore console, and the underwater information, including the video image information and each ROV's sensor information, is monitored in real time displayed on the screen.

## 3  Control System

### 3.1  ROV's Control System Structure

The control system of this ROV is divided into two sub-control systems, onshore console control system and underwater ROV body control system. The two control system is connected by umbilical cable to transmit signals and power. The control system structure is shown in Fig. 3, the onshore console which includes joystick, control buttons, monitor, and IPC (Industrial Personal Computer), etc., realizes the display of communication data and the issue of control instructions. The data on the control panel is collected by the console control system, packaged and sent to the underwater ROV body control system. ROV body receives control instruction from onshore console control system and adopts embedded microcontroller to control the propellers, underlights, manipulator, camera and other parts, and to collect data from the sensors so as to sending these data to the onshore monitor for operators to watch.

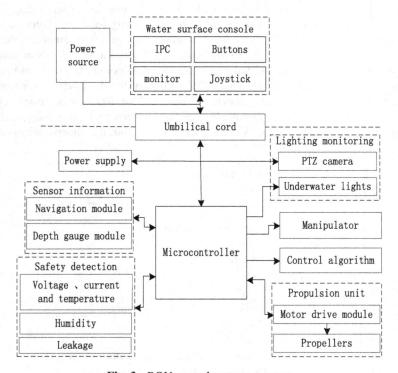

**Fig. 3.** ROV control system structure

## 3.2    ROV's Control Algorithm

For the ROV to achieve its basic operational capability, it must have the functions of fixed navigation determination, and need to have more accurate control ability of the underwater propeller, and the closed-loop control of the propeller must be realized. PID (proportional, integral, differential) control is a control algorithm based on classical control theory to estimate past, present and future information. PID control strategy has simple structure, good stability, high reliability and easy implementation. The block diagram of PID control algorithm with double closed-loop [9] for fixed navigation is shown Fig. 4.

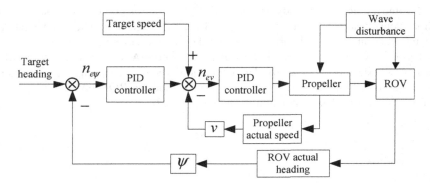

**Fig. 4.** Fixed navigation double closed loop PID control algorithm

# 4    Human Robot Interaction System

## 4.1    Visual Interaction

The visual interaction system consists of two parts: the onshore monitor and the high-definition underwater camera (see Fig. 5). The monitor is mounted on an onshore console, and the engineers can see the images and video taken by the underwater camera through the monitor.

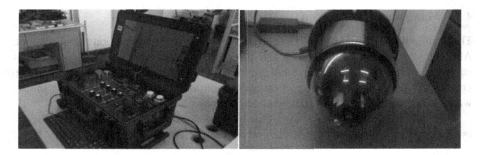

**Fig. 5.** Monitors on the console and underwater camera

The ROV onshore console sends the control command directly to the microcontroller on camera cradle via network communication to control the camera rotation, which enables the ROV to observe all directions in real time without moving. The microcontroller can control the camera movement to achieve the focus function. The camera housing is made of transparent acrylic ball with a thickness of 5 mm. Its compressive strength is up to 300 m. A light is mounted below the camera to illuminate the subject. Flange is left at the back of the camera for easy installation.

### 4.2 Data Interaction

In order to realize the teleoperation, the data interaction between the onshore console and the underwater robot body is necessary. The control command is sent by the onshore console to the robot body to control the robot's action. The robot feeds the state information, video, pictures and other data to the console to realize the communication between console and underwater robot body. A user operating interface is independently developed to realize data interaction. The user operating interface on the console can display data from the onshore console and the ROV body.

The structure of data interaction is shown in Fig. 6.

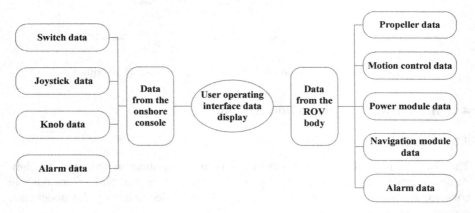

**Fig. 6.**  Data interaction structure

### 4.3 Manipulator Interaction

The manipulator is an important part of the underwater operation of the robot. Although the manipulator used on the ROV has only one degree of freedom, it is equipped with two kinds of manipulator (see Fig. 7). The manipulator can perform underwater grasping and cutting operations, such as grasping attachments on underwater structures and cutting ropes wrapped around propellers.

The engineer controls the action of the manipulator through the buttons (see Fig. 8) on the onshore console to realize the grab or cutting operation.

**Fig. 7.** Two kinds of manipulator

**Fig. 8.** The onshore console

# 5 ROV Underwater Tests

The ROV underwater tests were conducted on a pool and the Qiandao Lake respectively. These tests show that underwater robots can meet the requirements of Human-Robot-Interaction system and teleoperation underwater operating.

## 5.1 Visual Interaction Test

When the robot dived to water in the Qiandao Lake test shown in Fig. 9, the sensor data was normal, and the sharpness of underwater images has improved compared to previous ones after improving the camera's pixels. The stability and reliability of the robot

**Fig. 9.** ROV test in the lake

are preliminarily verified and the robot can successfully complete the direct navigation, turning bow, rolling and other motion postures in the lake (Figs. 10 and 11).

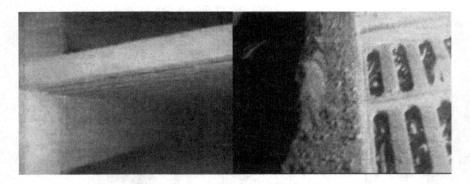

**Fig. 10.** Previous underwater images

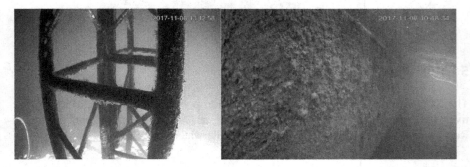

**Fig. 11.** Improved underwater images

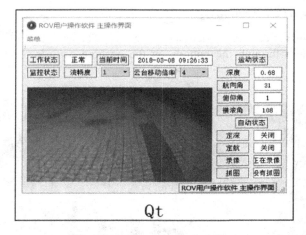

**Fig. 12.** User operation interface

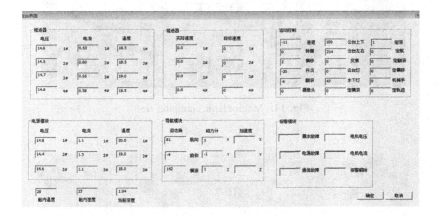

**Fig. 13.** Background data

## 5.2 Data Interaction Test

In order to display images obtained by underwater cameras and various data of the ROV in real time, a user operating interface based on Qt was independently developed. Due to the large amount of data to be displayed, it is impossible to display images and all data in one interface at the same time. Therefore, all data are displayed in the background, and users can get these data with one click. In this test, the images and data displayed on the interface are all normal.

## 5.3  Manipulator Interaction

The test of the manipulator is carried out in the pool. The engineer controls the action of the manipulator through the buttons on the onshore console to realize the grab operation.

**Fig. 14.**  Manipulator clamping test

**Fig. 15.**  Setting yaw of ROV

ROV in Qiandao Lake trials conducted on navigation test, as shown in Fig. 12, setting the initial heading angle at 326°, and the experimental data can be seen from Fig. 13. Because of the influence of the flow, the heading angle of underwater robot exists dithering when navigating in directional heading angle, but the robot can quickly adjust to set course, meet the navigation requirements (Figs. 14 and 15).

In the test, the deviation of heading angle is large. Due to the strong nonlinearity of underwater robot and the complex underwater environment, the inertial navigation devices have errors accumulated over time, which disturb the performance of the underwater robot (Fig. 16).

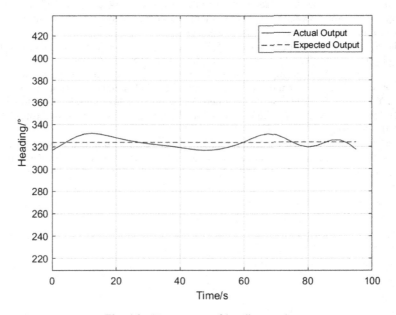

**Fig. 16.** Data output of heading angle

# 6   Conclusion

This paper introduces the general compositions of teleoperation underwater safety inspection and operational ROV "METI-01", and introduces the control system structure and control algorithm of the ROV. The Human-Robot-Interaction system of this ROV was designed to realize underwater inspection and operating through visual interaction, data interaction and manipulator interaction. The control system and Human-Robot-Interaction system were verified through the test of ROV conducted in pool and Qiandao Lake. It proves the teleoperated ROV's underwater inspection and operating capability.

# References

1. Wu, J.-M., Xu, Y., Tao, L.-B., Yu, M., Dou, Y.-Z.: An integrated hydrodynamics and control model of a tethered underwater robot. China Ocean Eng. **32**(05), 557–569 (2018)
2. Anonymous: China's 'Sea Dragon' ROV Reaches 5,630-Meter Depth. Ocean News & Technology (2018)
3. Bruno, F., Lagudi, A., Barbieri, L., Rizzo, D., Muzzupappa, M., et al.: Augmented reality visualization of scene depth for aiding ROV pilots in underwater manipulation. Ocean Eng. **168**, 140–154 (2018)
4. Zhang, J., Li, W., Yu, J., Feng, X., Zhang, Q., Chen, G.: Study of manipulator operations maneuvered by a ROV in virtual environments. Ocean Eng. **142**, 292–302 (2017)
5. Zhang, W.K., Wang, G.X., Xu, G.H.: Development of control system in abdominal operating ROV. Chin. J. Ship Res. **12**(2), 124–132 (2017)
6. Soylu, S., Proctor, A.A., Podhorodeski, R.P., Bradley, C., Buckham, B.J.: Precise trajectory control for an inspection class ROV. Ocean Eng. **111**, 508–523 (2016)
7. Sato, S., Adachi, Y.: Development of ROV for limestone cave control system and position estimation method investigation. In: The Proceedings of Conference of Kanto Branch (2017)
8. Yang, Y., Hirose, S., Debenest, P., Guarnieri, M., Izumi, N., Suzumori, K.: Development of a stable localized visual inspection system for underwater structures. Adv. Robot. **30**(21), 1415–1429 (2016)
9. Mai, C., Pedersen, S., Hansen, L., Jepsen, K., Yang, Z.: Modeling and control of industrial ROV's for semi-autonomous subsea maintenance services. IFAC Papers OnLine **50**(1), 13686–13691 (2017)

# Detecting Untraversable Regions
# for Navigating Mobile Robot
# on Pedestrian Lanes

Jiatong Bao[1]([✉]), Xiaomei Yao[1], Hongru Tang[1], and Aiguo Song[2]

[1] Yangzhou University, Yangzhou 225000, China
jtbao@yzu.edu.cn
[2] Southeast University, Nanjing 210096, China
http://www.yzuralab.cn

**Abstract.** The abstract should summarize the contents of the paper using at least 70 and at most 150 words. It will be set in 9-point font size and be inset 1.0 cm from the right and left margins. There will be two blank lines before and after the Abstract. ... Pedestrian lane following for autonomous navigation without pre-built maps in unconstrained outdoor environments is investigated. We extend the occupancy grid based mapping method which is dominantly applied in indoor environments to more open outdoor environments with far fewer surrounding objects. A stereo camera with middle ranging capability is used to capture color and depth data of road scenes. The color images are semantically parsed into different regions by using a pre-trained convolutional neural network (CNN). By taking advantages of the depth data, all 3D points of the image regions with non-road class labels are determined as untraversable ones and processed into pseudo laser scans. The pseudo laser scans are further projected into obstacle cells of the local occupancy grid map. By proposing a virtual wall and following it, the robot can autonomously move along the unconstrained pedestrian lanes and keep to the right. We test the navigation system in outdoor and indoor environments using the TurtleBot2 platform. The good performance of occupancy grid mapping and the effectiveness of lane following are validated by the blind test results.

**Keywords:** Outdoor navigation · Lane following · Untraversable region detection · Occupancy grid mapping

## 1 Introduction

Autonomous navigation is a critical capability for truly autonomous robot systems. There have been remarkable developments in approaches and technologies of mapping, localization and path planning for mobile robots in indoor and outdoor environments. In structured indoor environments where have walls and furniture, proximity sensors such as laser range finders, depth cameras like Kinect,

This research work is partially supported by the National Natural Science Foundation of China (No. 61806175) and the Postdoctoral Science Foundation of Jiangsu Province (No. 1601006C).

© Springer Nature Switzerland AG 2019
H. Yu et al. (Eds.): ICIRA 2019, LNAI 11741, pp. 661–671, 2019.
https://doi.org/10.1007/978-3-030-27532-7_58

**Fig. 1.** Overview of the proposed method. Given an input scene image (a), a pre-trained convolutional neural network is used to parse it semantically (b). By taking advantages of the depth data come from the stereo camera, all 3D points of the image regions with non-road class labels are determined as untraversable ones and processed into pseudo laser scans (c). The pseudo laser scans are projected into obstacle cells for building local occupancy grid map and also used for locating a virtual wall to the right side of the robot. The robot continuously follows the virtual wall and keeps a specified distance to them, which means the robot can move along the pedestrian lane and keep to the right safely (d).

etc, are commonly used to detect obstacles and build maps. However, this poses a challenge in unstructured outdoor environments, because they are more open with far few surrounding objects for mapping.

In the literature on outdoor navigation based on mapping, building offline maps with high resolutions is one of the main categories of methods, which is highly promoted by developing self-driving cars. For mapping motorized vehicle roads that are much regulated, multi-layer laser range finders are used to build high-resolution maps with lanes and other objects which are then annotated by humans. This method always need high-cost sensors and too much efforts to label the map data. It would be infeasible for much unconstrained pedestrian roads.

Many researches are focusing on finding more specific features for mapping and localization. One approach relies on detecting the curbs on roadways through the laser range finder [7]. The robot builds the map of the curbs and the map is used for tracking and localization. However, road curbs are always not so obvious to detect because of the inherent variance in shapes, sizes and textures. For example, the two sides of pedestrian lanes are always connected with lawns where may be unsafe for the robot, it is hard for the proximity sensors to detect. Fueled by deep learning, it becomes a good choice to employ pixel-wise semantic scene segmentation method to detect curbs based on color images [12]. Another category of approaches is visual simultaneous localization and mapping (Visual SLAM) [3,9]. It focuses on building the feature point based maps by using monocular, stereo or RGB-D cameras. However, the mapping performance can be affected by environmental illumination, and especially the built sparse point based map cannot be directly used for path planning and navigation.

Outdoor navigation, not limited to a pre-built map, is another main concern. The key idea is to enable mobile robots to keep following lanes safely. One kind of approaches is to represent the road as a set of lines extrapolated from the detected image contour segments [1,11]. However, there may exist many noise lines in unknown outdoor environments. The road situations where may be untraversable for the robots cannot also be recognized. Without strong geometric assumptions, others approaches employ end-to-end deep learning methods to estimate lanes or generate motion velocities directly when feeding with a new scene image [6].

This paper studies the outdoor pedestrian lane following problem without a pre-built map, but with a real-time local occupancy grid map benefit from visual semantic detection of untraversable regions. A stereo camera with middle ranging capability is used to capture color and depth information of scenes in the field of view (FOV) of our robot. The color images are constantly parsed into different regions with corresponding object class labels by using a pre-trained convolutional neural network (CNN). By taking advantages of the depth data, all 3D points of the image regions with non-road class labels are determined and processed into pseudo laser scans, which are further projected into obstacle cells of the local occupancy grid map. Based on the local map, a virtual wall is then located. By following it, the robot can autonomously move along the unconstrained pedestrian lanes and keep to the right with a desired distance.

The main contribution of this paper is that we extend the occupancy grid based mapping method which is dominantly applied in indoor environments to outdoor environments, and propose a virtual wall following strategy to navigate the robot moving along the lane and keeping to the right.

## 2   Method Description

### 2.1   Visual Semantic Detection of Untraversable Regions

Benefit from the success of deep architectures for scene parsing in soft real time, the ERFNet [10] based CNN with the encoder-decoder architecture as shown in Fig. 2 is implemented. The encoder produces downsampling feature maps, while the decoder upscales feature maps to match input resolution. The downsampling operation is performed by convolving the feature map with $3 \times 3$ kernels followed by max-pooling. The residual layers are designed based on 1D spatial factorizations of the convolutional kernels using the non-bottleneck version, which aim at collecting more context information. The encoder's output is then upscaled by using transposed convolutions. The corresponding residual layers are also designed. The linear classifier are finally deployed to estimate multiple classes each image pixel belongs to.

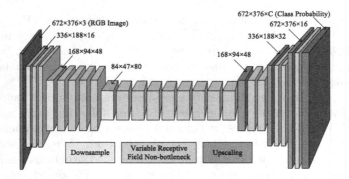

**Fig. 2.** The encoder-decoder semantic scene parsing CNN implemented in our navigation system.

## 2.2 Local Occupancy Grid Mapping

The main task of local mapping is to project the image pixels marked as untraversable to the 3D points within the robot base coordinate system. Figure 3 shows the pixel coordinate frame $\{U\}$, the image coordinate frame $\{I\}$, the camera coordinate frame $\{C\}$ and the robot base coordinate frame $\{R\}$. The stereo camera is attached to the robot at some constant relative pose and is to estimate 3D positions of the untraversable points in the scene. Suppose an arbitrary scene point $^CP = (^Cx_P, {}^Cy_P, {}^Cz_P)$ with respect to $\{C\}$ is projected to the rectangular image pixel $^Up = (u_p, v_p)$ with respect to $\{U\}$, i.e., the image point $^Ip = (^Ix_p, {}^Iy_p)$ with respect to $\{I\}$, by employing the pinhole camera model, the relationship between $^CP$ and $^Up$ can be determined by

$$^Cz_P \begin{bmatrix} u_p \\ v_p \\ 1 \end{bmatrix} = \begin{bmatrix} \frac{f}{dx} & 0 & u_0 \\ 0 & \frac{f}{dy} & v_0 \\ 0 & 0 & 1 \end{bmatrix} \begin{bmatrix} ^Cx_P \\ ^Cy_P \\ ^Cz_P \end{bmatrix} = K \begin{bmatrix} ^Cx_P \\ ^Cy_P \\ ^Cz_P \end{bmatrix} \tag{1}$$

where $(u_0, v_0)$ is the pixel coordinate of the principal point relative to $\{I\}$, $f$ is the focal length, $(dx, dy)$ represent the physical lengths of one pixel along the $x$ and $y$ directions, and $K$ is also called calibration matrix of the camera.

Therefore, given any pixel $^Up$ marked as untraversable by the visual semantic detection module as well as the measured spatial distance $^Cz_P$ between its corresponding 3D point and the camera, the untraversable 3D point $^CP$ with respect to $\{C\}$ can be calculated by Eq. (1). Meanwhile, suppose $^R\xi_C = \begin{bmatrix} R_{3\times3} & t_{3\times1} \\ 0_{1\times3} & 1 \end{bmatrix}$ denotes the pose of $\{C\}$ relative to $\{R\}$, the point $^RP$ with respect to $\{R\}$ can be described as

$$\begin{bmatrix} ^Rx_P \\ ^Ry_P \\ ^Rz_P \end{bmatrix} = \begin{bmatrix} R_{3\times3} & t_{3\times1} \end{bmatrix} \begin{bmatrix} u_p \cdot {}^Cz_P \\ v_p \cdot {}^Cz_P \\ ^Cz_P \\ 1 \end{bmatrix} \tag{2}$$

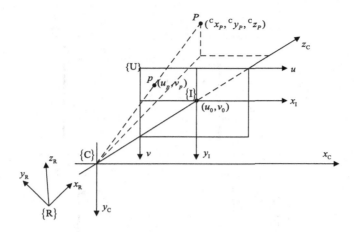

**Fig. 3.** Coordinate frames in the robot system.

By now, considering $\{R\}$ is rigidly attached to the centroid of the robot base, with its x-axis pointing forwards, y-axis pointing leftwards and z-axis pointing upwards, and the local map coordinate frame is defined the same as $\{R\}$, the obstacles in the local map can be directly located at $\left({}^{R}x_P, {}^{R}y_P\right)$ for every detected untraversable point in $\{{}^{R}P\}$, which results in a pseudo laser scan as well as a local scaled occupancy grid map.

### 2.3  Pedestrian Lane Following

With the understanding of its surrounding environments, the robot should keep moving on the pedestrian lane safely by taking advantage of the real-time local map, which means the robot can not move off the lane and should avoid collision with the obstacles such as pedestrians, cars, etc. It will be preferred if the robot can obey the traffic rules, e.g., driving on the right side of the road.

In our case, the pedestrian lanes are divided into lane segments by the global path planner [1] according to GPS coordinates of road intersection waypoints. The robot only need to move along the lane until achieving road intersections. A virtual wall following strategy is proposed to navigate the robot moving along the lane and keeping to the right. Firstly, the obstacles to the right of robot which are the lane borders in most cases are detected as the virtual wall base on the local map. When the virtual wall is detected, as shown in Fig. 4, the distance $d$ between the robot and the virtual wall and the relative heading angle $\theta$ can be calculated. The robot is then controlled to achieve the state with the desired distance $d = d_0$ and heading angle $\theta = 0$.

Suppose the virtual wall is represented by $Ax + By + C = 0$ within the robot base coordinate system, $k = -\dfrac{A}{B}$ denotes its slope, $d_0$ is a distance tolerance, $\omega_{max}$ is the maximal angular velocity, and $\delta(x)$ outputs 1 when $x > 0$ and 0 otherwise. An applicable control law of angular velocity is

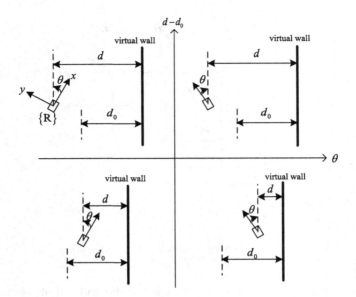

**Fig. 4.** Situations for control of the robot following a virtual wall.

$$\omega_c = \begin{cases} \delta(0.5 - k) \cdot (d_0 - d)\omega_{\max}, & d > d_0 + d_\sigma \\ \delta(k + 0.2) \cdot (d_0 - d)\omega_{\max}, & d < d_0 - d_\sigma \\ k \cdot \omega_{\max}, & other \end{cases} \tag{3}$$

where 0.5 and 0.2 are configurable constants used for adjusting the robot's heading to a desired value when moving toward and far from the virtual wall, respectively. Then, the linear velocity for control is determined accordingly by

$$v_c = \exp\left(-\lambda_v \left|\omega_c\right|\right) v_{\max} \tag{4}$$

where $v_{\max}$ is the maximal linear velocity, and $\lambda_v$ is a tunable parameter.

In addition, the robot would purely guided by the global goal assigned by the global path planner [1] when the virtual wall is not detected. The robot also reacts to the obstacles by using the dynamic window approach [4].

## 3   Experimental Results

### 3.1   Experimental Platform

A two-wheel differential driving mobile robot, TurtleBot2, was used as the mobile platform shown in Fig. 5. It can provide with the odometry based on the inner gyro and motor encoders. The ZED stereo camera which has $90°(\text{H}) \times 60°(\text{V})$ field of view (FOV) and up to 20 m depth ranges was equipped on the top for perceiving the environment. We implemented the semantic untraversable region detection algorithm based on an open-source semantic segmentation framework [8]. Currently, we trained the CNN for scene parsing only with the Cityscapes dataset [2] which provides with labeled outdoor scenes. After processing the 3D points which correspond to the image pixels with non-road class labels into pseudo laser scans, the GMapping [5] which is a highly efficient Rao-Blackwellized particle filter to learn global grid maps from the range data was employed. All modules and algorithms are implemented on the onboard Nvidia Jetson TX2 computer with the Robot Operating System (ROS).

**Fig. 5.** The TurtleBot2 platform with ZED stereo camera and Nvidia Jetson TX2 computer attached.

### 3.2   Semantic Detection of Untraversable Regions for 2D Mapping

Figure 6 shows two outdoor places where 2D mapping based on semantic detection of untraversable regions was performed. The first place is a pedestrian lane with shape like S. The lane is set to the only traversable region. All other objects such as curbs, grasses, trees, etc., are deemed as obstacles. The second place is a wood bridge with multiple corners. The solid wood floor is the traversable region while the others are not. Since this type of experiments was designed to see how the semantic detection of 3D obstacles and the mapping perform, the robot was manually driven with a joystick in the mapping process.

Figure 7 shows the 2D mapping result of the first place. In the evolving mapping process, the robot constantly captured a color image and segmented it to regions with corresponding class labels. All 3D points of the image regions with non-road classes were then processed into the pseudo laser scans, which were further projected into the obstacle cells of the local map. The global map was also built by the GMapping [5] algorithm. It should be noticed that the map cannot be obtained by traditional methods that use laser range finder to detect obstacles. This is because most curbs and grasses where may be dangerous cannot be directly detected by the sensors, which shows the importance of semantic detection of possibly unsafe regions.

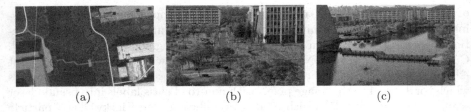

(a)                    (b)                    (c)

**Fig. 6.** Two experimental environments for 2D mapping. Two places are marked in (a) with red circles, (b) and (c) show the pictures of the real scenes. (Color figure online)

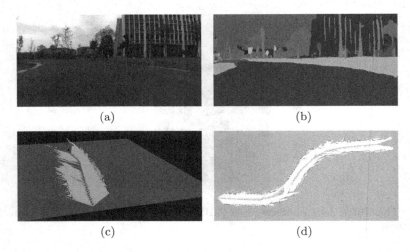

(a)                                    (b)

(c)                                    (d)

**Fig. 7.** Semantic detection of untraversable regions for 2D mapping in the first environment. An input RGB image (a) was segmented to the semantic image (b) where each colored patch represents a specific category of object. All image patches except the road were deemed as untraversable, and their corresponding 3D points were processed into the pseudo 2D laser scans, shown as the white dots and lines in (c), within the camera coordinate system. The scan data were further used for 2D local mapping within the robot base coordinate system. (c) shows the robot was doing global mapping and the map (d) was finally generated. (Color figure online)

Figure 8 shows the mapping result in another environment. All regions except from the wood floor were successfully detected as obstacles and the generated map has a high consistence with the real environment.

### 3.3    Automatic Lane Following

Figure 9 shows the lane following results in a curved outdoor lane environment and an indoor lab environment. The robot trajectory estimated based on odometry and map alignment is display on the map. The kept distances to the virtual wall were set to 1 m and 0.4 m in two environments respectively. The tolerance distances were both set to 0.2 m.

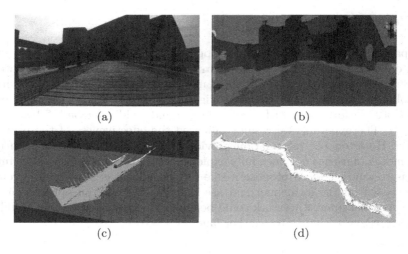

**Fig. 8.** Semantic detection of untraversable regions for 2D mapping in the second environment. (a)–(d) show an input RGB image, its corresponding semantic image, the corresponding pseudo 2D laser scans when the robot was doing mapping, and the final map, respectively.

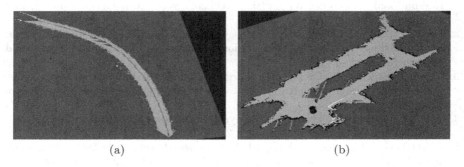

**Fig. 9.** Lane following results in a curved outdoor lane environment (a) and an indoor lab environment (b). The robot trajectories estimated based on odometry and map alignment are displayed on the generated map.

The results show that the robot trajectories are smooth and the robot can move along the lane and keep to the right with a desired distance. The lane following result in indoor environments also shows the trained CNN has a good transfer capability for parsing the indoor environments, especially in the aspect of recognizing the grounds. In both environments, benefit from the good performance of scene parser, the corresponding 3D points of the non-ground regions were successfully detected. By taking advantage of the generated local map, the robot can finally perform well as expected. The experiment videos are available on http://www.yzuralab.cn/research/sr/.

# 4   Conclusions

This paper investigates whether it is applicable to build occupancy grid maps based on semantic detection of untraversable regions in unconstrained outdoor environments, and to navigate the robot moving along the lane by using a virtual wall following strategy. The overall navigation system was implemented on the TurtleBot2 platform with ZED stereo camera and Nvidia Jetson TX2 computer attached. The experimental results validated the effectiveness of the proposed method. However, the information provided by the built local map with middle/remote ranges has not been fully exploited yet in this work. A possible future work is to study how to propose a safe foremost local goal at middle/remote ranges based on the local map and use that goal to plan an optimal path to follow. Another interesting work could be crossroad identification that could tell the robot when to change to another lane.

# References

1. Bao, J., Yao, X., Tang, H., Song, A.: Outdoor navigation of a mobile robot by following GPS waypoints and local pedestrian lane. In: Proceedings of the IEEE International Conference on CYBER Technology in Automation, Control, and Intelligent Systems (2018)
2. Cordts, M., et al.: The cityscapes dataset for semantic urban scene understanding. In: Proceedings of the IEEE International Conference on Computer Vision and Pattern Recognition (2016)
3. Engel, J., Stückler, J., Cremers, D.: Large-scale direct SLAM with stereo cameras. In: IEEE/RSJ International Conference on Intelligent Robots and Systems, pp. 1935–1942 (2015)
4. Fox, D., Burgard, W., Thrun, S.: The dynamic window approach to collision avoidance. IEEE Robot. Autom. Mag. 4(1), 23–33 (2002)
5. Grisetti, G., Stachniss, C., Burgard, W.: Improved techniques for grid mapping with Rao-Blackwellized particle filters. IEEE Trans. Robot. 23, 34–46 (2007)
6. Kim, J., Park, C.: End-to-end ego lane estimation based on sequential transfer learning for self-driving cars. In: Proceedings of the IEEE Conference on Computer Vision and Pattern Recognition Workshops, pp. 1194–1202 (2017)
7. Kim, S.H., Roh, C.W., Kang, S.C., Park, M.Y.: Outdoor navigation of a mobile robot using differential GPS and curb detection. In: Proceedings of the IEEE International Conference on Robotics and Automation (2007)
8. Milioto, A., Stachniss, C.: Bonnet: an open-source training and deployment framework for semantic segmentation in robotics using CNNs. In: Proceedings of the IEEE International Conference on Robotics and Automation (2019). https://arxiv.org/abs/1802.08960
9. Mur-Artal, R., Tardós, J.D.: ORB-SLAM2: an open-source slam system for monocular, stereo, and RGB-D cameras. IEEE Trans. Robot. 33(5), 1255–1262 (2017)
10. Romera, E., Álvarez, J.M., Bergasa, L.M., Arroyo, R.: ERFNet: efficient residual factorized convnet for real-time semantic segmentation. IEEE Trans. Intell. Transp. Syst. 19(1), 263–272 (2018)

11. Siagian, C., Chang, C., Itti, L.: Mobile robot navigation system in outdoor pedestrian environment using vision-based road recognition. In: Proceedings of the IEEE International Conference on Robotics and Automation, pp. 564–571 (2013)
12. Yang, K., Bergasa, L.M., Romera, E., Sun, D., Wang, K., Barea, R.: Semantic perception of curbs beyond traversability for real-world navigation assistance systems. In: Proceedings of the IEEE International Conference on Vehicular Electronics and Safety (2018)

# A Prediction Method of Contact Force in Precise Teleoperation with Time Delay

Pengwen Xiong[1,2](✉), Aiguo Song[1], Jianqing Li[1], and Yao Lei[2]

[1] School of Instrument Science and Engineering,
Southeast University, Nanjing 210096, China
[2] School of Information Engineering,
Nanchang University, Nanchang 330031, China
steven.xpw@ncu.edu.cn

**Abstract.** The precise teleoperation is still a hard and hot research topic in the teleoperation area, because of much higher requirement of transparency and stability. With the current teleoperation systems, the operator usually could not precisely feel the exact force he imposed to the master hand controller, and also the contact force generated by the slave robot during the interaction with the environment. In this paper, in order to provide an accurate contact force to the operator in the master robot side, a prediction method of contact force was presented based on our previous work. The operator was considered as the core part in the whole system. The relationship of the electromyography signal on the operator's arm and the gesture of the hand controller and the corresponding contact force, was explored and mapped with the generalized regression neural network. Based on the predicted force in the relationship function, a non-time based precise teleoperation control method was brought in to ensure the control stability of the teleoperation with time delay. A special experimental platform was established to conduct puncture experiment under a non-time based variable z with four different materials. The result of comparison with the prediction contact force by information fusion, corrected value by non-time based control and the real value shows the prediction method could get an accurate value of contact force in precise teleoperation with time delay.

**Keywords:** Teleoperation · Precise working · Contact force

## 1 Introduction

Teleoperation technology is a combination of the robot technology [1, 2], information technology and bilateral control technology, which can help people, even substitute people at some special situation, to perform tasks conveniently in the long-distance and dangerous environment where people are not able to deal with the task well by themself or even could not enter. The teleoperation system's application becomes wider and wider in the engineering area, and is currently being developed and applied in nuclear power [3], space [4, 5] and telemedicine [6, 7] and also other areas due to its important scientific value and social significance.

The transparency and stability during the teleoperation process are always the most important research points and the evaluation of the control algorithm [8, 9]. One key

© Springer Nature Switzerland AG 2019
H. Yu et al. (Eds.): ICIRA 2019, LNAI 11741, pp. 672–686, 2019.
https://doi.org/10.1007/978-3-030-27532-7_59

point of teleoperation is how to make the operator get the force information which is generated when the slave robot interfaces with the environment, and make the slave robot follow the movement of the master hand controller in an accurate and timely manner, which requires a more stable human-robot interaction system [10, 11].

So far, most teleoperation system establish virtual model of the operation environment in the slave robot side as a human-robot interface [12, 13]. However, it is difficult to estimate an accuracy model and ensure a precise predictive control especially when the slave robot works in the unknown unstructured environment. Furthermore, with the current teleoperation systems, the operator could sense the approximate force by touching a simple force feedback system with a certain force feedback model in the master hand controller side, and then estimate the contact force information in the slave robot side. However, the operator could not sensor the exact force he imposed to the master hand controller (the reactive force according to the Newton's third law) by himself, let alone the contact force generated by the slave robot during the interface with the environment. To take an example, in some special refinement operation, as for a teleoperation for the eye, heart and other vital organs surgery, it is the operator in the master side which plays the most important role in the whole process, and the operator should have a good perception of the action of the end effector of the slave robot in the remote side immediately. In case of bringing a irreparable hurt to the organs, at the moment when the operation knife reaches the target point, the operator need to know clearly and precisely the location of the operation knife on the end of slave robot and also how much force the robot has imposed to the organs via the operation knife. However, the teleoperation system may take some error information in the operator's remote operation, including system error or the error from force feedback model, which may influence or even confuse the operator's action. Thus it is very worthy to get an accurate prediction of contact force information during the operation from the end effector of the slave robot directly.

Several researchers have proposed ways to improve operator perception in teleoperation system [14–16]. In [14] a variable motion mapping method is proposed to improve the stiffness identification of remote objects. In this method, the motion mapping coefficient is adjusted according to the stiffness of the object, so that the operator can perceive the stiffness difference of the remote object to improve the sensing ability of the contact force of the slave robot. In [15] a new reconstruction method of remote object virtual model is proposed. The method builds a remote robot system based on augmented reality technology, which uses the position and force information of the remote robot to continuously update the dynamic parameters such as damping and stiffness of the virtual model and then feedbacks the real-time force to the operator through the virtual model. [16] proposed to use vibrating tactile and auditory display instead of force feedback, and not only solved the delay problem, but also the vibrational touch and auditory display are better sensors for operator compared with the traditional bilateral force feedback.

Although the above methods could improve the operator's perception ability, they are not able to enable the operator to accurately sense the contact force of the slave robot during his operation. In order to get a solution for this problem to increase the transparency, a prediction method that could accurately sense the contact force is presented based on our previous work in this paper. After the offline training prediction based on information fusion, in order to ensure the stability of the precise teleoperation with random time delay, the online prediction result is used as input in a non-time based control method. The rest of this paper is organized as follows: In the second section, it mainly introduce the system frame structure that includes teleoperation system and EMG signals sampling system. The third section introduces an information fusion based on GRNN, and a non-time based control method. Section four mainly describes the process of the experiment, and also the experimental data processing and analysis. The section five gives a conclusion.

## 2  The System Structure

In order to help the operator accurately feel the contact force information on the end effector of the slave robot during precise operation, a force perception system is built by teleoperation robot platform, in which the operator is the core point. As shown in Fig. 1, the whole structure includes two parts: the classical teleoperation system and the EMG signals sampling system, and it is easy to find the operator himself is the only intersection part of the two parts. The EMG sensors are well attached and placed on the operator's arm, and the EMG signal could be detected while the operator is imposing force to move the handle of the master hand controller, in the meantime, the master hand controller send the command and control the slave robot to interactive with the target object. With a certain and fixed force feedback model, the operator could feel the approximate feedback force and impose the reacting force to the handle of the hand controller. The operator could get subjective judgments based on this information to adjust the position of the handle of master controller to send the control command to the slave robot, and then conduct the precise operation on the target object.

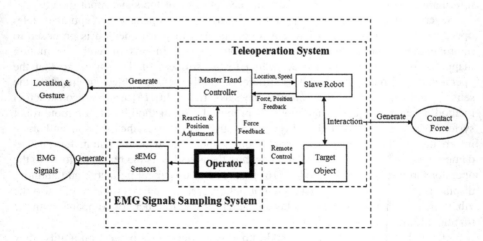

**Fig. 1.** System frame structure

The purpose of the teleoperation system is to extend human perception and ability. Teleoperation system consists of five parts: the operator, the master side, the slave side, communication channel and operation environment. The master side transmit information such as the position and speed to the slave side with a certain distance through the communication channel when the operator controlling the controller in the master side, and make the end effector in the slave side interactive with the object to conduct operation. In the meantime, the position, velocity and contact force from environment interaction and other information in the slave side will also be transmitted through the communication channel to the master side. It means that the operator could indirectly interact with the operation environment by sensing the feedback information from the active side.

## 2.1 Location and Gesture Detecting

A Phantom Omni controller with six degrees of freedom that includes the XYZ axis movement and rotation is used as master robot, as shown in Fig. 2.

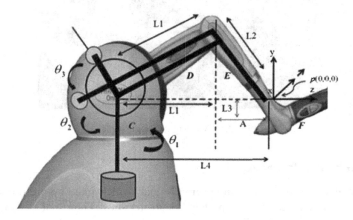

**Fig. 2.** Phantom Omni controller [17]

The attitude information, collected through the Phantom Omni controller, needs to be transformed by the Phantom Omni kinetic equation, as shown in Fig. 2. The kinematic equation is as follows [17]:

$$x_m = -\sin\theta_1(L_2\sin\theta_3 + L_1\cos\theta_2) \tag{1}$$

$$y_m = -L_2\cos\theta_3 + L_1\sin\theta_2 + L_3 \tag{2}$$

$$z_m = L_2\cos\theta_1\sin\theta_3 + L_1\cos\theta_1\cos\theta_2 - L_4 \tag{3}$$

Where $L_1$ = 133.35 mm, $L_2$ = 133.35 mm, $L_3$ = 23.35 mm, $L_4$ = 168.35 mm. $L_1$ and $L_2$ is the length of links 1 and 2, $L_3$ and $L_4$ is the workspace transform offset between the starting point of the terminal actuator and the first joint.

The Canadian company Thalmic Labs R & D's MYO arm ring with eight electrodes is used to collect the operator's information, as shown in Fig. 3. It not only collects EMG signals, but also collects acceleration and displacement, which be used to adjust the location and gesture of the handle.

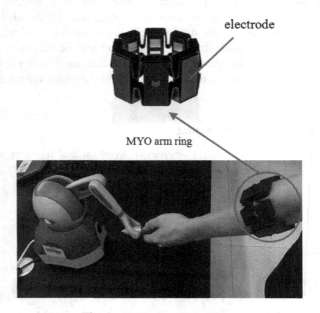

electrode

MYO arm ring

**Fig. 3.** EMG signal acquisition

## 2.2    EMG Signal Processing

The measured EMG signal is a time-series signal, which must be pre-processed and feature extraction that describing the hand characteristics. The usual methods of time domain feature extraction includes average absolute value (MAV), variance (VAR), zero crossing (ZAC) and Williamson amplitude (WA). However, with our previous work we found the MAV and VAR is conflict sometimes. Therefore, here only three main feature is used and the mathematical equations extracted are as follows:

$$MAV_i = \frac{1}{N}\sum\nolimits_{j=i-N+1}^{i}|x_i| \tag{4}$$

$$ZAC_i = \sum\nolimits_{j=i-N+1}^{i}\mathrm{sgn}(x_j \cdot x_{j-1}) \tag{5}$$

$$WA_i = \sum\nolimits_{j=i-N+2}^{i}f(x_j - x_{j-1}) \tag{6}$$

Where $x_j$ is the sample data of $j$, N is the total number.

## 2.3    Force Sensing

The Denso Company's manipulator platform with force feedback is used as slave robot, as shown in Fig. 4, and a three-dimensional force sensor with the maximum value of 30N from ATI is placed and fixed between the end effector via designed flange. Surely, the end effector could be changed flexibly with knife, needle and other useful tools.

Force sensor

**Fig. 4.**  The end of robot

# 3    Algorithm and Theory

Here we regarde the whole teleoperation system in Fig. 1 as a black box with input and output, and the location and gesture of the handle in the master side and the EMG signal on the operator's arm are fused as the input of the black box, while the contact force produced from the interface between the end effector and target object is the output.

Now what we are trying to do is to find the relationship between the input valve and output value, and anything in the intermediate process in the black box, including the different kind of force feedback model, the random time delay during the teleoperation and other complicated variables, would not need to focus on.

## 3.1    Information Fusion Based on GRNN

With the relationship between the input and output of the black box, in the same system the operator is able to sense how much force he has imposed on the end effector just by his action, but not the status of the system any more.

Here information fusion based on Generalized Regression Neural Network (GRNN) is brought in to attempt to map the relationship. GRNN is a kind of radial basis neural network, which was proposed by American scholar Specht [18] in 1991. It is mainly used to solve nonlinear problems and superior to other algorithms on the accuracy and learning speed, because it has the advantages of nonlinear mapping ability, high degree of fault tolerance and robustness.

GRNN network structure from the input layer, model layer, sum layer and output layer composition. The number of neurons in the input layer is equal to the number of input dimensions in the sample, where each neuron is a simple distribution unit that directly passes the input to each neuron in the mode layer. The number of neurons in the mode layer is equal to the number of samples, and the number is n, where each neuron corresponds to a different sample. The number of neurons in the output layer is equal to the dimension of the output vector in the sample. The output of each neuron in the sum layer is divided with the output of the sum layer.

## 3.2    Non-time Based Force Control

After the relationship has been restructed, the operator could predict the contact force by his action in the master side, and the transparency has been increased. Then another problem comes out, which is that there is always random time delay [19] during the teleoperation process, and most control method for teleoperation was based on time t, which make the control of the end effector potentially unstable. Therefore, a non-time based precise force control method [20] is used here to decrease the influence of random time delay.

Based on our previous work, let a non-time based variable z to be a reference variable in the non-time based control method, and in order to ensure the teleoperation system's stability, z should be nondecreasing over time. Here the predicted contact force could be marked as $F_e(z)$, and the corrected status of the end effector with action reference and the real value could be marked as $y_c(z)$ and $y(z)$ individually, and the status of the end effector could be regarded as $y = (p, F)$, where p is the position of end effector, and F is the contact force. The position p and contact force F could be divided by the stiffness of the target object as follow:

$$\dot{p} = v^*$$
$$\dot{F} = k\dot{p} = kv^* \tag{7}$$

where $v^*$ is the movement velocity of the end effector.

As shown in Fig. 5, when the operator feel the feedback force, the contact force will be controlled as the following:

$$F_e(z+1) = f(D(z)) + K_z \cdot (y_c(z) - y(z)) \tag{8}$$

Where $f$ is the GRNN transfer function, and $D$ is the feature set of EMG, and $K_z$ is a scale factor.

In order to make the operation more precise, an action reference $v(z)$ is brought in, which could be expressed as:

$$v(z) = \begin{cases} \frac{\dot{F}_c - (F - F_c)}{k} & k \neq 0 \\ \dot{p}_c - (p - p_c) & k = 0 \end{cases} \tag{9}$$

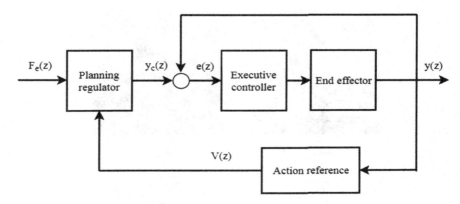

**Fig. 5.** The architecture of non-time based control [20]

In the whole control process, the time $t$ is never considered, and if substitute $v(z)$ into the $v^*$ in (7), it is easy to find that when $t \to \infty$, the error between the predict contact force and real force approaches to zero.

## 4    Experiment and Data Analysis

In order to verify the feasibility of prediction method of contact force in precise teleoperation, a special experiment platform is constructed as shown in Fig. 6. The operator hold the handle of Phantom Omni, and attempt to puncture the organized different points on the target object. Series of puncture experiment with four different materials, including "Paper box", "Foam board", "Sheet metal spring plate" and "Glass spring plate", was conducted via the experiment platform. During each group experiment, the EMG signal data on the operator's arm, Phantom Omni attitude information and contact force information data at the end of the slave robot were synchronously collected.

Every group of experiments collected ten thousands sets of data, in which EMG information had eight electrode data and could be extracted three eigenvalues of MAV, ZAC and WA in the time domain, and Phantom Omni gesture information has three different features, which respectively correspond to the position information of the XYZ axes of the coordinate system. The experimental data were tested by GRNN algorithms. Firstly, ten thousands sets of data were randomly selected as the training set. Then, nineteen features of EMG and Phantom Omni attitude information are taken as input, the contact force of end robot is used as output to train the algorithm model, and the best algorithm model is selected by cross-validation.

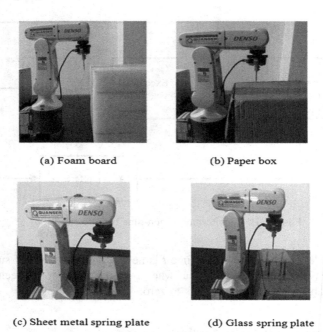

(a) Foam board                (b) Paper box

(c) Sheet metal spring plate        (d) Glass spring plate

**Fig. 6.** Puncture experiment with four kinds of materials

After the best algorithm model is well trained, the contact force could be predicted in time-based coordinate system. Then the operator control the slave robot move under non-time control mode. With the adjustment by action reference, a corrected status of the end effector, including the position and force information, is sent to the executive controller, and executive controller produces the next movement in z + 1 according to and real status.

As shown in Fig. 7, prediction value of contact force based on GRNN algorithm with four different materials is compared with the real value. Take the root-mean-square error (RMSE) as an accuracy index, the paper box's RMSE is 0.31, and the Foam board's RMSE is 0.22, and the Sheet metal spring plate's RMSE is 0.26 and the Glass spring plate's RMSE is 0.25.

Based on the prediction contact force, the corrected value is obtained and compared with the real value, as shown in Fig. 8. The paper box's RMSE is 0.20, and the Foam board's RMSE is 0.16, and the Sheet metal spring plate's RMSE is 0.21 and the Glass spring plate's RMSE is 0.11.

Through comparison result of the four kinds of materials in Figs. 7, and 8, it can be concluded that the prediction method could accurately sense contact force during the precise teleoperation in the teleoperation system with time delay.

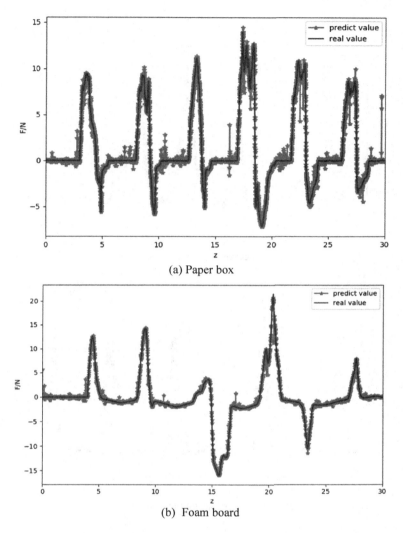

(a) Paper box

(b)  Foam board

**Fig. 7.**  (*continued*)

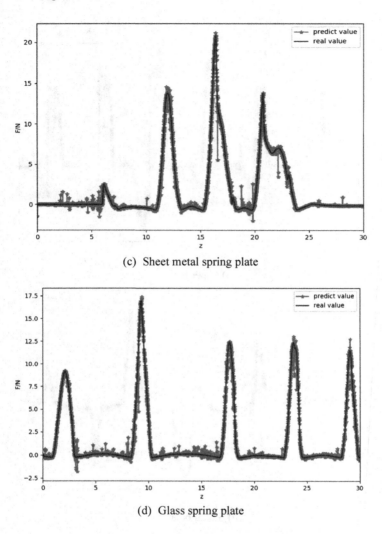

(c)  Sheet metal spring plate

(d)  Glass spring plate

**Fig. 7.** Prediction of contact force based on GRNN

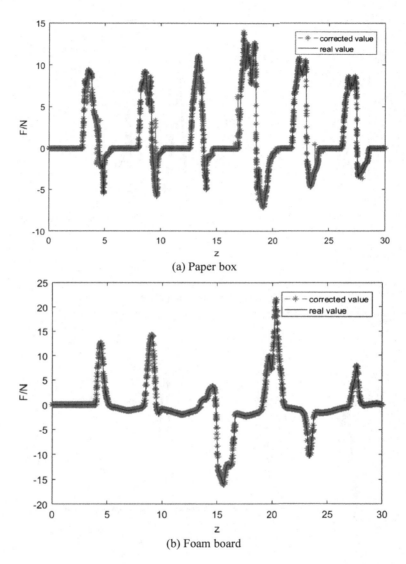

(a) Paper box

(b) Foam board

**Fig. 8.** (*continued*)

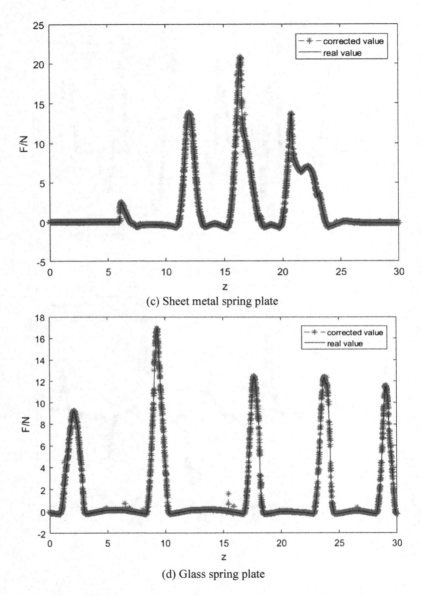

(c) Sheet metal spring plate

(d) Glass spring plate

**Fig. 8.** Corrected contact force under non-time based control

## 5   Conclusion

Precise teleoperation has high requirements on the transparency and the stability of the teleoperation. The operator plays a quite important roles in performing the task, and he needs accurately sense the contact force from the operation interface. A prediction method of contact force is proposed based on our previous work, which increase the transparency of teleoperation. Furthermore, a non-time based control method is proposed to increase the stability of teleoperation with random time delay. Puncture experiment with four different materials is designed, and in order to ensure the reliability of the experimental data, puncture action was performed at different points in every kind of material. The experimental results show that the operator could accurately sense the contact force information on the end effector during teleoperation, and also verify the effectiveness and feasibility.

**Acknowledgment.** This work was partially supported by the National Natural Science Foundation of China under Grants (61663027), and the Jiangxi Natural Science Foundation (20181BAB211019), China Postdoctoral Science Foundation (2018M642137) and the Jiangsu Province Postdoctoral Research Funding Plan (2018K024A).

# References

1. Suzumura, A., Fujimoto, Y.: Generalized design of position-based bilateral control parameterized by complementary sensitivity functio. IEEE Trans. Ind. Electron. **65**(11), 8707–8717 (2018)
2. Nagatani, K., Kiribayashi, S., Okada, Y., Otake, K., Yoshida, K., Tadokoro, S., et al.: Emergency response to the nuclear accident at the Fukushima Daiichi nuclear power plants using mobile rescue robots. J. Field Robot. **30**(1), 44–63 (2013)
3. Liu, C.Z., Yan, Z., Deng, J.S., Zhang, B.J., Guo, L.: Study on accident response robot for nuclear power plant and analysis of key technologies. Nucl. Sci. Eng. **33**(1), 97–105 (2013)
4. Luo, J.J., Zong, L.J., Wang, M.M., Yuan, J.P.: Optimal capture occasion determination and trajectory generation for space robots grasping tumbling objects. Acta Astronautica **136**, 380–386 (2017)
5. Hu, T.J., Huang, X.X., Tan, Q., Huang, J.Y.: Error feedback controller for autonomous space teleoperation. Procedia Eng. **29**, 1142–1149 (2012)
6. Alonso, S.C., Philippe, P., Etienne, D., Arianna, M.C., Paolo, D.: A design framework for surgical robots: example of the Araknes robot controller. Robot. Auton. Syst. **62**(9), 1342–1352 (2014)
7. Sharifi, I., Doustmohammadi, A., Talebi, H.A.: A safe interaction of robot assisted rehabilitation, based on model-free impedance control with singularity avoidance. IAES Int. J. Robot. Autom. **4**(2), 155–167 (2015)
8. Choussein, S.Z., Srouji, S.S., Farland, L.V., et al.: Robotic assistance confer ambidexterity to laparoscopic surgeons. J. Minim. Invasive Gynecol. **25**(1), 76–83 (2018)
9. Doris, A.B., Michael, F., Felix, S., Markus, K., Klaus, S.: Teleoperation of an industrial robot in an active production line. IFAC-PapersOnLine **48**(10), 159–164 (2015)
10. Dix, A.: Human-computer interaction, foundations and new paradigms. J. Vis. Lang. Comput. **42**, 122–134 (2017)
11. Juan, W.: Human-computer interaction system based on GRBF & HMM, part A. Phys. Procedia **24**, 769–773 (2012)
12. He, Z.M., Chang, T., Lu, S.Y., Ai, H., et al.: Research on human-computer interaction technology of wearable devices such as augmented reality supporting grid work. Procedia Comput. Sci. **107**, 170–175 (2017)

13. Cela, A., Yebes, J.J., Arroyo, R., Bergasa, L.M., et al.: Complete low-cost implementation of a teleoperated control system for a humanoid robot. Sensors **13**, 1385–1401 (2013)
14. Liu, L.Z., Zhang, Y.R., Liu, G.Y., Xu, W.L.: Variable motion mapping to enhance stiffness discrimination and identification in robot hand teleoperation. Robot. Comput.-Integr. Manufact. **51**, 202–208 (2018)
15. Zhao, Z., Huang, P.F., Lu, Z.Y., Liu, Z.X.: Augmented reality for enhancing tele-robotic system with force feedback. Robot. Auton. Syst. **96**, 93–101 (2017)
16. Massimino, M.J., Sheridan, T.B.: Sensory substitution for force feedback in teleoperation. IFAC Proc. Volumes **44**(1), 109–114 (2011)
17. Silva, A.J., Ramirez, A.D., Vega, V.P., et al.: PHANToM OMNI haptic device: kinematic and manipulability. In: CERMA Proceedings Volumes, pp. 193–198 (2009)
18. Specht, D.F.: The general regression neural network-Rediscovered. Neural Netw. **6**(7), 1033–1034 (1993)
19. Zhang, Y.K., Li, H.Y., Huang, R.X., Liu, J.H.: Shared control on lunar spacecraft teleoperation rendezvous operations with large time delay. Acta Astronautica **137**, 312–319 (2017)
20. Xi, N.: Event-based motion planning and control for robotic systems. Washington University (1993)

# A Neural Network Based Method for Judging the Rationality of Litigation Request

Huifang Cheng, Tong Cui, Feng Ding$^{(\boxtimes)}$, and Sheng Wan

China Electronic Science and Technology Group,
China Justice Big Data Institute Co., Ltd., 15th Floor, Building 4, Beijing
Information Technology Building, No. 54 Shijingshan Road, Beijing, China
{chenghuifang, cuitong, dingfeng, wansheng}@cjbdi.com

**Abstract.** With the advancement of the construction of the intelligence court, artificial intelligence technology has become more and more significant in the litigation risk analysis. The reasonable prediction of the litigation request can guide the parties to form a reasonable litigation expectation and guide the case diversion; it can also provide intelligent risk warning to assist judges. The current litigation request reasonable prediction method has a low accuracy rate, and lacks a method for rationalizing the expectation of heterogeneous and diverse cases; at the same time, based on machine learning methods, some research focus on the rationality judgment of litigation requests. However, the rationality of litigation request feature design, selection and model are still to be explored. In this paper, we propose a rationality prediction framework for litigation requests based on multi-party evidence correlation model and neural network. Firstly, based on the judicial knowledge of litigation request and the multi-party evidence association model, the judicial characteristics of the reasonableness of litigation request is designed. Then we train and predict the judicial features based on the deep neural network model. Finally, the prediction and evaluation of the reasonableness of litigation is realized.

**Keywords:** Deep neural network · Litigation request · Rationality prediction · Multi-party evidence association model

## 1 Introduction

Previous scholars believe that the factors affecting litigation risk are as follows. In 2000, Clemenz et al. conducted a survey of civil cases in Austria during 35 years. After analysis, it was concluded that macroeconomic development has a greater impact on litigation cases. It also reflected the improvement of the economic system and the promotion of the company's internal governance level [1].

In 2002, Gul et al. found that the company's handling accrual level was positively related to the level of creditor's rights. The company's handling accrual level was higher in countries where creditors' legal protection and law enforcement were poor, and weakened in countries with strong legal protection and law enforcement. The results of the study showed that effective legal protection and enforcement can reduce the risk of litigation arising from the company's breach of the debt contract [2].

© Springer Nature Switzerland AG 2019
H. Yu et al. (Eds.): ICIRA 2019, LNAI 11741, pp. 687–701, 2019.
https://doi.org/10.1007/978-3-030-27532-7_60

In 2002, Zhang Weiying and Ke Rongzhu analyzed 620 judgments of civil and commercial cases in the grass-roots courts in Beijing, and found that regional differences had a significant impact on the probability of winning. That is to say, there was a local protectionist tendency in the civil trial, and it significantly affected the possibility of the company's litigation [3].

In 1997, Skinner found that companies with loss news were more likely to be prosecuted. It showed that the company's business situation and litigation risk were positively related to a certain extent [4]. However, if management early disclosure the bad news about company's earnings, the litigation costs could be reduced [5].

In 2002, Johnson et al. found that the correlation between accounting conservatism and litigation risk was negative, and the correlation between insider trading and litigation risk was positive [6]. The study by Du Charme in 2002 concludes that there was a positive correlation between the degree of earnings management and the risk of shareholder litigation [7].

In 2013, the research results of Mao Xinshu and Meng Jie show that the number and amount of company complaints were negatively correlated with the effectiveness of internal control. Among them, internal supervision and environmental construction had played a major role. The types of litigation cases mainly included: contract disputes, arrears disputes, company infringement liability disputes, equity transfer disputes, asset agreement disputes, securities false statements disputes, and so on. These lawsuits were closely related to corporate governance structure [8]. The research by Lin Bin et al. also supported the above viewpoints and draws a view that the quality of internal control was significantly negatively correlated with corporate litigation [9]. Therefore, the company can effectively prevent litigation risks by improving internal control [10].

The company's litigation risk was related to its financial status. In 2016, Wang Yanchao et al. studied the financial distress and the company's characteristic variables and found that the potential litigation risk of the firm was positively related to the debt financing cost, and this relationship was more obvious in the areas where litigation execution costs were high [11].

The company's litigation risk is related to its internal governance structure. In 2016, Guan Zhonghui found that the difference in actual controllers caused listed companies to have different enforcement laws in violation of penalties and litigation. Non-state-owned enterprises were more vulnerable to violations or legal proceedings than state-owned enterprises [12]. In 2017, Zhao Kangsheng et al. used the propensity score matching method (PSM) to analyze the relationship between the shareholding of large shareholders and litigation risk based on the corporate governance literature. The study utilized the 2007–2014 China A-share listed company as the initial research sample. The results showed that the company's litigation risk was significantly reduced, with the increase in the shareholding ratio of the largest shareholder [13].

Litigation risks can have the following economic consequences. First, the level of litigation risk of the company has a greater impact on the audit work. For example, the level of corporate litigation risk will change the auditor's preferences. In 1998 Defond found that auditors tended to adopt a sound accounting policy when the company's litigation risk was high [14]. Second, companies with high litigation risks changed their auditors more frequently. In 1997, Jagan and Jayanthi found that the auditor would decide to lift the customer relationship due to the pressure of litigation risk when the audited unit's financial situation and major events were abnormal. In 2000, Susan's study also supported the above conclusions [15, 16].

In 2012, Atanasov found that high-reputation venture capital institutions had a low probability of filing a lawsuit [17]. In the same industry, the involved institutions were more uncertain in their future operations, and there may be risks of declining performance. If the institution had a good reputation, the decline was even more pronounced.

In 2014, Liu Qiliang et al. found that when the company's litigation risk was high, the media negative reports faced by the company increased with the increase of litigation cases, and the audit fees also increased. Conversely, if the company was in low litigation risk, its correlation was not obvious [18].

In 2016, Dai Yiyi, Peng Zhen and Pan Yue used the data of A-share listed companies from 2006 to 2012 to study the impact of litigation risk on corporate charitable donations. The study subjects were divided into two samples, ST and non-ST. The results showed that in the ST sample, the higher the risk of corporate litigation, the higher the possibility of donation and the level of donation; in the case of non-ST samples, the opposite is true. The result reflected the difference in the impact of litigation risk on charitable donations, and charitable donation had become a self-salvation behavior in a high litigation risk environment to a certain extent [19].

In conclusion, the rationality analysis of the litigation risk can guide the parties to form a reasonable litigation expectation and guide the case diversion; at the same time, it can also provide intelligent risk warning for the judge to assist in the case. In summary, the rationality analysis of litigation risk is of great significance.

The rationality of current litigation requests is facing the following two difficulties and challenges. Firstly, the accuracy of rationality and prediction for current litigation requests based on Chinese laws and regulations is not high, and it is difficult model the rationalization of heterogeneous and diverse cases. Secondly, there are few studies on the rationality judgment of litigation requests based on the machine learning method, and the feature design, selection and model of litigation request rationality are still to be explored.

This paper proposes a rationality prediction framework based on multi-party evidence association model and neural network. Firstly, we design the judicial characteristics of litigation request rationality based on the judicial knowledge and multi-party evidence association model of litigation request. Then we train and predict the judicial characteristics based on the deep neural network model [20].

The main contributions and innovations of this paper include the following aspects:

1. This paper proposes a method for judging the rationality of litigation requests based on neural networks, and further realizes the goal of intelligent litigation by machine learning.
2. A multi-party evidence network node is constructed in this paper. Based on the multi-party evidence association model, the judicial characteristics of litigation request rationality are designed, which lays a foundation for the rationality of subsequent litigation requests.
3. In this paper, the multi-evidence association model and the neural network method are combined to construct a reasonable prediction framework for litigation requests. Firstly, we design the judicial characteristics of litigation request rationality based

on the judicial knowledge and multi-party evidence association model of litigation request. Then we train and predict the judicial characteristics based on the deep neural network model. Finally we realize the prediction and evaluation of the rationality of litigation.

The paper is organized as follows. In the second section, the existing methods for the rational analysis of litigation requests is introduced. In the third section, the overall framework for the rationality of litigation requests based on neural networks is presented. In the fourth section, the multi-party evidence correlation model is introduced, including the factual decision chain, model structure, model output, model reasoning and other processes. In Sect. 5 we conduct the design and quantification of litigation features. Section 6 designs a predictive model of the neural network. In the seventh section, the above methods are tested and the experimental results are given. The final section summarizes the contributions, and further work plans of this paper.

## 2 Related Work

With the development of information technology, the research on the rationality of lawsuit claims is not only based on the traditional method of judging by experience, but also with the help of methods which using natural language processing (NLP) to understand semantics [21]. However, NLP based methods often have ambiguities in the process of lexical analysis, syntactic analysis, semantic analysis and so on. At present, the further development of neural network method is discriminating. The reasonableness of litigation claims has a positive impact, so this paper based on neural network to judge the reasonableness of litigation claims.

According to the historical development of neural networks, neural networks can be divided into basic neural networks, advanced neural networks and deep neural networks. Basic neural networks include single-layer perceptron, linear neural network, BP neural network, Hopfield neural network and so on. Advanced neural networks include Boltzmann machines, restricted Boltzmann machines, recurrent neural networks and so on. Depth neural network includes depth confidence network, convolution neural network, depth residual network, LSTM network and so on. The most representative neural network methods include the following:

### 2.1 LeNet5

In 1988, based on the BP neural network, LeCun published "A theoretical framework for Back-Propagation". A few years later, LeCun used BP algorithm to train multi-layer neural network to recognize handwritten postal codes (Handwritten Digit Recognition: Applications of Neural Net Chips and Automatic Learning). This work is said to be the pioneering work of CNN, which uses 55 convolution cores in many places. But in this article, LeCun only said that 55 adjacent areas were regarded as receptive fields, and did not mention convolution or convolution neural networks. In the following years LeCun continued to optimize and published many articles on handwriting recognition [22].

## 2.2 AlexNet

In 2012, Alex Krizhevsky published AlexNet (ImageNet Classification with Deep Convolutional Neural Networks), a deeper and broader version of LeNet, and won the difficult ImageNet contest by a notable advantage.

AlexNet was a classic work published in 2012, and achieved the best results of ImageNet that year. After that year, more and deeper neural networks were proposed.

## 2.3 VGG-Net

In 2014, the VGG network from Oxford University (Very Deep Convolutional Networks for Large-Scale Image Recognition) was the first network to use smaller 3 * 3 filters in each convolution layer and combine them into a convolution sequence for processing.

## 2.4 R-CNN, Fast R-CNN, Faster R-CNN

RCNN (Regions with CNN features) is a milestone in the application of CNN method to target detection. It was proposed by the young and promising RBG. With the help of good feature extraction and classification performance of CNN, the problem of target detection can be transformed by RegionProposal method [23].

Inspired by SPPnet, RBG published Fast R-CNN in 2015. It has exquisite conception, more compact process and greatly improves the speed of target detection. Compared with R-CNN, the training time of Fast R-CNN is reduced from 84 h to 9.5 h and the testing time is reduced from 47 s to 0.32 s on the same largest network. The accuracy on PASCAL VOC 2007 is almost the same, ranging from 66% to 67%.

"Faster R-CNN: Towards Real-Time Object Detection with Region Proposal Networks" was proposed to improve Fast R-CNN. Because the test time in Fast R-CNN articles did not include search selective time, and a large part of the test time was spent on the extraction of candidate regions, Faster R-CNN was proposed to solve this problem.

## 2.5 GoogLeNet

Christian Szegedy from Google seek to reduce the computational overhead of in-depth learning networks, and designed Google LeNet, the first Inception architecture, Google LeNet.

## 2.6 ResNet

New changes took place in December 2015 as Inception V3 did. ResNet had a simple idea: supply the output of two consecutive convolution layers and pass the input into the next layer.

## 2.7    SqueezeNet

In 2016, SqueezeNet (SqueezeNet: AlexNet-level accuracy with 50x fewer parameters and <0.5 MB model size) was recently released, and the architecture reprocessed the concepts in ResNet and Inception. Better architecture design requires a smaller network model and no complex compression algorithm for parameters [24].

## 3    Framework

The framework of reasonableness discrimination of litigation claims based on neural network is shown in Fig. 1, which includes document data processing, evidence feature design and feature quantification, in-depth training of neural network model, and litigation risk assessment [25].

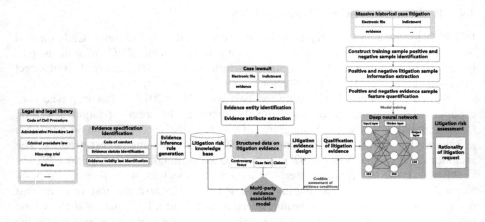

**Fig. 1.** The framework of reasonableness discrimination of litigation claims based on neural network

Firstly, the identification of evidence norms is carried out according to the library of laws and regulations, which includes civil procedure law, administrative procedure law, criminal procedure law, nine-step trial law, judicial documents and other legal and regulatory documents. The identification of evidence norms includes the identification of behavior norms, the identification of limitation of evidence law and the identification of evidence validity law. Then the evidence reasoning rules are identified and generated according to the evidence norms to form a knowledge base of litigation risk. The electronic files, indictments and evidence are used to identify the evidence entity and extract the evidence attributes. Combing the structured data of procedural evidence obtained from the knowledge base of litigation risk, the characteristics of procedural evidence are designed and quantified by using the key model of multi-party evidence and the structured data of procedural evidence. Using massive litigation documents of historical cases to construct training data to identify positive and negative cases, we extract information from positive and negative litigation cases and quantify their characteristics. Combining the characteristic design and quantification of litigation evidence, the deep neural network simulation training is carried out. Finally, the litigation risk assessment results confirm the rationality of litigation claims.

## 4   Multi-party Evidence Association Model

The multi-party evidence association model is about to construct a multi-party evidence network node, which is divided into three steps: 1. the template for corresponding fact-determination chain is selected according to the type of documents involved; 2. pattern recognition and information extraction methods to extract evidence elements and evidence attributes for the documents involved, through the use of clauses, word segmentation, syntactic analysis, entity identification, entity relationship extraction NLP technology; 3. Classification and reasoning of the evidence elements into evidence elements of the plaintiff, evidence of the defendant, evidence of judicial appraisal, and third-party evidence [26]. At the same time, the elements of evidence are classified and reasoned according to the facts of the evidence. The following three steps are described in detail (Fig. 2):

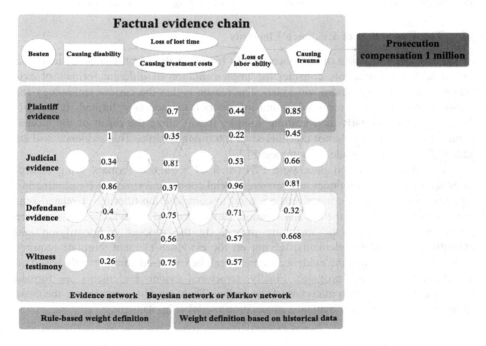

**Fig. 2.** Principle of multi-party evidence association model

## 4.1    Factual Judgment Chain

Based on the experience of experts, the factual judgment chain for different types of cases is determined. After in-depth analysis of civil, criminal, administrative and other types of litigation support chain, Fig. 3 gives an example of the factual chain of civil cases [27]. The factual decision chain can effectively support litigation requests. Multiple types of factual decision chains can form a judicial knowledge base.

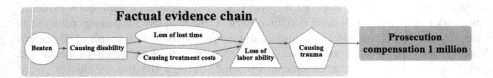

**Fig. 3.**  Example of a factual decision chain

For example, in this case, if the fact that "beating - causing disability - causing medical expenses - incapacity to work - causing trauma", if any, can support the claim for compensation. The judgment of facts needs the support of evidence. In this paper, the factual decision chain is used to guide the reasoning of the evidence chain.

## 4.2    The Extraction of Evidence Elements

At present, the extraction of evidence mainly based on the identification of text data and information extraction, consider the implementation of different formats of evidence, such as photos, audio and video. The reason is that the current technology for photo, audio and video recognition and information extraction is limited. If the evidence is added too early as a training sample, it will affect the result of the model. Therefore, the evidence is not considered as a training sample. This evidence will be added after the basic model is completed [28].

Fast extract plain text data from PDF or TXT evidence formats using natural language extraction techniques and remove special control information. By eliminating semantic noise, the triggering words are used to complete the filtering of related sentences from the text, and the key information is extracted and the evidence elements are identified according to the matching pattern. In the process of identifying and extracting the evidence elements, relying on the evidence element template requires artificial effort, and then the evidence elements can be extracted automatically based on the template utilization program. Finally, structured evidence elements are formed according to the litigation materials of the parties. These evidence entities are the basic elements in a multi-party evidence association model (Fig. 4).

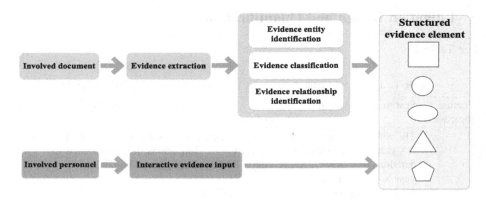

**Fig. 4.** Schematic diagram of structural evidence extraction

## 4.3 Evidence Element Classification Reasoning

The Bayesian Evidence Network or Markov Network is mainly used for multi-party and multi-class weak evidence reasoning, trying to find the most credible and persuasive evidence chain from multiple categories, multiple mutually-tested or contradictory evidences. It is expected that a combination of multiple weak evidences will be combined into a credible evidence chain to play a strong evidence role. Based on the multi-party evidence association model with multi-party evidence and evidence transfer probability, the genetic algorithm and other optimization methods are used to reason the multi-party evidence association network, and all possible evidence chain combinations are calculated [29]. According to the probability value of each evidence chain, we choose the probability. The largest chain of evidence serves as the most credible chain of evidence. The principle is shown in the Fig. 5.

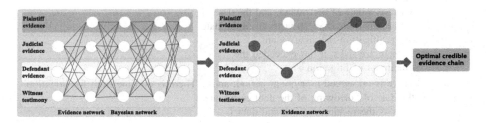

**Fig. 5.** Evidence chain reasoning based on multi-party evidence association mod

# 5   Litigation Design and Quantification

See Table 1

**Table 1.** Design and quantification of litigation characteristics of loan cases

| Feature dimension | Feature quantization | Characteristic meaning |
|---|---|---|
| 0 | The withdrawal is scheduled for XXXX XX XX date before repayment/repayment date/loan term XXXX XX XX day - XXXX year XX XX day and so on. There is an agreed repayment period, and the agreed repayment period has exceeded the two-year date of the litigation risk assessment. 1, there are risks: it has exceeded the timeliness of litigation. | There is a risk of statute of limitations: it has exceeded the timeliness of litigation. |
|  | The withdrawal is scheduled for XXXX XX XX date before repayment/repayment date/loan term XXXX XX XX day - XXXX year XX XX day and so on. There is an agreed repayment period, and the agreed repayment period does not exceed 2 years from the date of the litigation risk assessment. 0, no statute of limitations. | There is no time limit for litigation. |
| 1 | There is no agreed repayment period, and the date of borrowing of the debt certificate such as the receipt, receipt, and debt is drawn (e.g., contract signing date, date of loan, etc.). There is a date of borrowing, and the date of the loan is more than 20 years from the date of the litigation risk assessment. 1, there are risks: it has exceeded the timeliness of litigation. | There is a risk of statute of limitations: it has exceeded the timeliness of litigation. |
|  | There is no agreed repayment period, and the date of borrowing of the debt certificate such as the receipt, receipt, and debt is drawn (e.g., contract signing date, date of loan, etc.). There is a date of loan, the date of the loan is not more than 20 years from the date of the risk assessment of the litigation, and the time for collecting the dunning is not more than 2 years from the date of the risk assessment. 0, no statute of limitations. | There is no time limit for litigation. |

(*continued*)

**Table 1.** (*continued*)

| Feature dimension | Feature quantization | Characteristic meaning |
|---|---|---|
| | There is no agreed repayment period, and the date of borrowing of the debt certificate such as the receipt, receipt, and debt is drawn (e.g., contract signing date, date of loan, etc.). There is a date of borrowing, the date of the loan is not more than 20 years from the date of the risk assessment of the litigation, and the dunning time is taken to the date of the litigation risk assessment for more than 2 years. 1, risk: has exceeded the statute of limitations. | There is a risk of statute of limitations: it has exceeded the statute of limitations. |
| | There is no agreed repayment period, and the date of borrowing of the debt certificate such as the receipt, receipt, and debt is drawn (e.g., contract signing date, date of loan, etc.). There is a date of borrowing, the date of the loan is not more than 20 years from the date of the risk assessment of the litigation, and the dunning time is not drawn. −1, Risk: It is not possible to determine whether the statute of limitations has expired. | There is a statute of limitations: It is impossible to determine whether the statute of limitations has expired. |
| 2 | There is no agreed repayment period, no loan date, and whether the information of the indictment, the loan supporting evidence (witness testimony, WeChat/Alipay/SMS, etc.) is collected by the creditor, and the debtor has no intention to repay the semantics and time. There is a dunning time, and the dunning time is more than 2 years from the date of the litigation risk assessment. 1, risk: has exceeded the statute of limitations. | There is a risk of statute of limitations: it has exceeded the statute of limitations. |

(*continued*)

**Table 1.** (*continued*)

| Feature dimension | Feature quantization | Characteristic meaning |
|---|---|---|
| | There is no agreed repayment period, no loan date, and whether the information of the indictment, the loan supporting evidence (witness testimony, WeChat/Alipay/SMS, etc.) is collected by the creditor, and the debtor has no intention to repay the semantics and time. There is a dunning time, and the dunning time does not exceed 2 years from the date of the litigation risk assessment. 0, no statute of limitations. | There is no time limit for litigation. |
| | There is no agreed repayment period, no loan date, and whether the information of the indictment, the loan supporting evidence (witness testimony, WeChat/Alipay/SMS, etc.) is collected by the creditor, and the debtor has no intention to repay the semantics and time. The dunning time was not extracted. −1, Risk: It is not possible to determine whether the statute of limitations has expired. | There is a statute of limitations: It is impossible to determine whether the statute of limitations has expired. |

## 6  Neural Network Prediction Model

The prediction of litigation rationality, litigation effectiveness and litigation rationality involve litigation risk knowledge, which are suitable for complex depth model for forecasting. The litigation feature vector combines the multi-party evidence association map and the litigation risk knowledge base. The evidence and the focus of the dispute provided by the parties can be used to represent the structural elements of each litigation risk (disputed focus, litigation request, case fact). Discriminant characterization. Using the deep neural network multi-layer sensor, the litigation feature vector is input into the predictive model, and whether the validity of the litigation and the litigation rationality are valid and the effective probability is predicted respectively [30].

The input to this model is the feature vector designed in Table 1, and the output is the predictive label for whether the litigation request is reasonable (Fig. 6).

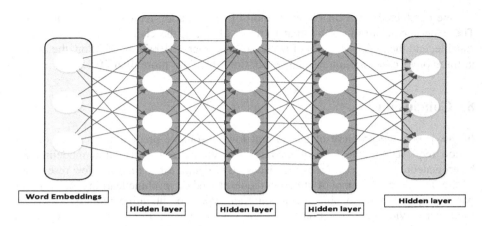

**Fig. 6.** Principle of neural network prediction model

## 7    Experimental Evaluation

The data set is derived from the real data crawled by the referee's paperwork. We manually determined that the loan case was selected for experimental analysis. At the same time, our judicial business experts marked three categories of dimensional features in the case and quantified the features; subsequently, the two groups of experts cross-checked the evidence features marked by the other party. These labeled evidence features can be used as real values to test the effectiveness of our multi-evidence association model. Then use the deep neural network to learn according to the marked evidence characteristics, and obtain the litigation risk assessment results to confirm the rationality of the litigation request.

This paper uses Java language and MATLAB mixed programming, the experiment uses DELL Optiplex 7040 model machine, memory 64 GB, the operating system is CentOS 10, JDK1.7 version.

The experimental results are shown in Table 2:

**Table 2.** Evaluation results of predicting the reasonableness of litigation requests in the case of lending

| No. | Evaluation result | Reasonable result |
|-----|-------------------|-------------------|
| 1   | 1.00              | Yes               |
| 2   | 1.00              | Yes               |
| 3   | 0.988             | Yes               |
| 4   | 0.963             | Yes               |
| 5   | 0.915             | Yes               |
| 6   | 0.836             | Yes               |
| 7   | 0.658             | Yes               |
| 8   | 0.381             | No                |
| 9   | 0.492             | No                |
| 10  | 0.525             | No                |
| 11  | 0.824             | Yes               |

We conducted a reasonable evaluation of the litigation request for 11 loan cases. The experimental results show that in these 11 cases, the claims of 8 cases are reasonable, and the reasonableness of two cases has reached 100%. In addition, the claims in three other cases are unreasonable, both of which are more than 60%.

## 8  Conclusion

In this paper, the problem of the current low reasonable prediction accuracy of litigation request, and the lack of methods for rationalized expectation modeling for heterogeneous and diverse cases are discussed in depth. Since there are few researches on the rationality judgment of litigation request based on machine learning method, this paper proposes a reasonable prediction framework for litigation requests based on multi-party evidence association model and neural network. Firstly, we design judicial knowledge based on litigation request and multi-party evidence association model and the judicial characteristics of litigation request rationality. Then prediction the judicial characteristics is trained based on the deep neural network model, and finally realized the prediction and evaluation of litigation plausibility. In the future, the author will increase the number of input parameters in the deep neural network learning process and study the accuracy of the evaluation results.

**Acknowledgement.** Thanks to the reviewers for their helpful feedback. The project is derived from the sub-project of "Research on litigation risk intelligence analysis and result prediction technology for multi-party evidence correlation analysis" in the national key R&D plan "Integrated convenience service technology and equipment research for litigation whole process", project number: 2018YFC0830200, sub-project number: 2018YFC0830202.

## References

1. Clemenz, G., Gugler, K.: Macroeconomic development and civil litigation. Eur. J. Law Econ. (9), 215–230 (2000)
2. Gul, F.A, Tsui, J.S.L., Su, X., Min, R.: Legal protection, enforceability and tests of the debt hypothesis: an international study. Working Paper, no. 22, 1259–1273 (2002)
3. Zhang, W., Ke, R.: Adverse selection and interpretation in the process of litigation—an empirical study of the basic court judgment of contract dispute. Chin. Soc. Sci. (2), 34–42 (2002)
4. Lev, B.: Information disclosure strategy. Calfornia Manage. Rev. **34**(4), 9–32 (1992)
5. Johnson, M., Nelson, K.K., Adam, C.: Pritchard in resilicon graphics securities litigation: shareholder wealth effects of the interpretation of the private securities litigation reform act? Plead. Stand. Univ. Michigan Lawand Econ. (4), 99–118 (2002)
6. Du, C., Malatesta, P., Sefcik, S.: Earnings management, stock issues and shareholder lawsuits. University of Washington, (3), 77–92 (2002)
7. Mao, X., Meng, J.: Internal control and litigation risks. Manage. World (11), 155–165 (2013 )
8. Lin, B., Zhou, M., Shu, W.: Internal control, corporate litigation and debt contract: an empirical study based on a-share market. Audit Econ. Res. (3), 3–11 (2015)
9. Luo, G.: Analysis on the Risk Prevention of Corporate Litigation in Internal Control. J. Wuxi Inst. Commer. Technol. (4), 17–20 (2014)

10. Wang, Y., Lin, B., Xin, Q.: Market environment, civil litigation and earnings management. China Acc. Rev. (1), 21–40 (2008)
11. Guan, Z.: An empirical study of the impact of internal defects on listed companies' violations and litigation risks. Nanjing University, Nanjing (2016)
12. Zhao, K., Zhou, P., Yan, N.: Empirical analysis of large shareholders' shareholdings and corporate litigation risks based on Chinese listed companies. Foreign Econ. Manage. (1), 84–90 (2017)
13. DeFond, M.L., Lennox, C.S.: The effect of SOX on small auditor exits and audit quality. J. Acc. Econ. 52(1), 21–40 (2011)
14. Krishnan, J., Krishnan, J.: Litigation risk and auditor resignations. Acc. Rev. (4), 539–560 (1997)
15. Susan, H.: Measuring the cost of corporate litigation: five case studies. J. Legal Stud. (2), 377–399 (2000)
16. Atanasov, V., Ivanov, V., Litvak, K.: Does reputation limit opportunistic behavior in the VC industry? Evidence from litigation against VCs. J. Financ. 67(6), 2215–2246 (2012)
17. Liu, Q., Li, W., Zhao, C., et al.: Media negative reports, litigation risks and audit fees. Acc. Res. (6), 81–88 (2014)
18. Dai, Y., Peng, Z., Pan, Y.: Corporate charitable donation: self-salvation under the risk of litigation. J. Xiamen Univ. (2), 122 (2016)
19. Ma, X., Di, X.: The paradox and dispelling of criminal misjudged cases in the background of artificial intelligence. Huxiang Forum 32(02), 37–48 (2019)
20. Liu, P., Chen, L.: Unified evidence standard for dataization. J. Natl. Procur. Coll. 27(02), 129–143 (2019)
21. Shi, M.: Civil justice in the age of blockchain. East Methodol. (03), 110–120 (2019)
22. Editorial Department of the Journal: General Catalogue. J. Southwest Univ. Polit. Sci. Law 20(06), 136–137 (2018)
23. Hong, D.: How does justice face technological innovations such as "Internet +" and artificial intelligence. Law (11), 169–180 (2018)
24. Gao, X.: Construction of legal knowledge map of artificial intelligence civil justice application—based on the factual type of civil judgment. Legal Syst. Soc. Dev. 24(06), 66–80 (2018)
25. Qian, D.: The Chinese process of judicial artificial intelligence: functional substitution and structural strengthening. Jurisprud. Rev. 36(05), 138–152 (2018)
26. Lu, T., Guo, Y., Liu, Y.: 2018 intellectual property nanhu forum - a summary of the international symposium on "new age technology revolution and intellectual property". Electron. Intell. Prop. (06), 94–99 (2018)
27. Li, X.: Thoughts on the legislative model of criminal proof standard "Chinese-Western Use". Polit. Legal Forum 36(03), 127–141 (2018)
28. Yang, Y.: Review, reflection and prospect of China's patent system in the 40 years of reform and opening-up. Chongqing Soc. Sci. (04), 32–40 (2018)
29. Lü, W., Yang, Q.: Prediction of engineering dispute litigation results based on CBR-RBR. Comput. Eng. Appl. 49(23), 228–234 (2013)
30. Xiong, M.: From legal argument to litigation argument—talking about the transformation of the object of legal argument logic. Seek. Truth (06), 24–27 (2007). 131

# Design of a Wireless Six-Axis Wrist Force Sensor for Teleoperation Robots

Wanglong Chen, Shuyan Yang, Quan Hu, and Aiguo Song[(✉)]

School of Instrument Science and Engineering,
Southeast University, Nanjing, Jiangsu, China
a.g.song@seu.edu.cn

**Abstract.** The six-axis force sensor is an indispensable component for the teleoperation robot to realize force sensing. It can be used to detect the force and moment generated when the robot is in contact with the target. In order to satisfy the usage requirements of teleoperation robots, a miniaturized wireless six-axis force sensor based on the principle of resistance strain is proposed in this paper. Firstly, the stepped cross beam structural elastic body is designed, and the optimal structural size of the sensor is determined by simulation analysis using ANSYS software. Secondly, the bridge circuit, amplifier circuit, signal processing and transmitting circuit of the sensor are designed to realize the wireless transmission of sensor data, which improves the flexibility and environmental adaptability of the sensor. The experimental results show that the indoor transmission distance of the sensor can reach 8 m, and the class I and class II errors reach the high precision standard of the six-dimensional force sensor.

**Keywords:** Teleoperation robots · Six-axis force sensor · Elastomer · Wireless transmission · Decoupling

## 1 Introduction

Teleoperation robots are suited for tasks in some special environments, and have played an increasingly important role in robotics field recently [1]. However, their intelligence degree and sensory ability are still not satisfactory. Actually, the sensory ability is particularly important, especially in some complex environments such as high risk, high temperature and strong radiation. In most cases, the operator controls robots and make decisions mainly through the information of image, position, and status of the actuator. But this control method has a poor linkage effect and low efficiency. Moreover, visual information is prone to errors in some unstructured environments, and it greatly limits the application of teleoperation robots [2].

Force perception is one of the most important environmental perception technologies [3]. Considering the above problems, the force sensor is a necessary component to realize effective interaction, and to improve operational efficiency. It is used to detect the force and moment between the robot and the target, and can be divided into different types, such as wrist force sensor, fingertip force sensor and joint force sensor [4]. Among them, the wrist force sensor needs to detect the force components of three axes $(F_x, F_y, F_z)$ and the torque components of three axes $(M_x, M_y, M_z)$ at the

© Springer Nature Switzerland AG 2019
H. Yu et al. (Eds.): ICIRA 2019, LNAI 11741, pp. 702–713, 2019.
https://doi.org/10.1007/978-3-030-27532-7_61

wrist of the mechanical arm, so a six-axis force sensor is needed. The design requirements of this kind of sensor are high sensitivity, high resolution, high linearity and high stability [5].

Usually, the working environment of teleoperation robots is pretty complex. "Zeus" [6] is one of the typical early application cases of teleoperation robots in the medical field. Liu [7] and Dong [8] proposed two kinds of teleoperation robots for detection in nuclear radiation environments. Besides, teleoperation robots have also been used in the aerospace field. In 2017, China Aerospace Center used teleoperation technology to complete the docking task of "Tianzhou No.1" and "Tiangong No.2" [9]. Because of the complex application environment, the design of six-axis force sensor has higher requirement. Firstly, the overall volume of the sensor should be as small as possible. In addition, the wiring should be as minimal as possible, and the transmitted signal is preferably digital. Enhancing the portability and reliability of the sensor can ensure it works properly in complex environment.

In order to satisfy the application of teleoperation robots, a six-axis force sensor which is based on the principle of resistance strain and has a stepped cross beam is designed. We install the circuit inside the sensor and transmitted the measurement result wirelessly through Bluetooth. The static calibration experiment method is designed and the decoupling algorithm based on coupling error modeling and piece-wise fitting is optimized, as well. After decoupling, the sensor reaches high precision standard.

## 2 Structure Design

### 2.1 Design and Analysis of the Elastomer

**Structure Design**
In order to make the sensor meet the requirements of small size and high precision, we propose a stepped cross beam structure based on the integral spoke-type cross beam structure. The structure is fixed and supported by four symmetrical rims. The cross beam consists of four prismatic main beams, and every main beam is connected to the rim through a floating beam. In particular, the end of the main beam which is near the floating beam is narrower, forming a stepped beam structure. According to analysis and test, this structure can reduce the inter-dimensional coupling of the sensor and improve the measurement accuracy. The strain gauges are glued around the four beams. They form strain bridges to sense the force components of three axes ($F_x$, $F_y$, $F_z$) and the torque components of three axes ($M_x$, $M_y$, $M_z$). Its structure is shown in Fig. 1. As the figure shows, 1 is the central cube, 2, 3, 4, 5 are the main beams, 6, 7, 8, and 9 are the floating beams, and 10, 11, 12, and 13 are the rims. The x-y-z coordinate system is right-handed.

**Finite Element Analysis**
After determining the elastomer structure, we should run finite element analysis to find the proper parameters. ANSYS is a user-friendly software for finite element analysis, and we use it to finish this job.

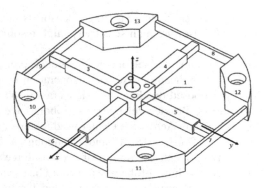

**Fig. 1.** The elastomer structure of the sensor

Firstly, the rough volume of the elastomer should be determined according to the application environment, i.e. the diameter and thickness. At a certain volume, the range and sensitivity of the sensor are contradictory, mainly affected by the thickness and length of the floating beam and the main beam. Actually, the sensitivity is positively related to the length of the main beam and the floating beam, and negatively related to the thickness, while the range is exactly opposite. Therefore, it is necessary to comprehensively consider the volume, sensitivity, overload capacity, etc. We constantly resize and simulate, and finally find the proper parameters as Table 1 shows.

The elastomer of the sensor is made of LY12. It is a kind of hard aluminum alloy with high hardness and fatigue resistance [10]. Its elastic modulus E is $72 \times 10^9$ Pa, and Poisson's ratio $\mu$ is 0.33.

**Table 1.** Parameters of the elastomer (mm)

|          | Main beam | Floating beam | Central cube | Center hole | Rim   | Rim screw hole |
|----------|-----------|---------------|--------------|-------------|-------|----------------|
| Length   | 27        | 32            | 10           |             |       |                |
| Width    | 3.8       | 1             | 10           |             |       |                |
| Height   | 3.8       | 3.8           | 8            | 8           | 8     | 8              |
| Diameter |           |               |              | 5           | 74/58 | 3.2            |

We use SOLIDWORKS 2017 to build the model, and import it into ANSYS 12.1. Select high-precision solid element SOLID95 and do meshing. The finite element model is shown in Fig. 2.

Then, load and solve. By analyzing the stress and strain, find the best placement of strain gauge and determine whether the structure meets the strength requirement.

Due to the symmetry of the structure, the stress and strain are the same when force or torque along the X and Y directions are loaded. Therefore, there are only four directions i.e. $F_x, F_z, M_x, M_z$ which need to be loaded and analyzed. The load value is determined by the design requirements. In the application scenario of this paper, we set the measurement range as: $F_{xy,z} = \pm 200$ N, $M_{xy,z} = \pm 2$ Nm, and the overload

**Fig. 2.** Finite element model of the elastomer

capacity as: $F_{x,y,z} = \pm300$ N, $M_{x,y,z} = \pm4$ Nm. Solving each load separately, we get the results shown in Fig. 3. The darker the color in the figure is, the greater the strain at that point is.

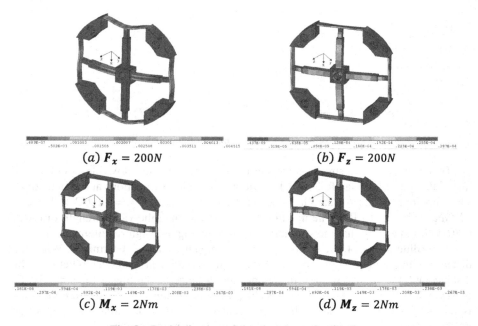

**Fig. 3.** Strain diagram of the elastomer after loading

The strain gauge is pasted on the main beams, and we need to find the exact position by the path mapping technique of ANSYS. The path is set to the surface of the main beam, and the strain of the main beam is mapped to it. We still load and solve separately in each dimension, and the result is shown in Fig. 4. In the figure, the horizontal axis represents the distance from the center cube to each point on the path, and the vertical axis represents the strain.

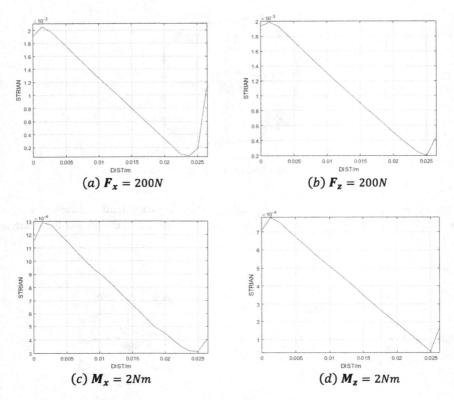

(a) $F_x = 200N$

(b) $F_z = 200N$

(c) $M_x = 2Nm$

(d) $M_z = 2Nm$

**Fig. 4.** Strain on the path mapped on the main beam

To ensure that the stress of the elastomer is within the allowable stress of the material, we need to load full-scale force/moment in all six directions at the same time. The maximum strain on the elastomer is $2.932 \times 10^{-3}$, $\varepsilon \times E = (2.932 \times 10^{-3}) \times 72$ GPa $\approx 211.104$ MPa. The maximum stress is less than the yield strength of LY12 (380 MPa), meaning that the structure meets the strength design requirements.

According to Fig. 4, the position of the strain gauges can be determined. When the distance is in the interval of 5 mm to 20 mm, there is a linear relationship between the distance and the strain. Besides, the shorter the distance is, the bigger the strain is. To increase the sensitivity as much as possible, the strain gauges which measure the force is attached about 4 mm away from the center cube, and the strain gauges which measure the torque is attached about 10 mm away from the center cube.

## 2.2  Packaging and Assembly

The structure of other mechanical parts is designed based on the assembly requirements and the parameters of the elastomer. The mechanical parts include the base, the top cover, the bottom cover and the force shaft. Figure 5(a) is a photograph of the six-axis force sensor, and Fig. 5(b) is an exploded view. Its overall height is 50 mm and outer diameter is 94 mm.

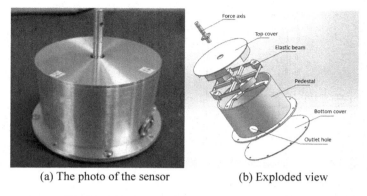

(a) The photo of the sensor        (b) Exploded view

**Fig. 5.** The six-axis force sensor that we design

# 3   Circuit Design

The six-axis force sensor consists of the elastomer, metal strain gauges, the measuring circuit and other mechanical parts. Figure 6 shows the system diagram of the sensor.

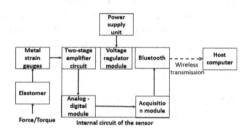

**Fig. 6.** System diagram of the sensor

## 3.1   Strain Bridge

The working principle of the resistance strain sensor is based on the resistance strain effect [11]. Each force/torque dimension of the sensor is measured through a four-arm full-bridge circuit. According to the analysis in Sect. 2.1 - **Finite element analysis**, the positions of strain gauges are shown in Fig. 7(a), and the bridge circuit is shown in Fig. 7(b) (take the force in X direction as example).

We choose the strain gauge BF350 for our sensor. Its initial resistance value R0 is 350 Ω and the sensitivity coefficient K is 2.10. According to the theoretical calculation [12] based on the actual position of the strain gauge, when the supply voltage of the bridge is ±5 V, the voltages of each direction at full scale are:

$$F_x(F_y): 15.57 \text{ mV}; \quad F_z: 21.69 \text{ mV};$$

$$M_x(M_y): 6.55 \text{ mV}; \quad M_z: 8.31 \text{ mV}$$

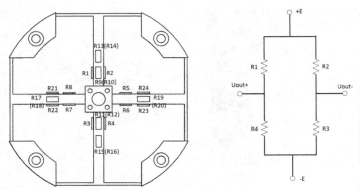

(a) Patch position of the gauges (b) The bridge circuit (X direction force)

**Fig. 7.** Patch position of the gauges and bridge circuit

## 3.2 Two-Stage Amplification Circuit

The output of the strain bridges is a six-channel differential voltage value in the millivolt range. To improve the sensitivity of the sensor, we use the amplification circuit to amplify the differential voltage to about ±9 V. According to the theoretical full-scale output of the bridges calculated in Sect. 2.1, the amplification factor of the six-channel amplifier circuit can be determined: 610 times in $F_x(F_y)$ directions, 438 times in $F_z$ direction, and 1451 times in $M_x(M_y)$ directions, 1143 times in $M_z$ direction.

Since the amplification factor of the circuit is relatively large, single-stage amplification may cause significant distortion of the signal. So the two-stage amplification circuit is considered.

We choose AD620 as the core of the first-stage amplification circuit, and its gain formula is:

$$G = \frac{49.4 \text{ k}\Omega}{R_G} + 1 \tag{1}$$

where $R_G$ is the external gain resistor. To prevent excessive noise, the magnification is set to about 100 [13].

TL084 is used as the core of the second-stage amplification circuit, and the same operational amplifier circuit amplifies the signal to ±9 V eventually [14].

## 3.3 Signal Processing Circuit

The signal processing circuit is designed based on the microcontroller STM32F103ZET6, including A/D conversion, data processing and transmission functions.

The 16-bit ADC - AD7606 can sample 6 voltage data of the sensor simultaneously at a speed of 200KSPS. The wireless transmission of the signal is performed by the master-slave HC-06 Bluetooth. And the entire signal processing circuit is embedded inside the sensor to achieve miniaturization and productization.

The procedure is written based on the platform of STM32F103. Firstly, set a 2-10 ms timer interrupt. The interrupt service function queries the data received by the serial port to determine whether to enable the SPI timing and collect the voltage of the AD7606. If data is received, apply the moving average filtering to obtain the final value. After decoupling, transmit the data of force/torque to PC by Bluetooth. The flow chart of the whole system is shown in Fig. 8. The collecting rate of the signal is up to 500 Hz, and the transmission distance is up to 8 m.

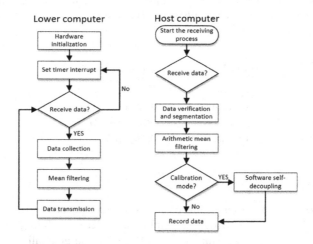

**Fig. 8.** Flow chart of the collection system

# 4    Calibration and Decoupling

## 4.1    Static Calibration Experiment

The static calibration method is carried out by using the weight. This kind of method is sample, stable and can apply load in one direction accurately. The calibration table we use is shown in Fig. 9, and accuracy grade of the weight is M1.

The linearity error in each dimension is shown in Table 2.

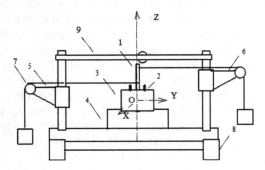

**Fig. 9.** Calibration table and the loading method. 1 is Force transmission shaft, 2 is force column, 3 is sensor, 4 is Indexing plate, 5(6) is left (right) slider, 7 is pulley, 8 is bench base, 9 is additional slider

**Table 2.** Linearity error in all directions

| Direction | $F_x$ | $F_y$ | $F_z$ |
|---|---|---|---|
| Linearity error % | 0.32 | 0.52 | 0.23 |
| Direction | $M_x$ | $M_y$ | $M_z$ |
| Linearity error % | 0.32 | 0.22 | 1.22 |

## 4.2  Decoupling

We improve the decoupling algorithm of six-axis force sensor proposed by our laboratory [15] which is based on modeling coupling and piecewise fitting. Compared with the traditional decoupling algorithm which is based on the generalized inverse of the solution matrix [16], the former has a small amount of calculation and does not produce ill-conditioned matrixes.

Due to the inter-dimensional coupling, the output of each channel is related to the force/torque of all dimensions. It is necessary to subtract the component of the coupling direction.

We improve and adopt a stepped decoupling method. Instead of calculating each substep independently, the calculation results of each substep are used in the following substeps. The process of decoupling can be expressed by Eqs. (2) and (3). And compared with the original algorithm, it makes the precision higher.

$$\begin{cases} U'_1 = U_1 \\ U'_2 = U_2 - \sum_{i=1,i\neq2}^{2} h_{2_i}(U'_i) \\ U'_3 = U_3 - \sum_{i=1,i\neq3}^{3} h_{3_i}(U'_i) \\ U'_4 = U_4 - \sum_{i=1,i\neq4}^{4} h_{4_i}(U'_i) \\ U'_5 = U_5 - \sum_{i=1,i\neq5}^{5} h_{5_i}(U'_i) \\ U'_6 = U_6 - \sum_{i=1,i\neq6}^{6} h_{6_i}(U'_i) \end{cases} \tag{2}$$

$$\begin{cases} D_1 = k'_1 U'_1 \\ D_2 = k'_2 U'_2 \\ D_3 = k'_3 U'_3 \\ D_4 = k'_4 U'_4 \\ D_5 = k'_5 U'_5 \\ D_6 = k'_6 U'_6 \end{cases} \tag{3}$$

where $h_{j_i}(U_i), j \in [1,6], i \in [1,6]$ represents the voltage component in j direction which is caused by force/torque in $i$ direction; $D_1$ to $D_6$ represent the force/torque value after decoupling. $k'_1$ to $k'_6$ represent linear coefficients of six directions.

A large number of experimental data show that the inter-dimensional coupling in the positive and negative directions is different. Therefore, we need to do decoupling separately. After zero calibration, the fitting result can be expressed as:

$$\begin{cases} h_{j_i}(U_i) = \begin{cases} f_{j_i}(U_i) & U_i \geq 0 \\ g_{j_i}(U_i) & U_i < 0 \end{cases} \\ f_{j_i}(U_i) = a_{j_i} U_i^2 + b_{j_i} U_i \\ g_{j_i}(U_i) = b'_{j_i} U_i^2 + b'_{j_i} U_i \end{cases} \tag{4}$$

### 4.3  Error Analysis

The error of the six-axis force sensor can be divided into two types: class I error and class II error. Class I error (non-linearity error) reflects the linearity of the sensor, and class II error (coupling error) reflects the inter-dimension coupling error. The definition of the two kinds of errors can be expressed by Eq. (5) where, $e_{i(max)}$ refers to the maximum deviation between the measured value and the actual value in the $i$ direction, $y_{i(F.S)}$ refers to the force/torque of full scale in the $i$ direction, $y_{ij(max)}$ to $y_{in(max)}$ respectively mean the maximum value measured in the $i$ direction when a single force/torque is applied in the j(k, l, m, n) direction.

$$
\begin{cases}
\textit{Class I error} = \left|\dfrac{e_{i(max)}}{y_{i(F.S)}}\right| \\[4mm]
\textit{Class II error} = \sqrt{\dfrac{\left|y_{ij(max)}\right|^2 + \left|y_{ik(max)}\right|^2 + \left|y_{il(max)}\right|^2 + \left|y_{im(max)}\right|^2 + \left|y_{in(max)}\right|^2}{\left|y_{i(F.S)}\right|^2}}
\end{cases}
\tag{5}
$$

Calculate the class I error and class II error of the six-axis force sensor according to Eq. (5), the result is shown in Table 3. It can be seen that, after decoupling, the class II error of the sensor is greatly reduced. And the coupling error is less than 3%, having been up to the standard of high precision.

**Table 3.** Precision comparison (Before decoupling & After decoupling) (%)

|  |  | $F_x$ | $F_y$ | $F_z$ | $M_x$ | $M_y$ | $M_z$ |
|---|---|---|---|---|---|---|---|
| *Class I error* | Undecoupled | 0.38 | 0.29 | 0.25 | 0.30 | 0.27 | 1.18 |
|  | Decoupled | 0.438 | 0.29 | 0.25 | 0.30 | 0.27 | 1.18 |
| *Class II error* | Undecoupled | 3.01 | 2.02 | 2.37 | 102.45 | 107.41 | 3.25 |
|  | Decoupled | 0.59 | 2.02 | 2.15 | 2.57 | 0.42 | 2.32 |

## 5 Conclusion

Aiming at the design requirements of high precision, miniaturization and simple wiring, we design a miniaturized wireless six-axis force/torque sensor for teleoperation robots. The optimization of the mechanical structure effectively reduces the volume of the sensor. And make it satisfy the application requirement of various teleoperation robots. We embed the MCU inside the sensor and use Bluetooth to transmit the signal. Real-time collection and wireless transmission avoid interference when the robot is in complex environment. At the same time, the static calibration method and the decoupling algorithm are used to reduce the inter-dimension coupling error of the sensor and be up to the standard of high precision.

## References

1. Song, A.G.: Force-sensing teleoperation robot (1): the development and current status of technology. J. Nanjing Univ. Inform. Sci. Technol. **5**(01), 1–19 (2013)
2. Yi, R.Z., Li, H.L., Song, A.G.: Man-machine interaction system for robot tele-operation based on multiple sensors. Meas. Control. Technol. **37**(09), 56–59 (2018)
3. Zhou, C.F., Wang, L.: Welding information acquisition system of tele-operation welding robot. Weld. Join. **07**(01), 1–6 (2018)
4. Song, A.G.: Research on the technology of human-computer interaction and tele-presence tele-operation robot. Sci. Technol. Rev. **33**(23), 100–109 (2015)
5. Song, A.G., Ni, D.J.: Force tele-presence tele-robot (4): evaluation of operational performance. J. Nanjing Univ. Inform. Sci. Technol. **6**(03), 211–220 (2014)

6. Ni, Z.Q., Miao, W., Liu, Z.D.: Survey on medical robotics. J. Mech. Eng. **51**(13), 45–52 (2015)
7. Liu, M.Z., Tuo, X., Li, G.Z., et al.: Research on the application of robots in comprehensive monitoring in nuclear emergency radiation environment. Robot. Appl. **03**(01), 21–23 (2011)
8. Dong, Y.C., Liu, Q.S., Qian, J.H.: Research on characteristics and test methods of robots used for disaster relief in nuclear power plants. Robot. Appl. **05**(01), 33–35 (2013)
9. Zhao, J.C.: China's first cargo spacecraft, Tianzhou-1, successfully docked with Tiangong No. 2 space laboratory. Science **03**(01), 31 (2017)
10. Vanko, B., Stanček, L., Čeretka, M., et al.: Properties of EN AW-2024 wrought aluminum alloy after casting with crystallization under pressure. Sci. Proc. Fac. Mech. Eng. **23**(1), 58–65 (2015)
11. Payo, I.: Six-axis column-type force and moment sensor for robotic applications. IEEE Sens. J. **18**(17), 6996–7003 (2018)
12. Li, A.: Design and application of miniaturized multi-dimension force sensor. Southeast University, Electronic Engineering (2017)
13. Zhang, Y.Q.: The impact analyses of zero drift in differential amplifier circuit. Metrol. Measure. Technol. **37**(05), 51–52 (2017)
14. Wang, W.M., Fan, X.Z.: Signal detection system based on TL084C. Electron. Compon. Device Appl. **12**(06), 24–26+30 (2010)
15. Mao, C., Song, A.G., Gao, X., Xu, G.Z.: Research and application of static decoupling algorithm for six - axis force/torque sensor. Chin. J. Sens. Actuators **28**(02), 205–210 (2015)
16. Wu, X.X., Song, A.G., Wang, Z.: The study on static decoupling algorithm for six-axis force sensor and static calibration. Chin. J. Sens. Actuators **26**(06), 851–856 (2013)

# Autonomous Control of Unmanned Aircraft Systems

# Reorientation Control for a Microsatellite with Pointing and Angular Velocity Constraints

Zhen-xin Feng[✉], Jian-guo Guo, and Jun Zhou

Institute of Precision Guidance and Control,
Northwestern Polytechnical University, Xi'an 710072, China
zxfeng@mail.nwpu.edu.cn

**Abstract.** An attitude reorientation control is proposed for a microsatellite with pointing and angular velocity constraints. In order to guarantee the measure performances of the optical instruments equipped on the microsatellite, these optical instruments are required to point their boresight along a target direction while keeping away from direct exposure to the bright celestial bodies. However, the limited space of the microsatellite may lead to a more complicated attitude path planning compared with the traditional large spacecrafts. In this paper, a reorientation control method integrating the logarithmic convex potential function with the fixed barrier Lyapunov function is introduced to solve the attitude path planning issue. Comparing with the existing on-line path planning methods, the proposed method can efficiently reduce the computation burden and is very fit for the microsatellite with low computation ability. Moreover, the angular velocity constraints caused by saturation limitation of low-rate gyro or mission specification requirement are also well tackled by the proposed method. The ultimate uniformly stabilization for the closed-loop system is achieved without violating the considered constraints. Finally, the simulations are verified in order to demonstrate the effectiveness of the proposed reorientation control method for a microsatellite.

**Keywords:** Reorientation control · Microsatellite · Attitude constraint · Angular velocity constraint

## 1 Introduction

During the past two decades, hundreds of microsatellites are launched and applied in technology demonstrations, scientific researches and even commercial applications in the world. The microsatellites are playing more and more important role in modern space exploring fields due to their low cost and fast response ability. However, with the increasing complicated mission requirements, the constraints required by the actuators, payloads, and sensors equipped on the microsatellite within the limited space may lead to the path planning rather difficult compared with the large spacecraft. For instance, the optical instruments such as optical camera or star tracker are required to point their boresight along a target direction while avoiding the bright objects directly enter into the limited field of view. In addition, the physical limitations such as the angular rate

© Springer Nature Switzerland AG 2019
H. Yu et al. (Eds.): ICIRA 2019, LNAI 11741, pp. 717–726, 2019.
https://doi.org/10.1007/978-3-030-27532-7_62

measurement and the control torque should also be taken into account. Owing to the perspective development for microsatellite, the attitude reorientation control issue with multi-constraints has attracted many research interests [1, 2].

For attitude reorientation, [3] proposes the attitude control method which can avoid bright objects and maintain communications with ground station by creating ideal tangential paths around forbidden zones using a unit sphere. [4] presents a two-stage approach by using heuristic methods for time-optimal attitude constrained control. In [5], the unit sphere is discretized into a polyhedron-based graph and a constrained attitude A* pathfinding control method for microsatellites is proposed. However, the aforementioned methods are almost on-line path planning approaches and may lead to heavy computation burden with the increasing number of constraints. Moreover, [6, 7] construct a convex parameterization of forbidden and mandatory zones and propose a strictly convex logarithmic potential function for feedback control in order to solve the pointing constraints. For actuator and rate limitations, Shen et al. [8] propose a rigid-body attitude tracking control under actuator faults and angular velocity constraints. [9] proposes a nonlinear control under the constraints of assigned velocity and actuator.

Inspired by the aforementioned work, the guaranteed boundaries and performance control method is proposed for a microsatellite with pointing constraints and angular velocity limits simultaneously in this paper. The logarithmic-type convex potential function is introduced to solve the attitude path planning issue. It can efficiently reduce the computation burden compared with the on-line slew maneuver methods. Thereby, it is very fit for the microsatellite with low computation ability. In addition, the angular velocity constraints caused by the saturation limitation of low-rate gyro or instruments equipped on the microsatellite are well tackled by the fixed barrier Lyapunov function. The ultimate uniformly stability is maintained for the closed-loop control system under multiple constraints by the proposed method.

The organization of this paper is outlined as follows. In Sect. 2, the microsatellite kinematics and some preliminaries are given. In Sect. 3, the constrained attitude stabilization control is designed and analyzed. Subsequently, the numerical simulations are performed to verify the proposed method, conclusions are drawn at last.

**Notations:** $\otimes$ denotes the quaternion multiplication operator, $\times$ denotes the vector cross product. $\nabla(\cdot), \nabla^2(\cdot)$ imply the gradient and Hessian of function $(\cdot)$ respectively. The operator $\text{Vec}(\cdot)$ denotes the vector part of $(\cdot)$, and $(\cdot)^*$ represents the complex conjugate of $(\cdot)$.

# 2 Problem Formulation and Preliminaries

The microsatellite kinematics in terms of the unit quaternion are given as follows

$$\dot{Q} = \frac{1}{2}Q \otimes v(\omega) = \frac{1}{2}\begin{bmatrix} -q^{\mathrm{T}} \\ S(q) + q_0 I_3 \end{bmatrix}\omega \tag{1}$$

where $\omega = [\omega_x, \omega_y, \omega_z]^{\mathrm{T}}$ is the inertial angular velocity vector of the microsatellite with respect to an inertial frame and expressed in the body frame $B$. The function is defined as the mapping $v(\omega) = [0 \quad \omega^{\mathrm{T}}]^{\mathrm{T}}$, and the matrix $S(x) \in \Re^{3\times3}$ is a skew-symmetric matrix satisfying $S(x)y = x \times y$ for any vectors $x,y \in \Re^3$.

The attitude dynamics of rigid microsatellite are described by Euler's rotational equation

$$J\dot{\omega} = R(\omega)J\omega + u \tag{2}$$

where $J = \mathrm{diag}\{J_x, J_y, J_z\}$ denotes the inertia matrix of microsatellite in the body frame, $u = [M_x, M_y, M_z]^{\mathrm{T}}$ represents the control torque input vector about the body axes. $R(\omega)$ is

$$R(\omega) = \begin{bmatrix} 0 & \omega_z & -\omega_y \\ -\omega_z & 0 & \omega_x \\ \omega_y & -\omega_x & 0 \end{bmatrix} \tag{3}$$

As depicted in Fig. 1, the attitude pointing constraints can be illustrated as follows: $x$ denotes the bright object (e.g. the Sun) vector in the inertial coordinate. $y$ represents the boresight vector of optical instrument equipped on the microsatellite in the body axis. In order to ensure the observation performance of the optical instrument, the vector $y$ must keep away from direct exposure to the bright object vector $x$.

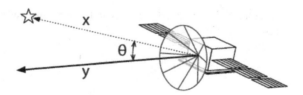

**Fig. 1.** The illustrate of attitude forbidden zone [7]

Therefore, the relationship between $x$ and $y$ can be expressed by the minimum exclusion cone angle $\theta$

$$x \cdot y' < \cos\theta \tag{4}$$

where

$$y' = Q \otimes y \otimes Q^* = y - 2(q^{\mathrm{T}}q)y + 2(q^{\mathrm{T}}y)q - 2q_0(y \times q) \tag{5}$$

Furthermore, After some algebraic manipulations, we thus obtain

$$Q^{\mathrm{T}}(M - \cos\theta I_4)Q = Q^{\mathrm{T}}\widetilde{M}Q < 0 \tag{6}$$

where

$$M = \begin{bmatrix} x^{\mathrm{T}}y & (y \times x)^{\mathrm{T}} \\ y \times x & xy^{\mathrm{T}} + yx^{\mathrm{T}} - (x^{\mathrm{T}}y)I_{3\times3} \end{bmatrix} \tag{7}$$

**Lemma 1** [7]: Consider a logarithmic-type convex potential function:

$$V(Q) = -k_1 \|Q - Q_d\|^2 \log\left(-\frac{Q^{\mathrm{T}}\tilde{M}Q}{2}\right) \tag{8}$$

It satisfies the following conditions: ①. $V(Q_d) = 0$. ②. $V(Q) > 0$, for all $Q \in Q_p \backslash \{Q_d\}$. ③. $\nabla^2 V(Q)$ is positive definite for all $Q \in Q_p$. Where $Q_d$ denote the desired attitude. The proof can be seen in [7].

**Remark 1:** Similarly, the attitude reorientation problem with multiple forbidden zones can also be illustrated by the logarithmic-type convex potential function as follows.

$$V_M(Q) = -k_1 \|Q - Q_d\|^2 \sum_{j=1}^{m} \sum_{i=1}^{n} \log\left(-\frac{Q^{\mathrm{T}}\tilde{M}_i^j Q}{2}\right) \tag{9}$$

where $i = 1, 2, \ldots, n$ denotes the $i$ th forbidden bright object, $j = 1, 2, \ldots, m$ represents the $j$th instruments.

In addition, the angular velocity must vary in a limit range owing to the gyro measurement and sensor requirements.

$$\mathcal{W} = \left\{ \omega \in \Re^3 \middle| |\omega_i| \leq \omega_{i,\max} \right\} \tag{10}$$

where $i = x, y, z$.

Therefore, the control objective of this paper is to design a control law that can satisfy the attitude pointing accuracy without transgressing the angular velocity constraints and attitude forbidden zones.

## 3    Control Law Design

In this section, the controller is designed with both pointing constraints and angular velocity constraints, then the stability analysis is given by Lyapunov stability theorems.

## 3.1    Constraint Control Design

The gradient of (9) is

$$
\nabla V_M = \left[ -k_1 \frac{\partial \|\boldsymbol{Q} - \boldsymbol{Q}_d\|^2}{\partial \boldsymbol{Q}} \sum_{j=1}^{m} \sum_{i=1}^{n} \log\left( -\frac{\boldsymbol{Q}^{\mathrm{T}} \tilde{\boldsymbol{M}}_i^j \boldsymbol{Q}}{2} \right) + \|\boldsymbol{Q} - \boldsymbol{Q}_d\|^2 \frac{2k_1 \boldsymbol{Q}^{\mathrm{T}} \tilde{\boldsymbol{M}}}{\boldsymbol{Q}^{\mathrm{T}} \tilde{\boldsymbol{M}} \boldsymbol{Q}} \right]
$$
$$
= \left[ (2k_1 \boldsymbol{Q}_d^{\mathrm{T}}) \sum_{j=1}^{m} \sum_{i=1}^{n} \log\left( -\frac{\boldsymbol{Q}^{\mathrm{T}} \tilde{\boldsymbol{M}}_i^j \boldsymbol{Q}}{2} \right) + \|\boldsymbol{Q} - \boldsymbol{Q}_d\|^2 \frac{2k_1 \boldsymbol{Q}^{\mathrm{T}} \tilde{\boldsymbol{M}}}{\boldsymbol{Q}^{\mathrm{T}} \tilde{\boldsymbol{M}} \boldsymbol{Q}} \right]
\tag{11}
$$

To ensure both pointing and angular velocity constraints, we choose a Lyapunov candidate combining (9) with a logarithmic-type barrier Lyapunov function [12]

$$
V_2 = V_M(\boldsymbol{Q}) + \frac{1}{2} \sum_{i=1}^{3} \log\left( \frac{\omega_{\mathrm{max}}^2}{\omega_{\mathrm{max}}^2 - \omega_i^2} \right)
\tag{12}
$$

The derivation of (12) is

$$
\dot{V}_2 = \nabla V_M^{\mathrm{T}} (\dot{\boldsymbol{Q}}) + \boldsymbol{\omega}^{\mathrm{T}} \Xi \dot{\boldsymbol{\omega}}
\tag{13}
$$

where $\Xi = \mathrm{diag}\left\{ 1/(\omega_{\mathrm{max}}^2 - \omega_{\mathrm{x}}^2), 1/(\omega_{\mathrm{max}}^2 - \omega_{\mathrm{y}}^2), 1/(\omega_{\mathrm{max}}^2 - \omega_{\mathrm{z}}^2) \right\}$, and $\omega_{\mathrm{max}}$ denotes the maximum feasible angular velocity.

Substitute (1), (9) into (13), it obtains

$$
\dot{V}_2 = \nabla V_M^{\mathrm{T}} \left( \frac{1}{2} \boldsymbol{Q} \otimes v(\boldsymbol{\omega}) \right) + \boldsymbol{\omega}^{\mathrm{T}} \Xi \boldsymbol{J}^{-1} [R(\boldsymbol{\omega}) \boldsymbol{J} \boldsymbol{\omega} + \boldsymbol{u}]
\tag{14}
$$

Further, we have

$$
\dot{V}_2 = \boldsymbol{\omega}^{\mathrm{T}} \mathrm{Vec}\left( -\nabla V_M^* \otimes \frac{1}{2} \boldsymbol{Q} \right) + \boldsymbol{\omega}^{\mathrm{T}} \Xi \boldsymbol{J}^{-1} [R(\boldsymbol{\omega}) \boldsymbol{J} \boldsymbol{\omega} + \boldsymbol{u}]
\tag{15}
$$

Thereby, the stabilization control law is designed as

$$
\boldsymbol{u} = \boldsymbol{J} \Xi^{-1} \left( -k\boldsymbol{\omega} + \mathrm{Vec}\left( \nabla V_M^* \otimes \frac{1}{2} \boldsymbol{Q} \right) - \Xi \boldsymbol{J}^{-1} R(\boldsymbol{\omega}) \boldsymbol{J} \boldsymbol{\omega} \right)
\tag{16}
$$

## 3.2    Stability Analysis

**Theorem 1:** For (1), (2), with the control law (16), the control system achieves ultimate uniform stability without violating the pointing and angular velocity constraints.

**Proof:** Substitute (16) into (15), it obtains

$$\dot{V}_2 = -k\omega^{\mathrm{T}}\omega \le 0 \tag{17}$$

Since $\dot{V}_2 \le 0$ and $V_2 > 0$, this implies that $\omega$ and $Q$ are bounded, and then $V_2$ is bounded. Then using Barbalat's lemma [10], one has $\omega \to 0$ as $t \to \infty$. Furthermore, by using LaSalle's invariance principle [11], it will lead to $Q \to Q_d$ as $t \to \infty$. By using the Lemma 1 it is clear that the pointing constraints are guaranteed. Moreover, within the Lemma in [12], which implies that if $\omega$ is bounded then $\omega$ is varying in its specified range without violation due to the unboundedness properties of the barrier Lyapunov function. Therefore, both the pointing constraints and the angular rate constraints can be guaranteed by the proposed method. This complete the proof.

## 4    Numerical Simulations

In this section, numerical simulations are demonstrated in order to verify the effectiveness of the proposed method. It is assumed that a microsatellite carries an optical payload with a fixed boresight in the microsatellite body axes directly along the Z direction. The initial simulation parameters can be seen in Table 1, and it is assumed that there exist four constrained objects in the attitude slew path. In the simulation, the all the constrained objects satisfy that $Q_0^{\mathrm{T}}\tilde{M}_i Q_0 < 0$ and $Q_0^{\mathrm{T}}\tilde{M}_i Q_0 < 0$, where $i = 1, 2, 3, 4$. It indicates that the initial attitude and desired attitude located outside the forbidden zones and this can be the precondition of the proposed method. The microsatellite's moment of inertia is $J = \mathrm{diag}\{[1.25, 9.65, 9.65]\}\mathrm{kg} \cdot \mathrm{m}^2$.

**Table 1.** Simulation Parameters

| Parameters | Value |
|---|---|
| Initial attitude | $[-0.470, -0.187, -0.735, -0.45]$ |
| Desired attitude | $[0.382, 0.592, -0.675, -0.215]$ |
| Initial angular rate vector | $[0, 0, 0]$ |
| Maximum angular velocity | $5°/s$ |
| Constrained object 1 | $[0.174, -0.934, -0.034]$ |
| Constrained object 2 | $[0, 0.707, 0.707]$ |
| Constrained object 3 | $[-0.853, 0.436, -0.286]$ |
| Constrained object 4 | $[-0.122, -0.14, -0.983]$ |

### 4.1    Single Attitude Constraint

In this subsection, we firstly assume that the microsatellite slew from the initial attitude to the desired attitude while avoiding the constraint object 1 with the exclusion angle of $40°$. In the simulation, the method in reference [7] is compared in order to validate the effectiveness of our proposed method. The control law in reference [7] is following

$$u = -k\omega + \mathrm{Vec}\left(\nabla V_M^* \otimes \frac{1}{2}Q\right) \tag{18}$$

In order to make the comparison as fair as possible, the control gains are chosen as the same where $k = 20, k_1 = 4.8$. In Fig. 2(a), both the proposed method (dotted line) and method in reference [7] (solid line) can achieve that the attitude converge to the desired attitude eventually almost at the same speed. At the same time, we can clearly see that the Index $<0$ in Fig. 2(b) with both methods, which means the constrained zone is avoided successfully owing to the (6).

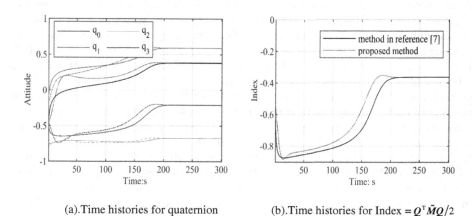

(a).Time histories for quaternion          (b).Time histories for Index $= Q^T \tilde{M}Q/2$

**Fig. 2.** Time histories for quaternion

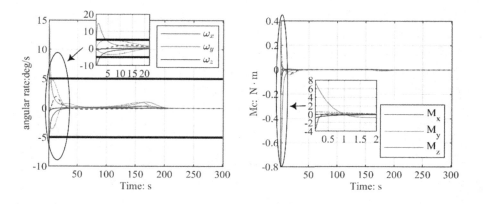

(a).Time histories for angular velocities          (b).Time histories for control torque

**Fig. 3.** Time histories for angular velocities

However, the angular velocities vary within the limited range under our proposed method (dotted line) whereas the control law in [7] cannot prevent the angular rates from violating the constraints (solid line) in Fig. 3(a). Moreover, It is also clear that the consumption of the control torque is larger within control method in [7] compared with our proposed method in Fig. 3(b). In other words, the angular velocity constraints are ensured and the control consumption requirements can be properly fulfilled simultaneously within our proposed method.

## 4.2 Multiple Attitude Constraints

In this subsection, we assumes that there exist four constrained zones in Table 1 and the exclusion angle is 40°, 40°, 30°, 20° respectively. Similar to Subsec. 4.1, we introduce the method in reference [7] to compare the effectiveness of our proposed method under multiple constrained zones where the control gains are the same where $k = 15, k_1 = 0.2$. In Figs. 4 and 5, The dotted line and solid line represent the simulation results under the reference [7] and the proposed method respectively. In Fig. 4(a), the attitude slew to the desired attitude eventually under both methods. At the same time, all the forbidden zones are avoided (in Fig. 4(b)). However, under the same control gains, the proposed method can achieve fast convergence rate than the method in reference [7]. Although the angular rates vary in their specified set with $|\omega_i| \leq 5°/s, i = x, y, z$ all the time In Fig. 5(a), the histories of the control torque are varying in different way comparing with the two methods. The proposed method requires less control torque and is more fit for the microsatellite with less control ability. Therefore, our proposed method can guarantee both the pointing constraints and angular velocity constraints and need less control torque.

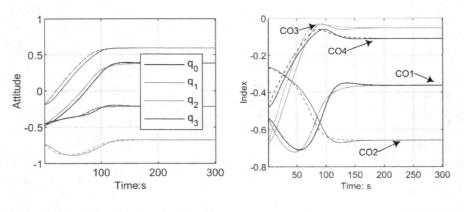

(a).Time histories for quaternion        (b).Time histories for Index $= Q^{\mathrm{T}}\tilde{M}Q/2$

**Fig. 4.** Time histories for quaternion

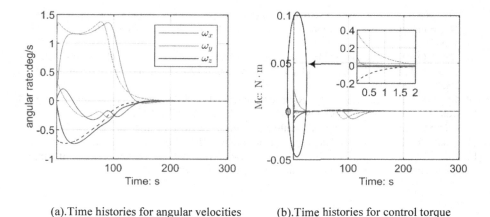

(a).Time histories for angular velocities     (b).Time histories for control torque

**Fig. 5.** Time histories for angular velocities

## 5  Conclusions

In this paper, an attitude reorientation control method is presented for microsatellite with pointing and angular velocity constraints simultaneously. The convex potential function is developed to address the pointing constraints as the attitude slewing. Moreover, the fixed barrier Lyapunov function method is inserted into the control law in order to guarantee the angular velocity without transgressing the constraints. Numerical simulations demonstrate that the proposed method can guarantee both the pointing constraints and angular velocity constraints while maintaining the desired attitude eventually. Future directions main focus on the microsatellites with external disturbances and control input nonlinearities.

## References

1. McInnes, C.R.: Large angle slew maneuvers with autonomous sun vector avoidance. J. Guidance Control Dyn. **17**(4), 875–877 (1994)
2. Wie, B., Lu, J.: Feedback control logic for spacecraft eigenaxis rotations under slew rate and control constraints. J. Guidance Control Dyn. **18**(6), 1372–1379 (1995)
3. Hablani, H.B.: Attitude commands avoiding bright objects and maintaining communications with ground station. J. Guidance Control Dyn. **22**(6), 759–767 (1999)
4. Melton, R.G.: Hybrid methods for determining time-optimal, constrained spacecraft reorientation maneuvers. Acta Astronaut. **94**, 294–301 (2014)
5. Kjellberg, H., Lightsey, E.: Discretized constrained attitude pathfinding and control for satellites. J. Guidance Control Dyn. **36**(5), 1301–1309 (2013)
6. Kim, Y., Mesbahi, M., Singh, G., Hadaegh, F.: On the convex parametrization of spacecraft orientation in the presence of constraints and its applications. IEEE Trans. Aerosp. Electron. Syst. **46**(3), 1097–1109 (2010)

7. Lee, U., Mesbahi, M.: Feedback control for spacecraft reorientation under attitude constraints via convex potentials. IEEE Trans. Aerosp. Electron. Syst. 50(4), 2578–2592 (2014)

8. Shen, Q., Yue, C., Goh, C.H., Wu, B., et al.: Rigid-body attitude tracking control under actuator faults and angular velocity constraints. IEEE/ASME Trans. Mechatron. 23(3), 1338–1349 (2018)

9. Hu, Q.L., Li, B., Zhang, Y.M.: Robust attitude control design for spacecraft under assigned velocity and control constraints. ISA Trans. 52(4), 480–493 (2013)

10. Slotine, J.J.E., Li, W.: Applied Nonlinear Control. Prentice Hall, New Jersey (1991)

11. Khalil, H.K.: Nonlinear Systems, 3rd edn. Prentice Hall, New Jersey (2002)

12. Tee, K.P., Ge, S.S., Tay, E.H.: Barrier Lyapunov functions for the control of output-constrained nonlinear systems. Automatica 45(4), 918–927 (2009)

# Real-Time Trajectory Replanning for Quadrotor Using OctoMap and Uniform B-Splines

Jia Hu, Zhaowei Ma, Yifeng Niu$^{(\boxtimes)}$, Wenli Tian, and Wenchen Yao

National University of Defense Technology, Changsha 410073, China
niuyifeng@nudt.edu.com

**Abstract.** In this paper, we present a real-time local trajectory replanning method for quadrotors in unknown cluttered environment. In the process of following the global trajectory, an octree-based environment map is built using the onboard sensor. The map is stored in a fixed-size three-dimensional circular buffer to build a local map, which is centered on the quadrotor and updated in real time with the movement of the quadrotor. Based on the local map, we adopt a sampling-based path planning method to find the initial safe path passing through obstacles, and then use uniform b-spline to convert the path consisting of line segments into a smooth and dynamical feasible trajectory. The local trajectory replanning is performed at 0.5 s intervals until reaching the target point. Through simulation experiments and comparison with existing methods, we verify the effectiveness of the method we proposed.

**Keywords:** Local Octomap · Uniform B-splines · Trajectory replanning

## 1 Introduction

Micro aerial vehicles (MAVs), such as the quadrotor, has been widely used in many applications such as aerial photography, inspection, logistics and rescue due to its high agility, high maneuverability and easy control [1]. In most cases, the mission environment of MAV is unknown or there are unpredictable obstacles. To meet the need for autonomous flight in unknown environment, real-time local replanning is of great significance in producing smooth and dynamical feasible trajectories.

When the quadrotor is performing a task, such as logistics, it is first necessary to plan a global trajectory from the starting point to the target point for the drone with the situation of no environmental information. Then, when the quadrotor following the global trajectory, the onboard sensor detects the environment in real time and performs local trajectory replanning to respond quickly to the newly observed obstacles, ensuring that the trajectory is collision-free.

Based on the perception from onboard sensors, an environmental description can be established. We gradually build an octree-based environment occupancy map (Octo-Map) [2] during the flight. Since the perception range of the sensor is limited, a bounded

© Springer Nature Switzerland AG 2019
H. Yu et al. (Eds.): ICIRA 2019, LNAI 11741, pp. 727–741, 2019.
https://doi.org/10.1007/978-3-030-27532-7_63

map is needed for local replanning to ensure efficient and fast collision detection. We use a fixed-size three-dimensional circular buffer to build the local octomap [3]. The local octomap is centered on the quadrotor and moves together with the quadrotor.

Given a three-dimensional environment occupancy map, a sample-based path planning approach can be used to find a collision-free path. The path is often not smooth enough for quadrotors to follow. Researchers generally adopt polynomial or b-splines to fit waypoints to generate a smooth and feasible trajectory.

Mellinger et al. [4] proposed that the quadrotor system has the differential flatness characteristic that can reduce the full state space to the 3-D positions and the yaw angle and their derivatives. The differentiability of b-spline allows it to be followed by a suitably designed geometry controller [14].

According to this feature of b-spline, we design a novel method for local trajectory replanning. The method employs an RGB-D camera mounted on quadrotor to sense the environment and build local octomap. Then use the RRT* algorithm to search the initial security path and get the waypoints. A uniform b-spline method is used to fit the waypoints to obtain a smooth trajectory that can be followed by quadrotor. The smoothed trajectory will deviate from the initial path, causing the quadrotor to collide with the obstacle when following the trajectory. To solve this problem, we use the method of increasing waypoints to ensure the safety of the trajectory. A local trajectory replanner is designed using the method proposed above. The planner combines the local octomap to perform local trajectory replanning at a fixed period until reaching the target point. We summarize our contributions as follows:

(1) A method for building local octomap by using circular buffer is designed.
(2) We design a local trajectory planner, which combines an RRT*-based path planning method to find an initial safe path and a b-spline based method to convert the path to a smooth and dynamical feasible trajectory. The planner can generate collision-free trajectories in real time in an unknown environment.

We discuss the related research in Sect. 2, and introduce the approach of build local map in Sect. 3. Our local trajectory replanning method is detailed in Sect. 4. In Sect. 5, simulation experimental results which display autonomous flight of quadrotor in unknown environments are given. The paper is concluded in Sect. 6.

## 2  Related Work

In this section, we introduce the related research on collision-free trajectory planning. First, we discuss the different representations of 3D environment mapping. Then we discuss the existing methods of generating collision-free trajectories and applications on the quadrotor.

## 2.1  Environment Representation

To implement collision detection, a representation of the environment occupancy information is required. A voxel-based environment representation is used in [3]. This approach divides the space into regular voxel grids, where each of them stores information about its occupancy. The advantage of this method is that it can quickly access any element while the disadvantage is its large memory-occupancy. To solve this problem, Nießner et al. [5] proposed a voxel hash algorithm, which only divides voxels on the surface of the measured scene, thereby reducing memory usage. A voxblox system was developed in [6], which builds Truncated Signed Distance Field (TSDF) and Euclidean Signed Distance Field (ESDF) for optimization-based planning. The ESDF built by voxblox was used in [7] to obtain collision cost and gradient.

Another way to represent environment is to use an octree-based probabilistic 3D mapping framework (OctoMap) [2], which can model arbitrary environments without prior assumptions about it and is possible to add new information or sensor readings at any time. The octomap has the advantages of high storage efficiency and flexible expression, which is widely used in trajectory planning.

## 2.2  Trajectory Planning

The methods for local obstacle avoidance are mainly divided into two categories. The first is purely reactive methods that does not require the environmental map but plan directly using the sensor data [8, 9]. Although these methods are very fast, they do not work well in cluttered environment. The second is local trajectory planning methods, which generate collision-free trajectories through local map built from the sensor data. The method proposed in our work belongs to this category. Trajectory planning methods can be mainly divided into a sampling-based method and an optimization-based method.

Rapidly-exploring random tree (RRT) was proposed by LaValle [10]. The method guides the tree to grow to the target by randomly selecting sampling points in the state space, and avoids the modeling of space by collision detection of sampling points. However, RRT has a problem of excessive computational cost. Researchers have proposed various improvements to RRT to solve this problem, such as RRT-Connect [11] and Dynamic-RRT [12]. The RRT-Connect simultaneously generate two trees from the initial point and the target point to improves the efficiency of the algorithm. Dynamic RRT removes invalid nodes by using pruning and merging operations. Another problem of RRT is that it is not asymptotically optimal. Karaman and Frazzoli [13] summarized sampling-based algorithms for asymptotically optimal motion planning, including RRT* algorithm, PRM* algorithm and so on. Webb et al. [14] proposed a dynamic RRT* method that extends the RRT* method by using a fixed-final-state-free-final-time controller to ensure asymptotically optimal and increase the convergence speed.

Although the sampling-based method can find safe path, it is often necessary to optimize the path to generate smooth trajectory that can be followed by the quadrotor. Mellinger et al. [4] proposed a minimum snap trajectory generation algorithm, which formulated the trajectory generation problem as a quadratic programming problem

(QP) and obtained the optimal trajectory by minimizing the cost function composed of the norm of snap (the fourth derivative of position). The trajectory is represented by piecewise polynomial functions. Richter et al. [16] reconstructed the constrained QP problem into an unconstrained QP problem, thus eliminating the process of solving the constrained QP and improving the computational efficiency. Continuous time trajectory optimization method is proposed by Oleynikova et al. [17], which is adopted to design a local replanner that runs at a high rate and continuously recalculates the local safety trajectory. However, this method cannot deal with the local minima problem in the optimization process. Fei Gao et al. [18] proposed an online trajectory planning framework for quadrotor based on gradient information, which follows [17] 's formulation and has a 100% success rate to find collision-free trajectories. Oleynikova [7] presented a complete system for local trajectory generation, which tries to avoid local minima in the optimization through an exploration-inspired intermediate goal finding strategy. The method proposed in this paper does not involve the minimization of the cost function, thus avoiding the problem of local minima.

## 3  Local Map Building Using OctoMap and Circular Buffer

### 3.1  OctoMap Building

We use RGB-D cameras to get pointcloud. There are overlaps in the camera's multiple viewing angles, and there are large numbers of closely spaced points in the overlapping area, which occupy lots of storage space. We use a voxel filter to downsample the pointcloud, which guarantees that there is only one point in a fixed-size voxel without destroying the geometry of the pointcloud itself.

Since the pointcloud map is large and cannot handle moving objects, we convert it into an octree-based grid map (OctoMap). When the effective depth data of a point is obtained, it indicates that the point is occupied.

For a more accurate representation, OctoMap takes the form of a probability to indicate whether the point is occupied. The occupied probability is represented by $x \in (0, 1)$, and the greater the probability is, the more likely the point is occupied. We use $y \in R$ to indicate the state of the point. When the point is perceived to be occupied, the value of $y$ is increased; otherwise, the value of $y$ is decreased. The conversion relationship between $x$ and $y$ is defined as follows:

$$y = \log it(x) = \log\left(\frac{x}{1 - x}\right) \in (-\infty, +\infty) \tag{1}$$

$$x = \log it^{-1}(y) = \frac{\exp(y)}{\exp(y) + 1} \in (0, 1) \tag{2}$$

when $y$ changes from $-\infty$ to $+\infty$, correspondingly, $x$ changes from 0 to 1. Through probabilistic logarithmic transformation, we can update the map in real time and dynamically model obstacles in the environment.

## 3.2  Local Octomap Building Using Circular Buffer

A bounded map is required to perform local trajectory replanning. We used a method in [3] to build a local map by using a three-dimensional circular buffer. In addition to representing the occupancy information of the environment, the buffer also needs to clear some unnecessary data with the movement of the quadrotor to reduce memory usage and query time.

The circular buffer is made up of a three-dimensional array of size $N(N = 2^p)$. We suppose the resolution of octomap is $r$, which divides the three-dimensional space into cubes of size $r$. We need to map the point $p(x, y, z)$ from 3D space to the point $p'(x', y', z')$ in the buffer. The mapping process is as follows:

$$
\begin{cases}
x' = x/r \\
y' = y/r \\
z' = z/r
\end{cases}
\tag{3}
$$

The mapping is reversible. Assuming the center of the buffer is $O(o_1, o_2, o_3)$, with this information, we can check whether a point is in the buffer:

$$
insideBuffer(p') = \left(0 \leq x' - o_1 < \frac{N}{2}\right) \& \left(0 \leq y' - o_2 < \frac{N}{2}\right) \& \left(0 \leq z' - o_3 < \frac{N}{2}\right)
\tag{4}
$$

To ensure that the buffer is centered on the quadrotor, it is necessary to constantly change the value of $O$ with the quadrotor's movement. Assuming the coordinate of the quadrotor is $Q(q_1, q_2, q_3)$, the initial position of the buffer's center is the starting point of the quadrotor. With the flight of quadrotor, when $q_i - o_i > 0$, $o_i = o_i + d$; otherwise, $o_i = o_i - d$, $d$ is the moving step size of the buffer's center.

# 4  Real-Time Local Trajectory Replanning

## 4.1  RRT*-Based Waypoints Generation

We utilize the RRT* algorithm to generate waypoints. The RRT* can quickly find the initial path, and then continuously optimize the path as the sample point increases until the target point is found or the number of iterations is reached. The RRT* algorithm is progressively optimized and it is not possible to find the optimal path in limited time. Therefore, the convergence time of the RRT* is a prominent research problem. But it is undeniable that the cost of the path calculated by the RRT* is much lower than that of the RRT.

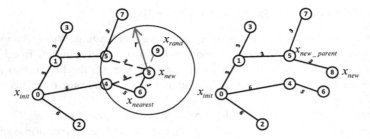

**Fig. 1.** The process of finding parent node of $x_{new}$ in RRT*. The cost of path 0-1-5-8 is 9, the cost of path 0-4-8 is 10, and the cost of path 0-4-6-8 is 12. Therefore, node 5 is selected as the parent node of $x_{new}$.

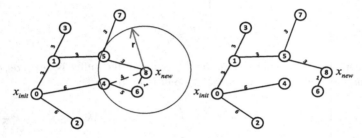

**Fig. 2.** The process of rewiring in the RRT* algorithm. The cost of path 0-1-5-8-6 is less than path 0-4-6. Therefore, the parent node of 6 is changed from 4 to $x_{new}$.

The pseudo code of the RRT* algorithm is shown in Algorithm 1. First, initialize the tree to produce the first node $x_{init}$, and a random point $x_{rand}$ will be generated during each iteration. Then, we traverse all the nodes in the tree and calculate the distance between them and the random point to find the node closest to the random point, which is denoted as $x_{nearest}$. Next, a new node $x_{new}$ is generated in the direction of the connection between $x_{nearest}$ and $x_{rand}$. RRT* searches for neighboring nodes within the specified range near the $x_{new}$ as choices to replacing its parent node, and finally selects the node that minimizes the path cost as the parent of $x_{new}$, as shown in Fig. 1. In addition, RRT* reduces the path cost by rewiring the tree, as shown in Fig. 2.

---

**Algorithm 1: RRT\***

---

1  T ← InitializeTree();

2  T.init_node( $x_{init}$ );

3  **for** $i = 1$ to $K$ **do**

4      $x_{rand}$ ← Random_State();

5      $x_{nearest}$ ← Nearest_Neighbor( $x_{rand}$ ,T);

6      $x_{new}$ ← Steer( $x_{rand}$ , $x_{nearest}$ );

7      **if** ( $\| x_{new} - x_{goal} \| < d$ ) **then**

8              **break;**

9      **endif**

10     **if** CollisionFree( $x_{nearest}$ , $x_{new}$ ) **then**

11             $X_{near\_neighbor}$  ← Find_Near(T, $x_{new}$ ,r);

12             T.add_node( $x_{new}$ );

13             $\cos t_{min}$ ← Cost( $x_{init}$ , $x_{nearest}$ ) + Cost( $x_{nearest}$ , $x_{new}$ );

14             **foreach** $x_{near} \in X_{near\_neighbor}$ **do**

15                     **if** CollisionFree( $x_{near}$ , $x_{new}$ ) $\wedge$ (Cost( $x_{init}$ , $x_{near}$ )+Cost( $x_{near}$ , $x_{new}$ )< $\cos t_{min}$ ))

16                             $x_{new\_parent}$ ← $x_{near}$ ;

17                             $\cos t_{min}$ ← Cost( $x_{init}$ , $x_{near}$ ) + Cost( $x_{near}$ , $x_{new}$ );

18                     **endif**

19             T.add_edge( $x_{new\_parent}$ , $x_{new}$ );

20             **foreach** $x_{near} \in X_{near\_neighbor}$ **do**

21                     **if** CollisionFree( $x_{near}$ , $x_{new}$ ) $\wedge$ (Cost( $x_{init}$ , $x_{new}$ )+Cost( $x_{new}$ , $x_{near}$ )<Cost( $x_{near}$

))

22                             $x_{parent}$ ← Parent( $x_{near}$ );

23                     **endif**

24             T.delete_edge( $x_{parent}$ , $x_{near}$ ) $\wedge$ T.add_edge( $x_{new}$ , $x_{near}$ );

25     **endif**

26  **end**

27  **return T;**

---

## 4.2  Trajectory Generation Using Uniform B-Spline

We adopt uniform b-spline method to fit the waypoints found by RRT\* to generate a smooth trajectory. The value of a b-spline of degree $k - 1$ can be expressed using the following formula:

$$p(t) = \sum_{i=0}^{n} p_i B_{i,k}(t) \tag{5}$$

where $p_i \in R^3$ is the control point of the b-spline at time $t_i, i \in [0, \ldots, n]$ and $B_{i,k}(t)$ is the basis function that can be calculated by the De Boor-Cox formula [19].

$$\begin{cases} B_{i,1}(t) = \begin{cases} 1 & t_i < t \le t_{i+1} \\ 0 & else \end{cases} \\ B_{i,k}(t) = \frac{(t-t_i)B_{i,k-1}(t)}{t_{i+k-1}-t_i} + \frac{(t_{i+k}-t)B_{i+1,k-1}(t)}{t_{i+k}-t_{i+1}} \end{cases} \tag{6}$$

There is a fixed time interval $\Delta t$ between uniform b-spline's control points, which simplifies the calculation of the basis function. In the case of uniform b-spline of degree $k - 1$, at time $t \in [t_i, t_{i+1})$, the value of $p(t)$ depends only on $k$ consecutive control points, namely $[p_i, p_{i+1}, \cdots, p_{i+k-1}]$.

$$u(t) = \frac{t - t_i}{t_{i+1} - t_i} = \frac{t - t_i}{\Delta t}, t \in [t_i, t_{i+1}] \tag{7}$$

According to the matrix representation of the De Boor-Cox formula, the formula (5) can be written as follows:

$$p(u(t)) = \begin{pmatrix} 1 \\ u \\ u^2 \\ \vdots \\ u^{k-1} \end{pmatrix}^T M^k \begin{pmatrix} p_i \\ p_{i+1} \\ p_{i+2} \\ \vdots \\ p_{i+k-1} \end{pmatrix} \tag{8}$$

where $M^k$ is a matrix of size $k \times k$.

$$M_{i,j}^k = \frac{1}{(k-1)!} C_{k-1}^{k-1-i} \sum_{s=j}^{k-1} (-1)^{s-j} \times C_k^{s-j}(k - s - 1)^{k-s-i} \tag{9}$$

$P$ is defined as $[p_i, p_{i+1}, \cdots, p_{i+k-1}]^T$. According to the formula (8), we can calculate the velocity (first derivative of position) and acceleration (second derivative of position) at any time of the trajectory.

$$\begin{cases} p'(u(t)) = \frac{1}{\Delta t} \begin{bmatrix} 0 & 1 & u & u^2 & \cdots & u^{k-2} \end{bmatrix} M^k P \\ p''(u(t)) = \frac{1}{\Delta t^2} \begin{bmatrix} 0 & 0 & 1 & u & \cdots & u^{k-3} \end{bmatrix} M^k P \end{cases} \tag{10}$$

An important feature of the b-spline is local control. We call $[t_i, t_{i+1})$ a single span, which is only controlled by the $k$ control points $[p_i, p_{i+1}, \cdots, p_{i+k-1}]$. That means a span of the b-spline curve is only controlled by $k$ control points, and any control point can only affect $k$ spans. This feature makes the b-spline more suitable for local trajectory planning because the insertion of control points affects only a small portion of the trajectory.

To enable the trajectory to be followed by the quadrotor, the dynamic constraints of the drone need to be satisfied. As shown in [16] and [2], the trajectory must continue to the fourth derivative of the position (snap). We use quantic uniform b-splines to represent the trajectory.

The smoothed trajectory still exists the danger of collisions, because it will deviate from the initial path, as shown in Fig. 3(a). We solve this problem by adding midpoint to the path segment, as shown in Fig. 3(b). $p_1$, $p_2$ and $p_3$ are the waypoints planned by the RRT*, $m_1$ and $m_2$ are the midpoints of line segments $p_1p_2$ and $p_2p_3$ respectively. The midpoint is collision-free because it is located on the optimal piecewise linear path returned by the RRT* search algorithm. Then we calculate the midpoint $p_2'$ of $m_1m_2$. If line segments $p_1p_2'$ and $p_2'p_3$ do not intersect the obstacle, replace the $p_2$ in the path with $p_2'$. We adopt the method of increasing the waypoint to solve the problem that the b-spline trajectory intersects the obstacle after smoothing, and the process is repeated if necessary.

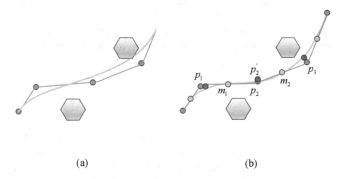

(a)                                        (b)

**Fig. 3.** Description of the trajectory planning method. The red line is the initial path obtained by the RRT* algorithm. The green line is the trajectory generated by the b-spline, which is still the possibility of collision with the obstacle, as shown in (a). The method of increasing waypoints as shown in (b). (Color figure online)

### 4.3  Real-Time Local Trajectory Replanning

Due to the limited sensing range of the onboard sensor, we design a real-time local trajectory replanning strategy. Before the flight begins, set the target point and use the method in [16] to get the global trajectory which reach the target. During the flight, a local planner is used to replan local trajectories online based on the local map built in real time, as shown in Fig. 4.

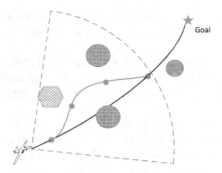

**Fig. 4.** Illustration of the real-time local trajectory replanning strategy. The global path is shown in black. The blue area represents the local map we built. The trajectory obtained by local replanning is indicated in orange. See Sect. 4.3 for details. (Color figure online)

We use a timer that performs local trajectory replanning every t seconds. The target point of each replanning is the position on the global trajectory at the corresponding moment to ensure the replanned trajectory does not deviate from the global trajectory. In the local planner, first use RRT* to find waypoints in the local octomap, and then insert waypoints as control points into the b-spline. If the target point is occupied or exceeds the range of the local map, the plan is abandoned and the last waypoint is copied into the b-spline. This is to allow the drone to remain hovering at the last control point when local planner does not generate new waypoints.

## 5   Results

We use the rotors_simulator system in gazebo to build an experimental platform to verify the local trajectory replanning approach we proposed. The onboard sensor we use is an RGB-D camera that provides pointcloud of images. The simulation environment is shown in Fig. 5. We provide the position, velocity, and acceleration data that we calculate to the controller developed in [15] to control the flight of the quadrotor.

**Fig. 5.** The simulation environment

## 5.1 Local Map Building Results

We discussed the build of local map in Sect. 3. To evaluate the effectiveness of the downsampling method, we recorded the number of points in the pointcloud before and after downsampling and the time required to insert the pointcloud into the map. We set the size of the mesh in the voxel filter to $0.2\,m \times 0.2\,m \times 0.2\,m$. There are 192 data received during the entire flight of the quadrotor, which are represented in the form of histogram, as shown in Fig. 6. The number of points after downsampling is an order of magnitude less than before filtering. The time it takes to insert it into the map is also reduced by half.

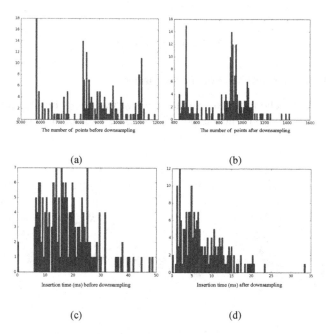

**Fig. 6.** Comparison of the number of points in the pointcloud before and after downsampling and the time it takes to insert the map. (a) and (b) are histograms of the number of points in the pointcloud, and (c) and (d) are histograms of the insertion time.

We set the size of the circular buffer to a three-dimensional array of length 64, which can be changed as needed. The resolution of octomap is set to $0.2\,m^3$, and the experimental results are shown in Fig. 7.

**Fig. 7.** Result of local octomap.

## 5.2    Trajectory Planning Method Performance

We utilize the RRT* algorithm to search for initial waypoints on OctoMap, and then use the uniform b-spline to fit the waypoint to generate a smooth trajectory, as shown in Fig. 8(a).

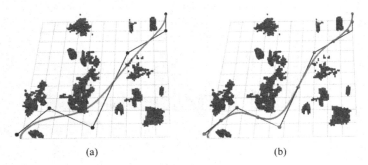

(a)                                    (b)

**Fig. 8.** Results of trajectory planning strategy. The red line indicates the initial path obtained by RRT*. The green curve represents the trajectory after fitting using the b-spline, (a) shows the curve and the green point is calculated by the method showing in Fig. 3(b). (Color figure online)

It can be seen from Fig. 8(a) that the smoothed trajectory deviates from the initial path and collides with the obstacle. We solve this problem by adding waypoints, as shown in Fig. 8(b).

We compare the method proposed in this paper with Richter et al. [16]. We all use the RRT* algorithm to get the waypoints, but they use polynomials to represent the trajectories. To compare the two methods, we use them to fit the same waypoint in the same map. The result is shown in Fig. 9.

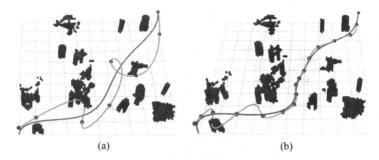

(a)                                    (b)

**Fig. 9.** Comparison of b-splines and polynomials. The red point represents the waypoint obtained by the RRT*. Blue indicates the polynomial trajectory, while green represents the b-spline trajectory. The number of waypoints in (a) is 7 and in (b) is 17. (Color figure online)

Both methods give a smooth trajectory. The characteristic of the polynomial is that it passes through all waypoints, but it also makes its trajectory not flexible enough. It can be seen from Fig. 9 that the polynomial may not obtain a reasonable result in the case of a small number of waypoints or irregular distribution. Therefore, the trajectory generated by the b-spline may be more suitable for the quadrotor.

### 5.3   Real-Time Local Trajectory Replanning Result

We present the simulation results of the real-time local trajectory replanning method in Fig. 10. In the experiment, the quadrotor was ordered to fly to the target point. First, a global trajectory is planned. Since the environment is unknown, the global trajectory may intersect with the obstacle. A local octomap is built by inserting the pointcloud obtained by the RGB-D camera into the circular buffer and then using it for local trajectory replanning.

Local map building, collision detection, and trajectory generation are all performed online, without any prior information about the environment. The time interval of the local planner is 1 s, and the minimum distance between the quadrotor and the obstacle is set to 0.5 m. As can be seen from Fig. 10, the local map is updated in real time with the movement of the quadrotor. The local trajectory of the collision-free region is consistent with the global trajectory, but when intersecting with the obstacle, a smooth trajectory is generated to avoid the obstacle.

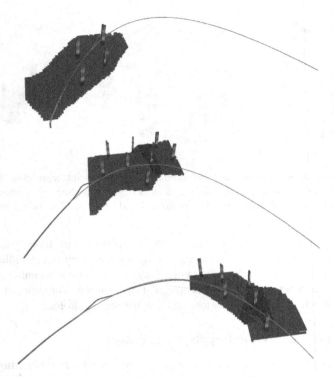

**Fig. 10.** Illustration of real-time local trajectory replanning. The preplanned global trajectory is represented by purple, and the local replanned trajectory is shown in green. (Color figure online)

## 6   Conclusion and Future Work

We propose a method for real-time local trajectory replanning. The method first pre-plans a global trajectory and commands the quadrotor to follow it. Then we design a local trajectory planner to avoid unknown obstacles in the environment. The planner divides the local trajectory replanning problem into sampling-based path planning and b-spline based trajectory generation. The octree-based local map is built by using the circular buffer to implement obstacle mapping and collision detection. The local trajectory planning is carried out online with the flight of the quadrotor. We verified the proposed method through experiments in the simulation environment. In future work, we plan to validate our approach in a real environment. And improve the method to apply to more complex environments, such as large-scale or dynamic environments.

**Acknowledgments.** This work was supported by National Nature Science Foundation (NNSF) of China under Grant 61876187.

# References

1. Nonami, K., et al.: Autonomous flying robots: unmanned aerial vehicles and micro aerial vehicles. Springer, Heidelberg (2010). https://doi.org/10.1007/978-4-431-53856-1
2. Hornung, A., et al.: OctoMap: an efficient probabilistic 3D mapping framework based on octrees. Auton. Robots **34**(3), 189–206 (2013)
3. Usenko, V., et al.: Real-time trajectory replanning for MAVs using uniform B-splines and a 3D circular buffer. In: 2017 IEEE/RSJ International Conference on Intelligent Robots and Systems (IROS). IEEE (2017)
4. Mellinger, D., Kumar, V.: Minimum snap trajectory generation and control for quadrotors. In: 2011 IEEE International Conference on Robotics and Automation IEEE (2011)
5. Nießner, M., et al.: Real-time 3D reconstruction at scale using voxel hashing. ACM Transact. Graph. (ToG) **32**(6), 169 (2013)
6. Oleynikova, H., et al.: Voxblox: Building 3d signed distance fields for planning. *arXiv* (2016): arXiv-1611
7. Oleynikova, H., et al.: Safe local exploration for replanning in cluttered unknown environments for microaerial vehicles. IEEE Robot. Autom. Lett. **3**(3), 1474–1481 (2018)
8. Hu, J., Niu, Y., et al.: Obstacle avoidance methods for rotor uavs using realsense camera. In: 2017 Chinese Automation Congress (CAC). IEEE (2017)
9. Ma, Z., et al.: A saliency-based reinforcement learning approach for a UAV to avoid flying obstacles. Robot. Auton. Syst. **100**, 108–118 (2018)
10. LaValle, S.M.: Rapidly-exploring random trees: A new tool for path planning (1998)
11. Kuffner Jr, J.J., Steven, M.: LaValle. RRT-connect: an efficient approach to single-query path planning. In: ICRA, vol. 2 (2000)
12. Shan, E., et al.: A dynamic RRT path planning algorithm based on B-spline. In: 2009 Second International Symposium on Computational Intelligence and Design, vol. 2. IEEE (2009)
13. Karaman, S., Frazzoli, E.: Sampling-based algorithms for optimal motion planning. Int. J. Robot. Res. **30**(7), 846–894 (2011)
14. Webb, D.J., Van Den Berg, J.: Kinodynamic RRT*: asymptotically optimal motion planning for robots with linear dynamics. In: 2013 IEEE International Conference on Robotics and Automation. IEEE (2013)
15. Lee, T., Leok, M., McClamroch, N.H.: Geometric tracking control of a quadrotor UAV on SE (3). In: 49th IEEE conference on decision and control (CDC). IEEE (2010)
16. Richter, C., Bry, A., Roy, N.: Polynomial trajectory planning for aggressive quadrotor flight in dense indoor environments. In: Inaba, M., Corke, P. (eds.) Robotics Research. STAR, vol. 114, pp. 649–666. Springer, Cham (2016). https://doi.org/10.1007/978-3-319-28872-7_37
17. Oleynikova, H., et al.: Continuous-time trajectory optimization for online UAV replanning. In: 2016 IEEE/RSJ International Conference on Intelligent Robots and Systems (IROS). IEEE (2016)
18. Gao, F., Lin, Y., Shen, S.: Gradient-based online safe trajectory generation for quadrotor flight in complex environments. In: 2017 IEEE/RSJ International Conference on Intelligent Robots and Systems (IROS). IEEE (2017)
19. Qin, K.: General matrix representations for B-splines. Visual Comput. **16**(3), 177–186 (2000)

# Research on Safety Control Method of Multi-rotor Unmanned Aerial Vehicle Under Super-Strong Wind Field

Yongqiang Hou[1,2,3(⊠)], Yuqing He[2,3,4,5], Wei Huang[1,2,3],
Qianhan Wang[1,2,3], and Hao Zhou[2,3]

[1] Northeastern University, Shenyang 110819, China
houyongqiang@sia.cn
[2] State Key Laboratory of Robotics, Shenyang Institute of Automation,
Chinese Academy of Sciences, Shenyang 110016, China
[3] Institutes for Robotics and Intelligent Manufacturing,
Chinese Academy of Sciences, Shenyang 110016, China
[4] Shenyang Institute of Automation (Guangzhou),
Chinese Academy of Sciences, Guangzhou 511458, China
[5] Shenyang Institute of Automation,
Chinese Academy of Sciences, Shenyang 110016, China

**Abstract.** Due to the simple structure and lightweight of the Multi-rotor Unmanned Aerial Vehicle (UAV), it is easy to be affected by the wind field environment. The super strong wind may even cause the multi-rotor UAV to crash, so it is very important to ensure the safe of the multi-rotor UAV under the super-strong wind environment. However, researchers focus on improving the anti-disturbance performance of multi-rotor UAVs in wind field, and there are relatively few researches on safety control methods. Therefore, the research on safety control when the multi-rotor UAV cannot resist the wind is of significance. Firstly, this paper takes the lead in the behavior of multi-rotor UAVs in super-strong wind field. Secondly, the research proposes a wind-driven safety control method based on wind and an altitude-security control method based on online estimation. At last, the ways have verified by experiments that the safety of the aircraft has effectively ensured.

**Keywords:** Multi-rotor unmanned aerial vehicle · Super strong wind field · Wind-driven safety control method · Online estimation

## 1 Introduction

Due to its vertical takeoff and landing, fixed-point hovering, and strong maneuverability [1–3], multi-rotor unmanned aerial vehicle are widely used in civil and military field. However, the multi-rotor unmanned aerial vehicle is easy to affect by the wind

Supported by the Science and Technology Planning Project of Guangdong Province (2017B010116002).

field environment because of the small size, lightweight and the structural characteristics [4, 5]. Moreover, the variability of the wind field environment sometimes leads the multi-rotor unmanned aerial vehicle directly to crash due to the stall of the propeller. Therefore, it is of great significance to study the safety control problem of multi-rotor unmanned aerial vehicle in super-strong wind environment.

The design of safety control strategy for multi-rotor unmanned aerial vehicle in super-strong wind environment mainly includes two aspects: the design of the body safety control and the design of the altitude anti-disturbance control. For the safety control problem of multi-rotor unmanned aerial vehicle in super-strong wind environment, researchers are mostly focusing on the research of anti-disturbance control methods, but there are few studies on the safety control methods of the aircraft. In 2003, Civita linearized the multi-rotor unmanned aerial vehicle model at multiple equilibrium points and achieved a wide range of stability by designing the controller, effectively achieving disturbance suppression [6]. However, the performance of multi-rotor unmanned aerial vehicle has greatly affected by local linearization. In recent years, the three-dimensional fuzzy PID method adopted by researchers has realized the stable control of the attitude and the precise trajectory tracking control, and effectively realized the disturbance suppression of the output signal [7], but this method has only used to suppress the disturbance caused by the parameter fluctuation. The ability to suppress external environmental disturbances is not strong. In addition, the combination of intelligent algorithms and UAVs can also achieve the suppression of disturbances. In 2014, Lee [8] proposes an inversion technique for dynamic models based adaptive neural networks, which effectively improves the performance of PD controllers and improves them. The anti-disturbance capability of the multi-rotor unmanned aerial vehicle system. In the same year, by combining the genetic algorithm with the identification of multi-rotor UAV model parameters, the influence of external disturbance on the parameters of multi-rotor UAV model is greatly reduced, and the multi-rotor UAV model is guaranteed to be reliable, which is proposed by Yang [9]. However, the calculation time of the intelligent algorithm is long, and it is not applicable to the UAV system with high real-time requirements. Therefore, it is urgent to propose a safety control method and a high anti-disturbance control method in a super-strong wind environment to ensure the flight safety of the multi-rotor UAV.

The paper takes the design of the safety control method of multi-rotor UAV in super-strong wind environment as the research topic. Firstly, a complete safety control strategy have proposed for the safety control of multi-rotor UAV in super-strong wind environment. Then two strategy have proposed to ensure the flight safety, the method of body safety control has used to ensure the attitude safety of the multi-rotor UAV, an altitude safety constant control method has used to ensure the altitude safety of the multi-rotor UAV during flight, and the reliability of the scheme has fully verified by experiments in various parts.

## 2   The Design of Safety Control Strategy

The multi-rotor UAV should remain altitude constant and attitude stable for practical flight in the super-strong wind field. Therefore, the core of the safety control strategy is to ensure that the aircraft's own attitude is stable and altitude constant.

In order to achieve this design goal, first, it is necessary to distinguish the control loop structure that should has added and abandoned at this time. When the multi-rotor UAV is working in the super-strong wind environment, if the UAV cannot resist the disturbance of wind, the field is no longer suitable for mission execution, and UAV should turn to ensure the safety of the aircraft. The effect of the wind field disturbance on the UAV is mainly to affect the output of the UAV's velocity control loop and the output of the attitude control loop. While in the safety control, the wind field should have changed to the attitude control loop. The output disturbance has regarded as the driving force, so that the three-axis torque has determined by the wind field, and the posture angle and the flight speed have reduced by actively adjusting the attitude angle to adapt to the direct effect of the wind field force on the body. In addition, the wind in the vertical direction will eventually act on the multi-rotor UAV in the form of force, which will eventually change the altitude of the UAV and intimidate to the safe of the UAV. Therefore, the altitude change of the multi-rotor UAV should has reduced as much as possible In the process of safety. Therefore, the wind force at this time should be a disturbance power that needs to suppress instead of the driving force.

The designed safety control scheme show in Fig. 1, and $\tau_h$ indicates the disturbance caused by the wind field disturbance to the altitude control loop of the multi-rotor UAV, $\tau_z$ indicates the disturbance torque generated by the wind field disturbance to the attitude control loop of the multi-rotor UAV.

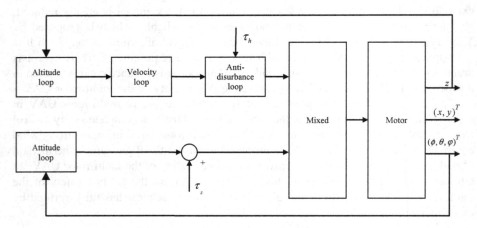

**Fig. 1.** The design of security control schemes.

## 3   Design of Body Safety Control Method

### 3.1   The Method Design of the Body Safety

The influence of wind field force on the multi-rotor UAV includes mainly two aspects. One is to change the induction speed at the propeller paddle, and the other is to change the force directly acting on the body. For both of them, the angle between the propeller and the wind is directly determined, that is to say, the attitude angle of the multi-rotor UAV has determined. Therefore, the wind field force has relationships with the attitude angle.

Because the wind field is unpredictable and changes frequently, the wind field force is uncontrollable. However, since the wind field force has relationships with the attitude angle, the attitude angle can adjust to adapt to the wind field to reduce the influence of the wind field to the multi-rotor UAV. Therefore, it is possible to adjust the attitude to adapt to the wind field force to ensure the safety of the multi-rotor UAV.

Assuming that the wind field force is $T$ and the influence of the wind field environment to the multi-rotor UAV all acts on the pitch channel. Which leads the multi-rotor UAV to generating acceleration $a_x$ along the axis $x$ of the body coordinate system and acceleration $a_y$ along the axis $y$ of the body coordinate system, and the multi-rotor UAV has a tensile force $F$ due to the high-speed rotation of the propeller. The force analysis diagram shows in Fig. 2.

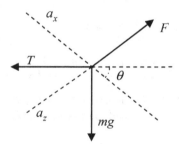

**Fig. 2.**  Diagram of wind analysis

Due to the combination of the wind field force, the pulling force generated by the propeller and the gravity, the acceleration along the axis $x$ and $y$ of the body coordinate system has generated. In order to analyze the wind field force, the acceleration has decomposed parallel to the horizontal direction and perpendicular to the horizontal direction as shown in Fig. 3.

Two equations of Eqs. (1) and (2) have obtained.

$$T - F \sin \theta = m(a_x \cos \theta + a_z \sin \theta) \tag{1}$$

$$F \cos \theta - mg = m(a_x \sin \theta - a_z \cos \theta) \tag{2}$$

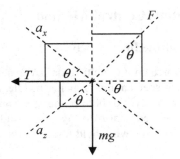

**Fig. 3.** Diagram of wind analysis

The above two equations can be solved in tandem to obtain an expression about the wind field force, as shown in Eq. (3).

$$T \cos \theta - mg \sin \theta = ma_x \tag{3}$$

Assuming that the combined force of wind field force and gravity is $T_\infty$, and the Eq. (4) can have obtained.

$$T_\propto = \sqrt{(mg)^2 + (T)^2} \tag{4}$$

Moreover, the Eq. (5) can have obtained.

$$\frac{T}{T_\propto} \cos \theta - \frac{mg}{T_\propto} \sin \theta = \frac{ma_x}{T_\propto} \tag{5}$$

Assuming that the angle between the force produced by the wind field and the gravity is $\beta$. Moreover, the Eqs. (6) and (7) have obtained.

$$T_\propto \sin \beta = T \tag{6}$$

$$T_\propto \cos \beta = mg \tag{7}$$

The Eq. (8) has simplified by the Eq. (5) as shown below.

$$\sin \beta \cos \theta - \cos \beta \sin \theta = \frac{ma_x}{T_\propto} \tag{8}$$

The expression obtained by the above equation to obtain the pitch angle is as shown in the Eq. (9).

$$\theta = \beta - \arcsin \frac{ma_x}{T_\propto} \tag{9}$$

However, the attitude angle has relationships with the wind field force. To adapt to the wind field by the attitude angle to reduce the fluctuation of the attitude angle of the multirotor UAV, it is necessary to be able to determine the magnitude of the wind field force at any time. Therefore, The kinematic equation of the multi-rotor UAV must have analyzed with the wind filed.

$$m\dot{v} = -RF + mge_z + Te_x \tag{10}$$

Since the wind field force is horizontal, the kinematics equation in the horizontal direction is as follows.

$$ma_x = -e_x^T RF + T \tag{11}$$

The magnitude of the wind field force can have solved as shown in Eq. (12).

$$T = ma_x + e_x^T RF \tag{12}$$

The attitude angle of the multi-rotor UAV can maintain under the wind field can have calculated from the Eqs. (5) and (12). The multi-rotor UAV can adjust the attitude angle in time to adapt to the current wind field.

### 3.2 Experimental Design and Data Analysis

Two sets of experiments are required to verify the reliability under super-strong wind conditions, and one set of experiments represented the situation corresponding to the UAV trying to maintain the current position even if it had subjected to the super strong wind environment. The actual situation corresponding to another set of experiments is that the multi-rotor UAV feels that the wind is too large to give up the position automatically, and instead uses attitude control to ensure the safety of the multi-rotor UAV itself.

In order to simulate the super-strong wind environment, it is necessary to ensure that the wind speed is large enough. For this reason, we use the JGFS7-4 fan. Moreover, the wind turbine can generate wind speeds of 17.7 m/s, which is enough to simulate the super wind field.

In the actual experimental process, in order to simplify the research, the head of the UAV and axial flow of the fan keep parallel in the initial state. In addition, during the experiment, the wind field disturbance has kept as far as possible on the pitch channel of the multi-rotor UAV, so that the disturbance of the wind field to the multi-rotor UAV was all manifested by yaw. Among them, the yaw angle curves of the two sets of experiments have shown in Figs. 4 and 5, respectively.

Among them, the red line represents the desired heading angle; the black line represents the actual heading angle. For the first set of experiments, combined with Fig. 4 and the actual flight experiments, the fan has turned on at the end of 115 s. During the period of 115 s–149 s, the deviation between the actual heading angle of the multi-rotor UAV and the desired heading angle reaches 0.5 radians. In addition, the

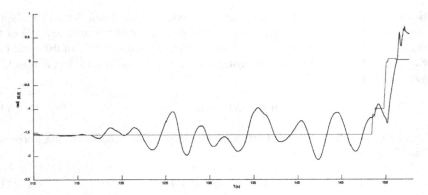

**Fig. 4.** Heading angle curve of the first set of experiments (Color figure online)

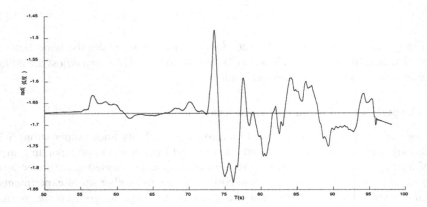

**Fig. 5.** Heading angle curve of the second set of experiments (Color figure online)

entire yaw angle showed a tendency to oscillate, which led to the loss of control of the multi-rotor drone at the end of 149 s, which eventually led to the crash of the UAV.

For the second set of experiments, combined with Fig. 5 and the actual flight experiments, it can be seen that the fan starts at the end of 70 s, and the deviation between the actual heading angle of the multi-rotor UAV and the desired heading angle reaches the maximum during the period of 70 s–77 s, which is 0.2 radians. And during the period of 77 s–98 s, the difference between the actual yaw angle and the expected yaw angle gradually decreases, and the yaw angle of the multi-rotor UAV exhibits a tendency to converge toward the desired yaw angle.

Combined with the actual experimental results, the multirotor UAV that always keeps the fixed point eventually crashes, and the multi-rotor UAV ensures the safety of the body by timely adopting the safety control method, further illustrating the reliability of the design method.

# 4  The Method Design of Altitude Constant Control

## 4.1  Feasibility Analysis of High Anti-disturbance

In order to collect wind speed data for the wind field, it is first necessary to select a reasonable anemometer. Here, we use the 3D anemometer sensor produced by Gill. Among them, the measurement accuracy of the three-dimensional anemometer sensor can be achieved 0.01 m/s, and the sampling frequency can be achieved 20 Hz.

During the sampling process, the wind speed sensor has first installed on a fixed iron frame with a length of 1.4 m, and then communicated with the computer through the serial port for data sampling. Moreover, the time fixes at 2 min each time.

Through the observation of the natural wind field for two months, which finally finds the regularity of the wind field data. For the data analysis, some data from 10:00 am to 3:00 pm on October 14, 2018 has selected as Table 1.

**Table 1.**  Wind field data sheet.

| x | Y | z | horize | horize/z |
|------|------|------|--------|----------|
| 2.25 | 2.51 | 0.28 | 3.37 | 12.2 |
| 2.07 | 2.13 | 0.5 | 2.97 | 5.89 |
| 2.30 | 2.51 | 0.89 | 3.41 | 3.83 |
| 1.52 | 1.45 | 0.33 | 2.1 | 6.34 |
| 2.35 | 1.88 | 0.09 | 3.01 | 32.35 |
| 1.41 | 1.1 | 0.42 | 1.79 | 4.27 |
| 0.73 | 0.84 | 0.51 | 1.11 | 2.18 |
| 1.35 | 6.99 | 1.15 | 7.12 | 6.19 |
| 2.79 | 0.72 | 0.11 | 2.88 | 25.25 |

Where *horize* represents the wind speed in the horizontal direction and its calculation formula is as shown in (13).

$$horize = \sqrt{x^2 + y^2} \tag{13}$$

It shows that the combined wind speed in the horizontal direction is at least double the wind speed in the vertical direction from the data. Due to this unevenness of the wind field, even the horizontal wind speed reaches a certain wind resistance limit due to the vertical wind speed. Vertical wind speed is relatively low, so there is still a large margin, so that the possibility of disturbance suppression of the height control loop of the multi-rotor drone in the wind field environment is greatly improved.

## 4.2  Design of Altitude Disturbance Control Method

He [10] proposed a disturbance suppression method based on first-order low-pass filter for low-frequency disturbance suppression of electromechanical systems in the robust and predictive control of nonlinear electromechanical systems, and achieved success through experiments. Therefore, with the help of similar ideas, this paper proposes an altitude control method based on online estimation. The online estimation of the altitude anti-disturbance control method directly compensates for the vertical acceleration by introducing a first-order low-pass filter to resist the wind field disturbance.

Assuming that the low-pass filter is $f_h$, the output tension of the vertical speed control loop is $F_h$, and the vertical acceleration generated after the disturbance is $a_z$, the altitude-disturbance control diagram shows in Fig. 6.

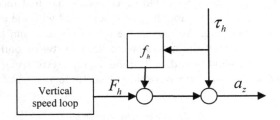

**Fig. 6.** Altitude anti-disturbance control chart

$F_h$ Can be decomposed into two parts of force, $F_m$ is used to balance gravity, and $F_a$ produces vertical acceleration. Among them, the expression is as shown in (14).

$$F_h = F_a + F_m \tag{14}$$

The equation shown in (15) can have obtained from the above transfer function.

$$F_a - f_h \tau_h + \tau_h = m a_z \tag{15}$$

The expression for simplification of the wind field disturbance shows in (16).

$$\tau_h = \frac{m a_z - F_a}{1 - f_h} \tag{16}$$

Thus, an expression of the amount of feedback of the disturbance has obtained as shown in the Eq. (17).

$$v_h = \frac{f_h}{f_h - 1} (m a_z - F_a) \tag{17}$$

Since $F_a$ and $F_h$ are related, an expression of the feedback amount $v_h$ can be further obtained as shown in the Eq. (18).

$$v_h = \frac{f_h}{f_h - 1} (m a_z + mg - F_h) \tag{18}$$

### 4.3  Determination of Low Pass Filter Parameter

In order to determine the low-pass filter parameters, data acquisition has performed on the wind field data at a distance of 2 m from the fan, and the spectrum of the wind field data is as shown in Fig. 7.

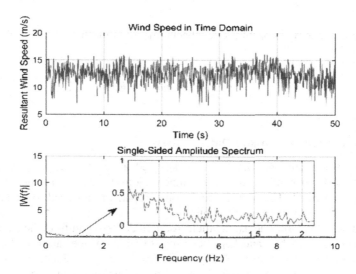

**Fig. 7.**  Spectrogram of wind

From Fig. 7, in addition to the large amplitude at the position where the frequency is zero, there is a relatively large amplitude at a frequency of 0.2 Hz, and the amplitude is small at other frequency segments. Taken together, to suppress wind disturbances, the frequency of suppression should not be lower than 0.2 Hz.

The form of the low pass filter $f_h$ is as shown in the Eq. (19).

$$f_h = \frac{a}{s+a} \tag{19}$$

The transfer function a of the wind field disturbance affecting the multi-rotor UAV is as shown in Eq. (20).

$$G_h = 1 - f_h = \frac{s}{s+a} \tag{20}$$

According to its frequency characteristics, $a$ is the cutoff frequency, and it has a good inhibitory effect on disturbances with a frequency below $a$. Since the wind disturbance of 0.2 Hz must have suppressed, the value of the cutoff frequency cannot be less than 0.2, so the cutoff frequency can take as six, as shown in the Eq. (21).

$$a = 6 \tag{21}$$

The form of $f_h$ is as shown in the Eq. (22).

$$f_h = \frac{6}{s+6} \tag{22}$$

Therefore, the expression of the feedback amount could have expressed as shown in the Eq. (23).

$$v_h = 6 \int (F_h - ma_z - mg)dt \tag{23}$$

### 4.4    Experimental Design and Data Analysis

During the experiment, the UAV can be hovered at the tuyere position, and then experiments with no wind disturbance compensation and wind disturbance compensation have performed. The altitude deviation comparison has used to judge the feasibility of altitude anti-interference control.

In the first set of experiments, the multi-rotor UAV flew 2 m from the axial fan and the altitude was about 1 m and kept hovering. In addition, the fan turned off after a period. Among them, the altitude change map drawn based on the data obtained by the experiment shows in Fig. 8. Among them, the black line represents the actual altitude curve of the UAV, and the red represents the desired altitude curve.

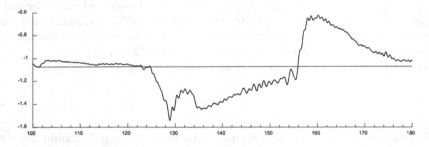

**Fig. 8.** Map of the altitude change without controller (Color figure online)

During the period of 100 s–124 s, the fan has not been turned on, and the multi-rotor UAV hovering around the desired altitude of 1 m, wherein the maximum deviation is 10 cm.

At the end of the 124 s, the fan has turned on, and the desired height does not change at this time, but the actual altitude is greatly deviated from the expected altitude. The maximum deviation is 50 cm, the average deviation is 30 cm, and it is always below the desired altitude. In addition, the altitude of UAV is extremely unstable.

In the second set of experiments, the multi-rotor UAV continue to keeping distance from 2 m to the axial fan and the altitude was about 1 m and kept hovering, and the altitude disturbance compensation has performed, and the fan had turned off after a period. Among them, the altitude change map drawn based on the data obtained by the experiment shows in Fig. 9.

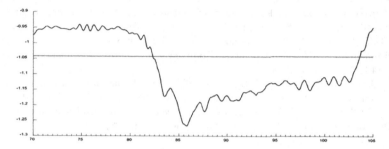

**Fig. 9.** Map of the altitude change with controller (Color figure online)

During the period of 70 s–82 s, the fan has not been turned on, and the multi-rotor UAV hovering around the desired altitude of 1 m, the maximum deviation is 10 cm.

At the end of the 82 s, the fan had turned on. The expected altitude did not change at this time, but the actual altitude began to change, but the deviation from the expected altitude was not large. Even the maximum deviation reached 20 cm, and the average deviation reached 15 cm.

This situation is clearly more stable than the first set of control experiments without altitude compensation. This further demonstrates the reliability of the design.

## 5    Conclusion

Based on the behavior analysis of multi-rotor UAV in super-strong wind environment, this paper proposes a safety control strategy for multi-rotor UAV in super-strong wind environment, and focuses on the methods of attitude stable control and altitude constant control. In the design of safety control method, a body safety control method based on wind driven adaptive wind field environment is proposed. In the design of altitude constant control method, an altitude anti-disturbance control method based on online estimation is proposed. The experimental results demonstrations of the two parts demonstrate the reliability of the proposed safety control scheme.

## References

1. Song, H.D., Hao, G.L.: Development and application of FourRotor aircraft (01), 134 (2018)
2. Xu, Y.Q.: Four-rotor aircraft flight control research. Xiamen University (2014)
3. Li, S.B.: Research on control technology of micro multi-rotor aircraft. Nanjing University of Aeronautics and Astronautics (2013)

4. Wang, F., Wu, J., Zhou, G.Q., et al.: Research on the development of multi-rotor UAV (13), 6–7 (2015)
5. Yu, C.: Development of civilian UAVs in China. Robot. Ind. **1**, 52–58 (2017)
6. La Civita, M., Papageorgiou, G., Messner, W.C., et al.: Design and flight testing of a gain-scheduled H∞, loop shaping controller for wide-envelope flight of a robotic helicopter. In: 2003 Proceedings of the American Control Conference, vol. 5, pp. 4195–4200. IEEE (2003)
7. Zhang, C., Zhou, X., Zhao, H., et al.: Three-dimensional fuzzy control of mini quadrotor UAV trajectory tracking under impact of wind disturbance. In: International Conference on Advanced Mechatronic Systems, pp. 372–377. IEEE (2017)
8. Lee, B.Y., Lee, H.I., Tank, M.J.: Analysis of adaptive control using on-line neural networks for a quadrotor UAV. In: International Conference on Control, Automation and Systems, pp. 1840–1844. IEEE (2014)
9. Yang, J., Cai, Z., Lin, Q., et al.: System identification of quadrotor UAV based on genetic algorithm. In: Guidance, Navigation and Control Conference, pp. 2336–2340. IEEE (2014)
10. He, Y.Q.: Robust and predictive control of nonlinear electromechanical systems. Shenyang Institute of Automation, Chinese Academy of Sciences (2008)

# Analysis of Disturbance Effect of a Cable on Underwater Vehicle

Zhandong Li[1(✉)], Jingkui Li[1], Jianguo Tao[2], Wei Wang[1], and Yang Luo[2]

[1] Shenyang Aerospace University, Shenyang 110136, Liaoning, China
lizhandong@sau.edu.cn
[2] Harbin Institute of Technology, Harbin 150001, Heilongjiang, China

**Abstract.** Aiming at the daily inspection and emergency repair of a nuclear power pool a cable underwater robot equipped with operation equipment was designed. The disturbance effect of the tail cable on the robot was studied to control precisely the robot. On the basis of the dynamic model the motion (including surge, heave, roll and yaw motion) of a robot with and without a cable was respectively simulated by a numerical method. The disturbance effect of a cable was quantified. The results shown that the maximum longitudinal velocity and displacement respectively decreased by 8.4% and 4.7%, the maximum vertical velocity and displacement respectively decreased by 8.64% and 6.25, and the maximum angular velocity of roll and yaw was reduced by 16.6% and 13.3%. This simulation method above can be used to evaluate the disturb effect on a robot, and provided a basis for the improved design and control strategy.

**Keywords:** Underwater robot · Dynamic model · Cable · Disturbance effect

## 1 Introduction

Nuclear energy [1] considered as a clean and efficient energy can alleviate the energy crisis, environmental pollution. However, after the Fukushima nuclear accident in 2011, nuclear safety has globally become a worldwide issue [2]. A nuclear power pool as a core part of the power plant is the key rescue area in the event of nuclear disasters. As an unmanned operation an underwater vehicle [3, 4] has been widely used in marine exploration [5], submarine geomorphology mapping [6] and deep-sea mining [7], which can provide a new idea for nuclear rescue.

In the event of a nuclear accident some cracks appeared in the nuclear power pool. If not repaired in time, a nuclear fuel leakage can happen. To repair the cracks of the nuclear power pool a robot with weld equipment was used. Underwater welding has the characteristics of high current. Hence the length-diameter ratio of the tail cable of the robot was larger than that of the cable used in ocean, which resulted in a more obvious the disturbance effect. An analysis of the disturbance effects of the tail was necessary to control the underwater robot accurately.

In the past research, scholars around the world have made a lot of explorations on the disturbance effect of a cable. Mai *et al.* [8] proposed the dynamic model of the

© Springer Nature Switzerland AG 2019
H. Yu et al. (Eds.): ICIRA 2019, LNAI 11741, pp. 755–764, 2019.
https://doi.org/10.1007/978-3-030-27532-7_65

underwater vehicle including the factors affecting the cables, and the influence of the cables on the various movements of the robot was analyzed. Eidsvik *et al.* [9] put forward the finite element model of a towing cable of an underwater vehicle to analyze the coupling effect between a cable and a robot. Zhu et al. [10] established a multi-rigid-body coupling dynamic model by lumped mass method to analyze the dynamic characteristics of the robot under cable disturbance. Fang *et al.* [11] established a dynamic model of an underwater vehicle, and obtained the trajectory changes of the robot in space motion with and without a cable to illustrate the disturbance effect of cables. Huo [12] deduced a two-dimensional dynamic model of a cable based on Euler-Bernoulli theory to study the coupling dynamics of a cable and an underwater vehicle. Wang *et al.* [13] applied the lumped mass method to describe respectively the dynamic motion of surface mother ship and an underwater towing cable, and then the motion response of the whole ship-cable system under different conditions was analyzed. Li *et al.* [14] established the motion mathematical model of an underwater towing cable and an underwater robot respectively, and solved the coupling problem between the two models by combining the two parts.

In this paper, an underwater robot with a cable was taken as the research object, and the disturbance effect of a cable on a robot was analyzed by a numerical simulation. Firstly, an overall design and a prototype of an underwater vehicle were introduced. Secondly the dynamic model of the underwater vehicle was established. Thirdly, the motion simulation of the robot without and without a cable was completed by numerical simulation. Finally, the disturbance effect of the tail cable on the robot was analyzed by comparison.

## 2  Underwater Robot

In this section, an omni-directional underwater vehicle with welding equipment and observation equipment was designed to repair the nuclear power pool in emergency state and inspect in daily state. The structure parameters of the robot were shown in Table 1.

**Table 1.** The structure parameters of an underwater robot

| Symbol | Numerical value | Remarks |
| --- | --- | --- |
| $L \times B \times H$ | 1.06 m $\times$ 0.65 m $\times$ 0.66 m | Length $\times$ width $\times$ height |
| $V$ | 0.21 m$^3$ | The volume of a robot |
| $M$ | 117 kg | The mass of a robot |

An underwater vehicle system included: a body, a control cabin, propellers, a cable and a winch, *etc.* The welding device and the inspection device were arranged inside the robot. A cable not only can transmit signals, but also can supply power for the robot and operating devices. Therefore, the length-diameter ratio was larger than that of ROV used in ocean. The cable consisted of outer sheath, armor, inner sheath, aluminum sheath, insulation layer, etc. The layout and withdrawal of a cable were conducted by a winch. The principle prototype of a robot and a winch was shown in Fig. 1.

**Fig. 1.** The prototype of a robot and a winch

## 3 Dynamic Model

To describe conveniently the position and attitude of the robot a fixed coordinate system E-$\xi\eta\zeta$ and a moving coordinate system O-$xyz$ were established as shown in Fig. 2. The origin $E$ and $O$ were respectively placed on the water surface and on the geometric center.

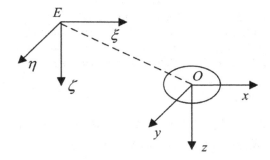

**Fig. 2.** The coordinate system of an underwater robot

In the fixed coordinate system the position and attitude of a robot was represented by a matrix $R = [L, \Lambda]^T$ which was the displacement vector $L = [\xi, \eta, \zeta]^T$ and the angular displacement vector $\Lambda = [\varphi, \theta, \psi]^T$. In the moving coordinate system, the velocity was expressed as a matrix $V = [V_G, \Omega]^T$ which was the linear velocity vector $V_G = [u, v, w]^T$ and the angular velocity vector $\Omega = [p, q, r]^T$. The force was expressed as a matrix $\tau = [\tau_1, \tau_2]^T$ which the force vector exerted on the robot was $\tau_1 = [X, Y, Z]^T$ and the moment vector was $\tau_2 = [K, M, N]^T$.

In order to control accurately a dynamic model was proposed based on Fossen [15]. According to the structural characteristics of a robot the dynamic model was as follows:

$$M\dot{V} + C(V)V + D(V)V + g(\lambda) = \tau \tag{1}$$

$M$ was an inertia matrix of body and added mass, which was expressed as:

$$M = \begin{bmatrix} m - X_{\dot{u}} & 0 & 0 & 0 & mz_G & -my_G \\ 0 & m - Y_{\dot{v}} & 0 & -mz_G & 0 & mx_G \\ 0 & 0 & m - Z_{\dot{w}} & my_G & -mx_G & 0 \\ 0 & -mz_G & my_G & I_x - K_{\dot{p}} & -I_{xy} & -I_{xz} \\ mz_G & 0 & -mx_G & -I_{yx} & I_y - M_{\dot{q}} & -I_{yz} \\ -my_G & mx_G & 0 & -I_{zx} & -I_{zy} & I_z - N_{\dot{r}} \end{bmatrix} \tag{2}$$

The mass of a robot was represented as m, the center of gravity was $x_G, y_G, z_G$, the moment of inertia of the axis was $I_x, I_y, I_z$, and the inertia product of the axis was $I_{xy} = I_{yz}, I_{xz} = I_{zx}, I_{yz} = I_{zy}$. The Coriolis force and centripetal force matrix of a robot and added mass was $C(V)$, in which the non-zero elements were:

$$\begin{cases} C(5,1) = -C(4,2) = mw + Z_{\dot{w}}w \\ C(4,3) = -C(6,1) = mv + Y_{\dot{v}}v \\ C(6,2) = -C(5,3) = mu + X_{\dot{u}}u \\ C(1,5) = -C(2,4) = mw - Z_{\dot{w}}w \\ C(3,4) = -C(1,6) = mv - Y_{\dot{v}}v \\ C(2,6) = -C(3,5) = mu - X_{\dot{u}}u \\ C(5,4) = -C(4,5) = I_{yz}q + I_{xz}p - I_zr + N_{\dot{r}}r \\ C(4,6) = -C(6,4) = I_{yz}r + I_{xy}p - I_yq + M_{\dot{q}}q \\ C(6,5) = -C(5,6) = I_{xz}r + I_{xy}q - I_xp + K_{\dot{p}}p \end{cases} \tag{3}$$

$D(V)$ was a damping matrix:

$$D(V) = -diag(X_u + X_{u|u|}|u|, Y_v + Y_{v|v|}|v|, Z_w + Z_{w|w|}|w|, \\ K_p + K_{p|p|}|p|, M_q + M_{q|q|}|q|, N_r + N_{r|r|}|r|) \tag{4}$$

In a fixed coordinate system, $g(\lambda)$ represented the force and moment generated by the restoring force.

$$g(\lambda) = \begin{bmatrix} (G - B)\sin\theta \\ -(G - B)\cos\theta\sin\varphi \\ -(G - B)\cos\theta\cos\varphi \\ -(y_GG - y_BB)\cos\theta\cos\varphi + (z_GG - z_BB)\cos\theta\sin\varphi \\ (z_GG - z_BB)\sin\theta + (x_GG - x_BB)\cos\theta\cos\varphi \\ -(x_GG - x_BB)\cos\theta\sin\varphi - (y_GG - y_BB)\sin\theta \end{bmatrix} \tag{5}$$

The gravity and buoyancy of a robot was respectively $G$ and $B$, the center coordinate of buoyancy was $x_B, y_B, z_B$. $\tau$ was the thrust and moment generated by propellers, which can be expressed as.

$$\tau = \begin{bmatrix} (-F_1 - F_2 + F_3 + F_4)\cos\alpha \\ (-F_1 + F_2 - F_3 + F_4)\sin\alpha \\ -(F_5 + F_6 + F_7 + F_8) \\ -F_5 D_{5x} + F_6 D_{6x} - F_7 D_{7x} + F_8 D_{8x} \\ F_5 D_{5y} + F_6 D_{6y} - F_7 D_{7y} - F_8 D_{8y} \\ \left( \sum_{i=2,3} F_i (D_{ix}\sin\alpha + D_{iy}\cos\alpha) - \sum_{i=1,4} F_i (D_{ix}\sin\alpha + D_{iy}\cos\alpha) \right) \end{bmatrix} \qquad (6)$$

The thrust generated by propellers can be represented by $F_i$ ($i = 1, 2, \ldots 8$), and the distance between the propeller axis and the coordinate axis was represented by $D_{ij}$ ($j = x, y, z$).

In formula (2)–(4) inertia hydrodynamic coefficients $X_{\dot{u}}, Y_{\dot{v}}, \ldots$, viscous hydrodynamic coefficients $X_u, Y_v, \ldots$, and coupling hydrodynamic coefficient $X_{u|u|}, Y_{v|v|}, \ldots$ can be obtained by empirical formula, simulation, test and parameter identification, which were not introduced in detail.

## 4  Motion Simulation

In this section the dynamic model of an underwater robot was regarded as a set of ordinary differential equations of velocity and time $t$. The motion of a robot was obtained by MATLAB. The dynamic equations of the underwater vehicle with and without a cable were solved respectively. By comparing the results, the disturbance effect of the tail-end cable on the robot was analyzed.

### 4.1  A Motion Simulation of a Robot Without a Cable

A robot was subjected to force including the thrust, the hydrodynamic force, gravity and buoyancy without the disturbance effect of cables. When the robot was in direct longitudinal motion, the initial position and velocity were respectively set as $\lambda = [0, 0, 0, 0, 0, 0]^T$ and $V_G = (0, 0, 0, 0, 0, 0)^T$. Under the maximum longitudinal thrust, the curve of the longitudinal velocity and displacement of the robot was shown in Fig. 3.

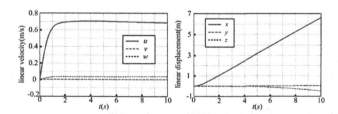

**Fig. 3.** The velocity and displacement of a robot under maximum longitudinal thrust

The robot moved in a vertical direction under the top thruster, at this time the curve of vertical linear velocity and displacement with time was shown in Fig. 4.

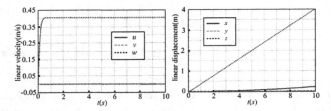

**Fig. 4.** The velocity and displacement of the robot under maximum vertical thrust

To attach on the side wall of the nuclear pool a robot can roll about 90° under the maximum roll moment from the top thruster. The change of the roll angular velocity and displacement of a robot can be obtained by simulation shown in Fig. 5.

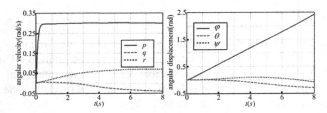

**Fig. 5.** The angular velocity and displacement of a robot under maximum roll torque

Under the maximum moment of bottom propellers the robot can yaw in the horizontal plane. The relationship between the yaw angular velocity, angular displacement and time can be obtained by simulation. The results were shown in Fig. 6.

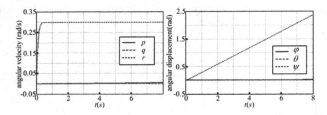

**Fig. 6.** The displacement change of the robot under maximum yaw torque

## 4.2    A Motion Simulation of a Robot with a Cable

The cable force was an important disturbance factor on a robot when moving in the pool. The disturbance effect acted on the body through a connecting point, which can result in a change of the motion state and trajectory of the robot. In a fixed coordinate system, the cable force can be expressed as:

$$\tau_{ct}(t) = \left[\tau_{ct\xi}\ \tau_{ct\eta}\ \tau_{ct\zeta}\ \tau_{cm\xi}\ \tau_{cm\eta}\ \tau_{cm\zeta}\right]^{T} \tag{7}$$

According to a transformation between a fixed coordinate and a motion coordinate, the normal shear force $S_b$, tension $S_t$ and normal shear force $S_n$ of a low-end point of a cable can be expressed as follows:

$$\tau_{ct}(t) = \begin{bmatrix} \tau_{ct\xi} \\ \tau_{ct\eta} \\ \tau_{ct\zeta} \end{bmatrix} = -\begin{bmatrix} S_b \cos\vartheta + S_t \sin\vartheta \cos\phi - S_n \sin\vartheta \sin\phi \\ -S_b \sin\vartheta + S_t \cos\vartheta \cos\phi - S_n \cos\vartheta \sin\phi \\ S_t \sin\phi + S_n \cos\phi \end{bmatrix} \tag{8}$$

The disturbance moment produced by a cable to robots was divided two parts: One was the moment exerted by a cable, which can be expressed as:

$$\tau_{cm1}(t) = \begin{bmatrix} \tau_{cm1\xi} \\ \tau_{cm1\eta} \\ \tau_{cm1\zeta} \end{bmatrix} = -\begin{bmatrix} M_b \cos\vartheta + M_t \sin\vartheta \cos\phi - M_n \sin\vartheta \sin\phi \\ -M_b \sin\vartheta + M_t \cos\vartheta \cos\phi - M_n \cos\vartheta \sin\phi \\ M_t \sin\phi + M_n \cos\phi \end{bmatrix} \tag{9}$$

The second was the disturbance moment produced by the cable force acting on the connection point. In a fixed coordinate system the coordinate of the connection point on the robot can be expressed as $r_c = (x_c,\ y_c,\ z_c)^T$, the second moment was as shown:

$$\tau_{cm2}(t) = \begin{bmatrix} \tau_{cm2\xi} \\ \tau_{cm2\eta} \\ \tau_{cm2\zeta} \end{bmatrix} = r_c \times \tau_{ct}(t) = \begin{bmatrix} x_c \\ y_c \\ z_c \end{bmatrix} \times \begin{bmatrix} \tau_{ct\xi} \\ \tau_{ct\eta} \\ \tau_{ct\zeta} \end{bmatrix} = \begin{bmatrix} y_c\tau_{ct\zeta} - z_c\tau_{ct\eta} \\ z_c\tau_{ct\xi} - x_c\tau_{ct\zeta} \\ x_c\tau_{ct\eta} - y_c\tau_{ct\xi} \end{bmatrix} \tag{10}$$

Under the bottom propellers the robot moved in a longitudinal acceleration. With the disturbance of the cable the linear displacement and linear velocity of the robot was shown in Fig. 7.

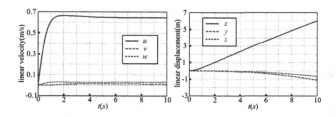

**Fig. 7.** The velocity and displacement of a cable robot under longitudinal maximum thrust

With the maximum thrust from the top thrusters the robot moved vertically. At this time under the disturbance of a cable the linear displacement and velocity of the robot can change with time $t$ as shown in Fig. 8.

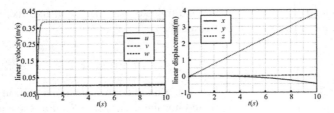

**Fig. 8.** The velocity and displacement of a cable robot under maximum vertical thrust

To attach to the side wall of the pool the robot will roll under the top thruster. At this time, the angular velocity and displacement of the robot can change with time $t$ under the cable disturbance as shown in Fig. 9.

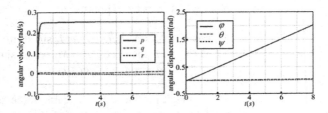

**Fig. 9.** The angular velocity and displacement of a cable robot under maximum roll moment

The robot can yaw under the bottom propellers. Under the disturbance of a cable, the angular velocity and displacement of the robot can be obtained by simulation as shown in Fig. 10.

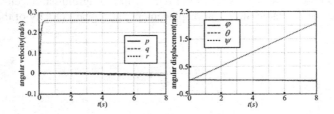

**Fig. 10.** The angular velocity and displacement of a cable robot under maximum yaw moment

From the observation of Fig. 7(a), we can see that when a robot moved with a longitudinal acceleration, the maximum longitudinal velocity reached 0.65 m/s after 0.75 s, while the lateral and vertical velocities were almost 0 m/s. From an observation of Fig. 7(b), the longitudinal displacement was about 6.0 m after 10 s, and the lateral and vertical displacements were less than 1 m. From an observation of Fig. 8(a), after 10 s the maximum vertical velocity can reach 0.38 m/s, while the lateral and vertical velocity was about 0 m/s. From an observation of Fig. 8(b), the vertical displacement was about

3.75 m, the longitudinal displacement was about 0.5 m and the lateral displacement was 0 m after 10 s. From the observation of Fig. 9(a), it can be seen that the maximum roll angular velocity of a robot was about 0.25 rad/s after 0.3 s of roll acceleration. From an observation of Fig. 9(b), after 6.3 s the robot can roll 90°, while the pitch and yaw angular displacement was about 0°. From an observation of Fig. 10(a), it can be seen that the maximum angular velocity was 0.26 rad/s after 0.35 s and the angular velocity of roll and pitch was about 0 rad/s. From an observation of Fig. 10(b), the angular displacement of yaw was about 2.05 rad after 8 s, while the angular displacement of pitch and roll was about 0 rad.

## 5   Conclusions

Based on the dynamic model of the underwater vehicle the motion of a robot with and without cable is obtained respectively with the thrust as the input condition. According to the analysis above the following conclusions can be drawn: To realize the daily inspection of nuclear power pools and the welding repair under an emergency condition, an omni-direction underwater vehicle with operation equipment was designed. When the robot moved in lined, the maximum longitudinal and vertical velocities were reduced by 8.4% and 8.64% respectively under the influence of a cable, and the displacements were respectively reduced by 4.7% and 6.25% within 10 s compared with those without a cable. Under the disturb of a cable, the maximum roll and yaw angular velocities of the robot were respectively reduced by 16.6% and 13.3%, while the roll time of 90° was increased by 17.3%.

## References

1. Sissine, F.: Renewable energy R&D funding history: a comparison with funding for nuclear energy, fossil energy, and energy efficiency R&D. Congressional Research Service Reports. Library of Congress, Congressional Research Service (2016)
2. Zheng, J., Tagami, K., Uchida, S.: Release of plutonium isotopes into the environment from the Fukushima Daiichi nuclear power plant accident: what is known and what needs to be known. Environ. Sci. Technol. **47**(17), 9584–9595 (2013)
3. Whitcomb, L.L.: Underwater robotics: out of the research laboratory and into the field. In: Proceedings of IEEE International Conference on Robotics and Automation, ICRA 2000, vol. 1, pp. 709–716. IEEE (2000)
4. Nomoto, M., Hattori, M.: A deep ROV "DOLPHIN 3 K": design and performance analysis. IEEE J. Oceanic Eng. **11**(3), 373–391 (2003)
5. Ramadass, G.A., Ramesh, S., Selvakuma, J.M., et al.: Deep-ocean exploration using remotely operated vehicle at gas hydrate site in Krishna-Godavari basin, Bay of Bengal. Curr. Sci. **99**(6), 809–815 (2010)
6. Salgado, J.T., Gonzalez, J.L., Martinez, L.F., et al.: Deep water ROV design for the Mexican oil industry. In: Oceans, pp. 1–6. IEEE (2010)
7. Park, S.J., Yeu, T.K., Yoon, S.M., et al.: A study of sweeping coverage path planning method for deep-sea manganese nodule mining robot. In: Oceans, pp. 1–5. IEEE (2011)

8. Mai, T.V., Choi, H.S., Kang, J., et al.: A study on hovering motion of the underwater vehicle with umbilical cable. Ocean Eng. **135**, 137–157 (2017)

9. Eidsvik, O.A., Schjølberg, I.: Time domain modeling of ROV umbilical using beam equations. IFAC PapersOnLine **49**(23), 452–457 (2016)

10. Zhu, K.Q., Zhu, H.Y., Zhang, Y.S., et al.: A multi-body space-coupled motion simulation for a deep-sea tethered remotely operated vehicle. J. Hydrodyn. Ser. B **20**(2), 210–215 (2008)

11. Fang, M.C., Hou, C.S., Luo, J.H.: On the motions of the underwater remotely operated vehicle with umbilical cable effect. Ocean Eng. **34**(8), 1275–1289 (2007)

12. Huo, C.F.: Dynamic analysis of undersea cables and its application to cable-remotely operated vehicle system. Shanghai Jiaotong University (2013). (in Chinese)

13. Wang, F.: Simulation and control research of marine towed seismic system. Shanghai Jiaotong University (2011). (in Chinese)

14. Li, Y.H., Li, X.B., Dai, J., Pang, Y.J., Xu, Y.R.: Calculation of coupling between the cable and the towed-body in the towed system. Ocean Eng. **20**(4), 37–42 (2002). (in Chinese)

15. Fossen, T.I.: Guidance and Control of Ocean Vehicles. Wiley, New York (1994)

# 3D UAV Path Planning Using Global-Best Brain Storm Optimization Algorithm and Artificial Potential Field

Qian Zhou[✉] and She-sheng Gao

School of Automatics, Northwestern Polytechnical University, Xian 710072, China
zqjmbt@sina.com, gshshnpu@163.com

**Abstract.** In this paper, the online obstacle avoidance path planning problem for UAV is studied. The global-best brain storming algorithm (GBSO) and artificial potential field (APF) method are applied to UAV path planning. The global-best brain storm optimization algorithm is applied for avoiding with fixed obstacles, which knowing at path planning stage. The pre-planning path can be obtained by the GBSO. When the sensors carried by the UAV identify the accidental obstacle during flight, the local path re-planning mechanism is triggered. In the re-plan stage, the artificial potential field method is applied for finding path with collision avoidance. The cubic B-spline curve is adopted for UAV 3D path planning. The maximum curvature and climb (or dive) angle constraints of path are taken into consideration in pre-planning stage. The simulation results demonstrate that the effectiveness of the proposed method for online UAV 3D path planning problem.

**Keywords:** Unmanned aerial vehicle (UAV) · Path planning · Global-best brain storm optimization algorithm · Artificial potential field

## 1 Introduction

In numerous areas, autonomous systems are replacing manual operation in some extent. UAVs are widely used in military and civilian applications due to the properties of simplicity, low cost, safety, flexibility and reliability, such as search and rescue missions [1,2], monitoring [3], missile launching, environmental protection, mailing and delivery [4]. Especially in dangerous, remote or harsh environments, the man-machine systems are replaced by UAVs. The methodology used to design unmanned aerial vehicle (UAV) path is one of the key factors that affect the level of autonomy [5]. The purpose of UAV path planning problem is to find the optimal or near-optimal solution that meets mission requirements under the shortest running time and safe conditions [6].

In literature, there are many researches concerning find an collision free and optimal path for UAV evading risk, such as visibility graph, rapidly-exploring

© Springer Nature Switzerland AG 2019
H. Yu et al. (Eds.): ICIRA 2019, LNAI 11741, pp. 765–775, 2019.
https://doi.org/10.1007/978-3-030-27532-7_66

random tree, probabilistic roadmap, dijkstras algorithm, A* algorithm, and D* algorithm. It proves that finding the optimal path is an nondeterministic polynomial time complete (NP-complete) problem. The meta-heuristic methods are effective approaches that have already been used to solve NP-complete problems. This kind of works contains: genetic algorithms (GA), particle swarm optimization (PSO) Algorithm, differential evolution (DE) algorithm, ant colony optimization (ACO) algorithm, artificial bee colony (ABC) Algorithm, design GA, design evolutionary algorithm (EA) and hybrid version of the above algorithms. Xu, Duan and Liu applied the ABC algorithm for 2D UAV path planning problem, the threat and the fuel cost were considered in their work [7]. In order to increase the applicability in real-world, the 3D situation, more objectives and constraints are taken into consideration. In [8], the GA and PSO have been used to cope the 3D UAV path planning problem. Chen and Yu et al. [6] adopted a modified central force optimization algorithm for 3D UAV path planning. In this work, the length, height and of path as well as the smoothness of the path were included in the cost function. Fu and Yu et al. [9] applied a designed EA to solve the path planning problem. The security, length and smoothness cost are used to guide the algorithms to find the optimal path.

In addition to the traditional heuristic algorithms, some recently proposed nature-inspired algorithms have received great attention in the field of UAV path planning. One typical example is the brain storming optimization (BSO) algorithm. The BSO algorithm was originally introduced in 2011 [10]. The BSO has been widely applied to solve optimization problems [11,12]. However, the basic BSO still has the drawback that easily traps into the local optimal and has a slow convergent speed [13]. To improve the performance of the original BSO algorithm, researchers have modified BSO from three different perspectives: clustering strategy [14], creating strategy [15] and selecting strategies [16]. The global-best guidance concept in PSO had been introduced [17]. The results show that the GBSO can get better performance than other previous BSO variants and global-best algorithms on benchmarks under the same conditions and encoding.

In dynamic and uncertain environment, the online UAV path planning has been considered as a fundamental and necessary mission. Although meta-heuristic methods are effective approaches for path planning, they cannot meet real-time path planning requirements when encounter the accidental obstacles or threats. For achieving real-time path planning, local path re-planning is necessary in complex and uncertain flight environment. In our work, the APF method is applied for local re-planning because of its advantages of being simple, practical and of high engineering practicality. On the other hand, the APF method is easy trapped in the local minimum points in path planning with a large number of obstacles [18,19]. That's the reason why the APF is only used for local path re-planning in our work.

The contributions of this paper are as follows. First, the method of global best pre-planning path integrate with local re-planning path is proposed for solving online path planning problem. Second, the GBSO was applied for 3D UAV path planning problem with consideration of the kinematics and dynamic constraints for UAV. Section 2 provides the proposed method for UAV path planning problem. The pre-planning path obtained using the GBSO, and APF method are presented in Sects. 3 and 4, respectively. The experimental results and discussion are presented in Sect. 5. Finally, some conclusions and further discussion are introduced in Sect. 6.

## 2    The Proposed Method for Online UAV Path Planning

The main objective of UAV path planning is to search a safe and flyable path to the destination with minimal cost.

$$p_s(x_s, y_s, h_s) \longrightarrow p_f(x_f, y_f, h_f) \tag{1}$$

subject to

$$(x^L, y^L, z^L) \leq p_i(x_i, y_i, z_i) \leq (x^U, y^U, z^U)$$
$$p_i(x_i, y_i, z_i) \cap \psi = \emptyset$$

where $p_s$ and $p_f$ are the start and end points of the task respectively, and $p_i(x_i, y_i, z_i)$ is the $i$-th waypoint of a specific path. $(x^L, y^L, z^L)$ and $(x^U, y^U, z^U)$ are the lower and upper boundaries of the search area. The full flowchart of the proposed method for 3D UAV path planning is shown in Fig. 1. The GBSO is applied for finding the optimal path with collision avoiding with fixed obstacles knowing at pre-planning stage. In the re-planning stage, the APF method is applied for finding local re-plan path with collision avoidance. The final path obtained by integrating the pre-planning path and local re-planning path, and cubic spline curves is used to smooth the path.

## 3    Pre-planning Path Using GBSO

In order to find the optimal path, a cost function is designed. In our method, the length and height of path, distance with obstacles (knowing at path planning stage) were introduced to the cost function. Our design cost function is as follows:

$$min : f_{cost} = w_1 * f_1 + w_2 * f_2 + w_3 * f_3 \tag{2}$$

where $f_1$ and $f_2$ penalize the longer path and the path with higher altitudes, and $f_3$ penalize the path collision with obstacles.

(1). Minimal path length

$$f_1 = \sum_{i=2}^{n} \left( \sqrt{(x_i - x_{i-1})^2 + (y_i - y_{i-1})^2 + (z_i - z_{i-1})^2} \right) \tag{3}$$

(2). Minimal flight altitude

$$f_2 = \sum_{i=1}^{n} z_i \tag{4}$$

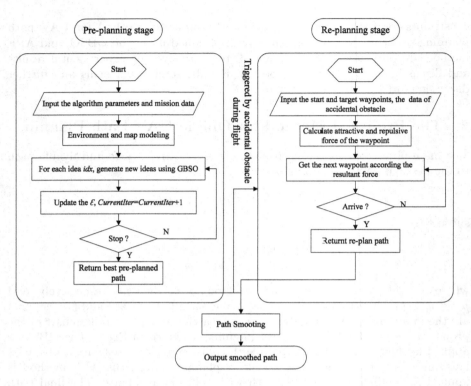

**Fig. 1.** The full flowchart of the proposed method for 3D UAV path planning

(3). Minimal distance with obstacles

The obstacles areas are modeled as cuboids $[a_m, b_m, c(x_m, y_m), l_m]$, $m = 1,...,Nt$. $(a_m, b_m)$ denote the length and width of the $m$-th obstacle, $c(x_m, y_m)$ denote the center of the $m$-th obstacle in the xy plane, $l_m$ denote the height of the $m$-th obstacle.

$$f_3 = \sum_{i=1}^{n} \left( f_3^i \right) \tag{5}$$

where

$$f_3^i = \begin{cases} \sqrt{(a_m - d_{x,m})^2 + (b_m - d_{y,m})^2 + (l_m - H_{\text{map}}(x_i, y_i))^2} & otherwise \\ 0 & if \ r_i(t) \cap \psi = \emptyset \end{cases}$$

where $f_3^i$ represents the cost function associated with collision obstacles. $d_{x,m}$ and $d_{y,m}$ are the distance between the path and the center of m-th obstacle in the x, y direction, respectively. $H_{map}(x_i, y_i)$ is the height of terrain at $(x_i, y_i)$.

(4). Terrain constraint

$$G_1 = \sum_{i=1}^{n} (g_1^i) \tag{6}$$

where

$$g_1^i = \begin{cases} 0 & if \ z_i \geq H_{map}(x_i, y_i) + h_{\min} \\ z_i - (H_{map}(x_i, y_i) + h_{\min}) & others \end{cases}$$

where $g_1^i$ represents the degree of violation for terrain constrain. $h_{min}$ is the minimum safe value of flight path above terrain.

(5). Maximal curvature constraint

$$G_2 = \sum_{i=3}^{n} (g_2^i) \tag{7}$$

where

$$g_2^i = \begin{cases} 0 & if \ k_i \leq k_{\max} \\ k_i - k_{\max} & otherwise \end{cases}$$

where $g_2^i$ represents the degree of violation for curvature constraint, $k_i$ and $k_{max}$ are approximate curvature of path and the maximum curvature constraint for UAV, respectively.

(6). Maximal climb (or dive) angle constraint

$$G_3 = \sum_{i=2}^{n} (g_3^i) \tag{8}$$

where

$$g_i^3 = \begin{cases} 0 & if \ |\theta_i| \leq \theta_{max} \\ |\theta_i| - \theta_{max} & others \end{cases}$$

$$\theta_i = \arctan(\frac{z_i - z_{i-1}}{\sqrt{(x_i - x_{i-1})^2 + (y_i - y_{i-1})^2}})$$

where $g_3^i$ is represents the degree of violation for climb (or dive) angle constrain of path. $\theta_{max}$ is the maximum climb (or dive) angle constraint of path for UAV. The 3D path planning for UAV is regard as constrained single-objective optimization problem, and the detailed procedure of the GBSO as in [17]. Furthermore, the improved $\epsilon$ level comparison method is introduced to handle constrains [20]. This method can balance the search between feasible regions and infeasible regions by adjusting the value of $\epsilon$ adaptively.

## 4   Local Path Re-planning Using Artificial Potential Field

APF method is a theory based on the principle of interaction between electric charges. When UAV approaches the obstacle, the UAV will be forced by a repulsive force opposite to its own direction of motion achieving collision avoidance with the obstacle. The UAV control by the resultant force from the target and obstacles.

$$F(X, X_f, X_o) = F_{att}(X, X_f) + F_{rep}(X, X_o) \tag{9}$$

where the $F(X, X_f, X_o)$ is the resultant force forced by UAV, $F_{att}(X, X_f)$ and $F_{rep}(X, X_o)$ are the attractive and repulsive force, respectively. The $X$, $X_f$ and $X_o$ are the location of UAV, target and obstacle, respectively.

(1). The attractive potential function

$$U_{att}(X, X_f) = \frac{1}{2}\alpha\rho^2(X, X_f) \tag{10}$$

where the $\alpha$ is the coefficient constant of the attractive potential function, and $\rho(X, X_f)$ is the distance between UAV and target.

(2). The repulsive potential function

$$U_{rep}(X, X_o) = \begin{cases} \frac{1}{2}\beta[\frac{1}{\rho(X, X_o)} - \frac{1}{\rho_o}]^2 & if \rho(X, X_o) \le \rho_o \\ 0 & others \end{cases} \tag{11}$$

where the $\beta$ is the coefficient constant of the repulsive potential function, and $\rho(X, X_o)$ is the distance between UAV and obstacle. $\rho_o$ is the effect range of obstacle. The attractive and repulsive force of the UAV are the negative gradient of the attractive and repulsive potential function.

(3). The attractive force

$$F_{att}(X, X_f) = -grad[U_{att}(X, X_f)] = \alpha\rho(X, X_f) \tag{12}$$

(4). The repulsive force

$$F_{rep}(X, X_o) = \begin{cases} \beta[\frac{1}{\rho(X, X_o)} - \frac{1}{\rho_o}]\frac{1}{\rho^2(X, X_o)} & if \rho(X, X_o) \le \rho_o \\ 0 & others \end{cases} \tag{13}$$

The waypoints are decided by the resultant force from target and obstacles in the re-planning stage.

## 5    Simulation

In this section, the virtual environment, the fixed obstacles (which knowing at path planning stage) and accidental obstacle are designed. The simulation results of path planning problems based on MATLAB R2016a are given, which proved that the effectiveness of proposed method. The mission area of the UAV is 1000 m long, 600 m wide, 100 m high with known terrain. The maximum curvature and climb (or dive) angle for UAV are set 1/30 and 30 in pre-planning stage. The maximum number of function evaluations are set as 10000. The detailed parameters are show in Table 1.

**Table 1.** The parameters of different algorithms

| Algorithm | Related parameters |
|---|---|
| GBSO | 25 ideas, the number of clusters $m = 5$, $C$ varies from 0.2 to 0.8 linearly, $p\_onecluster = 0.8, p\_onecenter = 0.4, p\_twocenters = 0.5$ |
| BSO | 100 ideas, the number of clusters $m = 10$, $perc_e = 0.1, p_e = 0.2, p_{one} = 0.8$ |
| DE | 40 population, $F$ varies from 0.2 to 0.8 linearly, $Cr = 0.9$ |
| APF | $\alpha = 30$, $\beta = 60000$, $\rho_o = 100$ |

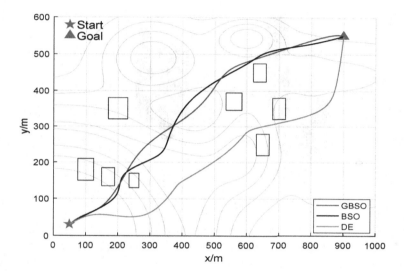

**Fig. 2.** The 2D path obtained by three algorithms in pre-planning stage

In order to test the performance of the GBSO algorithm for UAV path planning, brain storm optimization (BSO) and DE are tested for comparison. The 2D and 3D pre-planning path is shown in Figs. 2 and 3, respectively. The figures show three algorithms all can find safe path from starting point to destination. The length and height of the path obtained by GBSO algorithm is 1037.75 m and 2072.98 m, and they are all superior than the results of BSO and DE under the same test condition. Note that the result meet the restraints of path for UAV, so the $G1$-$G3$ are zero. The required time of GBSO, BSO, DE are more than 175s, this results show that the heuristic algorithms are incapable of solving path planning problem under real-time in this manner (Table 2).

**Table 2.** The results of three algorithms in pre-planning stage

| Algorithm | Length (m) | Height (m) | Required time (s) |
|-----------|-----------|-----------|-------------------|
| GBSO | 1037.75 | 2072.98 | 175.23 |
| BSO | 1050.81 | 2296.65 | 177.08 |
| DE | 1115.43 | 4248.72 | 178.60 |

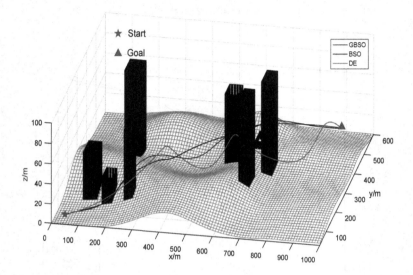

**Fig. 3.** The 3D path obtained by three algorithms in pre-planning stage

For achieving path planning in dynamic environment, the local path replan is necessary. If an unexpected obstacle pops up, the re-planning is triggered online using APF method to find obstacle avoidance path. In order to test the effective of APF, the accidental obstacles are designed. The accidental obstacles are considered as spheres. The location of accidental obstacles are (300 m, 245 m, 20 m) and (350 m, 300 m, 20 m). The radius of the spheres are 20 m and 30 m, respectively. The 2D and 3D of the final path obtained by the proposed method are shown in Figs. 4 and 5, respectively. The time required for local re-planning is 1.325 s, and the length of final path is 1054.05 m.

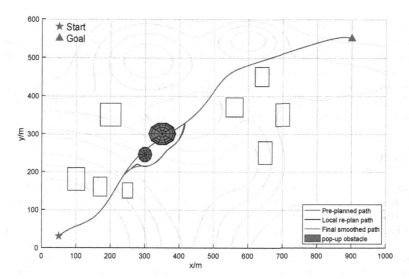

**Fig. 4.** The 2D final path obtained by the proposed method

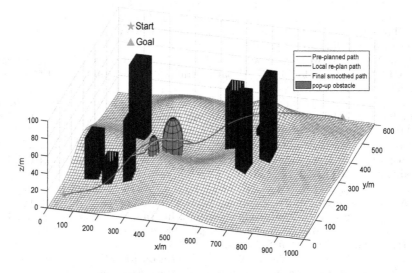

**Fig. 5.** The 3D final path obtained by the proposed method

## 6    Conclusion

In this paper, the problem of designing path with obstacles avoidance property for UAV in 3D scenes is studied. The global-best brain storm optimization algorithm is applied for avoiding fixed obstacles, which knowing at path planning stage. When the sensors carried by the UAV identify the accidental obstacle during flight, the local path re-planning mechanism is triggered. In the re-plan stage, the artificial potential field method is applied for finding path with collision avoidance. Although the results give a promising research direction for UAV online path planning problems, it is based on the sensors carried by the UAV can identify the size of obstacle. As further investigation, how to improve the performance of the proposed method is being considered. Furthermore, the swarm UAVs path planning problems are interesting research direction.

# References

1. Adams, S.M., Friedland, C.J.: A survey of unmanned aerial vehicle (UAV) usage for imagery collection in disaster research and management. In: 9th International Workshop on Remote Sensing for Disaster Response, vol 8 (2011)
2. Erdos, D., Erdos, A., Watkins, S.E.: An experimental UAV system for search and rescue challenge. IEEE Aerosp. Electron. Syst. Mag. **28**(5), 32–37 (2013)
3. Eschmann, C., Kuo, C.M., Kuo, C.H., Boller, C.: Unmanned aircraft systems for remote building inspection and monitoring. In: Proceedings of the 6th European Workshop on Structural Health Monitoring, Dresden, Germany, vol. 36 (2012)
4. Yan, R.J., Pang, S., Sun, H.B., Pang, Y.J.: Development and missions of unmanned surface vehicle. J. Mar. Sci. Appl. **9**(4), 451–457 (2010)
5. Besada-Portas, E., de la Torre Cubillo, L., M-de la Cruz, J., de Andres-Toro, B.: Evolutionary trajectory planner for multiple UAVS in realistic scenarios. IEEE Trans. Rob. **26**(4), 619–634 (2010)
6. Chen, Y., Yu, J., Mei, Y., Wang, Y., Su, X.: Modified central force optimization (MCFO) algorithm for 3D UAV path planning. Neurocomputing **171**, 878–888 (2016)
7. Xu, C., Duan, H., Liu, F.: Chaotic artificial bee colony approach to uninhabited combat air vehicle (UCAV) path planning. Aerosp. Sci. Technol. **14**(8), 535–541 (2010)
8. Roberge, V., Tarbouchi, M., Labonté, G.: Comparison of parallel genetic algorithm and particle swarm optimization for real-time UAV path planning. IEEE Trans. Industr. Inf. **9**(1), 132–141 (2013)
9. Fu, Z., Yu, J., Xie, G., Chen, Y., Mao, Y.: A heuristic evolutionary algorithm of UAV path planning. Wirel. Commun. Mob. Comput. **2018**, 1–11 (2018)
10. Shi, Y.: Brain storm optimization algorithm. In: Tan, Y., Shi, Y., Chai, Y., Wang, G. (eds.) ICSI 2011. LNCS, vol. 6728, pp. 303–309. Springer, Heidelberg (2011). https://doi.org/10.1007/978-3-642-21515-5_36
11. Aldhafeeri, A., Rahmat-Samii, Y.: Brain storm optimization for electromagnetic applications: continuous and discrete. IEEE Trans. Antennas Propag. **67**(4), 2710–2722 (2019)
12. Guo, Q., Xue, Z., Zhang, L., Lu, X., Yin, Y., Huang, C.: Wind turbine unit power prediction based on wavelet neural network optimized by brain storm optimization algorithm. In: 2018 IEEE 7th Data Driven Control and Learning Systems Conference (DDCLS), pp. 664–669. IEEE (2018)
13. Qiu, H., Duan, H.: Receding horizon control for multiple UAV formation flight based on modified brain storm optimization. Nonlinear Dyn. **78**(3), 1973–1988 (2014)

14. Cao, Z., Shi, Y., Rong, X., Liu, B., Du, Z., Yang, B.: Random grouping brain storm optimization algorithm with a new dynamically changing step size. In: Tan, Y., Shi, Y., Buarque, F., Gelbukh, A., Das, S., Engelbrecht, A. (eds.) ICSI 2015. LNCS, vol. 9140, pp. 357–364. Springer, Cham (2015). https://doi.org/10.1007/978-3-319-20466-6_38

15. Yang, Y., Shi, Y., Xia, S.: Advanced discussion mechanism-based brain storm optimization algorithm. Soft Comput. **19**(10), 2997–3007 (2015)

16. Yu, Y., Gao, S., Wang, Y., Cheng, J., Todo, Y.: ASBSO: an improved brain storm optimization with flexible search length and memory-based selection. IEEE Access **6**, 36977–36994 (2018)

17. El-Abd, M.: Global-best brain storm optimization algorithm. Swarm Evol. Comput. **37**, 27–44 (2017)

18. Tazibt, C.Y., Achir, N., Muhlethaler, P., Djamah, T.: UAV-based data gathering using an artificial potential fields approach. In: 2018 IEEE 88th Vehicular Technology Conference (VTC-Fall), pp. 1–5. IEEE (2019)

19. Rostami, S.M.H., Sangaiah, A.K., Wang, J., Liu, X.: Obstacle avoidance of mobile robots using modified artificial potential field algorithm. EURASIP J. Wirel. Commun. Netw. **2019**(1), 70 (2019)

20. Fan, Z., Fang, Y., Li, W., Yuan, Y., Wang, Z., Bian, X.: LSHADE44 with an improved $\epsilon$ constraint-handling method for solving constrained single-objective optimization problems. In: 2018 IEEE Congress on Evolutionary Computation (CEC), pp. 1–8. IEEE (2018)